Lecture Notes in Artificial Intelligence 8609

Subseries of Lecture Notes in Computer Science

LNAI Series Editors

Randy Goebel
University of Alberta, Edmonton, Canada
Yuzuru Tanaka
Hokkaido University, Sapporo, Japan
Wolfgang Wahlster
DFKI and Saarland University, Saarbrücken, Germany

LNAI Founding Series Editor

Joerg Siekmann
DFKI and Saarland University, Saarbrücken, Germany

Dominik Ślęzak   Ah-Hwee Tan
James F. Peters   Lars Schwabe (Eds.)

Brain Informatics and Health

International Conference, BIH 2014
Warsaw, Poland, August 11-14, 2014
Proceedings

 Springer

Volume Editors

Dominik Ślęzak
University of Warsaw
and Infobright Inc., Poland
E-mail: slezak@mimuw.edu.pl

Ah-Hwee Tan
Nanyang Technological University, Singapore
E-mail: asahtan@ntu.edu.sg

James F. Peters
University of Manitoba, Winnipeg, MB, Canada
and Adiyaman University, Turkey
E-mail: james.peters3@ad.umanitoba.ca

Lars Schwabe
University of Rostock, Germany
E-mail: lars.schwabe@uni-rostock.de

ISSN 0302-9743   e-ISSN 1611-3349
ISBN 978-3-319-09890-6   e-ISBN 978-3-319-09891-3
DOI 10.1007/978-3-319-09891-3
Springer Cham Heidelberg New York Dordrecht London

Library of Congress Control Number: 2014945234

LNCS Sublibrary: SL 7 – Artificial Intelligence

Typesetting: Camera-ready by author, data conversion by Scientific Publishing Services, Chennai, India

Printed on acid-free paper

Springer is part of Springer Science+Business Media (www.springer.com)

Preface

This volume contains the papers selected for presentation at the 2014 International Conference on Brain Informatics and Health (BIH 2014), held as part of the 2014 Web Intelligence Congress (WIC 2014) at the University of Warsaw, Poland, during August 11–14, 2014. The conference was organized jointly by the Web Intelligence Consortium, the University of Warsaw, the Polish Mathematical Society, and Warsaw University of Technology.

The series of Brain Informatics conferences began in China in 2006 with the International Workshop on Web Intelligence Meets Brain Informatics (WImBI 2006). The next events were held in China, Canada, and Japan. Since 2012, the conference topics have been extended with major elements of health informatics in order to investigate some common challenges in both areas. In 2014, this series of events visited Europe for the first time ever.

BIH 2014 received 101 paper submissions, in the areas of foundations of brain understanding, brain-inspired problem solving, brain and health data management, biomedical decision support, brain and health data analytics, healthcare systems, biomedical technologies, as well as applications of brain and health informatics. After a rigorous evaluation process, 29 papers were selected as regular contributions, giving an acceptance rate of 28.7%, and are grouped into the first seven sections of this volume.

The last five sections of this volume contain 23 papers selected for oral presentations in BIH 2014 special sessions. Additionally, the first paper in the last section corresponds to one of the WIC 2014 tutorials. We would like to thank all special session organizers and all authors who contributed their research results to this volume.

The congress provided a very exciting program with a number of keynote talks, regular and special sessions, workshops, tutorials, panel discussions and social programs. We greatly appreciate our keynote speakers: Andrew Chi-Chih Yao, Karl Friston, Henryk Skarżyński, Stefan Decker, Robert Kowalski, Sadaaki Miyamoto, Yi Pan, John F. Sowa, and Andrzej Szałas. We would also like to acknowledge all tutorial and panel speakers for preparing high-quality lectures and conducting inspiring research discussions.

A program of this kind would not have been possible without the dedication of Marcin Szczuka and the whole local Organizing Committee, the administrative support by Juzhen Dong, the strategic guidance by Andrzej Skowron, Ning Zhong, and Jiming Liu, as well as all other chairs, Program Committee members, and external reviewers.

We would also like to thank our institutional patrons: the Ministry of Science and Higher Education of the Republic of Poland and the Warsaw Center of Mathematics and Computer Science.

We wish to express our gratitude to our sponsors: Dituel (Main Sponsor), Google (Gold Sponsor), Human Brain Project, IOS Press (Web25 Event Sponsor), Core Technology, and Gemius. Without their generous support we would never have been able to make this conference such a success.

We are also grateful to the Committee on Informatics of the Polish Academy of Sciences, the Polish Artificial Intelligence Society, the World Wide Web Consortium (Web25 Anniversary initiative), the European Brain Council (Year of the Brain in Europe initiative), and the IEEE CIS ETTC Task Force on Brain Informatics for help with publicizing the congress.

Finally, we wish to acknowledge Andrzej Janusz and Marcin Możejko for taking over the job of putting this volume together. We extend our highest appreciation to Springer's LNCS/LNAI team for their generous support. In particular, we thank Alfred Hofmann, Anna Kramer, Ingrid Beyer, and Leonie Kunz for their help in coordinating the publication of this volume.

August 2014

Dominik Ślęzak
Ah-Hwee Tan
James F. Peters
Lars Schwabe

Organization

General Congress Chair

Andrzej Skowron   University of Warsaw, Poland

General Program Chair

Dominik Ślęzak   University of Warsaw and Infobright Inc.,
Poland

BIH 2014 Program Co-chairs

Ah-Hwee Tan   Nanyang Technological University, Singapore
James F. Peters   University of Manitoba, Canada
Lars Schwabe   University of Rostock, Germany

Workshop Chairs

Lipika Dey   TATA Consultancy Services, India
Adam Krasuski   Main School of Fire Service, Poland
Marek Reformat   University of Alberta, Canada

Tutorial Chairs

Hiranmay Ghosh   TATA Consultancy Services, India
Radosław Katarzyniak   Wrocław University of Technology, Poland
Christina Schweikert   St. John's University, USA

Publicity Chairs

Shinichi Motomura   Maebashi Institute of Technology, Japan
Piotr S. Szczepaniak   Technical University of Łódź, Poland
JingTao Yao   University of Regina, Canada

Publication Chairs

Marcin Dziubiński   University of Warsaw, Poland
Andrzej Janusz   University of Warsaw, Poland

Financial Chair

Juzhen Dong   Web Intelligence Consortium, Japan

Local Organizing Committee

Marcin Szczuka   University of Warsaw, Poland
Łukasz Sosnowski   Dituel, Poland
Henryk Rybiński   Warsaw University of Technology, Poland
Andrzej Jankowski   Warsaw University of Technology, Poland

Steering Committee Chairs/WIC Directors

Ning Zhong   Maebashi Institute of Technology, Japan
Jiming Liu   Hong Kong Baptist University, Hong Kong,
                                       SAR China

Steering Committee/WIC Technical Committee

Jeffrey Bradshaw   UWF/Institute for Human and Machine
                                       Cognition, USA
Nick Cercone   York University, Canada
Dieter Fensel   STI/University of Innsbruck, Austria
Georg Gottlob   Oxford University, UK
Lakhmi Jain   University of South Australia, Australia
Jianchang Mao   Microsoft, USA
Jianhua Ma   Hosei University, Japan
Pierre Morizet-Mahoudeaux   Compiegne University of Technology, France
Hiroshi Motoda   Osaka University, Japan
Toyoaki Nishida   Kyoto University, Japan
Vijay Raghavan   University of Louisiana at Lafayette, USA
Andrzej Skowron   University of Warsaw, Poland
Jinglong Wu   Okayama University, Japan
Xindong Wu   University of Vermont, USA
Yiyu Yao   University of Regina, Canada

BIH 2014 Program Committee

Samina Abidi   Dalhousie University, Canada
Juan Carlos Augusto   Middlesex University, UK
Luiz Baccala   University of Sao Paulo, Brazil
Sanghamitra Bandyopadhyay   Indian Statistical Institute, India
Andrzej Bargiela   University of Nottingham, UK

Alan J. Barton — Carleton University, Canada
Jan G. Bazan — University of Rzeszów, Poland
Przemysław Biecek — University of Warsaw, Poland
Katarzyna Blinowska — University of Warsaw, Poland
Piotr Bogorodzki — Warsaw University of Technology, Poland
Nizar Bouguila — Concordia University, Canada
M. Emre Celebi — LSUS, USA
Nick Cercone — York University, Canada
W. Art Chaovalitwongse — University of Washington, USA
Yiqiang Chen — Institute of Computing Technology, CAS, China
Yiu-ming Cheung — Hong Kong Baptist University, Hong Kong, SAR China
Andrzej Cichocki — RIKEN Brain Science Institute, Japan
Marek Druzdzel — University of Pittsburgh, USA
Frank Emmert-Streib — Queen's University Belfast, UK
Yuhong Feng — Shenzhen University, China
Philippe Fournier-Viger — University of Moncton, Canada
Richard Frackowiak — University of Lausanne, Switzerland
Wojciech Froelich — University of Silesia, Poland
Hassan Ghasemzadeh — Washington State University, USA
Consuelo Gonzalo-Martín — Universidad Politécnica de Madrid, Spain
Jerzy Grzymała-Busse — University of Kansas, USA
Yi-Ke Guo — Imperial College London, UK
Mohand-Said Hacid — Université Claude Bernard Lyon 1, France
Takahiro Hara — Osaka University, Japan
Aboul Ella Hassanien — University of Cairo, Egypt
Yong He — Beijing Normal University, China
Thomas Heinis — EPFL, Switzerland
Shoji Hirano — Shimane University, Japan
Andreas Holzinger — Medical University Graz, Austria
Daniel Howard — Howard Science Limited, UK
D. Frank Hsu — Fordham University, USA
Bin Hu — Lanzhou University, China
Zhisheng Huang — Vrije University Amsterdam, The Netherlands
Kazuyuki Imamura — Maebashi Institute of Technology, Japan
Tianzi Jiang — Institute of Automation, CAS, China
C.G. Johnson — University of Kent, UK
Hanmin Jung — KISTI, Korea
Igor Jurisica — University of Toronto, Canada
Ferath Kherif — CHUV/UNIL, Switzerland
Syoji Kobashi — University of Hyogo, Japan
Jacek Koronacki — Institute of Computer Science, PAS, Poland
Abbas Z. Kouzani — Deakin University, Australia
Yasuo Kudo — Muroran Institute of Technology, Japan
Bartosz Kunka — Gdańsk University of Technology, Poland

Gerald Schaefer	Loughborough University, UK
Christina Schweikert	St. John's University, USA
Abdulkadir Sengur	Firat University, Turkey
Arash Shaban-Nejad	McGill University, Canada
Hava Siegelmann	University of Massachusetts Amherst, USA
Marek Sikora	Silesian University of Technology, Poland
Daniel L. Silver	Acadia University, Canada
Henryk Skarżyński	IFPS, Poland
Andrzej Skowron	University of Warsaw, Poland
Neil Smalheiser	University of Illinois, USA
Tomasz G. Smoliński	DESU, USA
Diego Sona	Italian Institute of Technology, Italy
Marcin Szczuka	University of Warsaw, Poland
Andrzej Świerniak	Silesian University of Technology, Poland
Ryszard Tadeusiewicz	AGH University of Science and Technology, Poland
Satoshi Takahashi	Okayama University, Japan
Xijin Tang	Academy of Mathematics and Systems Sciences, CAS, China
Teck-Hou Teng	Nanyang Technological University, Singapore
K. Thangavel	Periyar University, India
Jerzy Tiuryn	University of Warsaw, Poland
Shiro Usui	Toyohashi University of Technology, Japan
Sunil Vadera	University of Salford, UK
Egon L. van den Broek	Utrecht University, The Netherlands
Frank van der Velde	Leiden University, The Netherlands
Feng Wan	University of Macau, Macau, SAR China
Hongbin Wang	University of Texas, USA
Lipo Wang	Nanyang Technology University, Singapore
Konrad W. Wojciechowski	Silesian University of Technology, Poland
Limsoon Wong	National University of Singapore, Singapore
Michał Woźniak	Wrocław University of Technology, Poland
Daniel K. Wójcik	Nencki Institute of Experimental Biology, Poland
Jakub Wróblewski	Infobright Inc., Poland
Jinglong Wu	Okayama University, Japan
Yiyu Yao	University of Regina, Canada
Fabio Massimo Zanzotto	University of Rome Tor Vergata, Italy
Krzysztof Zaremba	Warsaw University of Technology, Poland
Yi Zeng	Institute of Automation, CAS, China
Wen Zhang	Institute of Software, CAS, China
Yanchun Zhang	Victoria University, Australia
Yanqing Zhang	Georgia State University, USA
Jiashu Zhao	York University, Canada
Ning Zhong	Maebashi Institute of Technology, Japan
Haiyan Zhou	Beijing University of Technology, China

Zhi-Hua Zhou	Nanjing University, China
Yangyong Zhu	Fudan University, China
Michal Żochowski	University of Michigan, USA
Xi-Nian Zuo	Institute of Psychology, CAS, China
Jacek M. Żurada	University of Louisville, USA

BIH 2014 External Reviewers

Xiangdong An	Ivan Lee
Joel P. Arrais	Antonio Moreno-Ribas
Andre Calero-Valdez	Vasile Palade
Nitesh V. Chawla	Jan Paralic
Janir da Cruz	Lior Rokach
Matthias Dehmer	Christin Seifert
Luca Dodero	Benyun Shi
Myunggwon Hwang	Gregor Stiglic
Taehong Kim	Sebastian Widz
Mei Kobayashi	Szymon Wilk
David Koslicki	Pinar Yildirim
Nada Lavrac	

Table of Contents

Regular Contributions

Brain Understanding

Cognitive Modelling

Brain Data Analytics

Health Data Analytics

Brain Informatics and Data Management

Semantic Aspects of Biomedical Analytics

Healthcare Technologies and Systems

Special Sessions

Extracting Knowledge from Symptoms in Neurodegenerative Disease (Parkinson)

Analysis of Complex Medical Data

Understanding of Information Processing in Brain

Neuroimaging Data Processing Strategies

Advanced Methods of Interactive Data Mining for Personalized Medicine

Neuronal Morphology Modeling Based on Microscopy Reconstruction Data in the Public Repositories

Yi Zeng, Weida Bi, Xuan Tang, and Bo Xu

Institute of Automation, Chinese Academy of Sciences, Beijing, China
{yi.zeng,weida.bi,xuan.tang,xubo}@ia.ac.cn

Abstract. Neuronal morphology modeling is one of the key steps for reverse engineering the brain at the micro level. It creates a realistic digital version of the neuron obtained by microscopy reconstruction in a visualized way so that the structure of the whole neuron (including soma, dendrite, axon, spin, etc.) is visible in different angles in a three dimensional space. Whether the modeled neuronal morphology matches the original neuron in vivo is closely related to the details captured by the manually sampled morphological points. Many data in public neuronal morphology data repositories (such as the NeuroMorpho project) focus more on the morphology of dendrites and axons, while there are only a few points to represent the neuron soma. The lack of enough details for neuron soma makes the modeling on the soma morphology a challenging task. In this paper, we provide a general method to neuronal morphology modeling (including the soma and its connections to surrounding dendrites, and axons, with a focus on how different components are connected) and handle the challenging task when there are not many detailed sample points for soma.

Keywords: Neuron Morphology Reconstruction, Neuronal Morphology Modeling, Soma Reconstruction.

1 Introduction

Reverse engineering the brain and simulation of brain activities at multiple scales in silicon will revolutionize the future of Information and Intelligence Science [1-5]. In order to understand the information processing mechanism of the brain at the micro level, biologically realistic neurons need to be visually modeled and simulated so that activities of different neuronal components can be simulated and observed. In addition, they are basic components to build neural pathways and neural networks for higher levels of modeling and simulations.

Neural morphology modeling is either conducted by using manually sampled morphological points data from researchers' own lab, or from neuron databases. In order to make our approach more applicable to general sources, we acquire morphological data from the NeuroMorpho Project. This project currently contains data about more than 10 thousand neurons, covering 21 types of animals, and 123 types of cells, with contributions from 120 laboratories[1].

---

[1] NeuroMorpho Project by the George Mason University: [http://neuromorpho.org]

D. Ślęzak et al. (Eds.): BIH 2014, LNAI 8609, pp. 1–11, 2014.

Most sampled morphological points data from various institutions follow the same rules for data representation. The SWC format is a widely adopted format [6], and all the morphological data from the NeuroMorpho Project can be downloaded as an SWC file [7]. The SWC files in the NeuroMorpho project repository often include concrete information on: the position and radius of soma, branch information (spatial position, radius, and how the sampled points are connected to each other) of dendrites and axons. The project provides a tool named 3D Neuron Viewer to observe the SWC file in a visualized environment, while the morphology shown by this tool is somewhat simplified. More detailed and realistic modeling can be made based on these data.

Compared to the information for dendrites and axons in different neurons, contributed data from different studies are always lack of detailed soma information. Especially how the soma and the dendrites, axons are connected are not clear in the reconstruction data. Hence in this paper, we provide a general process for neuronal morphology modeling based on the sampled data from the NeuroMorpho project, with a focus on how the different components of the neuron are connected.

Section 2 discusses the data selection principles for the neuronal morphology modeling based on NeuroMorpho data. Section 3 introduces the modeling process for dendrites and axons. Section 4 discusses how the soma is generated based on only a few sampled points. Section 5 discusses how different components of the neuron are bridged together and refined to be a unified structure. Section 7 discusses some related work. Section 8 concludes the paper.

2   Data Selection for Neuronal Morphology Modeling

As for neuron soma morphology modeling, some of the SWC files include more detailed points to provide a contour of the soma in two dimensions, as shown in Figure 1(a). This kind of data captures the morphology of the soma in a nicer way. While most of the SWC files in the NeuroMorpho project only provide three points, which capture much less morphological details of the soma. One of them indicates the center of the soma, while the other two are marked in the same line with the first one, indicating the approximate size of the soma, as shown in Figure 1(b).

Compared to Figure 1(b), it would be much easier using Figure1(a) to reconstruct the soma. But most of the data in the NeuroMorpho project repository follows the type of Figure 1(b). Hence, we select the type of data of Figure 1(b) for soma modeling (we try to recover many missing details), so that the proposed method can be applied to most of the sampled data from the NeuroMorpho project repository.

Since axons were cut by most of the brain slices in the data from the NeuroMorpho project, in this paper, we select the files which contain relatively complete information on dendrites and axons sampled points.

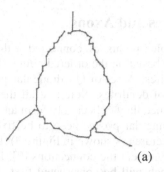
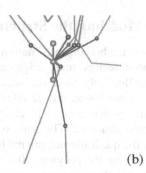

(a)   (b)

Fig. 1. Two Types of Descriptions of Neuron Soma. (a) A set of sampled points which provide the detailed contour of the soma in two dimensions as well as its connections with other components of the neuron, adopted from [8]. (b) Three sampled points in green, indicating the size of the soma, the data is from the file with NeuroMorpho ID: NMO_00941.

Some of the SWC files do not contain proper radius information. In this case, important morphology cannot be captured by the visualized neuron. For example, 49.1% of the morphology data in the NeuroMorpho project repository is reconstructed pyramidal neurons. There are two types of dendrites for this type of neuron, namely the basal dendrite and the apical dendrite. From the morphology perspective, the radius of the apical dendrite is much larger than the one of basal dendrite, while many of the SWC files ignore the difference on the radius of these two types of dendrites and set the radius values as the same. In this case, it will be hard to distinguish the types of dendrites (Figure 2 provides a comparative study on the reconstructed dendrites. Figure 2(a) is with the same radius value, while Figure 2(b) is with proper radius value. In Figure 2(b), it would be much easier to distinguish the apical dendrite from basal dendrites). In addition, improper radius value will have negative impact on the morphology modeling of the soma. Hence, when modeling the neuronal morphology, only the data with proper radius values on dendrites will be selected.

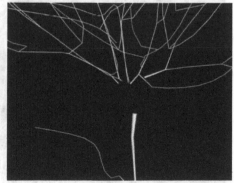

(a) The apical dendrite and the basal dendrites are with the same radius value (NeuroMorpho ID: NMO_06163)

(b) The apical dendrite and the basal dendrites are with the proper different radius (NeuroMorpho ID: NMO_00941)

Fig. 2. A Comparative Study on the Morphology of the Modeled Dendrites

3   Modeling the Structure of Dendrites and Axons

Based on the branch information on how the sampled points are connected with each other on dendrites, many edges can be constructed based on the ordered points. These edges collectively form the skeleton of the dendrites. A set of Quadrangular prisms are generated based on the edges and the radius of dendrites. Note that all the quadrangular prisms need to be connected together, since they collectively form an interconnected structure. The gaps between the quadrangular prisms need to be fixed so that all the quadrangular prisms form a unified structure (as shown in Figure 3). In our study, we use the polywire SOP in Houdini to implement the connections [9]. If two child nodes share the same parent node, one branch will be constructed first. There will be a gap on the first branch, and the second branch will be built starting from the location of the gap [8].

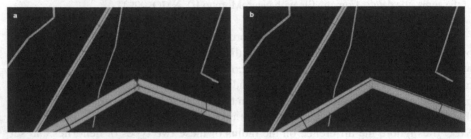

Fig. 3. The Gap between Quadrangular Prisms Before (marked in red) and After (marked in green) Smoothing (NeuroMorpho ID: NMO_00941)

Since the SWC file only contains the connections among sampled points for axons, the modeling process is similar to the process for dendrites. Figure 4 provides the modeled structures of dendrites and axons based on the upper discussed approach.

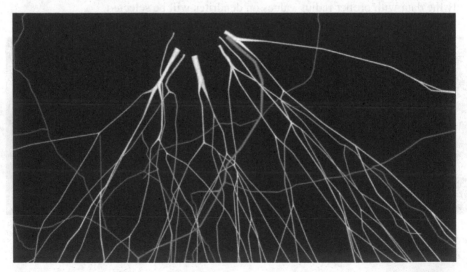

Fig. 4. The Modeled Structures of Dendrites and Axons (NeuroMorpho ID: NMO_00206)

The green lines describe the axon, while the white lines describe the dendrites. The Catmull-Clark subdivision algorithm is used for sub dividing the surfaces so that the cross sections of dendrites and axons are close to round [10].

4 Basic Soma Morphology Construction

For modeling the soma morphology, the first step is to fix the center of the soma in the three dimensional space. As for most SWC files in the NeuroMorpho project repository, the point between the other two for soma should be the center of the soma. The second step is to generate a sphere based on the radius and the central point of the soma. In order to lay a foundation for bridging the soma, the dendrites and the axon, the generated spherical soma is actually composed of many quadrilateral surfaces, as shown in Figure 5(a).

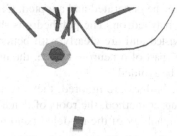

(a) Soma modeling by using half of its radius at first to avoid possible errors on the connections among the soma and the rest (NeuroMorpho ID: NMO_00941).

(b) Soma modeling based on the full radius, with a dendrite root stick into the soma body (NeuroMorpho ID: NMO_02000).

Fig. 5. The Generated Skeleton of the Soma and the Dendrites of a Neuron based on the Data from the NeuroMorpho Project Repository

Some coordinates of the dendrites are very close to the soma surface, which brings difficulties to rebuild the connections among soma and dendrites (as shown in Figure 5(b), if we use the full radius of the soma to generate the soma structure directly, one of the dendrite roots is into the soma.). Hence, firstly we use half of the radius to build the soma, as shown in Figure 5(a) (The dark pink structure is the soma rebuilt as the first step, the size of the soma will be extended to the size described in the light pink structure) in the later process.

5 Bridging the Soma, Axon and the Dendrites

5.1 Bridge Structure Generation

In Section 3 and Section 4, the basic structure of the soma, the axon and the dendrites are built. Nevertheless, they are not connected with each other. Since the root of axon and each dendrite is a surface with four edges, and the soma surface is also composed of many different sub surfaces with four edges, an extra four edges can be generated to connect the soma and the root of the dendrite or axon. The connected edges and surfaces form a polyhedron [11]. These polyhedrons serve as the bridge structures to connect the soma, the dendrites and the axon. Note that when trying to select the four-edged surface on the soma to be connected to the dendrite root surface, the candidate should have the shorted distance to the specific dendrite root surface. The bridge structure among the soma, the axon and the dendrites are similar, hence we discuss the generation of the bridge structure between the soma and the dendrite as an illustration. From the implementation perspective, the skin SOP in Houdini is used.

Note that the orientation of the surfaces of dendrite roots are stochastic, it is not possible for all of them to be parallel to the surface of the soma. Hence, the formed polyhedron is not necessarily a quadrangular prism, and the warped surfaces between the soma and the dendrites might have negative impact for modeling the neuron. Hence, we need to reconsider the order of the vertices on the root surface for dendrites so that polyhedrons with better shapes can be generated and adopted. Given two surfaces, there are four ways to construct the polyhedron. The polyhedrons shown as Figure 6(a) and Figure 6(b) seem not that twisted and are clearly with better shapes compared to Figure 6(c) and Figure 6(d) to be part of a neuron. Hence, the modeling similar to Figure 6(c) and Figure 6(d) need to be avoided.

Although within the original SWC file, the bridges are ignored, they are very important to shape the whole neuron. With the upper method, the roots of dendrites and the soma can be bridged together, and the morphology of the modeled neuron will be closer to the original data from the brain slice.

Even it seems that the bridges among the soma and the dendrites are seamlessly connected. In fact, the surfaces that connect the soma and the dendrites on the bridges only share the coordinates with them. Hence they are not truly connected (as shown in Figure 7 (a), the purple structure and the green structure share the same coordinates at the connection points, while they are actually identical structures). We fuse those points which share the same coordinates. With this step, the separated soma and dendrites structures are sutured together.

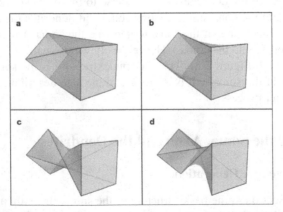

Fig. 6. Four Possible Polyhedrons based on the Two Surfaces from the Root of Dendrite and Soma ((a) and (b) are with better shapes to be adopted for connection reconstruction)

5.2   Weight Control Based Soma and Bridge Enlarge Process

In order to avoid possible errors, in our previous step, we use half of the radius to rebuild the soma. Since the bridging and suturing process has been finished, the size of the soma needs to be extended to its original size. There are two major considerations for the enlarge process: Firstly, if we only enlarge the size of the soma, there will be penetrations among the bridge surfaces and the soma. Secondly, if we enlarge the size of the soma and proportionally enlarge the bridge surfaces together, there will be penetrations among the bridge surfaces and the dendrites. In order to solve this problem, we introduce a weight (ω) to control the enlarge ratios:

$$\omega = 2 - \frac{D - r}{D_{max}}$$

where D is the distance of a point on the bridge to the center of the soma, D_{max} is the point on the bridge which holds the maximum value to the center of the soma. The weight distribution is shown in Figure 7(b). If $\omega = 1$, the surface will be in red, and if $\omega = 2$ the surface will be in yellow. After the enlarge process, a soma with its original size and its connected dendrites are shown in Figure 7(c).

Up until now, we have constructed a completely enclosed polygon mesh (composed of many quadrilateral surfaces) which describes the morphology of a neuron. This model can be widely applied to many three dimensional platforms for neuron reconstruction.

For a more realistic modeling, one may need even finer neuron models. In this case, the Catmull-Clark subdivision algorithm can be applied to divide all the quadrilateral surfaces into smaller ones [10], so that the surface will be smoother, Figure 7(d) shows a refined version of Figure 7(c) by using this method.

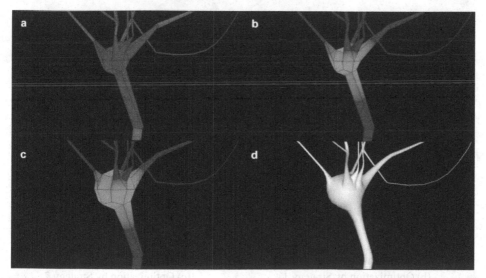

Fig. 7. Neuron sub-components Fusion and Refinement (NeuroMorpho ID: NMO_00941). (a) The soma, dendrites and their bridges; (b) The sutured neuron structure, with computed weights; (c) Enlarged structure based on the soma size and the weight control; (d) Surface refinement and smoothing process.

5.3   Optimization on the Penetration Structures

In the process of bridging the soma and the dendrites, when the roots of two dendrites are too close, they may be connected with the same four-edged surface on the soma. In this case, one bridged structure will be penetrated into the other one, as shown in Figure 8(a), the yellow branch penetrates into the blue one. This kind of penetration is visually very strange and is not a standard 3-D object representation method. Hence, it should be optimized. Here we provide two strategies to solve this problem.

Strategy 1: We rank the distances among the dendrite root surface and the candidate four-edge surfaces on the soma in reverse order. If the first and closest candidate has been picked up by another dendrite root, then the second one is chosen. Figure 8(b) is an optimized structure on Figure 8(a) based on this strategy.

Strategy 2: Refine the original four-edged surfaces by smaller ones, so that there will be more four-edge surfaces to be connected to. In this case, the possibility of having tow dendrites roots to be connected to one surface will be reduced. Figure 8(c) is an optimized structure on Figure 8(a) based on this strategy.

Nevertheless, Strategy 2 will have impact on the shape of the soma, since the size of the bridge surface has been changed, and the shape of the bridge structure will be changed respectively. Hence, Strategy 1 is preferred in most cases.

Figure 9 provides some screenshots on the full pictures of the modeled neuronal morphology based the SWC file with ID: NMO_00206 from the NeuroMorpho project repository (The green lines are axons, while the white lines are dendrites.

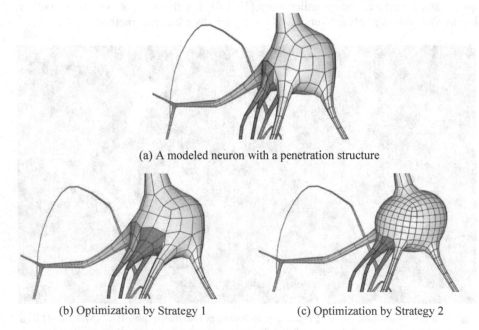

(a) A modeled neuron with a penetration structure

(b) Optimization by Strategy 1   (c) Optimization by Strategy 2

Fig. 8. A Penetration Structure and Its Optimizations (NeuroMorpho ID: NMO_00941)

Figure 9(a) is without the reconstructed soma, while Figure 9(b) is with a recon-structed soma.). It shows that the modeling in this work capture major morphological characteristics of the neuron, and the modeled neuron provides a foundation for build-ing complex neural pathways and neural networks.

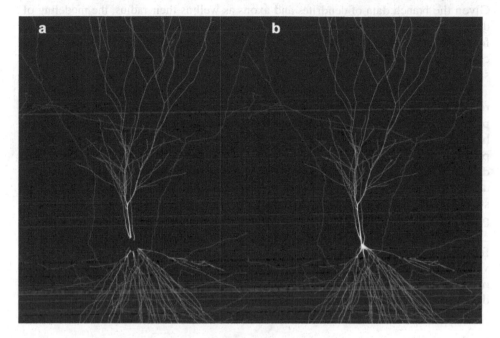

Fig. 9. Screenshots on the Full Pictures of the Modeled Neuronal Morphology

6   Related Work

Here we briefly discuss the relationship of our efforts compared to other related work. Neuronize is a tool for constructing realistic neuron morphologies [8]. The mass-spring deformation algorithm is used to handle the connection between the soma and the dendrites [12, 13]. Although the results are close to the original morphologies in brain slices, enough number of sub-surfaces needs to be generated. This might be challenging for the computing resources when the modeled neural network contains huge number of neurons.

Our method for handling the connections among the soma and the dendrites are re-lated to the work in [14]. Namely, we start with a sphere which is composed of not so many sub-surfaces, then the Catmull-Clark subdivision algorithm is used for refine-ment [10]. The difference between our work and the proposed method in [14] is that in their work, the soma is built at first, and the rest of the structures are extruded from the soma. While in our method, the modeling of dendrites, axons and the soma are in parallel, and the bridging structures are built after the modeling of these components.

7   Conclusion and Future Work

This paper provides a general process to neural morphology modeling based on manually sampled reconstruction data from public neuronal morphology repositories. Given the branch data of dendrites and axons as well as their radius, the modeling of dendritic and axonal structures are relatively intuitive. We provide a general method for soma reconstruction and how the soma connects to the rest of the neuron components, and this method is especially practical when there are only a few sampled points on the soma. Hence, it can be applied to most of the modeling tasks.

The data for modeling comes from the SWC files in the NeuroMorpho project reporsitory, and all the data within this repository share the same format. Hence, it is potentially effective to most of the data (In our study, we have conducted modeling of human, rat, and mouse neurons based on the data from this reporsitory by using the proposed method). Nevertheless, more modeling evaluation should be done on different animal species and different types of neurons. The whole modeling task is done by using the Houdini platform. Nevertheless, the concrete methods and strategies are platform independent, and can be adopted to any other three dimentional platforms. The neuron models can also be transformed to other platforms.

Current morphological data in NeuroMorpho repository only contain branch information of dendrites, while there is no information on dendritic spins which are very important for building synapses. In addition, when detailed modeling is needed on axons, morphological data for myelin sheaths are also needed. Hence, additional data from other sources need to be included for more detailed neuron modeling.

References

[1] Perry, W., Broers, A., El-Baz, F., Harris, W., Healy, B., Hillis, W.D., et al.: Grand challenges for engineering. National Academy of Engineering, Washington, DC (2008)

[2] Grand Challenges: Reverse-engineering the Brain. National Academy of Engineering, http://www.engineeringchallenges.org/cms/8996/9109.aspx

[3] The Human Brain Project: A Report to the European Commission (2012)

[4] Zhong, N., Bradshaw, J.M., Liu, J., Taylor, J.G.: Brain Informatics. IEEE Intelligent Systems 26(5), 16–21 (2011)

[5] Cauwenberghs, G.: Reverse engineering the cognitive brain. Proceedings of the National Academy of Sciences 110(39), 15512–15513 (2013)

[6] Cannon, R.C., Turner, D.A., Pyapali, G.K., Wheal, H.V.: An on-line archive of reconstructed hippocampal neurons. Journal of Neuroscience Methods 84(1-2), 49–54 (1998)

[7] Halavi, M., Polavaram, S., Donohue, D.E., Hamilton, G., Hoyt, J., Smith, K.P., et al.: NeuroMorpho.Org implementation of digital neuroscience: dense coverage and integration with the NIF. Neuroinformatics 6(3), 241–252 (2008)

[8] Brito, J.P., Mata, S., Bayona, S., Pastor, L., Defelipe, J., Benavides-Piccione, R.: Neuronize: a tool for building realistic neuronal cell morphologies. Frontiers in Neuroanatomy 7(15) (2013)

[9] Zerouni, C.: Houdini on the Spot: Power User Tips and Techniques. Focal Press (2007)

[10] Catmull, E., Clark, J.: Recursively generated B-spline surfaces on arbitrary topological meshes. Seminal graphics, pp. 183–188. ACM (1998)

[11] Shreiner, D., Sellers, G., Kessenich, J.M., Licea-Kane, B.M.: OpenGL Programming Guide: The Official Guide to Learning OpenGL, Version 4.3, 8th edn. Addison-Wesley Professional (2013)

[12] Terzopoulos, D., Platt, J., Barr, A., Fleischer, K.: Elastically deformable models. SIGGRAPH Comput. Graph. 21(4), 205–214 (1987)

[13] Nealen, A., Muller, M., Keiser, R., Boxerman, E., Carlson, M.: Physically based deformable models in computer graphics. Comput. Graph. Forum 25(4), 809–836 (2006)

[14] Lasserre, S., Hernando, J., Hill, S., Schumann, F., Anasagasti, P.M., Jaoude, G.A., et al.: A neuron membrane mesh representation for visualization of electrophysiological simulations. IEEE Transactions on Visualization and Computer Graphics 18(2), 214–227 (2012)

Ventral Stream Plays an Important Role in Statistical Graph Comprehension: An fMRI Study

Mi Li[1,2,4,5], Shengfu Lu[1,4,5], Jing Wang[1,4,5], Liwang Ma[1,4,5], Mengjie Zhang[1,4,5], and Ning Zhong[1,3,4,5]

[1] International WIC Institute, Beijing University of Technology
Beijing 100024, China
[2] The School of Computer and Communication Engineering
Liaoning ShiHua University, Liaoning 113001, China
[3] Dept. of Life Science and Informatics, Maebashi Institute of Technology
Maebashi-City 371-0816, Japan
[4] Beijing International Collaboration Base on Brain Informatics
and Wisdom Services, China
[5] Beijing Key Laboratory of MRI and Brain Informatics, China
limi135@gmail.com, lusf@bjut.edu.cn, zhong@maebashi-it.ac.jp

Abstract. Although statistical graph comprehension has been investigated in cognitive psychology, it has not been reported in cognitive neuroscience. The study designed an experimental condition, i.e., a statistical graph (SG), and two control conditions, i.e., a text (ST) and a statistical graph with text (SGT), where the ST is a verbal description of the information from the SG, and the SGT is a mixed graph + textual description. We used fMRI to analyze the brain activity of 36 normal subjects while they passively view the statistical information presented in any of SG, ST, and SGT. The results indicate that statistical graph comprehension requires the involvement of both ventral and dorsal streams, with more dependence on the ventral stream than the dorsal.

1 Introduction

Nearly 200 years ago, William Playfair (1786) first proposed the use of graphs to represent data. Thus, a statistical graph is considered a vital information carrier because it facilitates easy remembering and comprehension. The statistical graph is also widely used to represent quantitative data on science, business, and education, which is an important part of statistical data analysis. To date, most studies on statistical graph comprehension are limited to cognitive psychology [1–3]. Some of the early studies mainly concentrated on perceptual aspects in statistical graph comprehension, such as reading off a y-value from a bar or line graph or extracting a trend from a line graph [3, 4]. Recent studies argue that graph comprehension in reality is hierarchical: the represented data is explicitly read off first before the information is interpreted [5]. A number of common assumptions are given in the literature on graph comprehension [6]; however, these

D. Ślęzak et al. (Eds.): BIH 2014, LNAI 8609, pp. 12–20, 2014.

assumptions are rarely subjected to empirical test [7]. The main purpose of this paper is to provide neuroscience evidence on statistical graph comprehension through brain imaging.

A statistical graph is used to show spatial relationships among data, including both graphical and non-graphical elements. Specific elements include graphical components, such as X- and Y-axes and the entity (e.g., data point, bar, or line), and non-graphical components, such as category labels in the X-axis (e.g., the year or item's name), numerical labels in the Y-axis, and title of graphics. As most statistical graphs have titles and are accompanied by a linguistic context, comprehending them is constrained by a cognitive system that processes the graph and the language context in which the graph appears. To distinguish the cognitive systems involved in graphical and verbal processing, the elements of verbal description are extracted from the statistical graph, forming the text that is contextually consistent with the verbal description. That is, both text and statistical graph are expected to express the same statistical information, although the graph reflects a combination of graphics and verbal description, whereas the text only shows the verbal description. Thus, we select the text as a control task for the statistical graph to examine the brain basis better during statistical graph comprehension. To make the brain basis accurate, we designed another control task, i.e., statistical graph with text [i.e., combination of statistical graph and text, (SGT)], which can remove the low-level visual features. Previous studies show that while verifying text-graphical tasks, subjects read the text first before viewing the graphics [2, 8]. Other studies on SGT comprehension show similar results, suggesting that SGT comprehension is text oriented [9, 10]. In the current study, while observing the SGT stimuli, subjects first read data from the part of text before verifying them on the part of graph, weakening the graphical cognitive operation in SGT. The results from the cognitive subtraction between the statistical graph and SGT are then used to obtain the brain neural basis of statistical graph comprehension.

2 Methods

2.1 Participants

Thirty-six volunteers (eighteen female and eighteen male; mean age ± standard deviation (S.D.) = 22.5 ± 1.7) participated in this study. All of the subjects were right-handed and native-Chinese speakers. The subjects had no history of neurological or psychiatric illness, and no developmental disorders, including reading disablities. All of the participants gave their written informed consent, and the protocol was approved by the Ethical Committee of Xuanwu Hospital of Capital Medical University and the institutional Review Board of the Beijing University of Technology.

2.2 Stimuli

In the experiment, 60 high-familiarity statistical events taken from the Internet were used, with each described by a bar graph and a line graph to form 60 bar graphs (B_1-B_{60}) and 60 line graphs (L_1-L_{60}). Each statistical event was standardized and reorganized by verbal description, which includes the various items of the corresponding bar or line graphs to form 60 written texts (T_1-T_{60}). The same index of each task represents the same content of statistical information; e.g., B_i, L_i and T_i denote the i-statistics described by a bar graph, line graph, and text, respectively. In the current study, 40 bar graphs (B_1-B_{40}) and 40 line graphs (L_1-L_{40}) were selected for separate statistical graph tasks. The remaining 20 bar graphs, 20 line graphs, and 20 corresponding texts were combined into 20 bar graphs with text control tasks (BT_{41}-BT_{60}) and 20 line graphs with text control tasks (LT_{41}-LT_{60}). The 40 texts were selected as the control tasks (T_1-T_{40}).

To create statistical graphs with the same data complexity, we used statistical graphs with only 2 variables (only the x-axis and y-axis) and limited the number of objects in each statistical graph to 4-6. All the statistical graphs had the same size and brightness, same width for each bar in the bar graphs, same thickness for each line segment, and same size for each specifier (e.g., circle, square, and triangular) in the line graphs. The font and size of the labels in the statistical graphs were also set in balance.

2.3 Procedure

Each subject completed 60 tasks consisting of 20 SG tasks (10 bar graphs and 10 line graphs), 20 SGT tasks (10 bar graphs with text and 10 line graphs with text), and 20 ST tasks. The 40 subjects were divided into 4 groups, namely, G1, G2, G3, and G4; the stimuli were counterbalanced across subjects, no individual read the same event twice [11]. The distribution of the tasks is as follows: G1 = {B_1-B_{10}, L_{11}-L_{20}, BT_{41}-BT_{50}, LT_{51}-LT_{60}, T_{21}-T_{40}}, G2 = {B_{11}-B_{20}, L_1-L_{10}, BT_{41}-BT_{50}, LT_{51}-LT_{60}, T_{21}-T_{40}}, G3 = {B_{21}-B_{30}, L_{31}-L_{40}, BT_{51}-BT_{60}, LT_{41}-LT_{50}, T_1-T_{20}}, G4 = {B_{31}-B_{40}, L_{21}-L_{30}, BT_{51}-BT_{60}, LT_{41}-LT_{50}, T_1-T_{20}}.

These tasks were assigned into 3 sessions on average. The inter-session intervals between sessions were 120 s. The order of SG, SGT, and ST stimuli was pseudo-randomized in each session. Each SG, SGT, and ST stimulus was presented for a period of 14, 18, and 16 s, respectively. Presentation time was set according to the behavioral experiment prior to the fMRI study, in which participants could understand fully the statistical information. After a stimulus disappeared in each session, a question with two options was presented, and the subjects were required to press the selected buttons (i.e., the left button denotes the first option, and the right button denotes the second option). The time for the subjects to answer the question was limited to 8 s and that for the remaining tasks was limited to 6 s.

Prior to the experiment, the learning tasks of 2 SG tasks, 2 SGT tasks, and 2 ST tasks were prepared. To help the subjects fully understand their participation in the experiment, they were instructed to complete the practice tasks during the fMRI.

2.4   Image Acquisition

Blood oxygenation level-dependent fMRI signal data were collected from each participant using a Siemens 3-T Trio scanner (Trio system; Siemens Magnetom scanner, Erlangen, Germany). Functional data were acquired using a gradient-echo echo-planar pulse sequence (TR = 2000 ms, TE = 31 ms, FA = 90°,the matrix size = 64× 64 mm, Voxel = 4 × 4 × 4 mm, 30 slices, slice thickness = 4 mm, inter-slice interval = 0.8 mm, FOV = 240 × 240 mm). High-resolution T1-weighted anatomical images were collected in the same plane as the functional image using a spin echo sequence with the following parameters (TR = 130 ms, TE = 2.89 ms, FA = 70°, the matrix size = 320 × 320 mm, Voxel = 0.8 × 0.8 × 4 mm, 30 slices, slice thickness = 4 mm, inter-slice interval = 0.8 mm, FOV = 240 × 240 mm). Stimulus presentation and data synchronization were conducted using E-Prime 2.0 (Psychology Software Tools, Pittsburgh, USA). Prior to each run, the first two (10 s) discarded volumes were acquired to enable the stabilization of magnetization. The scanner was synchronized with the presentation of every trial in each run.

2.5   Data Analysis

Data were analyzed using SPM8 software (Welcome Department of Cognitive Neurology, London, UK, http://www.fil.ion.ucl.ac.uk). Images were collected to obtain the differences in the timing of slice acquisition, followed by rigid body motion correction. Data were realigned and normalized to the standard EPI template. The registration of the EPI data to the template was verified for each individual subject. All volumes were spatially realigned to the first volume. The fMRI data were then smoothed with an 8 mm FWHM isotropic Gaussian kernel. The hemodynamic response to the conclusion was modeled with the canonical hemodynamic response function used in SPM8. No scaling was implemented for the global effects. The resulting time series across each voxel was high-pass filtered with a cut-off of 128 s to remove section-specific low frequency drifts in the BOLD signal. An auto-regression AR (1) was used to exclude the variance explained by the pervious scan. The least squares parameter estimates of height of the best fitting synthetic HRF for each condition were used in pairwise contrasts and stored as a separate image for each subject. Using a random-effects model in the group analysis, these images were then tested against the null hypothesis that there is no difference between conditions using one-sided t-tests. To obtain an accurate comparison, a region was considered significant if it has 50 or more contiguous voxels (400 mm^3) and exceeds an alpha threshold of ($p <$ 0.05, corrected) and ($p <$ 0.001, uncorrected). The coordinates given by SPM8 were corrected to correspond to the atlas of Talairach and Tournoux (1988).

3   Results

As shown in Table 1 and Fig. 1(a), compared with the control tasks (ST), the SG tasks more significantly activated the ventral stream, including the lingual gyrus, fusiform gyrus, posterior parahippocampal gyrus, and middle temporal gyrus, as well as the dorsal stream, including the superior occipital gyrus, precuneus, and superior parietal lobule. In Table 1, the cluster size (mm^3) of activation in the ventral stream was greater than that in the dorsal stream. Based on the brain activation map [Fig. 1(a)], activity in the ventral stream was also stronger than that in the dorsal stream during statistical graph comprehension.

Table 1. Brain activations during SG compared with that during ST ($p < 0.05$, *corrected*)

Anatomical regions	Coordinates[a]			t	Cluster size (mm^3)
	x	y	z		
Ventral stream					26224
Lt. lingual gyrus (BA18)	-8	-74	2	12.01	1392
Rt. lingual gyrus (BA18)	8	-72	7	11.08	2112
Lt. fusiform gyrus (BA19)	-26	-68	-5	16.10	5896
Rt. fusiform gyrus (BA19)	26	-68	-5	12.12	2056
Lt. paraphippocampal cortex (BA37)	-32	-43	-8	20.10	9768
Rt. paraphippocampal cortex (BA19)	30	-55	-9	13.34	5000
Lt. middle temporal gyrus(BA19)	-40	-83	19	8.95	808
Rt. middle temporal gyrus(BA19)	42	-81	19	6.80	568
Dorsal stream				8456	
Lt. superior occipital gyrus (BA19)	-32	-82	24	9.55	2648
Rt. superior occipital gyrus (BA19)	34	-78	30	7.40	2072
Lt. precuneus (BA7)	-14	-68	44	7.74	2088
Rt. superior parietal lobule (BA7)	28	-66	46	6.98	1648

[a] The Talairach coordinates of the centroid and associated maximum t within contiguous regions are reported. SG: statistical graph; ST: text; BA, Brodmann area; Lt: left hemisphere; Rt: right hemisphere.

We also compared the SG with the SGT (SG vs. SGT). In Table 2 and Fig. Fig. 1(b), the results show that only the ventral stream, including the lingual gyrus, fusiform gyrus, and posterior parahippocampal gyrus, was activated more significantly, but there was no dorsal stream. The results indicate that the statistical graph comprehension is more dependent on the ventral stream than on the dorsal stream.

The ventral and dorsal streams are the two pathways for visual information processing. A large number of studies show that the ventral stream is related to the identification of the characteristics of objects (e.g., color, shape, and size),

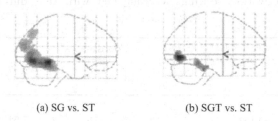

(a) SG vs. ST   (b) SGT vs. ST

Fig. 1. Whole-brain statistical activation maps directly comparing the tasks. (a) SG vs. ST: the contrast shows significant activation in the ventral and dorsal streams; (b) SG vs. SGT: the contrast shows that only the ventral stream is activated more significantly. SG: statistical graph; SGT: statistical graph with text; ST: text. All the Statistical Parametric Mapping t of the contrasts thresholded at (a) $p < 0.05$, corrected, Cluster size $\geq 400mm^3$; (b) $p < 0.001$, uncorrected, Cluster size $\geq 400mm^3$.

whereas the dorsal stream is used more in processing the spatial properties of objects [12–15]. The fusiform gyrus is involved in the shape analysis of both outline and fragmentation drawings [16], as well as object recognition. Activation in this region is increased gradually with a subjective rating of recognition [17]. The lingual gyrus is associated with spatial attention [18], in which the selective direction of visual attention is toward a location. Hopfinger et al. showed that the fusiform gyrus and lingual gyrus are significantly activated when target selection is compared with the clues [19]. These results suggest that the fusiform gyrus and lingual gyrus are related more to information selection and recognition in statistical graphs. Moreover, the parahippocampal gyrus responds to object-location associations [20, 21]. The dorsal stream, which consists of the precuneus, superior parietal lobule, and superior occipital gyrus, is involved in spatial processing [22]. Therefore, both ventral and dorsal streams are commonly involved in statistical graph comprehension, in which the extracting and recognition information (e.g., axis, label, bar, or line) engages the ventral stream in perception processing, and the integrating information engages the dorsal stream in space-related cognitive processing.

4   Discussion

Graph comprehension mainly includes three processes: encoding visual elements (e.g., identify a bar, line, or axis), translating the elements into patterns (e.g., noticing that one bar is higher than the other or the slope of a line), and mapping the patterns to the labels (e.g., determining the value of a bar graph) [23]. However, the study of Bertin did not indicate which step is involved in either perception operation or spatial processing. In future studies, the occurrence of spatial processing in statistical graph comprehension is still debatable in cognitive psychology.

Table 2. Brain activations during SG compared with that during SGT ($p <$ 0.001, *uncorrected*)

Anatomical regions	Coordinates[a]			t	Cluster size (mm^3)
	x	y	z		
Ventral stream					5272
Lt. lingual gyrus (BA18)	-6	-76	2	5.51	1416
Rt. lingual gyrus (BA18)	8	-74	6	4.60	832
Lt. fusiform gyrus (BA19)	-32	-41	-13	4.64	1248
Rt. fusiform gyrus (BA37)	38	-38	-18	4.34	616
Lt. paraphippocampal cortex (BA36)	-34	-32	-22	4.79	640
Rt. paraphippocampal cortex (BA36)	34	-28	-19	4.39	520

[a] The Talairach coordinates of the centroid and associated maximum t within contiguous regions are reported. SG: statistical graph; SGT: statistical graph + text; BA, Brodmann area; Lt: left hemisphere; Rt: right hemisphere.

The results of the comparison between the SG and ST tasks suggests that statistical graph comprehension requires the involvement of both ventral and dorsal streams, in which the ventral stream is related to perception operation, and the dorsal stream is associated with spatial processing. This result is consistent with that of the hierarchical framework model [5] and that of Trickett and Trafton's study [24],which demonstrates that spatial processing is involved in graph comprehension. In graph comprehension, the hierarchical framework model considers that the explicitly represented data are read off first before the information is integrated, which involves spatial processing. Trickett and Trafton [24] further demonstrated that spatial processing is involved in a range of graph tasks, regardless of the complexity of graphs.

Other studies also indicate that graph comprehension mainly depends on perceptual operation. For example, according to Pinker's model of graph comprehension [25], a reader first constructs a visual description of the display before forming conceptual messages or propositions about variables depicted in the graph. High-level inferential processes can operate conceptual messages. A similar research is that of Shah et al. [26], which proposes another model: perceptual processes are "bottom-up encoding mechanisms" that focus on the visual features of the display, whereas conceptual processes are equal to "top-down encoding processes" that influence interpretation.

All these theories imply that graph comprehension mainly depends on perceptual operation. However, in our study, the result in (SG vs. ST) suggests that statistical graph comprehension requires both perceptual processing and spatial processing, and the volume and response of activations in the ventral stream are higher than those in the dorsal stream. Moreover, the result in (SG vs. SGT) shows that the ventral stream is more activated, but there is no dorsal stream. Summing up these results indicates that statistical graph comprehension depends more on perceptual processing than on spatial processing. This finding is consistent with the description of a good statistical graph. The strength of good statistical graphs as a form of representation is that they can make implicit things explicit. Statistical graphs use location to group information about a single element, which may be "adjacent" to any number of other elements. When reading statistical graphs, the readers' working memory forms a series of visual chunks that support perceptual reasoning, making a direct comparison between visual chunks possible. In other words, in statistical graph comprehension, the perceptual operation comes first, followed by spatial processing.

Based on the experimental results, activation in the dorsal stream suggests that statistical graph comprehension requires the involvement of spatial processing; i.e., involving a certain degree of spatial analysis in graph comprehension is necessary. However, more activation in the ventral stream indicates that perceptual processing plays a dominant role in graph comprehension. Therefore, relative to the dorsal stream, the ventral stream is involved more in the process of graph comprehension.

Acknowledgements. This work is supported by the 973 Program (No. 2014CB744600), the International Science & Technology Cooperation Program of China (2013DFA32180), the National Natural Science Foundation of China (No. 61272345), the Beijing Natural Science Foundation(No. 4132023), the China Postdoctoral Science Foundation Funded Project (No. 2012M510298), Projected by Beijing Postdoctoral Research Foundation (No. 2012ZZ-04), Beijing Municipal Commission of Education and Beijing Key Laboratory of Magnetic Resonance Imaging and Brain Informatics, and Beijing lab of Intelligent Information Technology (IITLAB11201).

References

1. Kosslyn, S.M.: Understanding charts and graphs. Applied Cognitive Psychology 3, 185–226 (1989)
2. Carpenter, P.A., Shah, P.: A Model of the Perceptual and Conceptual Processes in Graph Comprehension. Journal of Experimental Psychology: Applied 4, 75–100 (1998)
3. Zacks, J., Tversky, B.: Bars and lines: A study of graphic communication. Memory and Cognition 27, 1073–1079 (1999)
4. Cleveland, W.S., Mcgill, R.: Graphical perception - theory, experimentation, and application to the development of graphical methods. J. Am. Stat. Assoc. 79, 531–554 (1984)
5. Ratwani, R.M., Trafton, J.G.: Making graphical inferences: a hierarchical framework. In: The 26th Annual Meeting of the Cognitive Science Society. Erlbaum and Associates, Chicago (2004)
6. Scaife, M., Rogers, Y.: External cognition: How do graphical representations work? Int. J. Hum-Comput. St. 45, 185–213 (1996)
7. Cheng, P.C., Lowe, R.K., Scaife, M.: Cognitive science approaches to understanding diagrammatic representations. Artif. Intell. Rev. 15, 79–94 (2001)

8. Lohse, G.L.: Eye Movement-Based Analyses of Graphs and Text: The Next Generation. In: Proceedings of the International Conference on Information Systems, 14th edn. ACM (1993)
9. Hegarty, M.: Mental animation: Inferring motion from static displays of mechanical systems. Journal of Experimental Psychology: Learning, Memory, and Cognition 18, 1084–1102 (1992)
10. Rayner, K., Rotelloa, C.M., Stewartb, A.J., Keira, J., Duffy, S.A.: Integrating Text and Pictorial Information: Eye Movements When Looking at Print Advertisements. Journal of Experimental Psychology: Applied 7, 219–226 (2001)
11. St George, M., Kutas, M., Martinez, A., Sereno, M.I.: Semantic integration in reading: engagement of the right hemisphere during discourse processing. Brain 122, 1317–1325 (1999)
12. Mishkin, M., Ungerleider, L.G., Macko, K.A.: Object vision and spatial vision - 2 cortical pathways. Trends Neurosci. 6, 414–417 (1983)
13. Haxby, J.V., Grady, C.L., Horwitz, B., Ungerleider, L.G., Mishkin, M., Carson, R.E., et al.: Dissociation of object and spatial visual processing pathways in human extrastriate cortex. PNAS 88, 1621–1625 (1991)
14. Shmuelof, L., Zohary, E.: Dissociation between ventral and dorsal fMRl activation during object and action recognition. Neuron 47, 457–470 (2005)
15. Valyear, K.F., Culham, J.C., Sharif, N., Westwood, D., Goodale, M.A.: A double dissociation between sensitivity to changes in object identity and object orientation in the ventral and dorsal visual streams: A human fMRI study. Neuropsychologia 44, 218–228 (2006)
16. Gerlach, C., Law, I., Paulson, O.B.: Shape configuration and category-specificity. Neuropsychologia 44, 1247–1260 (2006)
17. Bar, M., Tootell, R., Schacter, D.L., Greve, D.N., Fischl, B., Mendola, J.D., et al.: Cortical mechanisms specific to explicit visual object recognition. Neuron 29, 529–535 (2001)
18. Martinez, A., Anllo-Vento, L., Sereno, M.I., Frank, L.R., Buxton, R.B., Dubowitz, D.J., et al.: Involvement of striate and extrastriate visual cortical areas in spatial attention. Nature Neuroscience 2, 364–369 (1999)
19. Hopfinger, J.B., Buonocore, M.H., Mangun, G.R.: The neural mechanisms of top-down attentional control. Nature Neuroscience 3, 284–291 (2000)
20. Johnsrude, I.S., Owen, A.M., Crane, J., Milner, B., Evans, A.C.: A cognitive activation study of memory for spatial relationships. Neuropsychologia 37, 829–841 (1999)
21. Sommer, T., Rose, M., Weiller, C., Buchel, C.: Contributions of occipital, parietal and parahippocampal cortex to encoding of object-location associations. Neuropsychologia 43, 732–743 (2005)
22. Margulies, D.S., Vincent, J.L., Kelly, C., Lohmann, G., Uddin, L.Q., Biswal, B.B., et al.: Precuneus shares intrinsic functional architecture in humans and monkeys. PNAS 106, 20069–20074 (2009)
23. Bertin, J.: Semiology of graphs. University of Wisconsin Press, Madison (1983)
24. Trickett, S.B., Trafton, J.G.: Toward a comprehensive model of graph comprehension: Making the case for spatial cognition. In: Barker-Plummer, D., Cox, R., Swoboda, N. (eds.) Diagrams 2006. LNCS (LNAI), vol. 4045, pp. 286–300. Springer, Heidelberg (2006)
25. Pinker, S.: A Theory of Graph Comprehension. In: Freedle, R. (ed.) Artificial Intelligence and the Future of Testing, pp. 73–126. Lawrence Erlbaum Associates Ltd., Hillsdale (1990)
26. Shah, P., Freedman, E.G., Vekiri, I.: The Comprehension of Quantitative Information in Graphical Displays. Cambridge University Press, New York (2005)

Computational Neuro-Modeling of Visual Memory: Multimodal Imaging and Analysis

Mohammed Elanbari[1], Nawel Nemmour[2], Othmane Bouhali[1,3], Reda Rawi[1], Ali Sheharyar[3], and Halima Bensmail[1,*]

[1] Qatar Computing Research Institute,
Qatar Foundation, Qatar
{hbensmail,melanbari,rrawi}@qf.org.qa
[2] University of Surrey, UK
nn00070@surrey.ac.uk
[3] Texas A&M University, Qatar
{othmane.bouhali,ali.sheharyar}@qatar.tamu.edu
http://www.qcri.com

Abstract. The high dimensionality of functional magnetic resonance imaging (fMRI) data presents major challenges to fMRI pattern classification. Directly applying standard classifiers often results in overfitting or singularity, which limits the generalizability of the results. In this paper, we propose a "Doubly Regularized LOgistic Regression Algorithm" (DR LORA) which penalizes the voxels of the brain that are of no importance for the classification using the Alternating Direction Method of Multipliers (ADMM) and therefore alleviate this overfitting problem. Our algorithm was compared to other classification based algorithms such as Naive Bayes, Random forest and support vector machine. The results show clear performances for our algorithm.

Keywords: fMRI, Logistic Regression, Alternating Direction Method of Multipliers, LASSO, Classification.

1 Introduction

When people are looking at a magazine or browsing the Internet, they are attracted by some photographs and images. Often, one is interested to check what makes a generic photograph or image memorable? Brady et al. [1] showed that humans are extremely adept at remembering thousands of pictures and a surprising amount of their visual details. But whereas some images stick in our minds, others are ignored or quickly forgotten. Artists, advertisers and photographers are routinely challenged by the questions: what makes a picture memorable? Memorability qualifies something about the utility of a photograph toward our everyday lives for example: educational materials, logos, advertisement, book covers, websites etc. The quality of what makes an image memorable is hard to quantify, yet our preliminary result suggests that using fMRI and exposing

---

* Corresponding author.

D. Ślęzak et al. (Eds.): BIH 2014, LNAI 8609, pp. 21–32, 2014.
© Springer International Publishing Switzerland 2014

Fig. 1. What makes a picture memorable? Left panel: High memorable, right panel: low memorable. Courtesy of Aude's MIT group.

healthy individuals to structured images (scene versus faces) it is not an inexplicable phenomenon, and confirms that areas of the brain are activated for certain images [2]. People have the remarkable ability to remember thousands of pictures they saw only once [3] even when they were exposed to many other images that look alike. It seems that we do not just remember some pictures, but we are able to recognize which precise image we saw along with some of its details [4]. However, we can remember some images and forget others. In other words, some pictures stick in our minds whereas others are forgotten. The reasons why images are remembered may be highly varied; some pictures might contain friends, a fun event involving family members, or a particular moment during a trip. Other images might not contain any recognizable monuments or people and yet also be highly memorable [5].

Isola et al. [6] characterized an image memorability as the probability that an observer will detect a repetition of a photograph at various delays after exposition, when presented amidst a stream of images. This setting allowed to measure long-term memory performance for a large collection of images (see Fig.1 and Fig.2). With this approach they introduced a database for which they have measured the probability that each picture will be recognized after a single view. The database was mined to identify which features of the images correlate with memorability, and trained memorability predictors on these features. Their work constitutes an initial benchmark for quantifying image memorability. On the other hand, imagine waking up and not recognizing your own bedroom or your own house, being so lost as to be detached from space and time, and not knowing what to do next. This is the experience of millions of individuals with Alzheimer's disease who have effectively lost connection to their memories of space, are unable to retrieve past events and predict future ones. Any advances in basic understanding of the spatio-visual memory system will help focus the quest for therapies for Alzheimers disease, one of the most devastating brain

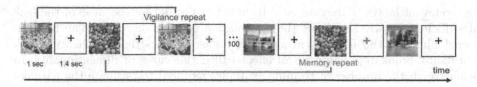

Fig. 2. Mechanical Turk workers played a Memory Game in which they watched for repeats in a long stream of images

diseases of the aging population. The challenge of mapping the brain systems involved in visual memory also motivates the development of methods that integrate spatial information from functional magnetic resonance imaging (fMRI) with the temporal dynamics provided by magnetoencephalography (MEG) and electroencephalography (EEG) into a single model of the brain organization and activity. Therefore, the application of pattern classification techniques for analyzing brain activity has increased and attracted machine learning community in recent years.

Pattern classification methods focus the activity distribution of the entire brain to discriminate different cognitive states or stimuli. The power of this brain classification approach is motivated from the idea that all voxels, including the ones with weak individual responses may carry important information when analyzed jointly. However, the high dimensionality of fMRI data and the interpretability of the classification weights remain as major challenges to this class of approaches. The fMRI signal intensity (or its average) at each voxel is usually taken as a feature (variable), with each brain volume (or each time) treated as a sample (observation). Since typical fMRI datasets consist of considerably more voxels (thousands) than brain volumes (hundreds) and subjects (tens), direct application of standard classifiers, such as Linear Discriminant Analysis (LDA), Quadratic discriminant Analysis (QDA), Regularized Discriminant Analysis (RDA) and Support Vector Machine (SVM) where all the voxels are used as variables, will likely result in overfitting and singularity. To reduce the dimensionality of the variables, a common strategy is to reduce the feature set to those voxels displaying significant expression or discriminant power. For example, principal component analysis (PCA) can be applied prior to classification, however, neither of these strategies considers the collective discriminant information encoded by the voxel patterns, and thus may result in suboptimal feature selection.

2 Method

The performance of a classifier depends significantly on the number of available examples, number of features and complexity of the classifier. A typical fMRI dataset contains far more features than the examples. In our dataset number of features are on the order of tens of thousands while the number of training examples are on the order of hundreds. Furthermore, many of the features may be irrelevant however they are still included in the dataset because of the lack of sufficient knowledge about the information content of voxels. The high dimensionality of the features in an fMRI dataset makes the classification task a difficult problem because of an effect called the curse of dimensionality. In other words the number of training examples required to estimate the parameters of a function grows exponentially with the number of features. The number of parameters of the classifier increases as the number of features increases. As a result, the accuracy and precision of the estimated parameters decrease, which usually leads to poor classification performance. Given n $p-$dimensional feature vectors, $\mathbf{x}_i$, forming the columns of a predictor matrix, $\mathbf{x}$, our goal is to find the corresponding $n \times 1$ response vector, $\mathbf{Y}$, containing the class label of $\mathbf{x}_i$. In the context of fMRI, the feature vector usually comprises either signal intensities or summary statistics of p image voxels, and the n samples are either the brain volumes or the subjects drawn from different populations. The problem of fMRI classification can thus be posed as that of subspace learning for finding a mapping that well separates feature vectors of different classes. Classification algorithms integrating network structure information have been demonstrated to improve variable selection accuracy to analyze functional magnetic resonance imaging [7] and microarray data [8,9].

In this paper, we propose a "Doubly Regularized LOgistic Algorithm" (DR LORA) that permits more general penalties, such as spatial smoothness in addition to sparsity, to be integrated. DR LORA constructs upon the realization that numerous standard classifiers can be reformulated and trained under a regression framework which enables direct deployment of standard regularization techniques, such as least absolute shrinkage and selection operator (LASSO) and elastic net [10]. Building on this regression framework, we employ two penalties, the first generates a sparse model which reduce the number of voxels, while the second (a quadratic part of the penalty) encourages grouping effect and stabilizes the regularization path, thus captures explicitly spatial correlations in brain activity.

2.1   DR LORA: Doubly Regularized Logistic Regression Algorithm

For $i = 1, ..., n$, let $\mathbf{y}_i$ and $\mathbf{x}_i = (x_{i1}, ..., x_{ip})^t$ be the response variable and a p-dimensional vector of features (or covariates or predictors) respectively. Consider the case of logistic regression where $\mathbf{y}_i | \mathbf{x}_i = x \sim \text{Bernoulli}(\pi(x))$, i.e., $\text{Binomial}(1, \pi(x))$, with

$$\log \left(\frac{\pi(x)}{1 - \pi(x)} \right) = \alpha + \sum_{j=1}^{p} \beta_j x_{ij}. \tag{1}$$

This is a generalized linear model with link function $g(\pi) = \log(\frac{\pi}{1-\pi})$ [17].

Estimation of the vector parameters $(\alpha, \beta_1, ..., \beta_p)$ is usually performed by maximizing the log-likelihood of the model, which is equivalent to minimizing the quantity

$$(\hat{\alpha}, \hat{\beta}) = \arg\min_{\alpha,\beta} \sum_{i=1}^{n} \left[\log(1 + \exp(\alpha + \mathbf{x}_i^t \beta)) - y_i(\alpha + \mathbf{x}_i^t \beta) \right]. \tag{2}$$

During the last decade, penalized methods have emerged as attractive approaches for high-dimensional regression problems. Many types of penalties have been proposed; most relevant are the Lasso, Ridge, Elastic-net, Smooth Lasso and Weighted fusion penalty. These penalties all introduce stability into high-dimensional models by penalizing large values of regression coefficients. They conduct variable selection as well, by shrinking some of the coefficients all the way to zero. Taking all these remarks into account, we propose to estimate the vector parameters by the penalized criterion

$$(\hat{\alpha}, \hat{\beta}) = \arg\min_{\alpha,\beta} \sum_{i=1}^{n} \left[\log(1 + \exp(\alpha + \mathbf{x}_i^t \beta)) - y_i(\alpha + \mathbf{x}_i^t \beta) \right]$$

$$+ \lambda_1 \sum_{j=1}^{p} |\beta_j| + \lambda_2 P_c(\beta), \tag{3}$$

where $\lambda_1 \geq 0$, $\lambda_2 \geq 0$ are tuning parameters, and

$$P_c(\beta) = \sum_{j=1}^{p-1} \sum_{i>j} \left\{ \frac{(\beta_i - \beta_j)^2}{1 - \rho_{ij}} + \frac{(\beta_i + \beta_j)^2}{1 + \rho_{ij}} \right\}, \tag{4}$$

ρ_{ij} denotes the (empirical) correlation between the ith and the jth predictors. The l_1 part of the penalty generates a sparse model, while the quadratic part of the penalty encourages grouping effect and stabilizes the l_1 regularization path.

It is also interesting to note that the penalty $P_c(\beta)$ can be written in a simple quadratic form

$$P_c(\beta) = \beta^t \mathbf{Q} \beta, \tag{5}$$

where $\mathbf{Q} = (q_{ij})_{1 \leq i,j \leq p}$ is a positive definite matrix with general term

$$q_{ij} = \begin{cases} 2 \sum_{s \neq i} \frac{1}{1-\rho_{is}^2} & \text{if } i = j \\ -2 \frac{\rho_{ij}}{1-\rho_{ij}^2} & \text{if } i \neq j. \end{cases} \tag{6}$$

As stated earlier, the advantage of our algorithm are: (1) Combine the strengths of all kind of LASSO-type models with a quadratic penalty designed to capture additional structure on the features (voxels) in high dimensional setting. (2) Develop an easy and fast algorithm using the "Alternating Direction Method of Multipliers" approach to find optimal estimator. Alternating Direction Method of Multipliers (ADMM) optimization is suited for distributed convex optimization and distributed computing for big data. In the following, we emphasize on the advantage of using ADMM on a general lasso-type model with a general penalty term and we will show that this approach is powerful as it provides fast and optimal solution. The problem formulation and its corresponding ADMM algorithm are considered in the following section.

2.2 Alternating Direction Method of Multipliers

Recently, the alternating direction method of multipliers (ADMM) has been revisited and successfully applied to solving large scale problems arising from different applications. In this section we give an overview of ADMM and its application to solve our problem.

Consider the following optimization problem:

$$\text{minimize } f(\beta) + g(\xi)$$
$$\text{subject to } \beta - \xi = 0, \tag{7}$$

where f and g are two convex functions and $\beta, \xi \in \mathbb{R}^p$. In this optimization problem, we have two sets of variables, with separable objective. The augmented Lagrangian for this problem is:

$$L_\tau(\beta, \xi, \delta) = f(\beta) + g(\xi) + \delta^t(\beta - \xi) + (\tau/2)\|\beta - \xi\|_2^2,$$

where δ is the dual variable for the constraint $\beta - \xi = 0$ and $\tau > 0$ is a penalty parameter.

The augmented Lagrangian methods were developed in part to bring robustness to the *dual ascent method*, and in particular, to yield convergence without strong assumptions like strict convexity or finiteness of f and g.

At iteration k, the ADMM algorithm consists of the three steps:

$$\beta^{k+1} := \arg\min_\beta L_\tau(\beta, \xi^k, \delta^k) \tag{8}$$

$$\xi^{k+1} := \arg\min_\xi L_\tau(\beta^{k+1}, \xi, \delta^k) \tag{9}$$

$$\delta^{k+1} := \delta^k + \tau(\beta^{k+1} - \xi^{k+1}). \tag{10}$$

In the first step of the ADMM algorithm, we fix ξ and δ and minimize the augmented Lagrangian over β. In the second step, we fix β and δ and minimize the augmented Lagrangian over ξ finally, we update the dual variable δ. Consider now the generic problem

$$\text{minimize } l(\beta) + \mu\beta^t \mathbf{Q}\beta + \lambda\|\beta\|_1, \tag{11}$$

where l is any convex loss function. In an ADMM form, this problem can be written as

$$\text{minimize } \tilde{l}(\beta) + g(\xi)$$
$$\text{subject to } \beta - \xi = 0, \tag{12}$$

where $\tilde{l}(\beta) = l(\beta) + \mu\beta^t \mathbf{Q}\beta$ and $g(\xi) = \lambda\|\xi\|_1$. The ADMM algorithm can be expressed on its scaled dual form as:

$$\beta^{k+1} := \arg\min_\beta \left\{ \tilde{l}(\beta) + (\tau/2)\|\beta - \xi^k + \eta^k\|_2^2 \right\}; \tag{13}$$

$$\xi^{k+1} := \arg\min_\xi \left\{ g(\xi) + (\tau/2)\|\beta^{k+1} - \xi + \eta^k\|_2^2 \right\}; \tag{14}$$

$$\eta^{k+1} := \eta^k + \beta^{k+1} - \xi^{k+1}. \tag{15}$$

The β-update is proximal operator evaluation. Since $\tilde{l}$ is smooth, this can be done using Newton-Raphson method. The ξ-update has a closed form solution given by

$$\xi^{k+1} := S_{\frac{\lambda}{\tau}}\left(\beta^{k+1} + \eta^k\right),$$

where

$$S_\kappa(a) = (1 - \kappa/|a|)_+ a = \begin{cases} a - \kappa \text{ if } a > \kappa \\ 0 \text{ if } |a| \leq \kappa \\ a + \kappa \text{ if } a < -\kappa \end{cases}$$

is the soft thresholding function introduced and analyzed by [11].

Stopping criteria
The primal and dual residuals at iteration k have the forms:

$$e_{pri}^k = (\beta^k - \xi^k), \quad e_{dual}^k = -\tau(\eta^k - \eta^{k-1}).$$

The ADMM algorithm terminates when the primal and dual residuals satisfy stopping criterion. A typical stopping criterion is when $\|e_{pri}^k\| \leq \epsilon^{pri}$, $\|e_{dual}^k\| \leq \epsilon^{dual}$. The tolerances $\epsilon^{pri} > 0$ and $\epsilon^{dual} > 0$ can be chosen using an absolute and relative criterion, such as $\epsilon^{pri} = \sqrt{p}\epsilon^{abs} + \epsilon^{rel} \max\{\|\beta^k\|_2, \|\eta^k\|_2\}$; and $\epsilon^{dual} = \sqrt{p}\epsilon^{abs} + \epsilon^{rel}\tau\|\eta^k\|_2$, where $\epsilon^{abs} > 0$ and $\epsilon^{rel} > 0$ are absolute and relative tolerances. A reasonable value for the relative stopping criterion is $\epsilon^{rel} = 10^{-3}$ or 10^{-4}, while ϵ^{abs} depends on the scale of the typical variable.

2.3 Grouping Effect

The following Lemma tells us that the proposed method enjoys the *grouping effect* property, which means that strongly correlated predictors tend to be in or out of the model together.

Lemma. Given data $(\mathbf{y}, \mathbf{x})$, where $\mathbf{x} = (\mathbf{x}_1, ..., \mathbf{x}_p)$ and tuning parameters (λ_1, λ_2), the response is centered and the predictors are standardized. Let $\hat{\beta}(\lambda_1, \lambda_2) = \hat{\beta}$ be the DR LORA estimate. If $\hat{\beta}_i\hat{\beta}_j > 0$ and $\rho_{kl} = \rho$, for all (k, l), then

$$\frac{1}{\|\mathbf{y}\|_2}\left|\hat{\beta}_j - \hat{\beta}_i\right| \leq \frac{1 - \rho^2}{2(p + \rho - 1)\lambda_2}\sqrt{2(1 - \rho)}.$$

$$(16)$$

Comment. When we have highly correlated voxels ($\rho_{ij} \to 1$) then the right hand side of (16) $\to 0$. This forces $\hat{\beta}_j \approx \hat{\beta}_i$ which shows that the proposed approach has the property of *grouping effect*.

3   Experiments

fMRI Data from seven healthy subjects were kindly made available by one of the authors of [2], Dr. Aude Oliva (an MIT's Computer Science and Artificial Intelligence Lab researcher). Data were used for validation of our proposed algorithm. Using Amazons Mechanical Turk, sequence of images were presented (2222 images) and memorability scores were collected (memorable and forgettable), as explained in [2]. Images and scenes were then categorized into four distinct conditions: LowFace, HighFace, LowScene and HighScene (see Fig.3). Out of a total of 2222, One hundred sixty fMRI images/scenes were presented in a block design grouped by stimulus type (16 seconds of high memorable faces (20 faces), 10 seconds rest (fixation), 16 seconds of low memorable scenes (20 scenes), 10 seconds rest (fixation), 16 seconds of low memorable scenes (20 faces), 10 seconds rest (fixation), etc). The fMRI protocol will allow us to use multivariate pattern analyses to see if/which brain regions are encoding memorability of an image, after a first exposure. The idea is to look at both cortical regions (that encode the type of visual stimuli) and subcortical medial temporal regions, that are associated with memory. Because memorability allows to predict later memory at the first exposure of the image, and predict which types of images or faces will be remembered or forgotten, it is an open question where and how memorability is represented in the brain. Memorability is a new tool that could be used for detecting memory deficits, either in short term memory, or in long term memory. Eight sessions were created for each participant referring to the eight runs (7-14), with 39 slices and repetition time: TR=2.5 seconds, and a TA (TA = TR (TR/N),)= 2.5 -

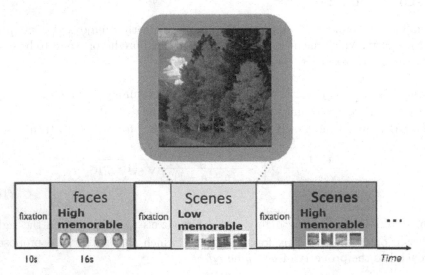

Fig. 3. During functional scanning, participants performed target detection on novel and repeated stimuli from 4 classes: high memorability faces, low memorability faces, high memorability scenes, low memorability scenes

(2.5 / 39) = 0.0641). Before looking for brain regions in which the experimental manipulation had an effect, we needed to preprocess data (realigning, filtering, spatial normalization etc.) and specify parameters involved such as a) timing parameters, b) data and design, c) subject and session to be able to do the inference. Data were preprocessed using SPM8 (Wellcome Department of Imaging Neuroscience, London, UK) [12] and custom Matlab routines. An artifact repair algorithm (http://cibsr.stanford.edu/tools/ArtRepair/ArtRepair.htm [date last accessed; 28 August 2007]) was first implemented to detect and remove noise from individual functional volumes using linear interpolation of the immediately preceding and following volumes in the time series. Functional images were then corrected to account for the differences in slice acquisition times by interpolating the voxel time series using sinc interpolation and resampling the time series using the center slice as a reference point. Functional volumes were then realigned to the first volume in the time series to correct for motion. A mean T_2^*-weighted volume was computed during realignment, and the T_2-weighted anatomical volume was coregistered to this mean functional volume. Functional volumes were high pass filtered to remove low frequency drift before being converted to percentage signal change in preparation for univariate statistical analyses or z-scored in preparation for our analysis. Figure 4 shows two 3D images of the statistical parametric mapping for group analysis between all subjects. It calculates the effect of image stimulus on brain after testing hypotheses about regionally specific effects in our data. Colored regions are activated brain regions due to the High-Scene stimulus. This is achieved by estimating the beta's in the model and testing the significance of each beta. The colored regions of the brain are related to a significant beta of a specific voxel.

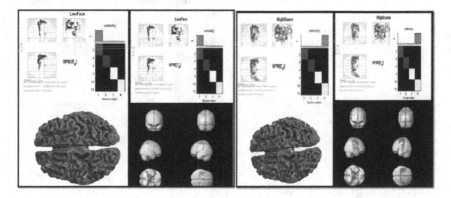

Fig. 4. Two 3D images of the statistical parametric mapping for group analysis between all subjects. Left panel: LowFace condition. Right panel: HighScene condition.

3.1   Evaluation of Classification Performance

The performance of DR LORA classifier on the memorability datasets in selecting relevant features was assessed by computing the sensitivity, false positive rate, accuracy in feature selection and the 10-fold cross-validation accuracy. To check the performance, we compared the algorithm to popular robust algorithms such as support vector classifier (SVC), Random Forest classifier (RFC), K-nearest neighborhood classifier (K-NNC) and Naive bayesian classifier NBC). We randomly split the data into a training set representing 75% of the data and the 25% remaining is considered as a test data designed to measure the performance of the different methods.

The performance metrics such as precision, recall and accuracy were computed as in Table 1. Let Y and $\hat{Y}$ be random variables representing the class and the prediction for a randomly drawn sample, respectively. We denote by $+1$ and -1 the Face and Scene class, respectively. Further, we use the following abbreviations for empirical quantities: P (# positive samples), N (# negative samples), TP (# true positives), TN (# true negatives), FP (# false positives), FN (# false negatives). We compare different classification methods using the

Table 1. Measures of performance

Measure of performance	Estimated by	SVC	RFC	K-NNC	NBC	DR LORA
$Accu$(Prediction)	TP/Total	0.9375	1.00	0.3750	0.4375	1.00
$prec$(Precision)	TP/(TP+FP)	1.00	1.00	0.67	0.67	1.00
rec(Recall)	TP/P	0.91	1.00	0.31	0.36	1.00

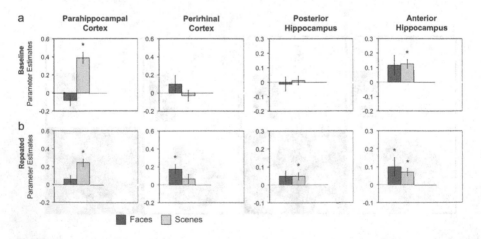

Fig. 5. Response to memorability content in anatomically defined MTL ROIs (PHc, PRc, posterior hippocampus, and anterior hippocampus). (a) Parameter estimates representing activation during content blocks relative to baseline. (b) Representing activation during content blocks relative to repeated event. Error bars represent standard error of the mean. Asterisks indicate significant differences from baseline ($P < 0.05$).

mentioned measures of performance. We can see from Table 1 that the best performances are given by the DR LORA, Random forest and support vector machines; the worst performances are given by k-nearest neighbors and naive Bayes classifier. In terms of model complexity, we note that DR LORA achieves its best performance using a subset of 22961 voxels (30% reduction of voxels) while the other competitors use the entire set of voxels which makes the interpretation very difficult.

When encoding runs were contrasted based on subsequent memory performance (high memorable > low memorable) for both faces and scenes, differential activation was observed in defined MTL ROIs (parahippocampal cortex, perirhinal cortex, posterior hippocampus, and anterior hippocampus), see Figure 5.

4 Conclusion

In this paper, we tried to answer to the question: why some images are consistently forgotten, while others are consistently remembered. For this end, we have adapted the *ADMM* algorithm for a doubly regularized logistic regression models. It has been demonstrated through the analysis of fMRI data set, that the proposed algorithm gives good performances in both prediction and feature selection viewpoints.

Acknowledgments. This work was supported by the qatar foundation QCRI FTRP13 award (Fast-Track Research Project). We thank our colleagues from MIT-CSAIL lab in particular Aude Oliva for sharing memorability data with us, Polina Golland for her insightful help and discussions, Ramesh Sridharan, Wilma Bainbridge, Radoslaw Cichy for their help.

References

1. Brady, T.F., Konkle, T., Alvarez, G.A., Oliva, A.: Visual long-term memory has a massive storage capacity for object details. Proc. Natl. Acad. Sci. (2008)
2. Isola, P., Parikh, D., Torralba, A., Oliva, A.: Understanding the intrinsic memorability of images. In: Advances in Neural Information Processing Systems (NIPS) (2011)
3. Standing, L.: Learning 10,000 pictures. Quarterly Journal of Experimental Psychology (1973)
4. Brady, T., Konkle, T., Alvarez, G., Oliva, A.: Are real-world objects represented as bound units? Independent forgetting of different object details from visual memory. Journal of Experimental Psychology: General (2012)
5. Konkle, T., Brady, T.F., Alvarez, G.A., Oliva, A.: Conceptual distinctiveness supports detailed visual long-term memory for real-world objects. JEP:G (2010)
6. Isola, P., Xiao, J., Parikh, D., Torralba, A., Oliva, A.: What makes a photograph memorable? IEEE Transactions on Pattern Analysis and Machine Intelligence (2014)

7. Grosenick, L., Klingenberg, B., Katovich, K., Knutson, B., Taylor, J.: Interpretable whole-brain prediction analysis with GraphNet. NeuroImage 72, 304–321 (2013)
8. Kim, S., Xing, E.: Statistical estimation of correlated genome associations to a quantitative trait network. PLoS Genetics 5(8), e1000587 (2009)
9. Tian, Z., Zhang, H., Kuang, R.: Sparse Group Selection on Fused Lasso Components for Identifying Group-Specific DNA Copy Number Variations. In: ICDM 2012, pp. 665–674 (2012)
10. Zou, H., Hastie, T.: Regularization and Variable Selection via the Elastic Net. J. Royal Stat. Soc. B67, 301–320 (2005)
11. Donoho, D., Johnstone, I.: Ideal Spatial Adaptation by Wavelet Shrinkage. Biometrika 81(3), 425–455 (1994)
12. Guillaume: SPM. Statistical Parametric Mapping, www.fil.ion.ucl.ac.uk/spm/ (retrieved July 18, 2013)
13. Isola, P., Xiao, J., Torralba, A., Oliva, A.: What makes an image memorable? In: IEEE Conference on Computer Vision and Pattern Recognition (CVPR) (2011)
14. Isola, P., Xiao, J., Parikh, D., Torralba, A., Oliva, A.: What makes a photograph memorable? IEEE Pattern Analysis and Machine Intelligence, PAMI (2014)
15. Bainbridge, W.A., Isola, P., Oliva, A.: The Intrinsic Memorability of Face Images. Journal of Experimental Psychology (in press)
16. Pedregosa, F., Varoquaux, G., Gramfort, A., Michel, V., Thirion, B., Grisel, O., Blondel, M., Prettenhofer, P., Weiss, R., Dubourg, V., Vanderplas, J., Passos, A., Cournapeau, D., Brucher, M., Perrot, M., Duchesnay, E.: Scikit-learn: Machine Learning in Python. In: JMLR 12, pp. 2825–2830 (2011)
17. McCullagh, Nelder: 198

When Are Two Visual Cognition Systems Better Than One?

Darius A. Mulia, Alfonso Vergara, Charles R. Skelsey,
Lihan Yao, and D. Frank Hsu

Laboratory of Informatics and Data Mining,
Department of Computer and Information Science,
Fordham University, New York, NY 10023
{dmulia, avergara, cskelsey, lyao1}@fordham.edu,
hsu@cis.fordham.edu

Abstract. Visual decision-making involving pairs of individuals tasked with determining the location of an object is a cognitive process combining independent systems together. Although it has been observed that combined systems can improve each of the individual systems, it remains a challenging problem to determine why and how this will occur. In this paper, we use Combinatorial Fusion Analysis (CFA) as a methodology through which we can effectively combine the decisions of two independent visual cognition systems. An experiment with 20 trials is performed in which participants are tasked with determining an object location, and stating the uncertainty factor for their decision. Our results demonstrate that the combination of two visual cognition systems using CFA can match or improve the performance of each individual system only if the pair of systems perform relatively well and are cognitively diverse.

Keywords: Combinatorial Fusion Analysis (CFA), Rank-Score Characteristic (RSC) Function, Cognitive Diversity, Visual Cognition System.

1 Introduction

The cognitive process of perceptual decision-making – the act of making a definitive judgment – involves the use of sensory systems (particularly visual cognition systems) and has been of great interest to many fields of science. When individuals make a cognitive judgment or decision based on visual sensory input, he/she is considered to be an independent visual cognition system. The use of combinations of independent visual cognition systems in making a joint decision has been an area of recent work [6–8],[15],[20]. The results of this research show that effective combinations of multiple visual cognition systems can be constructed to reach a more accurate joint decision than independent decisions alone.

Contemporary decision-making research focuses on human cognition systems and its use and interpretation of visually retrieved information [1],[5],[14],[18], with wide-reaching applications in areas such as virtual screening, image analysis, task allocation, etc. The work of Bahrami et al. [1] explores joint perceptual

D. Ślęzak et al. (Eds.): BIH 2014, LNAI 8609, pp. 33–44, 2014.

decision-making using multiple scoring systems, seeking a methodology to effectively combine two human visual cognition systems. Given a pair of participants tasked with reaching a joint image identification decision, Bahrami et al. [1] proposes Weighted Confidence Sharing (WCS) as a predictive method (compared to other decision-making methods) that best fit empirical data. The findings of this study show that joint decision accuracy, as well as pair performance, can be improved through communication between individuals. Ernst et al. [7] expanded Bahramis' study into a hypothetical example of two referees viewing a goal line, sharing information as to whether or not the ball crossed the line. Ernsts study also validates the effectiveness of WCS, since other predictive methods tend to omit information that leads to an optimal joint decision.

In contrast to Bahrami and Ernsts studies, Koriat [15] assumes no communication between participants when seeking an optimal joint decision. He showed that choosing the more confident participant in a pair, assuming conditions that prohibited information exchange between individuals, could outperform either participants individual performance. Other work has been done on the neural basis of decision making [9],[25] and combining sensory informatics [10].

Each of Batallones et al. [2, 3], McMunn-Coffran et al. [20, 21], and Paolercio et al. [23] expands upon the works of Bahrami and Ernst by further optimizing joint visual cognition decisions. In this paper, Ernsts hypothetical soccer ball experiment is implemented, with each of the 20 trials consisting of a pair of participants determining the location of an object thrown into a plane from a considerable distance. Each participant is separately asked to determine the objects landing position, and the uncertainty factor of their decision (recorded as a variably-sized radius about each participants respective decision location). Here, each participant acts as a visual cognition system, where their responses are collected as points on a two-dimensional Cartesian plane. These cognition systems are then analyzed using Combinatorial Fusion Analysis (CFA).

CFA is an emerging information fusion paradigm defined and studied by Hsu et al. [11–13]. It has been used successfully in several domain applications including sensor fusion selection and combination [4], information retrieval [11],[22], protein structure prediction [16], image recognition [17], target tracking [19], genomics sequencing [24], and virtual screening [25]. CFA entails a set of multiple scoring systems $A_1, A_2, \ldots, A_p$, such that each scoring system consists of a score function s_A. The rank function r_A is obtained by sorting the score function s_A. A rank-score characteristic (RSC) function, f_A, is obtained by composition of s_A with the inverse function of r_A, $s_A \circ r_A^{-1} = f_A$. In this paper, the Cognitive Diversity between two scoring systems A and B, $d(A, B)$, is measured by the area between f_A and f_B, $d(f_A, f_B)$.

Section 2 describes the approach to combining visual cognition systems. It also covers methods of combination including statistical means and the construction of scoring systems. Score and rank combinations are offered and criteria for positive vs. negative results are defined. Section 3 covers the results of the experiments, and Section 4 concludes the paper with a summary and discussion of further work.

2   Combinations of Two Visual Cognition Systems

2.1   Using Statistical Means

Pairs of participants (dyads) who base cognitive decisions on visual data are represented as two individual scoring systems P,Q. In each trial, the independent decisions of participants P, Q are each recorded as d_P, d_Q. These values represent the participant's decisions regarding the location they determine the object A to have landed. The uncertainty factors of their decisions, σ_P, σ_Q, are also recorded, where $\sigma = 0.5r$. Here, r is the radius (in inches) of a variably-sized circle centered about each participant's guess location.

As detailed by Bahrami et al. [1], meaningful predictions on the dataset can be generated by combining independent scoring systems using WCS. To numerically express the dyads' joint decision, we employ a modified WCS model for Ernst's hypothetical scenario, detailed further in [7]. The uncertainty factors are emphasized to varying degrees in the generation of joint decisions $M_i, i = 0, 1, 2, \ldots, n$, where higher values of i imply increased significance and weight on the uncertainty factor values of each participants' decision. In this study, we restrict M_i to $i = 0, 1, 2$, and calculate the joint decision as follows:

$$M_i = \frac{\frac{d_P}{\sigma_P^i} + \frac{d_Q}{\sigma_Q^i}}{\frac{1}{\sigma_P^i} + \frac{1}{\sigma_Q^i}}, \quad i = 0, 1, 2 \tag{1}$$

where d_P, d_Q are the individual decisions, and σ_P, σ_Q are the uncertainty factors.

2.2   Establishing a Common Visual Space

To treat each participant as a visual cognition system, we record their decisions as x- and y- coordinates. Each pair of visual cognition systems P, Q generates a 2-dimensional Cartesian plane containing (P_x, P_y), and (Q_x, Q_y). To evaluate this system, we treat the line $\overline{PQ}$ (the line between (P_x, P_y) and (Q_x, Q_y)), as the Common Visual Space (CVS).

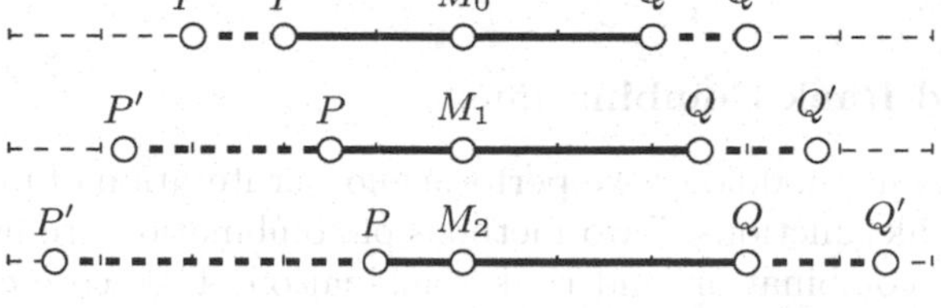

Fig. 1. Visualization of the CVS for M_0, M_1, and M_2. Here, the line $\overline{P'Q'}$ displays how the values $i = 0, 1, 2$ can affect the position of the statistical mean M_i in relation to P and Q.

Since the uncertainty factors σ_P, σ_Q can extend beyond $\overline{PQ}$, we extend the line to $\overline{P'Q'}$. To create this new line, we take the longer distance between $|PM_i|$ and $|M_iQ|$, appending 50% of this distance to the greater of the two. To preserve M_i as the center of the line segment, we append $|\overline{M_iQ'} - \overline{PM_i}|$ to P, thus generating P' (assume that $|M_iQ| > |PM_i|$ for the sake of this description)

2.3   Constructing Scoring Systems

To construct the scoring system for P,Q, the positions of P and Q on $\overline{P'Q'}$ and the uncertainty factors of P and Q are treated as the expected mean and the variance of P and Q, respectively. It is assumed that each individual assigns the highest score to the location where they believe the object landed. As we move away from this point, the score decreases at a rate influenced by the value of the observer's uncertainty factor. From the perspective of each individual scoring system, a higher score implies a higher probability that the object landed at that point, while a lower score implies a lower probability that the object landed at that point. The probability model by normal distribution is calculated as follows:

$$f(x, \mu, \sigma) = \frac{1}{\sigma\sqrt{2\pi}}e^{-\frac{(x-\mu)^2}{2\sigma^2}} \qquad (2)$$

where x is a normal random variable, μ is the mean, and σ is the uncertainty factor. Theoretically, a normal distribution spans to infinity, therefore our two scoring systems P and Q create overlapping distributions that span the entire visual space. Each of the 63 intervals $d_i, i \in [1, 63]$ has a score by P and a score by Q that range from 0 to 1. The values obtained by this method constitute our score function.

After we generate the scores for each interval d_i, we rank d_i from highest to lowest. The highest rank receives a smaller number, while the lowest rank receives the largest number, thus establishing our rank function.

The scoring systems P and Q are constructed from the two visual cognition systems P and Q, respectively. Each system is a score function s. The score of d_i by the score function s_P (or s_Q) is computed as the probability that the decision of the visual cognition system P or Q at location d_i contains the location of the object. Hence, we are able to score each guess of both visual cognition systems using a normal distribution $N(P, \sigma_P^2), N(Q, \sigma_Q^2)$, where σ_P^2 (or σ_Q^2) is the variance of P (or Q), and $i \in [1, 63]$.

2.4   Score and Rank Combinations

Adhering to CFA methodology, we perform another iteration of processing both the score and rank functions. Two methods of combination are used, which we refer to as score combination and rank combination. The score combination is defined as:

$$C(d_j) = \frac{\sum_{i=1}^{2} s_i(d_j)}{2}, \quad j \in [1, 63], \qquad (3)$$

where $s_i(d_j)$ is the score at each interval d_j. The rank combination function is defined as:

$$D(d_j) = \frac{\sum_{i=1}^{2} r_i(d_j)}{2}, \quad j \in [1, 63],\tag{4}$$

where $r_i(d_j)$ is the rank at each interval, $d_j, j \in [1, 63]$, and the score function and rank function are s and r respectively. For each of the 63 intervals, the score values and rank values of P and Q are combined respectively. The score combination of systems P and Q is labeled as C, and the rank combination of systems P and Q is labeled as D.

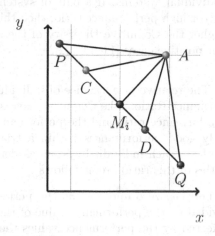

Fig. 2. An example of analysis using M, C, D, P, Q comparing distances to the actual A. Here, P and Q denote the individual systems, C and D represent score combination and rank combination respectively, and M_i represents the statistical mean.

Each interval d_i in C and D are ranked, where CFA considers the top-ranked intervals in C, D as optimal points (see Figure 2)

2.5   Cognitive Diversity and the Performance Ratio

Cognitive Diversity. The Rank-Score Characteristic Function (RSC) of the scoring system A is defined as (see [12, 13]):

$$f_A(i) = \left(s_A \circ r_A^{-1}\right)(i) = s_A\left(r_A^{-1}(i)\right)\tag{5}$$

where s_A and r_A are the score and rank functions of the scoring system A. The rank-score characteristics function can be computed by sorting the score values in $s_A(d_j)$ using the rank value as the key, where $j \in [1, 63]$. The RSC calculates the Cognitive Diversity by measuring the gap among Cognitive Diversity $d(A, B)$ of the two scoring systems A and B. Cognitive Diversity between two visual cognition systems, $d(P, Q)$, is defined by the two RSC functions f_P, f_Q of the scoring systems P and Q. Cognitive Diversity measures how distinct each scoring system is relative to the other paired scoring system, where we can calculate $d(P, Q) = d(f_P, f_Q)$ by

$$d(P, Q) = \sqrt{\frac{\sum_{i=1}^{63}[f_P(i) - f_Q(i)]^2}{63}} \qquad (6)$$

Yang et al. [25] defines positive and negative cases for pair combinations to describe whether the combinations outperform each of their constituent systems. Under a positive case, either score or rank combination has improved upon the performances of the individual systems. If a pair of systems P and Q exhibit Cognitive Diversity and/or high performance ratio, then this pair is likely to be a positive case. The higher the Cognitive Diversity of the scoring systems, the higher the likelihood for positive cases [11–13],[22].

Performance Ratio. The relative performance of individual systems within a trial is called the Performance Ratio. Like Cognitive Diversity, there is a direct relationship between performance ratio and the performance of the rank/score combinations. Relatively good performances within a trial implies that their combination will outperform each individual system as demonstrated by Yang et. al. [25]. The properties of this ratio are as follows:

1. The ratio value is between zero and one, as the performance value of the worse system is divided by the performance value of the better system
2. The ratio is not affected by the performance values themselves, but by the performance difference within a pair of systems. For example, it is permissible for two low performing systems to have a high performance ratio if the overall performance difference is low, and vice versa.

To generate the performance ratio, we first invert all current performance values, such that the performance values are directly related to actual performance (the higher the value, the closer to actual the system is). These inverted columns are normalized with respect to the largest value of all pairs. Normalization is the rescaling procedure for a set of values from their original range to the range $(0, 1]$. The performance ratio is derived by dividing the lower performing system by the higher performing system, where this ratio is normalized once more to the range $(0, 1]$.

3   Experiments

3.1   Data Collection

Our experimental data collection consists of twenty randomly selected paired participants in a public park, situated in a marked 25 by 30 feet grid. Each pair of participants stood 40 feet from a marked prop and stood 10 feet apart from one another. Parallel to the participants stood the head research coordinator with a 1.5 by 1.5 inch flat round object; the object was constructed of metal washers with a peculiar design to satisfy three criteria: first, a static landing with minimum residual movement; second, a satisfying visibility while airborne; and third, upon landing, minuscule enough to stay subtle once on the ground.

The participants were directed to observe the object as the object was propelled from the coordinators persons onto to the marked grid. Our grid is an emulation modeled after [2] with a slight visual enhancement for the observers. The perimeter of the marked grid is outlined using orange flags placed at 5 foot intervals. Two coordinators stood opposite of each other in the field, one top left of the grid and the other top right of the grid facing the participants. Two other coordinators stood next to each participant, respectfully.

Once the research coordinator throws the object, each participant, simultaneously and independently, instructs the far opposing researchers to the perceived location of the object, where a marker is planted on the ground at each participants' chosen location. Due to the complexity of individual visual cognition systems, the disparity between the location of the actual and the marker location of each participant can vary widely or slightly depending on internal and external factors, such as height, participant visual ability, weather conditions, and so on. After the markers are placed, we quantify the observers uncertainty factors using a tool similar to a divider caliper. This tool is introduced and explained to the participant, and the uncertainty factor is recorded by placing the tool over each participants marker location. The participants chose their uncertainty factors around his or her respective marker location by directing a coordinator to either increase or decrease the size of the tool. The tool emphasizes the shape of a circle expanding or contracting about the participants marker location, allowing the participant to decide how wide a circle is necessary to encapsulate both their respective marker location and the actual object location.

Measurements for the tool provided participant uncertainty factor values: a narrower circle radius yielded a smaller uncertainty factor value, while a wider circle radius yielded a larger uncertainty factor value. Here, smaller uncertainty values imply that a participant was confident in their decision, while larger uncertainty values imply the opposite. After the uncertainty factor values were recorded, the participants were shown their chosen marker locations and the location of the actual object.

At the conclusion of the experiment, eight values were recorded for each trial. The x- and y- coordinates for participants P and Q, the x- and y- coordinates for the object A, and the uncertainty value radii for participants P and Q. This methodology of data collection was performed a total of twenty times for this experiment. This data is labeled as #09/15/2013.

After the data was collected, the decisions of P and Q, marked as P (and Q), are used to obtain line segment PQ. We located the weighted confidence mean of M_0, M_1, and M_2 by using the uncertainty factor radii taken from P and Q as σ_P and σ_Q. We extend the line segment PQ to $P'Q'$. In order to join the two visual cognition systems, we need to establish a common ground that accounts for the visual space of both participants. The 63 intervals along the $\overline{P'Q'}$ line serve as the common visual space to be scored.

When the line segment $P'Q'$ is divided into 63 intervals for each $M_i, i = 0, 1, 2$, the intervals are scored according to the normal distribution of P and Q by using the location of P and Q as the mean and σ_P and σ_Q as the standard deviation, respectively. Both systems assume the set of common interval midpoints $d_i, i \in [1, 63]$. The score functions $s_P(d_i)$ and $s_Q(d_i)$ map each interval d_i to a score in systems P and Q. The rank function $r_P(d_i)$ and $r_Q(d_i)$ map each d_i to a positive integer from 1 to 63 by assigning 1 to the highest score and 63 to the lowest score for each d_i.

For each of the statistical means M_0, M_1, and M_2, we apply the score combination C and rank combination D given by formulas 3 and 4. The highest score combination in the interval is chosen as the score combination C and the lowest rank combination is chosen as the rank combination D. Then we calculate the performance of each system P, Q, Mi, C, D, for $i = 0, 1, 2$ by calculating the distance of these five points to the actual object A. The performances of each point are ranked from 1 to 5. The point with the shortest distance from the target is ranked 1.

3.2   Results and Analysis

In Figure 3, the first column labeled Trial is the specific trial that was analyzed. Column (a) provides the performances of P and Q in inches, which is the distance

Trial	(a): Per (P,Q)	(b): Un. Factors (P,Q)	(c): Rank			(d):Rank(P,Q,Mi,C,D) for i= 0,1,2														
			Mo	M1	M2	P	Q	Mo	C	D	P	Q	M1	C	D	P	Q	M2	C	D
Trial 1	(33.6,28.2)	(12,8)	1	2	3	4	2	1	2	4	5	2	1	2	2	4	3	1	4	2
Trial 2	(5.4,27.8)	(6,14)	2	1	3	1	5	4	1	1	2	5	1	2	2	4	1		4	3
Trial 3	(136.8,154.6)	(16.5,15)	3	2	1	1	4	3	4	1	1	5	2	3	3	1	5	2	3	3
Trial 4	(7.2,41)	(6,10)	3	2	1	1	5	4	1	1	2	4	3	4	1	2	4	3	4	1
Trial 5	(55.1,40.8)	(21,9)	1	2	3	4	2	1	2	4	5	2	1	2	2	4	3	1	4	2
Trial 6	(86,27.6)	(15,6)	3	2	1	4	1	3	1	4	4	2	3	4	1	4	3	1	4	2
Trial 7	(103.8,65.6)	(18,13.5)	1	2	3	4	1	3	1	4	4	1	3	4	2	4	1	3	4	2
Trial 8	(12,22.2)	(11,11)	3	2	1	1	4	3	4	1	1	4	3	4	1	1	4	3	4	1
Trial 9	(97.6,281.4)	(29,17)	3	2	1	1	4	3	4	1	1	5	3	1	4	1	5	3	1	4
Trial 10	(80.8,57.6)	(14.5,6)	3	2	1	4	1	3	1	4	5	2	4	1	3	5	2	4	1	3
Trial 11	(46,43.2)	(9,10)	3	2	1	3	1	2	3	3	3	1	2	4	4	5	1	2	3	3
Trial 12	(58,45.7)	(6,6)	3	2	1	3	1	2	3	3	3	1	2	3	3	3	1	2	3	3
Trial 13	(11,58.5)	(6,19)	2	1	2	1	4	3	1	4	1	4	3	4	2	3	4	1	4	2
Trial 14	(2,68.3)	(6,14)	1	2	3	1	4	3	1	4	1	5	4	1	1	2	4	3	4	1
Trial 15	(12,35.5)	(6,8)	2	1	3	1	5	4	1	1	2	4	3	4	1	2	4	3	4	1
Trial 16	(51.4,37.8)	(10,8)	1	2	3	4	1	3	1	4	5	2	4	1	3	5	1	4	2	2
Trial 17	(28,13.2)	(6,11)	3	2	1	3	2	1	3	3	5	1	3	1	4	5	1	3	1	4
Trial 18	(29.4,384.3)	(6.5,15)	1	2	3	1	3	2	3	3	1	3	2	3	3	1	3	2	3	3
Trial 19	(18.3,53.6)	(10,19.5)	1	2	3	1	5	4	1	1	2	4	1	4	3	2	4	1	4	3
Trial 20	(33.6,54.3)	(13,8)	2	3	1	2	4	1	4	2	2	5	1	2	4	1	5	3	1	4

Fig. 3. Summary of Experiment and Analysis of Results: (a): shows the performances of systems P and Q; (b) shows the uncertainty factors for P and Q; (c) ranks the performances of the statistical means M_0, M_1, M_2; (d) ranks the performances of the individual systems P and Q; score combination C, rank combination D, and the statistical means $M_i, i = 0, 1, 2$.

between P and the actual A, and the distance between Q and actual A. Column
(b) provides the uncertainty factor radii of P and Q.

In (b), there are green, white, and gray cells. The green cells indicate that
choosing the more confident system would lead to the more optimal decision
(by Koriats criteria). The gray cells indicate that uncertainty factor radii are
equal, implying that Koriats criteria does not apply. The white cells indicate
that choosing the more confident system (P or Q) does not lead to an optimal
decision. These cases exhibit situations opposite to Koriat's criterion.

Column (c) ranks the relative performance of weighted means M_0, M_1, and
M_2 against one another, within the scope of each trial. A yellow cell indicates
that the weighted mean is the highest ranked performer among P, Q, M_i, C,
and D. White cells indicate that the weighted mean is not the highest ranked
performer among its respective values of P, Q, M_i, C, and D.

Column (d) is broken up into 3 sub-columns. Each sub-column ranks P, Q,
M_i, C, and D in descending order of performance. The number 1 indicates the
best (or closest) performance to actual A, while the number 5 indicates the worst
(or farthest) performance from A. Multiple occurring values imply that a tie has
occurred for a performance ranking. If, for example, both C and D have the same
interval as their optimal decision, then they will share the same performance,
and subsequently the same performance rank. Red cells indicate when the score
combinations (D) (or the rank combination (C)) are superior to the individual
performances of P and Q. Gray cells indicate when C (or D) shares the same

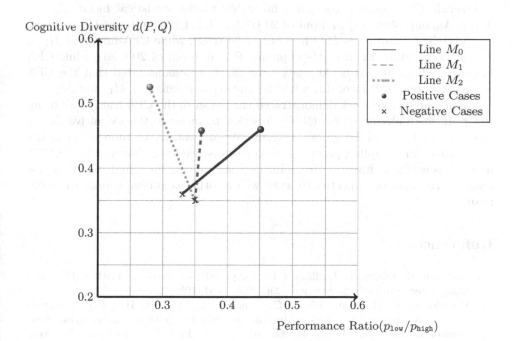

Fig. 4. Positive and Negative Cases on Cognitive Diversity vs Performance Ratio

performance as the best performer of P and Q. White cells (in the columns of C and D) indicate when C (or D) fails to provide a superior decision when compared to P and Q.

Figure 4 depicts positive cases and negative cases with respect to criteria, i.e. Cognitive Diversity vs. performance ratio calculated in Section 2.5. Circle "o" is the center of all positive cases where combinations of P and Q are better or equal to the best of P and Q. "x" denotes the center of all negative cases where the combined system of P and Q are but a positive case. Overall, we see that Cognitive Diversity and performance ratio can be used to discriminate positive vs. negative cases.

4   Discussion and Remarks

Our results demonstrate that CFA is a viable method to combine two visual cognition systems. 13 of the 60 trials (based on M_0, M_1, and M_2) show that C or D perform better than P and Q, while 45 out of the 60 total trials perform better than or equal to the best performer of P or Q. This gives an improvement rate of 75%. Koriat's criterion also gives a 75% correct rate (15 out of 20 trials). The only case not covered by Koriat's criterion or by the CFA framework is Trial 11. Trial 3, 9, 17, and 20, which cannot be covered by Koriat's criterion, can indeed be improved by the CFA method, while Trial 12 and 18, on which CFA does not perform well, can be covered by Koriat's criterion.

Overall, CFA method compares favorably to the statistical mean $M_i, i = 0, 1, 2$. M_0 improves P, Q in 4 out of 20 trials, while CFA improves M_0 in 13 out of 20 trials. M_1 improves P, Q in 5 out of 20 trials, while CFA improves M_1 in 11 out of 20 trials. Finally, M_2 improves P, Q in 6 out of 20 trials, while CFA improves M_2 in 10 out of 20 trials. Overall, it is demonstrated that the CFA framework compares favorably with the statistical means M_0, M_1, and M_2.

While our current work demonstrated the power of the CFA framework using the rank-score characteristic (RSC) function to measure the Cognitive Diversity between two visual cognition systems. We are working on more experiments to broaden our sampling practices. Nevertheless, we have shown that the CFA method is useful in investigating joint decision making on visual cognition systems. It can also be expected to work well in other cognitive neuroscience domains.

References

1. Bahrami, B., Olsen, K., Latham, P.E., Roepstorff, A., Rees, G., Frith, C.D.: Optimally interacting minds. Science 329(5995), 1081–1085 (2010)
2. Batallones, A., McMunn-Coffran, C., Sanchez, K., Mott, B., Hsu, D.F.: Comparative study of joint decision-making on two visual cognition systems using combinatorial fusion. In: Huang, R., Ghorbani, A.A., Pasi, G., Yamaguchi, T., Yen, N.Y., Jin, B. (eds.) AMT 2012. LNCS, vol. 7669, pp. 215–225. Springer, Heidelberg (2012)

3. Batallones, A., Sanchez, K., Mott, B., McMunn-Coffran, C., Hsu, D.F.: Combining Two Visual Cognition Systems Using Confidence Radius and Combinatorial Fusion. In: Imamura, K., Usui, S., Shirao, T., Kasamatsu, T., Schwabe, L., Zhong, N. (eds.) BHI 2013. LNCS, vol. 8211, pp. 72–81. Springer, Heidelberg (2013)
4. Deng, Y., Wu, Z., Chu, C.H., Zhang, Q., Hsu, D.F.: Sensor Feature Selection and Combination for Stress Identification Using Combinatorial Fusion. International Journal of Advanced Robotic Systems 10, 1–10 (2013)
5. Ernst, M.O., Banks, M.S.: Humans integrate visual and haptic information in a statistically optimal fashion. Nature 415(6870), 429–433 (2002)
6. Ernst, M.O.: Learning to integrate arbitrary signals from vision and touch. Journal of Vision 7(5), 1–14 (2007)
7. Ernst, M.O.: Decisions made better. Science 329(5995), 1022–1023 (2010)
8. Gepshtein, S., Burge, J., Ernst, M.O., Banks, M.S.: The combination of vision and touch depends on spatial proximity. Journal of Vision 5(11), 1013–1023 (2005)
9. Gold, J.I., Shadlen, M.N.: The neural basis of decision making. Annual Review of Neuroscience 30, 535–574 (2007)
10. Hillis, J.M., Ernst, M.O., Banks, M.S., Landy, M.S.: Combining sensory information: mandatory fusion within, but not between, senses. Science 298(5598), 1627–1630 (2002)
11. Hsu, D.F., Taksa, I.: Comparing rank and score combination methods for data fusion in information retrieval. Information Retrieval 8(3), 449–480 (2005)
12. Hsu, D.F., Chung, Y.S., Kristal, B.S.: Combinatorial fusion analysis: methods and practice of combining multiple scoring systems. In: Advanced Data Mining Technologies in Bioinformatics, pp. 1157–1181 (2006)
13. Hsu, D.F., Kristal, B.S., Schweikert, C.: Rank-score characteristics (RSC) function and cognitive diversity. In: Yao, Y., Sun, R., Poggio, T., Liu, J., Zhong, N., Huang, J. (eds.) BI 2010. LNCS, vol. 6334, pp. 42–54. Springer, Heidelberg (2010)
14. Kepecs, A., Uchida, N., Zariwala, H.A., Mainen, Z.F.: Neural correlates, computation and behavioural impact of decision confidence. Nature 455(7210), 227–231 (2008)
15. Koriat, A.: When Are Two Heads Better than One and Why? Science 336(6079), 360–362 (2012)
16. Lin, K.L., Lin, C.Y., Huang, C.D., Chang, H.M., Yang, C.Y., Lin, C.T., Hsu, D.F.: Feature selection and combination criteria for improving accuracy in protein structure prediction. IEEE Transactions on NanoBioscience 6(2), 186–196 (2007)
17. Liu, H., Wu, Z.H., Zhang, X., Hsu, D.F.: A skeleton pruning algorithm based on information fusion. Pattern Recognition Letters, 1138–1145 (2013)
18. Lunghi, C., Binda, P., Morrone, M.C.: Touch disambiguates rivalrous perception at early stages of visual analysis. Current Biology 20(4), R143–R144 (2010)
19. Lyons, D.M., Hsu, D.F.: Combining multiple scoring systems for target tracking using rank-score characteristics. Information Fusion 10(2), 124–136 (2009)
20. McMunn-Coffran, C., Paolercio, E., Liu, H., Tsai, R., Hsu, D.F.: Joint decision making in visual cognition using Combinatorial Fusion Analysis. In: 2011 10th IEEE International Conference on Cognitive Informatics & Cognitive Computing (ICCI* CC), pp. 254–261. IEEE (August 2011)
21. McMunn-Coffran, C., Paolercio, E., Fei, Y., Hsu, D.F.: Combining multiple visual cognition systems for joint decision-making using combinatorial fusion. In: 2012 IEEE 11th International Conference on Cognitive Informatics & Cognitive Computing (ICCI* CC), pp. 313–322. IEEE (August 2012)

22. Ng, K.B., Kantor, P.B.: Predicting the effectiveness of naive data fusion on the basis of system characteristics. Journal of the American Society for Information Science 51(13), 1177–1189 (2000)
23. Paolercio, E., McMunn-Coffran, C., Mott, B., Hsu, D.F., Schweikert, C.: Fusion of two visual perception systems utilizing cognitive diversity. In: 2013 12th IEEE International Conference on Cognitive Informatics & Cognitive Computing (ICCI* CC), pp. 226–235. IEEE (July 2013)
24. Schweikert, C., Brown, S., Tang, Z., Smith, P.R., Hsu, D.F.: Combining multiple ChIP-seq peak detection systems using combinatorial fusion. BMC Genomics 13(suppl. 8), S12 (2012)
25. Yang, J.M., Chen, Y.F., Shen, T.W., Kristal, B.S., Hsu, D.F.: Consensus scoring criteria for improving enrichment in virtual screening. Journal of Chemical Information and Modeling 45(4), 1134–1146 (2005)

Shift of Brain-State during Recovery from Discomfort Induced by Aversive Pictures

Yang Yang[1,3,4], Emi Tosaka[1], Xiaojing Yang[2,3,4], Kazuyuki Imamura[1], Xiuya Lei[5], Gang Wang[6], Bin Hu[7], Shengfu Lu[2,3,4], and Ning Zhong[1,2,3,4]

[1] Maebashi Institute of Technology, Maebashi, Japan
[2] International WIC Institute, Beijing University of Technology, Beijing, China
[3] Beijing Key Laboratory of MRI and Brain Informatics, Beijing, China
[4] Beijing International Collaboration Base on Brain Informatics and Wisdom Services, Beijing, China
[5] Department of Psychology, Beijing Forestry University, Beijing, China
[6] Mood Disorders Center, Beijing Anding Hospital, Capital Medical University, Beijing, China
[7] Ubiquitous Awareness and Intelligent Solutions Lab, Lanzhou University, Lanzhou, China
yang@maebashi-it.org, xiuyalei@bjfu.edu.cn, lusf@bjut.edu.cn,
{zhong,imamurak}@maebashi-it.ac.jp

Abstract. Regarding to aversive stimuli, previous studies on emotion response and formation are plentiful, whereas concentrations on the emotional recovery are comparatively insufficient. The present study focused on the discomfort induced by looking at aversive pictures, and the emotional self-regulation during the following recovery period. A functional magnetic resonance imaging (fMRI) experiment with prolonged paradigm was recruited to investigate how brain-state shifted across three stages: picture viewing, earlier resting period, and latter resting period. Comparing with neutral pictures, aversive pictures activated the caudate nucleus centric subcortical areas, which also kept firing during the resting period. Meanwhile an activation pattern gradually appeared in fronto-parietal regions that were found negatively correlated to subcortical areas. Our findings suggest that the emotional recovery from discomfort is also a procedure accompanied by the strategy shift from passively suppressing emotional response to actively controlling the attention.

1 Introduction

Numerous researches on emotional response and its modulation have been yielded along with the widespread use of the fMRI [1-3]. Compared with positive emotions, emotional experiences with negative valence induced by aversive stimuli are more instinctive, such as fear and disgust. Previous studies proposed specific circuits for fear and disgust respectively. In general, fear arouses a network composed of some prefronto-limbic areas including amygdala, insula, orbitofrontal cortex (OFC), and anterior cingulate cortex (ACC) [4]. On the other hand, the disgust-related processing is implicated to be associated with basal ganglia [5, 6]. However, the involvement of basal ganglia can't be completely excluded from the fear-related network when threat is perceived. Evidence revealed that the caudate nucleus and putamen that are the primary

D. Ślęzak et al. (Eds.): BIH 2014, LNAI 8609, pp. 45–56, 2014.
© Springer International Publishing Switzerland 2014

components of basal ganglia were activated during subjects observed the fearful body expressions [7]. Other neuroimaging studies specifically reported frontal activity together with subcortical activations during processing of threat-related facial expressions [8, 9]. In addition, concurrence of both fear and disgust appeared in some circumstances. Investigations on blood-injection-injury (BII) phobia, spider phobia, and contamination-related obsessive-compulsive disorder (OCD) suggested all these disorders were characterized by both fear and disgust [10, 11]. Given the debatable independence of fear-specific circuit and the tangled relationship between fear and disgust, we didn't put focus on how to establish the respective network for fear and disgust, but concerned on the experience and self-modulation in treating the discomfort induced by both fear and disgust.

Much of the progress has come from studies of aversive emotions, especially emotion conditioning based on the classic Pavlovian paradigm, in which the formation and learning procedure of aversive emotions are particularly highlighted while the aftermaths are always overlooked [4, 12]. Relative to the stress response or emotional contagion, researches on the recovery from emotional discomfort is insufficient. It is more valuable to work out the recovery mechanism to those people who are suffering from traumas. For such a research, the longitudinal design is more preferable. Eryilmaz, H. et al. [13] implemented an experiment by tracing the subsequent brain activity at the 90-second resting period following fearful movie clips. Their findings revealed that short emotional events may have prolonged effects on spontaneous brain states at rest. We employed a similar pattern that underlined the subsequent discomfort induced by aversive pictures. But the resting period was extended to 4 minutes since we supposed the recovery to be a slower and more gradual procedure.

It has come to light that people are inclined to monitor their mood state and self-regulate their emotion to comfortable levels [14]. Attention deployment and cognitive change are two effective strategies to modulate emotions [15]. The present study attempted to investigate the overall process of brain-state shift and emotional self-regulation during the dynamic recovery of subjects, from they began to perceive aversive stimuli until finished the following rest, and also to verify the involvement of strategies during the recovery when considering its role in mediating the emotional regulation.

2   Materials and Methods

2.1   Subjects

We recruited twenty right-handed healthy postgraduates (10 females) with the mean age of 25 ± 1.3 years and normal or corrected-to-normal vision, to participate in the experiment. None of them reported any history of neurological or psychiatric diseases. All the subjects signed the informed consent and this study was approved by the Ethics committee of Xuanwu Hospital, Capital Medical University.

2.2   Stimuli

Fifteen aversive pictures and fifteen neutral pictures were selected from the International Affective Picture System (IAPS) which is based on normative ratings in valence and arousal [16]. The contents of pictures involving snakes, spiders, attacks, bloody wounds, and dead bodies were adopted for the aversive stimuli, with the mean valence of 2.61 ± 1.60 and the mean arousal of 6.30 ± 2.14. In contrast, pictures of household items in simple contexts (e.g., a cup on a table) were used as the neutral stimuli, with the mean valence of 5.01 ± 1.13 and the mean arousal of 3.05 ± 1.94.

2.3   Experimental Design

A one-group, "pre-post" test-designed fMRI experiment was used (see Figure 1). We presented the neutral pictures only in the pre-test session, and aversive pictures only in the post-test session. In each session, fifteen emotional pictures were successively displayed for 1 minute, at a rate of 4 seconds per picture. Subjects were required to view all the pictures carefully. A four-minute resting period subsequently followed the picture viewing stage (PVS), in which subjects were asked to keep their eyes open and relax without thinking. In order to compare different phases, we divided the resting period into two parts factitiously: the first minute named early resting stage (ERS) and the last three minutes named later resting stage (LRS). The interval between the pre- and post- tests was 15 minutes.

2.4   MR Data Acquisition

A 3.0 T MRI system (Siemens Trio Tim; Siemens Medical System, Erlanger, Germany) and a 12-channel phased array head coil were employed for the scanning. Foam padding and headphone were used to limit head motion and reduce scanning noise. 192 slices of structural images with a thickness of 1 mm were acquired by using a T1 weighted 3D MPRAGE sequence (TR = 1600 ms, TE = 3.28 ms, TI = 800 ms, FOV = 256 × 256 mm^2, flip angle = 9°, voxel size = 1 × 1 × 1 mm^3). Functional images were collected through a T2 gradient-echo EPI sequence (TR = 2000 ms, TE = 31 ms, flip angle = 90°, FOV = 240 × 240 mm^2, matrix size = 64 × 64). Thirty axial slices with a thickness of 4 mm and an interslice gap of 0.8 mm were acquired.

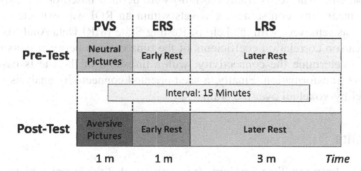

Fig. 1. Subjects should view 15 neutral pictures in the pre-test session and 15 aversive pictures in the post-test session separately. Each session started with a 1-minute PVS, followed by a 1-minute ERS and a 3-minute LRS subsequently. The interval of the two sessions was 15 minutes. Abbreviations: PVS: picture viewing stage, ERS: early resting stage, LRS: later resting stage.

2.5   Data Preprocessing

The preprocessing of fMRI data was implemented with SPM8 software (Wellcome Department of Cognitive Neurology, London, UK, http://www.fil.ion.ucl. ac.uk). The first two images have been discarded to allow the magnetization to approach dynamic equilibrium. The data format was converted to make the fMRI data available for the SPM software, then a series of stages followed: realignment that aimed at identifying and correcting redundant body motions, coregistering that merged the high resolution structural image with the mean image of the EPI series, normalization that adjusted the structural image to the MNI template and applied normalization parameters to EPI images, smoothing that had fMRI data smoothed with an 8 mm FWHM isotropic Gaussian kernel. After normalization, all volumes were resampled into $3 \times 3 \times 3$ mm^3 voxels. Head movement was less than 2 mm in all cases.

2.6   fMRI Analysis

Data from the two sessions were statistically analyzed by using SPM8. In one session, images of PVS, ERS, and LRS, and the contrasts among them were created individually based on the general linear model. In the group-level, paired t-tests were implemented for each stage to examine the different activated patterns between the pre-test and post-test. Moreover, one-sample t-tests were performed for the contrast images. For each session, the contrasts of ERS > PVS and LRS > PVS revealed the pattern of increased activation in the rest period compared with the picture viewing; the pattern of decreased activation was shown by the reverse contrasts. Activations reported survived an uncorrected voxel-level intensity threshold of $p < 0.001$ with minimum cluster size of $k > 30$ voxels. Regions of activation originally obtained in MNI coordinates were converted into Talairach coordinates with the GingerALE and labeled with Talairach Daemon (BrainMap Project, Research Imaging Center of the University of Texas Health Science Center, San Antonio, USA, http://brainmap.org).

Functional connectivity analysis was also applied to elicit the relationship between activation patterns. The ROIs (radius=6 mm) were defined based on the exploratory results. The mean time-course across voxels within an ROI was extracted after the linear trend was removed, with the help of Resting-State fMRI Data Analysis Toolkit [17]. The Pearson correlation coefficients of the time courses between pairs of ROIs were used to determine the connectivity, with a threshold of the t-tests based on a Fisher's r-to-z transformation. Finally, a seed-oriented connectivity analysis was performed voxel-by-voxel all over the brain.

3   Results

Paired t-Tests between Two Sessions. It was shown that the aversive pictures in the post-test induced stronger and more extensive activation, while the neutral pictures in pre-test activated nowhere but the visual cortex. Images were contrasted in couples between the two sessions for each stage including the picture viewing, early resting period, and latter resting period. Increased activation was identified only in the contrast of Post-test > Pre-test, which may be associated with the discomfort caused by the aversive stimuli (see Table 1). In the PVS, significant brain activation was observed in visual cortex, posterior cingulate cortex, striatal-thalamic areas, motor cortex, and frontal cortex including the opercular and orbital parts. Activated regions reduced obviously in the ERS, involving the left lingual gyrus, left caudate nucleus, right superior temporal gyrus, and posterior cingulate on the right. In the LRS, only activations of left lingual gyrus, left caudate nucleus, and the rostral portions of right middle frontal gyrus were detected (see Figure 2).

Table 1. Activated regions revealed by the paired t-tests. Loci of maxima are in Talairach coordinates in millimeters. All regions survived the statistical threshold of p < 0.001 (uncorrected), cluster size k > 30 voxels.

Stage (Post-test > Pre-test)	Region	BA	Cluster	Talairach Coordinates			T-score
				x	y	z	
PVS	L. MOG	19	805	-35	-67	-2	7.43
	L. IFG / PreCG	44 / 6	94	-32	-5	31	6.53
	L. MFG	46	10	-46	32	24	5.60
	L. PCun	31	28	-7	-69	15	5.54
	L. SOG	7	84	-18	-61	21	6.50
	L. Insula / CN		68	-21	19	17	6.62
	L. Thalamus		13	-23	-22	3	5.12
	L. STG	41	11	-40	-40	12	5.87
	R. FFG	37	34	32	-43	-15	6.62
	R. CN		72	18	24	21	7.63
	R. IFG	44	35	46	7	17	6.41
	R. OFC	47	30	46	31	1	4.61
	R. PoCG	4	42	46	-19	28	5.60
	R. PreCG	6	47	38	-5	27	6.62
	R. CG	31	29	12	-40	39	5.87
	L.R. SMA	6	27	-2	-11	64	5.33
	R. Thalamus		12	7	-10	18	5.75
	R. PCun	7	19	15	-57	38	4.88
ERS	L. LinG	19	416	-26	-73	-2	5.54
	L. CN		168	-23	19	17	5.01
	R. STG		46	27	-38	13	6.16
	R. PCC	30 / 31	33	13	-62	5	4.42
LRS	L.LinG	17	470	-18	-71	12	4.9
	L. CN		108	-18	22	7	4.93
	R. MFG	10	30	19	42	9	4.43

Abbreviation: MOG: middle occipital gyrus, IFG: inferior frontal gyrus, MFG: middle frontal gyrus, PCun: precuneus, SOG: superior occipital gyrus, CN: caudate nucleus, STG: superior temporal gyrus, FFG: fusiform gyrus, OFC: orbital frontal cortex, PoCG: postcentral gyrus, PreCG: precentral gyrus, CG: cingulate gyrus, SMA: supplementary motor area, LinG: lingual gyrus, PCC: posterior cingulate cortex.

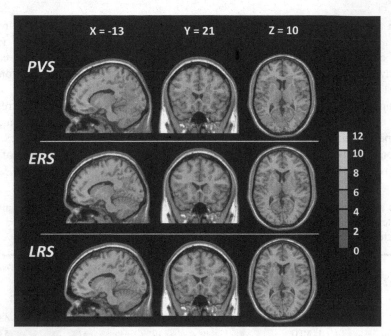

Fig. 2. Images were compared in couples between the two sessions for each stage with the paired t-tests. Increased activation was identified only in the contrast of Post-test > Pre-test with the threshold of p < 0.001 (uncorrected) and k > 30, revealed in MNI coordinates. The Color bar indicates the t-score. Abbreviations: PVS: picture viewing stage, ERS: early resting stage, LRS: later resting stage.

Shift of Brain-State in the Post-Test. The emotional arousal in each stage brought by aversive pictures was revealed by the paired t-tests. However, the apparent differences across the three stages could not be identified unless the three stages were contrasted mutually. Thus, the contrasts of ERS vs. PVS and LRS vs. PVS in the post-test session were performed to show the processing of self-regulation and the shift of brain-state when subjects responded to the emotional discomfort (see Table 2). The contrast of ERS > PVS brought about the increased activation in fronto-parietal areas including angular gyrus and middle frontal gyrus, and the decreased activation in visual-spatial processing-related regions and areas corresponding to emotional salience, such as insula and hippocampus. The contrast of LRS > PVS inherited a homologous pattern, but with stronger increased activation in the fronto-parietal circuit and milder decreased activation in subcortical-limbic regions (see Figure 3).

Relationship between Caudate and Fronto-Parietal Network. The activation in caudate nucleus (CN) and posterior cingulate cortex (PCC) can be observed throughout the whole course in the post-test (see Figure 2). However, the activation in PCC dropped off as time passed, while the condition of CN seemed to be sustained, especially the one on the left. On the other hand, from the early rest to the latter rest, the activation of the fronto-parietal network (FPN) gradually emerged (see Figure 3).

Table 2. Regions significantly activated following ERS vs. PVS and LRS vs. PVS. Loci of maxima are in Talairach coordinates in millimeters. All regions survived the statistical threshold of p < 0.001 (uncorrected), cluster size k > 30 voxels.

Contrast	Region	BA	Cluster	Talairach Coordinates x	y	z	T-score
ERS > PVS	L. AG	39 / 40	196	-46	-70	30	6.35
	R. AG	40	113	54	-56	30	5.95
	R. PCun	31	33	1	-70	31	4.38
	R. MFG	9	15	32	16	42	4.80
LRS > PVS	L. AG	39 / 40	65	-49	-56	31	4.82
	L. MFG	9	10	-32	22	39	4.67
	R. AG	39	21	54	-59	30	4.77
	R. SMG	40	33	43	-48	31	5.20
	R. MFG	9	38	29	19	40	4.76
ERS < PVS	L. MOG	18	967	-13	-96	7	7.35
	L. SPL	7	76	-27	-52	48	4.73
	R. MOG	19	602	24	-84	3	8.36
	R. SPL	7	215	23	-54	41	4.69
	R. Hipp	27	244	5	-36	-6	6.67
	R. Insula	13	153	40	-2	22	6.30
	R. Putamen		32	27	-8	-3	5.00
	R. PoCG	2	39	60	-23	36	4.50
LRS < PVS	L. MOG	18	1005	-15	-96	7	8.72
	R. MOG	18	643	24	-87	3	8.12
	R. PCun	7	121	29	-50	50	4.74
	R. PoCG	2	35	54	-30	47	4.49

Abbreviation: AG: angular gyrus, SMG: supramarginal gyrus, SPL: superior parietal lobule Hipp: hippocampus.

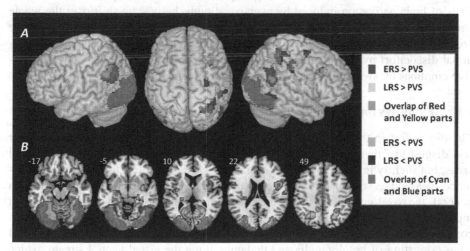

Fig. 3. Regions of activation were revealed by contrasts of ERS vs. PVS and LRS vs. PVS. (*A*) Both increasingly and decreasingly activated regions were rendered on the surface of brain. As increasingly activated regions, the fronto-parietal network (FPN) gradually emerged; (*B*) the decreased activation was presented in the axial view in MNI coordinates.

In order to understand the roles CN and FPN played during the recovery from emotional discomfort, and make out the interrelation between them, the functional connectivity analysis was performed. Firstly, five ROIs corresponding to left CN, bilateral middle frontal gyrus (MFG), and bilateral angular gyrus (AG) were selected. All the coordinates for the five ROIs were taken from the activated regions in the latter rest period in consideration of the instability of the other two stages. The ROIs were oriented at (-18, 22, 7), (-32, 22, 39), (29, 19, 40), (-49, -56, 31), and (54, -59, 30) respectively, in Talairach coordinates (see Table 1 and 2). The Pearson correlation coefficients of the time courses between any pair of the ROIs were calculated, followed by a t-test based on the Fisher's r-to-z transformation (see Figure 4). It turned out a significant negative correlation between left CN and right AG with the r value of -0.44 at two tailed 0.05 level. Connections between the left CN and other nodes could not be determined. In contrast, the other four nodes except CN demonstrated high correlation to each other, which may imply the existence of segregation between CN and other fronto-parietal nodes during the emotion recovery. At last, the voxel-based connectivity analyses were conducted, using the left CN (-18, 22, 7) and right AG (54, -59, 30) as the center respectively. A dissociable pattern with two separate networks was generated. The CN centric network primarily involved the subcortical-limbic system, extending posteriorly to the visual cortex, and dorsally to the motor cortex. The AG centric network seemed to be associated with the default mode network (DMN), but mixed with some regions of emotional modulation and cognitive control, such as OFG and MFG.

4   Discussion

The present study revealed an overall perspective from three aspects: different patterns of brain activation induced by aversive stimuli, brain-state shift over the whole course of emotional self-regulation, and the neural circuits involved in these processing. From perceiving the fearful and disgusting pictures to reducing the emotional discomfort by self-modulation, an intrinsic mode on how to deal with the aversive emotions by switching strategies spontaneously emerged.

4.1   Pathways for Transferring the Aversive Information and Discomfort

The discomfort in the experiment was triggered by a complex emotion blending fear and disgust together, which caused activation mainly in caudate centric subcortical areas, but slightly in amygdala. The generation of the discomfort followed the transference of aversive stimuli through the cortico-basal ganglia-thalamo-cortical loop. In general, the basal ganglia was described as a set of input structures that receive direct input from the cerebral cortex, and output structures that project back to the cerebral cortex via the thalamus [18]. In this case, aversive stimuli were passed to the subcortical areas consisting of basal ganglia and thalamus along the visual ventral stream, which can be evidenced by the connections between visual cortex and subcortical areas in the CN centric network (see Figure 4). However, the subcortical areas functioned not only as a relay station, but also a significant node for processing the emotional information.

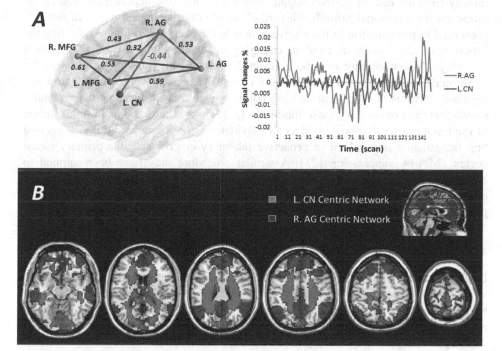

Fig. 4. Results of functional connectivity analyses. (*A*) A significant negative correlation was found between left CN and right AG with the r value of -0.44 at two tailed 0.05 level. The negative correlation can be seen from the blood oxygen level dependent (BOLD) signals extracted from the two ROIs. (*B*) Two networks were disassociated by voxel-based connectivity analysis. The left CN centric network primarily involved the subcortical-limbic system, together with the visual cortex, and motor cortex; the right AG centric network correlated with the default mode network (DMN), and extending to OFG and MFG.

In previous studies, the subcortical pathway was proposed to provide a quick analysis of the affective properties of stimuli that serves as an initial template for subsequent processing [19]. Moreover, evidence also exists linking the caudate nucleus with aversive learning. Especially lesions to this region have led to failure in conditioned emotional response, conditioned freezing and passive and active avoidance [20]. Thus, it is implied that the CN centric subcortical areas processed the aversive stimuli, and then delivered signals back to cerebral cortex accompanied with discomfort.

4.2   The Function of Caudate in Processing Discomfort

As a crucial element of the brain reward system that plays a critical role in the response to pleasure and pain, CN centric basal ganglia is directly activated in anticipation of aversive stimuli [21]. In this study, the role of right CN in emotional response can be inferred from the inhibitory activation when picture viewing finished (see Figure 2). Most activation in the frontal and temporal cortices including the right CN decayed rapidly from the resting periods began, which illustrated the dependence of such regions on the emotional stimuli. Nevertheless, the consistent activation in left CN presented its participation in the aftertreatment to the aversive emotion, indicating the function of some parts of caudate engaging in the modulation during emotional recovery. This processing may be connected to motor functions. In addition to the emotional functions, the primary function of basal ganglia is proposed to control and regulate activities of the motor and premotor cortical areas to promote the voluntary movements and manual response inhibition [22]. The striatum, the main input station of the basal ganglia, is considered as an important region for stopping. It is suggested that the striatum is involved in proactive inhibitory control over the primary motor cortex (M1) by suppression [23]. A similar procedure may have been applied to emotional self-regulation. Associating the connection to the regulation of aversive emotion, it is more likely that the CN centric basal ganglia modulate emotion by suppressing the emotional response to aversive stimuli.

4.3   The Switch of Strategies on Emotional Self-regulation

Different strategies can be applied to regulate emotional responses [15]. Over the whole course of post-test session, two dissociable networks were displayed supporting two different strategies on emotional self-regulation. The left CN centric network made up of subcortical areas, visual cortex, and motor cortex, referred to a passive "strategy" of suppression; the right AG centric network primarily based on the DMN network mixed with bilateral MFG and OFG, referred to a strategy of active control. These right AG related regions were highly consistent with the executive-control network (ECN) that has been verified to be connected to working memory and control processes [24]. During the recovery procedure, the connection between MFG and posterior parietal cortex (PPC) tended to be closer as time went on, with increasingly common activation in the relevant areas. As shown in Figure 3, the pattern of common activation can be revealed more conspicuously in the latter resting state than in earlier resting state through the longitudinal contrasts among stages. The involvement of DMN and ECN can be interpreted to the deployment of attention in the latter resting period, moving from concentration on aversive emotions to self-referential processes, such as mind wandering. The BOLD signal of the right AG rising after initiatory dropping suggested the effect of attention deployment was getting stronger in the latter resting period, and the discomfort caused by aversive stimuli was getting attenuated corresponding to the negative correlation between right AG and left CN. It is implied that subjects gradually shifted their concerns away from the turning point. Therefore, the emotional recovery from discomfort is also a procedure accompanied by the strategy shift from passively inhibiting emotional response to actively controlling the attention, although the both strategies were spontaneously utilized.

5   Conclusion

Two dissociable networks were revealed during the dynamic recovery from the discomfort induced by aversive pictures. The left CN centric subcortical network was found to be associated with the processing on aversive stimuli, and the right AG centric fronto-parietal network was related to attentional control. The spontaneous switch of the two networks underlaid the brain-state shift over the whole course of recovery, and enabled the transition of strategies from suppression to attention deployment, which facilitated the emotional self-regulation.

Acknowledgements. This work was supported by Beijing Municipal Commission of Education, Beijing Xuanwu Hospital, and funded by National Basic Research Program of China (2014CB744600), International Science & Technology Cooperation Program of China (2013DFA32180), and National Natural Science Foundation of China (61272345).

References

1. Davidson, R.J., Putnam, K.M., Larson, C.L.: Dysfunction in the neural circuitry of emotion regulation–a possible prelude to violence. Science 289, 591–594 (2000)
2. Dolan, R.J.: Emotion, cognition, and behavior. Science 298, 1191–1194 (2002)
3. Wager, T.D., Phan, K.L., Liberzon, I., Taylor, S.F.: Valence, gender, and lateralization of functional brain anatomy in emotion: a meta-analysis of findings from neuroimaging. NeuroImage 19, 513–531 (2003)
4. Sehlmeyer, C., Schoning, S., Zwitserlood, P., Pfleiderer, B., Kircher, T., Arolt, V., Konrad, C.: Human fear conditioning and extinction in neuroimaging: a systematic review. PloS One 4, e5865 (2009)
5. Barrett, L.F., Wager, T.D.: The Structure of Emotion: Evidence From Neuroimaging Studies. Current Directions in Psychological Science 15, 79–83 (2006)
6. Jabbi, M., Bastiaansen, J., Keysers, C.: A common anterior insula representation of disgust observation, experience and imagination shows divergent functional connectivity pathways. PloS One 3, e2939 (2008)
7. de Gelder, B., Snyder, J., Greve, D., Gerard, G., Hadjikhani, N.: Fear fosters flight: a mechanism for fear contagion when perceiving emotion expressed by a whole body. Proceedings of the National Academy of Sciences of the United States of America 101, 16701–16706 (2004)
8. Liddell, B.J., Brown, K.J., Kemp, A.H., Barton, M.J., Das, P., Peduto, A., Gordon, E., Williams, L.M.: A direct brainstem-amygdala-cortical 'alarm' system for subliminal signals of fear. NeuroImage 24, 235–243 (2005)
9. Muhlberger, A., Wieser, M.J., Gerdes, A.B., Frey, M.C., Weyers, P., Pauli, P.: Stop looking angry and smile, please: start and stop of the very same facial expression differentially activate threat- and reward-related brain networks. Social Cognitive and Affective Neuroscience 6, 321–329 (2011)
10. Cisler, J.M., Olatunji, B.O., Lohr, J.M.: Disgust, fear, and the anxiety disorders: a critical review. Clinical Psychology Review 29, 34–46 (2009)
11. Cavusoglu, M., Dirik, G.: Fear or disgust? The role of emotions in spider phobia and blood-injection-injury phobia. Turk Psikiyatri Dergisi = Turkish Journal of Psychiatry 22, 115–122 (2011)
12. Fox, M.D.: Sleeping with the enemy: Garfield and the National Heart, Lung, and Blood Institute. Pediatrics 118, 1257–1258 (2006)

13. Fox, M.D., Corbetta, M., Snyder, A.Z., Vincent, J.L., Raichle, M.E.: Spontaneous neuronal activity distinguishes human dorsal and ventral attention systems. Proceedings of the National Academy of Sciences of the United States of America 103, 10046–10051 (2006)
14. Thayer, R.E., Newman, J.R., McClain, T.M.: Self-regulation of mood: strategies for changing a bad mood, raising energy, and reducing tension. Journal of Personality and Social Psychology 67, 910–925 (1994)
15. Kanske, P., Heissler, J., Schonfelder, S., Bongers, A., Wessa, M.: How to regulate emotion? Neural networks for reappraisal and distraction. Cereb Cortex 21, 1379–1388 (2011)
16. Lang, P.J., Bradley, M.M., Cuthbert, B.N.: International affective picture system (IAPS): Affective ratings of pictures and instruction manual. Technical Report A-8. University of Florida, Gainesville, FL (2008)
17. Song, X.W., Dong, Z.Y., Long, X.Y., Li, S.F., Zuo, X.N., Zhu, C.Z., He, Y., Yan, C.G., Zang, Y.F.: REST: a toolkit for resting-state functional magnetic resonance imaging data processing. PloS One 6, e25031 (2011)
18. Alexander, G.E., DeLong, M.R., Strick, P.L.: Parallel organization of functionally segregated circuits linking basal ganglia and cortex. Annual Review of Neuroscience 9, 357–381 (1986)
19. LeDoux, J.: Fear and the brain: where have we been, and where are we going? Biological Psychiatry 44, 1229–1238 (1998)
20. White, N.M., Salinas, J.A.: Mnemonic functions of dorsal striatum and hippocampus in aversive conditioning. Behavioural Brain Research 142, 99–107 (2003)
21. Jensen, J., McIntosh, A.R., Crawley, A.P., Mikulis, D.J., Remington, G., Kapur, S.: Direct activation of the ventral striatum in anticipation of aversive stimuli. Neuron 40, 1251–1257 (2003)
22. Stocco, A., Lebiere, C., Anderson, J.R.: Conditional routing of information to the cortex: a model of the basal ganglia's role in cognitive coordination. Psychological Review 117, 541–574 (2010)
23. Zandbelt, B.B., Vink, M.: On the role of the striatum in response inhibition. PloS One 5, e13848 (2010)
24. Seeley, W.W., Menon, V., Schatzberg, A.F., Keller, J., Glover, G.H., Kenna, H., Reiss, A.L., Greicius, M.D.: Dissociable intrinsic connectivity networks for salience processing and executive control. The Journal of Neuroscience: The Official Journal of the Society for Neuroscience 27, 2349–2356 (2007)

Consciousness Study of Subjects with Unresponsive Wakefulness Syndrome Employing Multimodal Interfaces

Bartosz Kunka[1,*], Tomasz Sanner[1], Andrzej Czyżewski[1],
and Agnieszka Kwiatkowska[2]

[1] Multimedia Systems Dept., Gdansk Univ. of Technology, Gdansk, Poland
{kuneck,sanner,andcz}@sound.eti.pg.gda.pl
[2] Dept. of Individual Differences Psychology, Kazimierz Wielki Univ., Bydgoszcz, Poland
agnieszka.kwiatkowska06@gmail.com

Abstract. The paper presents a novel multimodal-based methodology for consciousness study of individuals with unresponsive wakefulness syndrome. Two interfaces were employed in the experiments: eye gaze tracking system – CyberEye developed at the Multimedia Systems Department, and EEG device with electrode placement in the international 10-20 standard. It was a pilot study for checking if it is possible to determine objective methods based on multimodal techniques which could replace or support current expensive and difficult to access neuroimaging techniques, like fMRI, PET, utilizing in evaluation of consciousness state. The multimodal-based methodology consists of several phases of research involving subjects. Hearing examination based on objective methods (OAE, ABR), consciousness test based on analysis of visual activity, examination of visual neural pathway with Steady State Visually Evoked Potentials and EEG-based comprehension test were proposed. The results obtained within conducted experiments and presented in this paper suggest that proposed objective-subjective methodology could potentially be introduced into clinical facilities after further validation.

Keywords: consciousness study, vegetative state, minimally conscious state, unresponsive wakefulness syndrome, gaze interaction, EEG, comprehension test.

1   Introduction

There has been important research utilizing EEG [1]–[3], positron emission tomography (PET) [4], [5] and fMRI technology [6], [7] in the diagnosis of consciousness disorders. Nevertheless, their role in clinical consciousness evaluation is still insignificant. In particular, PET and fMRI require specialist expensive equipment, so that their availability is very limited as a result. It is essential to point out that even when employing the standardized protocols like CRS-R, misdiagnosis of up to 40% regarding the

---

* Corresponding author.

D. Ślęzak et al. (Eds.): BIH 2014, LNAI 8609, pp. 57–67, 2014.

consciousness level of subjects in the vegetative state still occurs [8], [9]. Hence, we have developed the research method based on an eye-gaze tracking system and an EEG interface. Important advantages of the proposed approach are as follows: ease of performance, portability and cost. The paper includes the results of experiments utilizing our method to evaluate the consciousness state of 10 subjects diagnosed as VS subjects. We hypothesized that subjects in the vegetative state could be differentiated from those who manifest their consciousness by interacting with a computer employing multimodal interfaces. We believe that it is possible to decrease the ratio of misdiagnosis of subjects awaking from the coma basing on the approach that could be summarized in this context as "the absence of proof is not proof of the absence".

2   Methods

Employing two interfaces in the same experiments has contributed to idea of joining them together and to develop an integrated multimodal examination tool. Data fusion could deliver an added value associated with the integration of eye gaze tracking and EEG modules. In case of filtering and analysis EEG signals it is justified to utilize Kalman filtering, neural networks or soft computing algorithms. In the Subsection 2.1 multimodal interfaces employed in the conducted experiment were presented, separately. Nevertheless, the idea of creating an integrated multimodal examination platform is considered by Authors in the context of planned experiments.

2.1   Multimodal Interfaces

Hearing Examination
The assessment of each participant's hearing threshold was necessary to being confident that they can hear therapists' commands. The hearing of each subject was evaluated based on two objective methods: otoacoustic emission (OAE) and auditory brainstem response (ABR). Hearing examination was performed utilizing professional equipment of Vivosonic Integrity. In order to test the sound conducting mechanism and the efficiency of the cochlea click evoked otoacoustic emissions (TEOAE) were employed.

Eye-Gaze Tracking
All experiments based on subjects' gaze activity were conducted utilizing the eye-gaze tracking system called *CyberEye*. The CyberEye was developed at the Multimedia Systems Department of Gdansk University of Technology. Consequently, eye-gaze tracking technology became available in experiments carried out in cooperation with "Light" Residential Medical Care Facility in Torun. The CyberEye's angular resolution (3.3°) was less than best commercial eye-gaze trackers (ca. 0.5°). However, it was sufficient for the consciousness study of VS subjects and, more importantly, it was definitely inexpensive. More detailed information on the CyberEye software and hardware can be found in some previous publications [10]–[12]. Utilizing the CyberEye system in studies with VS subjects was shown in Fig. 1.

Fig. 1. The subject during the consciousness test session

The CyberEye is exploited in the so-called consciousness test in the first path of the proposed method. The consciousness test consists of twelve neuropsychological tasks based on gaze interaction. Assessment procedure of the level of single words understanding (comprehension of speech) or assessment of phonemic hearing is implemented in the software form.

The first task is preliminary and the subject's interaction with the CyberEye system and his/her visual field is studied. This stage of the test is significant in order to display the content in relevant parts of the monitor screen.

In addition, an essential aspect was the long-term nature of the experiments. These studies were conducted within 3 months.

Electroencephalography

EEG-based examination consisted of two steps according to the scheme shown in Fig. 4. Within the first step Steady State Visually Evoked Potentials (SSVEP) were recorded to assess if visual neural pathway is undegenerated. Within the second step of EEG-based examination a comprehension test was proposed. It enables to check if there is possible to confirm symptoms of subjects' consciousness in objective way based on 'names test'.

SSVEP is a continuous visual cortical response evoked by repetitive stimuli with a constant frequency on the central retina. The SSVEP assumes that the response signal contains the same fundamental frequency as the stimulus being considered as one of BCI paradigms. In the literature [13] there were shown results of the analysis of SSVEP signals registered for stimuli frequencies changing from 1Hz to 100 Hz with the constant increment of 1 Hz. Increase of energy for frequencies corresponding to stimuli frequency is clearly visible in the range from 5-60 Hz. Due to the literature [14]–[16] the main area responsible for generating SSVEP responses is the primary visual cortex. It is activated by visual stimuli regardless the flickering frequency.

Our experiments were conducted employing a professional EEG apparatus *Neuron-Spectrum 4/P* with 19 active electrodes. Subject's eyes were covered with a band and flashed with a LED stimulator on given frequencies as it was presented in Fig. 2. Flickering frequencies were chosen arbitrary as: 13, 15, 17 and 21 Hz. During recordings the international 10-20 system was used according to electrodes placement shown in Fig. 3.

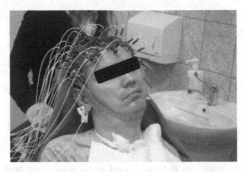

Fig. 2. The subject under EEG-based examination with usage of *Neuron-Spectrum 4/P*

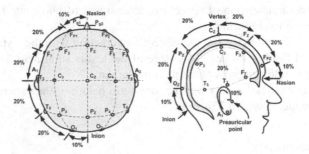

Fig. 3. Electrode placement in the international 10-20 standard [17]

Analysis of EEG recordings for SSVEP responses consisted of the following steps:

1. select fragments of EEG recordings (duration of 30 seconds) for neutral state (open eyes) and for each stimuli frequency,
2. filtrate signals with 10-25 Hz band-pass filter,
3. windowing – the Hamming window was selected,
4. determination of the amplitude spectra of selected fragments,
5. subtraction of the calculated neutral state spectrum from each stimuli frequency spectrum,
6. determination of the power spectra for each stimuli frequency.

Listed above steps were conducted for each subject involved in the experiment. Finally 3 subjects were not examined because of suspicion of epileptic tendencies.

In the second step of EEG-based experiment the comprehension test being the active paradigm was conducted. Exercise based on event related potentials (ERP) induced by counting names was conducted. Subjects were instructed to count their own names while the therapist reads a list of various names. According to the assumption, the P300 response should be larger when subject counts his/her own name in comparison to passive listening [18]. Thus, the comprehension test (names test) could be regarded as quick method for evaluation of subject's consciousness in objective way.

2.2   Subjects

This study was conducted in the "Light" Residential Medical Care Facility, Torun, Poland. Ten subjects were recruited from a group of 34 subjects residing in the center. (most of them with traumatic brain injury): three females and seven males. All of the subjects had been previously diagnosed as remaining in vegetative state and therapists had classified them into a group of 'good prognosis subjects'. Informed consent was obtained from the subjects' legal representatives. Table 2 presents the demographic and clinical data of the subjects, as well as the most important outcomes for CyberEye and EEG-based experiments.

2.3   Method

Eye-gaze tracking is related to one of two paths used for consciousness state evaluation by the therapist. The second path is the analysis of the brain's electrical activity, consisting of examination of visual neural pathway based on Steady State Visually Evoked Potentials (SSVEP), as well as comprehension test based on so-called *names test*. We consider that all subjects should be examined parallel in these two paths. However, in most cases it is impossible because of the different external and internal indispositions of subjects. The scheme of the method proposed and applied in our research is shown in Fig. 4.

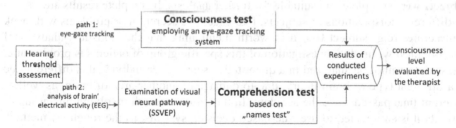

Fig. 4. The developed method of consciousness study utilizing multimodal interfaces

The tasks of the consciousness test based on the CyberEye system include simple neuropsychological tasks. The aim of the consciousness testing is to make a diagnosis followed by stimulation of cognitive, linguistic and communication functions, memory, understanding, logical and abstract thinking.

Within the EEG-based names test the sequence of 30 auditory stimuli were prepared. The sequence included first names – 10 times the subject's own name and 20 unfamiliar names. Names were presented for each subject in the same order. The inter-stimulus interval was set to 3000 ms. Data were collected at a sampling rate of 500 Hz. The ERPs were averaged as a function of the subject's own name and unfamiliar names. In order to ensure equivalent signal to noise ratios, the 10 unfamiliar names from each sequence were chosen. The total duration of EEG recording for each subject was 20 min.

3   Results and Discussion

All results of experiments based on the analysis of eye-gaze tracking and brain's electrical activity have been stored in the database. The outcomes obtained from the CyberEye system and the EEG interfaces were studied independently. The therapists evaluated the subjects' consciousness level based on three features: correctness of performed neuropsychological tasks related to gaze interaction, analysis of P300 responses in the comprehension test, as well as their subjective observations (each case is different).

3.1   Eye-Gaze Tracking Analysis

The main criterion of the consciousness test in the first path of the proposed method was the correctness of test task performance. The credibility of the data obtained from the CyberEye system requires many repetitions of the test. The parameter 'correctness' is a mean of all sums of correctly performed tasks of each examination session. Parameter 'correctness' is normalized and its maximum value is 1. Fig. 5 shows the box-whisker plot presenting the results of sessions based on the eye-gaze tracking during a 3-month observation period. We applied 'mean / standard error (SE) / 2·standard deviation (SD)' types of box-whisker plot. Values of the determined correctness parameters were included in Tab. 2. Unfortunately, the results of only 5 of 10 subjects were complete and suitable for further analysis. Incomplete results are caused by different indispositions of subjects, like excessive secretion or problems with neck contractures (e.g. subject 01). It is worth mentioning that the statistical analysis of data obtained within the investigation of this specific group of patients is problematic. These data cannot be analyzed in a quantitative sense. Each individual is different due to a different type of brain injury, due to damage of another area of brain, as well as different time passed since the accident. In the future research involving this group of patients it is anticipated to use rule-based decision systems, as the rough set method, because besides the diagnosis results, usually more information is available from a medical history of patients which can be used for reasoning about their actual condition and therapy prognosis.

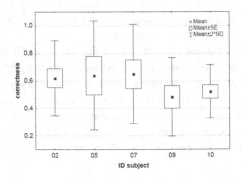

Fig. 5. Correctness of consciousness test performing within 3 months

According to the results presented in Fig. 5 three of patients revealed mean of all the tests at ca. 60% correctness. The other two patients achieved correctness of all tasks close to 50%. It should be mentioned that in case of vegetative patients the expected result equaled 0%.

3.2   EEG Analysis

The obtained results show in an objective way that each subject reacted for flickering frequencies with increase visual cortex response at precise stimulus frequency. The results obtained from occipital area placed electrodes for the particular subject are shown in Fig. 6. These results enable to assess that subjects' visual neural pathways are undamaged, so that they could participate in tests involving the CyberEye system. The results confirmed also that SSVEP are generated mainly in the occipital cortex (points O_1, O_2 and O_z). Moreover, the energies of recorded signal on the stimuli frequency compared to the energy of signal in 10-25 Hz frequency band could be expressed by formula (1):

$$E_{relative} = \frac{E_{ffy}}{E_{10-25Hz}},\qquad(1)$$

where: E_{ffy} – energy of signal at flickering stimuli frequency with tolerance of 0.5 Hz (i. e. for 13 Hz stimuli energy at 12.5–13.5 Hz frequency band);
$E_{10-25Hz}$ – energy of recorded signal at flickering stimuli in 10-25 Hz frequency band.

Energy of signal recorded during photo-stimulation rose minimum twice compared to records without any stimulation. After all, it also confirms that visual neural pathway of each subject participated in experiment has been preserved.

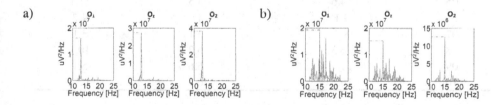

Fig. 6. Power spectra of SSVEP experiment for particular subject stimulated with selected flickering signals at a) 13 and b) 15 Hz, recorded from electrodes O1, O2 and Oz due to international 10-20 system of electrode placement

In the names test a significant higher P300 was obtained when the subject's own name had to be counted. The most significant electrodes were: C_3, C_4, C_z, P_3, P_z and P_4. In Fig. 7 the time plots for averaged ERP responses in period 0 – 1000 ms from stimuli presentation.

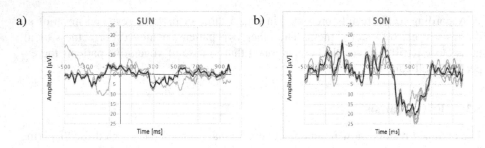

Fig. 7. Grand average of ERP responses for: a) unfamiliar names (SUN) and b) subject's own name (SON) (b). Gray lines denotes EEG signals from most significant electrodes (C_3, C_4, C_z, P_3, P_z, P_4) while black line denotes their weighted mean value.

In Tab. 1 there are presented event-related amplitudes (in μV) at P_z for P300 component in response to subject's own name (SON) and subject's unfamiliar names (SUN). The fourth column includes difference [μV] between amplitudes of SON and SUN. There is a hypothesis that level of subject's consciousness should be related to the value of this difference.

Table 1. Results of averaged ERPs amplitudes [μV] for each subject

Subject ID	SON response amplitude	SUN response amplitude	difference
01	12.6	5.1	7.5
02	6.8	3.8	3.0
03	7.6	5.4	2.2
04	12	5.7	6.3
05	14.6	3.5	11.1
06	9.1	4.9	4.2
07	8.2	5.1	3.1
08	16.3	6.2	10.1
09	11.7	6.6	5.1
10	16.6	6.4	10.2

Obtained results suggest that some of studied subjects are able to detect their own first name consciously. It is known that speech processing can be observed in unconscious state such as anesthesia or sleep [19], however using the active paradigm (counting subject's own name) reduces probability of getting inaccurate results. Tab. 2 contains general data related to participants, as well as results provided by the eye-gaze tracking system and EEG interface. Moreover, the therapists were able to assess more precisely subjects' consciousness state supported by multimodal interfaces.

Table 2. Demographic and clinical data and current diagnosis of the subjects

Subject ID	Sex	Age (years)	Cause	Interval post-ictus	EGT (average of correctness)	EEG (difference in [μV])	Post-experimental diagnosis
01	male	25	trauma	33 m	–	7.5	LIS
02	male	56	SCA	28 m	0.62	3.0	LIS
03	male	37	SCA	9 m	–	2.2	MCS
04	male	31	trauma	13 m	–	6.3	MCS+
05	female	40	trauma	72 m	0.64	11.1	LIS
06	male	32	trauma	72 m	–	4.2	MCS
07	female	19	trauma	15 m	0.65	3.1	MCS+
08	male	36	trauma	14 m	–	10.1	MCS
09	male	29	trauma	19 m	0.48	5.1	MCS+
10	female	33	SCA	11 m	0.52	10.2	LIS

SCA – sudden cardiac arrest; m – months; EGT – eye-gaze tracking

It is difficult to determine correlation coefficient between values of the results provided by the eye-gaze tracking and EEG interfaces and state of subjects' consciousness. Nevertheless, obtained values indicate unquestionably that the studied human beings are conscious.

4   Conclusions

The correct diagnosis of state of patients emerging from coma after acute brain injury is very complex, yet an essential problem. Therapists of most centers, especially in developing countries like Poland, where our patients reside, do not verify the diagnosis of VS patients even by CRS-R criteria. Our approach of consciousness evaluation does not require expensive technology application and it could be applied at the patient's bedside. Moreover, we can estimate the patient's state conducting one of two proposed paths of examination.

The results obtained from EEG experiments proved objectively that visual neural pathways of each subject from research group is undamaged and they could participate in therapy with the usage of CyberEye equipment. Moreover, results of the names test indicate that most subjects are able to detect their own first names correctly. It is worth stressing that the role of the therapist's subjective observation is significant in this approach because neither the eye-gaze tracking system, nor the EEG interface includes information on the patient's attitude and their different indispositions, like e. g. excessive secretion. Results presented in this paper suggest that our objective-subjective methodology could potentially be introduced into a clinical facilities after further validation. The next step of the analysis of the obtained results will be associated with using rough sets not only for interpretation of CyberEye's data but also for the whole diagnosis based on CyberEye's and EEG' results in order to support therapists and neurologists in a more efficient way.

Acknowledgements. The research was funded within the project No. POIG.01.03.01-22-017/08, entitled "Elaboration of a series of multimodal interfaces and their implementation to educational, medical, security and industrial applications". The project is subsidized by the European Regional Development Fund by the Polish State budget".

References

[1] Landsness, E., Bruno, M.A., Noirhomme, Q., Riedner, B., Gosseries, O., Schnakers, C., Massimini, M., Laureys, S., Tononi, G., Boly, M.: Electrophysiological correlates of behavioural changes in vigilance in vegetative state and minimally conscious state. Brain 134(pt. 8), 2222–2232 (2011)

[2] Lulé, D., Noirhomme, Q., Kleih, S.C., Chatelle, C., Halder, S., Demertzi, A., Bruno, M.-A., Gosseries, O., Vanhaudenhuyse, A., Schnakers, C., Thonnard, M., Soddu, A., Kübler, A., Laureys, S.: Probing command following in patients with disorders of consciousness using a brain-computer interface. Clin. Neurophysiol. 124(1), 101–106 (2013)

[3] Rosanova, M., Gosseries, O., Casarotto, S., Boly, M., Casali, A.G., Bruno, M.A., Mariotti, M., Boveroux, P., Tononi, G., Laureys, S., Massimini, M.: Recovery of cortical effective connectivity and recovery of consciousness in vegetative patients. Brain 135, 1308–1320 (2012)

[4] Laureys, S., Goldman, S., Phillips, C., Van Bogaert, P., Aerts, J., Luxen, A., Franck, G., Maquet, P.: Impaired effective cortical connectivity in vegetative state: preliminary investigation using PET. Neuroimage 9(4), 377–382 (1999)

[5] Noirhomme, Q., Soddu, A., Vanhaudenhuyse, A., Lehembre, R., Bruno, M.A., Gosseries, O., Demertzi, A., Maudoux, A., Schnakers, C., Boveroux, P., Boly, M., Laureys, S.: Functional neuroimaging approaches to the changing borders of consciousness. J. Psychophysiol. 24(2), 68–75 (2010)

[6] Laureys, S., Schiff, N.D.: Coma and consciousness: paradigms (re)framed by neuroimaging. Neuroimage 61(2), 478–491 (2012)

[7] Vanhaudenhuyse, A., Noirhomme, Q., Tshibanda, L., Bruno, M.A., Boveroux, P., Schnakers, C., Soddu, A., Perlbarg, V., Ledoux, D., Brichant, J.F., Moonen, G., Maquet, P., Greicius, M.D., Laureys, S., Boly, M.: Default network connectivity reflects the level of consciousness in non-communicative brain-damaged patients. Brain 133(pt. 1), 161–171 (2010)

[8] Monti, M.M., Laureys, S., Owen, A.M.: The vegetative state. BMJ 341 (2010)

[9] Monti, M.M., Vanhaudenhuyse, A., Coleman, M.R., Boly, M., Pickard, J.D., Tshibanda, L., Owen, A.M., Laureys, S.: Willful modulation of brain activity in disorders of consciousness. N. Engl. J. Med. 362(7), 579–589 (2010)

[10] Kunka, B., Czyzewski, A., Kwiatkowska, A.: Awareness evaluation of patients in vegetative state employing eye-gaze tracking system. Int. J. Artif. Intell. Tools 21(2), 1–11 (2012)

[11] Kunka, B., Kostek, B.: Objectivization of audio-visual correlation analysis. Arch. Acoust. 37(1), 63–72 (2012)

[12] Kunka, B., Kostek, B.: Exploiting audio-visual correlation by means of gaze tracking. Int. J. Comput. Sci. Appl. 7(3), 104–123 (2010)

[13] Herrmann, C.S.: Human EEG responses to 1–100 Hz flicker: resonance phenomena in visual cortex and their potential correlation to cognitive phenomena. Exp. Brain Res. 137(3–4), 346–353 (2001)

[14] Pastor, M., Artieda, J., Arbizu, J., Valencia, M., Masdeu, J.: Human cerebral activation during steady-state visual-evoked responses. J. Neurosci. 23(37), 621–627 (2003)
[15] Vialatte, F., Maurice, M., Dauwels, J., Cichocki, A.: Steady- state visually evoked potentials: Focus on essential paradigms and future perspectives. Prog. Neurobiol. 90, 418–438 (2010)
[16] Bayram, A.: Simultaneous EEG/fMRI Analysis of the Resonance Phenomena in Steady-State Visual Evoked Responses. Clin. EEG Neurosci. 42(2), 98–106 (2011)
[17] Sharbrough, F., Chatrian, G.-E., Lesser, R.P., Lüders, H., Nuwer, M., Picton, T.W.: American Electroencephalographic Society Guidelines for Standard Electrode Position Nomenclature. J. Clin. Neurophysiol. 8, 200–202 (1991)
[18] Lehembre, R., Gosseries, O., Lugo, Z., Jedidi, Z., Chatelle, C., Sadzot, B., Laureys, S., Noirhomme, Q.: Electrophysiological investigations of brain function in coma, vegetative and minimally conscious patients. Arch. Ital. Biol. 150, 122–139 (2012)
[19] Perrin, F., Garcia-Larrea, L., Mauguiere, F., Bastuji, H.: A differential brain response to the subject's own name persists during sleep. Clin. Neurophysiol. 110(12), 2153–2164 (1999)

Establishing a Baseline Value of Cognitive Skills among School-Aged Children in Upper Egypt Using Computer Based Cognitive Assessment Rehacom Program

Faten Hassan Abdelazeim and Shereen Ali Ameen

College of Physical Therapy, Cairo University, Egypt
Faten.hassan@pt.cu.edu.eg,
dr.shereena@yahoo.com

Abstract. Computer-based cognitive assessment programs for children have recently become increasingly popular. This assessment tool has many advantages over traditional assessment approaches including the option of offering an immediate feedback, the ability to systematize delivery of the test items and to modify the difficulty level and the ability to quantify progress. **Purpose:** the purpose of the study is to establish a reference baseline for the cognitive skills among Egyptian school-aged children. **Method:** This study is a cross-sectional prospective design. A sample of 223 healthy children of both sexes, of age ranged from 6-12 years, from urban areas' elementary schools in Upper Egypt were recruited. **Results:** Rehacom program tool produced a separate progress report for the individual progress of every child. **Conclusions:** Based on the study's results the executive function ability was the first to initiated followed by the logical reasoning and finally the topological memory and vigilance

Keywords: Cognitive, Assessment, Normal Children, Upper Egypt, Rehacom program.

1   Introduction

Cognition is the mental action of process of gaining knowledge through thought, experience and the senses, so the word cognition is a cover for all of the mental activities that we engage in; our thoughts and our thinking [1]. Cognition can be divided into different domains of ability, which can be tested separately; the most important of these are attention and concentration, memory and learning, language, visuospatial function and executive functions [2]. Cognitive assessment is considered to become an important component of diagnosing learning and behavior problems in children. Intellectual deficits and learning disabilities may have an adverse effect on a child's ability to comprehend and retain information [3]. It also plays an important role in academic placement decisions as it allows teachers, parents and clinicians to gain an understanding about a particular child's capabilities in order to facilitate informed (academic and training) decisions [4].

D. Ślęzak et al. (Eds.): BIH 2014, LNAI 8609, pp. 68–78, 2014.
© Springer International Publishing Switzerland 2014

Neuropsychological testing has been conducted in the past with paper and pencil test. Recently, more and more neuropsychological testing become computerized as computerization has made scoring much simpler and more accurate, it also allows for more complicated computations [5]. According to The American Psychological Association (APA), it identified six major benefits of computerized assessment including: (1) automated data collection and storage, (2) greater efficiency of use, (3) release of the clinician from test administration to focus on treatment, (4) greater sense of mastery and control for the client, (5) reduced negative self-evaluation among clients that experience difficulty on the computer and (6) greater ability to measure aspects of performance not possible through traditional means, such as latency, strength and variability in response patterns [6].

Socioeconomic status (SES) is a multidimensional construct that includes not only measure of maternal wealth, but also education and social prestige. Many studies displayed the effect of low SES of the families and poorly parental education on their children's cognitive skills. Parental SES can affect an individual from very early development in utero, as well as throughout life [7,8] . Stress, nutrition, parental care and cognitive stimulation have been suggested as some of the factors that mediate the impact of SES on both brain structures and cognitive functions across development [9,10].

Children in low income countries are exposed to several diseases and adverse conditions that affect brain development and cognition either through direct injury to the brain or lack of stimulating conditions [11, 12]. The goal of the ongoing paper is to assess the cognitive functioning of Egyptian school-aged children resident in urban areas, establishing a baseline value of cognitive skills among these children by using the Rehacom computerized program which is a method for assessment of cognitive domains among Egyptian school-aged children from families with low socioeconomic class. It is computer based software composed of several rehabilitation programs, designed to measure and rehabilitate different cognitive abilities.

2   Method

2.1   Subjects

The present study was conducted on 223 healthy school-aged children recruited from urban elementary schools. The purpose of the study was establishing cognitive norms for the Egyptian school-aged children. The children were randomly selected by the simple protocol of sealed envelope approach" each child has the same chance of being selected" in order to reduce the probability of imbalance in children selection according to the inclusive criteria. Initially, the study included 241 children. 18 children decided to quit before completion of the test procedures not because they did not want to complete but their parents had no time. The children age ranged from 6-12 years. The selection of children was based on their score in on "Draw a person test" and "Pediatric symptom checklist" to detect any mild cognitive impairment. They were able to follow instructions and understand commands during testing procedures. Children with history of mental, cognitive, neuromuscular disorders, epilepsy, visual, auditory defects or autistic features were excluded. All children were from families with low socioeconomic class and their parents had no or low level of education.

2.2   Testing Procedures

Prior to beginning testing, The Researches were provided approval from ethical committee faculty of physical therapy, Cairo university, school manager , and students` parents consent for agreeing about participating their children in the study and were informed of any limits to confidentiality according to American Psychological Association, (2002) and NAN, (2003). All tests administered and scored in a manner that is consistent with the test publisher directions as standardized procedures are critical to valid interpretation. The areas of cognitive domains of function assessed were including attention, memory, visual perception, executive functions. The children were given a brief demonstration of how the Rehacom programs is working in four tested domains , according to the research protocol , before starting the actual testing. Participants were informed that they could quit at any time during the test procedures. All subjects performed a preliminary test to familiarize them with the sit-up and testing procedures. All subjects were started with level 1 on Rehacom. The administration of the tests should be based on the standardized procedures outlined in testing manuals. The testing procedures were conducted in an environment free from any distraction and noise which may affects children`s performance.

2.3   Testing Protocol

For logical reasoning program
The type of test used is 'completion of a series'. By increasing the difficulty of the logic succession and increasing supposition of several logic structures, the child should figure out the concepts underlying each problematic situation and to use these concepts to solve the logic problem. In the testing procedure, a picture series is shown with simple graphic figures. The child must find the relationship between the individual links of the series and through Induction derive a rule (figure reasoning), which clarifies what the next link of the series is [13] . When the child has established what the rule is - he must then select the relevant picture from a matrix of pictures. The matrix of pictures can be used by the patient to check that he has derived the correct rule.

For vigilance Program
In the test, the child works as a high-quality controller at the end of a manufacturing line in a factory (drinks and/or canned food production, furniture industry, electronics manufacturing or production of budget subjects) .the task is to identify which objects are not identical to the specimens, and remove them from the conveyor at the point indicated The aim of the program vigilance is to evaluate the child`s performance in the area of tonic attention, with specific attention focused on maintaining visual vigilance, in difficult observation situations the child`s reaction skills are put under pressure in that they are also exposed to irrelevant information..

For topological memory
In this test, a varying number of cards (dependent on the level of difficulty) with concrete pictures or geometric figures are displayed on the screen. The child must memorize the location of the pictures. After a pre-set time – or manually, by pressing the OK button – the pictures in the matrix are hidden (turned face down). The objective

of this procedure is to evaluate the memory for visual-spatial information as by a means of ordering the pictures in a topological way, the possibility exists to elaborate and to consolidate, different memory strategies with the child.

For exploration program
The procedure allows assessment for visual exploration. The child is required to slowly search for a series - in locating these precise objects. Varieties of abstract and concrete stimuli are projected on a dark background Squares, triangles, circles, asterisks and other see symbols, numbers, letters, objects (flowers, cars etc.). The child has to search the surface for these various stimuli. The stimuli are arranged in lines and columns.

A circular cursor, which is the same size as a matrix unit, moves over the field line by line. In this way the exploration movements of the child can be controlled. Every time a previously defined stimulus is located, the child has to press the OK key on the Rehacom keyboard.

3   Data Analysis

Descriptive statistical analysis was used in the present study. Mean age for each level of each domain was calculated to conclude the progression for each ability with age (when it appeared on average, when it became stronger and when it peaked). A bar chart was used to display a comparison between the mean ages of first appearance of each domain. Another bar chart was used to display the rational development of the four cognitive domains.

4   Results

The study was conducted on 223 children of age ranging from 6 to 12 years with mean age 9.4538 years. Each child's level of performance on the Rehacom program domains (exploration, logical reasoning, topological memory and vigilance) was measured. We considered the level of performance as an indicator for the presence of the cognitive ability. Data were analyzed along the dimension of age and the mean scores on each level of the four cognitive domains. Regarding the age there were significant difference between 6 and 12 years in the level of performance on each domain which indicating developing of such domain of cognitive function. As described in (Table 1) & (Fig. 1) Exploration which is defined as the active searching of the field of vision for particular symbols: The levels ranged from 1 to 8, level 1 appeared at age 6 years and 9 months with mean age of 9.02 years. Level 8 appeared 11 years and 9 months with mean age 11.75 years.

Logical reasoning which is the ability to think and make relations between objects: Levels ranged from 1 to 7, level 1 appeared at age 7years with mean age of 9.23 years. Level 7 appeared at age 11 years and 9 months with mean age 11.75 years.

Topological memory which is the ability to remember pictures: Levels ranged from 1 to 3, level 1 appeared at age 8 years with mean age of 9.53 years. Level 3 appeared at age 11 years and 9 months with mean age 11.75 years.

Vigilance which is the ability to make sustained attention: Levels ranged from 0 1to 3, level 1 appeared at age 8 years with mean age of 9.35 years. Level 3 appeared at age 11 years and 2 months with mean age 11.02 years.

Table 1. The mean values of performance of children in four domains

level	Exploration	Logical reasoning	Topological memory	Vigilance
	Mean age			
1	9.02	9.23	9.53	9.35
2	9.52	10.04	10.25	10.43
3	9.93	9.97	11.75	11.02
4	10.32	10.53		
5	11.15	10.95	--------	---------
6	11.17	10.83		
7	-------	11.75	--------	---------
8	11.75			

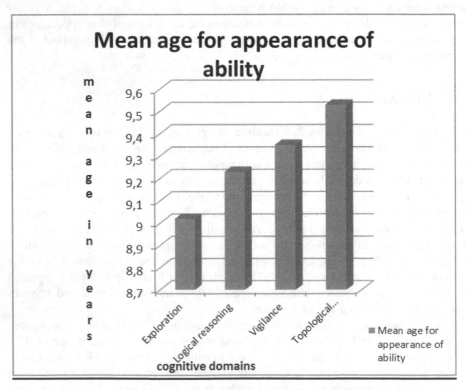

Fig. 1. Mean age for appearance of each ability

The development of the four cognitive domains with age
As shown in figure 1 :Exploration appeared first at mean age 9.02, became stronger at
mean age 9.93 and reached a peak at mean age 11.75.Then Logical reasoning appeared at mean age 9.23, became stronger at mean age 9.97 and reached a peak at
mean age 11.75. Vigilance appeared then at mean age 9.35, became stronger at mean
age 10.43 and reached a peak at mean age 11.02.At last Topological memory appeared at age 9.53, became stronger at mean age 10.25 and reached a peak at mean
age 11.75.

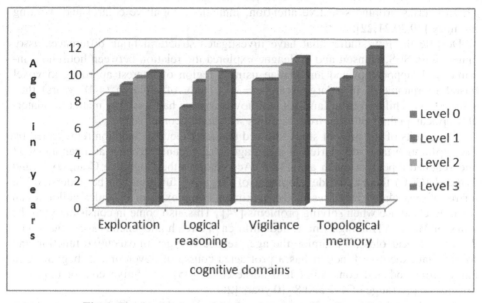

Fig. 2. The development of the four cognitive domains with age

5   Discussion

The present study was conducted on 223 healthy school-aged children recruited from
urban elementary school for the purpose of establishing cognitive norms for the Egyptian school-aged children. The study focused on gathering normative data regarding
the children's cognitive development in specific domains: sustained attention, topological memory, logical reasoning and executive functions. Choosing the study sample to include children aged from 6 -12 years supports the finding of Bjorklund who
stated that there is a huge amount of cognitive development that occurs after infancy,
after the pre-school years and during the elementary school ages and even into adolescence [14], and also this come in consistent with Coffey and his colleague who
argued that Cognitive development is an active and ongoing process that is influenced
by both internal and external stimuli from infancy to adolescence [15] . Almost all
aspects of cognition show marked development after the pre-school years and during
the elementary school ages: perception and attention, memory, conceptualizing,

problem solving and reasoning, symbolic processes. All of these have important implications for education and other practical activities [16] .

We worked with randomly selected children from families with low SES and poor educational level, in upper Egypt, to measure the children's cognitive abilities. These children suffer from poor nutrition, parental care and diseases, which influence the process of cognitive development and brain structures. Our work is related to the work of Hackman and Raizada who postulated that, at least three cognitive domains (i.e. language, executive function and memory) have been suggested to be influenced by SES [17,18], and low SES children also perform more than their peers from high SES on tasks probing selective attention, inhibition, cognitive control and working memory [19,20,21,22].

Despite the few studies that have investigated structural brain differences associated with SES, Hanson and colleague explored the relation between household income and hippocampi and amygladae using a region of interest approacg in voxel based morphometry in a large scale (n=317) study of children (4-18 years) they showed that, children from families with lower income had less gray matter in bilateral hippocampi than children from families with high income [23] .

The results of the present study showed that the executive function represented by the exploration task was started at mean age 9.02, became stronger at mean age 9.93 and reached a peak at mean age 11.75. According to the Cognitive Complexity and Control (CCC) theory, the development of executive function can be understood in terms of age-related increases in the maximum complexity of the rules children can formulate and use when solving problems [24] . This also come in consistent with the work of Mariette Huizinga who tested children in three homogeneous age groups (i.e., 7-, 11-, 15-year olds),to examine the age –related changes in executive function and found that executive function has a protracted course of development, beginning in early childhood and continuing into adolescence [25]. Executive control improves during the age range of 4–7 and 8–10 years [26].

In the logical reasoning domain, according to Vygotsky (1978) great importance was placed on a child's culture, he saw it as paramount to the emergence of reasoning skills [27]. Children from different cultures demonstrate differences in the timing of certain abilities, and in some cultures, formal operational reasoning may not appear at all because it has little bearing on everyday functioning [28,29]. The results of the present study showed that, it appeared at age 7 y with mean age 9.23, became stronger at mean age 9.97 and reached a peak at mean age 11.75. This comes in consistent with thoughts of piaget in Brophy and Van Sledright who stated that logical reasoning ability starts around age 7 years at time children begin to develop concrete operations-cognitive capacities that enable them to solve concrete problems logically, and at age 12 children begin to develop formal operations- cognitive capacities that enable them to engage in more abstract, hypothetical and purely symbolic thinking without being so dependent on direct experiences or concrete examples [30].

Memory refers to the complex process by which the individual encodes, stores, and retrieves information and for a memory to be useful one must be able to retrieve it [31] Memory is not unitary but rather consists of a variety of different forms, each mediated by different component processes which in turn are subserved by different neural mechanisms [32]. In response to the results of the memory domain in the present study it showed that, Topological memory representing the visuospatial skill which is the ability to produce and recognize figures and to form relationships among spatial locations, appeared at mean age 9.53, became stronger at mean age 10.25 and reached a peak at mean age 11.75, which means that working memory and cognitive control, develop throughout late childhood and adolescence and continue to mature until young adulthood [33] . Tests of working memory have demonstrated that there are three active stages of maturation: early childhood, middle childhood, and early adolescence [34].

Attention can be conceptualized as the gateway for information flow to the brain and it is a complex system of interacting components that allows the individual to filter relevant and irrelevant information in the context of internal drives and intentions, hold and manipulate mental representations and monitor/ modulate responses to stimuli [35] . Sustained attention is defined as the ability to stay on-task and to inhibit distracting stimuli over a prolonged period of time. It forms a component of the vigilance network, and is assessed through tasks that require a participant to remain prepared to respond to an infrequent target over an extended time [36]. The results of the present study showed that, Vigilance or sustained attention appeared then at mean age 9.35, became stronger at mean age 10.43 and reached a peak at mean age 11.02. These results are closely in line with those recently reported by Steele and colleague as they measured attentional performance in preschool children, with several tasks involving the capacity to sustain attention for a prolonged period of time (Go/No-Go task) to visually search targets among distracters and to benefit from a target presented in a position spatially congruent with the response they found that, attentional performance extends to ages later than preschool [37].

The Outcome results of the present study showed that, executive function ability is the first to develop early as it initiated at age 6y &9m. that matches level 1 on exploration domain on Rehacom and mastered at age 12 which is at level 8 (each domain on Rehacom program is ranged from 1 -24) . It considered as the base that control and regulate other behaviors, and therefore enable goal-directed behavior [24]. Shore claim that the years between three and five are especially important in the development of executive function because of changes in brain development during this period, particularly in the frontal cortex, which is responsible for regulating and expressing emotion [38]. The logical reasoning ability started little a bit later as it begins at age 7 years as it needs more maturation of the brain structures which occurred during late childhood and adolescence as piaget suggested that children from 7-11 years are concerned with knowing only the facts and therefore becomes confused when faced with the relative, probabilistic nature of human knowledge, children begin to apply mental operations to real, concrete problems, objects, or events [39]. Finally, sustained attention and topological memory are the latest domains to develop as they need more and more maturation of the brain they begin at 8y which comes in contact with Sowell and Gogtay Who stated that the cortex matures in a sequence that parallels cognitive development. Brain regions mediating motor and sensory functions mature first, followed by temporal and parietal areas (which primarily mediate language and spatial skills). Association areas (such as the prefrontal cortex and lateral temporal regions) mature last; these areas integrate information from sensory–motor regions and modulate processes like attention and working memory [40,41].

6   Conclusion

The present study was conducted in order to establish a baseline values for the cognitive abilities (executive function, logical reasoning, topological memory and vigilance) for Egyptian school-aged children using computerized cognitive program (Rehacom). Based on the study`s results the executive function ability was the first to initiated at 6 years and 9 months followed by the logical reasoning at 7 years and finally the topological memory and vigilance emerged at 8 years. The study suggests the usability of the computerized cognitive assessment tool "Rehacom" to detect the level of cognitive ability and variability of cognitive development patterns in school-aged children.

References

1. Taylor, L.: Introducing Cognitive Development, pp. 8–28. Psychology Press, Taylor & Francis (2005)
2. Richards, M., Shipley, B., Fuhrer, R., et al.: Cognitive Ability in Childhood and Cognitive Decline in Midlife: Longitudinal birth cohort study. British Medical Journal 29, 484–493 (2004)
3. Krishnamurthy, R.V., Creek, L., Kaslow, N.J., et al.: Achieving Competency in Psychological Assessment: Direction for education and training. Journal of Clinical Psychology 60, 725–739 (2004)
4. Sattler, J.M.: Assessment of Children: cognitive foundation, 5th edn., pp. 256–263. San Diego State University (2008)
5. Naglirei, J.A., Graham, J.R.: Handbook of Psychology, Assessment Psychology, pp. 45–451. John Wiley and sons (2003)
6. Woo, E.: Computerized Neuropsychological Assessments. CNS Spectr. 13(10 suppl.) 16, 14–17 (2008)
7. Sarsour, K., Sheridan, M., Jutte, D., et al.: Family Socioeconomic Status and Child Executive Functions: The Roles of Language, Home Environment, and Single Parenthood. Journal of the International Neuropsychological Society 17, 120–132 (2011)
8. Jednoro´g, K., Altarelli, I., Monzalvo, K., et al.: The Influence of Socioeconomic Status on Children's Brain Structure. Plos. One 7(8) (2012)
9. Hackman, D.A., Farah, M.J., Meaney, M.J.: Socioeconomic Status and the Brain: Mechanistic Insights From Human and Animal Research. Nat. Rev. Neurosci. 11, 651–659 (2010)
10. Tomalski, P., Johnson, M.H.: The Effects of Early Adversity On the Adult and Developing Brain. Curr. Opin. Psychiatry 23, 233–238 (2010)
11. Walker, S.P., Wachs, T.D., Gardner, J.M., Lozoff, B., Wasserman, G.A., et al.: Child development: Risk Factors for Adverse Outcomes in Developing Countries. Lancet 369, 145–157 (2007)
12. Olness, K.: Effects on Brain Development Leading to Cognitive Impairment: a worldwide epidemic. J. Dev. Behav. Pediatr. 24, 120–130 (2003)
13. von Cramon, D.Y., Matthes- von Cramon, G.: Reflections on the Treatment of Brain-Injured Patients Suffering from Problem-solving Disorders. Disorders. Neuropsychological Rehabilitation 2(3), 207–229 (1993)

14. Bjorklund, D.F.: Cognitive Development and Individual Differences Children's Thinking, 5th edn., pp. 7–31. Wadsworth/Cengage Learning, Belmont (2012)
15. Coffey, C.E., Brumback, R.A., Rosenberg, D.R., et al.: Pediatric Neuropsychiatry, 1st edn., pp. 50–62. Lippincott Williams and Wilkins (2006)
16. Pick Jr., H.L.: Implications, A Newsletter by Informe Design. A Web site for Design and Human Behavior Research 1(8) (2003)
17. Hackman, D.A., Farah, M.J.: Socioeconomic Status and The Developing Brain. Trends Cogn. Sci. 13, 65–73 (2009)
18. Raizada, R.D.S., Kishiyama, M.M.: Effects of Socioeconomic Status on Brain Development, and How Cognitive Neuroscience Contribute to Leveling the Playing Field. Front Hum., Neurosci. 4, 1–11 (2010)
19. Bradley, R.H., Corwin, R.F.: Socioeconomic Status and Child Development. Annu. Rev. Psychol. 53, 371–399 (2002)
20. Mezzacappa, E.: Alerting, Orienting, and Executive Attention: Developmental Properties and Sociodemographic Correlates in an Epidemiological Sample of Young, Urban Children. Child. Dev. 75, 1373–1386 (2004)
21. Kishiyama, M.M., Boyce, T., Jimenez, A.M., Perry, L.M., Knight, R.T.: Socioeconomic Disparities Affect Prefrontal Function in Children. J. Cogn. Neurosci. 21, 1106–1115 (2008)
22. Stevens, C., Lauinger, B., Neville, H.: Differences in the neural mechanisms of selective attention in children from different socioeconomic backgrounds: an event-related brain potential study. Dev. Sci. 12, 634–646 (2009)
23. Hanson, J.L., Chandra, A., Wolfe, B.L., Pollak, S.D.: Association Between Income and The Hippocampus. Plos ONE 6(5), e18712 (2011)
24. Zelazo, P.D., Muller, U., Frye, D., Marcovitch, S.: The Development of Executive Function in Early Childhood. Monographs of the Society for Research in Child Development 68(3), Serial No. 274 (2003)
25. Huizinga, M., Dolan, C.V., Maurits, W.: Age-related Change in Executive Function: Developmental Trends and a Latent Variable Analysis. Neuropsychologia 44, 2017–2036 (2006)
26. Reuda, M.R., Rothbart, M.K., McCandliss, B.D., et al.: Training, Maturation and Genetic Influences on Development of Executive Functions. Proc. Natl. Acad. Sci. U.S.A. 102, 14932–14936 (2005)
27. Vygotsky, L.: Interaction between Learning and Development. In: Mind and Society, pp. 79–91. Harvard University Press, Cambridge (1978)
28. Miller, P.J., Wiley, A.R., Fung, H., Liang, C.H.: Personal Storytelling as a Medium of Socialization in Chinese and American families. Child Development 68, 557–568 (1997)
29. Norenzayan, A., Choi, I., Peng, K.: Cognition and Perception. In: Kitayama, S., Cohen, D. (eds.) Handbook of Cultural Psychology, pp. 569–594. Guilford Publications, New York (2007)
30. Brophy, J.E., Sledright, V.: Teaching and Learning History in Elementary Schools, p. 11. Library of congress (1997)
31. Banich, M.T.: Cognitive Neuroscience and Neuropsychology, 2nd edn., pp. 412–420. Houghton Mifflin, Boston (2004)
32. Moscovitch, M., Fernandes, M.A., Davidson, P.S.R.: Contribution of Frontal and Temporal Lobe Function to Memory Interferences from Divided Attention at Retrieval. Neuropsychology 18, 514–525 (2004)
33. Casey, B.J., Tottenham, N., Liston, C., et al.: Imaging the Developing Brain: what have we learned about cognitive development? Trends Cogn. Sci. (Regul. Ed.) 9, 104–110 (2005b)

34. Brocki, K.C., Bohlin, G.: Executive functions in children aged 6 to 13: A Dimensional and Developmental study. Developmental Neuropsychology 26(2), 571–593 (2004)
35. Cohen, D.: Cultural Variation: Considerations and Implications. Psychological Bulletin 127, 451–471 (2001)
36. Guy, J.: Age-Related Changes in Visual and Auditory Sustained Attention, Inhibition and Working Memory in Preschool-Aged Children. In: Integrated Program in Neuroscience. McGill University, Montreal (2010)
37. Steele, A., Karmiloff-Smith, A., Cornish, K., Scerif, G.: The Multiple Subfunctions of Attention: Differential developmental gateways to literacy and numeracy. Child Development 83, 2028–2041 (2012)
38. Shore, S.: Beyond the Wall: Personal Experiences with Autism and Asperger Syndrome, 2nd edn., pp. 127–130. Shawnee Mission, Kansas (2003)
39. Piaget, J.: Plays, dreams, and imitation in childhood. Norton, New York (1962)
40. Sowell, E.R., Peterson, B.S., Thompson, P.M., et al.: Mapping Cortical Change Across the Human Life span. Nat. Neurosci. 6, 309–315 (2003)
41. Gogtay, N., Giedd, J.N., Lusk, L., et al.: Dynamic Mapping of Human Cortical Development during Childhood Through Early Adulthood. Proc. Natl. Acad. Sci. U.S.A. 101, 8174–8179 (2004)

Autocovariance Based PCA Method for fMRI Data

Dazhong Liu, Xuedong Tian, and Liang Zhu

School of Mathematics and Computer Science, Hebei University Baoding 071002, China
liudazhong@hbu.edu.cn

Abstract. There are various kinds of methods on activated regions detection, including model-driven method and data-driven method, univariate method and multivariate method, frequency domain analysis and time-domain analysis etc. We investigated the problems of principal component analysis applied to activated regions detection, an autocovariance based principal component analysis method was proposed. Firstly, the time series were converted to the autocovariance series, and then the principal component analysis was employed. Meanwhile, the tactic of principal component selection was discussed. The validity of the proposed method was illustrated by experiments on a synthetic dataset and a real dataset. It was shown that the error rate of the new approach was lower compared with the principal component analysis itself.

Keywords: Autocovariance, principal component analysis, functional Magnetic Resonance Imaging, statistic parameter mapping.

1 Introduction

FMRI data analysis can be roughly divided into two main categories: model-driven (hypothesis-driven) methods and data-driven methods. The general linear model (GLM) is most commonly used model-driven approach, which uses a canonical hemodynamic response function (HRF) as the priori hypothesis. Comparing to the classic statistical hypothesis testing approaches, Data-driven approaches do not make assumptions on the profile of the HRF. Like the Clustering, principal component analysis (PCA) [1-2], and independent component analysis (ICA) are the most widely discussed model-driven methods.

PCA is frequently applied in the research of data reduction and signals denoise, it has also been applied to face recognition and other fields. PCA is also an approach to functional brain connectivity analysis and data-preprocessing [3]. It is also suitable for the processing of multivariate data.

In PCA, the singular value decomposition (SVD) method is used for the computation of the covariance matrix to construct a series of corresponding components which are orthogonal to each other. The principal spatial variation of a signal can be represented by an image named eigenimage and temporal variation represented by the eigenvector [4-7]. We ranked these components in descending order of the amount of their variance, that is to say, the first principal component may correspond to the direction with the largest variance in data and can account for the major variance of

D. Ślęzak et al. (Eds.): BIH 2014, LNAI 8609, pp. 79–89, 2014.

signal change. We used the eigenimage chosen randomly to illustrate the transformation of signal space. The eigenimage is a similar description of the functional magnetic resonance imaging (fMRI) activation map. Each principal component indicates its corresponding distribution brain network. Different principal components are orthogonal and uncorrelated. As an exploratory multivariate statistical method, PCA has been previously used to analyze the fMRI data. Although PCA method is continuously making progress, its processing performance has to be improved. Baumgartner [8] found that fuzzy cluster analysis performs better than PCA, especially when signal-to-noise ratio (SNR) is low. Thomas [9] pointed out that the PCA has its limitation when analyzing fMRI data, since task-dependent component may mix into other physiology noise signals. Because sometimes the brain areas of task activated are small, its component may not in the first few components. Because of this, in order to improve PCA analysis performance, determining the related principal component has become a major problem we are faced with when trying to analyze fMRI data based on PCA method [10]. How to highlight the signal features and detect signal from noise is the key to the problem. To solve this problem, we proposed the autocovariance based PCA method.

This paper was organized as follows. In Section 2, we first gave our method and then introduced the dataset used in our experiment. In Section 3, experimental results of the simulated dataset were given. In Section 4, experimental results of the real dataset were described. Finally, Section 5 gave discussion and concluding remarks.

2   Methods and Materials

2.1   Method

Suppose the fMRI time-series data had a length of N, we used $\{x_n(k)\}$ to denote value of k_{th} voxel at time n. For each voxel, we computed its autocovariance series by formula (1).

$$R_l(k) = \frac{1}{N} \sum_{n=1}^{N-l} (x_{n+l}(k) - \mu(k))(x_n(k) - \mu(k)) \tag{1}$$

Where $\mu(k)$ denotes the mean value of time series for voxel k, and l is a lag time point [11]. Given m voxels in whole brain, the size of autocovariance series was p, we got an $m \times p$ matrix M. We then computed the singular value decomposition (SVD) of M, namely, SVD (M) =USV'. Let r be the rank of matrix M, r≤min (m, p). U and V are orthogonal matrices, where U is $m \times r$ and S is $r \times r$ diagonal matrix. The diagonal entries of matrix S are called singular value and they are ranked in descending order.

M can be expressed in another form: $M = \sum_{k=1}^{r} \lambda_k u_k v'_k$ where λ_k is singular value.

U'S is called principle component PCs, the variance of the column i of PC is denoted as s_{ii}^2, each column vector of V is called the loadings of PC, and is also called eigen time series. To determine the number of PCs, we need to take the following three conditions into consideration. First, one ratio α. The accumulating contribution rate α of first k principle components is defined as:

$$\alpha = \sum_{i=1}^{k} s_{ii}^2 \Big/ \sum_{i=1}^{r} s_{ii}^2 \qquad (2)$$

Generally speaking, the accumulating contribution rate of first four items is usually more than 50%. Let us assume that the threshold α equals to 50% or more, first k PCs larger than α will be considered further. Secondly, we can also draw eigenvalue spectra map of variance (or its logarithm) against the order of PC. The inflection point (elbow point) of the map is reference value. Lastly, we need to observe column vectors of V, which reflect changes in time series and are useful to determine whether their corresponding component is important. By choosing the largest 5 percent or the smallest 5 percent voxels in PCs, we can detect activation; the percentage can be adjusted according to the experiment. The methods are as follows:

Autocovariance based PCA (APCA) method for activation detection:

(1)   Data preprocessing and normalization;
(2)   Compute each voxel's autocovariance series using formula(1);
(3)   Form a mxp matrix M where m is the number of voxels and p is the size of autocovariance series;
(4)   Compute the singular decomposition M=USV';
(5)   Determine number of PCs by taking overall consideration;
(6)   Choose the largest or smallest 5 percent voxels in selected k PCs;
(7)   Display result in order of voxel position.

Here we compared the non-autocovariance PCA (NAPCA) method with APCA above. In the non-autocovariance method, there is no step 2 and in step 3, p is the length of original time series. The implementation of APCA made several references to method in [12-13].

2.2   Simulated Data and Real Data

The dataset selected one slice of real fMRI data containing N = 1963 brain voxels with the series length T = 200. The paradigm was a block design. Three small activation foci of 21 voxels were created, and the activation time courses were obtained by the convolution of the experimental condition time courses with the HRF of SPM sampled at TP = 2s. The synthetic dataset is shown in Fig.1. Furthermore, Gaussian noise of zero mean value and standard deviation varies from 0.2 to 3.5 corresponding to SNR from 0.93 to 0.22, which is in the range of the SNR of real fMRI data. The data was smoothed spatially as commonly done for fMRI (FWHM = 4.5 mm = 1.5 voxel) [14].

The real dataset was a typical dataset, an auditory dataset from the Wellcome Department of Imaging Neuroscience of the University College London. The data were acquired using a modified 2T Siemens MAGNETOM Vision system. Each acquisition consisted of 64 contiguous slices (64 x 64 x 64, 3mm x 3mm x 3mm voxels) (http://www.fil.ion.ucl.ac.uk/spm/data/). Acquisition took 6.05s, it consisted of 96 acquisitions made (TR= 7s) from a single subject in blocks of 6 (42 seconds), giving 16 42s blocks. The paradigm consisted of eight rest and auditory stimulation cycles, starting with rest. Auditory stimulation was bi-syllabic words presented binaurally at a rate of 60 per minute. The first complete cycle (12 scans) was discarded, leaving 84 scans to analysis.

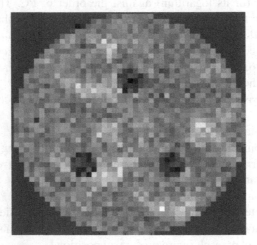

Fig. 1. The real baseline based synthetic dataset

3   Result of Simulated Data

The number of PCs in APCA was determined by overall consideration. We drew an eigenvalue spectra map of variance against the order of PC in Fig. 2. From the fig, the elbow point of the APCA is located at 3, and NAPCA is located at 2. And then we need to observe changes in time series to determine whether their corresponding component is important. Fig. 3 reflects first three eigen-timeseries of APCA. The period of the second eigen-timeseries (solid line) is the same as that of the stimulated time series (dotted line). The first four eigen-timeseries of NAPCA is shown in Fig. 4. From Fig.4, we can see that the third period of eigen-timeseries is the same as the stimulated time series. Although the elbow point of the NAPCA is 2, the first two eigen-timeseries are not enough and the third eigen-timeseries should be considered. By taking overall these considerations, we finally determined number of PCs as three. Both APCA and NAPCA computed error rate at its corresponding SNR, we computed error rate for each component and got their average value. The results are shown in Fig. 5. We can see that APCA performs better than NAPCA regardless of SNR.

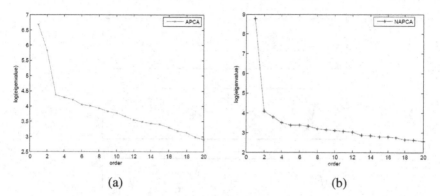

Fig. 2. The eigenvaluess of PCs for synthetic data. （a）APCA（b）NAPCA.

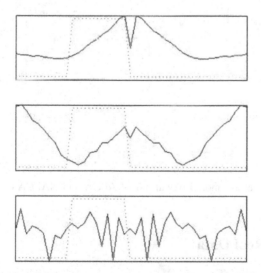

Fig. 3. The first three eigen-timeseries of APCA

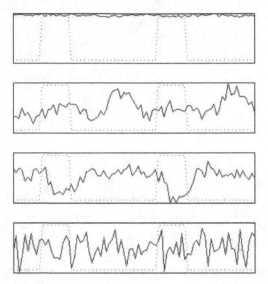

Fig. 4. The first four eigen-timeseries of NAPCA

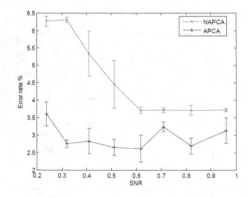

Fig. 5. The error rates and standard deviations of APCA and NAPCA on real baseline under different SNRs

4   Result of Real Data

For ACPA and NACPA, from Fig. 6, we had to take 4 PCs into consideration because of elbow points. The eigen time series of ACPA is shown in Fig. 7, where the form of first component was consistent with stimulation signal (shown in dotted line). The obtained activation map corresponding to the first principal component is shown in Fig. 9. The map is rendered by using xjView (http://www.alivelearn.net/xjview/). We got eigen time series in Fig. 8 by using NAPCA method. The form of the third component was consistent with stimulation signal (in dotted line), so we got activation map using the third principal component, shown in Fig. 10.

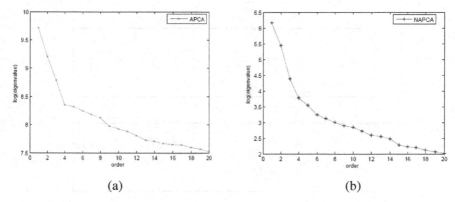

(a)   (b)

Fig. 6. The eigenvaluess of PCs for real data.（a）APCA（b）NAPCA.

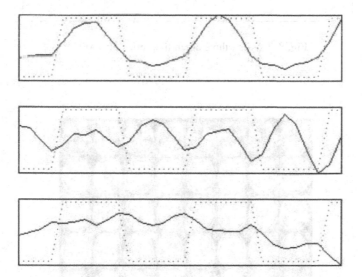

Fig. 7. The first three eigen-timeseries of APCA on auditory data

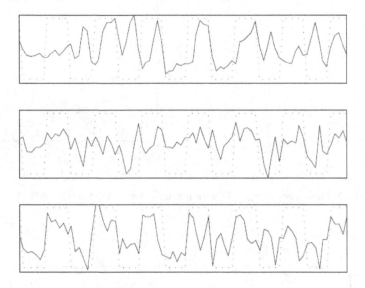

Fig. 8. The first three eigen-timeseries of NAPCA

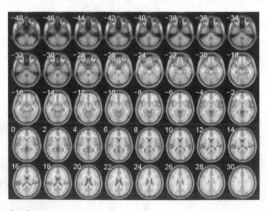

Fig. 9. The brain transverse overlay maps of activated results using APCA

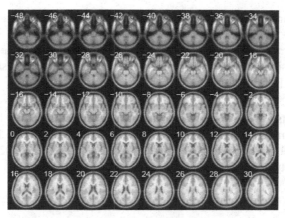

Fig. 10. The brain transverse overlay maps of activated results using NAPCA

5   Discussion and Conclusion

The result of NAPCA method had too many activation reports, especially at ocular regions, which might be false positive. The experiment shows that autocovariance based PCA method was effective. In addition, when choosing PCs, we had to take accumulating contribution rate, inflection of eigenvalue map and eigen time series into consideration at the same time.

PCA based method and clustering method both belong to the data-driven multivariate method. From the experiments above, we can see that PCA method may not perform well when simply using it without other methods. Some researchers compared fuzzy clustering method and general PCA method, they found out the following results [1]. Fuzzy clustering method and PCA method have a similar performance when researchers only take noises of device into consideration; however, clustering method is better if they also allow for physiology noise. Clustering method maintained the previous data, which is good for the interpretation of data; we can regard PCA method as a kind of cluster recognition.   PCA has some limitations, for it assume that each principal component is orthogonal to every other. However, signal and noise, as well as the components of signals, may not have such an orthogonal relationship with each other, clustering analysis doesn't have such a hypothesis.

Some literatures analyzed the limitations of using existing model-based methods. The problem they have in common is that we have to set the HRF in advance, which lead to a result that different regions of brain are supposed to be the same. However, studies have shown that there are differences between different regions of brain, which bring about the limitation when trying to analyze [14-16].

For model-free method such as some existing clustering methods, hierarchical clustering or K-means are usually adopted. Hierarchical clustering requires usually to determine exactly when to stop hierarchical tree and which layer should we choose. For K-means, we need to assign the cluster number in advance so it also has limitation. We proposed the autocovariance-based PCA activation detection method. Experiments had proved that this algorithm had a good performance; it also indicated that doing some data transformation beforehand was feasible for improving Performance of PCA.

There are several works to do, including seeking optimal size of the autocovariance series, using the simulated data [17] and doing further systematic study guided by Brain Informatics [18] in future.

Acknowledgments. The work is supported in part by the National Natural Science Foundation of China under Grant No. 61170039, No. 61375075, the Natural Science Foundation of Hebei Province (No. F2012201006), (No. F2012201020) and the NSF of Hebei University (2013-251).

References

1. Baumgartner, R., Ryner, L., Richter, W., Summers, R., Jarmasz, M., Somorjai, R.: Comparison of Two Exploratory Data Analysis Methods for fMRI: Fuzzy Clustering vs. Principal Component Analysis. Magnetic Resonance in Medicine 18, 89–94 (2000)
2. Hansen, L.K., Larsen, F.A., Nielsen, S.C., Strother, E., Rostrup, E., Savoy, R., Svarer, C., Paulson, O.B.: Generalizable Patterns in NeuroImaging: How Many Principal Components. NeuroImage 9, 534–544 (1999)
3. Friston, K.J., Frith, C.D., Liddle, P.F., Frackowiak, R.S.J.: Functional connectivity: the principal component analysis of large (PET) data sets. J. Cereb. Blood Flow Metab. 13, 5–14 (1993)
4. Friston, K., Phillips, J., Chawla, D., Buchel, C.: Revealing interactions among brain systems with nonlinear PCA. Hum. Brain Mapp. 8, 92–97 (1999)
5. Rogers, B.P., Morgan, V.L., Newton, A.T., Gore, J.C.: Assessing functional connectivity in the human brain by fMRI. Magn. Reson. Imaging 25, 1347–1357 (2007)
6. Ye, J., Lazar, N.A., Li, Y.: Sparse geostatistical analysis in clustering fMRI time series. Journal of Neuroscience Methods 199, 336–345 (2011)
7. Ecker, C., Reynaud, E., Williams, S.C., Brammer, M.J.: Detecting functional nodes in large-scale cortical networks with functional magnetic resonance imaging: A principal component analysis of the human visual system. Hum. Brain Mapp. 28, 817–834 (2007)
8. Baumgartner, R., Ryner, L., Richter, W., Summers, R., Jarmasz, M., Somorjai, R.: Comparison of Two Exploratory Data Analysis Methods for fMRI: Fuzzy Clustering vs. Magnetic Resonance in Medicine 18, 89–94 (2000)
9. Thomas, C.G., Harshman, R.A., Menon, R.S.: Noise reduction in bold-based fMRI using component analysis. NeuroImage 17(3), 1521–1537 (2002)
10. Andersen, A.H., Gash, D.M., Avison, M.J.: Principal component analysis of the dynamic response measured by fMRI: A generalized linear systems framework. Magn. Reson. Imaging 17, 795–815 (1999)
11. Liu, D.: Clustering Based Analysis for Human Brain Functional Magnetic Resonance Imaging dataset. Beijing University of Technology, China, doctoral dissertation (2012)
12. Bjerre, T., Henriksen, J., Rasmussen, P.M., Nielsen, C.H., Hansen, L.K., Madsen, K.H.: Unified ICA-SPM analysis of fMRI experiments - Implementation of an ICA graphical user interface for the SPM pipeline. In: Proceedings of BIOSTEC - BIOSIGNALS 2009 Conference (2009)

13. Metzak, P., Feredoes, E., Takane, Y., et al.: Constrained principal component analysis reveals functionally connected load-dependent networks involved in multiple stages of working memory. Hum. Brain Mapp. (2010)
14. Chuang, K., Chiu, M., Lin, C.C., Chen, J.: Model-free Functional MRI Analysis Using Kohonen Clustering Neural Network and Fuzzy C-means. IEEE Transactions on Medical Imaging 18, 1117–1128 (1999)
15. Kruger, G., Frahm, J., Kleinschmidt, A.: The cerebral blood oxygenation response to functional challenge: Differences between human motor and visual cortex. In: Proc. ISMRM 4th Annu. Meeting, New York, NY (1996)
16. Liu, D., Lu, W., Zhong, N.: Clustering of fMRI Data Using Affinity Propagation. In: Yao, Y., Sun, R., Poggio, T., Liu, J., Zhong, N., Huang, J. (eds.) BI 2010. LNCS, vol. 6334, pp. 399–406. Springer, Heidelberg (2010)
17. Dell'Arciprete, L., Murphy, B., Zanzotto, F.M.: Parallels between Machine and Brain Decoding. Brain Informatics, 162–174 (2012)
18. Zhong, N., Bradshaw, J.M., Liu, J., Taylor, J.G.: Brain informatics. IEEE Intell. Syst. 26(5), 16–21 (2011)

Balancing the Stability and Predictive Performance for Multivariate Voxel Selection in fMRI Study

Shulin Yan[1], Xian Yang[1], Chao Wu[1], Zhiyun Zheng[2], and Yike Guo[1,*]

[1] Department of Computing, Imperial College London, London, UK
{shu.yan09,xian.yang08,chao.wu,y.guo}@imperial.ac.uk
[2] School of Information Engineering, Zhengzhou University, Zhengzhou, Henan, China
iezyzheng@zzu.edu.cn

Abstract. Recently, the Multivariate Pattern Analysis (MVPA) studies for fMRI not only focus on cognitive state prediction, but also explore the interpretations of brain activity using model predictors (selected voxels). A model is considered to be good for interpreting brain activity if the selected voxels are all relevant to the specific cognitive state. Classical MVPA methods select voxels based on their prediction power; the selected ones are those that provide the best prediction performance. This precision based voxel selection method can guarantee the prediction performance, but it cannot ensure that all the selected ones are relevant. The interpretation of brain activity is therefore not ideal. This paper addresses this issue by introducing the concept of stability to the MVPA studies. If only the stability is emphasized in the selection process, the probability of selecting irrelevant voxels is highly reduced with the sacrifice of the prediction precision. We, therefore, propose a method to combine the stability assessment with the prediction precision assessment. In this paper, the proposed voxel selection method is integrated into a linear sparse predictor, Random Subspace Sparse Bayesian Learning (RS-SBL). The experiment results of simulation datasets demonstrate that our method can simultaneously reduce false positive and false negative rates while maintaining the prediction performance.

Keywords: functional MRI, linear sparse modelling, multivariate voxel selection, stability.

1 Introduction

Functional MRI (fMRI) is a neuroimaging technique to investigate the relationship between brain regions with specific cognitive functions by measuring changes in brain blood flow signal (BOLD). Conventional fMRI analyses focus on investigating the interpretation of neural activity with univariate analysis, such as General Linear Model (GLM) [1]. The univariate analysis methods work on isolated voxels and they determine active brain regions with the most statistically significant voxels in response to a cognitive task.

---

* Corresponding author.

D. Ślęzak et al. (Eds.): BIH 2014, LNAI 8609, pp. 90–99, 2014.

In contrast to univariate analyses, Multivariate Pattern Analysis (MVPA) of fMRI attempts to informatively decode patterns of brain activity [2]. By measuring multi-voxels simultaneously, MVPA is more sensitive and informative to the brain activity and robust to noise. Most recent MVPA methods [3-6] employ linear models that use individual voxels as predictors and time point volumes as samples. That is because the relevant voxels in response to cognitive states can be directly selected. As a result, the neural activity can be interpreted. The conventional MVPA methods select the voxels by considering their prediction powers that the selected ones are those that provide the most precise prediction. However, only take the prediction performance into consideration, the selected voxels are specific to particular dataset and irrelevant voxels may be wrongly selected. In consequence, with such selected voxels, even if the prediction performance can be guaranteed, the brain activity can be misunderstood. For this reason, an urgent problem for MVPA is to select voxels that can interpret the real neural activity and provide accurate cognitive state prediction.

Biomarker discovery, which aims to select biomarkers to differentiate disease from normal state, uses similar analysis methods and faces the same problems as fMRI analysis. That is because: 1. the training datasets are usually with high feature-to-sample ratio; 2. the selected predictors are expected to be predictive and meaningful, and the predictors are always sparse comparing with the high dimensional features; 3. correlations exist between predictors. In order to control the robustness of predictors, researchers (e.g. [7,8]) introduced the concept of stability to biomarker discovery techniques. They demonstrate that if the stability is higher, the predictors are more robust to noise and fewer noise predictors are selected. However, when predictors are fixed, the prediction performance is very poor. To deal with this, Kirk et al [9] investigated strategies to balance the robustness and prediction performance of biomarkers by optimizing both stability and predictive performance simultaneously.

In this paper, we introduce the concept of stability to fMRI MVPA analysis, which has not been considered in this field before. We explore the advantages of bringing stability into voxel selection and propose a novel multivariate voxel selection method that wraps a proposed selection strategy around a novel MPVA method, Random Subspace Sparse Bayesian Learning (RS-SBL) [10]. Our method aims to select voxels that can accurately discriminate different cognitive states as well as enable precision interpretation of brain activity. RS-SBL is implemented by incorporating linear Sparse Bayesian Learning (SBL) [11] with random subspace method. The linear SBL is a linear sparse model that can overcome the overfitting problem resulted from high dimensionality. It is an advanced Compressive Sensing (CS) method that can provide a useful sparse solution even when the design matrix is in poor condition and no parameter needs to be set by cross-validation. The random subspace [12] can further overcome the overfitting problem, and can improve the stability of voxel selection. By using our selection strategy, combining stability and prediction precision assessments, the probability of RS-SBL of selecting irrelevant voxels is highly reduced and only a small reduction of prediction precision is made.

The paper is organised as follows. In section 2, we introduce sparse linear modelling methods for fMRI MVPA study. In section 3, we first explain the voxel select function of RS-SBL and then describe our proposed method; experiment results of testing our method on simulation datasets are detailed in section 4. In the final section, we make a conclusion of this paper.

2   Linear Sparse Modelling for fMRI Analysis

In fMRI analysis, constructing models for brain cognition state prediction using the whole brain voxels faces a common problem that the number of voxels is several orders of magnitude of time points. This is especially the case when doing individual subject analysis. Classical machine learning methods [13] fail to solve this problem due to overfitting.

Sparse modelling avoids overfitting problem by constructing predictive models using a small subset of high dimensional features. A sparse model is expressed as:

$$y = \phi(x)w, \tag{1}$$

where $x \in R^{n \times p}$ is the design matrix composing of n observations and p features corresponding to a response vector $y \in R^n$, $\phi(x)$ is a fixed feature-space transformation, and w contains the coefficients of the model to be estimated.

The results of fMRI analysis show that active brain regions responding to a cognitive task are just a small part of the entire investigated area (e.g. whole brain). Motivated by this observation, the decoding problem can be formalized by linear sparse modelling, with which direct relevance of each voxel to the response can be obtained and no transformation of x is needed. This gives:

$$y = xw, \tag{2}$$

where the non-zero elements of $w \in R^p$ indicate their corresponding voxels are relevant to the cognitive state y. The total number of relevant voxels s, should be far less than the total number of voxels, that is $s \ll p$.

Given y and x, the decoding problem is to learn w. Constrained by the fMRI imaging technique, the number of samples n is always limited ($n \ll p$), making the estimation of w difficult. The CS technique [14] offers an opportunity to solve this underdetermined problem with sparse constraint on w as long as the number of samples satisfying $n \gg \rho s \, log \left(\frac{p}{s}\right)$, where ρ is a small constant [15]. Among them, least absolute shrinkage and selection operator (LASSO) is an efficient method for sparse linear regression:

$$min \frac{1}{2} ||xw - y||_2^2 + \eta ||w||_1, \tag{3}$$

where η controls the trade-off between estimation error and sparsity. Most compressive sensing algorithms (e.g. [16, 17]) have been proven to provide an accurate sparse solution if the design matrix satisfies the Restricted Isometry Property (RIP) condition. However, in the fMRI study, the spatial correlation of voxels leads to poor conditioned design matrix [10]. It is not easy to satisfy the RIP condition as well as mutual incoherence which is another condition required for exact sparse signal estimation [18]. When several columns of x are highly correlated, the estimation of their corresponding non-zero elements is difficult that only part of them may be selected.

To address this problem, the elastic net method is proposed to provide a relaxation on poor conditioned matrix by adding a ℓ_2 penalty to Equation 3 where the correlated voxels are highly grouped [4]. Another alternative approach, randomized ward lasso [6], is developed to reduce the spatial correlation by grouping correlated voxels together and using the average value of each cluster to construct design matrix. The former method considers the prediction power of the linear model while the latter one only focuses on the relevant voxel recovery. Moreover, the above methods involve penalty parameters that must be fixed beforehand using a hold-out method such as cross-validation.

Random Subspace Sparse Bayesian Learning (RS-SBL) [10] is another compressive sensing based linear sparse modelling method for fMRI analysis. It integrates the state-of-art compressive sensing method, Sparse Bayesian Learning, with random subspace assemble method to generate brain behavior predictors and prediction maps (constructed with selected voxels) from whole brain fMRI images. The random subspace method generates a set of subspace by randomly sampling a small subset of features, and a sparse model (constructed by linear SBL) is built for each subspace. With the implementation of random subspace method, the performance of linear SBL can be improved based on the following facts: 1. The correlation among features in a subspace can be tremendously reduced by random selection so that   better conditioned matrix can be produced; 2. Discrepancy between sample size and feature size in a subspace is highly reduced. As a consequence, linear SBL can provide robust predictors for subspaces, and a final strong predictor can be constructed via an aggregating process. Moreover, ensemble methods (e.g. random subspace) can increase the stability of predictors [12]. Benefiting from the linear sparse model, prediction maps are provided so that interpretation of neural activity can be investigated.

3   Methods

Instead of focusing on increasing the prediction power of the RS-SBL method, this paper makes special effort on the multivariate voxel selection process.

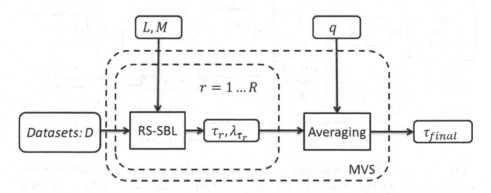

Fig. 1. Framework for RS-SBL Multivariate Voxel Selection (MVS)

Fig. 1 shows the framework for the multivariate voxel selection part of the RS-SBL method. Given an input fMRI dataset $D = \{x, y\}$, the RS-SBL method selects a subset of voxels τ as relevant voxels together with a weight vector λ_τ. The selected voxels are achieved by aggregating the voxels selected from all subspaces, which are the non-zero elements of the linear models. The weight of each selected voxel is proportional to the frequency of this voxel being selected by sparse modelling during the random sampling process. In order to reduce the influence of the sampling randomness, RS-SBL is repeated R times and the weights of selected voxels are averaged over repetitions. The final selected voxels τ_{final} are the top q voxels with highest weights.

After voxel selection, the Sparse Bayesian Learning with linear kernel (SBL-Lin) method [10] uses the selected voxels for making prediction. SBL-Lin is employed here as it has similar or even better prediction performance to SVM method, which is the most popular predictor for fMRI data analysis. In addition, no parameter needs to be optimized via cross-validation.

The conventional method for evaluating the selected voxels is to assess the performance of their predictive model when model parameters (e.g. L, M and q) are set to be optimal. Since cross-validation is often used to estimate the prediction power, different feature sets are selected for different partitioned sample subsets. These results in the selected voxels are not stable. For this reason, instead of using the conventional method, we optimize the voxel selection step with the introduction of stability assessment. Stable voxels are the ones that consistently selected across cross-validations, and irrelevant voxels are excluded via stability assessment as they are unstable. However, the prediction performance is poor if only stable voxels are used. Therefore, we propose a novel voxel selection strategy combining both stability and prediction precision assessments to select voxels stable in cross-validation process while returning robust prediction model.

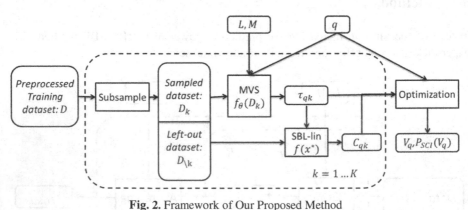

Fig. 2. Framework of Our Proposed Method

Fig. 2 illustrates the framework of our proposed multivariate voxel selection method. Given parameter $\theta = \{L, M\}$ and q, the multivariate voxel selection (MVS) works on a subset D_k, which is randomly sampled from the whole input fMRI dataset. After determining q selected voxels τ_{qk}, the prediction model is applied on the remaining dataset $D_{\backslash k} = D \backslash D_k$. The prediction performance is represented by the precision rate C_{qk}:

$$C_{qk} = \frac{1}{n^*}\sum_{i=1}^{n^*} \mathbb{I}(f(x_i^*) = y_i^*), \qquad (4)$$

where n^* is size of $D_{\backslash k} = \{x^*, y^*\}$, $f(\cdot)$ refers to the prediction model built by SBL-lin, and $\mathbb{I}(Z)$ is an indicator function, that $\mathbb{I}(Z) = 1$ if Z is true and 0 vice versa.

The Optimization process in the framework is to find an optimal set of voxels V_q from $K - \text{fold cross} - \text{validation}$ with the optimisation of both stability and prediction precision. This is achieved by maximising the joint probability [9]:

$$P_{SC}(V_q) = \mathbb{P}(\{select\ V_q\ \&\ model\ precision\}|f_\theta, q) = \frac{1}{K}\sum_{k=1}^{K} C_{qk} \mathbb{I}(V_q \subseteq \tau_{qk}). \quad (5)$$

However, this heuristic optimization process is intractable for high dimensional feature space, which is exactly the case in fMRI analysis. For this reason, an approximation method is applied by optimizing the following target function:

$$P_{SCI}(V_q) = \frac{1}{q}\sum_{v_i \in V_q} P_{SC}(v_i), \qquad (6)$$

where v_i is the ith element of the feature set V_q. This approach margins the selection and precision probability associated with individual voxel rather than voxel set (e.g. Equation 6). Our method returns a set of selected voxels with the associated P_{SCI} score. By searching all possible values of parameter θ and q, optimal relevant voxel set with the highest P_{SCI} score are selected.

4   Experiment Results

We test our methods on simulation datasets whose ground truth (i.e. w) is known. The simulation datasets are generated in the same manner as it is in [6] with $p = 8000$ and $n = 100$. In order to generate a design matrix x reflecting the key characteristic of fMRI image, which is spatial correlation of voxels, we construct x using a smoothed i.i.d Gaussian random matrix with a 2D Gaussian filter of standard deviation $\sigma = 0.8$. The s non-zero elements of w are grouped into different spatial clusters, and their values are randomly chosen from $\{-0.5, 0.5\}$. The response vector y is then generated by the linear model (i.e. Equation 2) with additive noises ($SNR = 0.9$). Three datasets are generated with different number of non-zero elements, $s = 16, 54, 128$ respectively.

In our experiment, the number of repetition time R is set to 50 and the parameter K in cross-validation is fixed to 10. The candidate values of parameter L and M used in random subspace process are selected from $L \in \{10, 40, 70, 100\}$ and $M \in \{\frac{1}{5}p, \frac{1}{3}p, \frac{7}{15}p, \frac{3}{5}p\}$ respectively. In order to demonstrate the recovery and prediction performance of our method, we compare our results with the results generated by other two optimization approaches:

- Stability. It selects the voxels with the highest stability score which is defined as $P_{SI}(V_q) = \frac{1}{q}\sum_{v_i \in V_q}(\frac{1}{K}\sum_{k=1}^{K} \mathbb{I}(v_i \subseteq \tau_{qk}))$. Same as P_{SCI}, it is an approximation of stability probability of voxel sets by margining the probabilities associated with individual voxels.
- Precision. It is a conventional optimization strategy to select voxels from prediction models. Under different parameter settings (e.g. θ, q), it calculates the precision score by $P_c = \frac{1}{K}\sum_{k=1}^{K} C_{qk}$ and selects the q most frequently selected voxels across K repetitions as relevant voxels.

The optimal values of parameters and relevant voxels are selected by maximizing the individual score of each approach. By defining real non-zero elements to be true positives, the performance of these approaches is represented by false positive rate, false negative rate, and precision from 10-fold cross-validation.

4.1   Performance Comparison of Different Parameter Settings

We use the simulation dataset 1 with parameter s equal to 16 to compare the performance of different methods under different parameter settings.

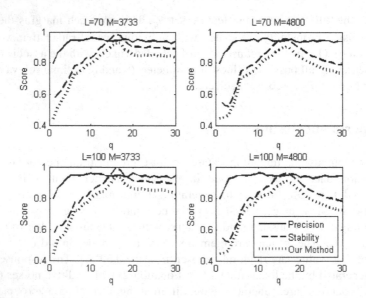

Fig. 3. Examples of Scores of Three Different Methods under Different Parameter Settings

Example results with selected settings of L and M are presented in Fig. 3. The number of selected voxels, q, in MVS ranges from 1 to 30. It is clear that, with a given value of L and M, the scores of our method and stability show similar trends: they both peak at $q = 16$, which is the true sparsity value of the dataset. Different from these two scores, the precision score becomes relatively stable when $q > 5$. This difference is caused by the strong correlation between relevant voxels. The sparse modelling method is to seek the minimal set of voxels that provide the best prediction performance, where only one out of closely correlated relevant voxels is usually chosen. The random subspace method enables the whole correlated voxel set to be selected, and the selected voxels are ranked by their prediction power. However, different training dataset D_k results in different voxel rank. As a result, when $q < s$, various subsets of correlated voxels are chosen across repetitions; the stability increase with the increase of q, because the selection of relevant voxels becomes covering the whole correlated relevant voxel set. Even the selected voxels are unstable; the prediction precision can still be maintained with partial correlated voxel set. When $q > s$, the stability decreases since some irrelevant voxels are wrongly selected.

Moreover, at the highest score point, both the stability and our method detect 16 relevant voxels correctly with the prediction accuracy of 0.944. On the other hand, the precision method only detect 14 relevant voxels but with higher prediction accuracy, 0.972. In addition, both the prediction and our methods find an optimal pair of (L, M), while the stability method finds four pairs having the highest score.

4.2   Comparison of Different Sparsity

The number of non-zero elements in the dataset used above is very small ($s = 16$) compared to the dimension of input voxels. The results show that the relevant voxels can be correctly detected with false positive rate equal to 0. In order to check the performance of our method on datasets with different number of non-zero voxels, we use another two simulation datasets with $s = 54\, q = 1 \ldots 70$ and $s = 128\, q = 150$ respectively.

Table 1. Optimial Results Achieved with highest Scores of Three Different Methods

Dataset		(L,M)	Q	Accuracy	FN	FP
Dataset 2	Stability	all pairs except (10,1600)	2	0.898	0.963	0
	Precision	(10,4800)	48	0.984	0.333	0.222
		(100, 2667)	49	0.984	0.148	0.056
		(70,3733)	57	0.984	0.167	0.222
		(70,3733)	59	0.984	0.167	0.259
	Our Strategy	(100,1600)	47	0.970	0.130	0
Dataset 3	Stability	(100,1600)	115	0.947	0.211	0.110
	Precision	(40,4800)	137	0.964	0.273	0.344
		(40,4800)	148	0.964	0.250	0.406
		(40,4800)	149	0.964	0.250	0.414
	Our Strategy	(100,1600)	129	0.951	0.172	0.180

Table 1 shows the optimal results from the three methods with the two datasets. The results demonstrate that the stability method can highly reduce the false positive rate while introducing high false negative rate (e.g. dataset 2), as some significant relevant voxels are unstable across repetitions. The precision method returns higher accuracy but introduces more noises. Among all three methods, our method makes the trade-off between relevant voxel selection accuracy and prediction performance. Compared to the precision method, our method can highly reduce the false positive and false negative rates with a small reduction in prediction precision. Moreover, the optimal values of parameters selected by our method are more stable that only one combination is selected. The other two methods, on the contrary, may select more than one optimal parameter settings.   Under these settings, the stability method select consistent voxel set, while the precision method returns different sets of voxels making difficult to decide which one to choose.

5   Conclusion

In fMRI analysis, MVPA has been the most popular method for brain cognitive state prediction. Previously, the MVPA studies mainly focus on the prediction power. Nowadays, it becomes popular to explore the interpretation of brain activity provided by the model predictors. Linear sparse modelling is an ideal approach, as the generated model weights are directly related to the voxels. Voxels with non-zero weights can be selected as relevant ones in response to a specific cognitive state. The conventional MVPA methods detect the relevant voxels only based on their prediction power. The selected voxels tend to be specific to particular datasets especially when the feature-to-sample ratio of dataset is very high, which is always the case in fMRI analysis. In consequence, the interpretation of brain activity is not perfect by exploring those selected voxels.

In this paper, we adopt the RS-SBL method for multivariate voxel selection and introduce the concept of stability to the selection process. The experiment results demonstrate that with the assessment of prediction precision, the sparse model selects voxels with the highest prediction power, but also those voxels contain irrelevant ones. Conversely, by employing the assessment of stability, the false positive selection is highly reduced, but it can result in the reduction in true positives and the prediction precision. Our method combines both assessments that false positive and false negative rates are reduced while the prediction performance is maintained. The successful application of our method on simulation datasets indicates the potential of using MVPA on real fMRI data to understand brain cognitive states.

Acknowledgements. This research is partially supported by the Innovative R&D Team Support Program of Guangdong Province (NO. 201001D0104726115), China.

References

1. Friston, K.J., Jezzard, P., Turner, R.: Analysis of Functional MRI Time-series. Human Brain Mapping 1, 153–171 (1994)
2. Haxby, J.V., Gobbini, M.I., Furey, M.L., Ishai, A., Schouten, J.L., Pietrini, P.: Distributed and Overlapping Representations of Faces and Objects in Ventral Temporal Cortex. Science 293, 2425–2430 (2001)

3. Yamashita, O., Sato, M., Yoshioka, T., Tong, F., Kamitani, Y.: Sparse Estimation Automatically Selects Voxels Relevant for the Decoding of fMRI Activity Patterns. NeuroImage 42, 1414–1429 (2008)
4. Carroll, M.K., Cecchi, G.A., Rish, I., Garg, R., Rao, A.: Ravishankar.: Prediction and Interpretation of Distributed Neural Activity with Sparse Models. NeuroImage 44, 112–122 (2009)
5. Ryali, S., Supekar, K., Abrams, D.A., Menon, V.: Sparse Logistic Regression for Whole-brain Classification of fMRI Data. NeuroImage 51, 752–764 (2010)
6. Varoquaux, G., Gramfort, A., Thirion, B.: Smallsample Brain Mapping: Sparse Recovery on Spatially Correlated Designs with Randomization and Clustering. In: Proceedings of the 29th International Conference on Machine Learning, vol. 4 (2012)
7. Abeel, T., Helleputte, T., de Peer, Y.V., et al.: Robust Biomarker Identification for Cancer Diagnosis with Ensemble Feature Selection Methods. Bioinformatics 26, 298–392 (2010)
8. Zuchnick, M., Richardson, S., Stronach, E.A.: Comparing the Characteristics of Gene Expression Profiles Derived by Univariate and Multivariate Classification Methods. Statistical Applications in Genetics and Molecular Biology 7(1) (2008)
9. Krirk, P., Witkover, A., Bangham, C.R., et al.: Balancing the Robustness and Predictive Performance of Biomarkders. Journal of Computational Biology 20, 979–989 (2013)
10. Yan, S., Yang, X., Wu, C., Guo, Y.: Integration of Sparse Bayesian Learning and Random Subspace for fMRI Multivariate Analysis. In: Submitted to the 36st Annual International Conference of the IEEE Engineering in Medicine and Biology Society (2014)
11. Tipping, M.E.: Sparse Bayesian Learning and the Relevance Vector Machine. The Journal of Machine Learning Research 1, 211–244 (2001)
12. Tao, D., Tang, X., Li, X., Wu, X.: Asymmetric Bagging and Random Subspace for Support Vector Machines-based Relevance Feedback in Image Retrieval. IEEE Transactions on Pattern Analysis and Machine Intelligence 28, 1088–1099 (2006)
13. Misaki, M., Kim, Y., Bandettini, P.A., Kriegeskorte, N.: Comparison of Multivariate Classifiers and Response Normalizations for Pattern-information fmri. NeuroImage 59, 1207–1223 (2006)
14. Donoho, D.L.: Compressed Sensing. IEEE Transactions on Information Theory 52, 1289–1306 (2006)
15. Baraniuk, R.G.: Compressive Sensing (lecture notes). IEEE Signal Processing Magazine 24, 118–121 (2007)
16. Candes, E.J., Romberg, J.K., Tao, T.: Stable signal recovery from incomplete and inaccurate measurements. Communications on Pure and Applied Mathematics 52(12), 5406–5425 (2006)
17. Tropp, J.A., Gilbert, A.C.: Signal Recovery from Random Measurements via Orthogonal Matching Pursuit. IEEE Transactions on Information Theory 53, 4655–4666 (2007)
18. Wainwright, M.J.: Sharp Thresholds for High-dimensional and Noisy Sparsity Recovery using l1-constrained Quadratic Programming (Lasso). IEEE Transactions on Information Theory 55, 2183–2202 (2009)

P3 Component Detection Using HHT

Improvement of EMD with Additional Stopping Criteria

Tomáš Prokop and Roman Mouček

Department of Computer Science and Engineering, University of West Bohemia, Univerzitní 8,
306 14, Pilsen, Czech Republic
{prokop,moucek}@kiv.zcu.cz

Abstract. This paper describes improvement of the Hilbert-Huang transform (HHT) for detection of ERP components in the EEG signal. Time-frequency domain methods, such as the wavelet transform or matching pursuit, are commonly for this task. We used a modified Hilbert-Huang transform that allows the processing of quasi-stationary signals such as EEG. The essential part of the HHT is an Empirical Mode Decomposition (EMD) that decomposes signal into intrinsic mode functions (IMFs). We designed additional stopping criteria for better selection of IMFs in the EMD. These IMFs positively affect later computed instantaneous attributes and increase classification success. We tested the influence of additional stopping criteria on classification reliability using the real EEG data acquired in our laboratory. Our results demonstrated that we were able to detect the P3 component by using the HHT with additional stopping criteria more successfully than by using the original implementation of modified HHT, continuous wavelet transform and matching pursuit.

Keywords: Electroencephalography, EEG signal processing, ERP detection, P3 component, Hilbert-Huang transform, HHT, Empirical Mode Decomposition, EMD, stopping criteria.

1 Introduction

Our research group widely uses the methods of electroencephalography (EEG) and event related potentials (ERP) in its experiments. One of the main difficulties during the EEG signal processing is detection of ERP components. This is important for the interpretation of experimental results. It is common to use time-frequency domain methods, such as the wavelet transform or matching pursuit (MP) to locate ERP components in the EEG signal. Another option is to use the Hilbert-Huang transform that was designed to process non-stationary signals and later modified for EEG signal processing.

The HHT consists of two algorithms – empirical mode decomposition and Hilbert spectral analysis (HSA). The EMD decomposes a signal into IMFs. The IMF is a function which fulfills the following condition: *The mean value of the envelope defined by the local maxima and the local minima is zero at any point [1,2,3].*

D. Ślęzak et al. (Eds.): BIH 2014, LNAI 8609, pp. 100–110, 2014.
© Springer International Publishing Switzerland 2014

The HSA applies the Hilbert transform on every IMF and allows us to compute the signal instantaneous attributes.

The original HHT is not fully suitable for the ERP detection because the EEG signal is quasi-stationary. During the EMD envelopes are created around the processed signal. This process suffers from an over/undershoot effect. The over/undershoot effect slows down the convergence of the EMD and causes the distortion of created IMFs. We already modified the HHT in [4] by improving the EMD algorithm. It decomposes the EEG signal into IMFs more precisely and minimizes the over/undershoot effect.

The improvement described in this article includes the process of IMFs selection. Appropriately selected IMFs more reflect the signal physical properties (amplitude and frequency) and this selection is essential for later instantaneous attributes computation and the subsequent ERP detection. The IMF selection is controlled with a stopping criterion of a sifting process. This process is a part of the EMD algorithm that acquires a single IMF from the signal.

Every IMF should fulfill the condition described above. However, it is very difficult to fulfill this condition strictly, it means to achieve the zero mean value of the envelope at any point. Therefore it is recommended to use one of the following stopping criteria - Cauchy convergence test [5] or standard deviation [6] in the sifting process. That is why we usually find only the estimation of ideal IMF using one of these stopping criteria. As a solution we designed two additional stopping criteria that help to find better IMFs and increase subsequent classification reliability.

The article is organized in the following way. A short introduction into EEG signal processing by the HHT is given in section 2. It includes the brief description of the EMD algorithm and the Hilbert transform. The next section describes the proposed additional stopping criteria. Testing data, classifiers, and achieved results are summarized in section 4. Conclusion is provided in the last section.

2   HHT and Its Application on the EEG Signal

2.1   Empirical Mode Decomposition

The most important part of the HHT is the EMD algorithm. The goal of the EMD is to decompose signal into IMFs and the residue. The EMD is a data driven method and IMFs are derived directly from the signal itself [7]. The IMF represents a simple oscillatory mode as a counterpart to a simple harmonic function, but it is much more general: instead of constant amplitude and frequency, as a simple harmonic component, the IMF can have a variable amplitude and frequency as the function of time [4]. The core of the EMD is the sifting process that acquires a single IMF from the signal. The EMD starts with the original (preprocessed) signal. In the sifting process we look for local extrema (minima and maxima) in the input signal and we create upper and lower envelopes by connecting local extrema with a cubic spline. Then we calculate the mean curve by averaging the upper and lower envelopes and subtract the obtained mean curve from the input signal. Finally, if a stopping criterion is met, we have found an IMF and the sifting process ends. In other case the sifting process continues with the next iteration. After acquiring an IMF the sifting is finished and the EMD continues with obtaining the residue by subtracting the IMF from the signal. If the residue has at least two extrema, we set the residue as the current input signal and continue with the next sifting process. Otherwise the EMD is over and we have a set of IMFs and the residue.

This basic algorithm is usable for both a general non-stationary signal and an EEG signal. We use the modified HHT (mHHT) to process the EEG signal. The EMD algorithm of the mHHT uses a modified mirror method [4] for the estimation of additional extrema to minimize or avoid the over/undershoot effect. Over/undershoot effect can occur when additional extrema are not well placed.

Local extrema detection is an important part of the EMD. Envelopes do not have to cover the whole signal when incorrect extrema are detected. The mHHT detects local extrema with a delta difference method [4] that locates correct local extrema. It allows ignoring insignificant changes in the amplitude and detecting local extrema, even when there is no inflection point.

2.2   Stopping Criteria

The stopping criterion (SC) controls the selection of IMF in the sifting process. As we are trying to fulfill the IMF condition, amplitude variations of the individual waves become more even. Therefore Standard deviation (SD) or Cauchy convergence test (CC) is usually used as the stopping criterion:

$$SD = \sum_{t=0}^{T} \frac{|h_{k-1}(t) - h_k(t)|^2}{h_{k-1}^2(t)}, \tag{1}$$

$$CC = \frac{\sum_{t=0}^{T} |h_{k-1}(t) - h_k(t)|^2}{\sum_{t=0}^{T} h_{k-1}^2(t)}. \tag{2}$$

A function in the current iteration of the sifting process is considered to be IMF, when the value of the stopping criterion is smaller than a threshold. The threshold value is selected empirically depending on the used stopping criterion and experimental design.

2.3   Hilbert Transform

The result of the EMD is an input to the Hilbert transform (HT). HT computes an analytical signal

$$Z(t) = X(t) + iY(t) = a(t)e^{i\theta(t)} \tag{3}$$

from every IMF, where $X(t)$ is the real part that represents the original signal, and $Y(t)$ is the imaginary part that represents the Hilbert transform of $X(t)$. The imaginary part contains original data with 90° phase shift. The analytical signal allows us to calculate signal instantaneous attributes:

$$a(t) = \sqrt{X(t)^2 + Y(t)^2}, \tag{4}$$

$$\theta(t) = arctan\left(\frac{Y(t)}{X(t)}\right), \tag{5}$$

$$\omega(t) = \frac{d\theta(t)}{dt}, \tag{6}$$

where $a(t)$ is the instantaneous amplitude, $\theta(t)$ is the instantaneous phase and $\omega(t)$ is the instantaneous frequency. The knowledge of amplitude and frequency is essential for ERP component detection.

3   Proposed Modifications

3.1   Additional Stopping Criteria

We designed two simple additional stopping criteria (ASCs) to help the sifting process to select IMFs that better correspond to the signal trend. A better decomposed signal positively affects computed instantaneous signal attributes and it should also significantly increase the classification reliability. The ASC is met if its value is smaller than a threshold. The threshold is selected empirically and differs for both ASCs.

New ASCs do not measure the convergence of the sifting process. They measure the distance of the mean curve from zero. We need to know if the sifting process converges to zero and how close the mean curve to zero is. The sifting process returns the IMF only if it meets both stopping conditions - standard SC and ASC.

3.2   Mean Value of Mean Curve

The first ASC is the simple mean value of the mean curve (MV):

$$ASC = MV = \frac{\sum_{i=1}^{N} x_i}{N}. \tag{7}$$

The mean value of the mean curve created from envelopes is zero if the mean value of envelopes is zero at any point. Of course, we are not trying to achieve the zero mean value strictly because of the effect described in 2.2.

3.3   Dispersion from Zero

The second ASC is based on the following standard deviation:

$$\sigma = \sqrt{\frac{\sum_{i=1}^{N}(x_i - \bar{x})^2}{N}}. \tag{8}$$

The standard deviation is a measure of the dispersion from the average. However, we are interested in how big dispersion from zero is, because the average of every IMF mean curve should be zero. We set $\bar{x}$ to zero and we get the formula for the second ASC:

$$ASC = ZD = \sqrt{\frac{\sum_{i=1}^{N} x_i^2}{N}}, \tag{9}$$

where ZD is the dispersion from zero.

3.4   Iterations and Number of Created IMFs

If we use ASC, the sifting process probably does more iterations to fulfill both conditions. The comparison of the average number of iterations and the average number of created IMFs is shown in Table 1. The number of iterations increases rapidly when the ASC threshold value is close to zero. The more iterations the sifting process does, the more IMFs are created.

Table 1. The average number of iterations and the average number of created IMFs during EMD

ASC	Threshold	Average number of iterations	Average number of IMFs
Without ASC	-	29.08	6,95
ZD	0.1	29.12	6,95
	0.01	30.54	7,075
	0.001	104.61	8
MV	0.01	29.16	6,95
	0.001	34.64	7,025
	0.0001	55.25	7,425

4   Results

4.1   Testing Data

We tested our EMD modification on the real EEG data acquired in our laboratory from 20 different subjects. We recorded the data using the BrainAmp device with the sampling frequency 1 kHz. We tried to detect the P3 component in all cases. The tests were performed on 1s (1000 samples) long epochs. The original data consist of 30 epochs of the target stimulus responses and 90 epochs of the non-target stimulus responses, though subsets of 30 epochs were selected randomly for the test. The testing data contained 30 averaged epochs. The first 100 data samples included in the average were used for the baseline correction.

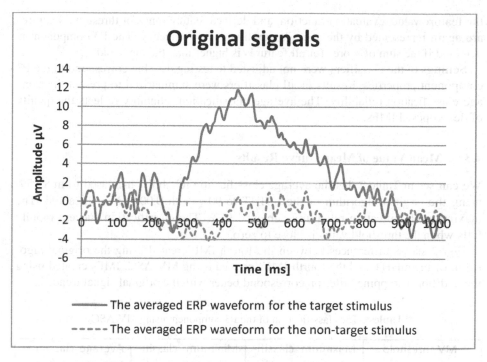

Fig. 1. The averaged ERP waveforms for the target stimulus (with the P3 component) and the non-target stimulus (without any P3 component)

We used the same data set, mHHT implementation, basic EMD settings and one classifier as in [4] to easy and objectively compare our results with the original implementation of the mHHT.

Typical averaged ERP waveforms for the target stimulus (creating the P3 component) and the non-target stimulus are shown in Fig. 1.

4.2   Classifiers

We used three simple classifiers with ten configurations in total to obtain the average classification reliability. All classifiers iterate through the IMFs and compute average amplitude and frequency between 150ms and 650ms after stimuli. The first classifier detects the P3 component when the average amplitude is higher than the threshold and the average frequency lies between 0.2Hz and 3Hz. The second classifier shifts a window over the signal and computes the average frequency and the average amplitude in this window. The window length is between 150ms and 250ms and the window shift is 10ms (10 samples). It detects the P3 component if the average amplitude is higher than the threshold and the average frequency lies between 0.2Hz and 3Hz in the current window. The last classifier assigns a score to every feature depending on the feature value, evaluation function, and defined feature range or threshold. Features are again represented by the average amplitude and frequency. The P3 component is detected if the sum of scores for all features is higher than the threshold.

Settings of the classifiers were not adjusted to testing data but correspond to the P3 component properties. Results of all classifiers were summarized to present the average classification reliability. The average classification reliability reflects the quality of decomposed IMFs.

4.3   Mean Value of Mean Curve Results

We can see in Table 2 that the average classification reliability increased from 89.5% using the original algorithm of the mHHT to 90% with 0.0009 MV threshold. The maximum classification reliability achieved 95%. The classification success rapidly falls when the threshold value is close to zero.

Fig. 2 shows differences between the fourth IMF created using the original algorithm of the mHHT and the fourth IMFs created using MV ASC. IMFs created using the additional stopping criterion correspond better with the original signal trend.

Table 2. The classification of the P3 component using MV ASC

MV threshold	Maximum classification success [%]	Minimum classification success [%]	Average classification success [%]
0,0009	92,5	87,5	90,00
0,001	92,5	87,5	89,75
0,025	92,5	87,5	89,75
0,04	92,5	87,5	89,75
0,05	92,5	87,5	89,75
0,075	92,5	87,5	89,75
0,09	92,5	87,5	89,75
Without ASC	92,5	87,5	89,50
0,005	90,0	85,0	88,75
0,0025	90,0	85,0	88,50
0,0005	95,5	85,0	88,25
0,00075	92,5	85,0	88,00
0,0004	95,0	82,5	87,00
0,004	87,5	82,5	86,25
0,0001	87,5	77,5	83,50
0,00025	85,0	77,5	81,25

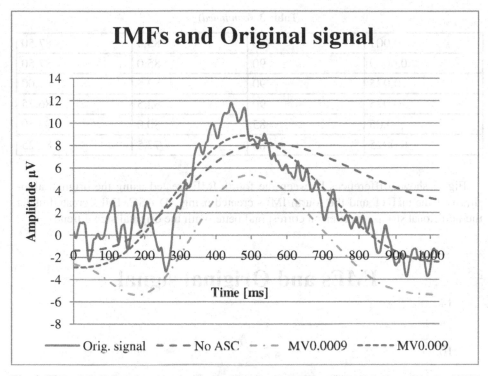

Fig. 2. The original signal and comparison of the fourth IMF created using the original mHHT with the fourth IMFs created using mHHT with MV ASC with 0,0009 and 0,009 thresholds

4.4 Dispersion from Zero Results

This additional stopping criterion seems to be more promising because it reflects more the IMF condition. We can see the classification results in Table 3. The maximum classification reliability increased to 95% in two cases and the average classification reliability is 4.25% higher in comparison with the original algorithm of the mHHT.

Table 3. The classification of the P3 component using ZD ASC

ZD threshold	Maximum classification success [%]	Minimum classification success[%]	Average classification success [%]
0,009	95,0	87,5	93,75
0,01	95,0	87,5	93,00
0,0075	92,5	87,5	91,25
0,09	92,5	87,5	90,00
Without ASC	92,5	87,5	89,50
0,005	92,5	85,0	89,25

Table 3. (*continued*)

0,001	90,0	85,0	87,50
0,0009	90	85,0	87,50
0,025	90	82,5	87,00
0,075	90	82,5	86,75
0,05	85	80,0	82,50
0,0025	85	77,5	81,25

Fig. 3 shows differences between the fourth IMF created using the original algorithm of the mHHT and the fourth IMFs created using ZD ASC. IMFs created using the additional stopping criterion correspond better with the original signal trend.

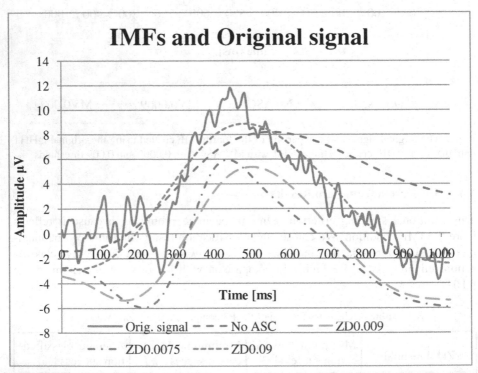

Fig. 3. The original signal and comparison of the fourth IMF created using the original mHHT with the fourth IMFs created using mHHT with ZD ASC with 0,009; 0,09 and 0,0075 thresholds

4.5   Comparison with CWT and MP

In Table 4 we can see the best classification results of the P3 component detection using CWT, MP modified for ERP detection [8], original HHT, mHHT and mHHT using ASC. The results of the mHHT are comparable to the results of widely used time-frequency domain algorithms. Modified HHT can achieve even better results by using ASC.

Table 4. Comparison of MP modified for ERP detection, CWT, original HHT and mHHT with mHHT using ASC. CWT, mHHT, MP and original HHT results rewritten from [4]

Method	Classification success [%]	The number of ERPs correctly detected	The number of no ERPs correctly detected
mHHT with ASC	95,0	20/20	18/20
CWT	92,5	18/20	19/20
mHHT	92,5	19/20	18/20
Matching pursuit	90,0	18/20	18/20
Original HHT	70,0	17/20	11/20

5   Conclusion

Our aim was to further improve the P3 component detection by the mHHT. We improved the EMD algorithm to better decompose the EEG signal into IMFs. We focused on the sifting process that is the core of the EMD algorithm. We tried to control the sifting process with the additional stopping criteria. It should assure that returned IMFs will better correspond to the original signal trend. We expected that better signal decomposition would positively affect computed instantaneous signal attributes and also the following classification results.

We designed two simple additional stopping criteria. The first is the simple mean value of the mean curve while the second is the dispersion of the mean curve around zero. Both additional stopping criteria measure the level of fulfillment of the IMF condition but not the convergence of the sifting process as the standard stopping criterion does.

We tested both ASCs on the real EEG data acquired in our laboratory during Odd-Ball experiments. IMFs created with the algorithm using ASC correspond more to the signal trend while the number of iterations of the sifting process does not rise rapidly for the most of usable threshold values. If the threshold value is very close to zero, it makes amplitude variations of the individual waves more even and we lose important information about the signal. Such threshold values produce the high number of iterations of the sifting process and negatively affect the classification success.

The average classification reliability is 0,5% higher for the MV ASC and 4,25% higher for ZD ASC than for the original mHHT algorithm that does not use ASC. The maximum classification success is 2,5% higher for both ASCs than for the original mHHT algorithm.

When we compare our best results with the best results of Continuous wavelet transform, Matching pursuit, original HHT and mHHT, we achieved even higher maximum classification success.

In the future we will focus on the development of the new classifier and integration of our modified HHT implementation into our EEG/ERP portal [9].

Acknowledgement. The work was supported by the UWB grant SGS-2013-039 Methods and Applications of Bio- and Medical Informatics.

References

1. Huang, N.E., Shen, Z., Long, S.R., Wu, M.C., Shih, H.H., Zheng, Q., Yen, N.C., Tung, C.C., Liu, H.H.: The empirical mode decomposition and the Hilbert spectrum for nonlinear and non-stationary time series analysis. Proceedings of the Royal Society of London Series A: Mathematical, Physical and Engineering Sciences 454, 903–995 (1971,1998)
2. Liu, R.: Empirical mode decomposition: A useful technique for neuroscience? (2002)
3. Yang, Z., Yang, L.: A new definition of the intrinsic mode function. A new definition of the intrinsic mode function. World Academy of Science, Engineering and Technology 60, 822–825 (2009)
4. Ciniburk, J.: Hilbert-Huang Transform for ERP Detection. Ph.D. thesis, Faculty of Applied Sciences, University of West Bohemia, Univerzitni 22, 306 14 Pilsen (2011)
5. Huang, N., Attoh-Okin, N.O.: The Hilbert-Huang Transform in Engineering. CRC Press (2005)
6. Huang, N.E., et al.: The empirical mode decomposition and the hilbert spectrum for nonlinear and non-stationary time series analysis. Proceedings of the Royal Society A: Mathematical 454 (1998)
7. Liang, H., Bresser, S., Desimone, R.: Empirical mode decomposition: a method for analyzing neural data. Neurocomputing 65, 801–807 (2005)
8. Řondík, T., Ciniburk, J., Mautner, P., Mouček, R.: Erp components detection using wavelet transform and matching pursuit algorithm. In: Proceedings of 3rd Driver Car Interaction Interface 2010 Conference (2010)
9. EEG/ERP Portal (2013), http://eegdatabase.kiv.zcu.cz/

A Novel Feature Extractor Based on Wavelet and Kernel PCA for Spike Sorting Neural Signals

Jun-Tao Liu[1], Sheng-Wei Xu[1], Ji-Yang Zhou[1], Mi-Xia Wang[1],
Nan-Sen Lin[1], and Xin-Xia Cai[1,2,*]

[1] State Key Laboratory of Transducer Technology, Institute of Electronics,
Chinese Academy of Sciences, Beijing 100190, China
[2] University of Chinese Academy of Sciences, Beijing 100190, China
xxcai@mail.ie.ac.cn

Abstract. Spike sorting is often required for analyzing neural recordings to isolate the activity of single neurons. In this paper, a new feature extractor based on Wavelet and kernel PCA for spike sorting was proposed. Electrophysiology recordings were made in Sprague-Dawley (SD) rats to provide neural signals. Here, an adaptive threshold based on the duty-cycle keeping method was used to detect spike and a new spike alignment technique was used to decrease sampling skew error. After spikes were detected and alimented, to extract spike features, their wavelet transform was calculated, the first 10 coefficients with the largest deviation from normality provided a compressed representation of the spike features that serves as the input to KPCA algorithm. Once the features have been extracted, k-means clustering was utilised to separate the features and differentiate the spikes. Test results with simulated data files and data obtained from SD rats in vivo showed an excellent classification result, indicating the good performance of the described algorithm approach.

Keywords: Spike sorting, kernel PCA, Wavelet, k-means clustering.

1 Introduction

NEURAL action potentials, also known as nerve impulses or spikes, play an important role in understanding the central nervous system. Nowadays, extracellular recording of neural spikes has been very popular in the neurophysiological research. As the tip is surrounded by many neurons, an electrode can simultaneously pick up spikes of an unknown number of neurons. Usually the experimenter tries to optimize the recording situation, so as to enhance the response of only one neuron. Unfortunately, experimental techniques are limited in achieving clear isolated recordings[1,2]. Therefore, to increase the data yield of each experiment, spike sorting is a crucial step to extract coherent signals of a single target neuron from this mixture of responses.

The spike sorting problem has received intense attention, and many solutions have been advanced. The basic algorithmic steps of spike classification are as follows:

---

* Corresponding author.

D. Ślęzak et al. (Eds.): BIH 2014, LNAI 8609, pp. 111–121, 2014.
© Springer International Publishing Switzerland 2014

(1) spike detection, (2) extraction of distinctive features from the spike shapes, and (3) clustering of the spikes by these features[3,4]. The clustering problem is widely known and there are many methods to solve it[5]. The performance of any clustering method relies on the original differences among the groups in the data. Hence, the efficiency of the feature extraction method in signifying those differences is crucial for the success of clustering.

Methods of spike sorting have been extensively studied during the last decades and a large number of techniques have been summarized in [5], such as the principal component analysis (PCA)[6,11], k-means clustering and Bayesian clustering[7], the wavelet based methods[4,8] , and filter-based methods[9].

The most common method of feature extraction and reduction is still the principal component analysis (PCA)[10]. PCA is a powerful method employed to automatically select features and use them to create feature vectors. PCA seeks an ordered set of orthogonal basis vectors, the principal components, which capture the directions in the data of largest variation. A smaller subspace created by some of the initial principal vectors is then used to make an approximate projection of the data. In this projection, clusters of different units in the data, corresponding to separate neurons, are revealed[11].

However, for some complicated cases in spike sorting with particularly nonlinear characteristics, PCA performs poorly due to its assumption that the process data are linear. A new nonlinear PCA technique for tackling the nonlinear problem, called kernel PCA (KPCA), has been in development in recent years [12,13].

KPCA is a type of kernel-based learning machine. PCA finds principal components minimizing data information loss in the input space, whereas KPCA searches them in the extended feature space[14]. KPCA can efficiently compute PCs in high-dimensional feature spaces by means of integral operators and nonlinear kernel functions. The basic idea of KPCA is to first map the input space into a feature space via nonlinear mapping and then to compute the PCs in that feature space[15].

Being linear in the feature space, but nonlinear in the input space, KPCA thus is capable of deriving low-dimensional features that incorporate higher order statistics. Compared to other nonlinear methods, the main advantage of KPCA is that it does not involve nonlinear optimization[16]; it essentially requires only linear algebra, making it as simple as standard PCA. Due to these merits, KPCA has shown better performance than linear PCA in feature extraction and classification in nonlinear systems.

In this paper, a new feature extractor based on Wavelet and kernel PCA for spike sorting was proposed. Electrophysiology recordings were made in Sprague-Dawley (SD) rats to provide neural signals. Here, an adaptive threshold based on the duty-cycle keeping method is used to detect spike and a new spike alignment technique was used to decrease sampling skew error. After spikes are detected and alimented, to extract spike features, their wavelet transform is calculated, the first 10 coefficients with the largest deviation from normality provided a compressed representation of the spike features that serves as the input to KPCA algorithm. Once the features have been extracted, k-means clustering is utilised to separate the features and differentiate the spikes. Test results with simulated data files and data obtained from SD) rats in vivo showed an excellent classification result, indicating the good performance of the described algorithm approach.

2   Methods

A schematic of the proposed methodology is depicted in Fig. 1. For this methodology, neuronal spikes are detected by the duty-cycle keeping method [17] and aligned at the peak points. Each aligned spike is subsequently transformed into a series of wavelet coefficients by a discrete wavelet transform. A set of selected wavelet coefficients is used to extract Spikes features through kernel principal component analysis. The proposed method was evaluated using MATLAB 7.0 (The MathWorks, Matik, MA, USA) based on the signals from SD rats.

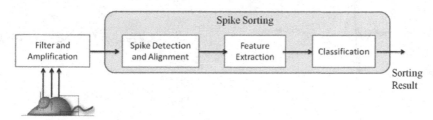

Fig. 1. A schematic of spike sorting flow based on wavelet an KPCA

2.1   Data Collection

2.1.1   Real Data

Electrophysiology recordings were made in Sprague-Dawley (SD) rats (from the Experimental Animal Center of Peking University), weighing 230 g. All animal experiments were carried out in accordance with the guidelines of the local animal welfare committee. The raw data were filtered and amplified before being analyzed at a 25 KHz sampling rate and stored. During off-line analysis of each recording session, original Spike signals were detected through threshold method. All these data analysis were made through   Multi Channel Systems Inc. (MCS, Germany).

Sensors used in electrophysiological experiments are homemade planar microelectrode array fabricated by the MEMS technique on silicon substrate[21,22]. The circular microelectrode sites with the diameter of 20 μm and distance of 100 μm were sputtered 250 nm platinum for recording. Working electrodes were lab-made CFME. The CFME is graphite monofilaments (Toary Industries, Japan) with the diameter of 6~7 μm, built in a borosilicate glass sheath to attain electrical insulation and mechanical. The carbon tip protruding from the sheathing by 10~100 μm provides an electroactive surface for electron transfer in electrochemical measurements. Reference/counter electrode is also homemade electrode painting with Ag|AgCl slurry which purchased from Dupont Co., Ltd (USA). The electrodes implanted in SD rats were under the guidance of stereotaxic frame (Stoelting, USA).

2.1.2   Simulated Data

The simulated signal has some advantages over the real signal for evaluating the performance of the algorithm, because it provides known solutions under different conditions, such as real templates, firing time and so on. The simulated spike train was designed by using five spike templates and background noise. The background noise was taken from a segment of a real recording. After the spike events were extracted from the recording of a selected electrode, the noise traces were concatenated and regarded as the background noise. In this work, two example data sets were employed to test our method. In data sets, several spike shapes were added to the background to generate simulated signal. The two spike shape groups were shown in Fig2.

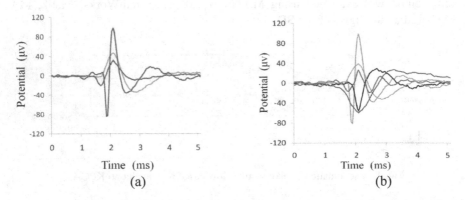

Fig. 2. Spike shape groups for adding to the datasets. (a) three spike shapes for addingto dataset1, (b) five spike shapes for addingto dataset1 dataset2.

2.2   Spike Detection and Alignment

In order to make a research on spikes, we need to detect spike signals from a large number of noise signals. The current methods for detection of spikes include threshold detection, peak value detection, nonlinear energy threshold detection, wavelet transform and other algorithms. The threshold detection method is the most widely used detection method. However, traditional adaptive threshold determined by multiples of the running root-mean-square (RMS) is unsusceptible to impede detection of lower-SNR neuronal spikes. As knowen, spike detection performance can be improved by adopting adaptive thresholds that are estimated from near spike-free background noises or using nonlinear operators to enhance spike-to-noise ratios[17].

In this work, an adaptive threshold based on the duty-cycle keeping method is used. As shown in Fig. 3, the duty-cycle of the signal, defined as the portion of data with larger magnitude than the duty-cycle threshold, is calculated. The error (ε) between the calculated duty-cycle and the desired value (15.85%) is used to adjust the duty-cycle threshold.

Usually, sampling skew is one of the main issues that causes the waveform distortion and results in the degradation of the sorting performance[18]. So spike segments are to be aligned at a particular point after detection. This method aligns spikes at the peak points, identified by the changing slope criterion(the sign of the slope of five sequential points changes when a new point is added on the right side and the first point on the left side is excluded). The spike data is a 128 dimensional vector and its peak appears at the 52th point.

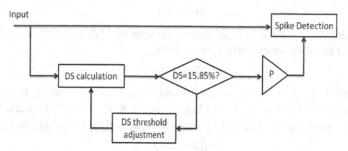

Fig. 3. The neuronal spike detectors incorporated with adaptive thresholds derived by duty-cycle (DS) keeping methods

2.3   Feature Extraction

In this study, we first implemented a four-level decomposition using Haar wavelets, which are rescaled square functions. Haar wavelets were chosen due to their compact support and orthogonality, which allows the discriminative features of the spikes to be expressed with a few wavelet coefficients and without a priori assumptions on the spike shapes. Then the lower wavelet coefficients were used to extract Spikes features through kernel principal component analysis.

2.3.1   Selection of Wavelet Coefficients

After spikes are detected and alimented, their wavelet transform is calculated, thus obtaining 128 wavelet coefficients for each spike. We implemented a four-level multiresolution decomposition using Haar wavelets. Each wavelet coefficient charac- terizes the spike shapes at different scales and times. The goal is to select a few coef- ficients that best separate the different spike classes. In our implementation, the first 10 coefficients with the largest deviation from normality were used. The selected set of wavelet coefficients provides a compressed representation of the spike features that serves as the input to KPCA algorithm.

2.3.2   The KPCA Algorithm

The basic idea of kernel PCA is to first map the input data into a feature space X via a nonlinear mapping and then perform a linear PCA in F. Given a imput set $X = \{x_1, x_2, ..., x_n\}$, where the examples $x_i \in R^m$,   There must be a nonlinear function $\emptyset: x_i \rightarrow \emptyset(x_i)$ to map the original input space X into a high-dimensional feature space F. The map $\emptyset$ and the space F are determined implicitly by the choice of a kernel function K , which computes the dot product between two input examples x_i and x_j mapped into F via

$$k(x_i, x_j) = \emptyset(x_i)^T \emptyset(x_j) \tag{1}$$

In space F, the covariance matrix of the mapped examples could be written as follow:

$$\bar{C} = \frac{1}{n} \emptyset^T \emptyset \tag{2}$$

Assuming that the data are centered in F, the eigenvalues λ and eigenvectors v could be found through

$$\lambda v = \bar{C} v \tag{3}$$

Since all solutions v with $\lambda \neq 0$ lie within the span of $\{\emptyset(X_1), \emptyset(X_2), \dots, \emptyset(X_n)\}$, we may consider the following equivalent problem:

$$\lambda \emptyset v = \emptyset \bar{C} v \tag{4}$$

and represent v in terms of an n-dimensional vector q as $v = \emptyset^T q$. Combining this with (3) and (4) and defining an n×n kernel matrix K by $K = \emptyset^T \emptyset$ leads to $n\lambda Kq = K^2 q$, The solution can be obtained by solving the kernel eigen-value problem:

$$n\lambda q = Kq \tag{5}$$

A justification of this procedure is given by Scholkopf[16]. Now, performing PCA in F is equivalent to resolving the eigen-problem of Eq. (5).

The PCs t of a test vector x are then extracted by projecting $\emptyset(x)$ onto eigenvectors v_k in F, where $k = 1, \dots, n$

$$t_k = \langle v_k, \emptyset(x) \rangle = \sum_{i=1}^{N} q_i^k \langle \emptyset(x_i), \emptyset(x) \rangle \tag{6}$$

Before applying KPCA, mean centering in the high-imensional space should be performed. The centered kernel matrix $\bar{K}$ can be easily calculated using the noncentered kernel matrix K:

$$\bar{K} = K - KE - EK + EKE \tag{7}$$

Where $E_{ij} = 1/n$.

There exist a number of kernel functions. Most widely used kernel functions contain Gaussian function, polynomial, sigmoidal, and inverse multiquadric type functions [19]. In our study, only a Gaussian function $\exp(-\|x - y\|^2/c)$ is considered to construct a statistical process model. Here, $\|\cdot\|$ is $l2$-norm and c is the width of a Gaussian function.

2.4   Classification (Using k-means Clustering)

Once the features have been extracted, k-means clustering is utilised to separate the features and differentiate the spikes. K-means clustering is a method that aims to partition the spikes (using the selected feature space) into k clusters, in which each spike belongs to the cluster with the nearest mean. This is generally implemented as an iterative algorithm that converges towards the solution. Depending on the feature types (and their dimensionality) the number of iterations required for convergence will vary. For all the classification presented herein, the Matlab ('kmeans') function was used. This has been used to ensure that all methods converge to a near-optimum classification accuracy.

3   Results

3.1   Feature Extraction

Fig.4 shows the wavelet coefficients for spikes in the data set shown in Fig.2. Coefficients corresponding to individual spikes are superimposed, each representing how closely the spike waveform matches the wavelet function at a particular scale and time. Coefficients are organized in detail levels (D_{1-4}) and a last approximation (A_4), which correspond to the different frequency bands in which spike shapes are decomposed. In Fig.4, we observe that some of the coefficients cluster around different values for the different spike classes, thus being well suited for classification. It is clear from this figure that coefficients showing the best discrimination are not necessarily the ones with the largest variance. In particular, the maximum variance criterion misses several coefficients from the high-frequency scales (D_{1-2}) that allow a good separation between the different spike shapes.

For the same data, the comparison between the separability of PCA, Wavelet and KPCA were showed in Figure 5. The best two-dimensional (2D) of PCA, Wavelet and KPCA were chosen to cluster spikes from dataset1(Fig.2a). We observed that using the KPCA, it is possible to clearly identify the three clusters. In contrast, when choosing the best two coefficients with Wavelet or the first two PCs from PCA, it is difficult to differentiate class1 and class2.

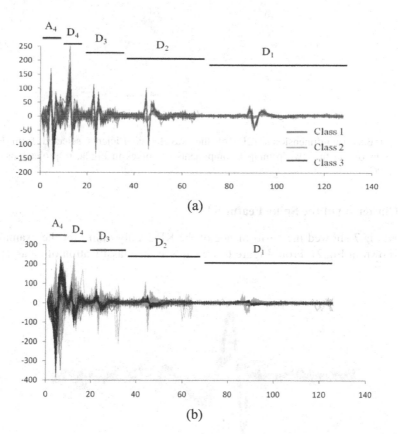

(a)

(b)

Fig. 4. Wavelet transform of the spikes from Figure 2a and Figure 2b (panes a and b, respectively)

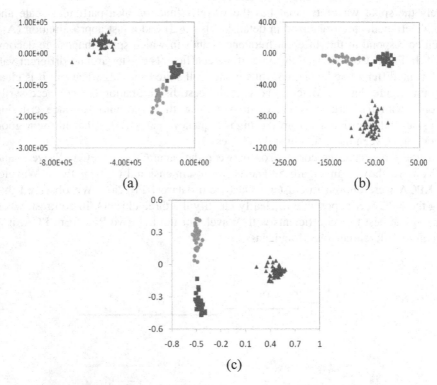

(a)

(b)

(c)

Fig. 5. (a) Best two-dimensional (2D) of the wavelet coefficients selected from Fig.4a, (b)projections of the first two principal components of spikes in Fig2a, (c)projections of the first two KPCs

3.2   Clustering of the Spike Features

Fig.6 and Fig.7 showed the performance of the KPCA algorithm for the example datasets (shown in Fig.2). From Figure 6, we can see the classification of dataset1 after

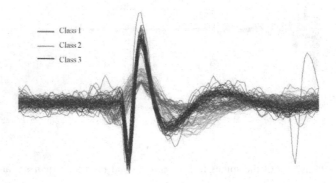

Fig. 6. Outcome of the clustering algorithm for Spikes from dataset1(Fig.2(a))

clustering. In this case, spike shapes are easy to differentiate, for there were only three spike clusters. In Fig.7, there are 5 spike clusters, it is difficult to differentiate class2, class3 from class5, class4 respectively. However, in all these cases, the classification errors were very low (see Table 1).

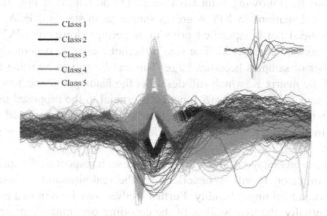

Fig. 7. Outcome of the clustering algorithm for Spikes from dataset2(Fig.2(b))

Errors of spike identification cumulatively derive from two sources: incorrect feature extraction and incorrect clustering. We compared the discrimination power of KPCA with other feature extraction methods using the same clustering algorithm, SPC. Specifically, we compared the outcome of classification with KPCA, wavelets, principal component analysis (using the first two principal components). Table 1 summarizes the results(examples 1 and 2 were shown in Fig.6 and Fig.7, respectively). Performance was quantified in terms of the number of classification errors. In general, the best performance was achieved by using KPCA algorithm. Since example 1 was easier to cluster, all of the three methods did a good job. In example 2, there were five spike cluster, classification errors by KPCA algorithm was smaller than the others.

Table 1. Number of Classification Errors for two Examples Obtained Using KPCA, PCA and WAVELET

Example	Number of Spike	Sorting error		
		This work	PCA	Wavelet
Dataset1	117	0	2	1
Dataset2	1428	8	16	14

4   Conclusion

In this paper, a new Spike sorting method based on Wavelet and KPCA was proposed. KPCA can efficiently compute PCs in high-dimensional feature spaces by means of integral operators and nonlinear kernel functions. Compared to other nonlinear methods, KPCA has the following main advantages: (1) no nonlinear optimization is involved; (2) the calculations in KPCA are as simple as in standard PCA, and (3) the number of PCs need not be specified prior to modeling. However, KPCA has some problems that must be considered. The size of kernel matrix K becomes problematic when the number of samples becomes large. This can be solved by using a sparse approximation of the matrix K, which still describes the leading eigenvectors sufficiently well [20]. The selection of the kernel function is crucial to the proposed method since the degree to which the nonlinear characteristic of a system is captured depends on this function; In this paper, the radial basis kernel function $\exp\left(-\|x - y\|^2/c\right)$ was considered.

We verified the advantage of the KPCA method with respect to the spike detection and classification error. It will be beneficial for the real situations, where the signal quality can be degraded unpredictably. Further studies may be required to clarify this statement. Eventually, the assessments of the decoding performance presented in this paper should be applied to a highly reliable experimental data.

Ackowledgement. This work was supported by National Basic Research Program of China (No. 2014CB744600 and 2011CB933202), Beijing Municipal Science & Technology Commission Project (NO. Z141102003414014 and NO. Z141100000214002), the National Natural Science Foundation of China (No. 61125105, 61101048, 61271147).

References

1. Pedreira, C., Martinez, J., Ison, M.J., Quiroga, R.Q.: How many neurons can we see with current spike sorting algorithms? Journal of Neuroscience Methods 211, 58–65 (2012)
2. Musial, P.G., Baker, S.N., Gerstein, G.L., King, E.A., Keating, J.G.: Signal-to-noise ratio improvement in multiple electrode recording. J. Neurosci. Methods 115, 29–43 (2002)
3. Paraskevopoulou, S.E., Barsakcioglu, D.Y., Saberi, M.R., Eftekhar, A., Constandinou, T.G.: Feature extraction using first and second derivative extrema (FSDE) for real-time and hardware-efficient spike sorting. Journal of Neuroscience Methods 215, 29–37 (2013)
4. Quiroga, R.Q., Nadasdy, Z., Ben-Shaul, Y.: Unsupervised Spike Detection and Sorting with Wavelets and Superparamagnetic Clustering. Neural Comput 16(8), 1661–1687 (2004)
5. Lewicki, M.: A review of methods for spike sorting: The detection and classification of neural action potentials. Network: Comput. Neural Syst. 9, 53–78 (1998)
6. Jung, H.K., Choi, J.H., Kim, T.: Solving alignment problems in neural spike sorting using frequency domain PCA. Neurocomputing 69, 975–978 (2006)
7. Bar-Hillel, A., Spiro, A., Stark, E.: Spike sorting: Bayesian clustering of non-stationary data. Journal of Neuroscience Methods 157, 303–316 (2006)

8. Kirn, K.H., Kirn, S.J.: A wavelet-based method for action potential detection from extracellular neural signal recording with low signal-to-noise ratio. IEEE Transactions on Biomedical Engineering 50(8), 999–1011 (2003)
9. Calabrese, A., Paninski, L.: Kalman filter mixture model for spike sorting of nonstationary data. Journal of Neuroscience Methods 196, 159–169 (2011)
10. Abeles, M., Goldstein, M.H.: Multispike train analysis. Proc. IEEE 65, 762–773 (1997)
11. Adamos, D.A., Kosmidis, E.K., Theophilidis, G.: Performance evaluation of PCA-based spike sorting algorithms. Computer Methods and Programs in Biomedicine 91, 232–244 (2008)
12. Scholkopf, B., Smola, A.J., Muller, K.: Nonlinear component analysis as a kernel eigenvalue problem. Neural Computation 10(5), 1299–1399 (1998)
13. Romdhani, S., Gong, S., Psarrou, A.: A multi-view nonlinear active shape model using kernel PCA. In: Proceedings of BMVC, Nottingham, UK, pp. 483–492 (1999)
14. Choi, S.W., Lee, I.-B.: Nonlinear dynamic process monitoring based on dynamic kernel PCA. Chemical Engineering Science 59, 5897–5908 (2004)
15. Mika, S., Scholkopf, B., Smola, A.J., Muller, K.-R., Scholz, M., Ratsch, G., Kernel, P.C.A.: de-noising in feature spaces. Advances in Neural Information Processing Systems 11, 536–542 (1999)
16. Scholkopf, B., Smola, A.J., Muller, K.: Nonlinear component analysis as a kernel eigenvalue problem. Neural Computation 10(5), 1299–1399 (1998)
17. Harrison, R.R.: A low-power integrated circuit for adaptive detection of action potentials in noisy signals. In: Proceedings of the 25th International IEEE EMBS Conference, pp. 3325–3328. IEEE, Cancun (2003)
18. Chen, Y.-Y., Chen, T.-C., Chen, L.-G.: Accuracy and power tradeoff in spike sorting microsystems with cubic spline interpolation. In: Proceedings of 2010 IEEE International Symposium on Circuits and Systems (ISCAS), pp. 1508–1511 (June 2010)
19. Müller, K.R., Mika, S., Rtsch, G., Tsuda, K., Schlkopf, B.: An introduction to kernel-based learning algorithms. IEEE Transactions on Neural Networks 12, 181–201 (2001)
20. Smola, A.J., Scholkopf, B.: Sparse greedy matrix approximation for machine learning. In: Proceedings of ICML 2000, San Francisco, pp. 911–918 (2000)
21. Song, Y., Lin, N., Liu, C., Luo, J., Wang, L., Cai, X.: Design and Fabrication of Microelectrode Array Sensor for Electrophysiological Recording In Vitro. Nanotechnology and Precision Engineering 9(3), 184–188 (2011)
22. Song, Y., Lin, N., Liu, C., Jiang, H., Xing, G., Cai, X.: A novel dual mode microelectrode array for neuroelectrical and neurochemical recording in vitro. Biosensors and Bioelectronics 38(1), 416–420 (2012)

Artifacts Reduction Method in EEG Signals with Wavelet Transform and Adaptive Filter

Rui Huang[1], Fei Heng[1], Bin Hu[1,2,*], Hong Peng[1], Qinglin Zhao[1], Qiuxia Shi[1], and Jun Han[3]

[1] The School of Information Science and Engineering, Lanzhou University, Lanzhou, China
[2] The School of Electronic Information and Control Engineering,
Beijing University of Technology, Beijing, China
[3] Chinese Academy of Sciences, China
{huangr12,hengf13,bh,pengh,qlzhao}@lzu.edu.cn,
shiqxjm@gmail.com, jhan@cashq.ac.cn

Abstract. This paper presents a method to remove ocular artifacts from electroencephalograms (EEGs) which can be used in biomedical analysis in portable environment. An important problem in EEG analysis is how to remove the ocular artifacts which wreak havoc among analyzing EEG signals. In this paper, we propose a combination of Wavelet Transform with effective threshold and adaptive filter which can extract the reference signal according to ocular artifacts distributing in low frequency domain mostly, and adaptive filter based on Least Mean Square (LMS) algorithm is used to remove ocular artifacts from recorded EEG signals. The results show that this method can remove ocular artifacts and superior to a comparison method on retaining uncontaminated EEG signal. This method is applicable to the portable environment, especially when only one channel EEG are recorded.

Keywords: electroencephalogram (EEG), ocular artifacts, adaptive filter, signal processing.

1 Introduction

Studies show clearly that mental health care represents a major cost to all nations and is increasingly becoming one of the most important aspects in Telecare and Telehealth projects. Researchers want to build a home care system based on EEG and it is designed to monitor levels of individual mental disorders and collect feedback during treatment using EEG signals. But the recorded EEG signal were contaminated by other potential bioelectricity interferences, such as Ocular artifact from eyemovement, electromyography (EMG) from muscle activity or baseline drift and power line interference, etc. [1]. These signals may be usually much higher than that of the neural signals, so it is necessary for these noises to be removed. Ocular artifact

---

* Corresponding author.

D. Ślęzak et al. (Eds.): BIH 2014, LNAI 8609, pp. 122–131, 2014.
© Springer International Publishing Switzerland 2014

from eye-movement is a major source of contamination of the EEG. So it is important to use effective methods to remove the ocular artifacts from recorded EEG signal.

Many traditional approaches have been proposed to remove or attenuate such ocular artifacts from recorded EEG in recent years. Widely used methods for attenuating ocular artifacts are based on time domain [2] or frequency domain [3] techniques. Independent Component Analysis (ICA) is a good method which is developed with respect to blind source separation and the aim is to obtain components that are approximately independent [4]-[6]. But to remove ocular artifacts, a reference signal is necessary which requires tedious visual classification of the components [7], [8]. Some methods have been used in the modeling of ocular artifacts components based on improved support vector machine (SVM) [9] to isolate them from the EEG [10]. Wavelet transform [11], [12] approach is becoming more and more popular for the analysis of biomedical data. Stationary Wavelet Transform (SWT) is a method which neither relies upon the reference ocular artifacts nor visual inspection. As frequency precision is also improved, researchers have often used SWT to detect the ocular artifacts region and then selected the correct threshold to remove the interferences [13]. However, the ocular artifacts, since they have an overlapping spectrum cannot be removed by SWT. These techniques are unlikely to provide sufficient accuracy to purify EEG signals.

In this paper, we proposed a method based on wavelet transform and adaptive filter to remove the ocular artifacts. Adaptive algorithms [15] play a very important role in many diverse applications, such as communications, acoustics, speech, radar, sonar, seismology, and biomedical engineering. In general, the adaptive filter adjusts its coefficients to minimize the squared error between its output and a primary signal. In stationary conditions, the filter should converge to the Wiener solution. Conversely, in non-stationary circumstances, the coefficients will change with time, according to the signal variation, thus converging to an optimum filter [14]. The transfer function of adaptive filter is adjusted according to an optimizing algorithm. The adaptation is directed by the error signal between the primary signal and the filter output. The optimizing criterion mostly used is the Least Mean Square (LMS) algorithm. In a portable environment, it is necessary to deal with contaminated EEG signal, especially when the recorded EEG signal has only one channel. We use wavelet transform to decompose contaminated EEG signal, then, apply effective threshold on the detail coefficients at last three levels, using wavelet transform again to reconstruct signal. We don't deal with all wavelet coefficients and only for three layers coefficients, because the last three levels coefficients contain the most information of ocular artifacts. So, we use this reconstructed signal instead of recorded electrooculogram (EOG) signal as the input reference signal of adaptive filter. This combination can do remove ocular artifacts from contaminated EEG signal well and this allows us to lever the biggest advantage of adaptive filter: it can follow the changes and automatically adjust its parameter to achieve optimal performance of the filter when the statistical properties of input signal are changing. Through the comparison results, the performance of the proposed method is better than comparison method on retaining the EEG signal without contaminated by ocular artifacts. It is effective even if the EEG signals have only one channel and hence is particularly suitable for portable applications.

The paper is structured as follows: Section 2 provides a detailed introduction with respect to the method in this paper. Section 3 presents the results of our study. In section 4 we discuss our results. Conclusion and the limitations of this study will be given in section 5. The data processing during the research is conducted through the MATLAB tool.

2   Methodology

EEG signals are contaminated by other biological signals, among them, the ocular artifacts have the greatest interferences. This contamination is considered to be an additive noise within the EEG signal. So we can get the following expression:

$$EEG_{rec}(t) = EEG_{true}(t) + k \cdot OAs(t) \tag{1}$$

where,

$EEG_{rec}(t)$: the recorded EEG signal,

$EEG_{true}(t)$: the EEG signal due to cortical activity and without interference,

$k \cdot OAs(t)$: the ocular artifacts due to eye movement.

We can get the $EEG_{rec}(t)$ from the $EEG_{true}(t)$ by removing the $k \cdot OAs(t)$ efficiently. In this paper, we applied a method which based on wavelet transformation and adaptive filter.

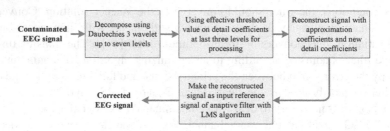

Fig. 1. Flowchart for correction of contaminated EEG

Using adaptive filter to remove the ocular artifacts from recorded EEG signal always needs a reference channel. Considering the more portable data recording environment, there is even no synchronous channel to record ocular artifacts signal, so here, we use wavelet transformation to obtain the reference ocular artifacts signal for adaptive filter. First, we apply wavelet decomposition to decompose the contaminated EEG signal, and select Daubechies 3 wavelet as mother wavelet function, because its coefficients are the simplest. Then approximation coefficients and detail coefficients are computed form seven levels of wavelet decomposition. Second, we use threshold value on detail coefficients at last three levels for processing. By analyzing the frequency spread of the EEG data, the ocular artifacts are mainly concentrated in the low frequency band, we can only process the last three levels detail coefficients with a hard threshold to extract the reference EOG signal, and use different threshold value to each level. The threshold value is an empirical value which based on the relationship of each level coefficients variance and mean. Third, we apply wavelet reconstruction on the new wavelet coefficients and obtain the reconstructed signal which contains a large amount of information of ocular artifacts and little information of EEG signal. Finally, we use adaptive filter to remove the ocular artifacts from recorded EEG signal, the reconstructed signal is used as the input reference signal of adaptive filter. Fig.1 shows the flowchart for correction of contaminated EEG with our method.

Adaptive filter algorithm have several choices, in this paper, we choose the most simple and commonly used algorithm: least mean square (LMS). An adaptive system based on the LMS algorithm has a good performance when the environmental noise is a stationary random signal. The LMS algorithm is outlined in the following set of equations [15]:

The error signal of adaptive filter is:

$$
\begin{aligned}
e(n) &= d(n) - y(n) \\
&= d(n) - x^{T}(n)w(n) \\
&= d(n) - w^{T}(n)x(n)
\end{aligned}
\tag{2}
$$

Where, $x(n)$ is the input signal, $y(n) = x^{T}(n)w(n) = w^{T}(n)x(n)$ is the output of adaptive filter, $d(n)$ is the reference signal, $w(n)$ is the filter's weight coefficients. Using the steepest descent method, we get the update recursive relation of filter weight coefficients:

$$
w(n+1) = w(n) + 2\mu x(n)[d(n) - x^{T}(n)w(n)]^{T}
\tag{3}
$$

Where, μ is the convergence factor. So:

$$
w(n+1) = w(n) + 2\mu x(n)e(n)
\tag{4}
$$

This is known as the iterative formula of filter weight coefficient based on LMS algorithm. The weight coefficient at the next time slice can be determined by the weight coefficient on current time slice and the error function for the proportion of input.

3   Results

EEG data with ocular artifacts are taken from the CHB-MIT Scalp EEG Database [16]. EEG recordings of 22 pediatric subjects with intractable seizures, are monitored for up to several days following withdrawal of anti-seizure medication to characterize their seizures and assess their candidacy for surgical intervention. The data are sampled at a rate of 256 samples per second. We chose an epoch without Seizures to validate our method. In the pre-processing part, we remove the baseline drift from the raw EEG signal and intercepted 1 to 40Hz from the chosen signals to avoid the influence of power line interference and baseline drift. Then we apply the method to the pretreatment EEG data. Fig. 2 shows the 'approximation' and 'detail' plot for the contaminated EEG signal. Fig.3 shows the reconstructed signal.

The process of detail coefficients at last three levels is carried out by using threshold. The choice of threshold is an empirical value which based on the relationship of coefficients standard deviation and coefficients mean. We extracted the last three levels coefficients and recorded as detail5, detail6 and detail7. The processed coefficients recorded as newdetail5, newdetail6 and newdetail7. The different thresholds used in this work are as follows:

(i)   **If**   the absolute value of detail5 coefficient value $>$ 2.3 $*$ the standard deviation of detail5
         then newdetail5 coefficient value = detail5 coefficient value
         else   newdetail5 coefficient value = 0

(ii)   **If**   the absolute value of detail6 coefficient value $>$ 1.5 $*$ the standard deviation of detail6
         then newdetail6 coefficient value = detail6 coefficient value
         else   newdetail6 coefficient value = 0

(iii)   **If**   the absolute value of detail7 coefficient value $>$ 0.4 $*$ the standard deviation of detail7
         then newdetail7 coefficient value = detail7 coefficient value
         else   newdetail7 coefficient value = 0

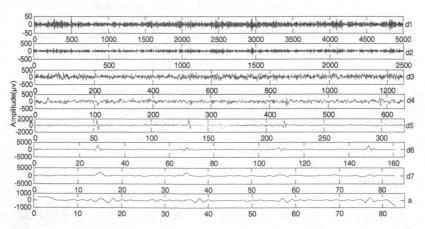

Fig. 2. 'Detail' (from the top down one to seven line) and 'Approximation' (the bottom line) plot. It is distinct that the information of ocular artifacts is almost contained in the detail coefficients at last three levels.

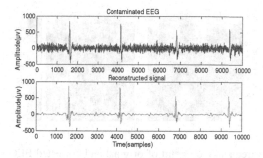

Fig. 3. The reconstructed signal

After threshold processing, we get the reference signal through wavelet reconstruction. Adaptive filter is used to remove ocular artifacts, the reconstructed signal is used as an input reference signal. In this paper, the order of adaptive filter is 5, and this not only reaches the purpose of noise removal, but also reduces the processing time of algorithm. Fig.4 shows the recorded EEG signal contaminated by ocular artifacts and the corrected EEG signal processed by our proposed method. In order to see clearly, only half of the signal is shown. Fig.5 shows the wave time-frequency diagram of original and corrected EEG signals. Fig.6 shows the power spectra of the contaminated EEG and corrected EEG. Note that the part of output in low frequency domain is attenuated and the high frequency part in more than 13 Hz is retained. This indicates that the ocular artifacts are actually removed. From the results, it can be seen that the ocular artifacts are reduced both in time and frequency domains. Particularly, in the frequency domain, a corrected EEG signal is generated which preserves the intrinsic components of the recorded EEG.

We also do a comparison with an existing method. The stationary wavelet transform (SWT) with threshold method described in [17] and our new model were applied to this contaminated EEG. The parameters of the adaptive filter remain unchanged. The results are shown in Fig.7. The SWT with threshold reduces the noise to a certain degree, but still leaves significant distortion in the EEG signal, at the same time, our method retains the EEG signal without ocular artifacts. We also can find similar result from the comparison of power spectral density in Fig.8.

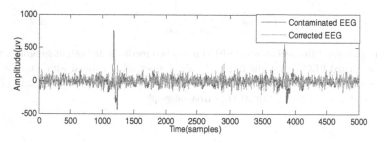

Fig. 4. The contaminated EEG signal and the corrected EEG signal in time domain. In order to see clearly, only a part of the signals are drawn.

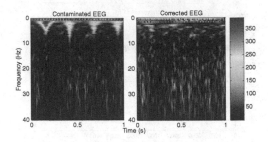

Fig. 5. The wave time-frequency diagram of original and corrected EEG signals. At the same time point, it is clearly that ocular artifacts in corrected EEG is much smaller than it in contaminated EEG.

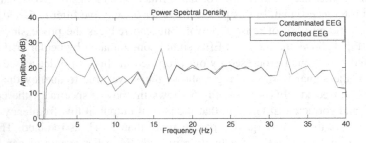

Fig. 6. Power spectral density plot

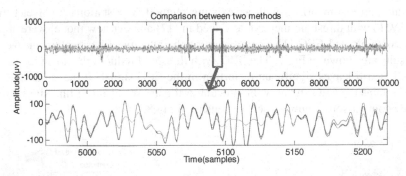

Fig. 7. Contaminated EEG and corrected EEG using two methods. In both of subgraph, the blue line is contaminated EEG signal, the red line is the corrected EEG signal with our new method and the green line is the corrected EEG signal with threshold method described in [18]. The second subgraph is the part amplification of first subgraph.

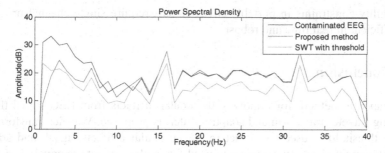

Fig. 8. The power spectral density of two corrected EEG signals. The SWT with threshold method in [17] has a large distortion in more than 13Hz frequency domain and the proposed method shows a beautiful tracking performance in this comparison.

4   Discussion

In this paper, we introduce a new method that combines wavelet transform with threshold and adaptive filter techniques to remove the ocular artifacts from contaminated EEG signals. We apply our methods on contaminated EEG signals and obtain good results. From the Fig.5, we can obviously see that the EEG signal part below 13Hz in frequency domain which includes ocular artifacts is greatly weakened and Fig.6 shows that the components above 13Hz are retained. We made a comparison power spectral density plot in Fig.6 shows that the powers of the in Fig.7 and Fig.8, the results show that the combination of wavelet transform and adaptive filter is superior to the method in [17].

EEG signal is composed by messes of frequency contents that vary as a function of time and recording site. Wavelet techniques can be employed to analyze such a non-stationary signal which facilitates multi-resolution analysis in the time–frequency plane. The most remarkable advantage of adaptive filter based on LMS algorithm is its adaptive preservation of components intrinsic to the EEG recordings. In addition, adaptive filter can adapt their coefficients to abrupt changes in the line frequency or modifications due to ocular artifacts. Our method proposed in this paper combines the two algorithms by keeping the merits of each algorithm to cancel ocular artifacts. We have demonstrated the effectiveness of our model in section two and shown how we can eliminate ocular artifacts even when their frequency band is overlapping with the EEG signal. By using wavelet transform to extract ocular artifacts reference signal avoids the trouble of recording ocular artifacts with another channel synchronously, which means significant pratical value to portable EEG equipment. From this perspective, employing such signal analytical processing together with portable EEG recording equipment is the necessary analytical processing, that is vitally important, especially for real-time application.

We therefore conclude that our new method is able to provide good attenuation levels for most types of ocular artifacts interference presents in EEG signals. The removal of ocular artifacts from EEG signals in projects, especially in portable environment Telecare and Telehealth project [18], is a promising application.

The usability constraints in portable environments require single channel processing that is efficient in real time and robust.

5   Conclusion

In this paper, a method, for removing the ocular artifacts from EEG signal through combining wavelet transform and adaptive filter, is proposed. Wavelet transform with effective threshold is used to extract reference ocular artifacts signal, and adaptive filter with extracted reference signal is used for ocular artifacts removal. The results indicate that the method in this paper can remove the interferences of ocular artifacts effectively and it is an efficient technique for improving the quality of EEG signals in biomedical analysis. The wave time-frequency diagram and power spectral density are used as performance metrics in this paper.

In future study, improvement of some parameters and algorithm will be the major considerations. Beyond that, we will apply this method on our portable project the EUFP 7 Project - Online Predictive Tools for Intervention in Mental Illness (OPTIMI).

Acknowledgment. This work was supported by the National Basic Research Program of China (973 Program) (No.2014CB744600, No.2011CB711000), the National Natural Science Foundation of China (grant No.61210010, No. 61300231), the Program of International S&T Cooperation of MOST (No.2013DFA11140), the EU's Seventh Framework Program OPTIMI (grant No.248544),Central Universities Fundamental Research Funds (grant No.lzujbky-2013-45) and   Natural Science Foundation of Gansu Province, China(1208RJZA127).

References

1. Jung, T.P., Makeig, S., Humphries, C., Lee, T.W., McKeown, M.J., Iragui, V., Sejnowski, T.J.: Removing electroencephalographic artifacts by blind source separation. Psychophysiology 37, 163–178 (2000)
2. Gratton, G., Coles, M.G.H., Donchin, E.: A new method for off-line removal of ocular artifact. Electroencephalography and Clinical Neurophysiology 55(4), 468–484 (1983)
3. Woestengurg, J.C., Verbaten, M.N., Slangen, J.L.: The removal of the eye movement artifact from the EEG by regression analysis in the frequency domain. Biological Physiology 16, 127–147 (1982)
4. Vigário, R.N.: Extraction of ocular artifacts from EEG using independent component analysis. Electroencephalography and clinical Neurophysiology 103, 395–404 (1997)
5. Hu, S., Stead, M., Worrell, G.A.: Automatic Identification and Removal of Scalp Reference Signal for Intracranial EEGs Based on Independent Component Analysis. IEEE Trans. Biomed. Eng. 54(9), 1560–1572 (2007)
6. Vigario, R., Sarela, J., Jousmaki, V., Hamalainen, M., Oja, E.: Independent component approach to the analysis of EEG and MEG recordings. IEEE Trans. Biomed. Eng. 47(5), 589–593 (2000)

7. Lu, W., Rajapakse, J.C.: ICA with reference. In: Proc. 3rd Int. Conf. Independent Component Analysis and Blind Signal Separation: ICA 2001, pp. 120–125 (2001)
8. Hyvärinen, A., Oja, E.: A fast fixed-point algorithm for independent component analysis. Neural Computation 9(7), 1483–1492 (1997)
9. Shen, K.-Q., Ong, C.J., Wilder-Smith, E., Li, X.-P.: Automatic EEG Artifact Removal: A Weighted Support Vector Machine Approach With Error Correction. IEEE Trans. Biomed. Eng. 56(2), 336–344 (2009)
10. Lins, O.G., Picton, T.W., Berg, P., Scherg, M.: Ocular artifacts in EEG and event-related potentials, I: Scalp topography. Brain Topography 6(1), 51–63 (1993)
11. Croft, R.J., Barry, R.J.: Removal of ocular artifact from the EEG: a review. Neurophysiologie Clinique/Clinical Neurophysiology 30, 5–19 (2000)
12. Peng, H., Hu, B., Qi, Y., Zhao, Q., Ratcliffe, M.: An Improved EEG De-noising Approach in Electroencephalogram (EEG) for Home Care. In: 2011 5th International Conference on Pervasive Computing Technologies for Healthcare (PervasiveHealth) and Workshops, pp. 469–474 (May 2011)
13. Krishnaveni, V., Jayaraman, S., Aravind, S., Hariharasudhan, V., Ramadoss, K.: Automatic Identification and Removal of Ocular Artifacts from EEG Using Wavelet Transform. Measurement Science Review 6(4), 45–57 (2006)
14. Widrow, B., Stearns, S.D.: Adaptive Signal Processing. Prentice-Hall, New Jersey (1985)
15. He, P., Wilson, G., Russell, C.: Removal of ocular artifacts from electro-encephalogram by adaptive filtering. Med. Biol. Eng. Comput. 42, 407–412 (2004)
16. Goldberger, A.L., Amaral, L.A.N., Glass, L., Hausdorff, J.M., Ivanov, P.C., Mark, R.G., Mietus, J.E., Moody, G.B., Peng, C.-K., Stanley, H.E.: Components of a New Research Resource for Complex Physiologic Signals. Circulation (June 2000)
17. Krishnaveni, V., Jayaraman, S., Malmurugan, N., Kandasamy, A., Ramadoss, D.: Non adaptive thresholding methods for correcting ocular artifacts in EEG. Academic Open Internet Journal 13 (2004)
18. Hu, B., Majoe, D., Ratcliffe, M., Qi, Y., Zhao, Q., Peng, H., Fan, D., Zheng, F., Jackson, M., Moore, P.: EEG-Based Cognitive Interfaces for Ubiquitous Applications: Developments and Challenges, vol. 26, pp. 46–53 (2011)

Utilizing Data Mining for Predictive Modeling of Colorectal Cancer Using Electronic Medical Records

Mark Hoogendoorn[1], Leon M.G. Moons[2], Mattijs E. Numans[3,4], and Robert-Jan Sips[5]

[1] VU University Amsterdam, Department of Computer Science
De Boelelaan 1081, 1081 HV, Amsterdam, The Netherlands
m.hoogendoorn@vu.nl
[2] Utrecht University Medical Center, Department of Gastroenterology and Hepatology
Heidelberglaan 100, 3584 CX Utrecht, The Netherlands
L.M.G.Moons@umcutrecht.nl
[3] Leiden University Medical Center, Department of Public Health and Primary Care
Hippocratespad 21, 2333 ZD Leiden, The Netherlands
M.E.Numans@lumc.nl
[4] Utrecht University Medical Center, Julius Center for Health Sciences and Primary Care,
Utrecht, The Netherlands
[5] IBM Netherlands, Center for Advanced Studies
Johan Huizingalaan 765, 1066 VH Amsterdam, The Netherlands
Robert-Jan.Sips@nl.ibm.com

Abstract. Colorectal cancer (CRC) is a relatively common cause of death around the globe. Predictive models for the development of CRC could be highly valuable and could facilitate an early diagnosis and increased survival rates. Currently available predictive models are improving, but do not fully utilize the wealth of data available about patients in routine care nor do they take advantage of the developments in the area of data mining. In this paper, a first attempt to generate a predictive model using the CHAID decision tree learner based on anonymously extracted Electronic Medical Records is reported, showing an area under the curve (AUC) of .839 for the adult population and .702 for the age group between 55 and 75.

1   Introduction

Colorectal cancer (CRC) is the second most common newly diagnosed cancer and the second most common single cause of death in the EU (cf. [2]). Survival is directly related to the stage of cancer at time of diagnosis. The 5-year survival ranges from >90% in stage I CRC (no lymphatic or haematogenous metastases) to 8-30% in stage IV CRC (distant metastases). It is therefore important to detect CRC at the earliest possible stage. In various countries, screening programs have been initiated. In the Netherlands for example, the entire population above 55 and below 75 is screened for blood in the stool followed by a colonoscopy when positive. This screening however, is far from optimal: attendance rates are relatively low (65% in a Dutch trial, 35% in Spain), and CRC is only detected in 6-7% of the patients that test positive for blood in the stool.

D. Ślęzak et al. (Eds.): BIH 2014, LNAI 8609, pp. 132–141, 2014.
© Springer International Publishing Switzerland 2014

It is clear that more effective screening methods are needed, so that the population at risk can be identified more easily. As the General Practitioner (GP) is the first to see such patients, risk models that utilize the information available to the GP already before seeing the patient are a natural starting point. Various prediction algorithms have been developed, including the QCancer prediction model [5] and the Bristol-Birmingham equation [9]. These approaches however apply more traditional statistical methods to come to a risk score, make use of information from questionnaires and are hypothesis driven. Alternative approaches, such as data mining have not yet been applied in this domain, and could potentially deliver valuable insights into more complex interactions between risk factors and the development of CRC.

In this paper, an anonymized Electronic Medical Records (EMR) dataset, shared from a network of GP's in the Utrecht region in the Netherlands, is used to create a first risk classification model for CRC using data mining techniques. The dataset consists of the patient records of over 140,000 patients from 2006 till 2011 of whom 492 became CRC cases during this time interval. Data include general characteristics of the patient (age, gender, observation time), structured and coded information on consults (dates, description of the findings such as symptoms and diagnoses in the form of ICPC codes, a structured coding approach used worldwide, see e.g. [7], medication (prescription data and ATC code of the type of medicine[1]), and information about referral to specialists. In this initial research, various subsets of the dataset have been used to evaluate the contribution of the different parts of the dataset. The algorithms deployed is the CHAID decision tree learning algorithm (cf. [6]) as the specialists need to be able to understand the resulting predictive models.

This paper is organized as follows. First, the dataset that has been obtained is described and analyzed in more detail in Section 2. Section 3 describes the preparation of the data to facilitate the learning and the choice of the algorithms. In Section 4 the results are shown, and finally, Section 5 is a discussion.

2   Dataset Description

This Section describes the characteristics of the dataset, which includes four parts in total. The first part of the dataset concerns the general characteristics of the patients. The dataset covers the period between January 1st 2006 and December 31st 2011. We only selected patients that were registered at one of the participating GP practices for a period of at least 6 months. This results in a total of 142,061 patients. Each patient is described by age, gender, ZIP code, practice code, the date of registration at the practice and the date of leaving (if available). The age distribution of the patients in the dataset is shown in Figure 1. The age distribution for the CRC patients is shown in Figure 2. Clearly, CRC occurs much more frequently among older patients.

---

[1] See http://www.whocc.no/atc/structure_and_principles/

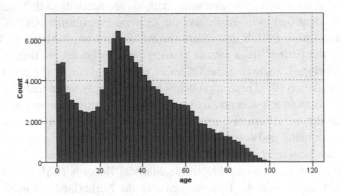

Fig. 1. Age distribution in dataset

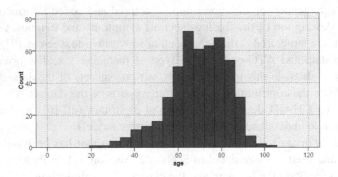

Fig. 2. Age distribution CRC patients

The second part of the dataset addresses the consultations of the patients referred to above with their GP. A total of 1.16 million coded consultations are present. From the consultations, the start date and ICPC code are only used. When looking at the distribution of the number of consults with a specific ICPC code (shown in Figure 3) a long tail distribution can be seen. A total of 691 distinct ICPC codes are present in the dataset covering the consults. Frequently occurring diagnosis include A97 (no disease, 5.25% of the consultations), A99 (general disease, non-specific, 3.51%), R44 (influenza vaccination, 2.67%), R74 (upper respiratory infection acute, 1.87%), and R05 (cough, 1.44%). Codes A97 and A99 are generally considered as "not meaningful", code R44 is linked with flue prevention that in general is taken by 1-20% of the patients in each practice. Figure 4 shows the number of consults per patient during their registration period organized in bins of size 2, clearly showing that patients with a limited number of visits to the GP are most common.

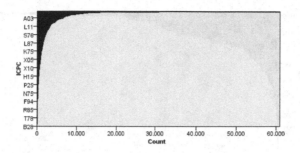

Fig. 3. ICPC consult distribution (number of records per ICPC code). Note that only a fraction of the ICPC codes is shown on the y-axis.

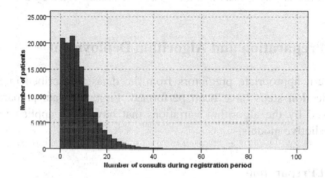

Fig. 4. The number of patients for a given number of consults

When focusing on medication (the third part), Figure 5 shows that the distribution of the ATC codes. The data used for this part includes the prescription date and the ATC code. Medication is a much larger dataset (around 3.9 million records). Frequently occurring codes here are N05 (psycholeptics, 7.4%); A02 (antacids, 5.1%), R03 (anti-asthmatics, 5.1 %) and C09 (agents acting on the renin-angiotensin system, 4.8%). A total of 92 distinct ATC codes (on level H2) are present in the dataset. The spread of the number of prescriptions per patient shows a similar distribution compared to the number of consults.

Finally data is present about the referral to medical specialists (referral date and specialism is used). Here, 92 unique forwarding specializations are present and around 30,000 records. Again, a long tail distribution is observed, with laboratory (32.7%), x-ray (10.2%) and physical therapy (10.1%) being the most frequently encountered specializations.

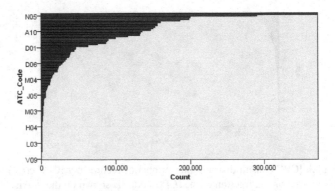

Fig. 5. ATC code (medication) distribution (number of records per ATC code).
Note that only a fraction of the ATC codes is shown on the y-axis.

3   Data Preparation and Algorithm Deployment

In order to learn appropriate predictors from the dataset described in Section 2, a
number of selection steps have been performed. First, the data preparation is discussed, followed by the algorithm variations that have been applied to enable the
learning of predictive models.

3.1   Dataset Preparation

Given the dataset that is available, the most relevant predictors occur or are registered within the period of 6 months of the diagnosis of CRC. As a result, for CRC
patients only the data is selected 6 months prior to the first diagnosis with CRC. For
patients that are not diagnosed with CRC a random period of 6 months during their
registration period is selected. The next step taken is to combine all the records of
individual patients (i.e. the basic patients data, the records per consult, for each medication prescribed and for each referral) into a single record. At this stage, the temporal nature of the data is no longer considered (it is future work to exploit this more
using temporal data mining techniques) as counts are just taken for each ICPC code,
ATC code, and referral during the six month period. Of course, the ICPC code for
CRC has been excluded from this dataset. As the data is rather sparse, additional
attributes have been added that count the number of records in certain groups, for
instance ICPC codes starting with a D are diagnoses associated with the digestive
system and ATC codes starting with an S concern medications for sensory organs.
Table 1 shows the overall resulting set of attributes per individual patient (as said, in
a single record).

Table 1. Description of patient record used for learning

Attribute	Values	Explanation
Age	Integer	The age of the particular patient
Gender	m/f	The gender of the patient
ICPC_A01, ..., ICPC_Z67	Integer	A total of 691 attributes including a count of the number of cases the specific ICPC code was recorded for the patient during the selected 6 month period.
ATC_A01, ..., ATC_V09	Integer	A total of 92 attributes including a count of the number of cases the specific ATC code was recorded for the patient during the selected 6 month period.
Referral_cardiology, ..., Referral_urology	Integer	A total of 92 attributes including a count of the number of cases a referral to a specific specialism was recorded for the patient during the selected 6 month period.
ICPC_Group_A,..., ICPC_Group_Z	Integer	A total of 17 attributes including a count of the number of cases an ICPC code from this group was recorded for the patient during the selected 6 month period.
ATC_Group_A,..., ATC_Group_V	Integer	A total of 14 attributes including a count of the number of cases an ICPC code from this group was recorded for the patient during the selected 6 month period.

3.2   Data Mining Algorithm and Setup

As this is the first endeavor to see whether interesting predictors can be found within the dataset, and it is essential for medical specialists to understand what the predictive model looks like a choice has been made to use the CHAID algorithm and create a decision tree. Tests with the C5.0 algorithm as proposed by (cf. [12]) have also been run but showed lower accuracies. It can be seen that the dataset is highly imbalanced (492 CRC cases in over 140,000 patients). As a result, a misclassification cost has been added for misclassifying an actual CRC patients as a non-CRC patient. The value thereof has been set proportional to the ratio between CRC cases and the total number of patients in the specific part of the dataset, the cost of misclassifying a non-CRC patient as a CRC patient has been set to 1. Furthermore, a maximum tree depth of 5 has been set, and the minimum number of records in a child branch has been set to 50. The significance level for splitting a node was set to 0.05.

For the learning, different sets of attributes are used as input for the learning algorithm to judge the benefits of using them:

- **Age.** As has been shown in the data analysis, age is a highly suitable predictor for CRC, therefore as a benchmark age as a single attribute it considered.
- **Age, gender, and all ICPC codes.** Age and gender combined with the ICPC codes on a detailed level. This provides all available information on the precise diagnoses the GP has registered for the patient.

- **Age, gender, and high level ICPC, ATC, and referrals.** This concerns the two standard attributes (age and gender) extended with the count for ICPC and ATC high-level categories as well as referrals.
- **All.** All the attributes listed in Table 1 are used.

Furthermore, two subsets were created covering different age ranges: the entire adult population (i.e. 18 or above, including all CRC cases) and the screening subpopulation (between 55 and 75, including 254 CRC cases). After selecting the appropriate subset, the dataset was split up into a training set of 60% of the patients and a test set of the remaining 40% each part having approximately the same percentage of CRC cases. As a means of evaluating the predictive capabilities an ROC curve is generated on the test set and the area under the curve (AUC) is calculated.

4   Results

The procedure described above (both the data preparation as the data mining) has been implemented in IBM SPSS Modeler and used to generate results. First, the results are presented which cover the entire adult population of patients (i.e. 18 or above). Table 2 shows the performance on the set-aside test set for the various setups of the attributes uses as input for the learning algorithm whereas a visualization of the simple decision tree performance is shown in Figure 6.

Table 2. Results of predictive model for entire adult population on test set

Attributes	AUC with CHAID
Only ICPC	.836
High level	.839
All	.834
Benchmark (pure age)	.778

In the graph and from the table it can be seen that age is already quite a good predictor for CRC, which makes sense when you see the age distribution of CRC patients compared to the entire population (Figures 1 and 2). However, using more information does clearly pay off although the differences between the more extended setups are quite marginal. More precisely, the difference between using pure age and the extensions is significant ($p < 0.05$, one-tailed test following [4]) whereas the differences between the extensions are not significant. When looking at the best tree which covers all the high level groups for ICPC and ATC codes (although the differences are very small) the aspects that play a crucial role in the decision tree that has been formed include (in order of importance): age, medication from the A (alimentary tract and metabolism), N (nervous system), and L (antineoplastic and immunomodulating agents) category. ATC code L medication is related with CRC through the indications ulcerative colitis or Crohn. ICPC categories T (endocrine/metabolic and nutritional), Z (social problems), D (digestive), U (urological), X (female genital), and L (musculoskeletal) are related to CRC. Hereby, some factors can be seen as confounding factors (e.g. medication signals that there is a problem which needs to be cured), but apparently these are better present in the data and provide a better predictive value than the underlying symptoms or disease. This could be due to two factors: (1) the registration of medication is better, or (2) the medication can be used to treat multiple diseases and the combination of these diseases is a better predictor.

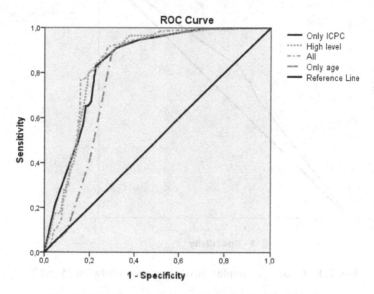

Fig. 6. ROC curve of simple CHAID for population > 18

Table 3 shows the performance for patients aged between 55 and 75 (i.e. the target population of screening approach) and Figure 7 shows the accompanying ROC curves. It is clear that CRC for this subset of patients is harder to predict. The differences in performance between the different variants are now much larger, here using solely the age does not result in a good predictive capability. Using all concepts is clearly best compared to the other variations of the subsets of attributes used. The approach performs significantly better compared to using only age or only ICPC ($p < 0.05$, one-sided test cf. [4]).

Table 3. Results of predictive model for age group between 55 and 75

Attributes	AUC with CHAID
Only ICPC	.579
High level	.658
All	.702
Benchmark (pure age)	.619

The predictive model for CRC that has been created no longer considers age as an important criterion, but the top five predictor with the highest importance are (again in order of importance): ATC codes L01 (antineoplastic agents), A03 (antispasmodic and anticholinergic agents and propulsuves), and B03 (antianemic preparations), and ICPC codes H70 (otitis externa), the high level S (skin) category. The association of these ICPC codes with CRC has to be studied.

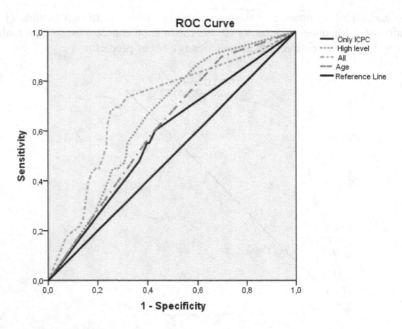

Fig. 7. ROC curve of simple CHAID for patients between 55 and 75

5   Discussion

In this paper a data mining approach has been deployed on a large set of medical records in order to create a predictive model for CRC. The results of a first exploration using a relatively straightforward approach show that a reasonable area under the curve can be obtained. Even for the difficult case where age is no longer a very distinguishing feature it has been shown that the approach can identify patients at risk. The area under the curve obtained in the general adult population was .839. When looking at the literature scores around .89 for females and .91 for males have been reported (cf. [5]), in [9] several datasets have been studied and the AUC's vary between 0.75 and 0.92. Clearly, the performance highly depends on the available information where the information most frequently used in related work includes lab results that have not been considered in this work at the moment.

For future work, we aim to apply more sophisticated algorithms that can derive more information from the data compared to the current algorithm. Hereby, a viable options is to take the temporal course of events into account (see e.g. [11], [8], and [10']). In addition, we would like to apply state-of-the-art data mining algorithms such as bagging approaches (cf. [1]). Initial attempts have shown a tendency that these approaches overfit the data, but more tweaking might result in improved performance, although this of course does take away part of the insightfulness of the results. Furthermore, learning on multiple levels of abstraction (by using medical ontologies) could provide valuable insights as well, as argued in [14]. Finally we would like to combine various datasets with the currently available information.

The idea is to combine the current dataset with nutritional and genetic data (e.g. as gathered in the EPIC longitudinal study, [13]) and also include specialist data.

Acknowledgements. We would like to thank the GPs sharing their anonymized routine healthcare data through the Julius GP network with us for the purpose of this study.

References

1. Breiman, L.: Bagging predictors. Machine Learning 26, 123–140 (1996)
2. Ferlay, J., Parkin, D.M., Steliarova-Foucher, E.: Estimates of cancer incidence and mortality in Europe in 2008. European Journal of Cancer 46(4), 765–781 (2010)
3. Grobbee, D.E., Hoes, A.W., Verheij, T.J., Schrijvers, A.J., van Ameijden, E.J., Numans, M.E.: The Utrecht Health Project: optimization of routine healthcare data for research. Eur. J. Epidemiol. 20(3), 285–287 (2005)
4. Hanley, J.A., McNeil, B.J.: The meaning and use of the area under a Receiver Operating Characteristic (ROC) curve. Radiology 143, 29–36 (1982)
5. Hippisley-Cox, J., Coupland, C.: Identifying patients with suspected colorectal cancer in primary care: derivation and validation of an algorithm. British Journal of GeneralPractice 37, e29–e37 (2012)
6. Kass, G. V.: An Exploratory Technique for Investigating Large Quantities of Categorical Data, Applied Statistics, Vol. 29, No. 2 (1980), pp. 119–127.
7. Lamberts, H., Wood, M., Hofmans-Okkes, I.M.: International primary care classifications: the effect of fifteen years of evolution. Fam. Pract. 9(3), 330–339 (1992)
8. Laxman, S., Sastry, P.: A survey of temporal data mining. In: SADHANA, Academy Proceedings in Engineering Sciences, vol. 31 (2006)
9. Marshall, T., Lancashire, R., Sharp, D., Peters, T.J., Cheng, K.K., Hamilton, W.: The diagnostic performance of scoring systems to identify symptomatic colorectal cancer compared to current referral guidance. Gut. 60(9), 1242–1248 (2011)
10. Patnaik, D., Butler, P., Ramakrishnan, N., Parida, L., Keller, B.J., Hanauer, A.: Experiences with Mining Temporal Event Sequences from Electronic Medical Records. In: Proc. of ACM SIGKDD, pp. 360–368 (2011)
11. Post, A.R., Harrison, J.H.: Temporal data mining. Clinics in Laboratory Medicine 28(1), 83–100 (2008)
12. Quinlan, R.: Data Mining Tools See5 and C5.0 (2003), http://www.rulequest.com
13. Riboli, E., et al.: European Prospective Investigation into Cancer and Nutrition (EPIC): study populations and data collection. Public Health Nutrition 5(6b), 1113–1124 (2002)
14. Zhang, J., Silvescu, A., Honavar, V.G.: Ontology-driven induction of decision trees at multiple levels of abstraction. In: Koenig, S., Holte, R. (eds.) SARA 2002. LNCS (LNAI), vol. 2371, p. 316. Springer, Heidelberg (2002)

Extracting Phenotypes from Patient Claim Records Using Nonnegative Tensor Factorization

Joyce C. Ho[1], Joydeep Ghosh[1], and Jimeng Sun[2]

[1] Electrical and Computer Engineering Department
The University of Texas at Austin, Austin, TX, 78712 USA
[2] College of Computing
Georgia Institute of Technology, Atlanta, GA 30332

Abstract. Electronic health records (EHRs) are becoming an increasingly important source of patient information. Unfortunately, EHR data do not always directly and reliably map to medical concepts that clinical researchers need or use. Some recent studies have focused on EHR-derived phenotyping, which aims at mapping the EHR data to specific medical concepts; however, most of these approaches require labor intensive supervision from experienced clinical professionals.

In this paper, we use Limestone, a nonnegative tensor factorization method to derive phenotype candidates from claims data with virtually no human supervision. Limestone represents the interactions between diagnoses and procedures among patients naturally using tensors (a generalization of matrices). The resulting tensor factors are reported as phenotype candidates that automatically reveal patient clusters on specific diagnoses and procedures. To the best of our knowledge, this is the first study that successfully extracts useful phenotypes by applying sparse nonnegative tensor factorization to a large, public-domain EHR dataset covering a broad range of diseases. Our experiments demonstrate the interpretability and the promise of high-throughput phenotypes generated from tensor factorization.

Keywords: EHR phenotyping, tensor factorization, dimensionality reduction.

1 Introduction

Electronic health records (EHRs), an important source of detailed patient information, are increasingly becoming prevalent within the U.S healthcare system, with federal incentives for meaningful use of EHRs serving as a major driving force. The complexity of the data stored in EHR systems has grown with the widespread adoption of EHRs. EHRs are composed of a diverse array of data, such as structured information (e.g. diagnosis, medications, lab results), molecular sequences, unstructured clinical progress notes, and social network information. Effective integration and efficient analysis of EHRs help physicians make informed clinical decisions; providers improve patient safety; and researchers discover new knowledge and facilitate investigations [1]. While

D. Ślęzak et al. (Eds.): BIH 2014, LNAI 8609, pp. 142–151, 2014.
© Springer International Publishing Switzerland 2014

data-driven approaches are revolutionizing the field of medical informatics [1–3], several formidable challenges arise from the application of EHR data to clinical research. These include: (i) diverse population, where the data cover patients from various providers who use different and incompatible EHR systems; (ii) heterogeneous and noisy information; (iii) sparsely sampled event sequences with varying time scales; (iv) modeling interactions amongst different data sources (types); and (v) reluctance of medical practitioners to act on any recommendations unless they can understand the findings and reconcile them with existing domain knowledge. The interpretability constraints arise because medical professionals are accustomed to reasoning based on concise and meaningful medical concepts, or phenotypes. Recent work has focused on EHR-based phenotyping, a process to map raw EHR data into meaningful medical concepts, Phenotyping approaches learn medically relevant characteristics of the data [4] and is crucial for supporting genome-wide association studies [5].

State of the art phenotype developments rely primarily on approaches that are heuristic, rule, and iterative based, and are a collaborative team effort between clinicians and IT experts [4, 6]. Examples of large-scale phenotyping efforts are typified by the Electronic Medical Records and Genomics (eMERGE) Network [7], which explores the use of EHRs to obtain phenotypic information at multiple medical institutions, and the Observational Medical Outcomes Partnership (OMOP) [8]. However, phenotypes are often disease-centric and the development of a phenotype for a single disease can take months [9]. Thus, data mining and machine learning tools have been leveraged for high-throughput phenotyping, or efficient and automated phenotype extractions to reduce manual development [4, 10]. Yet, current high-throughput methodologies cannot generate large amounts of candidate phenotypes and achieve good performance without human annotated samples [10]. Therefore, two major limitations of existing phenotyping efforts are (i) the need for human annotation of case and control samples, which take substantial time and effort and (ii) the lack of formalized methodology to derive novel phenotypes.

One possible approach for high-throughput phenotyping of EHR data is to use dimensionality reduction techniques [4]. The "ideal" phenotype (i) represents complex interactions between several sources, (ii) is concise and easily understood by a medical professional, and (iii) maps to domain knowledge. Thus, phenotyping can be viewed as a form of dimensionality reduction, where each phenotype forms a latent space [4]. Matrix factorization, a common dimensionality reduction approach, is insufficient as it cannot concisely capture structured EHR source interactions, such as multiple procedures performed to treat a single disease. A more natural transformation is tensor factorization, which utilizes the multiway structure to produce concise and potentially more interpretable results. We recently proposed *Limestone*, a nonnegative tensor factorization model, to simultaneously generate multiple phenotypes from EHR data with minimal human supervision [11] for the problem of characterizing heart failure. Our pilot study extracted 50 phenotypes from Geisinger Health System's EHRs that were

Table 1. List of notations used in this paper

Symbol	Definition
$\lambda, \mathbf{a}$	vector
$\mathbf{A}$	matrix
$\mathcal{X}, \mathcal{M}$	tensor
i	tensor element index $(i_1, i_2, \cdots, i_N)$
x_i	tensor element at index i
$\circ$	outer product

evaluated by an experienced cardiologist. The results were extremely promising, as 82% of the phenotypes generally mapped to a medical concept.

This paper briefly describes the Limestone model and evaluates the model on a publicly available, realistic set of claims data covering a much broader range of diseases. Our experimental results demonstrate the conciseness of the resulting phenotypes. Furthermore, we analyze the phenotypes associated with four common chronic disease conditions.

2   Preliminaries and Related Work

This section describes the preliminaries of matrix and tensor decomposition and related tensor factorization work. Table 1 provides a key for the symbols used in the paper. For indexing of matrix $\mathbf{A}$, we denote the $(i, j)^{\text{th}}$ element as a_{ij} and the jth column as $\mathbf{a}_j$.

Matrix Decomposition. Matrix factorization (MF) is a common dimensionality reduction approach, which represents the original data using a lower dimensional latent space. Standard MF approaches find two lower dimensional matrices that when multiplied together approximately produce the original matrix, $\mathbf{X} \approx \mathbf{WH}$. Although many matrix decomposition techniques exist, singular value decomposition and nonnegative matrix factorization (NMF) are two common algorithms used to reduce the feature dimension.

Tensor Decomposition. A tensor is a generalization of matrices to higher dimensions. Tensor representations are powerful because they can capture relationships for high-dimensional data. A tensor is rank-one if it can be written as follows:

Definition 1. *The outer product of N vectors, $\mathbf{a}^{(1)} \circ \mathbf{a}^{(2)} \circ \cdots \circ \mathbf{a}^{(N)}$, produces a rank-one, N^{th} order tensor $\mathcal{X}$ where each element $x_i = x_{i_1, i_2, \cdots, i_N} = a_{i_1}^{(1)} a_{i_2}^{(2)} \cdots a_{i_N}^{(N)}$.*

Tensor factorization (decomposition) is a natural extension of matrix factorization and utilizes information from the multiway structure that is lost when modes are collapsed to use matrix factorization algorithms [12, 13]. The CANDECOMP / PARAFAC (CP) [14, 15] model is a common tensor decomposition and can be viewed as a higher-order generalization of singular value decomposition [16]. The CP model approximates the original tensor $\mathcal{X}$ as a sum of R rank-one tensors and can be expressed as

$$\mathcal{X} \approx \sum_{r=1}^{R} \lambda_r \mathbf{a}_r^{(1)} \circ \ldots \circ \mathbf{a}_r^{(N)}$$
$$= [\![\boldsymbol{\lambda}; \mathbf{A}^{(1)}; \ldots; \mathbf{A}^{(N)}]\!].$$

Note that $[\![\boldsymbol{\lambda}; \mathbf{A}^{(1)}; \ldots; \mathbf{A}^{(N)}]\!]$ is shorthand notation to describe the CP decomposition, where $\boldsymbol{\lambda}$ is a vector of the weights λ_r and $\mathbf{a}_r^{(n)}$ is the rth column of $\mathbf{A}^{(n)}$. The CP tensor decomposition has been used for concept discovery [17], network analysis of fMRI data [18], and community discovery [19]. The details of computing the CP decomposition and other tensor decomposition models can be found in [16].

Some domain applications may desire nonnegative components, a higher-order generalization of NMF. Nonnegative tensor factorization (NTF) requires the elements of the factor matrices and the weights to be nonnegative. A broad survey of practical and useful NMF and NTF algorithms can be found in [20]. Our paper will focus on the nonnegative CP alternating Poisson regression (CP-APR) model to fit sparse count data [21]. For convenience, the CP-APR optimization problem is provided:

$$\min f(\mathcal{M}) \equiv \sum_{i} m_i - x_i \log m_i$$
$$\text{s.t } \mathcal{M} = [\![\boldsymbol{\lambda}; \mathbf{A}^{(1)}; ...; \mathbf{A}^{(N)}]\!] \in \Omega$$
$$\Omega = \Omega_\lambda \times \Omega_1 \times \cdots \times \Omega_N$$
$$\Omega_\lambda = [0, +\infty)^R$$
$$\Omega_n = \{\mathbf{A} \in [0,1]^{I_n \times R} \mid ||\mathbf{a}_r||_1 = 1 \; \forall r\},$$

where $\mathcal{M}$ is the CP tensor factorization that approximates the observed tensor $\mathcal{X}$, Ω is the sample space of $\mathcal{M}$, and I_n refers to the size of the nth mode. Details of the algorithm and model are presented in the paper by Chi and Kolda [21].

3   Limestone Overview

Limestone is a tensor factorization model to achieve high-throughput phenotyping from EHR data. The model is an extension of CP-APR to produce concise phenotype definitions for better interpretability. For this paper, we construct a tensor using the count of the co-occurrences between diagnoses and procedures. Thus, each tensor element denotes the number of times a procedure p is performed to treat diagnosis d for patient p. This third-order tensor is then approximated using the CP decomposition $\mathcal{M} = [\![\boldsymbol{\lambda}; \mathbf{A}^{(1)}, \mathbf{A}^{(2)}, \mathbf{A}^{(3)}]\!]$, shown in Figure 1. The factor matrix for the nth mode, $\mathbf{A}^{(n)}$, defines the elements from the

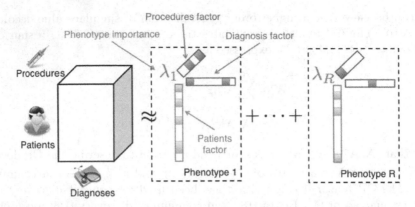

Fig. 1. Generating candidate phenotypes from the patient × diagnosis × procedure tensor using CP tensor factorization

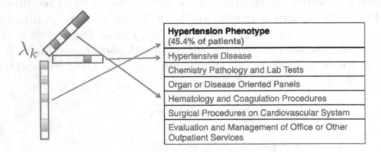

Hypertension Phenotype (45.4% of patients)
Hypertensive Disease
Chemistry Pathology and Lab Tests
Organ or Disease Oriented Panels
Hematology and Coagulation Procedures
Surgical Procedures on Cardiovascular System
Evaluation and Management of Office or Other Outpatient Services

Fig. 2. An example of the kth candidate phenotype produced from the tensor factorization, and the interpretation of the tensor factorization result. The green text, blue, and red text correspond to non-zero elements in the patient, diagnosis, and medication factors, respectively.

mode that comprise the candidate phenotypes. Limestone minimizes the presence of "minuscule and unnecessary" factor components via a hard-thresholding operator [22]. The hard-threshold constraint sets individual factor components $a_{jr}^{(n)}$ that are below a specified threshold (γ_n) to zero.

We provide an illustrative example of a Limestone phenotype from the claims record data in Figure 2. Given the kth phenotype, $a_{ik}^{(j)}$ represents the probability of seeing the ith element in the jth mode. In our example, hypertensive disease was the only non-zero element in the kth column of the diagnosis factor matrix while there are 5 non-zero elements in the kth column of the procedure factor matrix. The percentage of patients with the phenotype is calculated using the percentage of non-zero elements in the jth column of the patient factor matrix. The candidate phenotype shows that 45.4% of the patients had a non-zero element in the kth column.

4   Experimental Results

4.1   Data Description

The Centers for Medicare and Medicaid Services (CMS) provides the *CMS Linkable 2008-2010 Medicare Data Entrepreneurs' Synthetic Public Use File (DE-SynPUF)*, a publicly available dataset that contains inpatient, oupatient, carrier, and prescription drug event claims in addition to the patient summary files. The claim records have been synthesized from 5% of the 2008 Medicare population, spans 3 years, and is over 100 gigabytes (GB) in size . Although the relationships between some of the variables have been altered to protect the privacy of the beneficiaries, the data can still provide interesting and insightful phenotypes. A detailed description of the data can be found on the CMS website[1]. Our experiments focus on a random subset of 10,000 patients from Sample 1 (CMS released the data in 20 separate samples). The EHR tensor is constructed from the carrier claim records using the diagnosis and procedure codes. Since individual International Classification of Diseases (ICD-9) diagnosis codes and Healthcare Common Procedure Coding System (HCPCS) procedure codes capture fine-grained information, we grouped the codes using the Unified Medical Language System Metathesaurus[2], which contains the source vocabularies for over 150 sources, including ICD-9-CM and HCPCS. Aggregating the individual diagnosis codes and procedure codes results in a constructed tensor that is 10,000 patients by 129 diagnoses by 115 procedures.

4.2   Threshold Selection

Limestone uses predefined thresholds for each mode, γ_n, to zero out "probabilistically unlikely" elements. These thresholds provide a tunable knob to adjust the conciseness of the candidate phenotypes. Domain constraints can be used to determine the threshold values (e.g., a phenotype should only contain a maximum of 3 unique diagnoses). However, we explore the effect of the threshold on the number of non-zero phenotypes along the diagnosis and procedure modes. Figure 3 shows a boxplot of the number of non-zero elements per phenotype based on the various threshold values. Note that a low threshold ($\gamma = 0.001$) results in a large number of elements. As the threshold increases, the phenotypes become more concise and more easily interpretable. Based on the plots, the threshold of 0.05 was chosen to allow for slightly more complex phenotype definitions.

---

[1] The website URL is
http://www.cms.gov/Research-Statistics-Data-and-Systems/
Statistics-Trends-and-Reports/SynPUFs/DE_Syn_PUF.html
[2] Information about Metathesaurus is located at
http://www.nlm.nih.gov/research/umls/knowledge_sources/
metathesaurus/index.html

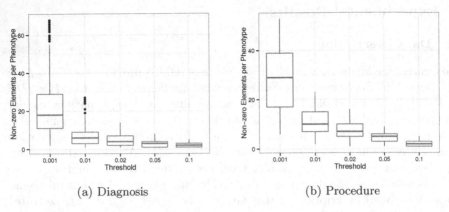

(a) Diagnosis   (b) Procedure

Fig. 3. The distribution of factor elements along the three CMS tensor modes. Zeros entries are omitted from the plot.

4.3 Chronic Disease Phenotypes

The United States spends more than 75% of its medical care cost on the treatment of chronic diseases [23]. Furthermore, 68.4% of the Medicare population suffers from 2 or more chronic diseases [24]. Thus, phenotypes relating to chronic disease factors such as heart failure, diabetes, and arthritis can help medical professionals tailor treatment options based on patient's phenotypes and reduce overall healthcare costs. The dataset provides chronic disease indicators that we will use to identify phenotypes associated with specific chronic diseases[3].

Table 2. Two phenotypes related to heart failure. The blue and red colors indicate the diagnosis and procedure elements respectively. Within each type, the elements are ordered in decreasing magnitude.

Heart Failure Phenotype 1 (36.7% of patients)
Other forms of heart disease
Complications of surgical and medical care
Hematology and Coagulation Procs.
Eval. and Mgmt. of Office or Other Outpatient Svcs.
Surgical Procs. on the Cardiovascular System
Chemistry Pathology and Laboratory Tests
Cardiovascular Procs.
Organ or Disease Oriented Panels

Heart Failure Phenotype 2 (30.9% of patients)
Other forms of heart disease
Ischemic heart disease
Hospital Inpatient Svcs.
Eval. and Mgmt. of Office or Other Outpatient Svcs.

Table 2 depicts two phenotypes related to heart failure. More than 1 in 3 Medicare patients exhibit the first phenotype while a smaller portion (but still substantial) have medical characteristics typified by the second phenotype. The

---

[3] A patient's chronic condition flag cannot be perfectly reproduced due to the synthetic claim process used.

Table 3. Four phenotypes related to diabetes and arthritis. The blue and red colors indicate the diagnosis and procedure elements respectively. Within each type, the elements are ordered in decreasing magnitude.

Diabetes Phenotype 1	**Diabetes Phenotype 2**
(34.8% of patients)	(33.1% of patients)
Diseases of other endocrine glands	Diseases of other endocrine glands
Other metabolic and immunity disorders	
Eval. and Mgmt. of Office or Other Outpatient Svcs.	Chemistry Pathology and Laboratory Tests
Surgical Procs. on the Cardiovascular System	Organ or Disease Oriented Panels
Ophthalmology Procs.	Hematology and Coagulation Procedures
Cardiovascular Procs.	Surgical Procs. on the Cardiovascular System
Urinalysis Procs.	Eval. and Mgmt. of Office or Other Outpatient Svcs.
Diagnostic/Screening Processes or Results	

	Arthritis Phenotype 2
	(38.6% of patients)
Arthritis Phenotype 1	Arthropathies and related disorders
(29.1% of patients)	Rheumatism, excluding the back
Arthropathies and related disorders	Eval. and Mgmt. of Office or Other Outpatient Svcs.
Physical Medicine and Rehabilitation Procs.	Surgical Procs. on the Musculoskeletal System
Eval. and Mgmt. of Office or Other Outpatient Svcs.	Surgical Procs. on the Cardiovascular System
	Cardiovascular Procs.
	Hematology and Coagulation Procs.

second phenotype suggests a higher degree of severity as there is an additional heart disease and it requires hospital inpatient services. The two phenotypes demonstrate the potential ability to derive novel phenotypes via a data-driven approach that could otherwise be difficult and time-consuming.

Table 3 depicts another four chronic-disease phenotypes relating to diabetes and arthritis. There are several other chronic disease phenotypes that were extracted, but due to space constraints are not shown in this paper. Note that these phenotypes shown are concise and easily interpretable. In particular, arthritis phenotype 1 contains just 1 diagnosis and 2 procedures and is exhibited in 29% of the population. The procedures are also consistent with known characteristics of the disease, as arthritis sufferers undergo rehabilitation to strengthen their joints. Similar to Table 2, the four phenotypes also demonstrate the power to automatically capture disease severity. Diabetes phenotype 1 suggests diabetes related complications that require cardiovascular surgery, while the second arthritis phenotype captures patients with multiple chronic conditions.

5   Conclusion

This paper shows that Limestone offers a data-driven solution to simultaneously generate multiple phenotypes from a diverse EHR population without expert supervision. The experimental results on 10,000 patient records from the CMS

De-SYNPUF dataset demonstrate the conciseness and interpretability of the tensor derived phenotypes. The phenotypes underscore the promise of Limestone for high-throughput phenotyping with minimal human intervention. Limestone can potentially be used to rapidly characterize, predict, and manage a large number of diseases, thereby promising a novel, data-driven solution that can benefit very large segments of the population. Future work will focus on generalizing the sparse nonnegative tensor factorization to multi-relational tensors [19] to incorporate multiple EHR data sources and examine quasi-Newton methods to improve computational speed of the algorithm [25].

Acknowledgements. This research is supported by the Schlumberger Centennial Chair in Engineering; Army Research Office under grant W911NF-11-1-0258; and Department of Defense award under award number 60036907.

References

1. Jensen, P.B., Jensen, L.J., Brunak, S.: Mining electronic health records: towards better research applications and clinical care. Nature Reviews: Genetics 13(6), 395–405 (2012)
2. Greengard, S.: A new model for healthcare. Communications of the ACM 56(2), 17–19 (2013)
3. Savage, N.: Better medicine through machine learning. Communications of the ACM 55(1), 17–19 (2012)
4. Hripcsak, G., Albers, D.J.: Next-generation phenotyping of electronic health records. Journal of the American Medical Informatics Association 20(1), 117–121 (2012)
5. Denny, J.C., Bastarache, L., Ritchie, M.D., Carroll, R.J., Zink, R., Mosley, J.D., Field, J.R., Pulley, J.M., Ramirez, A.H., Bowton, E., Basford, M.A., Carrell, D.S., Peissig, P.L., Kho, A.N., Pacheco, J.A., Rasmussen, L.V., Crosslin, D.R., Crane, P.K., Pathak, J., Bielinski, S.J., Pendergrass, S.A., Xu, H., Hindorff, L.A., Li, R., Manolio, T.A., Chute, C.G., Chisholm, R.L., Larson, E.B., Jarvik, G.P., Brilliant, M.H., McCarty, C.A., Kullo, I.J., Haines, J.L., Crawford, D.C., Masys, D.R., Roden, D.M.: Systematic comparison of phenome-wide association study of electronic medical record data and genome-wide association study data. Nature Biotechnology 31(12), 1102–1111 (2013)
6. Newton, K.M., Peissig, P.L., Kho, A.N., Bielinski, S.J., Berg, R.L., Choudhary, V., Basford, M., Chute, C.G., Kullo, I.J., Li, R., Pacheco, J.A., Rasmussen, L.V., Spangler, L., Denny, J.C.: Validation of electronic medical record-based phenotyping algorithms: results and lessons learned from the eMERGE network. Journal of the American Medical Informatics Association 20(e1), e147–e154 (2013)
7. McCarty, C.A., Chisholm, R.L., Chute, C.G., Kullo, I.J., Jarvik, G.P., Larson, E.B., Li, R., Masys, D.R., Ritchie, M.D., Roden, D.M., Struewing, J.P., Wolf, W.A.: eMERGE Team: The eMERGE Network: A consortium of biorepositories linked to electronic medical records data for conducting genomic studies. BMC Medical Genomics 4, 13 (2011)
8. Overhage, J.M., Ryan, P.B., Reich, C.G., Hartzema, A.G., Stang, P.E.: Validation of a common data model for active safety surveillance research. Journal of the American Medical Informatics Association 19(1), 54–60 (2012)

9. Hripcsak, G., Albers, D.J.: Correlating electronic health record concepts with healthcare process events. Journal of the American Medical Informatics Association 20(e2), e311–e318 (2013)

10. Chen, Y., Carroll, R.J., Hinz, E.R.M., Shah, A., Eyler, A.E., Denny, J.C., Xu, H.: Applying active learning to high-throughput phenotyping algorithms for electronic health records data. Journal of the American Medical Informatics Association 20(e2), e253–e259 (2013)

11. Ho, J.C., Ghosh, J., Steinhubl, S., Stewart, W., Denny, J.C., Malin, B.A., Sun, J.: Limestone: High-throughput candidate phenotype generation via tensor factorization. Journal of Biomedical Informatics (accepted)

12. Mørup, M.: Applications of tensor (multiway array) factorizations and decompositions in data mining. Wiley Interdisciplinary Reviews: Data Mining and Knowledge Discovery 1(1), 24–40 (2011)

13. Wang, D., Kong, S.: Feature selection from high-order tensorial data via sparse decomposition. Pattern Recognition Letters 33(13), 1695–1702 (2012)

14. Carroll, J.D., Chang, J.J.: Analysis of individual differences in multidimensional scaling via an N-way generalization of "Eckart-Young" decomposition. Psychometrika 35(3), 283–319 (1970)

15. Harshman, R.A.: Foundations of the PARAFAC procedure: Models and conditions for an "explanatory" multimodal factor analysis. UCLA Working Papers in Phonetics 16, 1–84 (1970)

16. Kolda, T.G., Bader, B.W.: Tensor decompositions and applications. SIAM Review 51(3), 455–500 (2009)

17. Kang, U., Papalexakis, E., Harpale, A., Faloutsos, C.: Gigatensor: Scaling tensor analysis up by 100 times-algorithms and discoveries. In: Proceeding of the 18th ACM SIGKDD International Conference on Knowledge Discovery and Data Mining (KDD), pp. 316–324. ACM (2012)

18. Davidson, I., Gilpin, S., Carmichael, O., Walker, P.: Network discovery via constrained tensor analysis of fMRI data. In: Proceeding of the 19th ACM SIGKDD International Conference on Knowledge Discovery and Data Mining (KDD). ACM (August 2013)

19. Lin, Y.R., Sun, J., Sundaram, H., Kelliher, A., Castro, P., Konuru, R.: Community discovery via metagraph factorization. ACM Transactions on Knowledge Discovery from Data (TKDD) 5(3) (August 2011)

20. Cichocki, A., Zdunek, R., Phan, A.H., Amari, S.I.: Nonnegative matrix and tensor factorizations: Applications to exploratory multi-way data analysis and blind source separation. Wiley (2009)

21. Chi, E.C., Kolda, T.G.: On tensors, sparsity, and nonnegative factorizations. SIAM Journal on Matrix Analysis and Applications 33(4), 1272–1299 (2012)

22. Bach, F., Jenatton, R., Mairal, J., Obozinski, G.: Optimization with sparsity-inducing penalties. Foundations and Trends in Machine Learning 4(1) (January 2012)

23. Centers for Disease Control and Prevention (CDC): Chronic diseases at a glance 2009. Technical report, CDC (2009)

24. Lochner, K.A., Cox, C.S.: Prevalence of multiple chronic conditions among Medicare beneficiaries, United State 2010. Preventing Chronic Disease: Public Health Research, Practice, and Policy (2013)

25. Hansen, S., Plantenga, T., Kolda, T.G.: Newton-Based Optimization for Nonnegative Tensor Factorizations. arXiv.org (April 2013)

Mining Professional Knowledge from Medical Records

Hen-Hsen Huang, Chia-Chun Lee, and Hsin-Hsi Chen

Department of Computer Science and Information Engineering, National Taiwan University
#1, Sec. 4, Roosevelt Road, Taipei, 10617 Taiwan
{hhhuang,cclee}@nlg.csie.ntu.edu.tw, hhchen@ntu.edu.tw

Abstract. The paper aims at two tasks of electronic medical record (EMR) processing: EMR retrieval and medical term extraction. The linguistic phenomena in EMRs in different departments are analyzed in depth including record size, vocabulary, entropy of medical languages, grammaticality, and so on. We explore various techniques of information retrieval for EMR retrieval, including five retrieval models with six pre-processing strategies on different parts of EMRs. The learning to rank algorithm is also adopted to improve the retrieval performance. Finally, our retrieval model is applied to extract medical terms from EMRs. Both coarse-grained relevance evaluation on department level and fine-grained relevance evaluation on treatment level are conducted.

Keywords: Learning to Rank, Medical Record Retrieval, Professional Information Access.

1 Introduction

Electronic medical records (EMRs) are a special kind of text corpus written by physicians. Medical text mining aims at extracting knowledge from EMRs, constructing a knowledge base (semi-)automatically, and finding new knowledge [1]. Mining medical text from an EMR database is important for case study. The course and treatments of similar cases provide important references, in particular, for medical students or junior physicians. There are many potential applications, e.g., comorbidities and disease correlations [2], acute myocardial infarction mining [3], assessment of healthcare utilization and treatments [4], outpatient department recommendation [5], virtual patient in health care education, and so on.

Finding relevant information is the first step to mining knowledge from diverse sources. Different information retrieval systems have been developed to meet these needs. This paper focuses on professional information access and addresses the supports for experts of medical domain. PubMed, which comprises more than 22 million citations for biomedical literature from MEDLINE, provides information retrieval engines for finding biomedical documents. Information retrieval on medical records has been introduced to improve healthcare services [5-6]. Medical records are similar to scientific documents in that both are written by domain experts, but they are different from several aspects such as authorship, genre, structure, grammaticality, source, and privacy. Biomedical literatures are research findings of researchers. The layout

D. Ślęzak et al. (Eds.): BIH 2014, LNAI 8609, pp. 152–163, 2014.

of a scientific paper published in journals and conference proceedings are often composed of problem specification, solutions, experimental setup, results, discussion and conclusion. To gain more impacts, scientific literatures are often made available to the public. Grammatical correctness and readability are the basic requirements for publication.

In contrast, medical records are patients' treatments by physicians when patients visit hospitals. The basic layout consists of a chief complaint, a brief history, and a course and treatment. From the ethical and legal aspects, medical records are privacy-sensitive. Release of medical records is restricted by government laws. Medical records are frequently below par in grammaticality. That is not a problem for the understanding by physicians, but is an issue for retrieval.

How to retrieve relevant EMRs effectively and efficiently is an essential research topic. TREC 2011 [7] and 2012 [8] Medical Records track provides test collections for patient retrieval based on a set of clinical criteria. Several approaches such as concept-based [9], query expansion [10], and knowledge-based [11] have been proposed to improve the retrieval performance. In this paper, we investigate medical record retrieval on an NTUH dataset provided by National Taiwan University Hospital. Given a chief complaint and/or a brief history, we would like to find the related EMRs, and propose examination, medicine and surgery that may be performed for the input case. Both basic IR models and learning to rank models are explored and discussed.

The structure of this paper is organized as follows. The characteristics of the domain-specific dataset are addressed and analyzed in Section 2. The basic retrieval models and the learning to rank approach are explored in Section 3. Section 4 describes the medical term extraction model and the finer grained relevance evaluation on course and treatment level. Finally, Section 5 concludes the remarks.

2   An Electronic Medical Record Dataset

The experimental materials come from National Taiwan University Hospital (NTUH). There are 113,625 EMRs in the NTUH dataset. Each EMR is composed of three major parts – say, a chief complaint, a brief history, and a course and treatment. A chief complaint is a short statement specifying the purpose of a patient's visit and the patient's physical discomfort, e.g., Epigastralgia for 10 days, Tarry stool twice since last night, and so on. It describes the symptoms found by the patient and the duration of these symptoms. A brief history summarizes the personal information, the physical conditions, and the past medical treatment of the patient. A course and treatment describes the treatment processes and the treatment outcomes in detail, where medication administration, inspection, and surgery are recorded.

There are 113,625 EMRs in the NTUH experimental dataset after those records consisting of scheduled cases, empty complaints, complaints written in Chinese, and treatments without mentioning any examination, medicine, and surgery are removed. Table 1 lists mean (μ) and standard deviation (σ) of chief complaint (CC), brief history (BH), course and treatment (CT), and EMR in terms of the number of words used in the corresponding part. Here a word is defined to be a character string separated by spaces. The patient and the physician names are removed from the dataset for the privacy issues. In general, the brief history is the longest, while the chief complaint is the shortest.

The 113,625 EMRs are categorized into 14 departments based on patients' visits. The statistics is illustrated in Table 2. Departments of Internal Medicine and Surgery have the first and the second largest amount of data, while Departments of Dental and Dermatology have the smallest amount. From the linguistic point of view, we also investigate the vocabulary size and entropy of the medical language overall for the dataset and individually for each department. Table 3 summarizes the statistics. Compared with the word entropy for general English, the entropy of the medical language used in NTUH dataset is 11.15 bits per word, a little smaller than Shannon entropy (i.e., 11.82 bits per word) [12] and larger than Grignetti entropy (i.e., 9.8 bits per word) [13]. Departments related to definite parts of body, e.g., dental, ear, nose & throat, ophthalmology and orthopedics, have lower entropy. Comparatively, departments related to generic parts have larger entropy. In particular, Department of Ophthalmology has the lowest entropy, while Department of Internal Medicine has the largest entropy.

Medical records are frequently below par in grammaticality. Spelling errors are very common in this dataset. Some common erroneous words and their correct forms enclosed in parentheses are listed below for reference: histropy (history), ag (ago/age), withour (without), denid (denied), and recieved (received). Some words are ambiguous in the erroneous form, e.g., "ag" can be interpreted as "ago" or "age" depending on its context. Besides grammatical problems, shorthand notation or abbreviation occurs very often. For example, "opd" is an abbreviation of "outpatient department" and "yrs" is a shorthand notation of "years-old". Furthermore, physicians tend to mix English and Chinese in the NTUH dataset. That makes medical record retrieval more challenging.

Table 1. Mean and Standard Deviation of NTUH EMRs in Words

component	mean (μ)	standard deviation (σ)
chief complaint (CC)	7.88	3.75
brief history (BH)	233.46	163.69
course and treatment (CT)	110.28	145.04
EMR	351.62	248.51

Table 2. Distribution of the NTUH EMRs w.r.t. Department Type

Dental	1,253	Dermatology	1,258	Ear, Nose & Throat	7,680
Internal Medicine	**34,396**	Neurology	2,739	Obstetrics & Gynecology	5,679
Oncology	4,226	Ophthalmology	3,400	Orthopedics	8,814
Pediatrics	11,468	Rehabilitation	1,935	Psychiatry	1,656
Surgery	**23,303**	Urology	5,818		

Table 3. Vocabulary Size and Entropy of the Medical Language w.r.t. Department Type

Vocabulary Size	Entropy	Vocabulary Size	Entropy	Vocabulary Size	Entropy
Dental		Dermatology		Ear, Nose & Throat	
15,036	**9.74**	26,914	10.32	48,452	**9.88**
Internal Medicine		Neurology		Obstetrics & Gynecology	
415,279	11.06	55,301	10.62	65,760	10.46
Oncology		Ophthalmology		Orthopedics	
101,361	10.81	27,765	**9.70**	47,082	**9.79**
Pediatrics		Rehabilitation		Psychiatry	
175,555	10.86	51,328	10.50	67,390	10.64
Surgery		Urology		Overall	
203,677	10.76	53,853	10.25	786,666	11.15

3   EMR Retrieval

Given a chief complaint and/or a brief history, physicians plan to retrieve the similar cases from the historical EMRs and reference to the possible course and treatments. Chief complaints and/or brief histories in the historical EMRs can be regarded as queries. Section 3.1 describes the basic models and Section 3.2 shows the experimental results. Section 3.3 introduces learning to rank [14] to EMR retrieval. Section 3.4 shows the results and compares them with the basic IR models.

3.1   Basic Models for EMR Retrieval

Words may be stemmed and stop words may be removed before indexing. Spelling checker is introduced to deal with spelling errors and typos. Besides words, medical terms are also recognized as indices. Different IR models can be explored on different parts of EMRs. In the empirical study, Lemur Toolkit is adopted and five retrieval models including TF-IDF, Okapi, KL-divergence, cosine similarity, and indri are experimented.

3.2   Results of the Basic Retrieval Models

In the experiments, 10-fold cross validation is adopted. Given a chief complaint, the output is the retrieved top-n EMRs. We aim to evaluate the quality of the returned n EMRs. There is no ground truth or relevance judgments available, surrogate relevance judgments are therefore used. Recall that each medical record belongs to a department. Let the input chief complaint belong to department d, and the departments of the top-n retrieved medical records be $d_1, d_2, ..., d_n$. Here, we postulate that medical record i is relevant to the input chief complaint, if d_i of medical record i is equal to d. In this way, we can compute precision@k, mean average precision (MAP), and nDCG as traditional IR.

Five retrieval models with six strategies (S1)-(S6) defined as follows are explored.

S1:   using chief complaints
S2:   S1 with stop word removal
S3:   S1 with porter stemming
S4:   S1 with both stop word removal and porter stemming
S5:   using chief complaints and the first two sentences in brief histories
S6:   S5 with porter stemming

For strategies S5 and S6, we extract gender (male/female), age (0-15, 16-45, 46-60, 61+), and other information from brief history besides chief complaints.

Top 5 and Top 10 EMRs are retrieved and compared. Table 4 shows the experimental results. Overall, the performance tendency is Okapi > TF-IDF > cosine > KL > indri no matter which strategies are used. Removing stop words tend to decrease the performance. Using porter stemming is useful when chief complaints are employed only. Introducing brief histories decreases the performance. The Okapi retrieval model with strategy S3 performs the best. In fact, Okapi+S3 is not significantly better than Okapi+S1, but both are significantly better than Okapi with other strategies (p value <0.0001) on MAP and nDCG. When S3 is adopted, Okapi is significantly better than the other models.

We further evaluate the retrieval models with precision@k shown in Table 5. The five retrieval models at the setting k=1 are significantly better than those at k=3 and k=5. Most of the precision@k are larger than 0.7 at k=1. It means the first medical record retrieved is often relevant. Okapi with strategy S3 is still the best under precision@k. Moreover, we examine the effects of the parameter n in the medical record retrieval. Only the best two retrieval models in the above experiments, i.e., TF-IDF and Okapi with strategy S3, are shown in Fig 1. We can find MAP decreases when n becomes larger in both models. It means noise is introduced when more medical records are reported. The Okapi+S3 model is better than the TF-IDF+S3 model in all the settings.

Table 6 further shows the retrieval performance in terms of MAP, nDCG and precision@k with respect to department type. Note four departments have entropy less than 10 shown in Table 3, i.e., Departments of Dental, Ear, Nose & Throat, Ophthalmology, and Orthopedics. The performances of query accesses to medical records in these departments are more than 0.8200 in all the metrics. In particular, the retrieval performances for Department of Ophthalmology are even more than 0.9155. Comparatively, Department of Internal Medicine, which has the largest entropy, achieves the average performance. Department of Oncology gets the worst retrieval performance because tumor may occur in different organs. The precision@1 to access medical records in this department is only 0.3685, which is the worst of all.

Table 4. MAP and nDCG of Basic Retrieval Models with Different Strategies

Model	Metric	S1	S2	S3	S4	S5	S6
				Top 5			
TF-IDF	MAP	0.6858	0.6776	0.6860	0.6780	0.6700	0.6685
	nDCG	0.7529	0.7456	0.7535	0.7461	0.7385	0.7370
Okapi	MAP	**0.6954**	**0.6871**	**0.6965**	**0.6875**	**0.6800**	**0.6774**
	nDCG	**0.7622**	**0.7545**	**0.7626**	**0.7551**	**0.7489**	**0.7469**
KL	MAP	0.6715	0.6634	0.6692	0.6612	0.6691	0.6654
	nDCG	0.7396	0.7316	0.7385	0.7305	0.7380	0.7350
cosine	MAP	0.6857	0.6818	0.6868	0.6827	0.6521	0.6503
	nDCG	0.7520	0.7485	0.7534	0.7488	0.7217	0.7203
indri	MAP	0.6638	0.6582	0.6604	0.6558	0.6557	0.6527
	nDCG	0.7328	0.7274	0.7305	0.7264	0.7251	0.7220
		S1	S2	S3	S4	S5	S6
				Top 10			
TF-IDF	MAP	0.6651	0.6584	0.6660	0.6590	0.6502	0.6487
	nDCG	0.7481	0.7420	0.7486	0.7422	0.7348	0.7330
Okapi	MAP	**0.6734**	**0.6672**	**0.6749**	**0.6678**	**0.6588**	**0.6566**
	nDCG	**0.7559**	**0.7498**	**0.7564**	**0.7498**	**0.7427**	**0.7404**
KL	MAP	0.6517	0.6444	0.6499	0.6430	0.6489	0.6465
	nDCG	0.7362	0.7297	0.7352	0.7285	0.7329	0.7307
cosine	MAP	0.6648	0.6611	0.6660	0.6622	0.6340	0.6331
	nDCG	0.7473	0.7437	0.7481	0.7447	0.7186	0.7181
indri	MAP	0.6446	0.6395	0.6422	0.6380	0.6365	0.6339
	nDCG	0.7305	0.7256	0.7285	0.7246	0.7221	0.7192

Table 5. precision@k of Retrieval Models on the Department Level with Different Strategies

Model	Precision @k	S1	S2	S3	S4	S5	S6
TF-IDF		0.7185	0.7103	0.7188	0.7105	0.7031	0.7013
Okapi		**0.7280**	**0.7197**	**0.7293**	**0.7203**	**0.7136**	**0.7109**
KL	k=1	0.7041	0.6958	0.7020	0.6933	0.7021	0.6984
cosine		0.7184	0.7138	0.7193	0.7149	0.6857	0.6827
indri		0.6960	0.6907	0.6926	0.6879	0.6880	0.6857
TF-IDF		0.6259	0.6196	0.6269	0.6204	0.6132	0.6117
Okapi		**0.6371**	**0.6316**	**0.6384**	**0.6326**	**0.6238**	**0.6231**
KL	k=3	0.6073	0.5997	0.6055	0.5988	0.6120	0.6105
cosine		0.6273	0.6236	0.6279	0.6245	0.5983	0.5970
indri		0.5986	0.5947	0.5967	0.5935	0.5986	0.5973
TF-IDF		0.5963	0.5911	0.5980	0.5928	0.5863	0.586
Okapi		**0.6072**	**0.6034**	**0.6099**	**0.6050**	**0.5973**	**0.5965**
KL	k=5	0.5775	0.5719	0.5770	0.5725	0.5842	0.5838
cosine		0.5972	0.5933	0.5984	0.5951	0.5741	0.5741
indri		0.5698	0.5670	0.5691	0.5676	0.5713	0.5702

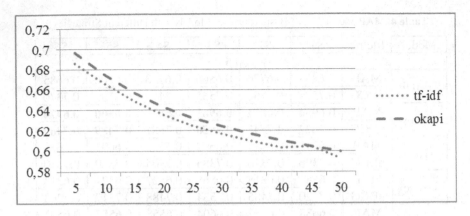

Fig. 1. MAPs of TF-IDF and Okapi under Different n's

Table 6. Retrieval Performance w.r.t. Department Type Using Okapi Retrieval Model and Strategy S3

Department	MAP @5	nDCG @5	MAP @10	nDCG @10	precision @1
Dental	**0.8545**	**0.8825**	**0.8295**	**0.8744**	**0.8755**
Dermatology	0.6531	0.7083	0.6263	0.7003	0.6901
Ear, Nose & Throat	**0.8443**	**0.8770**	**0.8282**	**0.8715**	**0.8640**
Internal Medicine	0.7001	0.7867	0.6695	0.7688	0.7381
Neurology	0.4843	0.5762	0.4612	0.5731	0.5232
Obstetrics & Gynecology	0.7779	0.8121	0.7635	0.8100	0.8000
Oncology	0.3233	0.3847	0.3236	0.4185	0.3685
Ophthalmology	**0.9265**	**0.9419**	**0.9155**	**0.9371**	**0.9377**
Orthopedics	**0.8518**	**0.8888**	**0.8326**	**0.8802**	**0.8736**
Pediatrics	0.6667	0.7278	0.6509	0.7290	0.6977
Rehabilitation	0.6088	0.6772	0.5921	0.6771	0.6390
Psychiatry	**0.8323**	**0.8631**	**0.8183**	**0.8608**	**0.8487**
Surgery	0.6120	0.6971	0.5889	0.6943	0.6535
Urology	0.7651	0.8035	0.7494	0.8037	0.7873

3.3   Ranking Models for EMR Retrieval

In addition to the fundamental retrieval models, we adopt the learning to ranking model to retrieve the EMRs. Assume a training set is composed of N medical records. Each medical record is regarded as a query. For each query q_i, we retrieval top 200 medical records, m_1, m_2, ..., m_{200}, with an IR model. Then, we extract features between q_i and m_1, q_i and m_2, ..., q_i and m_{200}. SVM rank along with these features is employed to learn a ranking model. We will use it to re-rank the initial retrieval results.

Table 7. Performance of Learn-to-Rank EMR Models

Model	Metric	BOW	MT	SYMP
TF-IDF	MAP	**0.6989**	**0.6997**	**0.7013**
	nDCG	**0.7620**	**0.7628**	**0.7640**
Okapi	MAP	†0.6957	†0.6964	*0.6992
	nDCG	†0.7593	†0.7597	*0.7618
KL	MAP	0.6970	†0.6968	†0.6977
	nDCG	†0.7595	†0.7592	†0.7604
cosine	MAP	†0.6939	†0.6933	†*0.6968
	nDCG	†0.7571	†0.7565	†*0.7597
indri	MAP	†0.6875	†0.6935	†*0.6954
	nDCG	†0.7516	†0.7567	†*0.7585

In the experiments shown in Section 3.2, the methodology of bag-of-words is adopted. Here we explore two more feature sets: medical terms and symptoms. The medical terms such as examination, medicine, and surgery are extracted from the course and treatment of the retrieved medical records. We describe the details of medical term extraction in Section 4.1.

Physicians often use some fixed patterns to describe symptoms. The following shows some examples for the JJ+NN+NN pattern: left breast pain, congenital heart disease, and bilateral neck mass. We formulate 20 common patterns as follows manually to capture symptoms: (1) JJ NN (and) NN NN, (2) JJ NN NN, (3) JJ (of) NN, (4) VBD NN, (5) NN NN (and) NN, (6) NN (and) NN, (7) JJ VBG NN, (8) VBG NN, (9) JJ NN (and) VBG, (10) NN (of) NN, (11) JJ NN, (12) JJ FW, (13) JJ VBG (and) VBG, (14) VBG (with) NN, (15) NN NN, (16) JJ VBG, (17) JJ JJ NN, (18) NN (with) VBG, (19) NN VBG, (20) NN. The longest-first strategy is adopted.

3.4 Results of the Ranking Models

Table 7 shows the performance of learning-to-rank electronic medical record retrieval models. Top 5 EMRs are retrieved and compared. BOW, MT, and SYMP denote bag-of-words, medical terms, and symptoms, respectively. From column part, using symptoms is better than using bag-of-words and using medical terms, where * denotes SYMP is better than BOW with $p<0.05$. From raw part, TF-IDF model is better than the other four models, where † denotes 95% confidence.

4   Medical Term Extraction

In Section 3, our methods for retrieving EMRs are shown. In addition to the evaluation at department-level, we extract the medical terms such as examination, medicine, and surgery from the course and treatment of the retrieved EMRs. This section shows our extraction models and their performances.

4.1   Extraction Models

To extract the relevant medical terms form EMR, the technology of medical term recognition [15] is required. In this work, Ontology-based and pattern-based approaches are adopted. The ontology-based approach adopts the resources from the Unified Medical Language System (UMLS) maintained by National Library of Medicine. The UMLS covers a wide range of terms in medical domain, and relations between these medical terms. Among these resources, the Metathesaurus organizes medical terms into groups of concepts. Moreover, each concept is assigned at least one Semantic Type. Semantic Types provide categorization of concepts at a more general level, and therefore are well-suited to be incorporated. The pattern-based approach adopts patterns such as "**SURGERY** was performed on **DATE**" to extract medical terms [16-17]. The idea comes from the special written styles of medical records. A number of patterns frequently repeat in medical records. The following lists some examples for the pattern "**SURGERY** was performed on **DATE**": **paracentesis** was performed on **2010-01-08**, **repositioning** was performed on **2008/04/03**, **incision and drainage** was performed on **2010-01-15**, and **tracheostomy** was performed on **2010/1/11**.

We follow the pattern-based approach to extract frequent patterns from medical record dataset and apply them to recognize medical terms. The overall procedure is summarized as follows.

(a)   Medical Entity Classification: Recognize medical named entities including surgeries, diseases, drugs, etc. by the ontology-based approach, transform them into the corresponding medical classes, and derive a new corpus.

(b)   Frequent Pattern Extraction: Employ n-gram models in the new corpus to extract a set of frequent patterns.

(c)   Linguistic Pattern Extraction: For each pattern, randomly sample sentences having this pattern, parse these sentences, and keep the pattern if there is at least one parsing sub-tree for it.

(d)   Pattern Coverage Finding: Check coverage relations among higher order patterns and lower order patterns, and remove those lower patterns being covered.

4.2   Results and Discussion

We evaluate the performance of medical term extraction as follows. The input is a chief complaint and a brief history, and the output is top-1 course and treatment selected from the historical NTUH medical records. Recall that examination, medicine and surgery are three key types of medical entities specified in a course and treatment. We would like to know if the retrieved medical record adopts the similar course and treatment as the input query. Thus the evaluation unit is the three types of entities. We extract examinations, medicines and surgeries from the courses and treatments of an input query and the retrieved medical record, respectively, by medical term recognition. They are named as GE, GM, and GS for ground truth (i.e., the course and treatment of the input query), and PE, PM, and PS for the proposed treatment (i.e., the course and treatment of the returned medical record), respectively. The Jaccard's coefficient between the ground truth and the proposed treatment is a metric indicating if the returned medical records are relevant and interesting to physicians. It is defined as: total number of common entities in the ground truth and the proposed answer divided by sum of the entities in the ground truth and the proposed answer for each query. The evaluation is done for each medical entity type. That is, Jaccard's coefficient for examination=|GE∩PE|/|GE∪PE|, Jaccard's coefficient for medicine=|GM∩PM|/|GM∪PM|, and Jaccard's coefficient for surgery=|GS∩PS|/|GS∪PS|. Note that the denominator will be zero, if both the ground truth and the proposed answer do not contain any medical entities of the designated type. In this case, we set Jaccard's coefficient to be 1. The average of the Jaccard's coefficients of all the input queries is considered as a metric to evaluate the performance of the retrieval model on the treatment level.

Table 8 lists the fine-grained relevance evaluation on the course and treatment level with Jaccard's coefficient. Total 663 examinations, 2,165 medicines, and 1,483 surgeries are used in the treatments. Total 54,679, 64,607, and 88,647 medical records mention examinations, medicines, and surgeries in their treatments. We count the number of the same examinations (medicines or surgeries) appearing in both ground

Table 8. Jaccard's Coefficients of Basic and Ranking Retrieval Models on the Course and Treatment Level

Strategy	Top-1	TF-IDF	Okapi	KL	cos	indri
S1	examination	0.3332	0.3448	0.4351	0.3362	0.4501
	medicine	0.2501	0.2995	0.2222	0.2846	0.2035
	surgery	0.1115	0.1406	0.0847	0.1358	0.0776
S2	examination	0.3109	0.3376	0.4017	0.3305	0.4202
	medicine	0.2445	0.2980	0.2370	0.2865	0.2257
	surgery	0.1154	0.1397	0.0961	0.1393	0.0898
S3	examination	0.3515	0.3499	0.4399	0.3437	**0.4535**
	medicine	0.2589	0.3000	0.2245	0.2897	0.2055
	surgery	0.1131	0.1394	0.0844	0.1339	0.0764
S4	examination	0.3289	0.3447	0.4076	0.3362	0.4259
	medicine	0.2539	0.2988	0.2389	0.2905	0.2267
	surgery	0.1168	0.1406	0.0950	0.1376	0.0879
S5	examination	0.3728	**0.3816**	0.3690	0.3814	0.3639
	medicine	0.3166	0.3289	0.3112	0.3292	0.3042
	surgery	0.1851	**0.1954**	0.1821	0.1882	0.1758
S6	examination	0.3727	0.3810	0.3679	0.3826	0.3636
	medicine	0.3147	0.3278	0.3101	0.3291	0.3035
	surgery	0.1835	0.1936	0.1803	0.1875	0.1743
Ranking	examination	0.3852	0.3852	0.3847	0.3890	0.3846
	medicine	0.3291	0.3301	0.3310	**0.3348**	0.3313
	surgery	0.2012	0.2007	**0.2013**	0.2005	0.1999

truth and the treatment of the top-1 returned medical record. The number is normalized by total number of examinations (medicines or surgeries) in both treatments for each query. If both do not recommend any examinations (medicines or surgeries), the Jaccard's coefficient is regarded as 1. The five retrieval models and the seven strategies used in the above experiments are explored again in the fine-grained evaluation. S1 to S6 are based on the basic retrieval models describe in Section 3.2. Ranking is the learning-to-rank model with symptom features shown in Section 3.3. Overall, the performance of examination prediction is larger than that of medicine prediction, which is larger than that of surgery prediction in all models. Considering brief history (i.e., strategies S5 and S6) benefits medicine and surgery prediction. Excluding the learning to rank approach, the Okapi model with strategy S5 achieves the best performance on medicine and surgery prediction (i.e., 0.3289 and 0.1954), and Indri with strategy S3 achieves the best performance on examination prediction (i.e., 0.4535). In other words, the information from brief history induces noises in examination prediction. The Comparison between S5 and the Ranking shows that the learning to rank approach improves the performances on all the examination, medicine, and surgery predictions in all the five models.

5   Conclusion

This paper aims at mining the professional knowledge from medical records. We compare different retrieval models under different strategies on department and course and treatment levels. In addition, ontology-based and pattern-based approaches are adopted to extract medical terms. Both coarse-grained and fine-grained relevance evaluations with various metrics are conducted.

Some linguistic phenomena in EMRs are identified. The medical records in medical languages of smaller entropy tend to have better retrieval performance. The departments related to generic parts of body such as Departments of Internal Medicine and Surgery may confuse the retrieval, in particular, for Departments of Oncology and Neurology.

In the experiments of basic retrieval models, five retrieval models and six index strategies are tested. The Okapi model achieves the best performance. Query accesses to the medical records in medical languages of smaller entropy tend to have better performance. The performance of departments related to generic parts of body such as Department of Oncology and Department of Neurology are worse than average performance. In the experiments of the learning to rank approach, we explore the ranking approach on five retrieval models and three index strategies. Under the learning to rank algorithm, the TF-IDF model with the symptoms strategy achieves the best performance. Applying learning to rank technique is significantly better than those models.

Our mining approach can be adopted in various applications. The medical record retrieval can be applied to create a search engine that delivers similar medical records for education and case study. The outpatient recommendation system is another application. For example, a patient can search for the appropriate outpatient department by inputting the patient's chief complaints. The medical term extraction can be applied to analyze the correlations between drug and symptoms. Moreover, a medical assistance system can be constructed to detect the anomalous treatments and remind the physicians to double-check their diagnosis.

Acknowledgements. This research was partially supported by Ministry of Science and Technology, Taiwan, under the grant 101-2221-E-002-195-MY3.

References

1. Jensen, L.J., Saric, J., Bork, P.: Literature mining for the biologist: from information retrieval to biological discovery. Nature Reviews Genetics 7, 119–129 (2006)
2. Goth, G.: Analyzing medical data. Communications of the ACM 55(6), 13–15 (2012)
3. Heinze, D.T., Morsch, M.L., Holbrook, J.: Mining free-text medical records. In: AMIA Annual Symposium, pp. 254–258 (2001)
4. Ramos, P.: Acute myocardial infarction patient data to assess healthcare utilization and treatments. ProQuest, UMI Dissertation Publishing (2011)
5. Huang, H.-H., Lee, C.-C., Chen, H.-H.: Outpatient department recommendation based on medical summaries. In: Hou, Y., Nie, J.-Y., Sun, L., Wang, B., Zhang, P. (eds.) AIRS 2012. LNCS, vol. 7675, pp. 518–527. Springer, Heidelberg (2012)
6. Hersh, W.: Information retrieval: A health and biomedical perspective, 3rd edn. Springer (2009)
7. Voorhees, E., Tong, R.: Overview of the TREC 2011 Medical Records Track. In: TREC (2011)
8. Voorhees, E., Hersh, W.: Overview of the TREC 2012 Medical Records Track. In: TREC (2012)
9. Koopman, B., Lawley, M., Bruza, P.: AEHRC & QUT at TREC 2011 Medical Track: A Concept-Based Information Retrieval. In: TREC (2011)
10. Dinh, D., Tamine, L.: IRIT at TREC 2011: Evaluation of Query Expansion Techniques for Medical Record Retrieval. In: TREC (2011)
11. Demner-Fushman, D., Abhyankar, S., Jimeno-Yepes, A., Loane, R., Rance, B., Lang, F., Ide, N., Apostolova, E., Aronson, A.R.: A Knowledge-Based Approach to Medical Records Retrieval. In: TREC (2011)
12. Shannon, C.E.: Prediction and entropy of printed English. Bell System Tech. J. 30(1), 50–64 (1950)
13. Grignetti, M.C.: A note on the entropy of words in printed English. Information and Control 7, 304–306 (1964)
14. Li, H.: A Short Introduction to Learning to Rank. IEICE Trans. Inf. & Syst. E-94D(10), 1–9 (2011)
15. Abacha, A.B., Zweigenbaum, P.: Medical entity recognition: a comparison of semantic and statistical methods. In: Workshop on Biomedical Natural Language Processing, pp. 56–64 (2011)
16. Chen, H.-B., Huang, H.-H., Chen, H.-H., Tan, C.-T.: A Simplification-Translation-Restoration Framework for Cross-Domain SMT Applications. In: 24th International Conference on Computational Linguistics, pp. 545–560 (2012)
17. Chen, H.-B., Huang, H.-H., Tjiu, J., Tan, C.-T., Chen, H.-H.: A statistical medical summary translation system. In: ACM SIGHIT International Health Informatics Symposium, pp. 101–110 (2012)

Predicting Flu Epidemics Using Twitter and Historical Data

Giovanni Stilo[1], Paola Velardi[1], Alberto E. Tozzi[2], and Francesco Gesualdo[2]

[1] Dipartimento di Informatica Sapienza Università di Roma, Italy
{stilo,velardi}@di.uniroma1.it
[2] Bambino Gesù Children Hospital, Roma, Italy
{alberto.tozzi,f.gesualdo}@gmail.com

Abstract. Recently there has been a growing attention on the use of web and social data to improve traditional prediction models in politics, finance, marketing and health, but even though a correlation between observed phenomena and related social data has been demonstrated in many cases, yet the effectiveness of the latter for long-term or even mid-term predictions has not been shown. In epidemiological surveillance, the problem is compounded by the fact that infectious diseases models (such as susceptible-infected-recovered-susceptible, SIRS) are very sensitive to current conditions, such that small changes can produce remarkable differences in future outcomes. Unfortunately, current or nearly-current conditions keep changing as data are collected and updated by the epidemiological surveillance organizations. In this paper we show that the time series of Twitter messages reporting a combination of symptoms that match the influenza-like-illness (ILI) case definition represent a more stable and reliable information on "current conditions", to the point that they can replace, rather than simply integrate, official epidemiological data. We estimate the effectiveness of these data at predicting current and past flu seasons (17 seasons overall), in combination with official historical data on past seasons, obtaining an average correlation of 0.85 over a period of 17 weeks covering the flu season.

Keywords: Twitter mining, epidemiological surveillance, predictability of health-related phenomena.

1   Introduction

Prediction of social phenomena in politics, finance, marketing and health is traditionally based on historical data of the same type, i.e. on time series $S(t) = (s_{t-n}, \ldots s_{t-1}, s_t)$ taken up until and including the time t in which the prediction is produced. These data are used to train predictors based on linear or non-linear regressions, machine learning, or model-based methods [1], the latter being the hardest way to do prediction since they require deep insight into the observed phenomenon. In recent research [2-11], it has been shown that better predictions can be obtained when augmenting historical data with social data, such as the frequency time series $K(t)$ of a keyword in web search data or in micro-blogs.

D. Ślęzak et al. (Eds.): BIH 2014, LNAI 8609, pp. 164–177, 2014.
© Springer International Publishing Switzerland 2014

Even though a correlation between observed phenomena and related social data has been demonstrated in many cases, yet the effectiveness of the latter for long-term or even mid-term predictions has not been shown. Furthermore, the usefulness of social observations is usually limited to recent values (k_t and k_{t-1}).

More related to the research described in this paper is the problem of predicting health-related phenomena, such as disease outbreaks. A seminal work in this area is [6], in which the level of influenza (influenza-like illness, ILI) in the U.S. is estimated using the relative frequency of search queries related to influenza-like illness. Similarly, in [7], the authors demonstrate that query search volumes associated to Dengue fever can predict the incidence of Dengue. Another recent study [8] analyses the problem of predicting the tendency of hand-foot-and-mouth disease (HFMD), clustering HFMD-related search queries, medical pages and news reports. In some cases, a correlation between search volumes and disease trends has been identified and, in 2008, a Google service, Flu Trends[1] (GFT), was developed to estimate and predict influenza activity by aggregating Google search query volumes. However, web search peaks can be completely unrelated to the incidence of a disease, as search behaviors change over time and discussions on traditional media may become reflected in search patterns. For example, GFT overestimated peak flu during the 2013 season[2], following breaking news on bird flu cases in China.

In [9,10] Twitter messages are used to predict flu trends. The advantage of Twitter (and micro-blogs in general) is that, unlike for user queries, a context is provided to distinguish cases in which a user is actually infected from those in which he/she is expressing fear of being infected. For example, Lamb et al. [9] separate tweets reporting infection (*flu*) from those expressing concerns and fear ("*a little worried about flu epidemic!*"), using a classifier trained with a number of specific linguistic features, like expressions of concern. The correlation of the related time series of Twitter messages with official ILI data published by the Center for Disease Control and Prevention[3] (CDC) is reported to be 0.98 in 2009 and 0.79 in 2011.

We note however that the studies mentioned so far do not actually "predict" disease trends, though they have been shown to correlate more or less well with available data on disease outbreaks provided by official epidemiological data. Rather, since both Twitter and GFT provide real-time data, methods based on these data are able to provide an "instant" forecast, while epidemiological data become available typically with one week of delay. A more interesting objective is to make a mid or long-term prediction, i.e. to be able to predict an influenza peak several weeks in advance. This objective is targeted in [11], where a model-based predictor is defined. The system uses an ensemble of SIRS[4] (susceptible-infected-recovered-susceptible) epidemic models to simulate the number of people infected with influenza in all major US cities. The authors use a data assimilation technique to adjust observable and non-observable

---

[1] http://www.google.org/flutrends/
[2] http://www.nature.com/news/when-google-got-flu-wrong-1.12413
[3] www.cdc.gov/
[4] en.wikipedia.org/wiki/Epidemic_model

model state variables. The predictor is based on historical data, along with real-time data on humidity, official CDC reports, and GFT estimates. The model has shown to accurately predict the influenza peak up to 9 weeks before in 2012. On week 52, prior to the influenza peak in all main cities, 63% of the city forecasts were accurate, where accuracy is computed in terms of precision at predicting the peak in a ±1 window.

The forecasting model described in [11] is by far the most complex and accurate presented in literature. However, the actual improvement obtained thanks to the use of GFT is not clear and, as a matter of facts, the authors note than in a previous study they used only GFT data, but then decided to employ an alternative metric that only in part relies on GFT. In this paper, we do not aim to define a better predictor, rather, our objective is to mitigate the causes for which a very complex calibration model is needed, as described in [11]. Infectious diseases models (such as SIRS) are very sensitive to current conditions, such that small changes can produce remarkable differences in future outcomes. Unfortunately, current or nearly-current conditions, e.g. the estimated number of infected individuals at time t, t-1.., as provided by the official surveillance organizations (for example, CDC), keep changing as data are locally collected and updated. On the other side web-based indicators, such as GFT, are stable but less reliable, since they might be affected by other phenomena (fear of being infected, information needs, etc.) than the one being observed. Furthermore, the case definition for ILI patients provided by CDC, requires a combination of symptoms[5] that cannot be mirrored accurately by GFT, as noted also in [11].

In this paper we show that the time series of Twitter messages reporting a combination of symptoms that precisely match the ILI case (hereafter denoted as *ILI-Tweets*) represent a stable and reliable information on "current conditions", to the point that they can reliably replace official ILI data (ILI^{CDC}). Using ILI-Tweets, we can produce reliable mid-term forecasts with a simpler model than the one in [11].

The paper is organized as follows: in Section 2, we summarize our method to extract ILI-Tweets. We also show that ILI^{CDC} data, as published weekly by CDC, are quite variable especially in the shot run (e.g. the current and past two-three values), but, when they eventually stabilize, there is a remarkably high correlation with our ILI-Tweets: in other terms, the ILI^{CDC} curve tends to overlap with our ILI-Tweets curve as official data gets stable. In Section 3 we present our forecasting model, based on ILI-Tweets and historical ILI^{CDC} data on past seasons. Section 4 is dedicated to evaluation: we both validate our model on current (on-going) 2013 flu season and retrospectively, on the past 17 seasons for which ILI^{CDC} data are available, including outlier seasons. Section 5 concludes the paper.

2   Using Twitter Data for Syndromic Surveillance

This section shortly described the algorithm used to extract ILI-related messages from Twitter. Further details can be found in [12-14].

---

[5] http://www.acha.org/ILI_Project/ILI_case_definition_CDC.pdf

2.1   Tracking Twitter Messages Reporting ILI Symptoms

Twitter mining algorithms used in previous health-related studies have measured the occurrence of single pre-specified terms, consisting of either the name or synonyms of a clinical condition (e.g: *H1N1* or *swine flu*) or of words, arbitrarily chosen by the authors, related to the clinical syndrome itself (e.g. *flu, vaccine, tamiflu*) and/or to specific expression, e.g. fear of infection [9]. However, this kind of approach may suffer from major biases, which we will illustrate with an example. Consider the following striking difference in the usage of terms describing the same health conditions, the first by a clinician, the second by a patient: *"Clinicians should maintain a high index of suspicion for this diagnosis in patients presenting with influenza-like symptoms that progress quickly to respiratory distress and extensive pulmonary involvement."*[6] *"For the past 3 days I have had a stuffy, runny nose, congested chest, fever, sore ears and throat and burning eyes. I've been taking cold and flu medication, and it doesn't help"*[7]. Clearly, the patient's symptoms should induce "a high index of suspicion", but the similarity between these symptom descriptions is not so obvious as to allow capture by an automated system, for two reasons: First, in blogs and forums, people are motivated by a communication need (frequently "one-to-one", between just two individuals), rather than by an information need, and therefore naïve language is often preferred to technical language. Thus, understanding the way people talk about medical terms (diseases, symptoms, and treatments) in "peer to peer" communications is crucial for an effective monitoring of health-related behaviors based on social data. Second, it is likely that, in their tweets, most users will describe a combination of symptoms rather than a diagnosis. An approach that takes into account only disease-related keywords can miss a large volume of messages in which users include a mix of signs and symptoms that may in reality be describing a clinical syndrome. With reference to the previous example, high co-occurrence rates of symptoms like *runny nose, congested chest, sore ears* etc. may be used to trigger an alarm in syndromic surveillance systems.

To cope with these issues, we adopted an entirely different approach. We first developed an algorithm to automatically learn a variety of expressions that people use to describe their health conditions, thus improving our ability to detect health-related "concepts" expressed in non-medical terms and, in the end, producing a larger body of evidence. We then implemented a Twitter monitoring instrument to finely analyze the presence and combinations of symptoms in tweets. We transformed five common syndrome definitions into a Boolean query, thereby basing our analysis on a combination of symptoms (each expanded with a set of correspondent naïve terms) rather than on a suspected or final diagnosis. For example, the Boolean query for influenza, matching at best the official CDC definition for ILI (see Section 1), is:

(1)   [(fever)∨(chills)) ∨ (malaise) ∨ (headache) ∨ (myalgia)] ∧ [(cough) ∨ (pharyngitis) ∨ (dyspnea)]

This query is extended replacing the technical terms with the disjunction of its correspondent naïve terms retrieved by our algorithm, for example: *malaise→ malaise, unease, discomfort, weakness, feeling of sickness, feel sick, bodily discomfort, body*

---

[6] www.ncbi.nlm.nih.gov/pubmed/20085663

[7] ehealthforum.com

aches, body pain, pain in body. Query expansion with naïve terms considerably increases the number of matches, thus providing a statistically reliable body of evidence. An example of tweet matching the ILI query is: *"If this is the flu! I am going to be so pissed: fever, nausea, neck pain, sore throat, all this coughing.. its back to bed!"*. Furthermore, we geo-localize our matching tweets using a variety of methods, not described here for sake of space (the interested reader is referred to our publications). Therefore, we can produce a reliable estimate of ILI cases in U.S. and even more fine-grained geographical distributions, for selected regions.

Detection of naïve language and symptom-driven keyword analysis (rather than disease-driven) represent a major difference with previous methods for syndromic surveillance. First, knowledge of naïve language provides a <u>considerably larger corpus of evidence</u>. Then, second, knowledge of patients' language allows fine-grained queries to be performed on the Twitter corpus, separating, for example, patients with simple cold symptoms from those with an allergy, or a "true" ILI, thus solving a "noise" problem pointed out in [11], and not considered, e.g. in [9]. Third, our methodology (similarly to [9]) is very reliable in selecting only tweets of people that actually complain of being infected, rather than people worried by the possibility of being infected. In fact, people may say *"I'm scared about this flu"* but they are unlikely to say *"I'm afraid to get fever, nausea, body aches, and cough!"*.

2.2   Creation of the ILI Tweets Dataset

We started collecting our ILI-related Twitter data since February, 2012. We used the available Twitter API[8] and a set of 78 disease-related naïve terms to track about 100% of the total traffic including these words. In peak periods (e.g. February 2013, January 2014), we collected over 3000 Tweets per day matching the ILI query (1). Additionally, we could monitor the higher or lower incidence of individual symptoms during a specific period under observation, e.g. *cough, pharyngitis* and *chills* have been the predominant symptoms complained of by influenza patients in past year (2012-13). The correlation of our data with official flu reports in the US during the past season 2012-13 was remarkably high (around 0.99%), and better, even, than Google Flu Trends (GFT) over the same period, however we started our collection after the peak period. For the current season, which we could monitor since the early beginning of the infection, the correlation is confirmed to be very high, as shown in Figure 1a. The correlation of ILI-Tweets was 0.965 against 0.947 of GFT. Notice also that both GFT and ILI-Tweets curves seems to be shifted one week in advance with reference to CDC. Figure 1b shows that, when shifting the ILI-Tweets curve one week to the right, there is an almost perfect overlapping with CDC. This is a phenomenon that we observed also during the past 2012-2013 season, and can be explained by the fact that patients' reaction on the web and on social media is instantaneous: they send a message as the symptoms occur. Instead, there might be a delay between the occurrence of the illness and the visit to a doctor, with subsequent registration of the case.

We also remark that our method is applicable to any frequent disease, not just flu, and is not prone to fluctuations in web search behaviors. These results makes our

---

[8] https://dev.twitter.com/docs/streaming-apis

ILI-Tweets data potentially more useful for ILI predictions than official CDC data, which are, instead, rather unstable as US States clean and submit additional ILI data from their healthcare providers. Figure 2 shows the ILI^{CDC} curves in subsequent CDC publications (e.g. Pub-46 means the CDC publication on week 47, including data up to week 46), and our ILI-Tweets curve, as on week 52. All curves are z-normalized[9] for comparison. Figure 2 shows that, as ILI^{CDC} values become stable, they get closer to our ILI-Tweets curve. Note also that the problem of data fluctuation is not considered in [11]; in this study, predictions ILI^{CDC} data, but at the end of the season. Even though the method is robust against fluctuations, we don't know if the quality of predictions would have been the same with varying ILI^{CDC} data.

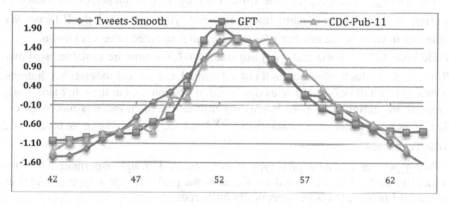

Fig. 1a. Final correlation during 2013-14 flu season, between CDC data (as on Pub-9), ILI Tweets (smoothed with Loess) and Google Flu (already smoothed). Correlation of GFT vrs CDC is 0.947, correlation' of ILI-Tweets vrs CDC is 0.965.

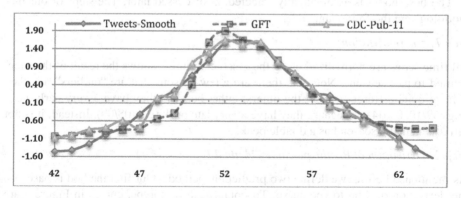

Fig. 1b. As for Fig. 1a, when shifting ILI-Tweets and GFT one week ahead

---

[9] http://stn.spotfire.com/spotfire_client_help/norm/norm_z_score.htm

3   Summary of Prediction Models

In this Section we describe our prediction model. More precisely, we consider the following available data sources:

1. $S(Y_{i-k}) = (x_{40}^{i-k}, x_{41}^{i-k}, ... x_{1}^{i-k}, ... x_{n}^{i-k})$, the time series of historical ILI data on past seasons i-k, where n=20 or 39[10];

2. $S(Y_i) = (x_{40}^i, x_{41}^i, ... x_{m-1}^i, ?, ? ... ?)$, the time series associated to the current year Y_i. We assume that in week m the official values from week 40 to week m-1 are publicly available.

3. $T(Y_i) = (y_{40}^i, y_{41}^i, ... y_m^i, ?, ? ..)$, the time series of Twitter messages associated to the current year Y_i, whose combination of reported symptoms match the ILI case. We assume that in week m the number of matching and associated tweets is known.

While both $S(Y_{i-k})$ $k \neq 0$ and $T_{(Y_i)}$ are stable, $S(Y_i)$ values are unstable, as shown in Figure 2. Such fluctuations, though not substantial, are critical for early predictions, i.e. when m is small (<7-8 values, as discussed in Section 4). On the other side, early predictions are definitively more interesting than late predictions: this motivates our choice of using Twitter data rather than $S(Y_i)$ values. Our predictor is based on 2 alternative models:

1. Prototype: we derive a prototype curve, obtained trough z-normalization and alignment of past curves, centered on the seasonal peak. The prototype provides an "average" ILI profile, but is not temporally anchored;

2. Fusion: A temporally anchored curve, obtained trough z-normalization of past seasons, similarity ranking and fusion of past seasons, as compared with available values of the season to be predicted, represented by the Twitter curve.

The best model is automatically selected, as discussed later. The steps of our methodology are the following:

Step 1: z-normalization

All time series are normalized using the z-score. Figure 3 shows the result of this step, limited to past seasons. Note that there are a few seasons that are "outliers", i.e. they behave quite differently from the others, either because they have a very early peak (e.g. 09/10, 03/04) or because they have a very late peak (e.g. 08/09). Instead, it is not infrequent that a season has a double peak.

Step 2: Derivation of Prototype curve (Method 1)

As mentioned before, we define two prediction methods. Our first method is based on the derivation of a prototype curve. To obtain such prototype, curves in Figure 3 are shifted to align their seasonal peak. An average ILI profile is then derived, as shown in Figure 4.

---

[10] National surveillance data goes from week 40 to week 20 of the subsequent year until season 2001-2002, while n=39 since 2002-2003.

The prediction is based on sliding the curve $T(Y_i)=(y^i_{40}, y^i_{41},...y^i_m, ?, ?..)$ on the Average ILI Profile (AIP), until the best match is found. The match is only based on values, not on temporal correspondence. For example, if the best match is along the crossed red points of Figure 4, the prediction from value $m+1$ is based on the subsequent values of the AIP curve. This method is used when the current season is classified as an outlier in its early or late stage. Outlier seasons exhibit absolute values exceeding of an experimentally determined threshold θ the correspondent values in the same weeks of the previous two seasons.

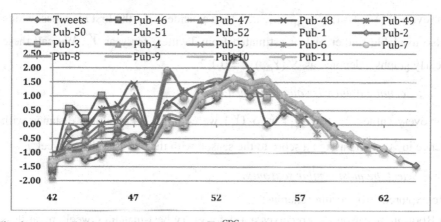

Fig. 2. z-normalized curves for subsequent ILI^CDC publications and (not smoothed) ILI Tweets, during early 2013-14 flu season

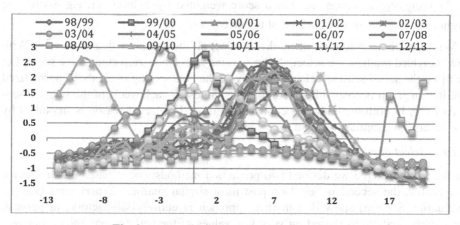

Fig. 3. z-normalized curves for past flu seasons

Step 3: Derivation of a Fusion curve (Method 2)

Our second prediction method is based on deriving a curve that is a fusion of past seasons, weighted according to similarity. The fusion curve is obtained by comparing the known (normalized) values of current season with corresponding values in past seasons, computing a similarity weight for each season and then generating a prediction curve based on combining these seasons. Known values in current season are represented by the known m values of $T(Y_i)$. Note that <u>another advantage of using</u> $T(Y_i)$ <u>rather than</u> $S(Y_i)$ <u>is that the</u> m-th <u>value is available in week</u> m, while ILI^{CDC} data, besides being subject to fluctuations, become available with one week of delay. We now describe the sub-phases of method 2. In what follows, for simplicity we use the same notation for normalized and not normalized time series.

Step 3.1: derive the "early graphs"

For every $S(Y_{i-k}) = (x_{40}^{i-k}, x_{41}^{i-k}, ...x_1^{i-k}, ...x_n^{i-k})$ we consider only the first m values, which are also available (either real or estimated from Twitter) for year Y_i. We call these the "early graphs", denoted as $S^e(Y_{i-k})$ $k = 0, 1, 2...$

Step 3.2: Compute point-wise quadratic distance

For every value x_j^i (or y_m^i) in $S^e(Y_i)$ we compute its quadratic distance with reference to x_j^{i-k} and assign a score to the season with the closest value in week j.

Step 3.3 Select the most similar season(s)

We explored two scoring schemas:

1) <u>Boolean</u>: a season Y_{i-k} receives a + 1 for every best-matching week, regardless of the week;

2) <u>Weighted</u>: a season receives a score weighted by $1/\ln(m-j)$, e.g. scores are higher for matches in weeks j closest to current week m.

With the Boolean scoring method, we select all the season with a score ≥ 1 .With the Weighted method, we select all the seasons with a non-zero cumulative score. Let [Y*] be the set of seasons selected by any of the two scoring methods. A normalized prediction graph is created by averaging the values, in each week, of the selected seasons [Y*]. In both methods, the contribution of each selected season is smoothed by the inverse of cumulated weight.

Step 4. Select best predictors

In Step 2 and Step 3 we defined two prediction methods: one is based on an average ILI profile, the second is based on past most similar seasons. Experiments (see the evaluation Section) show that neither approach is entirely satisfactory: in general, very early predictions (based on very few values of the early graph) and outlier seasons (as those shown in Figure 3) are better predicted using the average profile method, while when a certain number of week values are available, the similarity curve performs best. To select the best predictor we used a classifier to automatically select the best predictors, given the number of available weeks and the absolute distance between absolute values of previous seasons.

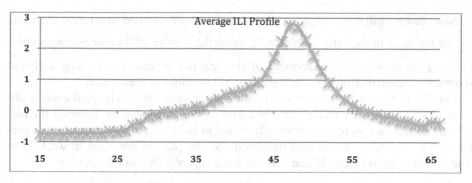

Fig. 4. Average ILI profile (z-normalized, not temporally anchored)

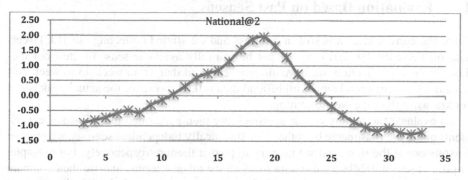

Fig. 5. Prediction of current flu season based on a fusion of most similar past seasons (using the Weighted scoring) with reference to an "early curve" derived from ILI-Tweets on week 2.

Step 5. Produce the final prediction

At the end of step 4 we obtain a prediction with z-normalized values. To produce the final prediction, we need to compute the absolute values for current season, based on selected most similar early graphs of past seasons. To re-weight the (predicted) new values, we use the following procedure. First, we compute the average number of total patients for the involved seasons ([Y*] and Y_i), in the period under analysis.

For example, if the season to be predicted is 13/14, and the selected most similar seasons are 02/03 and 98/99 (both with a score 2), and early graphs span from week 40 to 46, we denote these average values as $\mu_{13/14}, \mu_{02/03}, \mu_{98/99}$.

We compute two re-weighting factors as follows:

$$\delta^{13/14}_{02/03} = \frac{\mu_{13/14}}{\mu_{02/03}}, \delta^{13/14}_{98/99} = \frac{\mu_{13/14}}{\mu_{98/99}}$$

We then compute the season score factors $\xi^{13/14}_s$ as follows:

$$\xi^{13/14}_{02/03} = \frac{r_{02/03}}{\sum_{s\in\{02/03;98/99\}} r_s}, \xi^{13/14}_{02/03} = \frac{r_{98/99}}{\sum_{s\in\{02/03;98/99\}} r_s}$$

Finally, every predicted value for the new season is computed as follows

$$i=\{47...53,1...39\}: x^i_{13/14} = \sum_{s\in\{\substack{02\ 98\\03'99}\}} x^i_s * \delta^{\frac{13}{14}}_s * \xi^{13/14}_s$$

Note that a similar re-weighting procedure is initially applied to estimate the value y_k^i of flu cases in the early graph for Y_i, given the number of Twitter messages complaining flu in week k. Furthermore, if the selected similar seasons have different scores, their contribution to the computation is smoothed by their score.

Finally, in Figure 5 we show our prediction for year 13/14. The prediction is obtained using the Fusion method (method 2) with Weighted scoring, however the two scoring techniques were experimentally found to have no striking difference in performance. According to our real-time estimate, the peak is predicted in weeks 5-6. The season starts on week 48 and ends on week 16, for a total of 22 weeks.

4   Evaluation Based on Past Seasons

Since the current season is still in progress and we started collecting our ILI Tweets data on February 1st, 2013, we do not have a fully available season to test our method. In previous Section, we have already remarked that, from week 43 to week 2 of season 13/14, our correlation with official data is 0.94, however the actual peak is not yet known at the time we are writing.

To evaluate the quality of our approach, we then performed the following experiment: under the reasonable hypothesis of statistically independent seasons, we remove seasons one at the time, and we then try to predict them retrospectively. For example, to predict season 02/03 we use data from all the other seasons, and we then compare our prediction with the ground truth. Table 1 shows the correlation results obtained when using the method based on Fusion with Weighted scoring on the white rows, and Prototype on the orange rows. Note that selection of the method is automatically determined as described in step 4 of Section 3, however, season 08/09 (in yellow) was not recognized as an outlier, due to the late secondary peak (see Figure 2), therefore results are based on the Fusion method. In the Table 1, rows are the years to be predicted, and columns are the "m", e.g. "45" means that we predict week 45 for year Y_j based on weeks 40-45. Cells (j,k) are the Pearson's correlation between the predicted and actual curves for year j, from week 40 up to week k. The last row of Table 1 is the average correlation of all our predictions with reference to the actual values of the seasons to be predicted.

As already remarked, we do not actually have the $T(Y_j)$ values for years previous than 2013 (since, as previously noted, we started collecting flu-related tweets on February 2013). However, under the hypothesis that our method exhibits a stable and strong correlation with the flu seasons (as shown for partial but large fractions of seasons 12/13 [13-15] and 13/14), the effect of knowing $T(Y_j)$ is simulated simply by considering the correspondent known values for $S(Y_i)$.

Note also that, even though in this experiment the early curves for a year to be predicted are represented by the ILICDC values rather than by the Twitter estimate of these values (as it should be in our method), the correlation values in Table 1 are not necessarily optimistic, since, even if we could use stable ILICDC values for a year to be predicted (which, as already noted, is not the case) rather than un-official ILI-Tweets, still

ILI-Tweets keep an advantage over ILICDC data, since they provide an extra "real-time" value for week m. By comparing the values in cells (j,k) with (j,k+1) it is seen that one extra value almost always has a positive effect on performance.

Table 1 shows for example that, in week 48 (which may be considered a relatively early prediction, usually 4-8 weeks before the peak), the average obtained Pearson's correlation is 0,80. As expected, the correlation grows with the length of the available early curve, up to 0,94 on week 18. The average total correlation, i.e. the average of values in the last row, is 0,85.

Table 2 shows the average precision in predicting the peak over all historical data: the columns are the weeks in which the prediction is made, and precision for a season is computed as in [11]: 1 if prediction is accurate within ± 1 week of the observed ILI peak, else it is 0. Even though the comparison is based on uneven data (17 seasons US-wide in our case, season 12/13 and individual predictions for 108 cities[11], in [11]), we

Table 1. Retrospective prediction (using mixed approach)

Year / week	45	46	47	48	49	50	51	52	1	2	3	4	5	6	7	8	9	Avg
97/98	0,77	0,89	0,89	0,92	0,86	0,60	0,87	0,83	0,87	0,84	0,81	0,89	0,92	0,92	0,98	0,98	0,98	0,87
98/99	0,75	0,78	0,94	0,96	0,92	0,86	0,86	0,97	0,98	0,98	0,98	0,97	0,98	0,98	0,97	0,95	0,97	0,93
99/00	0,48	0,44	0,44	0,78	0,98	0,98	0,98	0,98	0,98	0,98	0,98	0,98	0,98	0,98	0,98	0,98	0,98	0,88
00/01	0,84	0,71	0,52	0,84	0,69	0,62	0,93	0,88	0,89	0,88	0,88	0,92	0,93	0,97	0,98	0,99	0,98	0,85
01/02	0,82	0,54	0,88	0,97	0,97	0,98	0,95	0,92	0,94	0,97	0,96	0,98	0,97	0,97	0,96	0,97	0,97	0,92
02/03	0,91	0,56	0,91	0,88	0,78	0,95	0,97	0,97	0,93	0,98	0,96	0,97	0,98	0,96	0,97	0,98	0,96	0,92
03/04	0,10	0,68	0,94	0,68	0,95	0,95	0,95	0,95	0,95	0,95	0,95	0,95	0,95	0,95	0,95	0,95	0,95	0,87
04/05	0,89	0,46	0,95	0,93	0,86	0,98	0,92	0,77	0,88	0,83	0,76	0,91	0,91	0,96	0,95	0,97	0,98	0,88
05/06	0,82	0,87	0,74	0,62	0,90	0,89	0,88	0,86	0,78	0,85	0,82	0,87	0,91	0,87	0,90	0,96	0,97	0,85
06/07	0,90	0,85	0,70	0,83	0,93	0,97	0,95	0,83	0,83	0,81	0,87	0,90	0,96	0,97	0,98	0,94	0,98	0,89
07/08	0,63	-0,19	0,73	0,51	0,81	0,90	0,97	0,79	0,86	0,88	0,91	0,95	0,90	0,93	0,89	0,91	0,92	0,78
08/09	0,44	0,54	0,50	0,64	0,63	0,38	0,35	0,29	0,45	0,53	0,54	0,52	0,58	0,53	0,63	0,61	0,59	0,52
09/10	0,66	0,66	0,76	0,84	0,88	0,94	0,96	0,94	0,95	0,95	0,93	0,97	0,96	0,98	0,98	0,99	1,00	0,90
10/11	0,99	0,87	0,93	0,88	0,93	0,98	0,95	0,96	0,96	0,85	0,91	0,92	0,87	0,88	0,96	0,94	0,97	0,93
11/12	0,69	0,85	0,77	0,84	0,78	0,77	0,68	0,84	0,80	0,78	0,73	0,84	0,86	0,85	0,85	0,88	0,89	0,81
12/13	0,60	0,45	0,85	0,69	0,89	0,86	0,78	0,88	0,88	0,93	0,91	0,92	0,97	0,99	0,99	0,99	0,99	0,86
Person Mean	0,70	0,62	0,78	0,80	0,86	0,85	0,87	0,85	0,87	0,87	0,87	0,90	0,91	0,92	0,93	0,94	0,94	0,85

Table 2. Precision at ± 1 peak prediction (retrospective, all seasons)

Week	43	44	45	46	47	48	49	50	51	52	1	2	3	4	5	6	7
Prec.	0,563	0,563	0,563	0,563	0,625	0,625	0,5	0,5	0,563	0,563	0,688	0,75	0,75	0,75	0,938	0,913	0,813

---

[11] Our data are hardly comparable with [11], since in that paper predictions are made separately for different cities. Unfortunately, even though we can more finely geo-localize our ILI Tweets, data at the city level are too few for a reliable prediction, because of the well known difficulty to obtain systematic and reliable location indicators in tweets.

note that in [11] (Table 2) the total % accuracy on week 52 is 0.631 against 0.563 in Table 2, on week 1 is 0.638 against 0.688, on week 5 is 0.739 against 0.938, and both predictions have a small drop on week 6 (0.733 and 0.913).

In [11] the authors also compute a total U.S. prediction accuracy obtained as an average of 10 regions, using the Health and Human Service (HHS) region scale: in this experiment, which is more comparable with our data, the accuracy of forecasts in year 12/13 ranged from 0.595 on week 52 to a high 0.90 in week 5, after the seasonal peak (the season last year had a rather anticipated peak). In the same year, our peak prediction on week 52 was 3 weeks after the actual peak, while since week 2 the prediction was correct (0 distance). Furthermore, the correlation of our Fusion curve with the actual ILI curve was 0.88 in week 52 and 0.97 on week 5 (see Table 1, last row). We finally note that correlation is a better performance measure than accuracy in peak prediction since, as previously shown in Figure 2 and 3, many seasons have more than one peak.

5   Conclusions

The major strength of the predictor presented in this paper is the reliability of values that represent the "current state" of the system, as demonstrated by Figures 1 (a and b) and 2 and in our previously published work [13-15].

We are not aware of previous studies that recognized (and solved) the problem of fluctuation of real-time ILI^{CDC} data publications, since all papers, including [11], do not actually predict in real-time, but only at the end of the season, when ILI^{CDC} data are eventually stable and reliable. Furthermore, ILI-Tweets collected according to our methodology overcome all the limitations of GFT data, also highlighted in [11], i.e.:

1. Media news may inflate GFT ILI estimates;
2. GFT ILI does not accurately model the CDC case definition for ILI, which requires a precise combination of symptoms (captured by ILI-Tweets). GFT estimates may then be affected by other types of respiratory diseases.

For truly real-time prediction, the problem of unreliable knowledge on "current conditions" is critical, since infectious diseases models are very sensitive to fluctuations, such that small changes can produce remarkable differences in future outcomes. If accurate data are available in real-time (as for our ILI-Tweets), even simpler predictors based on historical data may obtain good performance both in terms of correlation and peak prediction.

References

1. Yu, S., Kak, S.: A Survey of Prediction using Social Media (2012),
    http://arxiv.org/ftp/arxiv/papers/1203/1203.1647.pdf (retrieved)
2. Asur, S., Huberman, B.H.: Predicting the future with social media,
    http://www.hpl.hp.com/research/scl/papers/socialmedia/
    socialmedia.pdf (retrieved)

3. Radinsky, K., Horvitz, E.: Mining the web to predict future events. In: WSDM 2013, pp. 255–264 (2013)
4. Ruiz, E.J., Hristidis, V., Castillo, C., Gionis, A., Jaimes, A.: Correlating financial time series with micro-blogging activity. In: Proceedings of the Fifth ACM International Conference on Web Search and Data Mining, WSDM 2012, pp. 513–522. ACM, New York (2012)
5. Carrifere-Swallow, Y., Labbfe, F.: Nowcasting with Google Trends in an Emerging Market. Central Bank of Chile, Working Papers n. 588 (2010)
6. Ginsberg, J., Mohebbi, M.H., Patel, R.S., Brammer, L., Smolinski, M.S., et al.: Detecting influenza epidemics using search engine query data. Nature 457, 1012–1014 (2009)
7. Althouse, B.M., Ng, Y.Y., Cummings, D.A.T.: Prediction of Dengue Incidence Using Search Query Surveillance. PLoS Negl. Trop. Dis. 5(8) (2011)
8. Xu, D., Liu, Y., Zhang, M., Ma, S., Ciu, A., Ru, L.: Predicting Epidemic Tendency through Search Behaviour Analysis. In: Proc. of 22nd IJCAI (2011)
9. Lamb, A., Paul, M.J., Dredze, M.: Separating Fact from Fear: Tracking Flu Infections on Twitter. In: NAACL (2013)
10. Achrekar, H., Gandhe, A., Lazarus, R., Yu, S., Liu, B.: Predicting Flu Trends using Twitter Data. In: CPNS 2011 (2011)
11. Shaman, J., Karspeck, A., Yang, W., Tamerius, J., Lipsitch, M.: Real-time influenza forecasts during the 2012-2013 season. Nature Communications 4, 2837 (2013), doi:10.1038/ncomms3837
12. Gesualdo, F., Stilo, G., Agricola, E., Gonfiantini, M.V., Pandolfi, E., Velardi, P., Tozzi, A.E.: Influenza-like illness surveillance on Twitter through automated learning of naïve language. PloS One Public Library of Science One, Journal (2013)
13. Velardi, P., Stilo, G., Tozzi, A.E., Gesualdo, F.: Twitter mining for fine-grained syndromic surveillance. Artificial Intelligence in Medicine, Special Issue on Text Mining and Information Analysis (in press, 2014)
14. Stilo, G., De Vincenzi, M., Tozzi, A.E., Velardi, P.: Automated Learning of Everyday Patients' Language for Medical Blog Analytics. In: Proceedings of the Recent Advances in Natural Language Processing (RANLP 2013) Hissar, Hissar (Bulgaria), September 9-11 (2013)

A Hierarchical Ensemble of α-Trees
for Predicting Expensive Hospital Visits

Yubin Park and Joydeep Ghosh

The University of Texas at Austin, Austin TX 78712, USA
yubin.park@utexas.edu,
ghosh@ece.utexas.edu

Abstract. Hospital charges are determined by numerous factors. Even
the cost for the same procedure can vary greatly depending on a patient's conditions, complications, and types of facilities. With the advent
of Obamacare, estimating hospital charges has become an increasingly
important problem in healthcare informatics. We propose a hierarchical ensemble of α-Trees to delicately deal with this challenging problem. In the proposed approach, multiple α-Trees are built to capture the
different aspects of hospital charges, and then these multiple classifiers
are uniquely combined for each hospital. Hospitals are characterized by
unique weight vectors that explain the subtle differences in hospital spe-
cialties and patient groups. Experimental results based on the 2006 Texas
inpatient discharge data show that our approach effectively captures the
variability of hospital charges across different hospitals, and also provides
a useful characterization of different hospitals in the process.

Keywords: decision tree, α-divergence, ensemble classifiers, healthcare.

1 Introduction

One of the most notable and immediate impacts of the Patient Protection and
Affordable Care Act (PPACA, also called Obamacare) has been a surge of interest in modeling and predicting hospital costs in the USA. In particular, to set up
and run an Affordable Care Organization (ACO), a type of health care organization greatly encouraged by PPACA, being able to predict such costs is critical
since ACOs get reimbursed for a fixed amount per patient, which is dramatically
different from the fee-for-service model that has ruled healthcare in the USA all
these years. Recent studies have revealed that hospital bills in the United States
vary greatly across regions and hospitals [17,2,5]. Although such comparisons
may help bringing transparency to the current healthcare landscape, comparing
hospital charges based on procedure billing codes overlook the true nature of the
cost. The procedure codes used in billing systems are abstracted forms of actually performed procedures, and such codes do not capture the full information
about a patient's conditions, complications, and types of facilities. Regarding
the cost variation across hospitals, teaching hospitals tend to treat more critical

D. Ślęzak et al. (Eds.): BIH 2014, LNAI 8609, pp. 178–187, 2014.

patients. In essence, estimating hospital charges is a multi-faceted problem, and it is also important to discriminate costs that are legitimate versus those that are primarily due to bad practices/management, fraud, etc. Thus predictive and explanatory modeling of hospital costs has become a new and key challenge in health informatics.

In this paper, we classify expensive hospital charges using a novel, data-driven machine learning approach. Texas Department of State Health Services released inpatient discharge data ranging from year 1999 to 2007.[1] The datasets contain a wide range of billing information including patient demographics, types of diagnoses and procedures, length of stays, and hospital names. The demographic features cover patients' age, gender, ZIP codes, and their insurance plans. Our goal is to build a classification model for the expensive hospital bills, and to better explain the variability in hospital charges. Since many other states also provide similar discharge data, such a model will have national impact.

There have been several efforts to use statistical methods for predicting hospital charges, with generally weak results [23,8,11]. For the Inpatient Dataset, even a suitably regularized logistic regression model, fails to provide a comprehensive view on cost variations. First, most of the features are categorical variables; dummy-coding those variables results in a very high-dimensional design matrix[2]. Furthermore, we observed that interactions among variables have substantial effects on hospital costs. Including such interaction terms further increases the dimensionality of the design matrix.

In contrast, decision tree models are attractive candidates for this kind of dataset. Categorical variables and interaction terms are naturally handled in decision trees. We observed that classical decision trees (e.g. CART and C4.5) fit reasonably well to the data. However, the variations across hospitals are not adequately captured by these models. Also, most of the key splitting features are based on patient demographics and diagnosis. To better explain the variability across hospitals, a thorough exploratory analysis of the dataset was performed, which indicated that a multilevel (hierarchical) approach is needed.

To visualize this issue in more detail, consider a subset of the 2006 Texas inpatient data based on the ten most common diagnoses and ten biggest hospitals in Texas. Figure 1 (a) shows the histogram of hospital charges. As can be seen, the distribution of hospital charges is a mixture of several distributions. One main factor for the cost variation is, of course, the diagnosis variable. Figure 1 (b)

---

[1] Texas is chosen as it provides access to rich and comprehensive datasets. It is also appropriate since a very high profile and influential article by Atul Gawande, showing that one of its counties (McAllen) had inexplicably much higher Medicare costs than other counties, setting off a national debate on health costs in the USA [13].

[2] A dummy variable is an indicator variable that takes the value 0 for absence or 1 for presence of some categorical effect. For example, for a gender variable that takes a value from {Male, Female, Unknown}, dummy-coding creates two indicator variables $\mathbb{I}(\text{gender} = \text{Male})$ and $\mathbb{I}(\text{gender} = \text{Female})$.

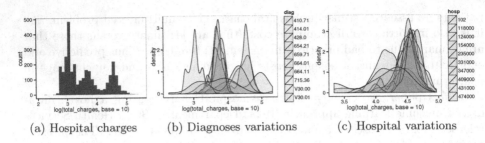

(a) Hospital charges   (b) Diagnoses variations   (c) Hospital variations

Fig. 1. Histograms and density plots for the 2006 Texas inpatient data. The horizontal axis represents the range of hospital charges in log-scale (base 10).

shows the cost distributions grouped by the diagnosis variable. The major peaks of the mixture distribution are well captured by the diagnosis variable. Although subtle, the cost distributions are also affected by the hospital variable. Figure 1 (c) shows the cost distributions grouped by the hospital variable for the coronary atherosclerosis diagnosis. We notice that some hospitals exhibit different cost distributions from the others, but the hospital effect is less noticeable compared to the diagnosis variable.

This paper proposes a hierarchical mixture of decision trees to delicately deal with such issues. To describe the overall idea, let us assume that we have a set of three different decision trees $\{\mathcal{T}_1, \mathcal{T}_2, \mathcal{T}_3\}$, where each decision tree captures different aspects of the data. For example such trees may be obtained using a different subset of features, as in a Random Forest. If we ignore the hospital effect, a uniform ensemble is given as:

$$Y = \frac{1}{3}\mathcal{T}_0(X) + \frac{1}{3}\mathcal{T}_1(X) + \frac{1}{3}\mathcal{T}_2(X) \tag{1}$$

where X and Y represent the feature and class random variables respectively. As shown in Figure 1 (c), each hospital has a slight different pricing mechanism and patient group. Thus, instead of mixing the decision trees with uniform weights, one could estimate a hospital-specific weight vector $\begin{bmatrix} w_0(H) & w_1(H) & w_2(H) \end{bmatrix}^\top$ where H represents hospital. Using a link function f, our hierarchical ensemble is written as:

$$Y = f(w_0(H)\mathcal{T}_0(X) + w_1(H)\mathcal{T}_1(X) + w_2(H)\mathcal{T}_2(X)) \tag{2}$$

where the weight vector characterizes a hospital specific pricing mechanism.

Although the proposed idea is simple, we have not addressed the critical building blocks of the algorithm: obtaining distinct decision trees that capture different aspects of the data. The diversity of bagging-based decision trees is somewhat limited when the size of training data is big; decision trees from sub-samples remain almost the same. Random Forests [4] is also not a good solution, since it typically requires hundreds of trees and lacks interpretability.

Instead, we use a novel and effective alternative for producing diverse trees by varying the splitting criteria. Specifically, we use the α-Tree [18,19], which is a generalization of C4.5 that uses α-divergence splitting criterion. By adjusting α, one can obtain different splitting criteria, and hence different tree structures. The information gain criterion of C4.5 is a special case of the α-divergence splitting criterion. An extension of the α-divergence splitting criterion also covers Gini (from CART) and DKM [10] splitting criteria. In this paper, we extensively use α-Tree to build a set of diverse classifiers. We then propose a hierarchical ensemble of α-Trees which can capture the subtle cost variability across hospitals using the Texas inpatient data.

2   Background

Decision trees are rule-based classification algorithms that can be obtained through:

1. selecting a splitting feature based on a certain criterion,
2. partitioning input data based on the selected splitting feature, and then
3. recursively repeating this process until certain stopping criteria are met.

Decision trees use different splitting criteria, e.g. C4.5 and ID3 use Information Gain and Information Gain Ratio [20], CHAID uses the Chi-squared test, and CART [3] uses the Gini impurity measure. There are numerous other impurity measures such as misclassification rate and Hellinger distance. It is generally believed that no single splitting criterion is guaranteed to outperform over the other criteria [12, p. 161].

A divergence, $D_\alpha(P\|Q)$, is a function that measures the distance between two distributions: P and Q. There exists many different kinds of divergences such as f-divergence [9] and β- and γ-divergences [7]. α-Tree uses α-divergence [1,24], defined as follows:

$$D_\alpha(P\|Q) = \frac{\int_x \alpha P(x) + (1-\alpha)Q(x) - P(x)^\alpha Q(x)^{1-\alpha} dx}{\alpha(1-\alpha)} \tag{3}$$

where P and Q are two probability distributions, and α is a real number. The α-divergence was introduced by Chernoff [6] to upper-bound the theoretical error probability of classification tasks. The mathematical form of α-divergence is closely related to those of Renyi entropy [21], Tsallis entropy [22], and generalized diversity index [16]; all four share the exponent term α.

If both P and Q are proper probability density functions (i.e. $\int_x P(x)dx = \int_x Q(x)dx = 1$), then Equation (3) simplifies to:

$$D_\alpha(P\|Q) = \frac{1 - \int_x P(x)^\alpha Q(x)^{1-\alpha} dx}{\alpha(1-\alpha)}. \tag{4}$$

Some special cases are:

$$D_{-1}(P\|Q) = \frac{1}{2}\int_x \frac{(Q(x) - P(x))^2}{P(x)}dx \tag{5}$$

$$\lim_{\alpha \to 0} D_\alpha(P\|Q) = KL(Q\|P) \tag{6}$$

$$D_{\frac{1}{2}}(P\|Q) = 2\int_x (\sqrt{P(x)} - \sqrt{Q(x)})^2 dx \tag{7}$$

$$\lim_{\alpha \to 1} D_\alpha(P\|Q) = KL(P\|Q) \tag{8}$$

$$D_2(P\|Q) = \frac{1}{2}\int_x \frac{(P(x) - Q(x))^2}{Q(x)}dx \tag{9}$$

Equation (7) is Hellinger distance, and Equations (6) and (8) are KL-divergences. Note that α-Divergence is always positive and is zero if and only if P = Q. Hence, α-divergence can be used as a (dis)similarity measure between two distributions.

α-Tree is a generalization of several decision trees, such as C4.5 and CART. The impurity reduction criterion in C4.5 can be written as a divergence maximization criterion as follows:

$$\begin{aligned}
\min_x \quad & \sum_x P(x)H(Y \mid x) \\
= \max \quad & H(Y) - H(Y \mid X) \\
= \max \quad & \sum_{x,y} P(x,y)\log\frac{P(x,y)}{P(x)P(y)} \\
= \max \quad & KL(P(X,Y)\|P(X)P(Y)) \\
= \max \quad & \lim_{\alpha \to 1} D_\alpha(P(X,Y)\|P(X)P(Y))
\end{aligned}$$

Replacing the KL divergence with the α-divergence yields the α-Tree algorithm, outlined in Algorithm 1. Thus, the **α-divergence criterion** selects a splitting feature which gives the maximum α-divergence between $P(X,Y)$ and $P(X)P(Y)$. The C4.5 splitting criterion can be obtained using $\alpha = 1$.

The α value determines the selection of splitting features, and different values can yield distinct splitting features. This property was used to increase the diversity of base trees in an ensemble framework [19].

3   Hierarchical Ensemble of α-Trees

Before building a hierarchical ensemble of α-Trees, we introduce some notation. An array of α-Trees is defined as:

$$\mathbf{T}(X) = \begin{bmatrix} \mathcal{T}_{\alpha_1}(X) & \mathcal{T}_{\alpha_2}(X) & \cdots & \mathcal{T}_{\alpha_A}(X) \end{bmatrix}^\top \tag{10}$$

Algorithm 1. α-Tree

Data: $\mathcal{S} = \{(X, Y)\}, \alpha$
Result: $\mathcal{T}$
$X_{i^*} = \arg\max_{X_i} D_\alpha(\mathrm{P}(X_i, Y) \| \mathrm{P}(X_i)\mathrm{P}(Y))$;
if *stopping_criteria(S)=True* then
$\quad E[Y \mid \mathcal{S}]$;
else
$\quad \mathcal{T}_{\text{left}} = \alpha\text{-Tree}(\{(X, Y) \mid X_{i^*} = 0\}, \alpha)$;
$\quad \mathcal{T}_{\text{right}} = \alpha\text{-Tree}(\{(X, Y) \mid X_{i^*} = 1\}, \alpha)$;
end
$\mathcal{T} = \{\mathcal{T}_{\text{left}}, \mathcal{T}_{\text{right}}\}$;

---

where A is the number of α-Trees, and $\alpha_i \neq \alpha_j \ \forall \ i \neq j$. For a specific data point $\mathbf{x}_i$, $\mathbf{T}(\mathbf{x}_i)$ is an A-dimensional real-valued vector. A basic Ensemble of α-Trees averages the outputs of the constituent trees $\mathbf{T}(X)$:

$$\mathrm{EAT}(X) = \begin{bmatrix} \frac{1}{A} & \frac{1}{A} & \cdots & \frac{1}{A} \end{bmatrix} \mathbf{T}(X) \tag{11}$$

The performance of EAT can be improved by using a convex combination of the tree outputs:

$$\mathrm{CEAT}(X) = \begin{bmatrix} w_{\alpha_1} & w_{\alpha_2} & \cdots & w_{\alpha_A} \end{bmatrix} \mathbf{T}(X) = \mathbf{w}^\top \mathbf{T}(X) \tag{12}$$

where CEAT stands for Convex Ensemble of α-Trees. The weights are estimated by maximizing the log-likelihood function:

$$\mathcal{L}^C(\mathbf{w}) = \sum_i y_i \log f(\mathbf{w}^\top \mathbf{T}(\mathbf{x}_i)) + (1 - y_i) \log(1 - f(\mathbf{w}^\top \mathbf{T}(\mathbf{x}_i))) \tag{13}$$

where $\mathbf{x}_i$ and y_i represent the feature vector and class label of the ith data point. We use a logic function for the link function f. CEAT, which is newly introduced in this paper, takes into account the performance difference of different trees. For example, if $\mathcal{T}_{\alpha_1}$ performs better than $\mathcal{T}_{\alpha_2}$, CEAT weights $\mathcal{T}_{\alpha_1}$ more than $\mathcal{T}_{\alpha_2}$.

A Hierarchical Ensemble of α-Trees (HEAT) is a generalization of CEAT where the weight vector can vary across hospitals. Mathematically, HEAT is written as follows:

$$\mathrm{HEAT}(X) = \begin{bmatrix} w_{\alpha_1}(H) & w_{\alpha_2}(H) & \cdots w_{\alpha_A}(H) \end{bmatrix} \mathbf{T}(X) = \mathbf{w}^\top(H)\mathbf{T}(X) \tag{14}$$

where H is a hospital random variable. The hospital-specific weight vector is estimated by maximizing the log-likelihood function:

$$\mathcal{L}^H(\mathbf{w}(H)) = \sum_i y_i \log f(\mathbf{w}^\top(h_i)\mathbf{T}(\mathbf{x}_i)) + (1 - y_i) \log(1 - f(\mathbf{w}^\top(h_i)\mathbf{T}(\mathbf{x}_i)))$$

$$\tag{15}$$

In addition, a regularization term $\sum_i (1 - w_{\alpha_i}(H))^2$ can be added to the above equation so that a maximum *aposteriori* solution is obtained instead. For our problem which involved a very large data set, this term had little effect and was subsequently ignored.

HEAT is summarized in Algorithm 2.

Algorithm 2. HEAT
_____
Data: $\mathcal{S} = \{(X, Y)\}$
Result: $\mathcal{T}_\alpha, \{\mathbf{w}(H)\}$
for α *in* $0 : A$ **do**
$\quad \mathcal{T}_\alpha = \alpha\text{-Tree}(\mathbf{X}, \mathbf{y}, \alpha);$
end
$\{\mathbf{w}(H)\} = \arg\min \mathcal{L}^{\mathrm{H}}(\mathbf{w}(H));$

---

4   Experimental Results

We use Texas Inpatient Public Use Data File from the Texas Department of State Health Services (DSHS). Hospital billing records collected from 1999 to 2007 are publicly available through their website. Each yearly dataset contains about 2.8 millions events with more than 250 features. Specifically, we use the inpatient records from the fourth quarter of 2006. Except for a few exempt hospitals, all the hospitals in Texas reported inpatient discharge events to DSHS. In this paper, any hospital charges above 50,000 dollars are defined as an expensive hospital charge, setting up a two-class problem. The expensive hospital charges are predicted among the patients who stayed one day in hospitals. Patients who stayed for more than one day are excluded from our study, since the hospital charges for the longer stays are dominated by hospital accommodation charges. Identifying the differences in hospital accommodation charges is a slightly different problem, and is not our focus in this paper.

Different values of α produce different decision trees. Figure 2 shows three α-Trees by setting $\alpha = 0, 1, 2$. For simplicity, we only showed the first level, and one side of the second level splits. As can be seen, these three trees have different splitting features. The first α-Tree with $\alpha = 0$ splits based on the age variable[3], and then drills down to the specialty unit variable. The second α-Tree with $\alpha = 1$ first looks for whether a patient is in his twenties, and then checks whether a patient received an implantation of cardiac resynchronization defibrillator (ICD-9 procedure code: 00.51). The last α-Tree with $\alpha = 2$ first examines the expensive procedure code (00.51), and then asks the age of a patient. Note that these three α-Trees highlight different aspects of the data.

Figure 3 (a) shows the pair-wise correlation between α-Trees. The values of α are 0, 1, 2, 4, 8, 16, and 32. As expected, the correlation between trees with similar values of α tends to be higher. Note that after $\alpha > 8$, changing α doesn't

---

[3] The age variable is binned. age=1 represents that a patient is a teenager, and age=2 means that a patient is in his twenties.

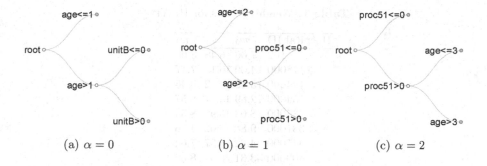

(a) $\alpha = 0$ (b) $\alpha = 1$ (c) $\alpha = 2$

Fig. 2. Different tree structures obtained by changing the value of α. For simplicity, we only showed the first level, and one side of the second level splits.

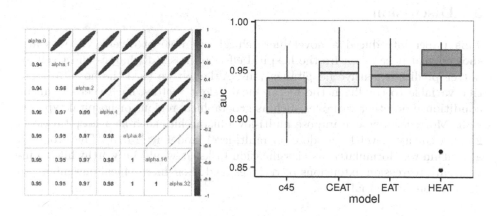

Fig. 3. (a) Pair-wise correlation between α-Trees (left) and (b) AUC comparison on hold-out datasets (right)

produce different tree structures. In this paper, we used three α-Trees with $\alpha = 0, 1, 2$ respectively. To be able to estimate the weights of CEAT and HEAT, the trees need to be linearly independent.

In this example, we partitioned the Texas data into training (90%) and test (10%) sets, and measured hold-out Areas Under the Receiver Operating Characteristics Curves (AUC). Figure 3 (b) shows the results obtained from 30 random partitions of training and test sets. As can be seen, the median AUC values are ordered as: HEAT > CEAT > EAT > C4.5. Table 1 shows the estimated HEAT weight vectors. Observe that each hospital has a unique weight vector. For example, the hospital charges from Hospital 431000 are explained almost purely by $\mathcal{T}_0$, while the charges from Hospital 102 require all three classification trees: $\mathcal{T}_0$, $\mathcal{T}_1$, and $\mathcal{T}_2$.

Table 1. Weight Vectors for HEAT

Hospital ID	w_0	w_1	w_2
102	7.06	16.48	8.60
118000	14.00	10.13	7.17
124000	13.18	-4.82	0.45
154000	12.89	13.81	8.57
235000	8.03	15.92	8.54
331000	9.88	6.02	4.56
347000	4.62	15.37	7.64
409000	-3.31	20.91	8.52
431000	29.14	-0.83	5.32
474000	-4.03	1.72	-0.03

5   Discussion

This paper introduced a novel hierarchical ensemble of diverse α-Trees and showed that it can capture the hospital effect on hospital charges effectively to better predict expensive hospitalizations. Although we used the hospital identity variable to condition the hierarchical weight vectors, such vectors can be conditioned on other variables such as geographical regions or hospital types as well. Moreover, one can impose multi-level hierarchies such as a hospital (level 2) in a county (level 1), as done in multi-level modeling [14,15]. The proposed algorithm was formulated as classification tasks. It would be worthwhile to investigate regression extensions of α-Trees, and their hierarchical ensembles, to directly predict actual costs.

References

1. Amari, S.: Integration of stochastic models by minimizing α-divergence. Neural Computation (2007)
2. Block, M., Cox, A., McGinty, J.C., Ericson, M.: How much hospitals charge for the same procedures (May 2013),
   http://www.nytimes.com/interactive/2013/05/08/business/
   how-much-hospitals-charge.html?ref=business&version=meter+at+8&
   region=FixedCenter&pgtype=Multimedia&priority=true&
   module=RegiWall-Regi&action=click
3. Breiman, L.: Classification and regression trees. Wadsworth International Group (1984)
4. Breiman, L.: Random forests. Journal of Machine Learning 45(1), 5–32 (2001)
5. Centers for Medicare and Medicaid Services: Medicare provider charge data. online (January 2014),
   http://www.cms.gov/Research-Statistics-Data-and-Systems/
   Statistics-Trends-and-Reports/Medicare-Provider-Charge-Data/index.html
6. Chernoff, H.: A measure of asymptotic efficiency for tests of a hypothesis based on the sum of observations. The Annals of Mathematical Statistics (1952)

7. Cichocki, A., Ishi Amari, S.: Families of alpha- beta- and gamma- divergences: Flexible and robust measures of similarities. Entropy (2010)
8. Cipriano, L.E., Steinberg, M.L., Gazelle, G.S., Gonzalez, R.G.: Comparing and predicting the costs and outcomes of patients with major and minor stroke using the boston acute stroke imaging scale neuroimaging classification system. American Journal of Neuroradiology 30, 703–709 (2009)
9. Csiszar, I.: Information-type measures of difference of probability distributions and indirect observation. Studia Scientiarum Mathematicarum Hungarica (1967)
10. Dietterich, T., Kearns, M., Mansour, Y.: Applying the weak learning framework to understand and improve c4.5. In: Proceedings of the Thirteenth International Conference on Machine Learning, pp. 96–104 (1996)
11. Diringer, M.N., Edwards, D.F., Mattson, T., Akins, P.T., Sheedy, C.W., Hsu, C.Y., Dromerick, A.W.: Predictors of acute hospital costs for treatment of ischemic stroke in an academic center. Stroke 30, 724–728 (1999)
12. Duda, R.O., Hart, P.E., Stork, D.G.: Pattern Classification. Wiley (2001)
13. Gawande, A.: The cost conundrum (June 2009),
    http://www.newyorker.com/reporting/2009/06/01/
    090601fa_fact_gawande?currentPage=1
14. Gelman, A., Hill, J.: Data Analysis using Regression and Multilevel/Hierarchical Models. Cambridge University Press (2007)
15. Goldstein, H.: Multilevel Statistical Models, 4th edn. Wiley (2010)
16. Jost, L.: Entropy and diversity. Oikos (2006)
17. Meier, B., McGinty, J.C., Creswell, J.: Hospital billing varies wildly, government data shows (May 2013),
    http://www.nytimes.com/2013/05/08/business/
    hospital-billing-varies-wildly-us-data-shows.html
18. Park, Y., Ghosh, J.: Compact ensemble trees for imbalanced data. In: Sansone, C., Kittler, J., Roli, F. (eds.) MCS 2011. LNCS, vol. 6713, pp. 86–95. Springer, Heidelberg (2011)
19. Park, Y., Ghosh, J.: Ensembles of α-Trees for Imbalanced Classification Problems. IEEE Transactions on Knowledge and Data Engineering 26(1), 131–143 (2014)
20. Quinlan, J.R.: C4.5: prgrams for machine learning. Morgan kaufmann (1993)
21. Renyi, A.: On measures of information and entropy. In: Proceedings of the Fourth Berkeley Symposium on Mathematics (1961)
22. Tsallis, C.: Possible generalization of boltzmann-gibbs statistics. Journal of Statistical Physics (1988)
23. Wang, J., Li, M., Hu, Y., Zhu, Y.: Comparison of hospital charge prediction models for gastric cancer patients: neural network vs. decision tree models. BMC Health Services Research 9 (2009)
24. Zhu, H., Rohwer, R.: Information geometric measurements of generalization. Tech. Rep. 4350, Aston University (1995)

Text Analysis and Information Extraction from Spanish Written Documents

Roberto Costumero[1], Ángel García-Pedrero[1], Consuelo Gonzalo-Martín[1],
Ernestina Menasalvas[1], and Socorro Millan[2]

[1] Universidad Politécnica de Madrid - Centro de Tecnología Biomédica,
Madrid, Spain
{roberto.costumero,consuelo.gonzalo,ernestina.menasalvas}@upm.es,
am.garcia@alumnos.upm.es
[2] Universidad del Valle, Colombia
marta.millan@correounivalle.edu.co

Abstract. Despite of the spread of Electronic Health Records (EHRs) in
Spanish hospitals and Spanish occupying the second place in the ranking
of number of speakers, to the best of our knowledge there are no natural
language processing tools for medical texts written in Spanish.

This paper presents an approach based on OpenNLP to process natural language texts written in Spanish for information extraction. The
main goal is to integrate our development with cTAKES. As cTAKES
has been specifically trained for the clinical domain, in this paper we will
train the main modules from a general purpose annotated Spanish corpus
and an in-house corpus developed with medical documents, testing both
on a set of medical documents. Best performance of individual components when tested with medical documents: Sentence boundary detector
accuracy = 0.872; Part-of-speech tagger accuracy = 0.946; chunker =
0.909.

Keywords: Natural Language Processing, Electronic Health Record,
Machine Learning.

1 Introduction

Despite of Spanish occupying the second place in the raking of number of speakers with more that 500 million speakers (according to [4]) as far as our knowledge there is no natural language tool for Spanish processing. In particular in
the health domain those tools exist for English but not for Spanish even though
the adoption of hospital Electronic Health Record (EHR) technology is currently
significantly growing and expected to grow. According to [1], back in 2009, Spain
was the second on EHR adoption, with roughly 60%, meanwhile it was projected
to have an adoption of 83% by 2013, with Nordic countries leading and US dou-
bling its adoption in the 2011-2013 period. Electronic Health Records contain
both structured and not structured information such as: the patient's medical
history, diagnoses, medications, treatment plans, immunization dates, allergies,

D. Ślęzak et al. (Eds.): BIH 2014, LNAI 8609, pp. 188–197, 2014.

radiology images, and laboratory and test results. This information is being collected and managed by a health care provider or organization. The access to textual information is crucial for clinical trials design, or patients retrieval by a certain criteria to name just a few.

Thus, in this paper we present a first approach towards integrating Spanish processing language capabilities in cTAKES [20]. In fact we start by adapting the sentence detector (SD), part-of-speech (PoS), and chunker modules of OpenNLP [16]. The paper contributions are as follows: i) modules for sentence detector, PoS, and chunker are trained with a general purpose and an Spanish corpus; ii) a set of Spanish medical related texts is manually annotated; iii) implementation of the OpenNLP modules (Sentence Detector, Part-of-speech, and Chunker) for Spanish are tested on the annotated texts.

The rest of the paper has been organized as follows: In section 2 a review of the tools for Natural Language Processing (NLP), specially in the medical domain, is done. The basic modules of OpenNLP in which our approach is based, the approach to train the models with Spanish texts, and the performance of the models are presented in section 3. To end with, section 4 presents the main conclusions obtained so far as well as the future lines of development.

2 Related Works

Patient medical records contain valuable clinical information expressed in narrative form. Meystre et al. in [15], analyze different uses of information extraction from textual documents in the EHR. According to them, this process implies a special challenge because, for instance, they contain telegraphic and shorthand phrases, abbreviations, acronyms and spelling errors.

The rapid and increasing growth of EHR or EMR (Electronic Medical Record) has generated a significant development in Medical Language Processing systems (MLP), Information Extraction techniques and applications [20], [15], [10], [27], [7], [8], [6], [9], [11], [3]. MLP systems have been contructed to analyze different types of medical reports (e.g. radiology, mammography, pathology, discharge summaries, biopsy).

To process radiology reports, a medical text processor is described in Friedman et al. [10]. Clinical documents are analyzed in order to transform them into terms belonging to a controlled vocabulary. In [7] the MedLEE system is presented. MedLEE was developed to extract structures and to encode clinical information from textual patient reports. The first version of MedLEE was evaluated in chest radiology reports. MedLEE was extended to work on mammography reports and discharge summaries [8], electrocardiography, echocardiography and pathology reports [9]. In [11], the performance of MedLEE using differents lexicons (LUMLS, M-CUR, M+UMLS) was evaluated.

Patient discharge summaries (PDS) are processed using MENELAS [27] to extract information from them. MENELAS can analyze reports in French, English and Dutch. cTAKES, a clinical Text Analysis and Knowledge Extraction System is introduced in [20]. cTAKES is an open-source NLP system that uses rule-based and machine learning techniques to process and extract information to support clinical research. The cTAKES components are sentence boundary detectors, tokenizers, normalizers, part-of-speech (PoS) taggers, shallow parsers and named entity recognition (NER) annotators. HITEx (Health Information Text Extraction) [13], an open-source application based on Gate framework, were developed to solve common problems in medical domains such as diagnoses extraction, discharge medications extraction and smoking status extraction. HITEx has been also used in [26] to extract the main diagnosis from a set of 150 discharge summaries. Co-morbidity and smoking status showed a positive performance.

MedTAS/P [3] is a system based on the open source framework that use NLP techniques, machine learning and rules to automatically map free-text pathology reports into concepts represented by CDKRM (Cancer Disease Knowledge Representation Model) for storing cancer characteristics and their relations. Fiszman et al. [6] introduce Sym Text, a NPL tool to extract relevant clinical information from radiology (Ventilation/Perfusion lung scan) reports. Sym Text was also evaluated on chest radiograph reports in order to establish if the expression "central venous catheter" is mentioned in the report [25]. To evaluate the use of current NLP techniques in an automatic knowledge acquisition domain, a system is introduced in Taboada et al. [21]. The system reuses OpenNLP, Stanford parsers, SemRep and UMLS NormalizeString service as building blocks, all of them open-source tools. Using an ontology, clinical practice guidelines documents are enriched. In Thomas et al., [24] a NLP program to identify patients with prostate cancer and to retrieve pathologic information from their EMR is evaluated. The results show that NLP can accurately do it.

To process clinical text in German, some systems have been developed [18], [12]. To parser summary sections of cytopathological findings reports an approach called Left-Associative Grammar (LAG) was used in MediTas [18], a Medical Text Analysis System for German. For the German SNOMED II version another parser is presented in [12] a NLP. The parser divide a medical term into fragments which might contain other SNOMED terms.

A multilevel annotated corpus for Catalan and Spanish known as AnCora (ANnotated CORporA) [14], [23], [2], [19], is available (http://clic.ub.edu/corpus/). It has almost half a million words ready to test NLP systems. The 3LB-CAT/ESP corpora [17], [22] was expanded and enriched with semantic information in order to generate AnCora.

3   Method

In the incoming sections we detail the process followed to train models that can be later used to extract information from medical Spanish texts. Our process trains models from OpenNLP [16] to extract information on medical texts. As there is no medical Spanish corpus we have used a general purpose AnCora [22] corpus as it is already annotated to train the models and later, a process of manually annotating medical texts has been followed so to be able to test and calculate the performance of the models. Firstly, we present the main components of OpenNLP; then we present the corpus used and finally the measures we will use to validate the trained models and their results.

3.1 Preliminaries

Apache OpenNLP [16] library supports the most common NLP tasks, such as tokenization, sentence segmentation, part-of-speech tagging, named entity extraction, chunking, parsing, and coreference resolution. These tasks are usually required to build more advanced text processing services. OpenNLP also includes maximum entropy and perceptron based machine learning. We describe below the components that we have trained in this paper:

- **Sentence detector:** The OpenNLP Sentence Detector can detect if a punctuation character marks the end of a sentence or not. In this sense a sentence is defined as the longest white space trimmed character sequence between two punctuation marks. The first and last sentence make an exception to this rule. The first non whitespace character is assumed to be the begin of a sentence, and the last non whitespace character is assumed to be a sentence end. Usually sentence detection is done before the text is tokenized.
- **Tokenizer:** The OpenNLP Tokenizers segment an input character sequence into tokens. Tokens are usually words, punctuation, numbers, etc.
- **Part-of-speech (PoS) tagger:** The Part of Speech Tagger marks tokens with their corresponding word type based on the token itself and the context of the token. A token might have multiple PoS tags depending on the kind of token and its context. The OpenNLP PoS Tagger uses a probability model to predict the correct PoS tag out of the tag set. To limit the possible tags for a token, a tag dictionary can be used which increases the tagging and runtime performance of the tagger.
- **Chunker:** Text chunking consists of dividing a text in syntactically correlated parts of words, like noun groups, verb groups, but does not specify their internal structure, nor their specific role in the main sentence.

3.2 Corpus

AnCora [22] consists of a Catalan corpus (AnCora-CA) and a Spanish corpus (AnCora-ES), each of them of 500,000 words (the Spanish version actually has 547,212 words, 17,375 sentences and 1,635 different documents). The corpus is annotated at different levels: i) Lemma and Part-of-speech, ii) Syntactic constituents and functions, iii) Argument structure and thematic roles, iv) Semantic classes of the verb, v) Denotative type of deverbal nouns, v) Nouns related to WordNet synsets, vi) Named Entities, vii) Coreference relations. AnCora corpus is mainly based on journalist texts.

Due to the lack of annotated resources for the clinical domain in Spanish, we have built our own gold standard dataset with linguistic annotations. The set is composed by 29 documents containing 745 sentences and 10,241 words, from which 2,259 words are unique.

Three different Computer Science experts assisted by a Physician and a Computational Linguistic expert performed the annotation task on the generated corpus. For this aim an in-house platform was generated to avoid errors in the annotation process. The annotation was done using the EAGLES [5] tags. To measure the quality of the in-house developed annotations, we report a method for inter-annotator agreement (IAA) similar to the one used in [20]. The method basically computes for those cases of disagreement in the annotation of a particular term the possible tags that have been assigned to that tag in any other sentences and then decides on the most frequent annotation.

3.3 Evaluation Metrics

Two kind of metrics have to be defined: on the one hand, the metrics to evaluate the performance of the training and testing models, and on the other hand, the parameters to run OpenNLP. In the first case, the standard metrics: precision, recall, accuracy, and F-Measure have been used [20].

The validation of all the models is done on the basis of a 10-fold cross-validation with 80/20 split as in [20] where 80% is used for training and 20% for testing.

On the other hand, OpenNLP requires to set the values for: i) *number of iterations* which is the number of times the training procedure should iterate when to find the best the model's parameters; ii) *cut-off* that is the number of times a feature must have been seen in order to be considered into the model.

3.4 Training the Models

The process that has been developed is depicted in figure 1. The process is composed of the following phases:

1. AnCora training models construction. In a first step models for the Sentence Detector, PoS and Chunker are obtained using the AnCora corpus. Note that the tokenizer is not trained as AnCora already provides tokens.
2. Manual annotation of the in-house corpus. A program for sentence detection is used to split the corpus into sentences. Starting from there, by means of a tools developed for this task three independent persons annotate the medical corpus. The tool makes it possible for annotators to correct the sentence detection, tag the PoS and perform the chunker annotation.
3. Medical corpus training models (from now on called in-house corpus). The set of documents annotated are splited into training and evaluation datasets. The training set will be used to train models with the same 10-fold cross-validation method used for the AnCora corpus.

Note that OpenNLP's Tokenizer is not trained. Instead, we have built a tokenizer in order to extract the tokens in the medical texts to annotate, in which

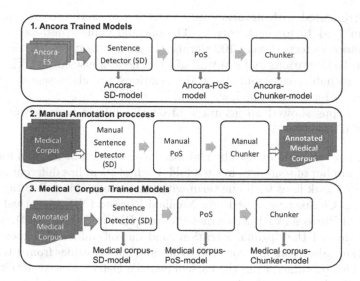

Fig. 1. Training the models

we have taken into account punctuation symbols, multiple spaces and line breaks
to determine the tokens.

In what follows we detail how the Sentence Detector, the PoS, and the Chunker
have been trained. An aggregated view of the results is found in table 1.

Sentence Boundary Detector. Experiments were conducted splitting the
training dataset into ten folds of an equivalent number of documents inside each
fold. In order to be trained by OpenNLP, each fold has its documents separated
by blank lines with one sentence per line.

We experimented with iteration values ranging from 100 to 600 and cut-off
values from 1 to 16 for each fold. The optimal values resulted to be 600 iterations
and a cut-off of 16 for the AnCora corpus, and 475 iterations and a cut-off of 7
for the in-house corpus (these corresponds to the values of iterations and cut-off
to which models generated have in average the highest F-Measure).

For these values, the best models obtained performed for AnCora corpus with
a precision of 0.948, a recall of 0.963 and a F-Measure of 0.955. For the in-house
corpus the performance values obtained are precision of 0.827, a recall of 0.714
and a F-Measure of 0.766.

The main source of errors in this particular component were due to headings
or sentences that did not use proper punctuation symbols, so the models were
not able to reproduce the sentences correctly.

Part-of-Speech Tagger. As in the Sentence Detector, the experiments were
conducted by splitting the training dataset into ten folds of an equivalent number
of documents inside each fold. The tokens used were generated using an in-house
developed platform to easily generate EAGLES [5] tags.

We experimented with iteration values ranging from 100 to 400 and cut-off values from 1 to 10 for each corpus. The optimal values (obtained as in the case of Sentece Detector) were 100 iterations and a cut-off of 2 for the AnCora corpus, and 100 iterations and a cut-off of 1 for the in-house corpus. The medical documents include great amounts of abbreviations and short sentences, so the cut-off value is intended to be low.

Ancora corpus showed an accuracy of 0.921 while in-house corpus got an accuracy of 0.774.

Chunker. For this component, the training dataset was split into ten folds of an equivalent number of sentences in each fold. Each of them has different sentences separated by blank lines with one term with the corresponding PoS tag and the Chunker tag. Chunker tags used are: Nominal Phrases (NP), Adjetival Phrases (AP), Verbal Phrases (VP), Adverbial Phrases (RP) and Others (O).

We determined the optimal iterations and cut-off values by experimenting with iteration values ranging from 100 to 400 and cut-off values from 1 to 10. The optimal values (obtained as in the case of Sentece Detector) were 100 iterations and a cut-off of 3 for the AnCora corpus, and 150 iterations and a cut-off of 3 for the in-house corpus.

The precision, recall an F-Measure for the Ancora corpus were 0.908, 0.907, and 0.907 respectively. In-house corpus performed with a precision of 0.852, a recall of 0.860, and a F-Measure of 0.856.

Table 1. General Precision, Recall, F-Measure and Accuracy values obtained

	AnCora	In-house corpus
Sentence Detector		
Precision	0.948	0.828
Recall	0.963	0.714
F-Measure	0.955	0.766
Part of Speech		
Accuracy	0.921	0.774
Chunker		
Precision	0.908	0.852
Recall	0.907	0.860
F-Measure	0.907	0.856

3.5 Comparison of the Models

Once the models have been generated, both with the manual annotated medical corpus and with the general purpose AnCora corpus, we compare the results. The main goal behind the experiment is to detect how models behave and to be able to analyze whether domain specific annotated corpus help to create new models ourperforming or not models generated with generic corpora.

Trained models are intended to be applied in the medical environment. This way, the comparison is done with the following process: i) From the ten models generated for the best iterations and cut-off values for each corpus in each component (Sentence Detector, PoS, and Chunker), the one with the best F-Measure and accuracy is the one selected to evaluate; ii) The medical texts that have not been used in the training of in-house corpus' selected model for each component are the ones used to evaluate both the AnCora and in-house corpus; iii) Results are gathered from the evaluation and can be observed in the table 2.

Table 2. Values comparison when evaluating the models with medical texts

	AnCora	In-house corpus
Sentence Detector		
Precision	0.904	0.904
Recall	0.842	0.842
F-Measure	0.872	0.872
Part of Speech		
Accuracy	0.946	0.836
Chunker		
Precision	0.904	0.891
Recall	0.914	0.894
F-Measure	0.909	0.893

Once the results have been analyzed, it can be seen that the training on the Sentence Detector is the same when the maximal values are obtained and the best model for those values is selected for evaluation, so the differences in the corpora are not significant for the delimitation of the phrases in a general corpus or a medical one for Spanish texts. The results for both corpora have obtained a precision of 0.904, a recall of 0.842 and a F-Measure of 0.872.

However, performance is more important when analyzing the Part of Speech and the Chunker, because of all the medical concepts and the huge differences in the way physicians write texts. AnCora corpus outperforms the in-house corpus on the Part of Speech, while both performed similarly in the Chunker. Accuracy for the AnCora corpus in the Part of Speech was 0.946, while in-house corpus performed 0.836. In the Chunker evaluation, the results are similar: the AnCora corpus showed a precision of 0.904, a recall of 0.914 and a F-Measure of 0.909. In-house corpus performed with a precision of 0.891, a recall of 0.894 and a F-measure of 0.893 for the same component.

4   Conclusions

This paper has presented a first approach towards integration of new Spanish Natural Language Processing models into cTAKES modules. Results presented have shown the performance of the models applied to a set of medical documents. These results show so far that general purpose corpora with hundreds of thousands of terms outperform specific domain corpora in Spanish texts, but particularly trained models can perform similarly. Note that these results comply with the results presented in [20]. Future work on building a bigger in-house corpus and comparing with other general purpose corpora will be done, together with the integration of these models into cTAKES.

References

1. Accenture: Overview of international emr/ehr markets (2010),
   http://www.accenture.com/SiteCollectionDocuments/PDF/
   Accenture_EMR_Markets_Whitepaper_vfinal.pdf
2. Aparicio, J., Taulé, M., Martí, M.A.: Ancora-verb: A lexical resource for the semantic annotation of corpora. In: LREC (2008)
3. Coden, A., Savova, G.K., Sominsky, I.L., Tanenblatt, M.A., Masanz, J.J., Schuler, K., Cooper, J.W., Guan, W., de Groen, P.C.: Automatically extracting cancer disease characteristics from pathology reports into a disease knowledge representation model. Journal of Biomedical Informatics 42(5), 937–949 (2009),
   http://dblp.uni-trier.de/db/journals/jbi/jbi42.html#CodenSSTMSCGG09
4. de la Concha, V.G., Salamanca, R.R.P., Prados, L., Fernández, F.M., Iglesias, M., Vítores, D.F., Rivilla, R.G.: El español: Una lengua viva
5. EAGLES Computational Lexicons Working Group: Preliminary recommendations on semantic encoding. Tech. rep., EAGLES (1996),
   http://www.ilc.pi.cnr.it/EAGLES96/rep2/
6. Fiszman, M., Haug, P., Frederick, P.: Automatic extraction of pioped interpretations from ventilation/perfusion lung scan reports. In: Proceedings of the AMIA Symposium, pp. 860–864 (1998)
7. Friedman, C., Hripcsak, G., DuMouchel, W., Johnson, S., Clayton, P.: Natural language processing in an operational clinical information system. Natural Language Engineering 1(1), 83–108 (1995),
   http://journals.cambridge.org/action/
   displayAbstract?fromPage=online&aid=1313068
8. Friedman, C.: Towards a comprehensive medical language processing system: methods and issues. In: Proceedings of the AMIA Annual Fall Symposium, p. 595. American Medical Informatics Association (1997)
9. Friedman, C.: A broad-coverage natural language processing system. In: Proceedings of the AMIA Symposium, p. 270. American Medical Informatics Association (2000)
10. Friedman, C., Alderson, P.O., Austin, J.H., Cimino, J.J., Johnson, S.B.: A general natural-language text processor for clinical radiology. Journal of the American Medical Informatics Association 1(2), 161–174 (1994)
11. Friedman, C., Liu, H., Shagina, L., Johnson, S., Hripcsak, G.: Evaluating the umls as a source of lexical knowledge for medical language processing. In: Proceedings of the AMIA Symposium, p. 189. American Medical Informatics Association (2001)
12. Hohnloser, J.H., Holzer, M., Fischer, M.R., Ingenerf, J., Günther-Sutherland, A.: Natural language processing and automatic snomed-encoding of free text: An analysis of free text data from a routine electronic patient record application with a parsing tool using the german snomed ii. In: Proceedings of the AMIA Annual Fall Symposium, p. 856. American Medical Informatics Association (1996)
13. i2b2: Health information text extraction,
   https://www.i2b2.org/software/projects/hitex/hitex_manual.html

14. Martí, M.A., Taulé, M., Bertran, M., Màrquez, L.: Ancora: Multilingual and multilevel annotated corpora (2007), http://clic.ub.edu/corpus/webfm_send/13
15. Meystre, S.M., Savova, G.K., Kipper-Schuler, K.C., Hurdle, J.F.: Extracting information from textual documents in the electronic health record: A review of recent research. IMIA Yearbook 2008: Access to Health Information 2008(1), 128–144 (2008),
    http://www.schattauer.de/en/magazine/subject-areas/journals-a-z/imia-yearbook/imia-yearbook-2008/issue/special/manuscript/9830/show.html
16. Apache OpenNLP: Apache software foundation (2011),
    http://opennlp.apache.org
17. Palomar, M., Civit, M., Díaz, A., Moreno, L., Bisbal, E., Aranzabe, M.J., Ageno, A., Martí, M.A., Navarro, B.: 3lb: Construcción de una base de datos de árboles sintáctico-semánticos para el catalán, euskera y castellano. Procesamiento del Lenguaje Natural 33 (2004),
    http://dblp.uni-trier.de/db/journals/pdln/
    pdln33.html#PalomarCDMBAAMNO4
18. Pietrzyk, P.: A medical text analysis system for german–syntax analysis. Methods of Information in Medicine 30(4), 275–283 (1991)
19. Recasens, M., Martí, M.A.: Ancora-co: Coreferentially annotated corpora for spanish and catalan. Language Resources and Evaluation 44(4), 315–345 (2010)
20. Savova, G.K., Masanz, J.J., Ogren, P.V., Zheng, J., Sohn, S., Kipper-Schuler, K.C., Chute, C.G.: Mayo clinical text analysis and knowledge extraction system (ctakes): architecture, component evaluation and applications. Journal of the American Medical Informatics Association 17(5), 507–513 (2010)
21. Taboada, M., Meizoso, M., Hernández, D.M., Riaño, D., Alonso, A.: Combining open-source natural language processing tools to parse clinical practice guidelines. Expert Systems 30(1), 3–11 (2013),
    http://dblp.uni-trier.de/db/journals/es/es30.html#TaboadaMHRA13
22. Taulé, M., Civit, M., Artigas, N., García, M., Màrquez, L., Martí, M.A., Navarro, B.: Minicors and cast3lb: Two semantically tagged spanish corpora. In: LREC. European Language Resources Association (2004),
    http://dblp.uni-trier.de/db/conf/lrec/lrec2004.html#TauleCAGMMNO4
23. Taulé, M., Martí, M.A., Recasens, M.: Ancora: Multilevel annotated corpora for catalan and spanish. In: LREC. European Language Resources Association (2008),
    http://dblp.uni-trier.de/db/conf/lrec/lrec2008.html#TauleMR08
24. Thomas, A.A., Zheng, C., Jung, H., Chang, A., Kim, B., Gelfond, J., Slezak, J., Porter, K., Jacobsen, S.J., Chien, G.W.: Extracting data from electronic medical records: validation of a natural language processing program to assess prostate biopsy results. World Journal of Urology 32(1), 99–103 (2014)
25. Trick, W.E., Chapman, W.W., Wisniewski, M.F., Peterson, B.J., Solomon, S.L., Weinstein, R.A.: Electronic interpretation of chest radiograph reports to detect central venous catheters. Infection Control and Hospital Epidemiology 24(12), 950–954 (2003)
26. Zeng, Q.T., Goryachev, S., Weiss, S., Sordo, M., Murphy, S.N., Lazarus, R.: Extracting principal diagnosis, co-morbidity and smoking status for asthma research: evaluation of a natural language processing system. BMC Medical Informatics and Decision Making 6(1), 30 (2006)
27. Zweigenbaum, P.: Menelas: an access system for medical records using natural language. Computer Methods and Programs in Biomedicine 45(1), 117–120 (1994)

Data-Brain Driven Documents Ranking
for Constructing Brain Informatics Provenances

Han Zhong[1], Jianhui Chen[2], Jian Han[1], and Ning Zhong[1,3,4]

[1] International WIC Institute, Beijing University of Technology
Beijing 100024, China
[2] Department of Computer Science and Technology, Tsinghua University
Beijing 100084, China
[3] Beijing Key Laboratory of MRI and Brain Informatics, Beijing, China
[4] Department of Life Science and Informatics, Maebashi Institute of Technology
Maebashi-City 371-0816, Japan
{z.h0912,hanjian0204}@emails.bjut.edu.cn, chenjhnh@mail.tsinghua.edu.cn,
zhong@maebashi-it.ac.jp

Abstract. The documents selection related brain information based on the data-brain ontology not only has an important significance in the promotion of data-brain ontology, but also lays the foundation for knowledge integration. However, traditional research of documents selection focuses on the concept, and cannot meet the requirement of the systematic Brain Informatics study. This paper analyzes the characteristics of source knowledge firstly with concepts, attributes and relations. Then, we calculate the weight of documents by using the improved method of VSM. Finally, the experiments using real documents associated with brain science are given and calculating the weight of each document achieves a better effect of ranking selection.

1 Introduction

Brain Informatics (BI) is an interdisciplinary field among computing science, cognitive science and neuroscience [11]. A systematic BI methodology includes four issues: systematic investigations for complex brain science problems, systematic experimental design, systematic data management and systematic data analysis/simulation [3] [12]. Meanwhile, systematic brain data management is a core issue of the systematic BI methodology, which effectively integrates multimode and closely-related brain big data for meeting various requirements coming from different aspects of the systematic BI study.

BI needs a Data-Brain to describe heterogeneous brain data and represents various relationships among multiple human brain data sources. On one hand, data-brain can provide a brain data knowledge framework based on the BI methodology to integrate various brain-data related domain ontology. On the other hand, obtaining the brain-data conceptual model from the data-brain provides machine-readable data description and guides relevant information collection. The data, information and knowledge are integrated together based on the

D. Ślęzak et al. (Eds.): BIH 2014, LNAI 8609, pp. 198–207, 2014.

model of methodology, which explicitly carries out systematic brain-data management, with respect to all major aspects and capabilities of human information processing systems (HIPS).

The Data-Brain is a domain-driven conceptual model of brain data, which represents multi-aspect relationships among multiple human brain data sources, with respect to all major aspects and capabilities of HIPS, for systematic investigation and understanding of human intelligence [3] [4].

Systematic investigations and systematic experimental design have resulted in a brain big data, including various primitive brain data, brain data related information, such as extracted data characteristics, related domain knowledge, *etc.*, which come from different research groups and include multi-aspect and multi-level relationships among various brain data sources [7]. It is necessary to realize systematic brain data management whose key problem is to effectively integrate multi-mode and closely-related brain big data for meeting various requirements coming from different aspects of the systematic BI study [12]. Brain informatics provenances provide a practical approach to realize the information-level (i.e. metadata-level) integration of brain big data. However, no matter what way, it needs to select brain informatics sources from a large amount of documents to meet the needs of systematic brain data management. How to determine which documents include the brain informatics sources? This is a question connecting the documents with required sources. In the final analysis, we need to find the required documents, that is to say, it is the question of documents ranking selection.

In order to solve the problem of documents ranking, as early as in 1997, Lee proposed the method of vector space model [9] and Egghe et al. proposed completing documents ranking using the fuzzy sets [6], which only consider the proportion of terms instead of the location of terms in the document. In 2001, Danilowicz et al. proposed the method based on Markov chain [5], discussing related documents ranking selection and considering the frequency or location of key words in the document. In 2007, Xing Jun et al. calculated the weights for document ranking through the method of ontology relation distance and neural network [10]. This paper analyzes the characteristics of concepts, attributes and relations of brain informatics sources based on the data-brain ontology and the weight of attributes is adopted to calculate the weight of a document for selecting sources.

In this paper we put forward a research on Brain Informatics provenances selection for the Data-Brain ontology. The remainder of this paper is organized as follows. Section 2 discusses the characteristics analysis of BI provenances. Section 3 describes the determination of the document level. Section 4 provides experimental analysis and results. Finally, Section 5 gives concluding remarks.

2   The Characteristics Analysis of BI Provenances

In brain science, the metadata describing the origin and subsequent processing of biological images is often referred to as "provenance". They are the metadata, which describe the origin and subsequent processing of various human brain data in the systematic BI study. As stated in our previous studies, BI provenances can be divided into data provenances and analysis provenances [12]. Data provenances describe the brain data origin by multi-aspect experiment information, including subject information, how experimental data were collected, and what instrument was used; etc. Analysis provenances describe what processing in a brain dataset has been carried out, including what analytic tasks were performed, what experimental data were used, what data features were extracted, and so on. Here, the acquisition of BI provenances is mainly related to the recognition of concepts, attributes and relations and the characteristics of BI provenances can be introduced as follows.

2.1   The Characteristics of Concepts

In order to effectively select concepts of BI sources, we need to solve the following problems. What are the characteristics of concepts? How to select them in the document?

Definition 1. Concepts, *they are key terms, which usually describe related equipments, operations, analysis and analytical results.*

The BI study can be mainly divided into two stages, experimental stage and analysis period. Each stage includes some key concepts. For example, it contains experimental tasks, experimental materials, experimental methods and so on in the experimental stage. Moreover, it contains analytical tasks, analytical tools, data feature, activations and so on in the analysis period. Here, there are some concepts which are commonly used but are not possible in the literatures. Hence, concepts can be divided into the abstract concepts and the informational concepts.

Definition 2. Abstract Concepts, *there are some real knowledge which cannot be used to reflect the terms in the experimental stage and analysis period. For example, Experimental-Group and Analytical-Process are the abstract concepts.*

Definition 3. Informational Concepts, *there are some real knowledge which can be used to reflect the terms in the experimental stage and analysis period. For example, Experimental-Task, Operator, Analytical-Tool, and so on are the informational concepts.*

2.2   The Characteristics of Attributes

There are some characteristics of attributes among BI sources in addition to some key concepts. So, we need to introduce the characteristics of attributes in order to increase the amount of data.

Definition 4. Attributes, *there are terms which describe detailed information of informational concepts among the experimental process and analytical process. For example, there are detailed information which describes that experimental-tasks contain the task-name, the designer, whether or not to press the key, the* *sensitive channel, the task-content, task-number, task-type and types-of-stimuli-presentation.*

2.3   The Characteristics of Relations

There are some characteristics of relations among BI sources in addition to some key concepts, attributes. So, we need to introduce the characteristics of relations in order to understand the meanings of BI sources.

Definition 5. Relations, *they are defined as the relationship between the concepts if two concepts appear at the same paragraph among BI sources. For example, the relationship between the Experiment and Brain-Data is this relation called has-result-data, which describes these two concepts that are Experiment and Brain-Data.*

3   The Determination of Documents' Level

In order to select the BI sources and understand the characteristics of BI sources, the documents' level is determined by the characteristics of BI sources. How to choose the documents is decided by the concepts, attributes, relations contained in the documents because the number of documents is an important problem. In a document, we use the weight of concepts, attributes and relations to evaluate the importance of this document. Hence, we adopt the VSM method combined with the characteristics of the BI sources to fix the weight of a document. Finally, the level of documents is decided through fixing the weight of documents.

3.1   The Weight of Concepts

The number of concepts in a document and the location appeared in the Data-Brain are considered to compute the weight of concepts. Meanwhile, the traditional VSM method combined with the characteristics of BI sources is improved to calculate the weight of concepts. In order to understand the location of concepts in a document, the definitions are introduced as follows:

Definition 7. The First of Text, *generally, the sum of introduction, background and related work is made into the first of text.*

Definition 8. The Tail of Text, *generally, the sum of conclusion and references is made into the tail of text.*

Definition 9. The Middle of Text, *generally, the rest of a document removing the first of text and the tail of text is the middle of text.*

The value of concepts is considered by the location and frequency in a document because concepts mainly concentrated in the text. Thus, we set the correlation coefficient of emergence position for m_1, m_2, m_3, representing the concepts that appear in the first of text, the middle of text and the tail of text and $m_1 + m_2 + m_3 = 1$. Generally, because the first of text is the background and related work, and the tail of text is the conclusion and references, the probability of appearing in above two parts is small relatively. Hence, set the correlation coefficient for $m_1=m_3=0.4$. The probability of concepts appearing in the middle of text is too large, so set the correlation coefficients in this area for $m_2=0.2$ [2]. Hence, the weight of concepts in a document is:

$$W_{d,c} = 1 + \ln(m_1 f_{1d,c} + m_2 f_{2d,c} + m_3 f_{3d,c}) \tag{1}$$

In this formula, $m_1 f_{1d,c}$, $m_2 f_{2d,c}$, $m_3 f_{3d,c}$ are the frequency of concepts that appear in the first of text, the middle of text and the tail of text. The weight of a document is shown as follows:

$$W_d^c = (1 - \alpha) + \alpha \frac{\sqrt{\sum_{c \in d} W_{d,c}^2}}{aver(\sqrt{\sum_{c \in d} W_{d,c}^2})} \tag{2}$$

Here, α is the slope and is usually 0.7. $aver(\sqrt{\sum_{c \in d} W_{d,c}^2})$ is the average number of documents [1]. It is very important to calculate the weight of a document according to concepts. By using the improved VSM method combined with the proportions of concepts in the Data-Brain, the weight of a document is computed. In the process of obtaining BI sources, the importance of concepts laid the foundation for the selection work.

3.2   The Weight of Attributes

The number of attributes in a document and the location appeared in the Data-Brain are considered to compute the weight of attributes. Meanwhile, the characteristics of concepts combined with the characteristics of BI sources are improved to calculate the weight of attributes. Generally, attributes belong to the concepts and we consider that attributes after concepts appeared in a document. Therefore, we set two coefficients. One is the coefficient of the weight of concepts, which is the proportion of total number of concepts. The other is the coefficient of the weight of attributes, which is the proportion of attributes in the total concepts. Therefore, put a document with symbol d and the attributes are represented by symbol a, then the weight of a in the d is:

$$W_{d,a} = q_c \cdot f_{d,a} \cdot q_a \tag{3}$$

In this formula, q_c is the coefficient of the weight of concepts and $q_c = \frac{c}{\sum_{i=1}^{n} c_i}$ (n is the number of concepts), q_a is the coefficient of the weight of attributes and $q_a = \frac{a}{\sum_{i=1, a \in c}^{m} a_i}$ (m is the number of attributes)

$$f_{d,a} = \begin{cases} 1, & if\ the\ attribute\ appears \\ 0, & otherwise \end{cases}$$

then, adopting (2) to calculate the weight of a document.

It is very important to calculate the weight of a document according to the attributes. The characteristics of attributes combined with the characteristics of BI sources are improved to calculate the weight of attributes. In the process of obtaining the BI sources, the attributes are very important for the selection work and calculating the weight of attributes greatly improves the accuracy of documents' weights.

3.3   The Weight of Relations

The relationship is the description between concepts based on the data-brain ontology and it is considered that we calculate the weights if the relationship between two concepts is in the same paragraph. There are many relationships between concepts among the BI sources and they are related as long as these two concepts appear in the same paragraph. There are two factors influencing the weight of relationships, one is the location which appeared in a document, and the other is the proportion of relations in the Data-Brain. The location of relations in a document refers to appearing in the same sentence, different sentences or a paragraph and different positions have different weights. Meanwhile, the proportion of relations in the Data-Brain also affects the weight of a document. In order to understand the location of relations in a document, the definitions are shown as follows:

Definition 10. The Distance d of Concepts, *two related concepts in a document appeared in the same sentence, different sentences and in the same paragraph with different relative weights, named d_1, d_2, d_3, and $d_1 > d_2 > d_3$.*
    The relation between concepts is r, the weight of relation is:

$$W_{d,r} = 1 + l \cdot \ln(d_1 f_{1d,r} + d_2 f_{2d,r} + d_3 f_{3d,r}) \qquad (4)$$

In this formula, $d_1 f_{1d,r}$, $d_2 f_{2d,r}$, $d_3 f_{3d,r}$ are the frequency of relation that appears in the same sentence, different sentences and in the same paragraph. l is the weight of relation in the data-brain. How to decide the weight of relations in the data-brain is a difficulty. The definition of [14] is more suitable and is shown as follows:

Definition 11. m or n is a concept, the relation between m and n is, *relation$(m,n) = \frac{1}{w+1}$ if m and n have indirect correlation through the number of w concepts;*
relation$(m,n) = 1$ if m and n have direct correlation.
    Then, we adopt (2) to calculate the weight of relations and calculate the weight of a document according to the relationship between concepts and the proportion in the data-brain ontology.

3.4   The Determination of Priority among the Documents

The determination of priority among the documents is fixed by the weight of concepts, attributes and relations from above analysis and is obtained by linear relationship. The weight of a document is: $W_d = oW_d^c + pW_d^a + qW_d^r$, the o, p, q is a constant respectively, $o+p+q=1$, W_d^c, W_d^a, W_d^r is the weight of concepts, attributes and relations respectively.

The determination of priority among the documents is obtained by the weight of concepts, attributes and relations. And the selection of BI sources meets the needs of the systematic brain-data management and realizes the document ranking.

4   Experimental Analysis and Results

The concepts, attributes and relations are identified in a document based on the data-brain ontology in order to verify above methods to select documents, including 15 concepts and 90 attributes, as shown in Figure 1. We recognize the concepts from the first, the middle, the tail of text based on the most manual rules and a few dictionary rules. The attributes such as the number of experimental-task, the type of stimulus-presentation are identified according to the knowledge of named entity recognition. There are relationships and statistics if two concepts appeared in the same paragraph.

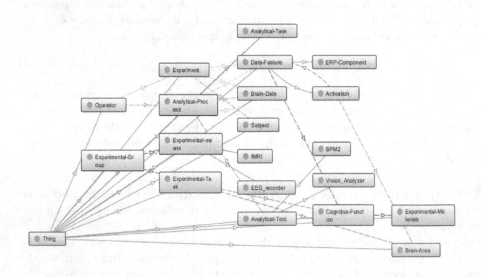

Fig. 1. The ontology of the data-brain

The description algorithm of experimental process is shown as Table 1:

Table 1. The description algorithm of experimental process

Algorithm 1 The Description of Experimental Process
Input: sample set S of literatures, the number n of paragraphs, the number m of sentences
Output: the weight of the document of S
1. For i in S
2. Extracting the information of paragraph of literature I;   3. Recognizing the first, the middle, the tail of the text;   4. End for   5. For j=1 to n
6. Recognizing concepts, counting the number of concepts, calculating the weight of concepts;
7. Recognizing attributes, counting the number of attributes, calculating the weight of attributes;
8. For k=1 to m
9. Recognizing relations, counting the number of relations, calculating the weight of relations;   10. Calculating the weight of documents;   11. End for

This paper mainly uses the data set which are real documents associated with the field of BI. Moreover, we download some literatures from the MEDLINE/PubMed, testing 50 documents and generating the weight of documents [8]. The weight of documents is shown as Table 2. At the same time, we calculate the weight of concepts, attributes, relations and the weight of documents, seeing as the second, third, fourth, fifth column in Table 2. Meanwhile, we design a questionnaire of experts which is composed of ten categories problems and has 100 the total score based on the BI provenance model to verify the correctness of the weight [13]. Then the experts judge the documents and the result is shown as the sixth column in Table 2. At last, we can see the order of documents is consistent using this method compared with the judge of experts. From above analysis, we can see that the method of selecting the required documents is effective.

Table 2. The comparison between the value of a document and experts' decision

The number (1)	The weight of concepts (2)	The weight of attributes (3)	The weight of relations (4)	The weight of a document (5)	Experts' decision (6)
1	3.01106	0.35807	0.55999	1.21454	61
2	2.15205	0.35807	0.51717	0.98745	59
3	2.01465	0.35289	0.15722	0.79273	57.5
4	2.15201	0.35444	1.51244	1.24111	61.5
5	1.86524	0.33370	0.51480	0.84749	58
6	1.51244	0.32022	0.66202	0.78043	57
7	0.64242	0.30104	0.30000	0.40315	51
8	1.86525	0.32852	1.28995	1.07798	60
9	1.70000	0.30207	0.83827	0.88231	58.5
50	1.28995	0.30830	0.66202	0.70891	56.5

5   Conclusions

Research on BI provenances selection for the Data-Brain ontology is a new project. This paper proposes a selection method based on the data-brain ontology through the analysis of characteristics and experimental results show that this method is effective. It is also the key technology of selecting BI sources. Furthermore, the obtained documents can be used to support sources-selection, provenances mining, the process planning of systematic brain data analysis; etc. All of these will be studied in our next work.

Acknowledgements. The work is supported by National Key Basic Research Program of China (2014CB744605), China Postdoctoral Science Foundation (2013M540096), International Science & Technology Cooperation Program of China (2013DFA32180), National Natural Science Foundation of China (61272345), Research Supported by the CAS/SAFEA International Partnership Program for Creative Research Teams, the Japan Society for the Promotion of Science Grants-in-Aid for Scientific Research (25330270).

References

1. Vo Ngoc, A., de Kretser, O., Moffat, A.: Vector-space Ranking with Effective Early Termination. In: Proceedings of ACM Sigir Forum, pp. 35–42. ACM Press, New York (2001)
2. Atsushi, M.: Effect of Relationships between Words on Japanese Information Retrieval. ACM Transactions on Asian Language Information Processing 5(3), 264–289 (2006)
3. Chen, J.H., Zhong, N.: Data-Brain Modeling Based on Brain Informatics Methodology. In: Proceedings of the 2008 IEEE/WIC/ACM International Conference on Web Intelligence, WI 2008, pp. 41–47. IEEE Computer Society, Sydney (2008)
4. Chen, J.H., Zhong, N.: Data-Brain Modeling for Systematic Brain Informatics. In: Zhong, N., Li, K., Lu, S., Chen, L. (eds.) BI 2009. LNCS, vol. 5819, pp. 182–193. Springer, Heidelberg (2009)
5. Danilowicz, C., Balinski, J.: Document Ranking based upon Markov Chains. Inf. Proc. and Manage. 37(4), 623–637 (2001)
6. Egghe, L., Michel, C.: Construction of Weak and Strong Similarity Measures for Ordered Sets of Documents Using Fuzzy Set Techniques. Inf. Proc. and Manage. 39(5), 771–807 (2003)
7. Howe, D., Costanzo, M., Fey, P., Gojobori, T., Hannick, L., Hide, W., Hill, D.P., Kania, R., Schaeffer, M., St Pierre, S., Twigger, S., White, O., Rhee, S.Y.: Big Data: The Future of Biocuration. Nature 455(7209), 47–50 (2008)
8. http://pubmed.gov/
9. Lee, D.L., Chuang, H., Seamons, K.: Document Ranking and The Vector-space Model. Software IEEE 14(2), 67–75 (1997)
10. Xing, J., Han, M., Zhou, K.P.: Research and Implementation of Ontic Information Source Selection. Journal of Dalian University of Technology 47(4), 598–604 (2007)
11. Zhong, N., Bradshaw, J.M., Liu, J., Taylor, J.G.: Brain Informatics. IEEE Intelligent Systems Special Issue on Brain Informatics 26(5), 16–21 (2011)

12. Zhong, N., Chen, J.H.: Constructing a New-style Conceptual Model of Brain Data for Systematic Brain Informatics. IEEE Transactions on Knowledge and Data Engineering 24(12), 2127–2142 (2011)
13. Zhong, H., Chen, J., Kotake, T., Han, J., Zhong, N., Huang, Z.: Developing a Brain Informatics Provenance Model. In: Imamura, K., Usui, S., Shirao, T., Kasamatsu, T., Schwabe, L., Zhong, N. (eds.) BHI 2013. LNCS, vol. 8211, pp. 439–449. Springer, Heidelberg (2013)
14. Zhu, L.J.: Research of Information Resource Management Model Based on Domain Knowledge in the Web Environment. China Agricultural University (2004)

A Brain Informatics Research Recommendation System

Jian Han[1], Jianhui Chen[2], Han Zhong[1], and Ning Zhong[1,3,4]

[1] International WIC Institute, Beijing University of Technology
Beijing 100024, China
[2] Department of Computer Science and Technology, Tsinghua University,
Beijing 100084, China
[3] Beijing Key Laboratory of MRI and Brain Informatics, Beijing, China
[4] Department of Life Science and Informatics, Maebashi Institute of Technology
Maebashi-City 371-0816, Japan
{hanjian0204,z.h0912}@emails.bjut.edu.cn,
chenjhnh@mail.tsinghua.edu.cn, zhong@maebashi-it.ac.jp

Abstract. Finding and learning related research is a necessary work in Brain Informatics studies. However, the keyword-based search on brain and mental big data center often brings a large amount of unnecessary results. It is very difficult to find needed research from those results for researchers. This paper proposes a Brain Informatics research recommendation system based on the Data-Brain and BI provenances. By choosing interest aspects from the Data-Brain and applying the unification of search and reasoning based on Data-Brain interests, the more accurate search can be realized to find really related literatures for supporting systematic Brain Informatics studies.

1 Introduction

Brain informatics (BI) is an interdiscipline of computer science, cognitive science and neuroscience, and it proceeds to a systematic study from the macro and micro perspectives on human information processing mechanism [9,10]. The systematic BI methodology includes four aspects: systematic investigation for complex brain science problems, systematic design of cognitive experiments, systematic brain data management and systematic brain data analysis/simulation [1,11]. Such a systematic study involves with various experimental design methods and analytical methods. The researchers often need to search a large amount of literatures, which are closely related to their studies, for comprehending the experimental design methods and analytical methods.

A brain and mental big data center has been developed to support the systematic research of Brain Informatics. The researchers can search related study on this system based on Data-Brain and BI provenances. However, the keyword-search often brings a lot of unnecessary results. In current, the brain and mental big data center stores 98 literatures. After submitting the word "Induction" on the system to find research about the human cognitive function "Induction", the

D. Ślęzak et al. (Eds.): BIH 2014, LNAI 8609, pp. 208–217, 2014.

number of results is 36. This is a very large proportion. When this system collects a large amount of data, It will be a serious problem to researchers. Researchers have to take a long time to find their really needed research. Like on PubMed, after submitting the word "Induction" on it to find literatures about the human cognitive function "reasoning", the number of results is 435269. Therefore, this paper proposes a Brain Informatics research recommendation system.Four element classes are selected from the Data-Brain to acquire the uses' interests. Then, a more accurate search are realized by applying the unification of search and reasoning based on the obtained interests.

The remainder of this paper is organized as follows. Session 2 gives the discussion of background and related work. a more accurate search are realized by applying the unification of search and reasoning based on the obtained interests. Based on the preparations, Session 5 proposes a research interests based strategy for refining the literature query. Furthermore, a case study is provided in Session 6 to introduce the experiments and the results. Finally, Section 7 gives concluding remarks.

2   Background and Related Work

2.1 The Data-Brain and BI Provenances

In order to support systematic BI studies, the Data-Brain has been proposed to represent functional relationships among multiple human brain data sources, with respect to all major aspects and capabilities of human information processing system [1,2]. It is domain driven and can be constructed by a BI methodology based approach [1,2]. In our previous studies, a prototype of the Data-Brain has been constructed by using the Web Ontology Language(OWL).

BI provenances are the metadata describing the origin and subsequent processing of various human brain data in the systematic BI study [4]. It includes data provenances and analysis provenances. The BI data provenances focus on the origin of BI data and involves with multi-aspect experimental information, including subject, experimental processes, measuring equipments, etc. In our previous studies, a Data-Brain based approach has been developed to construct BI provenances. By this approach, multi-aspect experimental information can be extracted from literatures and stored into the BI data provenances by using the Resource Description Framework (RDF). These BI data provenances become a kind of new metadata about literatures which can describe researches more detail than tiles of literatures.

2.2 The Interests-Based Unification of Search and Reasoning

In the past few years, we have developed the interests-based unification of search and reasoning (I-ReaSearch) [5], which has a deeper analysis on the interests comparing with additional research service systems. This method treats the keywords of literature titles as interests. However, those title-based interests cannot precisely express the BI research interests because titles are too simple to describe the whole studies.

By extending the I-reaSearch method, we develop a research recommendation system based on the Data-Brain and BI provenances. We define interest aspects based on the Data-Brain and acquire users' research interests from BI provenances. By using these research interests and the I-reaSearch method, the BI research recommendation system can provide a more accurate literature search. From the data-brain and the BI provenances of literatures, we can precisely express the interests of brain informatics researchers, and we can accurately express the main content of literatures.

3   The Brain Informatics Interest

Adding users' interests into the literature search can effectively improve the accuracy of results. Because the users' current research interests have a close relationship with his past research interests. they can be obtained based on users' published literatures.

In our previous studies [5], keywords of literature titles were treated as interests. However, as stated above, BI data provenances are the metadata of literatures which can describe researches more detail than tiles of literatures. Hence, they are better information sources for defining users' research interests than titles of literatures. Based on the Data-Brain and BI provenances, new definitions about research interests can be given as follows.

*An **Interest aspect**, denoted by $e(k)$, is a hierarchy of concepts in the Data-Brain, which describes a kind of focuses in systematic BI experiments.*

*An **Interest**, denoted by $t_{e(k)}$ (i), is a concept in the interest aspect $e(k)$, which describes a focus in systematic BI experiments.*

Owing to the BI methodology based modeling approach, the Data-Brain includes four dimension, the function dimension,the experiment dimension, the data dimension and the analysis dimension, corresponding to the four aspects of BI methodology, respectively. Each dimension includes a or several sub-dimensions which describe different sub-aspects of systematic BI studies. According to the definitions about dimensions of the Data-Brain, the experiment dimension binding the function dimension is used to describe systematic design of cognitive experiments. Hence, for developing this BI research recommendation system, users' research interests should be selected from the sub-dimensions in the experiment dimension and the function dimension, including Cognitive Function, Device Type, Perceptional Channel and Subject Type [3,12].

Cognitive function is a sub-dimension of function dimension in the Data-Brain. It includes multiple subclasses, such as Attention, computation, Reasoning. It is an important research content of BI. Different cognitive functions result to different experimental designs and different analytical methods. Therefore, the cognitive function is chosen as an interest aspect for defining similar researches in the BI research recommendation system.

Device type is a sub-dimension of experiment dimension in the Data-Brain. It contains multiple subclasses, for example, fMRI, ERP, Eye-Movement. It is an important factor in BI studies and affects the experimental design and the choice of analytical methods. Therefore, the device type is an indispensable interest aspect for defining similar researches in the BI research recommendation system.

Perceptional channel is a sub-dimension of experiment dimension in the Data-Brain. It includes Visual, Auditory and other subclasses. Different perceptional channels need different experimental designs and analytical methods. Therefore, researchers must consider the perceptional channel when they search the similar researches. It is also chosen as an interest aspect.

Subject type is a sub-dimension of experiment dimension in the Data-Brain. It contains Normal-Subject, Patient-Subject and College-Student, etc. It is also an important influence factor for the design of experiments and analysis. Therefore, the BI research recommendation system takes the subject type as an interest aspect.

4   Measuring Research Interests

In this section, a series of formulas stated in [5] will be refined to quantize the research interests for the BI research recommendation system. Let i, j, k be positive integers $(i, j \in I^{\,|})$, $y_{t_{e(k)}}(i), j$ be the number of literatures in BI data provenances that involved in interest $t_{e(k)}(i)$ during the time interval j.

Cumulative interest[7], defined as $CI\left(t_{e(k)}(i), n\right)$, is the sum of appearing times of interest $t_{e(k)}(i)$ during the n time intervals. It can be expressed as:

$$CI\left(t_{e(k)}(i), n\right) = \sum_{j=1}^{n} y_{t_{e(k)}}(i), j \tag{1}$$

It is assumed the appearing times of the $t_{e(k)}(i)$ during the considered n time intervals. This represents the users' research interests in the past, and can affect the users' current research interests.

The users' research interests during the n time intervals can be acquired by means of the researchers' cumulative interests. However, because the research interests of users dynamically change over time, the research interests during the time interval j may be different from research interests during the previous time interval $j - 1$ and during the next time interval $j + 1$. Therefore, the users' current research interests cannot be simply considered as research interests in the past. The impact of departed research interests on the users' current has to be discuss based on our previous studies [6,7].

The topics that researchers are interested in dynamically change over time. The researcher maybe lose interests in some topics and generate interests in other topics in sudden. The retained interests have a close relationship with the researcher's current interests. This phenomenon is similar with the forgetting mechanism of cognitive memory. Therefore, a model about retained interest can be developed according to the power function of cognitive memory retaining.

$$RI\left(t_{e(k)}\left(i\right),n\right) = \sum_{j=1}^{n} y_{t_{e(k)}}\left(i\right),j \times AT_{t_{e(k)}\left(i\right)}^{-b} \tag{2}$$

In which $T_{t_{e(k)}(i)}$ is the duration of interest $t_{e(k)}\left(i\right)$. $y_{t_{e(k)}}\left(i\right),j$ is the appearing times of interest $t_{e(k)}\left(i\right)$ during every time interval j, and $\sum_{j=1}^{n} y_{t_{e(k)}}\left(i\right),j \times AT_{t_{e(k)}(i)}^{-b}$ is the value of retained interest of $t_{e(k)}\left(i\right)$ during contained n time intervals.

Because retained interests are closely related to the users' current interests, we can predicate the current interests by means of retained interests. The parameters "A" and "b" are used to calculated this kind of correlation. "A" controls the difference of retained interest with current interest, and makes them have minimum difference. "b" is used to control the decaying speed on lost interests. In this study, the value of "A" is 0.855, and the "b" value is 1.295.

Some topics maybe have a high value on retained interests but a low value on cumulative interests, because these topics is current interests but in the past the research isn't interested on it.

5 A Framework of Unifying Search and Reasoning in Brain Informatics Research Recommendation System

Based on the above definition and measurement about research interests, an framework of unifying search and reasoning can be proposed to develop a BI research recommendation system. It can improve the accuracy of literature searches based on users' research interests. The details are introduced as follows.

The system provides four query conditions for searching needed literatures. Each condition is corresponding to an interest aspect. Users can choose a query condition and submit a keyword to start a query. After receiving the query request, the BI recommendation system will the other three aspects' interests which are BDI_1, BDI_2, BDI_3 will be obtained from the BI Provenances that extracted from the users' literatures in the brain and mental big data center system.

Here we come up with a unification of search and reasoning method based on brain informatics, which is named "BDI-ReaSearch". The process of BDI-ReaSearch can be expressed as below:

$$hasInterests(U, BDI_1, BDI_2, BDI_3), hasQuery(U, Q), executesOver(Q, D),$$
$$\neg contains(Q, BDI_1, BDI_2, BDI_3)$$
$$\rightarrow BDIReaSearch(BDI_1, BDI_2, BDI_3, Q, D) \tag{3}$$

In which the meaning of $hasInterests(U, BDI_1, BDI_2, BDI_3)$ is that the user "U" has a serious of interests "BDI_1, BDI_2, BDI_3" to brain informatics. $hasQuery(U, Q)$ denotes that user "U" inputs a query "Q" to acquire similar research. $executesOver(Q, D)$ denotes that the query "Q" which user inputs executes over database "D". The meaning of $\neg contains(Q, BDI_1, BDI_2, BDI_3)$ is

that query "Q" does not contain the research interests "BDI_1, BDI_2, BDI_3".
$BDIReaSearch(BDI_1, BDI_2, BDI_3, Q, D)$ denotes that user carry out the unification of search and reasoning method based on the brain informatics interests
BDI_1, BDI_2, BDI_3.

However, how to proceed $BDIReaSearch(BDI, Q, D)$ unification of search and reasoning? The following we select the strategy that redefines query "Q".
The BI research recommendation system calculates the users' retained interests
by the formula $RI\left(t_{e(k)}(i), n\right)$. Then this system makes use of users' interests
to refine the query so that it contains research interests "BDI". The process of
BDI-ReaSearch can be further expressed as below:

$$hasInterests(U, BDI_1, BDI_2, BDI_3), hasQuery(U, Q), executes(Q, D),$$
$$\neg contains(Q, BDI_1, BDI_2, BDI_3) \rightarrow$$
$$refinedas(Q, Q'), contains(Q', BDI_1, BDI_2, BDI_3), executesOver(Q', D) \quad (4)$$

In which $refinedas(Q, Q')$ denotes that the query "Q" inputted by user is refined
as "Q'". $contains(Q', BDI_1, BDI_2, BDI_3)$ denotes that the query "Q'" contains
users' research interests "BDI_1, BDI_2, BDI_3" to BI Provenances. The meaning
of $executesOver(Q', D)$ is that the refined query "Q'" executes over database
"D".

In the BI research recommendation system, the algorithm of research recommendation is shown in Table 1.

Table 1. The algorithm of research recommendation

Algorithm Research Recommendation
Input: cognitiveFunctionValue, username
Output: literatureResults
1. literatures = getLiterature(username)
2. Ror each interest aspect
3.   For each interest of interest aspect
4.   interests = getInterest(Literatures)
5.   retainedInterestValue = getValue(interests)
6.   End For
7.   Initialize maxRetainedInterestValue(j) = retainedInterestValue(1)
8.   For each interest of interest aspect
9.   If(retainedInterestValue(i)> retainedInterestValue(i-1)) then
10.   maxRetainedInterestValue(j) = retainedInterestValue(i)
11.   End If
12.   End For
13. End For
13. literatureResults = getResult(cognitiveFunctionValue, maxRetainedInterestValue(1), maxRetainedInterestValue(2), maxRetainedInterestValue(3))
14. return literatureResults

6   Experiments and Results

In this section, a realistic use case will be used to illustrate the proposed frame-work of unifying search and reasoning. A prototype of BI research recommendation system was developed based on a group of BI data provenances, which are extracted from 98 literatures, as shown in Fig.1.

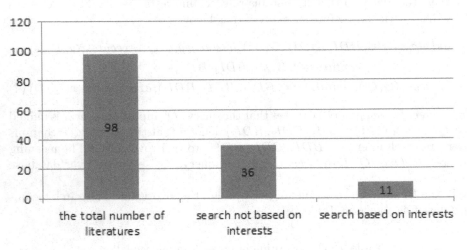

Fig. 1. The number of results

BI researchers can search related researches based on this prototype. For example, Dr. Liang is a BI researcher. He want to search researches about the human cognitive function "Inductive Reasoning". When he directly performs a query on those BI data provenances based on a query condition "Cognitive Function = Induction", a group of research information can be obtained. Fig.2 is the corresponding SPARQL query and Table 3 gives the query results including 36 research information. The BI research recommendation system can improve the accuracy of this query. The system provides the four interest aspect,including Cognitive Function, Device Type, Subject type and Perceptional Channel, as query conditions. When Dr. Liang chooses Cognitive Function as the query condition and input the keyword "Induction", the system automatically take other three query conditions as interest aspects to calculate the values of retained interests, respectively. The Table 2 gives the results of calculation. As shown in this table, the interests "fMRI", "Normal-Subject' and "Visual" have the biggest values of retained interest in those three interest aspects. Using these three interests to perform the redefinition algorithm of query stated in Section 5, a group of research information can be obtained shown in Table 4. The number of results is shown in Fig.1.

Table 4 includes 11 research information. Comparing with Table 3, 25 results are removed. The reason is to take Dr. Liang' current research interests into

PREFIX waasb: <http://www.semanticweb.org/ontologies/2011/11/DataBrain.owl#>
PREFIX rdf: <http://www.w3.org/1999/02/22-rdf-syntax-ns>
PREFIX owl: <http://www.w3.org/2002/07/owl#>
PREFIX rdfs: <http://www.w3.org/2000/01/rdf-schema#>
select distinct ?Literature_Name ?Cognitive_Function_Type ?Device_Type ?Subjects_Type ?Perception_Channel
where{
?Cognitive_Function rdf:type "Induction".
?Experimental_Group waasb:has-experimental-task ?Experimental_Task.
?Experimental_Task waasb:has-experimental-purpose ?Cognitive_Function.
?Experimental_Task waasb:sensory-channel ?Perception_Channel.
?Cognitive_Function waasb:type ?Cognitive_Function_Type.
optional {?Experimental_Group waasb:introduced-by ?Literature.
    ?Literature waasb:name ?Literature_Name.}
?Experimental_Group waasb:has-experimental-means ?Experimental_Means.
?Experimental_Means waasb:type ?Device_Type.
?Experimental_Group waasb:has-subjects ?Subjects.
?Subjects waasb:type ?Subjects_Type.
}
Order By ?Literature_Name
Limit 100|

Fig. 2. The SPARQL query

Table 2. The values of retained interests in three interest aspects

Device Type	Value	Subjects Type	Value	Perceptional Channel	Value
fMRI	1.078	Normal-Subject	1.448	Visual	1.546
ERP	0.535	Patient-Subject	0.166	Visual	0

Table 3. The results returned by the simple query

ID	title	Cognitive Function	Device Type	Subject Type	Perceptional Channel
1	ERP characteristics of sentential inductive reasoning in time and frequency domains	Inductive Reasoning	ERP	Normal-Subject	Visual
2	An fMRI study of the numerical Stroop task in individuals with and without minimal cognitive impairment	Inductive Reasoning	fMRI	Patient-Subject	Visual
...	...	...	...	...	...
36	The Role of Category Label in Adults' Inductive Reasoning	Inductive Reasoning	fMRI	Normal-Subject	Visual

account. As shonw in Table 2, Dr. Liang is focusing on fMRI experiments of visual tasks, which adopt normal subjects.

From the experiment above, we know that this BI research recommendation system can greatly shorten the time of brain researchers querying literatures. As a result, it can make researchers find appropriate articles more quickly.

Table 4. The results returned by the BI research recommendation

ID	title	Cognitive Function	Device Type	Subject Type	Perceptional Channel
1	the FMRI research: the inductive reasoning of figure	Inductive Reasoning	fMRI	Normal-Subject	Visual
2	Dynamics of Frontal, Striatal, and Hippocampal Systems during Rule Learning	Inductive Reasoning	fMRI	Normal-Subject	Visual
...	...	...	...	...	...
11	The Role of Category Label in Adults' Inductive Reasoning	Inductive Reasoning	fMRI	Normal-Subject	Visual

7   The Conclusion and Future Work

This paper concerns mainly on the researchers' interests in brain informatics, and takes advantage of them for research recommendation. In the brain informatics research recommendation system, we select the cognitive function, device type, perceptional channel and subject type as interest aspects. We have quantified the departed research interests. And to the dynamic change of research interests, we study retained interest according to the forgetting mechanism of cognitive memory. The retained interests closely relate with the users' current research interests, and they have been quantified. In addition, we have come up with the unification of search and reasoning based on Data-Brain and BI provenances named as "BDI-ReaSearch". Using the users' research interests, we redefine the sparql statement.

In this paper, we do not take the weight of literatures level into consideration. In future study, we will consider it and add it into calculation. And we should add the most popular research contents of the users' research domain to their interests. Then we can provide better services for brain science research.

Acknowledgements. The work is supported by National Key Basic Research Program of China (2014CB744605), China Postdoctoral Science Foundation (2013M540096), International Science Cooperation Program of China (2013-DFA32180), National Natural Science Foundation of China (61272345), Research Supported by the CAS/SAFEA International Partnership Program for Creative Research Teams, the Japan Society for the Promotion of Science Grants-in-Aid for Scientific Research (25330270).

References

1. Chen, J.H., Zhong, N.: Data-Brain Modeling Based on Brain Informatics Methodology. In: Proceedings of the 2008 IEEE/WIC/ACM International Conference on Web Intelligence, WI 2008, pp. 41–47. IEEE Computer Society, Sydney (2008)

2. Chen, J.H., Zhong, N.: Data-Brain modeling for systematic Brain Informatics. In: Zhong, N., Li, K., Lu, S., Chen, L. (eds.) BI 2009. LNCS, vol. 5819, pp. 182–193. Springer, Heidelberg (2009)
3. Chen, J.H., Zhong, N., Liang, P.P.: Data-Brain Driven Systematic Human Brain Data Analysis: A Case Study in Numerical Inductive Reasoning Centric Investigation. Cognitive Systems Research 15-16, 17–32 (2012)
4. Simmhan, Y.L., Plale, B., Gannon, D.: A survey of data provenance in e-Science. Sigmod Record 34(3), 31–36 (2005)
5. Zeng, Y., Zhou, E.Z., Wang, Y., Ren, X., Qin, Y.L., Huang, Z.S., Zhong, N.: Research interests: their dynamics, structuresand applications in unifying search and reasoning. J. Intell. Inf. Syst. 37(2011), 65–88 (2011)
6. Zeng, Y., Yao, Y.Y., Zhong, N.: Dblp-sse: A dblp search support engine. In: Proceedings of the 2009 IEEE/WIC/ACM International Conference on Web Intelligence, WI 2009, pp. 626–630 (2009)
7. Zeng, Y., Zhong, N., Wang, Y., Qin, Y.L., Huang, Z.S., Zhou, H.Y., Yao, Y.Y., Harmelen, F.V.: User-centric query refinement and processing using granularity based strategies. Knowledge and Information Systems 27(3), 419–450 (2011)
8. Zeng, Y., Zhou, E.Z., Qin, Y.L., Zhong, N.: Research interests: Their dynamics, structures and applications in web search refinement. In: Proceeding of the 2010 IEEE/WIC/ACM International Conference on Web Intelligence, pp. 639–646 (2010)
9. Zhong, N., Liu, J., Yao, Y., Wu, J., Lu, S., Qin, Y., Li, K., Wah, B.W.: Web Intelligence Meets Brain Informatics. In: Zhong, N., Liu, J., Yao, Y., Wu, J., Lu, S., Li, K. (eds.) Web Intelligence Meets Brain Informatics. LNCS (LNAI), vol. 4845, pp. 1–31. Springer, Heidelberg (2007)
10. Zhong, N.: Ways to develop human-level Web Intelligence: A Brain Informatics perspective. In: Franconi, E., Kifer, M., May, W. (eds.) ESWC 2007. LNCS, vol. 4519, pp. 27–36. Springer, Heidelberg (2007)
11. Zhong, N., Chen, J.H.: Constructing a New-style Conceptual Model of Brain Data for Systematic Brain Informatics. IEEE Transactions on Knowledge and Data Engineering 24(12), 2127–2142 (2012)
12. Zhong, N., Chen, J.H.: Constructing a New-style Conceptual Model of Bain Data for Systematic Brain Informatics. 2011 IEEE, 1041–4347 (November 26, 2011)

Hadoop for EEG Storage and Processing:
A Feasibility Study*

Ghita Berrada, Maurice van Keulen, and Mena B. Habib

University of Twente,
The Netherlands
{g.berrada,m.vankeulen,m.badiehhabibmorgan}@utwente.nl

Abstract. Lots of heterogeneous complex data are collected for diagnosis purposes. Such data should be shared between all caregivers and, often at least partly automatically processed, due to its complexity, for its full potential to be harnessed. This paper is a feasibility study that assesses the potential of Hadoop as a medical data storage and processing platform using EEGs as example of medical data.

Keywords: EEG,Hadoop, medical data storage and processing.

1 Introduction

The diagnosis process often involves multiple clinicians/specialists and a large number of ordered tests. As a result, huge amounts of heterogeneous data are gathered and scattered in many locations (or islands of data). Table 1 shows the scale of data produced in and spread across the healthcare system. To further compound the problem, different locations often use non-interoperable systems and file formats, if the data is indeed digitized. A McKinsey Global Institute (MGI) report on the US healthcare system ([1]) shows that up to 30% of data that includes medical records, laboratory and surgery reports, is not digitized and that the video and monitor feeds that make up most of the clinical data produced are not stored but used real time. Such a setting makes it hard for caregivers to access a patient's full history and get a full picture of his/her condition. As it stands, needless tests may be ordered and diagnoses delayed and/or missed, not to mention data security more easily breached. The prevalence of misdiagnoses is estimated to be up to 15% in most areas of medicine ([2]). And a study of physician-reported diagnosis errors ([3]) finds most cases are due to testing (44%) or clinician assessment errors (32%).

A case from The Washington Post exposes all those issues ([4]). A patient struggling with depression is diagnosed with a meningioma[1], unrelated with the

---

* The EEGs used in this paper were kindly provided by Prof. Dr. Ir. Michel van Putten (Dept. of Neurology and Clinical Neurophysiology, Medisch Spectrum Twente and MIRA, University of Twente, Enschede, The Netherlands), who we also thank for useful comments on the paper.

[1] A brain tumor.

D. Ślęzak et al. (Eds.): BIH 2014, LNAI 8609, pp. 218–230, 2014.
© Springer International Publishing Switzerland 2014

patient's depression and not in need of monitoring, according to the attending clinician at the time. Four years, many moves across US states and many consultations (with other clinicians) later, and with her condition steadily worsening, the patient is hospitalized and the meningioma, gone under the radar for years, is finally rediscovered and pinpointed as the cause of the patient's near-fatal condition. This case stresses the necessity of care continuity and easy access to patient history: had the meningioma been known to clinicians after the initial diagnosis, the patient may have been spared years of misery, a possible fatal outcome and enjoyed a better quality of life.

To solve such issues, authorized caregivers need fast and reliable access to a shared medical data repository containing tests' data and their interpretations. An international data repository would ideally be needed but is unlikely to be created in the foreseeable future for legal reasons. So national scale repositories should at least be created. The MGI report cited earlier ([1]) argues that sharing medical data offers huge premiums such as a drastic reduction of healthcare costs and waste and improved patient outcomes and quality of life through allowing remote patient monitoring, easing comparative effectiveness studies and clinical decision systems deployment and increasing data transparency.

Sharing data would also provide a trove of data on which competing automated medical data interpretation methods can easily be tested, compared, interpreted and reproduced. So far, the automated medical data interpretation methods aiming at reducing the clinicians' workload and easing the diagnosis process have been of limited use as they are tested on distinct, usually small data, making them hard to reproduce and interpret with any certainty.

The MGI report ([1]) also points out there are critical technical hurdles to overcome before medical data can be shared, analyzed properly and its full potential uncovered,e.g standardizing formats, ensuring systems' interoperability, integrating pre-existing, fragmented and heterogenous datasets and providing sufficient storage. So any potential design for a medical repository should take into account the distributed nature of the data[2], its heterogeneity and size and the diversity of file formats and platforms used across healthcare institutions. The data should also be easy to access for further, complex processing.

In this paper, we show that a rather low cost technical solution (and possible storage platform for medical data) that fits those constraints and requires minimal changes to current state of the art storage and processing techniques already exists: the Hadoop platform. In what follows, we will take EEG data as example of medical data.

The rest of this paper is organized as follows. We introduce Hadoop, explain why it is a good fit for medical data storage and show how EEGs can be stored with Hadoop (Section 2). The example of EEG feature selection by exhaustive search is then used to lay out why complex data processing should also be done with Hadoop (Sections 3 and 4).

---

[2] Healthcare institutions are unlikely to let their data be stored externally.

Table 1. Medical data statistics (2009 data, last year for which records are available) from [5]

	Netherlands	USA	OECD[5]
EEG[3]	100,000/167GB	N/A	N/A
MRI[4]	726,000/15.9TB	28 million/614TB	42 million/921TB
CT[4]	1.1 million/36.7TB	70 million/2.3PB	104.5 million/3.4PB

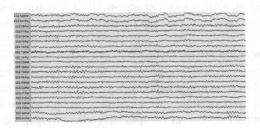

Fig. 1. EEG showing an adult's normal eyes-closed EEG segment

Contributions. In this paper, we give a proof of concept for an EEG repository by :
- explaining why Hadoop fits the constraints imposed on potential medical data repositories
- showing how to store EEG data in a Hadoop framework
- proving that EEG data can be analyzed on national scale on Hadoop by designing and benchmarking a representative machine-learning algorithm

1.1 Related Work

Hadoop has been found a viable solution for storing and processing big data similar to medical data, such as images in astronomy ([6]) or power grid time series, which unlike medical time series, are unidimensional time series ([7]).

[8] is, to the best of our knowledge, the first paper to consider storing medical data and EEGs in particular with Hadoop and show it is a promising solution in need of more testing. [8] suggest exploring the "design and benchmarking of machine learning algorithms on [the Hadoop] infrastructure and pattern matching from large scale EEG data." and this is one of the goals of our paper.

---

[3] Assuming standard 20-minute EEGs in EDF+ format. File average size: 13.7MB.

[4] Assuming average size of 23MB per MRI and 35MB per CT.

[5] Based on data from OECD countries with available data from exams performed in and outside of hospitals i.e the USA, Greece, France, Belgium, Turkey, Iceland, Luxembourg, the Netherlands, Canada, Denmark, Estonia,the Czech Republic, the Slovak Republic, Chile, Israel and South Korea.

2 Hadoop: A Good Fit for Medical Repositories' Constraints

2.1 Introduction to Hadoop

Hadoop, an open source platform managed by the Apache open source community, has 2 core components: the Hadoop Distributed File System (HDFS) and the job management framework or MapReduce framework. The HDFS is designed to reliably store huge files on all cluster machines. Each HDFS file is cut into blocks and each block then replicated and stored at different physical locations in the cluster to ensure fault tolerance. The HDFS has a master/slave architecture with one master server called *Namenode* managing the filesystem namespace and regulating the file access by clients and multiple slave servers (one per cluster node) called *Datanodes* managing the storage in the nodes they run on. The *Namenode* maps the file blocks to the *Datanodes* and gives the *Datanodes* instructions to perform operations on blocks and serve filesystem clients' read and write requests. The Hadoop MapReduce framework also has a master/slave architecture with a single master called *jobtracker* and several slave servers (one per cluster node) called *tasktrackers*. MapReduce jobs are submitted to the *jobtracker*, which puts the jobs in a queue and executes them on first come/first serve basis. The *jobtracker* assigns tasks to the *tasktrackers* with instructions on how to execute them.

2.2 Hadoop and Parallel Data Processing: The Mapreduce Model

MapReduce is a programming model for data-intensive parallelizable processing tasks (introduced in [9]) designed to process large volumes of data in parallel, with the workload split between large numbers of low level commodity machines. The MapReduce framework, unlike parallel databases, hides the complex and messy details of load balancing, data distribution, parallelization and fault-tolerance from the user in a library, thus making it simpler to use the resources of a large distributed system to process big datasets. The MapReduce model relies on 2 successive functions to transform lists of input data elements into lists of output data elements: a *mapper* function and a *reducer* function. Each input data element is transformed into a new output data element by the *mapper*. The transformed elements are then aggregated by the *reducer* to return a single output value. A simple example is files word count: in this case, the *mapper* associates a number of words to each of the input files while the *reducer* function sums the values obtained during the mapping step.

2.3 Hadoop for Medical Data Storage

The Hadoop platform provides a solution to the technical hurdles outlined by the MGI report ([1]) described earlier (Section 1).

First of all, Hadoop was designed to scale with large data. It is currently being used at Facebook to store about 100PB of user data, i.e data much bigger than national scale medical data which ranges from dozens of terabytes (e.g. the

Netherlands) to petabytes of data (e.g. the USA) annually as shown in Table 1. So Hadoop can easily handle national scale amount of medical data.

Moreover, Hadoop can store heterogeneous formats of data, in particular unstructured data, and if there is a method to extract the data from the files that store it[6], the data can then be fed to Hadoop MapReduce for further analysis and processing.

Hadoop is also tolerant to node failure. The HDFS relies on replication (by default 3 copies on 3 Datanodes per file block) to ensure file blocks are not lost if a data server fails. If a Datanode fails and some data blocks have less than a set minimum of copies, the Namenode orders the replication of the affected blocks in some available Datanodes to bring back the replication factor of the blocks to safer levels. The probability of losing a block in a 4000 nodes' cluster in a day (respectively in a year) in the case of uncorrelated failures of multiple nodes is about 5.7×10^{-7} (respectively 2.1×10^{-4}) ([10]). At Yahoo! in 2009 for example, only 641 blocks were lost out of 329 million on 17720 nodes i.e a loss rate of $1.9 \times 10^{-4}\%$ ([10]). The only problem left is the Namenode as the HDFS is unusable if the Namenode fails. Namenode crashes rarely occur though ([11])(1 in 4 years at Facebook) and solutions limiting the crash impact are already being deployed. One such solution is the AvatarNodes in use at Facebook: 2 AvatarNodes, an active and standby one, replace the unique Namenode and receive the Datanodes messages in its stead. The Standby AvatarNode thus contains up-to-date information about block locations and can be started in under a minute to replace the Namenode (or Active AvatarNode) if it fails. This solution cuts cluster planned downtime by 50%. Data stored with Hadoop will therefore be constantly available.

Hadoop was built for parallel processing (via MapReduce described in Section 2.2) and we study the feasibility EEG data processing with Hadoop with the example of feature selection by exhaustive search in Section 3.

2.4   Hadoop and EEG Storage

An EEG is a multidimensional time series obtained by capturing the brain's electric activity with scalp electrodes. Figure 1 shows an example of EEG. The increasingly popular EDF+ format is used to store EEGs and contains all the information about the EEG recording, both metadata in a header encoded in UTF-8 and raw data in binary format. The metadata includes patient information and EEG signal technical attributes (e.g. equipment details and sampling rate). Annotations on the EEG, such as context of recording or EEG events labels, may also be stored in the EDF+ file. See [12] for format details.

HDFS does not call for any set file format, so we store EEGs in EDF+ in HDFS. We anonymize EEGs before storage for security reasons. Keeping EEGs as EDF+ files has many advantages. No additional data formatting is needed and existing tools for EDF+ files, eg. visualization tools, can still be used. And

---

[6] Such methods currently exist at the sites where the different types of data are stored. There is,at most, a need to translate those methods into Java, Python, Perl or any other language that can be interfaced with Hadoop.

as EDF+ files are mainly binary files, the size of the stored EEGs is small: 2500 EDF+ files (dataset 1 in Section 4 and Table 2(a)) i.e to about 2 years of EEG data at the local hospital take up 46.5GB whereas the same data[7] would take up 1TB when in a relational database.

3 EEG Feature Selection with Hadoop

EEG interpretation is arduous even for trained specialists due to the mass of data to interpret[8] and non-specific, age or context-dependent patterns and artifacts. For example, the patterns for a chewing artifact and an epileptic seizure are similar. Machine learning-based methods ([14,15]) are being developed to ease the interpretation for clinicians, though the methods' scalability remains an issue. Instead of reducing algorithm complexity as in most studies aiming to lower the computational cost of machine-learning methods, we opt for using more commodity hardware with Hadoop and show, here, with EEGs as example, that parallelizable machine learning tasks and translatable to a sequence of *map/reduce* can be run in manageable times.

3.1 Feature Selection as Example EEG Machine Learning Algorithm

Most automated EEG data interpretation methods classify or cluster EEGs and select suitable features for classification/clustering (eg. fractal dimension in [14,16]) prior to it. Other approaches ([17]) select, quantify, visualize some "relevant" EEG features through time and present them to a practitioner who then interprets them and their variations to derive conclusions on the EEG. So the key task in the automated interpretation of EEG is feature selection so we pick a feature selection algorithm on EEG as example of machine-learning algorithm to determine whether Hadoop is suitable for medical data processing compared to other more traditional frameworks. We purposely choose an algorithm with exponential complexity for feature selection (exhaustive search) as achieving manageable execution times with Hadoop for this worst-case algorithm would entail achieving even more reasonable execution times for more common less computationally expensive algorithms. The goal of this study is not to evaluate the accuracy of the feature selection algorithm but to test whether running feature selection (as a sample machine-learning algorithm) on Hadoop has any benefits compared to using more traditional processing platforms.

3.2 Tested Features and Rationale for the Choice of Features

To test the feature selection algorithm, we choose a mix of 9 clinically-relevant and more general time-series features shown to be relevant for EEG

---

[7] With one table for metadata, one table for raw data and one tuple per raw data point.

[8] A routine 20 minute EEG fits in 109 A4-pages with the guidelines of the American Clinical Neurophysiology Society [13]

processing in literature: 4 features computed in the time domain (fractal dimension, mean amplitude, amplitude standard deviation, normalized Hjorth mobility and complexity[9]) and 5 in the frequency domain (frequency bands percentages (α band,β band,θ band,δ band)[10], the α to δ ratio, high to low frequency ratio (high frequency being frequencies above 25Hz), brain symmetry index (BSI) and spectral entropy). These features detect many pathologies and patterns: EEG asymmetries as in focal seizures or hemispheric ischemia with the BSI defined in [18], temporal lobe seizure with the Hjorth mobility and complexity([15]), high frequency artifacts with the high to low frequency ratio ([19]), hypofunctional patterns with the α to δ ratio and iso-electric ([19]), low-voltage EEGs with the mean amplitude ([19]). The fractal dimension separates normal sequences and other sequence types ([16]) and normal EEGs and Alzheimer patients EEGs ([14]). An extra feature, the nearest neighbour synchronization (mNNC) (defined in [17]), used to detect seizures ([19]), sleep or encephalopathies ([17])[11] is computed in the feature computation step (to measure scalability) but not used for classification.Each of the 9 features can be picked alone or in combination with a variable number of the other features. So there are $\sum_{i=1}^{9} C_9^i = 511$ distinct possible ways to pick a feature set from the 9 features. This paper doesn't aim to assess the classification performance of the chosen features. The features were only picked as sample EEG features for scalability tests so others may have been selected for this study.

3.3   Performing EEG Feature Selection with Exhaustive Search

We evaluate each of the 511 possible feature combinations to select the best feature combination for our classification problem. Figure 2 summarizes the feature evaluation steps. For simplicity, we choose KNN as classifier but the same principle applies to other classifiers. We then implement this algorithm in 4 steps in MapReduce:

1. Map: Extract the segments of interest from the original EEG files and compute all features for each of the segments
2. Reduce: Build one dataset per feature combination
3. Map: Train the classifier and assess its performance for each feature set
4. Reduce: Choose the feature set that maximizes mean accuracy (for all classes).

Details on the classifier and EEG segments of interest are found in Section 4.1.

4   Experiments

This section describes the experiments performed and their setup. Table 2 summarises the hardware and software properties of the experimental servers.

---

[9] 2-dimensional feature.

[10] The EEG waves are grouped by frequency in 4 main bands: δ band for frequencies from 0.5 to 4 Hz, θ band for frequencies from 4 to 7 Hz, α band for frequencies from 7 to 12 Hz and β band for frequencies from 12 to 30 Hz. The frequency band percentage is therefore a 4-dimensional feature.

[11] The mNNC value increases in seizures and decreases in sleep or encephalopathies.

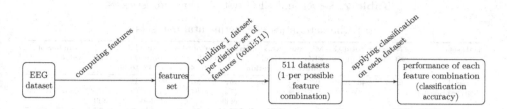

Fig. 2. EEG feature selection steps

4.1 Details on EEG Classification

EEG labeling hinges on properties such as sequence type and patient age so feature selection can be done only on segments of similar properties. Only eyes-closed segments from adult EEGs are used in this paper. The feature selection principle is unchanged for other age groups and segment types. We use KNN as a classifier. We assess a feature set's performance by the mean classification accuracy (mean of the accuracy for all classes) and run 3 rounds of the Shuffle and Split cross-validation, with 30% of the data used as training set per iteration, to reduce overfitting and minimize the prediction error. We have 3 EEG classes: normal, normal but for increased β wave (often due to medication) and abnormal.

4.2 Dataset Description

We use a dataset of 2500 EEGs for the experiments. This amount of data is about 30% of the EEG data collected monthly[12] in the Netherlands and about 2 years of data from the local hospital[13]. All EEGs in the dataset were recorded on patients in a hospital setting following the International 10/20 System with Ag/AgCl electrodes and using a common average reference. Only the 19 channels common to all EEGs are kept for calculations, with each channel sampled at 250Hz. All 9 features from Section 3.2 and mNNC are computed on the whole dataset (hereafter named dataset 1-Table 2(a)) to check the scalability of feature computation. To test feature selection by exhaustive search, we use a subset of 1000 files from dataset 1 for which the class label is known precisely (hereafter named dataset 2). The EEGs in both datasets predominantly represent standard EEGs (15 to 40 minutes' EEGs) i.e the most common EEGs in clinical practice (91.6% of the EEGs recorded per year at the local hospital).

4.3 Benchmarking the EEG Exhaustive Search Feature Selection

Setup. We test EEG feature selection with python and with Hadoop Streaming. To speed up the python code, we use the joblib library to parallelize parts of the

---

[12] And about a third of the annual Dutch data in filesize.
[13] Medisch Spectrum Twente, Enschede, The Netherlands.

Table 2. Server and EEG test file characteristics

(a) Characteristics of experimental datasets

Dataset	Number of files	Total size of files	Minimum EEG duration	Maximum EEG duration	Number of files of duration <15mn	15 to 40 mn	40mn to 1h	1 to 2h	>2h	Number of values
dataset 1 (feature computation only)	2500	46.51GB	10s	3h 9mn	204 (7.4% of files)	2201 (79.5% of files)	90 (3.25% of files)	253 (9.14% of files)	19 (0.69% of files)	578,648,474,500
dataset 2 for classification subset of dataset1	1000	16.06GB	10s	2h 8mn 50s	73 (5.6% of files)	909 (69.9% of files)	33 (2.54% of files)	35 (2.69% of files)	1 (0.08% of files)	6,828,505,000

(b) Characteristics of the servers used in the experiments

Server	OS	Software used	Processor	RAM	Number of nodes
Server for Parallel Python experiments	openSUSE 12.3 Milestone 2(x86-64) Kernel version 3.6.3-1-desktop	Python 2.7.3 with joblib 0.7d library scikit-learn 0.14 scikit-learn 0.14	AMD Opteron® Processor 4226 (6 cores) 2 processors	64GB	1
Hadoop cluster	Ubuntu 12.04.2 LTS(x86-64) Kernel version 3.2.0-40-generic	Python 2.7.3 with scikit-learn 0.10 Hadoop streaming jar from Cloudera Hadoop CDH3u6	Intel® Xeon® CPU E3110@3.00GHz (2 cores) 1 processor	7.8GB	15

feature selection: features are computed EEG by EEG with several tasks running concurrently and several feature combinations are tested for classification at the same time. The number of jobs running concurrently is RAM-bound.

We selected Hadoop Streaming as Hadoop interface as we can write python code with it. This allows us to reuse most of the code from the python with joblib approach, thus easing the performance comparison between both approaches tested. There are 30 available map slots in the Hadoop cluster (2 maps per node) so that up to 30 maps run at the same time until the Hadoop map jobs are done. Similarly there are 30 possible reduce slots. Unless otherwise stated, we run 2 maps per node for the Hadoop Streaming jobs. We compute all features over windows of 1800 ms in both Hadoop and Python approaches. 1800 ms of EEG data equals 450 points per channel with the standard frequency of EEG signal i.e 250Hz and about 9 eye blink artifacts (shortest known EEG events).

Experiment 1: Feature computation In the first set of experiments, we only perform the first step of feature selection (described in Section 3.3), i.e EEG segment extraction and feature computation, on part or all of dataset 1. For each experiment, execution times are recorded. Figures 3(a), 3(b), and 3(d) were obtained using all of dataset 1. Figure 3(d) explores the evolution of feature computation times when the number of cores of the Python server is made to vary. Feature computation execution times grow linearly with the size of processed files for both Hadoop and Python solutions (Figure 3(e)) but the Python execution times grow 4.5 times faster than the Hadoop ones. Therefore, feature extraction with Hadoop is especially beneficial for large files and scales to a national scale amount of data. Based on the interpolations of Figure 3(e), extracting the 10 features from Section 3.2 for the whole annual Dutch EEG data(i.e 167GB-Table

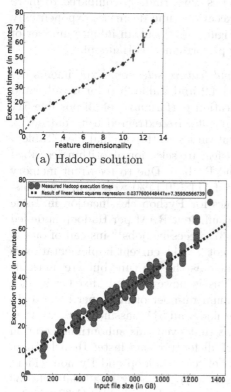

(a) Hadoop solution

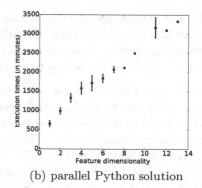

(b) parallel Python solution

(c) Evolution of Hadoop classification execution times with classification input file size (1 file per combination)

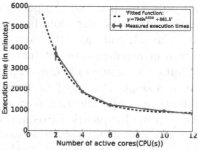

(d) Evolution of features' computation execution times (parallel Python) with number of active cores

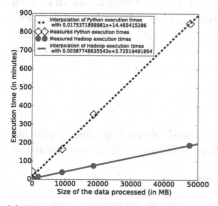

(e) Variation of feature computation execution times with EEG file size

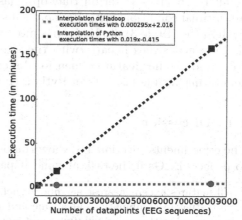

(f) Variation of classification execution times with number of data points (test and training sets)

Fig. 3. Impact of several factors on features' computation and classification execution times

1) would take about 11 hours and 7 minutes with Hadoop compared to more than 2 days with Python. The Python execution time decreases exponentially with the number of active cores/CPUs (Figure 3(d)) but an infinite number of CPUs would be needed to reach the same performance as Hadoop!

Experiment 2: Brute-force classification and feature selection Experiments described here all use dataset 2 (see Section 4.2 and Table 2(a) for details) and test the time it takes to assess the classification performance of all possible 511 feature combinations [14]. 253295 EEG segments are extracted from dataset 2, i.e 113,982,750 values or 1.67% of the total values in the original files. Table 3 summarises the results of implementing the feature selection algorithm described in Section 3.3 with Hadoop Streaming and Python. Due to recurrent memory errors, only 154 feature combinations out of 511 (30.14%) were tested for classification with Python. The execution times for Python classification in Table 3 are estimates based on available data. Insufficient RAM per Hadoop node led to all 511 combinations being tested with 37 successive jobs[15] instead of one so that only 1 map would run per node and not 2. The current implementation is clearly subpar as map slots become available as the job runs but are unusable until the job ends and the next starts. This is however easily fixed, with the right user privileges, by setting the maximum number of maps per node to 15 so that at any time only one map runs per node: all 511 classifications can then run in a single Hadoop job. Table 3 shows that even this suboptimal solution evaluates the classification performance of all feature sets faster than Python. The gap in classification execution times between Hadoop and Python widens with the size of datasets to classify (Figure 3(f)). For very small datasets (33 training and 67 test points), Python outperforms Hadoop slightly (1.82 minutes for Python and 2.4 minutes with Hadoop to test all 511 combinations). Hadoop has overall a clear edge over Python as dataset size rises: the classification runs about 64.76 times faster on Hadoop. Classifying dataset 2's sequences, even in suboptimal conditions with Hadoop, runs 29.9 to 34.16[16] times faster than with Python (see Table 3). So Hadoop is more suited for large datasets' classification. Hadoop also scales linearly with the size of classification input files[17] (Figure 3(c)) and handles feature dimensions' increase better than Python (about 2 orders of magnitude faster than Python (Figures 3(a) and 3(b))).

4.4   Discussion

The experiments (Section 4.3) show Hadoop as a scalable and promising solution to process EEGs if the task at hand it parallelizable (e.g. feature computation)

---

[14] All features except nearest neighbor synchronization.
[15] 36 testing 14 combinations at a time and 1 testing 7 combinations at a time.
[16] Compared to the estimated upper and lower bounds for the Python job respectively.
[17] Files obtained by extracting all eyes closed segments from the original EDF+ files and applying each of the 9 tested features on the extracted segments.
[15] Result of 37 successive jobs instead of only one job testing all 511 combinations
[16] Estimates based on data available.

Table 3. Execution times for whole feature selection process on dataset 2 and each of its steps

		Segment extraction& feature computation only	Feature computation and formatting for classification	Classification only	Complete feature selection
Execution time	Hadoop streaming	30.35min	1h7min20s	32h25min52s[9]	33h33min12s
	parallel Python	97.9min	97.9min	estimated lower bound: 11 days 47min[10] estimated upper bound: 12 days 14h34min	estimated lower bound: 11days2h25min estimated upper bound: 12 days 16h2 min

even if it is CPU-intensive and RAM-bound (classification with all possible feature combinations). It goes to prove that a cluster of commodity hardware (15 machines with Dual core processors and only 7.8GB of RAM here) is better at processing complex data than a single highly specialized powerful server if the task is a series of (semi-)independent steps that can run in parallel. Hadoop has also been shown to be able to process a national scale amount of data with a quite small number of cluster machines. This is also a rather cheap solution: a cluster like the experimental one costs 10000 to 20000 euros i.e 1000-1500 euros per machine as compared to above 3000 euros per machine for the type of server used in the Python experiments. Owning a Hadoop cluster is in theory not needed as web services like Amazon Elastic Map Reduce (EMR) offer access to Hadoop clusters tailored for diverse processing needs. This is not doable, though, given the sensitivity of medical data. And we can boost the Hadoop performance further by optimizing the code we wrote by mostly reusing the Python one, via for example, changing the Hadoop configuration parameters to solve memory issues or using other Hadoop Python frameworks like mrjob or Dumbo that don't require map/reduce inputs and outputs to be strings passed via stdin/stdout and should thus need less processing RAM or using machine-learning algorithms optimized for the platform (Mahout library).

5 Conclusions

Hadoop is a promising solution for EEG storage and processing. Computation times for complex parallelizable machine-learning algorithms are notably reduced compared to more traditional means of computation and become manageable. The gain in computation times grows with data amount to process, Hadoop scaling easily with national scale data. So it would seem that it is better to process data with many commodity machines rather than with one extremely powerful server, when the processing task is parallelizable. In future, we would like to extend this work to other medical data types such as MRI or CT and study how to integrate data from computations run on diverse types of medical data (e.g. MRI and EEG). We would also like to run more tests on medical data querying (especially natural language querying). And Hadoop data security also needs to be explored further.

References

1. Manyika, J., Chui, M., Brown, B., Bughin, J., Dobbs, R., Roxburgh, C., Byers, A.H.: Big data: The next frontier for innovation, competition, and productivity. Technical report, Mc Kinsey Global Institute (June 2011)
2. Berner, E.S., Graber, M.L.: Overconfidence as a cause of diagnostic error in medicine. Am. J. Med. 121(5), S2–S23 (supplement) (2008)
3. Schiff, G.D., Hasan, O., Kim, S., Abrams, R., Cosby, K., Lambert, B.L., Elstein, A.S., Hasler, S., Kabongo, M.L., Krosnjar, N., Odwazny, R., Wisniewski, M.F., McNutt, R.A.: Diagnostic error in medicine: Analysis of 583 physician-reported errors. Arch. Intern. Med. 169(20), 1881–1887 (2009)
4. Boodman, S.G.: Medical mystery: Depression and possible dementia masked the real problem. The Washington Post (December 23, 2013)
5. OECD: Medical technologies. In: Health at a Glance 2011: OECD Indicators. OECD Publishing (2011)
6. Wiley, K., Connolly, A., Gardner, J.P., Krughof, S., Balazinska, M., Howe, B., Kwon, Y., Bu, Y.: Astronomy in the cloud: Using mapreduce for image coaddition. CoRR abs/1010.1015 (2010)
7. Bach, F., Çakmak, H.K., Maass, H., Kuehnapfel, U.: Power Grid Time Series Data Analysis with Pig on a Hadoop Cluster compared to Multi Core Systems. In: Proc. of PDP 2013 (2013)
8. Dutta, H., Kamil, A., Pooleery, M., Sethumadhavan, S., Demme, J.: Distributed storage of large-scale multidimensional electroencephalogram data using hadoop and hbase. In: Grid and Cloud Database Management, pp. 331–347. Springer (2011)
9. Dean, J., Ghemawat, S.: Mapreduce: Simplified data processing on large clusters. In: OSDI, pp. 137–150. USENIX Association (2004)
10. Chansler, R.J.: Data availability and durability with the Hadoop Distributed File System 37(1), 16–22 (2012)
11. Borthakur, D., Gray, J., Sarma, J.S., Muthukkaruppan, K., Spiegelberg, N., Kuang, H., Ranganathan, K., Molkov, D., Menon, A., Rash, S., Schmidt, R., Aiyer, A.: Apache hadoop goes realtime at facebook. In: Proc. of SIGMOD, pp. 1071–1080 (2011)
12. Kemp, B., Olivan, J.: European data format 'plus' (EDF+), an EDF alike standard format for the exchange of physiological data. Clin. Neurophysiol. 114, 1755–1761 (2003)
13. American Clinical Neurophysiology Society: Guideline 8: Guidelines for recording clinical EEG on digital media. J. Clin. Neurophysiol. 23, 122–124 (2006)
14. Goh, C., Hamadicharef, B., Henderson, G.T., Ifeachor, E.C.: Comparison of Fractal Dimension Algorithms for the Computation of EEG Biomarkers for Dementia. In: Proc. of CIMED (2005)
15. Cecchin, T., Ranta, R., Koessler, L., Caspary, O., Vespignani, H., Maillard, L.: Seizure lateralization in scalp EEG using Hjorth parameters. Clin. Neurophysiol. 121(3), 290–300 (2010)
16. Berrada, G., de Keijzer, A.: An IFS-based similarity measure to index electroencephalograms. In: Huang, J.Z., Cao, L., Srivastava, J. (eds.) PAKDD 2011, Part II. LNCS, vol. 6635, pp. 457–468. Springer, Heidelberg (2011)
17. van Putten, M.J.: The Colorful Brain: Visualization of EEG Background Patterns. J. Clin. Neurophysiol. 25(2), 63–68 (2008)
18. van Putten, M.J.: Extended BSI for continuous EEG monitoring in carotid endarterectomy. Clin. Neurophysiol. 117(12), 2661–2666 (2006)
19. Cloostermans, M., de Vos, C., Heida, T., de Keijzer, A., van Putten, M.: Monitoring the brain in the adult ICU. In: Proc. of the 4th Annual Symposium of the IEEE/EMBS Benelux Chapter, pp. 128–130 (November 2009)

Supervised Learning for the Neurosurgery Intensive Care Unit Using Single-Layer Perceptron Classifiers

Chad A. Mello[2], Rory Lewis[1,2], Amy Brooks-Kayal[1], Jessica Carlsen[1], Heidi Grabenstatter[1], and Andrew M. White[1]

[1] Departments of Pediatrics & Neurology, University of Colorado Denver, Anschutz Medical Campus, Aurora, CO, 80045, USA
[2] Department of Computer Science, University of Colorado at Colorado Springs, Colorado Springs, CO USA 80918, USA

Abstract. In the continuing goal to merge the fields of computational neuroscience with medical based neurodiagnostic clinical research this paper presents advancements on machine learning Big Electroencephalogram (EEG) Data. The authors' clinical decision-support systems (CDSS) presented in previous work was able to distinguish, within minutes, pathological oscillations hidden in terabytes of complex signal analysis. This paper presents training and learning elements that compliment and advance this previous work. This paper shows how perceptrons, that predate modern-day neural network constructs, remain relevant in many modern classification applications where a clear linear separation is present in the data. Furthermore, the perceptrons also compliment the domain adaptation covariant shifts later used when the system is used in the neuroICU (Intensive Care Unit). Accordingly, we present supervised learning for the neuroICU using single-layer perceptron classifiers.

1 Introduction

In a healthy human brain there is a precise interaction of neural activities that renders multiple types of normal oscillatory synchronization [1] [2] [3] [4]. Conversely, when one develops a neurological illness (pathology) this synchronization is disrupted where some of these disorders have hypersynchronous oscillations while others have general alterations in synchronization. These abnormal synchronization processes are found in the pathological oscillations associated with several neuropsychiatric disorders including epilepsy [5], acute brain injury [6], Alzheimer's [7] [8], autism [9], post-neurosurgery Intensive Care Units (ICU) seizures [10], stroke [11], schizophrenia[12], dementia [13] and, in particular, basal ganglia disorders such as Parkinson's disease [14]. Additionally, both the aforementioned pathological states and normal states have superimposed noise and artifact that a robust machine learning system needs to discern and ignore. Accordingly, we present advances in neuroclustering that convert Big EEG Data into a machine learning state that will improve the efficiency of learning and detecting these aforementioned pathologies.

D. Ślęzak et al. (Eds.): BIH 2014, LNAI 8609, pp. 231–241, 2014.

In previous work the authors have shown that theoretical domain adaptation, which seeks to relate patterns in new patients to those in the larger established database, has shown some promise for neurosurgeons where there is a critical need to have the learning performed on a large previous distribution of neuro-ICU patients and then quickly train on a new neuro-ICU patient [15] [16] [17]. If the issue of using domain adaptation was resolved, *the second challenge* would be to overcome the complexities of EEG signals in the human brain in order to develop classification rules which can accurately detect *pathological* oscillations. These complexities include the subjective nature of what constitutes a pathological oscillation [18], and the huge dimensionality of the human brain, which has approximately 100 billion neurons each having about 1,000 connections (synapses)[19]. Moreover, neurological pathological activity may manifest itself differently from animal to animal or individual to individual [20] [21]. Because of this, it is necessary to not only collect large distributions of data sets in order for a machine to learn, but also a unique set of classification rules for each individual.

1.1   Big EEG Data

The authors are focused on developing a system to monitor patients recovering from surgery in the neuroICU ward. A single central server will need to be capable of monitoring and detecting pathological oscillations in all the patients from all the neuroICU wards across the country. Each day 320 neurosurgeries are performed in the US [22] where the average stay is for three days, Each patient is monitored with either sub-dural or dural electrodes at 1200 hz on 21 channels. This means that at any time there are 320 x 3 = 960 patients being monitored x 21 channels = 20,160 channels operating at 1200 hz = 24 million signals per second need to be disseminated and identified as pathological or artifact. Furthermore, these 24 million signals per second need to be constantly compared against hundreds of terabytes of stored neuro data from previous clients.

To overcome these challenges the authors have developed a system called *neuroClustering*^{TM} that is capable of dynamically ignoring artifact and converting complex signal analysis (*see* Fig.1 §I) into singular x, y points that constitute machine-learning-friendly clusters (*see* Fig.1 §III) . This is illustrated in Fig.1 where in a domain of time versus amplitudinal strength (*see* Fig.1 §II-c) in EEGs of a person during seizure (pathological oscillations also include specific types of oscillations neurosurgeons are interested in), artifact remain stationary in continuous clustered segments (*see* Fig.1 §III-i) while pathological oscillation activity should move in contrast thereof (*see* Fig.1 §III-k). To validate the hypothesis one needs to show that random amplitudinal distribution of artifact should be low during periods of normal neural activity because it is not coherent. The authors have already started patenting, and illustrated in detail, this technique, called *neuroClustering*, [23] [24] [15] and it is therefore not the subject matter of this paper.

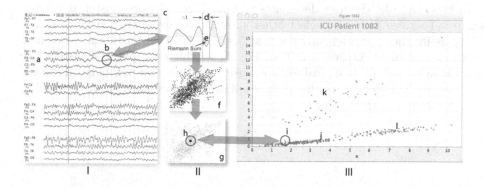

Fig. 1. neuroClustering: (Illustrates portion of patient's original EEG shown in §I. S II illustrates the 3 steps of *neuroClustering*™ which yield the final *neuroCluster*™ of the patient. §I-a shows shows one of the 18 EEG signals. §I-b illustrates one portion of the EEG extrapolated in §II-c which is with a spline to extract △ time§II-d and amplitudinal area values §II-e. Each point in §II-f represents one instance per 0.333 seconds. §III-h is the centroid of cluster in §II-g & II-f and is instantiated onto §III showing the point at §III-i which is in the normal cluster §III-j & §III-k being a pathological oscillation and §III-l being artifact.

2 Classifying Feature Clusters

We begin training the system with a typical EEG as shown in Fig.2(a). After applying the neuroClustering algorithm, we see the results instantiated on the scatter plot as shown in Fig.2(b). The window at the bottom contains a black line bisected by a red line. This black line is called the *feature line*; it represents the *temporally sequential* layout of the scatter plot above it. The bisecting red line running through the feature line is a running average of that line, and is referred to as the *feature threshold*; anything falling below this threshold is automatically ignored by our identification algorithm. As Fig.2(c) and (d) show, the feature line is used by the users (human clinical experts) of the system to classify pathological as well as non-pathological oscillations.

The next step in classification is for the user to click inside desired segments above the feature threshold to be assigned a classification. For example, if a user identifies a seizure, and wishes to classify it as such, the user will click on the related feature that rises above the feature threshold, at which point the program fills in the clicked area with a shade of white as shown by arrow 1 in Fig.2(c). Note that the individual cluster points associated by this white shaded area are highlighted in a new color, in this case purple. This cluster is known as the *feature cluster*. Additionally, upon selecting the feature area below, the centroid to the feature cluster is calculated and displayed in red, as indicated by arrow 2 in Fig.2c). This cluster can now be classified, and later used to train the system.

In this example, the user designates this particular feature cluster as being a seizure. The user may also select other surrounding segments that are artifact and classify them as such, arrows 3 & 5 in Fig.2d, that instantiate two new centroids shown by arrows 4 & 6 in Fig.2d. In this example, the system has now classified one pathological feature cluster and two non-pathological feature clusters. With these feature clusters marked, we can now continue on to training the system as shown in Fig.3.

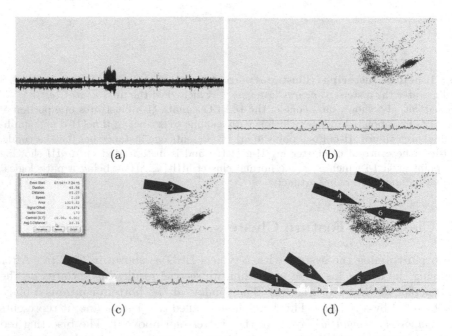

(a)   (b)

(c)   (d)

Fig. 2. Classifiying pathological oscillations vs. artifact: Original EEG comprising both a pathological oscillation and artifact (a), converted to neuroClusters (b), classifying a pathological oscillation (c), and classifying artifact (d).

3   Linearly Separable Attributes in Feature Clusters

After user has finished classifying pathological and artifact as illustrated in Fig.2(c) & (d), those feature clusters are stored so that the information can later be used to train the system. The system will be trained against two different single-dimensional hyperplanes based on two-dimensional (X,Y), linearly separable attributes culled from these feature clusters. The first hyperplane is based on two attributes: the *are length* (X) vs. *feature area* (Y). These two attributes, when used together, have high covariance above the feature threshold. Turns out that the covariance between X and Y is different between pathological feature clusters and artifact feature clusters; therefore, the data is linearly separable in most cases. The second hyperplane has similar properties to the first, and incorporates two additional features: *cDistance* and *pCount*. cDistance is a number indicating the average distance between a feature cluster's points and its centroid, while pCount is simply the number of points a feature cluster contains. If we take $X = \frac{pCount}{cDistance}$ vs. $Y = \frac{area}{cDistance}$, together these features give us data that is linearly separable.

4   The User Training Tool

The system's training tool, as shown in Fig.3 (a), instantiates a plot of *all* the previously classified feature clusters, which includes both pathological and artifact. This is illustrated by all of the selected feature clusters having checks as shown on the left hand side (*see* Fig.3 (a) arrow 1). Staying on Fig.3 (a); arrow 2 points to the blue points which represent the pathological oscillations classified in Fig.2(c) & (d) while arrow 3 points to smaller green points that represent artifact in Fig.2(c) & (d). Upon selecting the "train" button on the bottom left-hand corner of the training tool, the system calculates the linear classifier that separates the feature clusters, illustrated by the red line pointed to by arrow 4. In this particular case though, the data is distributed linearly in one easy-to-discern set of pathological feature clusters to the right of the line and another on the left-hand side of the line representing artifact.

Considering that the classifier line in the hyperplane shown in Fig.3 is a line that was trained on the *feature area* (X) versus *arc length* (Y), there may be times when there is conflicting pathological oscillations and artifact in the plane that cannot be differentiated one from the other. This prevents the learning algorithm from converging, thus rendering it unable to create a hyperplane. In these cases we can deselect the outliers in this plane that are classified as artifact, excluding them from the training set, as shown in Fig.3(b). While this allows convergence in this plane, the system is now vulnerable to misclassification, potentially causing false negatives or false positives.

For this reason, we must also train against the other plane based on $X = \frac{pCount}{cDistance}$ vs. $Y = \frac{area}{cDistance}$, including the artifact that was excluded from the previous plane. Creating a hyperplane here allows us to express the difference in density between pathological feature clusters and feature clusters representing artifact. Therefore, if the perceptron trained on the first plane activates on incorrect information, the second perceptron is very likely to not activate on that information in the second plane, which greatly reduces the likelihood of false positives (see Fig. 3(b)).

5   The Perceptron Learning Algorithm (PLA)

There is limited use for a single-layer perceptron having only two inputs, as this is typically a scenario designed for teaching students in an academic environment; however, our approach clearly demonstrates that the simplest of constructs can indeed be a potent annex. Much of the motivation behind this implementation is based on the notion that complexity should be introduced into a system only when the simplicity of that system impedes the production of meaningful results.

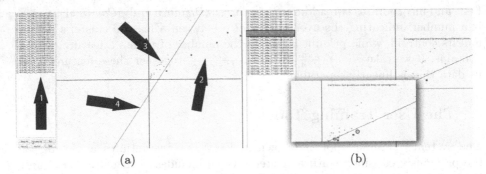

(a)   (b)

Fig. 3. Training Window: (a) Listed trained elements (arrow 1), Pathological oscillation (arrow 2), artifact (arrow 3) and perceptron classifier (arrow 4) *b* Different data in same plane, but showing elimination of outliers from the plane in the foreground.

Our version of the perceptron was purposely limited to two dimensions, as we only require a single dimension hyperplane for data classification. Once trained, the perceptron formula $h \in \mathcal{H}$ is expressed as:

$$h(X) = \operatorname{sgn}\left(\left(\sum_{i=1}^{2} \mathcal{W}_i \mathcal{X}_i\right) + \theta t\right) \tag{1}$$

where θt is the bias and $\mathcal{W}_i$ is the weight vector. Converting to vector form, the perceptron definition becomes $h(X) = \operatorname{sgn}(W^T X + b)$ where the *sgn* function is the binary decision maker, concluding the algorithm:

$$\operatorname{sgn}(x) = \begin{cases} 1 & \text{if } x > 0 \\ -1 & \text{otherwise} \end{cases} \tag{2}$$

The perceptron algorithm lends itself well to supervised classification. Our learning algorithm accepts a set of input vectors **X** where each vector has a predetermined classification (created through the classification tool), pathological oscillation (1) or artifact (-1), as training data. The predetermined classification is considered the *desired output* of **sgn(x)**. The algorithm receives user-identified training data constructed using the software's classification tool. As Fig. 3 demonstrates, the algorithm creates a single-dimensional hyperplane upon convergence. This is accomplished by adjusting weight vectors and a bias until the algorithm correctly classifies each element in the training set - i.e. the independent classification of sgn(x) matches the desired output states. To contend with the possibility of non-convergence, we limit our algorithm to a specified max epoch where, if reached, the algorithm is abandoned, and therefore never converges; the training data is considered not to be linearly separable.

Algorithm 1. Perceptron Learning Algorithm (PLA)

Accepts: training vectors **X**[], **float learningRate, int maxEpoch**
Returns: weight vectors **W**[], **bias**
Initialize variables, use arbitrary weights to start
W[1]=1.0f, W[2]=1.0f, float bias=0f, int epoch=0, float accuracy=0f
while (epcoh <maxEpoch and *accuracy* ≠ 1) **do**
    for each vector vx in vectors X **do**
        $(y \leftarrow sgn((W[1] * vx.X) + (W[2] * vx.Y) + bias)$
        if $(y \neq vx.Class)$ **then**
            make adjustments for the next pass
            $bias \leftarrow (bias + (learningRate * vx.Class) * 1)$
            $W[1] \leftarrow (W[1] + (learningRate * vx.Class) * vx.X)$
            $W[2] \leftarrow (W[2] + (learningRate * vx.Class) * vx.Y)$
        end if
        check accuracy and increment epoch
        $accuracy \leftarrow ComputeAccuracy(X, W, bias)$
        $epoch + +$
    end for
end while

---

6 The Data Attributes

To recap, our identification process incorporates two individual, single-layered perceptrons each trained against a different plane culled from the resultant data found in our scatter plot. The first perceptron is trained against vectors representing feature area over the arc length of the feature cluster. The feature area is derived from the temporally sequential graph of the scatter plot where the points are between when the graph first crosses above the feature threshold line and when if falls back below the line. Fig.2(c) illustrates this in the white highlighted area pointed to by arrow 1. In this case the summation of the Trapezoidal Rule was applied to calculate the approximate area: TRAP = (LEFT+RIGHT)/2

$$\int_a^b f(x)\,\mathrm{d}x \approx \sum_{i=0}^n \left(\frac{f(x_{i-1}) + f(x_i)}{2} \right) \Delta x_i \tag{3}$$

This was favored over performing actual integration, since the level of accuracy obtained through the integral was deemed unnecessary and expensive. The arc length calculation was performed using the summation of Euclidean distance between vector positions over the course of an event:

$$\mathrm{d}(\mathbf{q}, \mathbf{p}) = \sqrt{\sum_{i=1}^n (q_i - p_i)^2} \tag{4}$$

Fig.2(c) illustrates such an event where arrow 2 directs attention to the points in purple belonging to the highlighted cluster. A high degree of covariance exists between the area and arc length during events surrounding pathological oscillation, showing vectors as being farther away from the origin. For artifact, area tends to progress more slowly relative to arc length, forcing vectors to remain closer to the origin. Using our data, we discovered that even with reasonably good training in this plane, the degree of false positives can be as high as 15% in signals containing a high degree of noise combined with artifact.

The authors introduced another perceptron based on a different plane that would examine additional attributes after the first perceptron activates. Here we trained the second perceptron on attributes: feature area over average distance from centroid vs. point count of the feature cluster over average distance from centroid as shown in equation 4. This data allows the perceptron to gauge the density of the cluster being evaluated.

7   Experiments

The authors' goal was to validate the hypothesis that single-layer, two-dimensional perceptrons could, in fact, be trained to identify pathological brain oscillations with a high degree of sensitivity and precision. Our experiment was set up using a customized software suite built and tailored specifically for this research. The dataset consisted of twenty-two EEG files that spanned almost 120 days of data collected from four individual laboratory rats, and amounted to over forty-two gigabytes in total size. All of these files were processed through our software algorithms. For this experiment, data normalization was not performed.

It should be noted here that during the perceptron training process, it was necessary to modify the training set several times per animal. Because our perceptron algorithm does not produce an optimal hyperplane, it is easily overtrained so that there exists no optimal margin between the two classes of data. In most cases, less training data worked best so long as the sampling was good, keeping the training set to an average of five seizures and fifteen non seizure events. The algorithm processed one tenth of the data, which was then re-examined by the trainer for sensitivity, precision, and effectiveness. After the trainer identified false positives, and/or false negatives, several of those misclassified events were used to re-train the system. This process was repeated up to three times per rat before the entire dataset was processed, after which we recorded the final results of the experiment; they were as shown in Table 1.

8   Results

This experiment was performed using data from epileptic rats, however, this research is aimed towards addressing human epileptic seizures. Human data, while similar to the rat data, has its own set of challenges with respect to artifact and epileptiform pattern drift. There were a total of four animals for which EEG data sampled at 1000 Hz was analyzed. The animal subjects were labeled 246, 288, 307, and 309. In addition to the EEG data were Excel spreadsheets, created by trained researchers, identifying all the seizures within each file for each animal. The goal here was to have the system automatically identify epileptiform activity, and match all of the seizure entries perviously identified by trained researchers contained in the spreadsheets for each animal. To ensure proper comparison to other seizure identification methods, a standard of performance measurement was adopted here:

- *True positive* (TP): correctly classified as an epileptiform event.
- *True negative* (TN): correctly classified as a non-epileptiform event.
- *False positive* (FP): incorrectly classified as an epileptiform event.
- *False negative* (FN): incorrectly classified as non-epileptiform event (a miss).
- *Sensitivity* is defined as: $S=\frac{TP}{TP+FN}$
- *Specificity* is defined as: $K=\frac{TN}{TN+FP}$

In our results, the true negatives were not tracked. Essentially, everything not classified as a seizure qualifies as being TN. As such, actual specificity cannot be provided here. In its stead, we present *precision*: $P=\frac{TP}{TP+FP}$.

Out of the four animals, animal 246 was the most difficult to train for. The EEG was plagued with much artifact and other anomalous frequency drift throughout. In fact, the initial results for 246 were 89.6% sensitivity with precision of only around 85% due to false positives. In this case, a differential filter was applied to 246 EEG. The final results for animal 246 saw improvement in both sensitivity (95.6%) and precision (89.7%).

Table 1. Results of identifying pathological oscillations representing seizures in rats from 42 gb of EEG data

Rat	Sensitivity	False Positives	Precision
307	267 out of 281 = 95.00%	8	(281/289) = 97.00%
288	136 out of 141 = 96.40%	0	100.00%
246	108 out of 113 = 95.60%	12	(108/120) = 90.00%
309	311 out of 316 = 98.40%	28	(311/339) = 91.70%
Total results	822 out of 851 = 96.60%	48	(822/870) = 94.50%

Out of the 42gb of total data for all animals, 822 of the 851 pathologic oscillations were identified which equals a **96.60% sensitivity**. Out of the identified pathological oscillations there were 48 false positives, leaving us with a **94.50% precision** rate. The final results for each rat are shown in table 1. The identification routine was able to process almost 8gb of EEG per hour. This performance isn't all that bad, but can be improved upon in a big way. The current system places a lot of processing power towards displaying graphical information the entire time it is processing. If the graphical processing were taken out, it is estimated that performance could be increased by over 2x. Other simple improvements to the efficiency of the algorithms could get us close to processing the entire 42gb used in this experimentation within an hour or less.

9   Conclusions and Future Work

The experiments show that in terms of adding a classification rule based system onto the original neuroClustering developed by the authors is a viable option so long as it will also be in a form conducive to domain adaptation. Utilizing perceptrons in the manner described in this paper to aid the neurosurgeons selecting what kind of pathological oscillations they are interested in and what they want the machine to deem as artifact, has shown to be a viable option that certainly renders the need to continue honing and refining the perceptron based method illustrated and defined in this paper and these experiments. For our future work we will test various thresholds in the perceptron algorithms against large sets of data and see where the strengths and weaknesses of timing and confidence levels pan out. Overall the results of these experiments are encouraging and are a source to drill down deeper into the methodologies presented in these experiments.

References

1. Schnitzler, A., Gross, J.: Normal and pathological oscillatory communication in the brain. Nature Reviews Neuroscience 6(4), 285–296 (2005)
2. John, E., Prichep, L., Fridman, J., Easton, P.: Neurometrics: Computer-assisted differential diagnosis of brain dysfunctions. Science (1988)
3. Dumas, G., Nadel, J., Soussignan, R., Martinerie, J., Garnero, L.: Inter-brain synchronization during social interaction. PLoS One 5(8), e12166 (2010)
4. Ferrarelli, F., Sarasso, S., Guller, Y., Riedner, B.A., Peterson, M.J., Bellesi, M., Massimini, M., Postle, B.R., Tononi, G.: Reduced natural oscillatory frequency of frontal thalamocortical circuits in schizophrenia. Archives of General Psychiatry (2012)
5. Timofeev, I., Steriade, M., et al.: Neocortical seizures: initiation, development and cessation. Neuroscience 123(2), 299 (2004)
6. Mordekar, S., Prasad, M., Smith, N., Vyas, H., Ross, C., Jaspan, T., Whitehouse, W.: Favorable outcome from alpha coma in a 15-year-old with traumatic brain injury. Journal of Pediatric Neurology 10(2), 137–141 (2012)
7. Dauwels, J., Srinivasan, K., Ramasubba Reddy, M., Musha, T., Vialatte, F., Latchoumane, C., Jeong, J., Cichocki, A.: Slowing and loss of complexity in alzheimer's eeg: two sides of the same coin? International Journal of Alzheimer's Disease 2011 (2011)
8. Adeli, H., Ghosh-Dastidar, S., Dadmehr, N.: A spatio-temporal wavelet-chaos methodology for eeg-based diagnosis of alzheimer's disease. Neuroscience Letters 444(2), 190–194 (2008)
9. Bernier, R., Dawson, G., Webb, S., Murias, M.: Eeg mu rhythm and imitation impairments in individuals with autism spectrum disorder. Brain and Cognition 64(3), 228–237 (2007)
10. Shah, A., Agarwal, R., Carhuapoma, J., Loeb, J.: Compressed eeg pattern analysis for critically iii neurological-neurosurgical patients. Neurocritical Care 5(2), 124–133 (2006)
11. Yan, M., Hou, Z., Gao, Y.: A bilateral brain symmetry index for analysis of eeg signal in stroke patients. In: 2011 4th International Conference on Biomedical Engineering and Informatics (BMEI), vol. 1, pp. 8–11. IEEE (2011)

12. van der Stelt, O., Belger, A., Lieberman, J.A.: Macroscopic fast neuronal oscillations and synchrony in schizophrenia. Proceedings of the National Academy of Sciences of the United States of America 101(51), 17567–17568 (2004)
13. Jeong, J.: Eeg dynamics in patients with alzheimer's disease. Clinical Neurophysiology 115(7), 1490–1505 (2004)
14. Hutchison, W.D., Dostrovsky, J.O., Walters, J.R., Courtemanche, R., Boraud, T., Goldberg, J., Brown, P.: Neuronal oscillations in the basal ganglia and movement disorders: evidence from whole animal and human recordings. The Journal of Neuroscience 24(42), 9240–9243 (2004)
15. Lewis, R., Mello, C.A., Carlsen, J., Grabenstatter, H., Brooks-Kayal, A., White, A.M.: Autonomous neuroclustering of pathologic oscillations using discretized centroids. In: 8th International Conference on Mass Data Analysis of Images and Signals with Applications in Medicine, New York, USA, July13-16 (2013)
16. Lewis, R., Mello, C.A., Ellenberger, J., White, A.M.: Domain Adaptation for Pathologic Oscillations. In: Ciucci, D., Inuiguchi, M., Yao, Y., Ślęzak, D., Wang, G. (eds.) RSFDGrC 2013. LNCS, vol. 8170, pp. 374–379. Springer, Heidelberg (2013)
17. Lewis, R., Ellenberger, J., Williams, C., White, A.M.: Investigation into the efficacy of generating synthetic pathological oscillations for domain adaptation. In: IX International Seminar on Medical Information Processing and Analysis, pp. 89220E–89220E. International Society for Optics and Photonics (2013)
18. Williams, P.A., Hellier, J.L., White, A.M., Staley, K.J., Dudek, F.E.: Development of spontaneous seizures after experimental status epilepticus: Implications for understanding epileptogenesis. Epilepsia (Series 4) 48, 157–163 (2007)
19. Williams, R.W., Herrup, K.: The control of neuron number. The Annual Review of Neuroscience 11, 423–453 (1988)
20. Zhang, X., Jiang, W., Ras, Z.W., Lewis, R.: Blind music timbre source isolation by multi- resolution comparison of spectrum signatures. In: Szczuka, M., Kryszkiewicz, M., Ramanna, S., Jensen, R., Hu, Q. (eds.) RSCTC 2010. LNCS, vol. 6086, pp. 610–619. Springer, Heidelberg (2010)
21. Lewis, R.A., White, A.M.: Seizure detection using sequential and coincident power spectra with deterministic finite automata. In: BIOCOMP, pp. 481–488 (2010)
22. CDC: Centers for disease control and prevention (cdc). cdc/nchs national hospital discharge survey (2010),
http://www.cdc.gov/nchs/data/nhds/2average/2010ave2_firstlist.pdf
(accessed: March 14, 2014)
23. Lewis, R., Mello, C.A., White, A.M.: Tracking epileptogenesis progressions with layered fuzzy k-means and k-medoid clustering. Procedia Computer Science 9, 432–438 (2012)
24. Carlsen, J., Grabenstatter, H., Lewis, R., Mello, C.A., Brooks-Kayal, A., White, A.M.: Identification of seizures in prolonged video-eeg recordings. In: 66th American Epilepsy Society Annual Meeting, San Diego, CA, USA, November 30 - December 4 (2012); Poster

Data and Information Granule Rules Retrieval: Differences of Activation in Parietal Cortex

Wei Zhao[1], Hongyu Li[1], Gue Gu[2], Xiuzhen Wang[1,*], Guohui Zhou[1,*], Jiaxin Cui[3,4,*], Weiquan Gu[5,*]

[1] College of Computer Science and Information Engineering, Harbin Normal University, Harbin, China
xzhnwang@gmail.com, zhou_ghui@163.com
[2] Software College, Northeast Agricultural University, Harbin, China
[3] State Key Laboratory of Cognitive Neuroscience and Learning & IDG/McGovern Institute for Brain Research, Beijing Normal University, Beijing, China
[4] Center for Collaboration and Innovation in Brain and Learning Sciences, Beijing Normal University, Beijing, China
cuijiaxin@gmail.com
[5] Harbin Normal University, Harbin, China
guweiq.gu@gmail.com

Abstract. Efficient encoding of Roman rules is based on the neural bases of mathematical cognitive abilities. The present imaging studies have shown that information granule representing a form of Roman rules is associated with arithmetical domain-sensitive parietal cortex, indicating a switch from the data to the information granule retrieval of memory rules. So far, however, little is known about the developing neural substrate for the establishment of rules from data to information granule. The aim of the present fMRI study is to investigate whether and how mathematical intelligence might be enhanced from data to information granule of Roman arithmetic rules in the parietal cortex. Concerning the same rules, the paired t-test analysis indicated that different activation in the bilateral parietal lobule associated with different retrieval levels. In conclusion, the present study yielded some evidence that a successful model for knowledge-building of rules is accompanied by modifications of brain activation patterns.

Keywords: data, information granule, experiential knowledge, parietal lobule, mathematical intelligence.

1 Introduction

When we face a new problem our eagerness to solve it often leads us to accept the experiential response that comes to mind, so that we implement it with delay. Very often this will not be the most effective solution available. The best approach, particularly with conceptual rule problems, is to form an information granule from which we can perfectly constitute the rule of data and associated semantic information fusion [1].

---

* Corresponding authors.

D. Ślęzak et al. (Eds.): BIH 2014, LNAI 8609, pp. 242–251, 2014.

Cognitive and psychological studies converge in the view that the experiential knowledge can influence problem perception [2, 3]. So far, only a few functional MRI studies have investigated the information processing machines of arithmetic learning along with the parietal areas [4, 5]. These results support the view that the parietal regions are associated with mental operations including guessed results (data retrieval) based on background knowledge [6]. From previous studies, the inferior parietal lobule contributes to attentional selection and orientation for a number processing circuit [7]. The right inferior parietal lobule has been specifically linked to the representation of quantity [8] and relatively specific for episodic memory [9]. The stronger activation within the left superior parietal lobule in mnemonic retrieval has been interpreted as reflecting attentional processes differentially engaged as a result of perceived familiarity [10]. It can be concluded that the network involved in skilled mathematics performance in educated adults has been well established.

The present study investigated how information granule is formed by comparing information rules (after learning, namely post-test) with syntax and semantics to data rules (before learning, namely pre-test) with background knowledge using the same tasks (e.g. III × VII) during fMRI. On the practice phase, participants were asked to learn the Roman rules, and produce the result from memory to solve Roman arithmetic tasks with two-digit Roman operators. These were presented on a computer for a total duration of approximately 2 h before entering the second scanner (post-test). In pre-test (before learning), rules with data form (without syntax and semantics and with background knowledge) showed greater activation in the right parietal areas, right angular, right precuneus and left precueus (BA 7/31) than information granules of the same rules subsequently. Granular rules, on the other hand, showed greater activation in the left superior parietal lobule and the left precuneus (BA 19) than rules with data form. This shift of activation within the parietal lobe from a set of subareas in parietal cortex predominance to another set of subareas in the parietal cortex was interpreted to represent a shift from processing unsure symbolic relations to processing sure symbolic relations. The post-test could show that the observed relative decrease of action in the right parietal areas was specifically related to semantic and logical relations among elements in a Roman problem. This finding was interpreted to be because of uncertain relations between elements for the choice of a dominant background strategy as a solution strategy for tasks with data form. It is more likely that training effects in rules resulted from the storage of interdependencies among elements. A study on retrieving the simpler mathematical fact [6] also indicated that the parietal areas are closely linked to the representation of information stored in encoded memory. These results suggest that training leads to different brain activation patterns in the encoding of memory depending on background knowledge as well as on the time of training.

The studies reviewed so far investigated information- encoded changes in brain activation patterns once learning had taken place. It is unclear, however, how the storage changes take place from data to information granule. In the present brain imaging study, the process of encoding itself is investigated for healthy participants performing a Roman task. The twice tests investigated here consisting similarly of 28 Roman trials (e.g. III × VII), took place during the scanning session itself. Training consisted of a large number of tasks with two-digit Roman operator (e.g. XII × IX) in a higher frequency of repetition for one set of problems until participants had mastered them perfectly. After training, subjects took part in a post-test scanning. A difference between an information granule retrieval test and a data retrieval test is that in the previous studies, the comparison was between data retrieval (unstored rules) and granule retrieval (rules to be stored in memory) in decision-making processes [11] while in the present study the problems solved were compared data to information by mathematical rules. In particular, we expected to specify the nature of the information granule processes mediated by parietal and other brain regions. We did so by measuring in data and granular tasks not only the effects of background knowledge on neural activity but also the effects of accumulated information. Although the same tasks could explain greater activity for data than for information retrieval, these two ways of same rules retrieval can be expected to have different effects on accuracy.

2   Method

2.1   Participants

Eight of twelve right-handed healthy young adults (5 female, mean age=23.6±3.3) performed both pre-test (before learning, namely data retrieval) and post-test (after learning, namely granule retrieval). All were right-handed and native Chinese speakers with normal or corrected-to-normal vision. Written informed consent was obtained from all participants in accordance with the Ethical Commission of MRI center of Beijing Normal University. Participants received monetary in compensation for participation. One subject was omitted because of unsuccessful data acquisition and excessive head motion. Two subjects were removed from imaging analyses due to correct answer exceeding 90% and one other subject was removed due to body reason without the recording of the second imaging data. This fMRI resulted in 8 subjects for imaging analyses.

2.2   Stimuli and Procedure

The entire experiment was divided into three phases: the first phase involved acquiring functional MRI data for unknown rules guessing; the second entailed learning and training until mastering the Roman rules perfectly; and the third phase involved obtaining functional MRI images during mnemonic retrieval of Roman rules. On a single day, a participant guessed Roman rules before learning (pre-test, namely Phase 1), learned and training the Roman rules (phase 2), and demonstrated the ability to store the rules after learning (post-test, namely phase 3). Functional MR scans were acquired before and after learning, and these data form the basis of the current report.

The subject response recordings were performed using E-Prime software package. The participants' task was to guess and solve the same 28 Roman problems in a scanner (i.e. V× VII). In a previous study, Masataka et al. had investigated that the neuronal correlates of reading Roman numerals and the results revealed that the alphabetical symbols had numeric meaning [12]. To examine neural mechanisms of Roman rules, we present a set of stimuli repeatedly and examine how the brain's response to the same rules change over time.

Twenty-eight Roman rules made up the fMRI test. Making the two tasks for the comparison of memory encoding the same ensured that the differences in results between data and information granule retrieval could not be due to differences between tasks, but were only due to the quality of the retrieval of information encoded effects. The sequence of the twenty-eight Roman problems varied randomly from trial to trial through the test. Before the pre-test scanning, the participants were given a tutorial on Roman problem guessing. On the practice phase, before post-test fMRI scanning, participants were introduced to these Roman rules. They solved large numbers of Roman problems until mastering them perfectly.

A trial began with the presentation of the red star for 0.5 s, the presentation of the condition items for 3.5 s, then the Roman problem for not more than 2 s and a pause (white cross in the center) for (5.5-RT) s (RT: reaction times of choosing answer). RT was measured from the onset of the presentation of the given answer. The 2 s was given to ensure that participants could complete the guess, for unknown Roman problems, or the solving for well-known Roman problems from the very beginning of the choosing answer. During answer was presented, participants were requested to respond by pressing cither the left or right button with right-hand for selecting right answer on a 2-button handheld device. There was a (5.5-RT) s rest interval for before the next trials began.

2.3   Magnetic Resonance Methods

The study was performed using a 3.0-Tesla Siemens Scanner (Magnetom Trio, Erlangen, Germany) with a receive-only whole head coil in the MRI center of Beijing Normal University. Firm foam padding was used in order to minimize and restrict head motion. Axial multisclice T2* weighted EPI images with BOLD contrast were obtained (TR=2000 ms, TE=30 ms, flip angle=90°, matrix= 64×64, 4-mm slice thickness and slice gap=0.6 mm, in plane resolution 3.125×3.125 mm, 33 axial slices parallel to anterior commissure–posterior commissure (AC–PC) plane). For anatomic localization, a structural scan was obtained for each participant using a T1-weighted sequence. Scanning parameters were as follows: TR=2530 ms, TE=3.39 ms; flip angle=7°, acquisition matrix= 256×256, isotropic resolution =1×1 mm. slice thickness = 1.3 mm, number of slices = 144.

2.4   Data Processing and Statistics Analysis

All preprocessing and statistical analyses were conducted using SPM8. Slice timing correction was first applied to the EPI images, adjusting slice timing based on the middle slice. Next, the fMR images were realigned and co-registered to the participant's own T1-weighted MR images. The anatomical image was processed using a unified segmentation procedure combining segmentation, bias correction, and spatial normalization to the MNI template [13]; the same normalization parameters were then used to normalize the fMR images. Finally, a Gaussian kernel of 6 mm FWHM was applied to spatially smooth the images in order to conform to the assumptions of the GLM implemented in SPM8.

Statistical analysis was based on the general linear model (GLM) on individual subjects' data. First-level analyses estimating contrasts of interest for each subject were modeled by a series of impulses convolved with a canonical hemodynamic response function. The first-level multiple regression model included one condition at encoding for each participant, given by the crossing of "data retrieval" [correct and incorrect responses by unconfident judgment (pre-learning rules) and "information granule" [correct responses followed by confident judgment (post-learning rules)].

The group analysis concerned whole-brain contrasts between stimulus-driven effective related to the retrieval of the target object by performing t tests on these images, treating each subject as a random effect. A within-subject paired samples t-test modeled the two relevant events types [correct and incurrent trials vs. correct trials]. Our standard statistical threshold was set to p < 0.05, FDR uncorrected at the voxel level. We note that no voxels met the standard threshold on some occasions, For this, the results obtained when the statistical threshold is relaxed to p < 0.001 uncorrected with cluster-level correction for multiple comparisons at p <0.05. Region of interest (ROI) on the parietal voxel showed a significant effect with the MARSBAR toolbox for use with SPM8.

3   Results

3.1   Behavioral Data

When comparing data with granule retrieval, tests revealed significant differences in accuracy (63.0% vs. 95.0%, t = −8.5, P< 0.0001), and not significantly different for button-press tasks nor for correct responses when comparing the two tasks.

3.2   Brain Activation Patterns

The fMRI analyses tested for regions showing an effect of successful granule after learning, comparing correct/sure trials (post-test) minus all trials (pre-test). This revealed a significant cluster of activation in the left precuneus (BA 19)/Superior parietal lobule (BA 7) (x, y, z = -36, -72, 39; Figure 1). Activity in the right inferior parietal lobule/angular gyrus/precuneus (BA 39) (x, y, z = 45, -66, 39; Figure 1), the left precuneus (BA 31/7) (x, y, z = -6,-63, 27; Figure 1) and the left precuneus (BA 7) (x, y, z = -6, -60, 39; Figure 1) at data processed whether the target object would be unconfidently guessed at retrieval, highlighting confidence of stimulus processing at granular level. At a lower uncorrected level of significance, the reversed comparison showed activation also in other regions of the active network (Table 1).

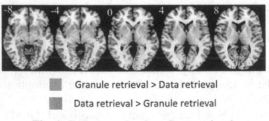

▮ Granule retrieval > Data retrieval

▮ Data retrieval > Granule retrieval

Fig. 1. Granule retrieval vs. Data retrieval

Table 1. Differential brain responses to data and information retrieval in stereotactic space

Side	Brain region (BA)	Vol.	T	x	y	z
I. Information processing > Data processing						
L	STG(BA 22)/Insula(BA 13)	47	4.78	-48	-18	-3
L	MTG/(BA 37/21)	44	3.15	-57	-45	-6
R	Lentiform Nucleus/ Claustrum)	40	2.86	30	-9	0
L	Precuneus(BA 19)/ SPL(BA 7)	52	2.85	-36	-72	39
L	Anterior Cingulate (BA 24)	42	2.63	-6	24	12
			2.51	0	18	12
II. Data processing> Information processing						
L	IFG/BA 47	137	6.09	-39	24	-6
L	Insula(BA 13)/IFG(BA 45/47)		4.45	-33	21	3
L	IFG/BA 47		4.39	-27	21	-9
R	IPL/ AG/ Precuneus(BA 19)/BA 39	180	6.04	45	-66	39
R	MTG(BA 39)/STG(BA 39)		4.34	45	-63	27
R	AG(BA 39)/SOG(BA 19)MTG(BA 39)		3.64	42	-72	27
R	IFG/BA 47)	80	5.65	33	27	-9
R	MFG(BA 11/47)/IFG(BA 47)		4.50	30	36	-6
R	SG(BA 34/25)/ Hypothalamus		2.31	39	33	3
R	SG(BA 34)/Hypothalamus	58	5.27	6	0	-9
L	SG(BA 34/25)/ Hypothalamus		4.69	-6	0	-9
L	Culmen/ PG(35/30/28/27)	49	5.05	-15	-30	-6
R	Culmen	100	4.99	6	-30	-12
R	Anterior Lobe		4.44	6	-36	-21
R	Culmen/PG(BA 35)		3.89	15	-27	-9
R	MFG/BA 46	58	4.79	45	18	21
R	MFG (BA 9)/ Precentral Gyrus(BA 9)		2.65	33	21	33
L	Cingulate Gyrus(BA 31)	220	4.76	-21	-30	42
L	Precuneus(BA 31/7)		3.86	-6	-63	27
L	Precuneus(BA 7)		3.70	-6	-60	39
L	Precentral Gyrus(BA 46/6)	93	4.63	-54	6	9
L	Insula(BA 13)		2.61	-45	9	15
L	Insula(BA 13/22)		2.49	-42	-3	3
L	MFG(BA 8)/SFG(BA 8)	174	4.43	-24	12	63
L	SFG/BA 6		2.95	-21	12	48
L	MFG(BA 9)/ AC(BA 32)	57	3.44	-3	39	27
L	Anterior Cingulate(BA 32/24)		3.21	-6	36	12
L	MFG(8/6/9)/Cingulate Gyrus(BA 32)		2.12	-3	30	36
		57	2.92	9	-27	-30
			2.87	0	-33	-33
L	Posterior Lobe		2.61	-9	-36	-36

Height threshold: p<0.05, uncorrected. Extent threshold: k=30 voxels. Voxel size: 3×3×3mm^3. The brain region in the parenthesis refers to the activated region center without maximum peak. STG:Superior Temporal Gyrus; MTG: Middle Temporal Gyrus; SPL:Superior Parietal Lobule; IFG:Inferior Frontal Gyrus; IPL: Inferior Parietal Lobule; SOG:Superior Occipital Gyrus;MTG: Middle Temporal Gyrus;MFG: Middle Frontal Gyrus; PG: Parahippocampal Gyrus; SFG:Superior Frontal Gyrus; AG: Angular Gyrus; SG:Subcallosal Gyrus; AC:Anterior Cingulate; L: Left; R: Right; BA: Brodmann area; Coordinates (X,Y,Z) are given using the Talairach coordinates; Vol.: volume.

4   Discussion

4.1   Granular Effects in the Behavioral Data

For tasks with identical stimuli, retrieving information granule is hardly any easier in comparison to data retrieval dependent only on experience. The difference in key-pressing between data retrieval of Roman rules and information granule of Roman rules was not significant. The learning effects observed here are clearer than those for data retrieval tasks using the same rules. This might be for two reasons. First, the learning was more extensive semantic processing in information retrieval tasks than in data retrieval tasks. Second, perhaps more importantly, there was an additional 2 hours rehearsal between the two tests. The solution to coarse-grained rules could have been retrieved at error rate of less than 5%, and no answer could be given before the associated output value was retrieved. The accuracy might therefore reflect the learning effect in the case of granular rules.

4.2   Granular Effect in the fMRI Data

We observed changes in activation in the left parietal areas and other brain regions due to training, indicating a shift from a guess associated with more effort to information retrieval including the correlation among elements. While data retrieval of Roman arithmetic tasks are assumed to be solved by mathematically skilled participants via retrieving the result from experiential knowledge, which may be due to a lack of knowledge regarding information among elements in expression. Retrieving the same Roman rule from granule enables the participant to connect the result from rule presentations, building some or all of the intermediate associations required for the solution of an encoded problem. A systematic change in activation patterns consisting of an activation decrease in some brain areas and an activation increase in others can indicate that encoding induced the development of new cognitive processes or representations, or that the degree of logical communication of processing components involved in granularity has changed. The pattern of the change in brain activation observed here is compatible with a shift from guessing to granule retrieval for the Roman rules: parietal areas are assumed to support different functions necessary in mathematical thinking [14]. In the following, we will discuss this interpretation in detail.

Within the left parietal areas, we observed larger activations for granule rules within the left superior parietal lobule and the left precuneus (BA 19). These regions are engaged when information retrieval is accompanied by the recollection of event details [15]. The left superior parietal cortex activations have been reported to responsive to calculation [16], learning strategy [17], variability in experience dependent plasticity [18] and effect of calculation [19]. As expected, these findings suggest that developmental increases in simple relational retrieving abilities are associated with a shift from a laborious executive and working memory towards focal activation in superior parietal regions associated with more automatic and efficient problem solving. In initial studies, one hypothesis is that the precuneus participates as part of the mind's 'eye' to reinstate visual content during retrieval [20]. It has also been suggested assumed that precuneus activity influences elaborating highly integrated and associative information, rather than directly processing external stimuli [21], with an important role for precuneus in retrieval of episodic memory[9][22]. Here, we present evidence that the function of precuneus is particularly important for explicit representation associated with semantic and logical relations among elements in rules. Thus, learning increased the retrieval of highly correlative information among elements.

We further observed some region within the left parietal areas in the two tests. Activation within the left precuneus has been observed in number processing [3], and is assumed to cause acalculia and a selective deficit in arithmetic by lesion studies [23, 24]. Thus, left precuneus is a brain region critical to numerical ability [25]. Given these findings, one would predict that data and granule rules would overlap due to their common reliance on experiential knowledge. The different areas observed in the two tests are therefore compatible with our interpretation of a shift from direct guessing to result retrieval for the same rules. In contrast to previous results from training study [26], the left precuneus also referred to as the sensory cortices, which controls the right hand, was found to correspond to the manual module.

5   Conclusion

We investigated the specificity of parietal cortex activations by directly comparing activity during data and information granule retrieval using fMRI. We examined whether activity in the left superior parietal lobule and left precuneus (BA 19) during high-correlation elements would be specific to the granule retrieval. Our findings suggest that left superior parietal lobule and left precuneus (BA 19) activity during solving Roman problems is memory specific (i.e. associating elements) and is related to the explicit requirement of details among elements in rule processing. The results demonstrate that the left superior parietal lobule and precuneus (BA 19) correlated with the enhancing of human mathematical abilities. Simultaneously, the present study revealed different activity: the right inferior parietal lobule, the angular gyrus and bilateral precuneus showing greater activity for data than for information granule during data and granule retrieval of Roman rules. The results demonstrate that this parietal region responds most strongly to manipulations of representational difficulty relying on previous experience [27].

Acknowledgments. This work was supported by New Century Excellent Talents at Universities (NCET-07-0101), Fundamental Research Funds for the Central Universities (248-105565GK), Foundation of Heilongjiang Educational Committee (No. SEIE2013-04, 12541255, 12531211 and 12531190), Philosophy Social Sciences Program of Heilongjiang Province of China (No. 11D055, 12D067 and F201233), the training project (No.XKGP201201302) and the National Science Foundation of China (No. 60931003, 30870759, 41071262 and 13BTQ057).

References

1. Pedrycz, W.: Knowledge-based clustering: from data to information granules. Wiley Interscience (2005)
2. Schoenfeld, A.H., Herrmann, D.J.: Problem perception and knowledge structure in expert and novice mathematical problem solvers. J. Exp. Psychol. Learn. Mem. Cogn. 8, 484 (1982)

3. Kolb, D.A.: Experimental learning. Experience as the source of learning and development. Prentice-Hall, New Jersey (1984)
4. Baroody, A.J., Dowker, A.: The development of arithmetic concepts and skills: Constructive adaptive expertise. Routledge (2013)
5. Price, G.R., Mazzocco, M.M., Ansari, D.: Why mental arithmetic counts: brain activation during single digit arithmetic predicts high school math scores. J. Neurosci. 33, 156–163 (2013)
6. Ischebeck, A., Zamarian, L., Schocke, M., Delazer, M.: Flexible transfer of knowledge in mental arithmetic–an fMRI study. Neuroimage 44, 1103–1112 (2009)
7. Dehaene, S., Piazza, M., Pinel, P., Cohen, L.: Three parietal circuits for number processing. Cogn. Neuropsychol. 20, 487–506 (2003)
8. Simon, O., Mangin, J.-F., Cohen, L., Le Bihan, D., Dehaene, S.: Topographical layout of hand, eye, calculation, and language-related areas in the human parietal lobe. Neuron 33, 475–487 (2002)
9. Sandrini, M., Rossini, P.M., Miniussi, C.: The differential involvement of inferior parietal lobule in number comparison: a rTMS study. Neuropsychologia 42, 1902–1909 (2004)
10. Goel, V., Dolan, R.J.: Explaining modulation of reasoning by belief. Cognition 87, B11–B22 (2003)
11. Wagner, A.D., Shannon, B.J., Kahn, I., Buckner, R.L.: Parietal lobe contributions to episodic memory retrieval. Trends in Cog. Sci. 9, 445–453 (2005)
12. Masataka, N., Ohnishi, T., Imabayashi, E., Hirakata, M., Matsuda, H.: Neural correlates for learning to read Roman numerals. Brain Lang 100, 276–282 (2007)
13. Ashburner, J., Friston, K.J.: Unified segmentation. Neuroimage 26, 839–851 (2005)
14. Harvey, B., Klein, B., Petridou, N., Dumoulin, S.: Topographic representation of numerosity in the human parietal cortex. Science 341, 1123–1126 (2013)
15. Henson, R.N., Rugg, M., Shallice, T., Josephs, O., Dolan, R.: Recollection and familiarity in recognition memory: an event-related functional magnetic resonance imaging study. J. Neurosci. 19, 3962–3972 (1999)
16. Arsalidou, M., Taylor, M.J.: Is 2+ 2= 4? Meta-analyses of brain areas needed for numbers and calculations. NeuroImage 54, 2382–2393 (2011)
17. Delazer, M., Ischebeck, A., Domahs, F., Zamarian, L., Koppelstaetter, F., Siedentopf, C.M., Kaufmann, L., Benke, T., Felber, S.: Learning by strategies and learning by drill—Evidence from an fMRI study. NeuroImage 25, 838–849 (2005)
18. Matejko, A.A., Price, G.R., Mazzocco, M.M.M., Ansari, D.: Individual differences in left parietal white matter predict math scores on the Preliminary Scholastic Aptitude Test. NeuroImage 66, 604–610 (2013)
19. Simon, O., Mangin, J.F., Cohen, L., Le Bihan, D., Dehaene, S.: Topographical Layout of Hand, Eye, Calculation, and Language-Related Areas in the Human Parietal Lobe. Neuron 33, 475–487 (2002)
20. Newman, S.D., Carpenter, P.A., Varma, S., Just, M.A.: Frontal and parietal participation in problem solving in the Tower of London: fMRI and computational modeling of planning and high-level perception. Neuropsychologia 41, 1668–1682 (2003)
21. Fletcher, P.C., Frith, C.D., Baker, S.C., Shallice, T., Frackowiak, R.S.J., Dolan, R.J.: The mind's eye—precuneus activation in memory-related imagery. Neuroimage 2, 195–200 (1995)
22. Cavanna, A.E., Trimble, M.R.: The precuneus: a review of its functional anatomy and behavioural correlates. Brain 129, 564–583 (2006)

23. Kelley, W.M., Macrae, C.N., Wyland, C.L., Caglar, S., Inati, S., Heatherton, T.F.: Finding the self? An event-related fMRI study. J. Cogn. Neurosci. 14, 785–794 (2002)
24. Dehaene, S., Cohen, L.: Cerebral pathways for calculation: Double dissociation between rote verbal and quantitative knowledge of arithmetic. Cortex 33, 219–250 (1997)
25. Takayama, Y., Sugishita, M., Akiguchi, I., Kimura, J.: Isolated acalculia due to left parietal lesion. Arch. Neurol. 51, 286 (1994)
26. Baldo, J.V., Dronkers, N.F.: Neural correlates of arithmetic and language comprehension: A common substrate? Neuropsychologia 45, 229–235 (2007)
27. Iwamura, Y.: Somatosensory association cortices. International Congress Series, 3–14 (2003)

Multiple Inheritance Problem in Semantic Spreading Activation Networks[*]

Paweł Matykiewicz[1] and Włodzisław Duch[2]

[1] Division of Biomedical Informatics,
Cincinnati Children's Hospital Medical Center,
3333 Burnet Ave, Cincinnati OH 45220, USA
[2] Department of Informatics, Faculty of Physics,
Astronomy and Informatics, Nicolaus Copernicus University,
ul. Grudziadzka 5, 87-100, Torun, Poland
pawel.matykiewicz@cchmc.org, wduch@is.umk.pl

Abstract. Semantic networks inspired by semantic information processing by the brain frequently do not improve the results of text classification. This counterintuitive fact is explained here by the multiple inheritance problem, which corrupts real-world knowledge representation attempts. After a review of early work on the use of semantic networks in text classification, our own heuristic solution to the problem is presented. Significance testing is used to contrast results obtained with pruned and entire semantic networks applied to medical text classification problems. The algorithm has been motivated by the process of spreading neural activation in the brain. The semantic network activation is propagated throughout the network until no more changes to the text representation are detected. Solving the multiple inheritance problem for the purpose of text classification is similar to embedding inhibition in the spreading activation process – a crucial mechanism for a healthy brain.

Keywords: text classification, semantic networks, multiple inheritance problem, spreading activation networks, inhibition.

1 Introduction

The neurocognitive approach to language has not led to practical algorithms [1] in natural language processing (NLP). Semantic networks, inspired by the work on human semantic memory, are a convenient way to store general information about the world. Using graphical notation network nodes are identified with concepts, and edges with semantic relations, allowing for direct logical inferences [2]. This seemed to be an obvious improvement over the most popular representation of texts in form of vectors built by counting the number of distinct words in a "bag-of-words" approach [3].

---

[*] Authors would like to thank Drs. John P. Pestian, Imre Solti, Lawrence Hunter, K. Bretonnel Cohen, Karen M. Stannard, Guergana K. Savova, and Alan R. Aronson for their interest in this article.

D. Ślęzak et al. (Eds.): BIH 2014, LNAI 8609, pp. 252–265, 2014.

In [4], experiments with bag-of-words, stemmed words, noun phrases, stemmed noun phrases, key phrases, stemmed key phrases, WordNet synonyms, and WordNet hypernyms were presented. In WordNet [5], a huge lexical database of the English language, words are grouped together by their synonymy with basic semantic relations between them. An artificial intelligence scholar would call it one of the largest non-monotonic logical systems. Unfortunately, in [4] experiments did not demonstrate the superiority of using synonyms and hypernyms over a bag-of-words. Only certain combinations of phrases and words improved results. In case of a general purpose semantic network using synonyms and hypernyms does not help much. This was unacceptable and non-intuitive for many researchers. How can adding knowledge to a representation based on a simple word count degrade text classification performance? Isn't adding such associations the key to how brains work?

Let us think of a simple example: "Humans have two legs", "John is a human", "John has one leg". In this semantic network, "John" inherits multiple contradictory properties: having one leg and having two legs. Such a small semantic network exposes an important fact: in real life not all assertions about the world are true all the time. In such cases, how should the knowledge encoded in a semantic network be used for inference? While episodic memory may come to rescue [6], it would lead to significant complication of the algorithm. It took many years to find the answer to this problem. In essence, a general purpose semantic network must be pruned before it may be used to enhance a text representation. From the artificial intelligence and NLP perspective, one needs to solve the multiple inheritance problem before using a non-monotonic knowledge representation system.

Inspired by many findings relevant to neurolinguistics [7–9], our goal is to create a neurocognitive language processing approach inspired by the spreading neural activation over a large semantic brain network [6]. Thus far, we have developed a practical method for pruning semantic networks in a way that improves the results of text categorization. Our algorithm spreads activation from one term to the other, inferring facts not present in the text, but preserving only those facts that improve text classification, avoiding unnecessary inheritance. In this way relevant "pathways of the brain" [1] are discovered. **We will show that text classification with a pruned semantic network is significantly better than a baseline model, while using entire network does not lead to improvements.**

2   Background and Significance

Text classification is pursued by the statistical machine learning community; the term "multiple inheritance" comes from the field of artificial intelligence. Textbooks on artificial intelligence mention statistical learning, but the converse is rarely true. The multiple inheritance problem has been rarely addressed in literature on text classification. Google Scholar cites over 10,100 articles that mention "text classification" and some version of a semantic network. Only 127

Table 1. Text classification with semantic networks started in 1998 and continues today. This table summarizes only the early work. Multiple sources were used to create semantic networks, but none of the papers addressed the multiple inheritance problem.

Publication	Task	Semantic Network	Data set	Algorithm
[11]	Categorization	WordNet	Reuters	Ripper
—	—	WordNet	USENET	Ripper
—	—	WordNet	Digital Tradition	Ripper
[12]	Clustering	WordNet	Reuters	K-center
[13]	Clustering	WordNet	Reuters	K-center
[14]	Categorization	WordNet	Reuters	SVM
—	—	WordNet	Amazon	SVM
[15]	Clustering	MeSH	PubMed	K-center
—	—	MeSH	PubMed	Hierarchical
—	—	MeSH	PubMed	Suffix Trees
[16]	Categorization	Wikipedia	Reuters	SVM
—	—	Wikipedia	OHSUMED	SVM
—	—	Wikipedia	20 Newsgroups	SVM
—	—	Wikipedia	Movies Reviews	SVM
[17]	Categorization	WordNet	Reuters	AdaBoost
—	—	WordNet	OHSUMED	AdaBoost
—	—	MeSH	OHSUMED	AdaBoost
—	—	AgroVoc	FaoDoc	AdaBoost

of them mention "multiple inheritance". That is not to say that the term "multiple inheritance" is unknown to the language processing community. There are over 1,600 articles on "multiple inheritance" and "semantic networks". Most of them, however, discuss semantic similarity and dismiss the multiple inheritance problem by taking maximal, average or minimal paths between two terms [10]. Semantic similarity will not be discussed in this paper, the focus will be on text classification using semantic networks.

Typical work in this field follows four steps: choose a semantic network, match words from text with the elements from the semantic network, expand the text representation by adding or replacing semantically related elements, and then classify documents using the expanded representations (see Table 1). Using this scheme various research groups made important observations.

In [11], it was shown that more general terms give better categorization than less general terms. The optimal level of generalization, however, was different for each data set. In [12], the same was shown for clustering. In addition, it was concluded that it is better to keep terms from lower levels of hierarchy rather than just replace them with terms from higher levels. In [13], the results from [12] were replicated and mapping terms from WordNet was further studied. It was found that ambiguities present in WordNet might render it useless when adding hypernyms. It was concluded that part of speech tagging is insufficient for disambiguation of word senses. Taking the most frequent meaning, as in [12], is helpful but clearly not sufficient. In [14], mapping text to WordNet was improved by using the Steiner tree cost. The effect of sample size on levels of generalization was studied. First, it was found that adding hypernyms works better for small data, but the depth of generalization does not show any regularity. Second, it was discovered that as the sample size is increased, the behavior of different depths stabilizes and converges, but at the cost of decreased improvements.

WordNet was not the only source of adding semantics. In [15], Medical Subject Headings (MeSH) was used for representing the text and improving clustering. In [16], Wikipedia was used as a semantic network: Wikipedia's articles became concepts and links from the articles to most similar web pages became associative relations. In [17], WordNet, MeSH, and the United Nations Food and Agriculture multilingual agriculture thesaurus (AgroVoc) were used with marginal text categorization improvements.

Work in the early years of text classification with semantic networks lacked a mechanism vital to the healthy brain: inhibition. Google Scholar cites around 46,000 publications on inhibition in brains. Brain studies show that inhibition is crucial for normal functioning of associative memory [18], and too low inhibition may lead to epilepsy, schizophrenia and a "formal thought disorder" [19]. Surprisingly, the neurofunctional and neuroanatomical "lack of inhibition" has a long-lost brother in the field of artificial intelligence: the multiple inheritance problem in non-monotonic reasoning [20, p. 206]. A machine retrieves all related nodes from a semantic network with the same conviction as a patient with a formal thought disorder. Inheritance along all edges cannot be allowed because not every fact about the world is true or relevant in a given context. General solutions like "default logic", "circumscription", or "truth maintenance systems" require inference with negations, rules for overriding default values, closed-world assumption, or infinite computing power [2]. These requirements make them unsuitable for the large semantic networks that are currently available for automated text processing.

Evidently finding the ideal solution to the multiple inheritance problem is going to be quite difficult. In this paper an algorithm is proposed that removes just enough inference paths to significantly improve text classification performance. We contrast it with a scenario where no pruning of semantic network is done, and problems due to the multiple inheritance cancel advantages of added semantics, making classification improvements statistically not significant.

3   Databases and Document Collection

OHSUMED. The OHSUMED document collection, named after the Oregon Health and Science University School of Medicine, was created to benchmark information retrieval algorithms. It contains 348,566 PubMed papers published between 1987-1991 in 270 medical journals [21]. All papers have titles but only 233,445 have abstracts of an average length of 167 words. The papers have been manually indexed with 14,626 distinct Medical Subject Headings (MeSH). There are on average 253 papers per one MeSH. The inter-indexer consistency measured using 760 papers was between 61%-75% [22]. The challenge is to create

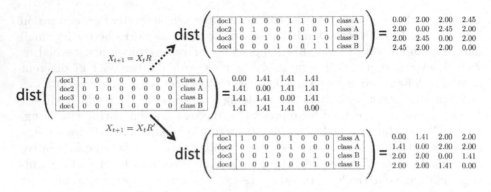

Fig. 1. Example of spreading activation matrices using semantic network with and without a solution to the multiple inheritance problem. The top right matrices show the features space and distances after entire semantic network has been applied (Figure 2 with all nodes and edges). The bottom right matrices show the feature space and distances after solving the multiple inheritance problem (Figure 2 without the dotted nodes and edges). Documents cluster according to the class labels only if the pruned semantic network is used.

an automated system that will do the indexing with competency comparable to human experts.

Researchers have created many such systems [23–25]. It is rare that someone would use all the data to develop and benchmark an algorithm but there is no consensus on how to split the data. One might say that the "Heart Diseases" (HD) subset is a common one. It has 12,417 training instances (years 1987-1990), 3,630 testing instances (1991 year), and 119 MeSH codes. The multiple inheritance problem is very complex so for clarity we have reduced the data set down to just ten MeSH codes. 4 of them, "endocarditis, bacterial", "aortic valve stenosis", "heart neoplasms", and "mitral valve stenosis" are used to develop the edge/node pruning algorithm and 6 of them, "mitral valve insufficiency", "atrial fibrillation", "aortic valve insufficiency", "cardiomyopathy, hypertrophic", "cardiomyopathy, congestive", and "heart arrest" are used for final benchmarking.

The UMLS Metathesaurus. The Unified Medical Language System (UMLS) is a set of tools, websites and databases created and maintained by the National Library of Medicine, a division of U.S. National Institutes of Health. The UMLS has two main components: implementation resources (software) and knowledge sources (databases). We are interested just in one knowledge source - Metathesaurus - and one implementation resource - MetaMap. In particular, we used the 2009AB version of the Metathesaurus as a source of medical semantic data and the 2009 version of MetaMap Transfer (MMTx) to map PubMed abstracts and titles to UMLS Metathesaurus medical concepts. After parsing the HD data set, MetaMap discovered 21,127 unique concepts out of the 2,181,062 available in the Metathesaurus. Every concept had to be part of one root branch of the semantic network: "clinical finding", "body structure", "substance", "procedure", or "pharmaceutical", otherwise the concept was discarded.

The 2009AB version of the UMLS Metathesaurus is a conglomerate of 101 individual biomedical semantic networks, also called "source vocabularies". Each sub-network has its own set of concepts and relations; when these are combined, it contains 26,762,104 relations. We followed the 21,127 concepts present in the HD data set along the following edge types: "other related" (RO), "related and possibly synonymous" (RQ), "similar or like relationship' (RL), "children" (CHD), "parent" (PAR), "broader" (RB), "narrower" (RN), and "source asserted synonymy" (SY). After 14 steps of spreading activation, we reached all 2,131,301 semantically related concepts using 11,250,022 distinct connections[1]. As a solution to the multiple inheritance problem, we proposed an algorithm that reduces the 11,250,022 connections to a bare minimum that improves automated indexing of PubMed citations.

4 Problem Identification and Methods of Solution

The Multiple Inheritance Problem. Let's start with an illustrative text categorization problem. There are four documents, each containing just one of the following medical terms: "aortic valve insufficiency", "aortic valve stenosis", "mitral valve insufficiency", "mitral valve stenosis". Let's say that the first two documents belong to the class "A" and the other two to the class "B". The vector space representation would look like the first matrix on the left in Figure 1. There would be equal distances between all documents, offering no learning generalization. Let's assume now that the four terms come from a semantic network like the one in Figure 2. As with every medical dictionary, a disease can be categorized by a location or by a pathophysiology. That is the case in our "small world" example: each disease inherits two concepts. Even though the inheritance by location and by pathophysiology is always true, it is not always relevant to the categorization task at hand. If unpruned network is used $(X_{t+1} = X_t R)$ the distances calculated for enhanced representation do not lead to good clusters (upper right matrix in Figure 1), and will lower the chances of correct classification.

On the other hand, if the **relative frequency** of a medical term in a class is used to denote its **belongingness**, we would find that certain edges connect medical terms from opposite classes. When that happens, documents from opposite classes become more similar and less distinguishable. In our example, connections to "valve insufficiency" and "valve stenosis" come from opposite classes. This situation can be repaired by removing at least one edge connecting "valve insufficiency" and at least one edge connecting "valve stenosis". Removing both edges will allow for removing also the nodes "valve insufficiency" and "valve stenosis". This leads to a reduced semantic network shown in Figure 2, without the elements marked with dotted lines. Spread activation $(X_{t+1} = X_t R')$ in the pruned network leads to a representation of documents from the same

---

[1] CHD = 2,137,767; PAR = 2,137,767; RB = 1,087,501; RL = 34,066; RN = 1,087,501; RO = 5,304,808; RQ = 287,280; SY = 49,846.

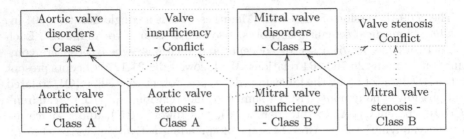

Fig. 2. Semantic network with an imposed document/term classification task. First, **relative frequency** is used to assign class to a node (see Figure 1). Second, edges that connect nodes belonging to different classes are identified. Third, conflicting nodes and edges (marked with dotted lines) are removed. This procedure prunes the semantic network, solving the multiple inheritance problem in text classification tasks.

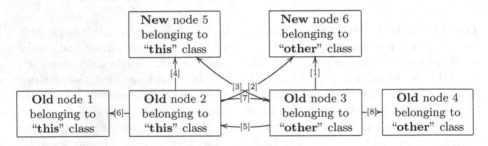

Fig. 3. Generalized semantic network with an imposed document/term classification task. Just by using **relative frequencies** we identify four types of nodes that receive activation and eight types of edges that carry the activation. We can empirically check which edge-pruning procedure improves the text classification task and use it as a heuristic solution to the multiple inheritance problem. Edges are enumerated in the order of their performances in Table 3.

class grouped tighter than documents from opposite classes (lower right matrix Figure 1). Is there a way to do this programmatically on a larger scale?

Edge Pruning. The conflict and non-conflict edge types shown in Figure 2, can be generalized for any binary classification problem. Let's call the positive class "**this**" and the negative class "**other**". The **relative frequency** will be used to assign class to a node. If we include spreading activation, it will give us four types of nodes: an **old** node belonging to the class "**this**", an **old** node belonging to the class "**other**", a **new** node belonging to the class "**this**", and a **new** node belonging to the class "**other**". If we exclude feedback loops, we will have eight edge types that connect the four node types, as shown in Figure 3. The learning process in a given context (here text categorization) should empirically determine which semantic associations should be inhibited. Therefore in the training phase a check is made to see if any improvement will result from removal of selected edge types. This will indirectly show whether the distances between vectors representing documents change in favor of or against the two-class separation. This is not an ideal solution, where all unnecessary nodes are removed, but it offers sufficient separation. Such pruning method allows for unattended spreading of concept activations.

What is meant here by "unattended spreading activations"? Let's say that f is a Heaviside step function. Our goal of pruning the semantic network is to get a map, $X_{t+1} = f(X_t R)$, that can be applied to the data iteratively until the document/term matrix stops changing $X_{n+1} = X_n$ for $n \gg 0$. This means that the pruning process has to be iterative. Let's say that P^i is a function that removes one type of edge, then $R' = P^i(X_{t+1}, X_t, R)$. If $R' \neq R$, then some edges were removed, and we need to reset the training matrix $X_t := X_0$ to its initial state. We keep applying $P^i(X_{t+1}, X_t, R)$ and resetting X_t until $R' = R$ for all t. Once the pruning procedure P^i is completed, the next procedure, P^j, is done, and so on. Which pruning procedures improve text categorization and the order in which pruning is applied should be empirically determined.

Text Categorization. After final representation is generated classification is done using the support vector machines (SVM) with cosine kernel. This way SVM becomes insensitive to very short or very long documents. Cosine kernel SVMs have only one parameter that has to be tuned by the user: "cost" of regularization. This parameter has been optimized checking results for its values from 2^{-1} to 2^5 with $2^{0.25}$ increments. All features are binary: the text either mentions the concept or it does not. The best models were selected using a 16-fold cross-validation, with classification quality measured by the F_1 score, a harmonic mean between precision and recall. Once the best model with the best pruning procedure was selected, it has been used for the final testing. All spreading activation models were compared to a model without the feature space enrichment and tested for significance.

Final Testing. The statistical significance of the F_1 score improvement is measured using a paired t-test [26]. For each classification label we have a total of 17 F_1 scores for the baseline model and the same number for the enhanced model, resulting in 17 pairwise comparisons. We used "endocarditis, bacterial", "aortic valve stenosis", "heart neoplasms", and "mitral valve stenosis" to find the best pruning procedure. Then we added "mitral valve insufficiency", "atrial fibrillation", "aortic valve insufficiency", "cardiomyopathy, hypertrophic", "cardiomyopathy, congestive" and "heart arrest" to see if the improvement generalized over different labels, a total of ten labels. Thus, the t-test across all experiments has 170 pairwise comparisons. The Pearson correlation coefficient is used to see if the data is improved by the same factor across different classes. If the baseline model is correlated with the enhanced model there is a stable improvement.

Concept Space Visualization. The changes to the semantic network rely on assigning medical concepts to a class based on the **relative frequency** measure. We use the class belongingness to identify edges connecting nodes from different classes. We can visualize the process. Each medical concept is represented by two

relative frequencies[2]: rf_{this}^3 and rf_{other}^3. If the semantic network separates two classes well, we should see concepts travel to the top-left corner and the bottom-right corner ($rf_{this}^3 \gg rf_{other}^3$ or $rf_{this}^3 \ll rf_{other}^3$). On the other hand, if the network does not separate classes, then most concepts will have similar **relative frequencies** ($rf_{this}^3 \approx rf_{other}^3$) and will lie along the $x = y$ line.

Relative frequency snapshots might not be enough to see a divergent or convergent trend, but if we follow the centers of the relative frequencies and connect them with arrows, the trend becomes apparent. If the arrows point outward, then the trend confirms separation by spreading activation. If the arrows are parallel to the $x = y$ line, then there is no separation trend, and spreading activation causes more harm than good.

5   Results

Spreading Activation without the Edge-Pruning Technique. First experiments had to determine which semantic relationships and their combinations yield the best results. Table 2 shows that only parent relationships ("is-a") improve classification performance. Other relationships or combinations tried did not improve the results. This finding is consistent with the work already published (Table 1). The vector feature space increases in size from 21,127 concepts to 40,134 concepts. Surprisingly, it takes almost 60 iteration steps before the feature space stabilized (lower right graph in Figure 4). Sixty multiplications of such huge matrix, even in a sparse format, is computationally demanding. It would be impractical for the full OHSUMED data set and impossible for the full PubMed database. If we look carefully at the relative frequency pathways, we notice a peculiar behavior where two classes initially diverge but then collapse (lower right graph in Figure 4). This is also congruent with others' work, where they would find a step of iteration with the largest separation, for example step 9, and use that for testing, sometimes without much success [11–14]. Other authors also reported that each class requires a different number of iterations, so this would not be a good source of generalization.

Figure 4 and Table 5 support evidence that 152,559 parent-child relations are enough to cause very complex behavior. There is some improvement in performance but not statistically significant (p-value=0.01259 at best, p-value=0.02618 overall). The improvement is almost random because it does not correlate well with the baseline model. The Pearson correlation coefficient between the baseline model and the enhanced model over all 170 runs of SVM is 0.66; it ranges between 0.29 and 0.81 depending on the class label. In summary, this means that 152,559 relations react differently to different classes, need more computational time and are not a reliable source of background knowledge.

Spreading Activation with Edge-Pruning Technique. This is uncharted territory. At the start 152,559 parent-child relations are included. Spreading activation and removing one edge type at a time requires restart of the process

---

[2] The power $= 3$ greatly enhances signal for concepts with $rf_{class} \approx 1$.

Table 2. Performance of various UMLS relation types after 60 steps of spreading activation without the edge-pruning technique. This table shows the SVM macro F_1 using 16-fold cross-validation, improvement when compared to a model with no spreading activation (δ), and the number of unique edges and unique nodes used during the 60 steps of activation. The best-performing relationship is PAR (parent), and it has been used for network pruning experiments.

REL Type	F_1^{CV} (δ^{CV})	Edges (Nodes)
RL + RB + SY	0.6286 (-0.1212)	129,003 (41,972)
RB + SY + PAR	0.6477 (-0.1021)	225,796 (51,672)
RL + RB	0.6523 (-0.0976)	116,592 (38,544)
RL	0.7064 (-0.0435)	35,231 (23,897)
RL + SY	0.7091 (-0.0408)	41,868 (25,870)
SY + PAR	0.7103 (-0.0395)	167,126 (43,354)
RB + PAR	0.7356 (-0.0143)	207,727 (47,888)
RB + SY	0.7488 (-0.0010)	78,939 (31,266)
RB	0.7498 (-0.0001)	68,270 (28,294)
SY	0.7509 (+0.0010)	24,437 (20,459)
PAR	**0.7758 (+0.0252)**	152,559 (40,134)

Table 3. Performance of PAR relationship after 60 steps of spreading activation with eight types of edge removal procedures. Edge types are defined in Figure 3. This table shows the SVM macro F_1 using 16-fold cross-validation, improvement when compared to a model with no spreading activation (δ), and the number of unique edges and unique nodes used during the 60 steps of activation. The best four edge types were chosen for permutation experiments.

Node A →	Node B	F_1^{CV} (δ^{CV})	Edges (Nodes)
Old Other →	Old Other [8]	0.7485 (-0.0014)	18,786 (18,782)
Old This →	Old Other [7]	0.7487 (-0.0012)	18,942 (18,844)
Old This →	Old This [6]	0.7535 (+0.0037)	19,375 (18,926)
Old Other →	Old This [5]	0.7593 (+0.0095)	19,618 (18,879)
Old This →	**New This [4]**	**0.7736 (+0.0237)**	147,857 (39,269)
Old Other →	**New This [3]**	**0.7740 (+0.0242)**	117,064 (32,946)
Old This →	**New Other [2]**	**0.7746 (+0.0247)**	139,621 (38,039)
Old Other →	**New Other [1]**	**0.7757 (+0.0258)**	63,957 (24,436)

Table 4. The best sequence of edge removal calculated using macro F_1 on classes "endocarditis, bacterial", "aortic valve stenosis", "heart neoplasms", and "mitral valve stenosis". Four out of eight removal procedures from Table 3 were permuted and the best sequence was chosen for final testing. Removing all edges that connect medical concepts that did not appear in any of the training documents worked best (edge types numbered 1-4 in Figure 3).

Node A	Node B	F_1^{CV} (δ^{CV})	Edges (Nodes)
(1) Old Other	New This [2]		
(2) Old Other	New Other[1]		
(3) Old This	New Other[3]		
(4) Old This	New This [4]	**0.7857 (+0.0358)**	51,405 (21,684)

Table 5. Final results using PAR relations without edge pruning. PAR relations without pruning offer poor improvement of the F_1 score on the cross-validation and the test sets. None of the improvements offers statistical significance when a paired t-test was used to compare models with and without the semantic enhancement. *Data used for finding the best types of semantic relationships and the best pruning procedures.

Class name (size)	$F_1^{CV}\ (\delta^{CV})$	$F_1^{TEST}\ (\delta^{TEST})$	p-value
aortic valve insufficiency (239)	0.6026 (-0.0267)	0.6226 (-0.0697)	0.91325
aortic valve stenosis* (341)	0.7725 (+0.0096)	0.6621 (-0.0281)	0.25232
atrial fibrillation (222)	0.6511 (+0.0463)	0.6713 (+0.0559)	0.05404
cardiomyopathy, congestive (253)	0.6009 (+0.0171)	0.6092 (-0.0211)	0.23898
cardiomyopathy, hypertrophic (192)	0.7799 (+0.0507)	0.7640 (+0.0140)	0.01259
endocarditis, bacterial* (310)	0.8242 (+0.0182)	0.7211 (+0.0017)	0.19099
heart arrest (405)	0.6952 (-0.0071)	0.6966 (-0.0234)	0.68066
heart neoplasms* (197)	0.7729 (+0.0275)	0.6512 (+0.1032)	0.17259
mitral valve insufficiency (295)	0.6007 (-0.0338)	0.6087 (+0.0259)	0.86898
mitral valve stenosis* (172)	0.7335 (+0.0485)	0.7627 (+0.0448)	0.07377
across all experiments	0.7034 (+0.0150)	0.6770 (+0.0103)	0.02618

Table 6. Final results using PAR relations with the best edge-pruning procedure. Edge pruning offers good improvement of the F_1 score on the cross-validation and the test sets. Four out of ten data sets achieved statistically significant improvement when a paired t-test was used to compare models with and without the semantic enhancement. *Data used for finding the best types of semantic relationships and the best pruning procedure. **Data with statistically significant categorization improvement.

Class name (size)	$F_1^{CV}\ (\delta^{CV})$	$F_1^{TEST}\ (\delta^{TEST})$	p-value
aortic valve insufficiency (239)	0.5924 (-0.0370)	0.6733 (-0.0190)	0.99374
aortic valve stenosis* (341)	0.7787 (+0.0158)	0.6853 (-0.0048)	0.15238
atrial fibrillation (222)	0.6731 (+0.0683)	0.7172 (+0.1019)	0.00088**
cardiomyopathy, congestive (253)	0.6363 (+0.0526)	0.6590 (+0.0287)	0.00240**
cardiomyopathy, hypertrophic (192)	0.7879 (+0.0587)	0.8235 (+0.0735)	0.00334**
endocarditis, bacterial* (310)	0.8149 (+0.0089)	0.7273 (+0.0078)	0.34398
heart arrest (405)	0.6886 (-0.0136)	0.6667 (-0.0533)	0.79991
heart neoplasms* (197)	0.8019 (+0.0565)	0.7229 (+0.1749)	0.01222
mitral valve insufficiency (295)	0.6262 (-0.0083)	0.6452 (+0.0624)	0.56264
mitral valve stenosis* (172)	0.7471 (+0.0621)	0.8062 (+0.0883)	0.00429**
across all experiments	0.7147 (+0.0264)	0.7127 (+0.0460)	0.00003

each time there is a change to the semantic network. After 60 iterations the algorithm stops. This means that $X_{t+1} = f(X_t R')$ and rf_{class} must be calculated on average between 73 and 1,082 times, depending on the edge type from Table 3. After that the four best-performing edge types are used and the order in which they are being applied to the semantic network is permuted. The best sequence of pruning (edge type 2, then 1, then 3, and then 4, see Table 4) requires on average 451 $X_{t+1} = f(X_t R')$ and rf_{class} operations, but reduces the initial 152,559 edges to a more modest 51,405, cutting the number of active concepts by half.

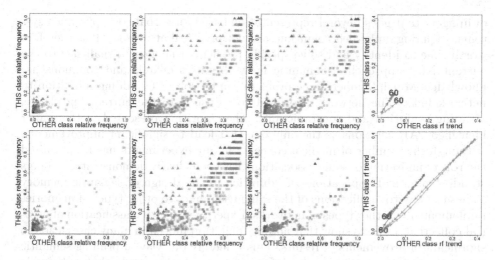

Fig. 4. Relative frequencies of the UMLS Metathesaurus concepts as they change with spreading activation steps. The X-axis and Y-axis have relative frequencies corresponding to the class "other" and the class "heart neoplasms", respectively. First three images show spreading activation on 1, 10 and 60 steps of the 1991 citation year data set. The top images show spreading activation using PAR relations that were pruned using the best edge-pruning procedure from Table 4. The bottom images show spreading activation using PAR relations that were not pruned in any way. The two images on the right show the 60-step pathway of the relative frequency centers as they move outward or inward and then settle down and stabilize around the 30th iteration with the pruning and around the 50th iteration without the pruning.

Figure 4 and Table 6 offer evidence that 51,405 parent-child relations create a predictable behavior. Spreading activation stabilizes around the 30th iteration. It has slightly better separation around ten iterations. After that, the relative frequency centers move back (upper right graph in Figure 4), but not nearly as much as in the case of spreading activation without edge pruning. The improvement is statistically significant in the case of four out of ten labels (best p-value 0.00088), three of which were not used during the best pruning sequence-seeking process. The improvement across all 170 subsets is statistically significant (p-value=0.00003). The Pearson correlation coefficient between the baseline model and the enhanced model over all 170 runs of SVM is 0.72 and ranges between 0.17 and 0.87, depending on the class label. In summary, the 51,405 parent-child relations offer good performance improvement, need less computational resources, and are a good source of background knowledge.

6 Conclusion and Discussion

Language competence at the human level may require detailed neurocognitive models that combine several kinds of memory: recognition, semantic, episodic and short-term working memory, in addition to the iconic spatial and other types of imagery that goes beyond representation based on verbal concepts. Such systems, requiring embodied cognition, are not practical at present. It is therefore worthwhile to identify and solve specific problems that pose a challenge to the current NLP approaches. Semantic network stores default and commonsense knowledge. Multiple inheritance problem can be solved by adding inhibition to network links. The network is pruned to adjust it to the current knowledge, avoiding confusion and contradictions. The algorithm presented in this paper identified PAR relations as the only one that lead to significant improvements. Although the number of medical concepts in our experiments has been limited the role of inhibition of some associations has been clearly demonstrated. Understanding practical applications of inhibition in the design of semantic memory shows the way to applications of the same techniques to other types of memories implemented by other types of networks. Experiments with classification of medical collections of texts show that adding inhibition indeed in many cases leads to significant improvements of results. This is merely one way of pruning semantic networks. Insights from granular information processing imply that a dynamic balancing of semantic generality and specificity could be a useful approach for subsequent refinements of the proposed method.

References

1. Lamb, S.M.: Pathways of the Brain: The Neurocognitive Basis of Language. John Benjamins Publishing Company (1999)
2. Russell, S.J., Norvig, P., Davis, E.: Artificial intelligence: a modern approach. Prentice Hall (2010)
3. Joachims, T.: A probabilistic analysis of the rocchio algorithm with tfidf for text categorization. In: Proc. of the 14th ICML, pp. 143–151. Morgan Kaufmann (1997)
4. Scott, S., Matwin, S.: Feature engineering for text classification. In: ICML 1999, pp. 379–388 (1999)
5. Fellbaum, C.: WordNet. Wiley (1999)
6. Duch, W., Matykiewicz, P., Pestian, J.: Neurolinguistic approach to natural language processing with applications to medical text analysis. Neural Networks 21(10), 1500–1510 (2008)
7. Billingsley, R.L., McAndrews, M.P., Crawley, A.P., Mikulis, D.J.: Functional MRI of phonological and semantic processing in temporal lobe epilepsy. Brain 124(6), 1218–1227 (2001)
8. Tivarus, M.E., Ibinson, J.W., Hillier, A., Schmalbrock, P., Beversdorf, D.Q.: An fMRI study of semantic priming: modulation of brain activity by varying semantic distances. Cogn. Behav. Neurol. 19(4), 194–201 (2006)
9. Duffau, H., Gatignol, P., Mandonnet, E., Peruzzi, P., Tzourio-Mazoyer, N., Capelle, L.: New insights into the anatomo-functional connectivity of the semantic system: a study using cortico-subcortical electrostimulations. Brain 128(4), 797–810 (2005)
10. Pedersen, T., Patwardhan, S., Michelizzi, J.: Wordnet::similarity: Measuring the relatedness of concepts. In: Demonstration Papers at HLT-NAACL, pp. 38–41. ACL (2004)
11. Scott, S., Matwin, S.: Text classification using WordNet hypernyms. In: Use of WordNet in Natural Language Processing Systems: Proc. of the Conference, pp. 38–44. ACL (1998)

12. Hotho, A., Staab, S., Stumme, G.: Wordnet improves text document clustering. In: Proc. of the 26th Annual International ACM SIGIR Conf. on Semantic Web Workshop, pp. 541–544 (2003)
13. Sedding, J., Kazakov, D.: WordNet-based text document clustering. In: COLING 3rd Workshop on Robust Methods in Analysis of Natural Language Data, COLING, pp. 104–113 (2004)
14. Mavroeidis, D., Tsatsaronis, G., Vazirgiannis, M., Theobald, M., Weikum, G.: Word sense disambiguation for exploiting hierarchical thesauri in text classification. In: Jorge, A.M., Torgo, L., Brazdil, P.B., Camacho, R., Gama, J. (eds.) PKDD 2005. LNCS (LNAI), vol. 3721, pp. 181–192. Springer, Heidelberg (2005)
15. Yoo, I., Hu, X.: A comprehensive comparison study of document clustering for a biomedical digital library MEDLINE. In: Proc. of the 6th ACM/IEEE-CS Joint Conference on Digital Libraries, pp. 220–229. IEEE (2006)
16. Gabrilovich, E., Markovitch, S.: Overcoming the brittleness bottleneck using wikipedia: Enhancing text categorization with encyclopedic knowledge. In: Proceedings of the 21st National Conference on AI, pp. 1301–1306 (2006)
17. Bloehdorn, S., Hotho, A.: Boosting for text classification with semantic features. In: Mobasher, B., Nasraoui, O., Liu, B., Masand, B. (eds.) WebKDD 2004. LNCS (LNAI), vol. 3932, pp. 149–166. Springer, Heidelberg (2006)
18. Khader, P., Knoth, K., Burke, M., Ranganath, C., Bien, S., Rosler, F.: Topography and dynamics of associative long-term memory retrieval in humans. Journal of Cognitive Neuroscience 19(3), 493–512 (2007)
19. Leeson, V.C., Simpson, A., McKenna, P.J., Laws, K.R.: Executive inhibition and semantic association in schizophrenia. Schizophrenia Research 74(1), 61–67 (2005)
20. Crevier, D.: AI: The tumultuous history of the search for artificial intelligence. Basic Books (1993)
21. Hersh, W., Hickam, D.: Use of a multi-application computer workstation in a clinical setting. Bulletin of the Medical Library Association 82(4), 382–389 (1994)
22. Funk, M.E., Reid, C.A.: Indexing consistency in MEDLINE. Bulletin of the Medical Library Association 71(2), 176–183 (1983)
23. Yang, Y., Pedersen, J.: A comparative study on feature selection in text categorization. In: Fisher, D. (ed.) Proc. of the 14th ICML, pp. 412–420. Morgan Kaufmann (1997)
24. Sebastiani, F.: Machine learning in automated text categorization. ACM Comput. Surv. 34(1), 1–47 (2002)
25. Joachims, T.: Text categorization with support vector machines: Learning with many relevant features. In: Nédellec, C., Rouveirol, C. (eds.) ECML 1998. LNCS, vol. 1398, pp. 137–142. Springer, Heidelberg (1998)
26. Demsar, J.: Statistical comparisons of classifiers over multiple data sets. The Journal of Machine Learning Research 7, 1–30 (2006)

Ontology-Based Text Classification for Filtering Cholangiocarcinoma Documents from PubMed

Chumsak Sibunruang and Jantima Polpinij

Intellect Laboratory, Faculty of Informatics, Mahasarakham University,
Mahasarakham, Thailand
{chumsak.s,jantima.p}@msu.ac.th

Abstract. PubMed is a search engine used to access the MEDLINE database, which comprises the massive amounts of biomedical literature. This an make more difficult for accessing to find the relevant medical literature. Therefore, this problem has been challenging in this work. We present a solution to retrieve the most relevant biomedical literature relating to Cholangiocarcinoma in clinical trials from PubMed. The proposed methodology is called ontology-based text classification (On-TC). We provide an ontology used as a semantic tool. It is called Cancer Technical Term Net (CCT-Net). This ontology is intergrated to the methodology to support automatic semantic interpretation during text processing, especially in the case of synonyms or term variations.

Keywords: PubMed, Ontology, CCT-Net, Text Classification, Cholangiocarcinoma.

1   Introduction

Cancer is a diseases that can affect any part of the body. The causes of cancer are various, complex, and only partially understood. One identifying feature of cancer is the rapid creation of unregulated cells that grow uncontrollably beyond their usual boundaries. Afterwards, the unregulated cells http://en.wikipedia.org/wiki/Cell_growthcan then attack adjoining parts of the body and spread to other organs. This is referred to as metastasis, and then metastases are the major cause of death from cancer. There are over 100 different types of known cancers that affect humans. At present, WHO reports that cancer becomes a leading cause of death worldwide, accounting for 8.2 million deaths in 2012 [1][2]. Furthermore, the worldwide burden of cancer rose to an estimated 14 million new cases per year. It can be found that the world's total new annual cases occur in Africa, Asia and Central and South America estimated at 60% [2].

In general, the previous knowledge relevant to cancer in clinical triala can offer the several benefits for further researches and clinical decisions. A solution to find this knowledge can be done through PubMed, where it is a search engine developed by the National Center for Biotechnology Information (NCBI). The purpose of PubMed is to use for retrieving biomedical information from MEDLINE database. Unfortunately, with the exponentially increasing rate of the medical literatures, large volume of

D. Ślęzak et al. (Eds.): BIH 2014, LNAI 8609, pp. 266–277, 2014.
© Springer International Publishing Switzerland 2014

search can be made more difficult for accessing to find the most relevant documents. This is because the traditional knowledge discovery from PubMed abstracts involves the use of several manual processes. The health professionals enter search terms into a web portal to produce a clinically relevant abstract retrieval [3].

To cope this problem, an easy-to-use retrieval tool is required to support clinicians with retrieving relevant information for clinical decision making. Therefore, this becomes the main motivation for this investigation. In this work, we not only present an application of content-based text classification (CBTC) to explore an enhanced solution for finding of the cancer documents, but also improve the method of CBTC by using our semantic tool, called Cancer Technical Term Net (CCT-net). This tool is used to support the semantics in the domain of text analysis. Finally, the improved methodology of CBTC is called ontology-based text classification (On-TC).

It is noted that our case study concentrates on the search of cancer documents relating to clinical trials in the particular domain of Cholangiocarcinoma (CHCA). This is because these documents can be used to support for advance researches or medical decisions of the clinicians. We are interested for CHCA, because it is one of the most common cancer in the Northeast Thailand. A main cause of CHCA in the Northeast Thailand is from the traditional habit of eating uncooked fish, repeated exposure to liver fluke, and consumption of nitrosamine-contaminated food [4]. These are major risk factors. Although CHCA is a rare cancer, especially in the Western countries, it has the world's highest prevalence in Northeastern Thailand.

2   Literature Reviews

There are some researches that mentioned in the problem of searching the relevant biomedical literature from PubMed. Firstly, PubMed is the biggest biomedical literature repository that contains more than 18 million articles and still keeps growing [5]. Large volume of search can be made more difficult for accessing to find relevant documents. Secondly, it is hard to express the specific relevance of users in the given keyword query [6]. Therefore, many results will be typically retrieved. As these problems mentioned, many researchers still pay attention to improve the quality of search on PubMed. However, biomedical researchers require not only an efficient search engine system, but also a tool used to automatically search for synopsis knowledge from PubMed. In reality, it is never easy to extract useful knowledge from PubMed. Traditionally searching for relevant knowledge from PubMed is a process that, the user reads the article's title to consider appropriateness and may then read the abstract to determine relevance. Indeed, this is time-consuming and labour-intensive, especially when a search returns a large number of abstracts and where each abstract contains a large volume of information [7].

In the last decade, the need for discovering the hidden knowledge from PubMed is also required, where automatic knowledge discovery allows the researchers to conduct quality work, avoid repetition, and generate new. Therefore, many researches also pay attention to study about how to extract knowledge from PubMed. For examples, [8] studied the possibility of utilizing the co-occurrence of MeSH terms in

MEDLINE citations associated with the search strategies optimal for evidence-based medicine. Afterwards, all evidence-based medicines will be stored as a knowledge base. Pustejovsky *et al.* [9] presented a system, called Acromed, which finds acronym-meaning pairs as part of as set of information extraction tools designed for processing and extracting data from abstract in the MEDLINE database. The results of this system are entered into a large, continuously updated database of acronyms for the biomedical literatures. Demner-Fushman & Lin [10] proposed a series of knowledge extractors, which employ a combination of knowledge-based and statistical techniques, for automatically identifying clinically relevant aspects of MEDLINE abstracts. The system started with an initial list of citations retrieved by PubMed, and then their system brings relevant abstracts into higher ranking positions. Finally, the MEDLINE abstracts will generate answer that directly responses to physicians' questions. They showed the experiments on a collection of real-world clinical questions that this approach significantly outperforms the already competitive PubMed baseline. Song et al. [11] proposed how to extract procedural knowledge rather than declarative knowledge. This technique applies machine learning method with deep language processing features.

3   Preliminary: The CCT-Net

Cancer Technical Term Net (CCT-Net) is the cancer technical terms set which is an association of cancer stage, modalities used, and specific drugs used. Also, the CCT-net it is organized by meaning and variation of terms, so cancer technical terms in close proximity are related. This ontology is firstly proposed in [12].

The background of the CCT-Net is from the problem of term variation. For examples, the term '*chemotherapy*' and '*radiotherapy*' can be changed by domain experts, when these terms are used together. These terms can be combined as '*chemoradiotherapy*', or '*chemoradiation*'. Sometimes, these terms are represented as abbreviations such as '*CTh/RTh*', '*CT/RT*', '*CTRT*'. If these terms are made understanding of human, the variation of these terms is not a problem. In contrast, if these terms are automatically analysed by a computing system, this becomes a significant problem, called 'the problem of ambiguity in language'.

As the problem mentioned above, we proposed the CCT-Net to handle the problem of term variations, where the pre-existing ontologies such the National Cancer Institute's Thesaurus and Ontology do not offer information relating to a domain specific variations in terms used by domain experts [13].

The entries of the CCT-Net are term-concepts mapping. It is applied from the basic idea of WordNet [14]. The associations in the mapping are conceptual and term-concept relations harness synonyms or term variations. For example, the concept '*specific drugs used*' is similar to the concept '*chemotherapy*' because chemotherapy describes a particular form of drug therapy. However, '*chemotherapy*' is also a distinct treatment concept contained within '*therapeutic modalities*'. These associations can be shown as Fig 1.

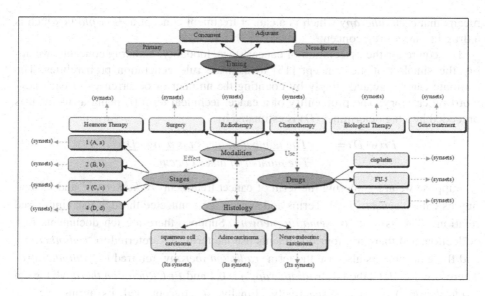

Fig. 1. The overview of the CCT-Net

In the CCT-Net, it consists of five main concept mappings: (1) histology, (2) disease stage, (3) therapeutic modalities, (4) timing of therapeutic modalities, and (5) specified drugs used. Each concept contains many sub-concepts that are shown as Table 1.

Table 1. Summary of the CCT-Net

List	Main Concept Name	Number of Sub-concepts	Examples
1	Histology	7	Squamous cell carcinoma Adenocarcinoma
2	Therapeutic modality	7	Surgery, Chemotherapy
3	Disease stage	5	0, I, II
4	Timing of therapeutic modality	3	Adjuvant, Concurrent
5	Specific drugs used	366	Cispatin, 5-FU

In this context, a concept can be expressed by many terms and each term can be synonymy or variation of term. For an example,

{*Treatment, surgery, chemotherapy, radiotherapy*}

{*Drugs, cisplatin, carboplatin, 5-FU, cyclophosphamide*}

The first example represents that the terms of '*surgery*', '*chemotherapy*', and '*radiotherapy*' are in the cancer treatment concept, meanwhile another represents that '*cisplatin*', '*carboplatin*', '*fluorouracil 5-FU*', and '*cyclo-phosphamide*' are in the cancer drugs concept. Meanwhile, one cancer technical term can be referred to other concepts or terms in another concept. For an example, {*chemotherapy, cisplatin*}, it means that *chemotherapy* which is a cancer treatment concept uses *cisplatin* which is a drug in cancer drug concept.

To acquire for the association of cancer stage, modality, and drug concepts, we apply the simple statistic concept [15] to estimate rule generation probabilities. The estimate can be created simply by counting the number of occurrences of each keyword by category. The probability of a cancer technical term (t) being a rule, if it is preceded by a tag determiner (D) is estimated by:

$$Pr(w \mid D) = \frac{\textit{The number of times t is a tag <D>}}{\textit{The number of times t occurs}} \qquad (1)$$

Suppose we are gathering the term of cancer treatment '*radiotherapy*' and its synonyms called '*synsets*' [15]. Terms and synsets are connected through meaning-based relations. This is a set of *semantic network*. Suppose there are ten documents in a collection, and there are four documents use the term '*RT*' referred to '*radiotherapy*' and three documents also use the term '*radiation therapy*' referred to '*radiotherapy*'. Therefore, *Pr* ('*RT*'| the tag '*radiotherapy*') is 0.4 and *Pr* ('*Radiation therapy*'| the tag '*radiotherapy*') is 0.3, respectively. Finally, a concept and its terms can be represented in format of the hierarchical tree. This example can be presented as in Fig 2.

```
< Therapeutic-modalities> chemotherapy
        <Synonyms> CTRT, CT/RT, CTN/RTN, Chemoradition, ... </synonyms>
        <Kind-of-modality> specific drugs used </kind-of-modality>
        <disease-stage> I, II, II, IV </disease-stage>
        <co-modalities> surgery, radiotherapy </ co-modalities >
    </therapeutic-modalities>
```

Fig. 2. An example of therapeutic modality concept in the CCT-Net

We developed the CCT-Net by using following sources: general information of cancer, cancer drugs, cancer staging, cancer treatment, documents of cancer, and so on. In this stage, we also obtained the cancer technical terms from more than 500 cancer documents that are gathered from PubMed.

4   The Method of Ontology-Based Text Classification

This section describes the details of our ontology-based text classification. It consists of three main processing steps.

4.1   Tokenization and Document Representation

In general, word segmentation [15] is the first and obligatory task in natural language processing because word is a basic unit in linguistics. We rely on the CCT-Net that is approached to select keyword features, where this ontology is used as a dictionary. These features can indicate to the relevant oncology documents. Afterwards, each word is weighted by *tf-idf* [15, 16]. It is used for providing a pre-defined set of features for exchanging information. Each unique word w_i corresponds to a feature with $tf(w_i, d_i)$, the number of times word w_i occurs in the document d_i, as its value. Refining the requirement representation, it has been shown that scaling the dimensions of the feature vector with their *inverse document frequency* $idf(w_i)$ leads to improved performance. $idf(w_i)$ can be calculated from the document frequency $df(w_i)$, which is the number of documents in which word w_i occurs. It is described as follows.

$$idf(w_i) = 1 + log(|D| / df(w_i)) \tag{2}$$

Finally, text contents on web sites are represented in a structured *"bag of words"* (as vector space model) [16] representation. The representation method is equivalent to an attribute value representation used in machine learning. It is noted that this work utilizes the CCT-Net to analyze the variations of each term. Then, these variations are in the same concept. For instance, consider these words *'radiotherapy'*, *'radiation therapy'* and *'RT'*. Although they are presented in different forms, they will be analyzed and interpreted as a feature having the same meaning if they are in the same concept.

4.2 Pruning the BOW Size

We consider that if some words occur very rarely and cannot be regarded as statistical evidence, they can be removed prior to classification as *rare words*. For a pre-defined threshold δ, a term word t is discarded from the representation, if $tf\text{-}idf(t) < \delta$. This approached was firstly found in [17]. This work applied the Mixed Min and Max model (MMM) to find the threshold δ that is a minimum term word weighting of the BOW. The MMM has been developed by Fox and Sharat [18]. There are two operations in the MMM: union and intersection. The union operation is used for finding a minimum, while the intersection operation is to find a maximum. Let T be the BOW and t be the term words that are weighted based on *tf-idf*. It can be determined that $t \in T$. The degree of membership for union and intersection are defined as follows:

$$T_{t_1 \cup t_2 \cup \ldots t_n} = \max(t_1, t_2, \ldots, t_n) \tag{3}$$

$$T_{t_1 \cap t_2 \cap \ldots t_n} = \min(t_1, t_2, \ldots, t_n) \tag{4}$$

The MMM algorithm attempts to soften the Boolean operation by considering the range of terms weight as a linear combination of the minimum and maximum term weighting. In this work, we interest only the minimum of the MMM. They can be computed as follows:

$$Min(\delta) = C_{or1} * max(tf\text{-}idf) + C_{or2} * min(tf\text{-}idf) \tag{5}$$

$$Max(\delta) = C_{and1} * max(tf\text{-}idf) + C_{and2} * min(tf\text{-}idf) \tag{6}$$

where C_{or1}, C_{or2} are "soften" coefficients of "or"operator, and C_{and1}, C_{and2} are softness coefficients of "and" operator. To give the maximum of the document weight more importance while considering "or" query and the minimum of the document more importance while considering "and" query. In general, they have $C_{or1} > C_{or2}$ and $C_{and1} > C_{and2}$. For simplicity, it is generally assumed that $C_{or1} = 1 - C_{or2}$ and $C_{and1} = 1 - C_{and2}$. The best performance usually occurs with C_{and1} in the range [0.5, 0.8] and $C_{or1} > 0.2$ [19]. In this our experiment, we select 0.5 of coefficients. Finally, we can get the threshold δ.

4.3   Searching of the Relevant Documents through Text Classification

The basic concept of text categorization may be formalized as the task of approximating the unknown target function $\Phi: D \times C \rightarrow \{T, F\}$ by means of a function $\Phi: D \times C \rightarrow \{T, F\}$ - called the classifier - where $C = \{c_1, c_2, ..., c_{|C|}\}$ is a predefined set of categories, and D is a set of documents. If $\Phi(d_i, c_j) = T$, then d_i is called a positive member of c_j, while if $\Phi(d_i, c_j) = F$, it is called a negative member of c_j. This work applies two algoriths for text classification model construction, called text classifier, and then text classifier will be used to find the most relevant CHCA docuemnts from PubMed.

4.3.1   kNN –Based Text Classification

k-Nearest Neighbor is one of the most popular algorithms for text categorization [20][21][22][23]. The kNN classifier is based on the assumption that the classification of an instance is most similar to the classification of other instances that are nearby in the vector space (or bag of words obtained from the step of text representation). In general, the idea behind k-Nearest Neighbor algorithm is quite straightforward. To classify a new document, the system finds the k nearest neighbors (as relevant documents) among the training documents, and uses the categories of the k nearest neighbors to weight the category candidates [20]. After k nearest neighbors are found, several strategies could be taken to predict the category of a test document based on them. However, a fixed k value is usually used for all classes in these methods, regardless of their different distributions. Equation (7) and (8) below are two of the widely used strategies of this kind method.

$$y(d_i) = \arg\max_k \sum_{x_j \in kNN} y(x_j, c_k) \tag{7}$$

$$y(d_i) = \arg\max_k \sum_{x_j \in kNN} Sim(d_i, x_j) y(x_j, c_k) \tag{8}$$

where d_i is a test document, x_j is one of the neighbors in the training set, $y(x_j, c_k) \in \{0, 1\}$ indicates whether x_j belongs to class c_k, and $similarity\ (d_i, x_j)$ is the similarity function for di and x_j. Equation (7) means that the predication will be the class that has the largest number of members in the k nearest neighbors; whereas equation (8) means the class with maximal sum of similarity will be the winner. The latter is thought to be better than the former and used more widely [24].

4.3.2 SVM –Based Text Classification

The basic concept of SVM [25] is to build a function that takes the value +1 in a "relevant" region capturing most of the data points, and -1 elsewhere. The dataset can be separated by the following primal optimization problem:

$$\text{Minimize:} \quad V(w, \xi, \rho) = \frac{\|w\|^2}{2} + \frac{1}{vl} \sum_{i=1}^{l} \xi_i - \upsilon \tag{9}$$

$$\text{Subject to:} \quad (w \cdot \Phi(x_i)) \geq \rho - \xi_i, \xi_i \geq 0 \tag{10}$$

where $v \in \{0,1\}$ is a parameter which lets one control the number of support vectors and errors, ξ is a measure of the mis-categorization errors, and ρ is the margin. When we solve the problem, we can obtain w and ρ. Given a new data point x to classify, a label is assigned according to the decision function that can be expressed as follows:

$$f(x) = \quad sign\ ((w \cdot \Phi\ (x_i) - \rho) \tag{11}$$

where α_i are Lagrange multipliers and we apply the Kuhn Tucker condition. We can set the derivatives with respect to the primal variables equal to zero, and then we can get:

$$W = \quad \Sigma \alpha_i \cdot \Phi(x_i) \tag{12}$$

There is only a subset of points x_i that lies closest to the hyperplane and has nonzero values α_i. These points are called support vectors. Instead of solving the primal optimization problem directly, the dual optimization problem is given by:

$$\text{Minimize:} \quad W(\alpha) = \frac{1}{2} \sum_{i,j} \alpha_i \alpha_j K(x_i, x_j) \tag{13}$$

$$\text{Subject to:} \quad 0 \leq \alpha_i \leq \frac{1}{vl}, \sum_i \alpha_i = 1 \tag{14}$$

where $K(x_i, x_j) = (\Phi(x_i), \Phi(x_j))$ are the kernels functions performing the non-linear mapping into the feature space based on dot products between mapped pairs of input points. They allow much more general decision functions when the data are nonlinearly separable and the hyperplane can be represented in a feature space. The kernels frequency used is polynomial kernels $K(x_i, x_j) = ((x_i \cdot x_j)+1)^d$, Gaussian or RBF (radial-basis function) kernels $K(x_i, x_j) = \exp(-\|x_i - x_j\|^2/2\sigma^2)$. We can eventually write the decision from equation (14) and (15) and the equation can be illustrated as follow:

$$f(x) = \quad sign\ (\Sigma\ \alpha_i K(x_i, x) - \rho) \tag{15}$$

For SVM implementation, we use and modify LIBSVM tools from the National Taiwan University [26] in our experiments, since we select the RBF kernels for model building.

5   The Experimental Results and Discussion

We estimated the common evaluation of text classifiers by using an accuracy measurement [16]. Consider the confusion matrix in Table 2.

Table 2. The confusion matrix

Document Retrieval		Expert judgment	
		Yes	No
System judgment	Yes	True Positive (TP)	False Positive (FP)
	No	False Negative (FN)	True Negative (TN)

Let *FP* be a *false positive* or α *error* (also known as Type I error) and *FN* be a *false negative* or β error (also known as Type II error). *TP* is a *true positive* and *TN* is a *true negative*. Then, a *FP* normally means that a test claims something to be positive, when that is not the case, while *FN* is the error of failing to observe a difference when in truth there is one. The accuracy can be calculated as follow:

$$Accuracy = \frac{TP + TN}{TP + FP + FN + TN} \tag{16}$$

We test with 300 cancer oncology documents as dataset. In this dataset, there are 100 documents of Cholangiocarcinoma. We also compare the techniques of document retrieval between the method of text classification that does not use the the CCT-Net and the method of the text classification with the CCT-Net (or the ontology-based text classification). The results of the ontology-based text classification by using the *k*NN can be shown in Table 3.

Table 3. The experimental results of *k*NN-based Text Classification

Method	Number of *k*	Accuracy (%)
Without CCT-net	3	77.40
	5	78.50
With CCT-net	3	83.50
	5	84.00

Consider Table 3, the method of the *k*NN-based text classification that did not use the CCT-Net returns the lower accuracy than the use of the ontology-based text classification method (On-TC). However, by using On-TC, it is more effective for retrieving the relevant documents from the dataset. Then, we experiment over the particular domain of Cholangiocarcinoma documents. This may demonstrate that if we apply this method to retrieve the documents from PubMed, the method may be more effectiveness in filtering and selecting the relevant oncology documents from PubMed.

However, by using *k*NN, *k* is the most important parameter in a text classification system based on *k*NN. In the classification process, *k* nearest documents to the test one in the training set are determined firstly. Then, the predication can be made according to the category distribution among these *k* nearest neighbors. Generally speaking, the class distribution in the training set is uneven. Some classes may have more samples than others. Therefore, the system performance is very sensitive to the choice of the parameter k. And it is very likely that a fixed k value will result in a bias on large categories. This should be improved in the future.

In addition, we also estimated the common evaluation of the SVM text classifier by using accuracy rates. It shows the results in Table 4. The SVM text classifier also shows a satisfactory accuracy because the solution of the SVM method gives an optimal hyperplane, which is a decision boundary between non-relevant and relevant information. The effectiveness of the SVM text classifier model can be increased with a small bag of words that consists of suitable features. However, it can be seen that, by using the CCT-Net, the accuracy is improved.

Table 4. The experimental results of SVM-based Text Classification

Method	Accuracy (%)
Without CCT-net	87.50
With CCT-net	92.50

As the results in Table 3 and 4, this would demonstrate that our method, called the ontology-based text classification method or On-TC, can achieve substantial improvements. However, the results of the On-TC methodology are still good in terms of accuracy but they show a failure rate. This is because some key-terms are used in other particular domains. For example, the key-terms of '*chemotherapy*' and '*radiotherapy*' can be found in other domains such as skin cancer or breast cancer. It may lead to misunderstanding during the process of text analysis and then this leads to poor accuracy of the On-TC methodology.

6   Conclusion and Future Work

PubMed provides literature resources to support their advance researches or medical decisions. Statistically, there are more than 18 millions biomedical related documents. In the last decades, it had been exponentially increasing in a vast amount of bibliographic information stored in electronic format. Therefore, PubMed becomes an accumulation of health information. This information covers different illnesses with a huge range of results regarding different disease types, symptoms, treatments, disease causing factors (genetic and environmental) as well as candidate genes that could be responsible for the onset of these diseases. Information regarding illness is dispersed over various areas such as health researches and disease treatment. Indeed, these health documents are valuable and costly

In this work, we present the method of ontology-based text classification used to retrieve the relevant documents from PubMed. The objective of this document retrieval is to find the Cholangiocarcinoma documents in clinical trials from PubMed. This is because these documents can be used to support for advance researches or medical decisions of the clinicians. Also, we provide Cholangiocarcinoma documents as the searching goal because in the Northeastern Thailand, this area is the world's highest prevalence. Our method of ontology-based text classification (ON-TC) has driven on two algorithms: kNN and SVM. The results of SVM-based On-TC is better than the results of kNN-based On-TC. Also, it can be seen that by using the CCT-Net as the semantic tool in ON-TC, the accuracy of Cholangiocarcinoma document retrieval is improved. After testing by F-measure, the experimental results can demonstrate that our proposal may provide a preliminary indication of more effectiveness in retrieving relevant documents from PubMed.

In our future work, we will use the CCT-Net to support the method of knowledge extraction from the Cholangiocarcinoma documents that are retrieved from PubMed.

Acknowlwedgement. This work is supported by Faculty of Informatics, Mahasarakham University, Thailand.

References

1. World Health Organization (WHO): GLOBOCAN 2012: Estimated Cancer Incidence, Morlality and Prevalence Worldwide in 2012. International Agency for Research on Cancer (2012), http://globocan.iarc.fr/Pages/fact_sheets_cancer.aspx
2. World Health Organization (WHO): Global battle against cancer won't be won with treatment alone Effective prevention measures urgently needed to prevent cancer crisis. International Agency for Research on Cancer (2014)
3. Hadzic, M., D'Souza, R., Hadzic, F., Dillon, T.: Thinking PubMed: an Innovative System for Mental Health Domain. In: The 21st IEEE International Symposium on Computer-Based Medical Systems, pp. 330–335 (2008)
4. Sawanyawisuth, K.: Genes and Cholangiocarcinoma, Department of Biochemistry, Faculty of Medicine, Khon Kaen University, Khon Kaen, Thailand (2009), http://www.tm.mahidol.ac.th/seameo/2009-40-4/05-4498.pdf
5. Hwanjo, Y., Taehoon, K., Jinoh, O., Ilhwan, K., Sungchul, K.: Relevance feedback retrieval system of PubMed. In: Proceedings of the 18th ACM Conference on Information and Knowledge Management (2009)
6. Hwanjo, Y., Taehoon, K., Jinoh, O., Ilhwan, K., Sungchul, K., Wook-Shin, H.: Enabling multi-level relevance feedback on PubMed by integrating rank learning into DBMS. BMC Bioinformatics (2010)
7. Vaka, H.G.G., Mukhopadhyay, S.: Knowledge Extraction and Extrapolation Using Ancient and Modern Biomedical Literature. In: International Conference on Advanced Information Networking and Applications Workshops, pp. 996–1001 (2009)
8. Mendonça, E.A., Cimino, J.J.: Automated knowledge extraction from MEDLINE citations. In: Proc. AMIA Symp. (2000)
9. Pustejovsky, J., Castafio, J., Cpchran, B., Kotecki, M., Morrell, M., Rumshisky, A.: Extraction and disambiguation of acronym-meaning pairs in MEDLINE. In: Proceedings of Medical Information (2001)
10. Demner-Fushman, D., Lin, J.: Answering Clinical Questions with Knowledge-Based and Statistical Techniques. Association for Computational Linguistics (2007)
11. Song, S.-K., Oh, H.-S., Myaeng, S.H., Choi, S.-P., Chun, H.-W., Choi, Y.-S., Jeong, C.-H.: Procedural knowledge extraction on MEDLINE abstracts. In: Zhong, N., Callaghan, V., Ghorbani, A.A., Hu, B. (eds.) AMT 2011. LNCS, vol. 6890, pp. 345–354. Springer, Heidelberg (2011)

12. Polpinij, J., Miller, A., Ghose, A.K., Dam, H.K.: Ontology-based Text Analysis Approach to Retrieve Oncology Documents from PubMed Relevant to Cervical Cancer in Clinical Trials. In: Industrial Conference on Data Mining – Workshops, pp. 157–169 (2010)
13. Golbeck, J., Fragoso, G., Hartel, F., Hendler, J., Oberthaler, J., Parsia, B.: National Cancer Institute's Thesaurus and Ontology. Journal of Web Semantics (2003)
14. Miller, G.A.: WordNet: An online lexical database. Int. J. Lexicograph 3(4), 235–244 (1990)
15. Dale, R., Moisl, H., Somers, H. (eds.): Handbook of Natural Language Processing. Mercel Dekker Inc., New York (2000)
16. Baeza-Yates, R., Ribeiro-Neto, B.: Modern information retrieval. ACM Press, New York (1999)
17. Polpinij, J., Ghose, A.K.: An Ontology-based Sentiment Classification Methodology for Online Consumer Reviews. In: 2008 IEEE/WIC/ACM International Conference on Web Intelligence (2008)
18. Fox, E.A., Sharat, S.: A comparison of two methods for soft Boolean interpretation in information retrieval. TR-86-1. Virginia Tech. Department of Computer Science (1986)
19. Lee, W.C., Fox, E.A.: Experimental Comparison of Schemes for Interpreting Boolean Queries. TR-88-27. Virginia Tech M.S. Thesis Department of Computer Science (1988)
20. Manning, C.D., Schutze, H.: Foundations of Statistical Natural Language Processing. MIT Press, Cambridge (1999)
21. Yang, Y., Liu, X.: A Re-examination of Text Categorization Methods. In: Proceedings of 22nd Annual International ACM SIGIR Conference on Research and Development in Information Retrieval, pp. 42–49 (1999)
22. Joachims, T.: Text Categorization with Support Vector Machines: Learning with Many Relevant Features. In: Nédellec, C., Rouveirol, C. (eds.) ECML 1998. LNCS, vol. 1398, pp. 137–142. Springer, Heidelberg (1998)
23. Baoli, L., Yuzhong, C., Shiwen, Y.: A Comparative Study on Automatic Categorization Methods for Chinese Search Engine. In: Proceedings of the Eighth Joint International Computer Conference, pp. 117–120. Zhejiang University Press, Hangzhou (2000)
24. Baoli, L., Shiwen, Y., Qin, L.: An Improved k-Nearest Neighbor Algorithm for text categorization. In: Proceedigns of 20th International Conference on Computer Processing of Oriental Language (2003)
25. Joachims, T.: Transductive Inference for Text Classification using Support Vector Machines. In: Proceedings of the International Conference on Machine Learning (ICML) (1999)
26. Chang, C.C., Lin, C.J.: LIBSVM: A Library for Support Vector Machines. Department of Computer Science and Information Engineering. National Taiwan University, Taipei, Taiwan (2004)

An Ontology Based Knowledge Preservation Model for Traditional Unani Medicines

Sobia Amjad[1], Talha Waheed[2], Ana M. Martinez Enriquez[3],
Muhammad Aslam[2], and Afraz Syed[2]

[1] Al-Khawarizmi Institute of Computer Science, UET Lahore, Pakistan
sobia.amjad@kics.edu.pk
[2] Dept. of Computer Science & Engineering, UET Lahore, Pakistan
{twaheed,maslam,afrazsyed}@uet.edu.pk
[3] Department of Computer Science, CINVESTAV, D.F. Mexico
ammartin@cinvestav.mx

Abstract. Traditional medicines can play a major role in global health care, due to its indigenous nature, easy access, and cost effectiveness. However, knowledge of this intellectual property is in danger of being lost. It is either undocumented or if documented, it is inaccessible and local in context. World Health Organization signifies the necessity to preserve and maintain this knowledge. Unani medicines, a subfield of traditional medicines, have been continuously practiced in Asia for about 2500 years, and it is facing the same situation of knowledge lost. To preserve knowledge of Unani medicines, initial kind of an effort has been done but a formal semantic structure, that is machine readable and reusable, is required to preserve this knowledge efficiently and effectively. This research focuses on conceptual structure of Unani medicines by presenting domain ontology which includes core principles and philosophy of Unani medicines, diseases, symptoms, diagnosis, drugs, and treatment. Knowledge about fundamentals is captured from expert interviews and books and then this knowledge is converted into ontologies using Protégé. Although it is not exhaustive domain ontology, however it may serve as a starting point for any knowledge based application of Unani medicines. In this research a semantic queries based case study along with a prototype expert system is also proposed.

Keywords: Traditional medicines, Unani medicines, Tibb Unani, domain ontology, knowledge management.

1 Introduction

In the whole world, the practice of traditional medicines is there since ancient times. It is a common belief that these have less side effects and less costly. Despite of their cultural roots, recent research signifies considerable medicinal benefits of herbs. However, traditional medicines need rigorous scientific investigation. As estimated by World Health Organization (WHO), 70% of the African and Asian population uses traditional medicines for their everyday health care needs [1] and 30% global population relies on traditional medicines [2]. In 2015, global market for traditional medicines will reach at US $ 114 billion [3].

D. Ślęzak et al. (Eds.): BIH 2014, LNAI 8609, pp. 278–289, 2014.

The importance of traditional medicines has been recently recognized by WHO. To enhance the role of traditional medicines in national healthcare of member countries, WHO suggested preserving the indigenous knowledge of traditional medicines, in its strategy [1]. Unfortunately this knowledge is mostly undocumented, and as the knowledgeable traditional healers are passing away, this great knowledge asset vanishes along with them. Whereas, documented knowledge is mostly in local languages, non-standardized, diverse, and inaccessible. In addition, if principles, practices, and concepts of traditional medicines are preserved and standardized, later it can be compared according to latest scientific methods [4] and included in national/international healthcare systems.

Unani medicines (aka Tibb e Unani) is a modified version of Greco-Arabic traditional medicines. It encompasses medical traditions of Greek, Arab, Persian, and Indian regions [5], in 2500 years of its practice. It is still being practiced in India, Pakistan, Iran, Afghanistan, Nepal, Bangladesh, Srilanka, Indonesia, Malaysia, Central Asia, and Arab countries. However, Unani Medicines still lacks a large scale scientific study. The Unani medicines have strong documented heritage. There are hundreds of books on its principles and treatment philosophy, herbal formulas, and therapies. Most of these books are written in Arabic, Persian, Hindi/Urdu, and local Indian languages. There are different constraints involved e.g. the content is multilingual, it is widespread time and space wise, its terminologies, and principles are non-standardized and above all lack of governmental interests.

Before conducting any scientific research, knowledge of Unani medicines needs preservation and translation into international languages so that access for this information across the globe becomes possible. In recent past, an effort from government of India to preserve knowledge of different domains of Indian traditional medicines including Unani medicines has been done [23], but it has its limitations. Efforts to preserve this knowledge systems of Japan [7], Korea [6], Thailand [8-11], China [15-22] and Africa [12-14] have been there since last decade. The concepts and practices of Unani medicines have some overlapping with other systems of traditional medicines, however it is fundamentally different with its own principles, concepts, and formulas that cannot be processed and represented with existing software applications of other traditional medicines domains, however, they can be compared and integrated later, if possible.

To compile, preserve and share knowledge of Unani medicines, a knowledge management framework is required. That needs to be based on Web services to store standard, semantically annotated multilingual, and reusable knowledge into a Web database. The proposed framework provides collaboration between domain experts of Unani medicines, researchers, traditional healers, and academicians, and it serves as an infrastructure for future computerization of Unani Medicines. In this framework, ontologies provide formal semantic structure. For the upcoming knowledge management framework, a domain ontology for Unani medicines along with semantic queries and prototype expert system is presented in this paper. This is the first effort of its kind in the domain of Unani medicines. The domain ontology contains upper level concepts of Unani medicines domain; their relationships with other concepts and data, and object properties. The objective of this work is to provide a framework to preserve, standardize, and validate this knowledge of Unani medicines as per modern scientific principles and then ultimately making it possible to include this system of traditional medicines in mainstream healthcare systems. The proposed ontology can be employed in design and development of intelligent applications like decision support system for diagnostics, prediction, and prescription.

Section 2 summarizes the related work already done by using ontologies in traditional medicines domain. In section 3, ontology modeling steps are listed along with the given ontology. Section 4 describes proposed expert system. In section 5, a case study of semantic queries is presented.

2   Literature Review

A survey of few ongoing efforts in knowledge management of traditional medicines using ontologies has been presented. However, this is not an exhaustive effort and chiropractic, reiki, massage, reflexology, meditation, and yoga like therapies are not included.

Ontology of traditional Korean medicines has been developed by Jang et al. for symptoms, diseases, and treatments [6]. An effort based on ontology for Japanese traditional medicines Kampo, is presented by Arita et. al. [7]. Some efforts to develop Thai herbal ontology can be seen in [8-11].

For African traditional medicines, an ontology is proposed by Atemezing and Pavon [12] which is further updated by Ayimdji et al. [13]. Another ontology was designed for African traditional herbs by Oladosu et al. [14]. Traditional Chinese medicines (TCM) seems rich in computational efforts, Chen [15] and Mao [16] proposed domain ontology for the problem of semantic heterogeneity. Multiple efforts on semantic Web and TCM domain modeling using ontology are available in [17-22].

Traditional Knowledge Digital Library abbreviated as TKDL [23] is a closely related application for the domain of Unani medicines and needs special focus. It is an online data base developed by the Indian government. It contains principles, formulations, definitions, and core concepts of different traditional medicines disciplines being practiced in India. It includes Ayurveda, Unani medicines, Yoga, and Siddha. In TKDL the local medicines knowledge in Hindi/Urdu, Arabic, Persia is translated into English, French, Spanish, German, and Japanese. In TKDL, around 0.25 million herbal formulas have been transcribed by 2011. TKRC, International Patent Classification (IPC) based classification system, has been specially evolved from this project.

Traditional medicines knowledge is encoded in TKRC using XML, Unicode, and Metadata. However, the database storing knowledge of TKDL is text-based [24] it has no formal semantic structure like ontologies, that limits its scope and it also lacks support of Web-services that is needed for integration with upcoming software applications. In TKDL, text based queries are allowed, but support for semantic queries is not available yet. Whereas, to get full benefits of semantic Web, a formal semantic structure similar to ontologies is needed i.e. structural data for reusability, extendibility, and automatic machine processing.

3   Ontology Modeling for Unani Medicines

During last decade for knowledge sharing and its organization, ontologies are being developed and used. Ontology is an explicit and formal specification of shared conceptualization, as defined by Gruber [25]. Every ontology mainly includes classes, attributes possessed by these classes, hierarchies, and link between individuals of the classes.

Huang[26] mentioned that in knowledge-based systems building and development of a domain model is an integral part. High level of analytical and abstract approach is required for building ontology. Noy and McGuiness suggested simple method for creating ontology [28]. Following are the steps involved in ontology development:

3.1   Determine the Domain and Scope of Ontology

Few simple and basic question are devised by Noy and McGuiness[28] which helps in this phase. First step of ontology building is limiting its scope and defining the domain. The domain of ontology is Unani medicines and scope is limited to core Unani medicines principles, related to symptom, diseases, diagnosis, and treatment.

3.2   Consider Reusing Existing Ontologies (if any)

Unani medicines domain ontology has been created first time according to our best possible knowledge so no other existing ontology can be used here. However, existing ontology of other traditional medicines can be of great help in integration and development of Unani medicines ontology at software level in future.

3.3   Enumerate Important Terms in the Ontology

Core concepts and terminologies of Unani medicines have been gathered both from explicit ways and by tacit knowledge. Explicit knowledge is enumerated from text and reference books of Unani medicines. However, tacit knowledge is acquired from experts by interviews, discussions, etc. This knowledge is then used in defining classes, attributes, and concepts of Unani medicines ontology.

3.4   Define Class and Class Hierarchy

In this phase hierarchy of core concepts (in the form of classes here), their super and sub classes has been defined as shown in Fig. 1. Gruber discussed different approaches in developing a class hierarchy [25]. Top level concepts are identified as super classes in our ontology. Proposed ontology is developed using Protégé [27].

The Identified Classes. The Unani_Medicines_Principle class is the most integral part of our ontology. It covers core philosophical concepts of Unani medicines. These concepts differentiates Unani medicines from other domains of traditional medicines.

Fig. 1. Class Hierarchy and Concepts

Unani medicines, takes a holistic approach towards the whole human body and soul and divides core concepts into seven components, known as Umoor-e-Tabiya [29] in Urdu language. These are Element (Arkaan), Temperaments (Mizaj), Humours (Akhlaat), Faculties (Quwa), Organs (Aa'za), Functions (Afa'al), and Pneumas (Arwaah). Fig. 2 explains all the relations that exist between Unani medicine principle class of our ontology.

Other classes includes Disease and Limitation which describes different diseases of patient, limitation of foods or medicines patient is allergic with or precautions for a specific disease. It also includes information about the risks and side effects. Whereas, class of Natural Products explains that drugs in Unani medicines can be obtained from four type of natural sources i.e. Animals, plants, minerals, and ecology. Class of Pulse Analysis is used in diagnosis process, an expert practitioner may judge different signs and symptoms by analyzing pulse rate and type of pulse. The class of Signs and Symptoms includes all the signs and symptoms that can possibly exist for diseases. In Unani medicines ontolgy mainly Eye color, tongue color, tongue coating color, skin color, etc are the important symptoms that are observed carefully by practitioners to diagnose the problems. Class of Stool and Urine Examination keeps the details of texture, color, and other features that can be useful for examination. Whereas, classes of Therapy and Treatment suggests drug to be used, therapies to be employed to treat the patient according to Unani medicine treatment practices.

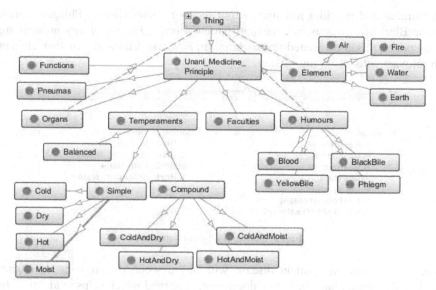

Fig. 2. Ontology Model

3.5   Define Class Properties (or Slots)

Classes and their hierarchy is not enough to preserve all the semantics of the domain. For this purpose, there exists an association between every instance of a class in the form of properties (or attributes).

The Data Properties. Data properties are of two types: simple or complex. Simple properties contains primitive data of concepts that comprises of strings, numbers, etc whereas a complex data property contains other objects. In proposed ontology there are four simple data properties as shown in Fig. 3.

- *Disease Full Name.* This property is of string type and it maintains the full name of the disease in English.
- *Disease Local Name.* It is of string type and saves the local name of the disease.
- *Herb Full Name.* It is also of string type and saves herb full name in local languages.
- *Herb Scientific Name.* It is saves the scientific name of herb in English.

The Object Properties. In ontology, two or more classes (or concepts) and their objects are linked to each other by defining object properties between them. Object properties can also exist independently in ontologies. A short description of used object properties is given in Fig. 3.

hasDisease associates symptoms with its diseases. Every symptom has a disease associated with it. *hasElement* relates any of Temperament value with related value of Element according to Unani Medicines principle. *hasHumour* relates temperament with humour and provides any one of four humour values (Blood, Phlegm, Yellow-Bile or BlackBile) that is in excess in patient's body. Excess of any humour may cause specific diseases related to that humour. *hasState* relates any of four elements with relevant value from four States.

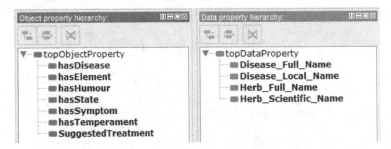

Fig. 3. Data and Object Properties

hasSymptoms relates patient disease with any associated Symptom for example having body temperature increased, decreased, or normal which helps in identification of Temperament or Disease, and ultimately in Diagnosis. *hasTemperament* links concept of Temperament with concept of Humour. *SuggestedTreatment* suggests treatment for diseases. For Example, in a treatment of any specific disease a practitioner may advise a simple or compound herb formulation to patients.

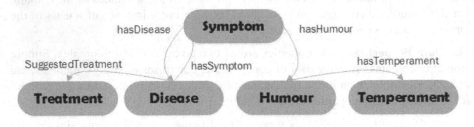

Fig. 4. Classes and its Relation

In Fig. 4, Symptom and Diseases are linked to each other using *hasSymptom* and *hasDisease* properties. The property *hasHumour* relates *Humour* to *Symptom*. Each *Humour* is associated to *temperament* through one to one relationship using *hasTemperament* property. Also, every disease has *suggestedTreatment* using *hasTreatment* property. After once defining all the classes, subclasses, data properties, object properties and facets, individuals are created. Individuals (or objects in object oriented paradigm) are like specific instances of classes.

4   Proposed Expert System

A prototype expert system is build after defining all of the concepts, properties, individuals and the relation that exist between them in Unani medicines ontology. In this section, it is explained that how proposed ontology of Unani medicines can be used in a clinical decision support system.

The architecture of this prototype system is presented in Fig. 5. There are mainly five components in our system; Domain Knowledge Acquisition, Unani Medicines Ontology, Database (OWL/RDF), Inference System, and User Interface. There are three associated roles of Knowledge Engineer, Domain expert and Users. Knowledge engineer acquires domain knowledge from the Unani medicines domain experts and practitioners, and text books. Domain ontology structure and representation has been created in Protégé editor. For inference, JENA API has been used to import and process ontology. Database fields have been populated with Unani medicines facts and information. The process starts when user requests through user interface which executes a query. It activates the inference system that infers the facts using rules based on Unani Medicines domain ontology.

Jena API is used for developing expert system based on our Unani medicines Ontology. Unani medicines expert system prototype takes the symptoms from user and returns the information of user Temperament and Humour. Then, after this result disease is diagnosed and treatment is suggested to patient.

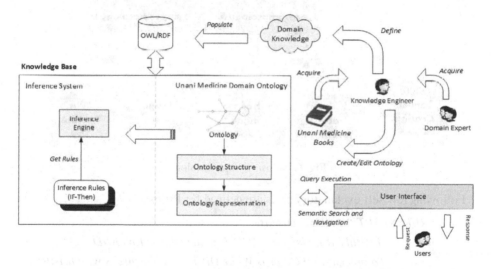

Fig. 5. Architecture of Proposed Expert System

Unani medicine expert system starts with the details of patient which are saved in a file. Then, first question is asked from the patient about its pulse rate. The answer selected by the user is saved in Java bean which can be accessed on all pages after this selection. The second question is about the Tongue. It has three types of questions related to tongue: color, coating color, and its texture. Third question is related to skin color and texture and fourth question is about eye color. After getting answers for all the questions, SPARQL query is executed with the above selected values and humour, temperament, disease, and treatment is returned based on selected symptoms.Expert system takes values from the selected radio buttons and generates query string based on those symptoms for getting a disease.

5   Case Study

Psilosis is a disease that can occur in both children and adults causing diarrhea. As case study of symptoms, treatment and cure for this intestinal disease are observed and its symptomatology is shown in Fig. 6. A weak pulse rate is observed for this disease. Color of tongue coating seems to be white and color of tongue itself is red. In symptomatology of Pilosis there exists AND relationship in three symptoms located at lower left position in diagram. These symptoms must need to exist for given disease as they have AND relationship between them. Optional symptoms have OR relationship with them, are related to texture of skin and tongue. Hence for Psilosis to be occurred our ontology has information about five symptoms in which three are compulsory and two are optional. Rules are then defined for the diagnosis of patient's disease after finalizing Symptomatology. These rules will help in query building.

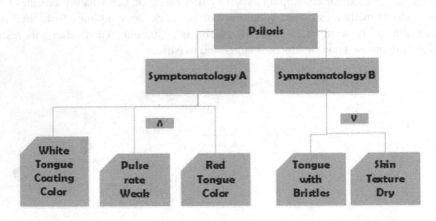

Fig. 6. Psilosis Symptomatology

Following few self explanatory rules are defined for Psilosis.

RULE 1: RULESTART " Psilosis Disease"

　　　　　IF (PulseRate is Weak AND TongueColor is Red AND

　　　　　TongueCoatingColor is White OR TongueTexture is with bristles

　　　　　OR SkinTexture is Dry)

　　　　　THEN Disease is Psilosis

　　　ENDRULE

Rule 1 explains that Disease will be diagnosed as Psilosis if above five mentioned symptoms exists in patient.

RULE 2: RULESTART "Isphagol_Husk SuggestedTreatment"

　　　　IF (Disease is Psilosis)

　　　　THEN suggestedTreatment is Isphagol_Husk

　　　ENDRULE

Rule 2 suggests the medicine named Isphagol_Husk for the treatment of disease Psilosis. Isphagol_Husk is a natural formulation according to Unani Medicines.

RULE 3: RULESTART "Phlegm Humour"

> *IF (PulseRate is Weak AND TongueColor is Red AND*
>
> *TongueCoatingColor is White OR TongueTexture is with_Bristles OR SkinTexture is Dry)*
>
> *THEN Humour is Phlegm*

ENDRULE

Rule 3 describes that Phlegm as Humour of the patient if symptoms exist.

RULE 4: RULESTART "ColdAndMoist Temperament"

> *IF (Humour is Phlegm)*
>
> *THEN Temperament is ColdandMoist*

ENDRULE

In rule 5, it is clear that if Phelgm is the Humour then Temperament of the patient would be ColdAndMoist. Temperament is linked to Humour using hasTemperament object property defined in Unani medicines. Temperament is one of the key concept to diagnose any disease according to core Unani medicines principles. While prescribing any medicine Unani practitioner carefully observes the temperament of patient.

In the same way, by using the proposed ontology, decision support system can infer facts from family history and signs and symptoms of disease, and helps in prescription of drugs for the treatment of Psilosis.

5.1   SPARQL Queries and Results

For executing queries in protégé SPARQL queries are developed for retrieving results according to selection criteria. For every RULE defined above, a query is presented against it. However, in this paper a single query is enough to present a method of building a query from rules.

```
SELECT ?subject ?object
    WHERE {
    Unani:Pulse_rate_Weak Unani:hasDisease ?object.
    Unani:Tongue_Color_Red Unani:hasDisease ?object .
    Unani:White_Tongue_Coating_Color Unani:hasDisease ?object.
    OPTIONAL{ Unani: Unani:hasDisease ?object .}
    OPTIONAL { Unani:Skin_Texture_Dry Unani:hasDisease ?object .}
    OPTIONAL{ Unani:Tongue_with_bristles Unani:hasDisease ?object .}
    OPTIONAL { Unani: Unani:hasDisease ?object .} }
```

Fig. 7. Query for Disease

Query for Getting Disease. SPARQL query in Fig. 7 is for selecting disease based on multiple symptoms build against Rule 1. Object property hasDisease is used for retrieving results. Optional symptoms for Psilosis are defined using "OPTIONAL" keyword.

6   Conclusion and Future Work

A domain ontology is proposed for knowledge preservation of Unani Medicines, a Traditional Medicines system practiced mainly in Asia. This is the first domain ontology of its kind build in this domain. Patient's disease, symptoms, diagnosis, treatment is covered by keeping the core principles of Unani Medicines. The ontology organizes common understanding for information of the domain both for human and for software agents; it serve as the base semantic structure that links concepts of Unani Medicines with each other, by restricting the types and values of each concept with semantic search and navigation. Thses above mentioned features are previously not possible in text-based databases, like traditional knowledge digital library, that have no built-in conceptual structure and offer only keyword based search. In future, ontology will be further expanded to broaden its depth and breadth and can be employed in knowledge management frameworks, clinical decision support systems and machine learning applications of Unani Medicines.

References

1. WHO: WHO traditional medicine strategy 2002–2005. WHO, Geneva (2002)
2. Patwardhan, B.: Traditional Medicine: Modern Approach for Affordable Global Health. WHO-Commission on Intellectual Property Rights Innovation and Public Health (CIPIH), Study Nine on TM, WHO, Geneva (2005)
3. Global Industry Analyst: Alternative Medicine: A Global Outlook. Report published by Global Industry Analyst, Inc. San Hose (2012)
4. Tinnaluck, Y.: Modern science and native knowledge: collaborative process that opens new perspective for PCST. J. Quark No. 32: April-June, Spain (2004)
5. Magnor, L.N.: A History of Medicine, 2nd edn. Taylor and Francis, USA (2005)
6. Jang, H., Kim, J., Kim, S.-K., Kim, C., Bae, S.-H., Kim, A., Eum, D.-M., Song, M.-Y.: Ontology for Medicinal Materials Based on Traditional Korean Medicine. Bioinformatics 26(18), 2359–2360 (2010)
7. Arita, M., Suwa, K., Yoshimoto, M., Hirai, A., Kanaya, S.: Ontology Checking and Integration of Crude-Drug and Kampo Information. In: 2nd Int. Conf. on BMEI, Tianjin, pp. 1–4 (2009)
8. Nantiruj, T., Maneerat, N., Varakulsiripunth, R., Izumi, S., Shiratori, N., Kato, T., Kato, Y., Takahashi, K.: An e-Health Advice System with Thai Herb and an Ontology. In: Proceeding of the 3rd International Symposium on Biomedical Engineering (ISBME 2008), Thailand, pp. 315–319 (2008)
9. Kato, T., Maneerat, N., Varakulsiripunth, R., Kato, Y., Takahashi, K.: Ontology-based E-health System with Thai Herb Recommendation. In: Proceeding of the 6th International Joint Conference on Computer Science and Software Engineering (JCSSE 2009), Thailand, pp. 172–177 (2009)

10. Kato, T., Maneerat, N., Varakulsiripunth, R., Izumi, S., Takahashi, H., Suganuma, T., Takahashi, K., Kato, Y., Shiratori, N.: Provision of Thai Herbal Recommendation Based on an Ontology. In: 3rd Int. Conf. on Human System Interaction (HSI 2010), Poland, pp. 217–222 (2010)
11. Izumi, S., Kuriyama, D., Itabashi, G., Togashi, A., Kato, Y., Takahashi, K.: An Ontology-based Advice System for Health and Exercise. In: Proceedings of the 10th International Conference on Internet and Multimedia Systems and Applications (IMSA 2006), pp. 95–100 (2006)
12. Atemezing, G., Pavon, J.: An Ontology for African Traditional Medicine. In: Corchado, J.M., Rodríguez, S., Llinas, J., Molina, J.M. (eds.) International Symposium on Distributed Computing and Artificial Intelligence 2008 (DCAI 2008), Salamanca. ASC, vol. 50, pp. 329–337. Springer, Heidelberg (2008)
13. Ayimdji, A., Koussoubé, S., Fotso, L.P., Konfé, B.O.: Towards a "Deep" Ontology for African Traditional Medicine. J. of the Intelligent Information Management, 244–251 (2011)
14. Oladosu, J.B., Adigun, M.O., Mbarika, V.: Towards a Pharmaceutical Ontology for African Traditional Herbs. In: Proceedings of the World Congress on Engineering and Computer Science (WCECS 2012), San Francisco, vol. I (2012)
15. Chen, H., Mao, Y., Zheng, X., Cui, M., Feng, Y., Deng, S., Yin, A., Zhou, C., Tang, J., Jiang, X., Wu, Z.: Towards Semantic e-Science for Traditional Chinese Medicine. BMC Bioinformatics 8(3) (2007)
16. Mao, Y., Wu, Z., Tian, W., Jiang, X., Cheung, W.K.: Dynamic sub-ontology evolution for traditional Chinese medicine web ontology. J. Biomed. Inform. 41(5), 790–805 (2008)
17. Cheung, K.H., Chen, H.: Semantic Web for data harmonization in Chinese medicine. J. of Chinese Medicine 5(2) (2010)
18. Levin, J.S., Jonas: Essentials of Complementary and Alternative Medicine. Chinese Traditional Medicine 88, 283–294 (2007)
19. Jokiniemi, J.: Ontologies and Computational Methods for Traditional Chinese Medicine, Master's Thesis, School of Science & Technology, Aalto University, Finland (2010)
20. Zhao, J.: Publishing Chinese medicine knowledge as Linked Data on the Web. J. of Chinese Medicine 5(27) (2010)
21. Qi, X., Meng, C., Cungen, C., Baoyan, L., Changlin, L., Hongguan, J.: Establishment of the TCM Meta Conceptual Model Based on Domain Ontology. J. of World Science and Technology Modernization of Traditional Chinese Medicine 11(4), 621–625 (2009)
22. Yu, T.: Ontology Engineering for Chinese Medicine - Connecting eastern and western medicine. Technical Report of CCNT DartGrid Group, Zhejiang University, Hangzhou, Zhejiang, China (2008)
23. Traditional Knowledge Digital Library, http://www.tkdl.res.in/
24. Samaddar, S.G., Chaudhary, B.D.: Development of a Framework for Traditional Knowledge Digital Library (TKDL-S) Semantic Web Portal for Santal Medicinal System. J. of Science and Culture 76(11-12), 544–551 (2010)
25. Gruber, T.R.: Toward principles for the design of ontologies used for knowledge sharing. International J. of Human-Computer Studies - Special Issue: The Role of Formal Ontology in the Information Technology 43(5-6), 907–928 (1995)
26. Huang, M.J., Chen, M.Y.: Integrated design of the intelligent web-based Chinese Medical Diagnostic System (CMDS) – Systematic development for digestive health. Expert Systems with Applications 32(2), 658–673 (2007)
27. Protégé Ontology Editor and Knowledge-base framework, http://protege.stanford.edu/
28. Noy, N.F., McGuiness, D.L.: Ontology Development 101: A Guide to Creating Your First Ontolotgy. Technical Report KSL-01-05, Stanford Knowledge System Laboratory (2001)

A Computational Study of Robotic Therapy for Stroke Rehabilitation Based on Population Coding

Yuki Ueyama

Department of Rehabilitation Engineering
Research Institute of National Rehabilitation Center for Persons with Disabilities
4-1 Namiki, Tokorozawa, Saitama 359-8555, Japan
ueyama-yuki@rehab.go.jp

Abstract. We evaluated the efficiency of robotic therapy for stroke survivors by using a computational approach in motor theory with a stroke rehabilitation model. In computational neuroscience, hand movement can be represented by population coding of neuronal preferred directions (PDs) in the motor cortex. We modeled the recovery processes of arm movement in conventional and robotic therapies as reoptimization of PDs in different learning rules, and compared the efficiencies after stroke. Conventional therapy did not induce complete recovery of stroke lesions, and the neuronal state depended on the training direction. However, robotic therapy reoptimized the PDs uniformly regardless of the training direction. These observations suggest that robotic therapy may be effective for recovery and not have a negative effect on motor performance depending the training direction. Furthermore, this study provides computational evidence to promote robotic therapy for stroke rehabilitation.

Keywords: Motor learning, Motor cortex, Preferred direction, Reinforcement learning, Reaching.

1   Introduction

The incidence of stroke was approximately 17 million in 2010, with 33 million people who previously had a stroke still being alive [1]. Most people survive a first stroke but often have significant morbidity. Loss of functional movement is a common consequence of stroke, for which a wide range of interventions has been developed including constraint-induced movement therapy (CIMT), electromyographic biofeedback, mental practice with motor imagery, and robotics. Some treatments show promise for improving motor recovery, particularly those that focus on high-intensity and repetitive task-specific practice. In particular, robotic devices are considered novel tools that can be used alone or in combination with novel pharmacological agents and other bioengineered devices. In addition, robotic devices can measure motor performance objectively and provide detailed insight into the process of stroke recovery. However, existing evidence is limited by poor trial designs [2].

On the other hand, the motor map of the motor cortex is not static. The motor cortex provides a substrate for adaptive changes during the acquisition of motor skills

D. Ślęzak et al. (Eds.): BIH 2014, LNAI 8609, pp. 290–300, 2014.

and functional recovery after lesions. Indeed, the neuronal circuitry creates a dynamic, adaptive map that generates the motor commands required to accomplish desired actions under different conditions [3, 4]. Thus, the motor cortex may be involved in the acquisition, retention, and recall of procedural skills. Task-oriented training with motor learning identified as robotic therapy can also induce plasticity changes in the cerebral cortex [5, 6]. A few studies have addressed the mechanisms underlying cortical reorganization of specific arm-rehabilitation methods, e.g., CIMT and bimanual training, in the context of voluntary motor activity in skill-learning scenarios [7, 8].

The present study investigated how robotic therapy influences recovery of motor performance in stroke survivors by using a computational model of motor control with a stroke model [9, 10]. Hand movement can be represented by population coding of neuronal preferred directions (PDs) based on computation in the motor cortex [11]. In addition, we postulated that a robotic device could generate a force that helps achieve a reaching task with maximal effort of subjects, and modeled conventional and robotic therapies as supervised learning and reinforcing learning, respectively. Conventional therapy did not induce complete recovery after a stroke lesion and the neuronal state depended on the training direction. However, robotics therapy reoptimized the PDs uniformly for all directions. In addition, the result persisted when training targets were limited. These observations suggest that robotic therapy is effective for recovery in stroke rehabilitation, and it does not have a negative effect on motor performance depending the training direction.

2   Computational Model

We considered a center-out arm-reaching task, and simulated hand movements according to a population vector (PV) with a stroke model [10]. The targets were randomly generated in eight directions uniformly aligned on a circle, i.e., target directions of $0°, 45°, 90°...315°$. We also performed simulations in which the targets were limited to impaired directions of $0°, 45°,$ and $90°$. The situation was assumed to involve training in arm extension movement. In both sessions, the rehabilitation process consisted of 1200 trials.

2.1   Motor Cortex Model

Motor learning can be divided into kinematic and dynamic components. A previous study of whole-arm reaching movement in monkeys indicated that the levels of activity of many motor cortex neurons change systematically with the direction of the external load even if the movement path does not change [12]. On the other hand, the PD of neurons shifts in the direction of applied force in the velocity-dependent curl force field, and shifts back in the oppose direction in the washout epoch [3]. Thus, the external force generated by robotic devices could change PDs in the motor cortex, and we modeled hand movement as a PV of motor cortex neurons.

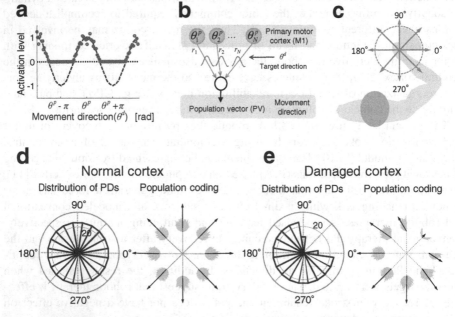

Fig. 1. Computational model of the motor cortex. (a) Example of a neuron's activation pattern as truncated cosine tuning. The red marks indicate activity, and the blue dotted line indicates the fitted cosine curve. (b) Illustration of population coding. (c) Movement directions in center-out reaching task. The gray zone indicates the movement direction impaired by stroke. Panels (d) and (e) show neuronal states in the motor cortex. Left panels show histograms of preferred directions. Right panels show neuronal population coding (gray lines) and population vectors (black arrows). (d) Normal motor cortex before stroke. (e) Damaged motor cortex after stroke.

Neural Model. The motor cortex contains neurons that are selectively activated depending on the direction of hand movement [11]. In particular, the direction of motion in which the neuron is maximally active is called the PD θ_i^p. In this study, we postulated that PDs are influenced by noise $n_i \sim N(0, \sigma_n^2)$ as $\theta_i^p + n_i$. In addition, the activity of the neuron (i.e., firing rate) is attenuated according to differences in the direction of movement from the PD fitting cosine curve (Fig. 1a). Therefore, the activity of a neuron, $u_i(\theta^d)$, can be modeled by a cosine function with the firing rate noise ε_i [13]:

$$u_i(\theta^d) = \left[\cos(\theta^d - \theta_i^p - n_i) + \varepsilon_i\right]_+ \quad (1 \le i \le N) \tag{1}$$

where θ^d and N are the desired movement direction and the number of neurons, respectively. The operator $[\cdot]_+$ is defined as $[\cdot]_+ \equiv \max\{\cdot, 0\}$. The firing-rate noise is given as signal-dependent multiplicative noise (SDN) [14]:

$$\varepsilon_i = v_i \left[\cos(\theta^d - \theta_i^p - n_i)\right]_+ \tag{2}$$

where v_i is Gaussian white noise with unity covariance, i.e., $v_i \sim N(0, \sigma_v^2)$. The SDN plays an important role in motor planning [15]. Note that we assumed the number of motor cortex neurons $N = 500$, with an initial uniform distribution of PDs (Fig. 1d, left), and set the noise parameters $\sigma_n = 0.022$, $\sigma_v = 0.15$, with reference to experimental observations [15, 16].

Population Coding of Movement. We postulated that hand movement can be represented by population coding of neuronal activities as the PV, which is a means by which information is encoded in a group of neurons [9] (Fig. 1b). According to population coding (Fig. 1d, right), the PV represented as $\mathbf{v}(\theta^d) \in R^2$ can be given by

$$\mathbf{v}(\theta^d) = \frac{1}{N}\sum_{i=1}^{N} u_i(\theta^d) \cdot \mathbf{p}_i \tag{3}$$

where $\mathbf{p}_i = [\cos(\theta_i^p + n_i), \sin(\theta_i^p + n_i)]^T$, which is the basis vector of the PD.

Reaching Impairment after Stroke. Stroke seems to affect movement only within a certain range of directions. The directional control of reaching after stroke can be simulated by cell death in a PV model of movement control [10]. To model the effect, we removed neurons with PDs in the first quadrant (Fig. 1c). This restricted the range of movement for the 45° direction, while movements the 0° and 90° directions deviated from the desired directions (Fig. 1e).

2.2   Effects of Rehabilitation

We modeled the effects of rehabilitation on motor function as motor adaptation. The aims of motor adaptation are to shift the actual encoded direction closer to the desired direction, i.e., active learning component, and to shift the PDs of the individual neurons toward the desired direction, i.e., passive learning component (self-organizing component). Thus, the leaning rule is described as the following cost function:

$$J = (\theta^d - \theta^h)^2 - \lambda \sum_{i=1}^{N} u_i(\theta^d)^2 \tag{4}$$

where θ^h and λ are the PV direction and free parameter, respectively. Through multiple rehabilitation trials, the PDs are updated in accordance with the learning rule. The updated rule is denoted using active and passive updating commands, w_a and w_p, respectively, by

$$\theta_i^p(t+1) = \theta_i^p(t) + w_a(t) + w_p(t) \tag{5}$$

where t is the number of trials. The passive component is derived from the deviation of the cost function with respect to a neuron's PD, i.e., $\partial J/\partial \theta_i^p$:

$$w_p(t) = \alpha_p \cdot u_i(\theta^d(t)) \cdot \sin(\theta^d(t) - \theta_i^p(t) - n_i(t)) \tag{6}$$

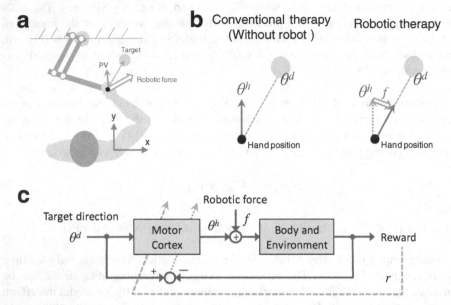

Fig. 2. Illustration of conventional and robotic therapies. (a) Arm movement training using robotic manipulandum. (b) Arm movements in the therapies. In conventional therapy, movement error is observed. In robotic therapy, there is no directional error, as the assistive robotic force is generated to reduce error. (c) Block diagram of active learning components. Blue dotted and red dashed arrows indicate supervised learning (conventional therapy) and reinforcement learning (robotic therapy) approaches, respectively.

where α_p is the learning rate, set equal to 0.002 according to a previous study [7]. Moreover, we defined the active updating command as different forms representing conventional and robotic therapies (Fig. 2).

Conventional Therapy. In previous studies [7, 8], the active learning component was defined as a supervised learning. Thus, we adapted supervised learning as conventional therapy in accordance with those studies (Fig.2b-c). Similar to the passive component, the active update component is derived from deviation of Eq. (4):

$$w_a(t) = \alpha_{aC} \cdot \frac{u_i(\theta^d(t))}{|\mathbf{v}(\theta^d(t))|} \cdot (\theta^d(t) - \theta^h(t)) \tag{7}$$

where α_{aC} is the learning rate, set equal to 0.05 in accordance with a previous study [7]. Notably, we adjusted the angular error between the desired and PV directions to fall within the interval $-\pi \leq \theta^d - \theta^h < \pi$.

Robotic Therapy. In robotic therapy, the robot generates assistive force to achieve the motor task, i.e., reduce error and increase the range of movement (Fig. 2a). Such training involves two interacting processes: the subject trying to move and the robot applying forces to the subject's arm. A fundamental principle of motor learning is that movement practice improves motor function; however, the role of applied robotic forces in improving motor function is still unclear. We assumed that the robotic therapy induced reinforcement learning rather than supervised learning because the task is always achieved with robotic support and a reward in the form of task achievement is presented, e.g., sound and explosion of targets (Fig. 2c). The explicit feedbacks may increase subjects' motivation to promote reinforcement learning [17]. We assumed that the robotic device would generate an assistive force to achieve the reaching task with maximal effort of the subject [21, 22].

Suppose that the expected cost-to-go function is

$$V(t) = \sum_{k=0}^{N-t} \gamma^k r(t+k) \tag{8}$$

for a general reward function $r(t)$, where the discount rate of reward γ is assumed to be 0.9. To solve this optimization problem, we adopted a temporal difference (TD) learning method. The TD learning updates the policy to minimize the reward prediction error known as TD error $\delta(t)$ given by

$$\delta(t) = r(t) + \gamma \hat{V}(t+1) - \hat{V}(t) \tag{9}$$

where $\hat{V}(t)$ is the estimated value. Then it is updated by

$$\hat{V}(t+1) = \hat{V}(t) + \beta \delta(t) \tag{10}$$

where the learning rate β is 0.05. In addition, the active component in the update rule is given by

$$w_a(t) = \alpha_{aR} \cdot \delta(t) \cdot n_i(t) \tag{11}$$

where α_{aR} is the learning rate, set equal to 10. A previous primate study suggested that dopamine cells in the basal ganglia appear to mimic the TD error signal [18]. Moreover, we defined the following reward function:

$$r(t) = 1 - \kappa f(t)^2 \tag{12}$$

where f is the affected robotic force and κ is the scaling parameter set equal to 10. The reward function requires subjects to improve the motor performance by reducing the affected force via the haptic interaction with the robotic manipulandum. In this study, we defined the robotic force according to the following simplified form:

$$f \equiv \theta^d - \theta^h \quad (-\pi \le f < \pi) \tag{13}$$

The assistive force in stroke rehabilitation plays a role in reducing the directional error (Fig. 2b: right).

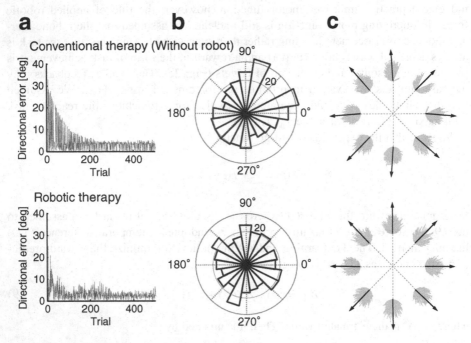

Fig. 3. Effects of rehabilitation in conventional and robotic therapies. The top and bottom rows show the results of conventional and robotic therapies, respectively. (a) Angular errors between the target position and PV during rehabilitation trials. (b) Reoptimization of PD distribution after rehabilitation. (c) Population coding of neurons.

The learning rule updates the policy that describes the "best" PD's rotation to maximize reward [16]. Notably, the best updating rule during trials was obtained from the iterative calculations.

3   Results

We carried out numerical simulations for the motor recover process in different rehabilitation approaches, i.e., conventional and robotic therapies. In both therapies (Fig. 3), directional errors decreased across trials (Fig. 3a). However, the PD of the neurons was reoptimized to different states depending on the approach used (Fig. 3b). In conventional therapy, no neurons had a PD of around 45°, as surrounding neurons were increased to make up for the deficit in neurons at 45°. As a result, the PVs directed toward the targets were modified, although they were detected in population coding. On the other hand, the robotic therapy made up for the deficits of other neurons. Loss of population coding recovered completely, and the directional error was smaller than with conventional therapy. We calculated the mean and standard distribution (SD) values for eight targets after rehabilitation (Fig. 4a). The errors (mean ± SD) were 2.7° ± 1.6° and 0.53° ± 0.46° in conventional and robotic therapies, respectively.

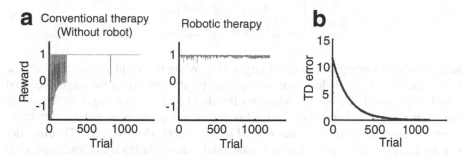

Fig. 4. Performance changes during conventional and robotic therapies. (a) Rewards during both therapies. Left and right panels indicate the profiles during conventional and robotic therapies, respectively. (b) Temporal difference (TD) error during robotic therapy.

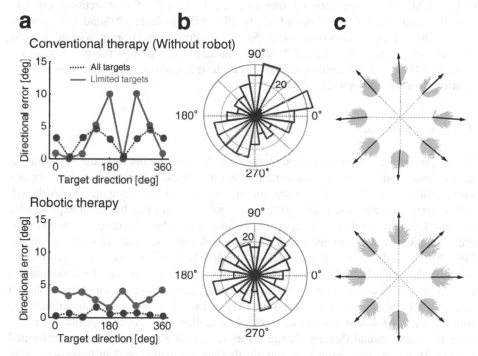

Fig. 5. Effects of rehabilitation for limited target directions after rehabilitation. The top and bottom rows indicate the results of conventional and robotic therapies, respectively. (a) Angular errors for several targets after rehabilitation of all targets (blue dotted lines) and limited targets (red solid lines). (b) Reoptimization of the distribution of preferred directions. (c) Population coding of neurons.

During conventional therapy, the reward value was gradually increased at early trials, and converged with 1 after about 300 trials (Fig. 4a: left). Notably we used following definition of the reward function $r_c(t)$ in conventional therapy:

$$r_c(t) = \begin{cases} 1 & |\theta^d - \theta^h| \leq \rho \\ -\kappa(\theta^d - \theta^h)^2 & |\theta^d - \theta^h| > \rho \end{cases} \qquad (14)$$

where ρ is the boundary threshold of target area. When the angular error between the target direction and PV is less than ρ, the hand position is within the target area and the task is achieved. We set the boundary threshold as 5° around target directions. In contrast, it was just below 1 with variability during robotic therapy, and the variability of reward remained during whole trials (Fig. 4a: right). However, the TD error denoted by Eq. (9) was decreased in an exponential manner during trials, and converged about 0 at late trials (Fig. 4b).

We also examined the situation when the presented targets were limited only to the first quadrant area (Fig. 5). After rehabilitation, the mean directional errors did not differ between the two approaches. However, the directional error varied markedly for different targets in conventional therapy, i.e., 3.7° ± 4.2°. The directional error of directions was greater in the second and fourth quadrants (e.g., 180° and 270°, respectively) than in other directions (Fig. 5a). In contrast, the error in robotic therapy showed smaller variation, i.e., 3.2° ± 1.0°. In addition, although robotic therapy recovered PDs in the impaired direction similar to the results for the eight targets, conventional therapy did not (Fig. 5b–c).

4   Conclusion

We evaluated the effects of robotic therapy for stroke survivors from the viewpoint of neural computation in the motor cortex. Hand movement was represented by population coding of neuronal PDs in the motor cortex based on computation. Although active assistance exercise is the primary control paradigm that has been explored for the development of robotic therapy, we postulated that the robotic device would generate an assistive force to achieve a reaching task with maximal effort of the subject [19, 20]. Indeed, we found that robotic therapy had advantages over conventional therapy. Although both therapies decreased directional error across the rehabilitation trials, conventional therapy did not recover loss of neurons in the area of the lesion. In contrast, robotic therapy reoptimized the PDs uniformly for movement directions. The robotic therapy showed smaller degrees of variability in directional errors compared with the conventional therapy. Large errors remained after rehabilitation for limited targets. However, the changes in robotic therapy were smaller than those seen with conventional therapy. In conclusion, we suggest that robotic therapy is an efficient means of generalizing motor function. Furthermore, this study provides computational evidence to promote the use of robotic therapy for stroke rehabilitation.

The understanding that recovery of brain function after stroke is imperfect has prompted decades of effort to achieve faster and better recovery through environmental manipulation using robotic devices [21]. In the search for an optimal method of training, the results presented here may encourage the use of robotic therapies for restoring motor function. Several strategies have been proposed, including assistive techniques, challenge-based methods, haptic simulation, and coaching. There is a need for head-to-head comparisons of control algorithms in randomized, controlled clinical trials, and for improved models of human motor recovery to provide a more rational framework for designing robotic therapy control strategies [22]. Recently, a linear dynamics model was developed to describe the trial-by-trial evolution of motor performance in chronic stroke survivors who underwent a rehabilitation protocol based on a robot-assisted arm extension task [23]. In future studies, we will combine the motor performance model with stroke rehabilitation models to develop an optimal robotic therapy approach.

Acknowledgement. This work was supported by JSPS KAKENHI Grant Numbers 25880031 and 26702023.

References

1. Feigin, V.L., Forouzanfar, M.H., Krishnamurthi, R., Mensah, G.A., Connor, M., Bennett, D.A., Moran, A.E., Sacco, R.L., Anderson, L., Truelsen, T.: Global and regional burden of stroke during 1990-2010: findings from the Global Burden of Disease Study 2010. The Lancet 383, 245–255 (2014)
2. Langhorne, P., Coupar, F., Pollock, A.: Motor recovery after stroke: a systematic review. The Lancet Neurology 8, 741–754 (2009)
3. Li, C.-S.R., Padoa-Schioppa, C., Bizzi, E.: Neuronal correlates of motor performance and motor learning in the primary motor cortex of monkeys adapting to an external force field. Neuron 30, 593–607 (2001)
4. Padoa-Schioppa, C., Li, C.-S.R., Bizzi, E.: Neuronal activity in the supplementary motor area of monkeys adapting to a new dynamic environment. J. Neurophysiol. 91, 449–473 (2004)
5. Molina-Luna, K., Hertler, B., Buitrago, M.M., Luft, A.R.: Motor learning transiently changes cortical somatotopy. Neuroimage 40, 1748–1754 (2008)
6. Nudo, R.J., Wise, B.M., SiFuentes, F., Milliken, G.W.: Neural substrates for the effects of rehabilitative training on motor recovery after ischemic infarct. Science 272, 1791–1794 (1996)
7. Han, C.E., Arbib, M.A., Schweighofer, N.: Stroke rehabilitation reaches a threshold. PLoS Comput. Biol. 4, e1000133 (2008)
8. Takiyama, K., Okada, M.: Recovery in stroke rehabilitation through the rotation of preferred directions induced by bimanual movements: a computational study. PLoS One 7, e37594 (2012)
9. Georgopoulos, A.P., Schwartz, A.B., Kettner, R.E.: Neuronal population coding of movement direction. Science 233, 1416–1419 (1986)
10. Reinkensmeyer, D.J., Iobbi, M.G., Kahn, L.E., Kamper, D.G., Takahashi, C.D.: Modeling reaching impairment after stroke using a population vector model of movement control that incorporates neural firing-rate variability. Neural Computation 15, 2619–2642 (2003)
11. Georgopoulos, A.P., Kalaska, J.F., Caminiti, R., Massey, J.T.: On the relations between the direction of two-dimensional arm movements and cell discharge in primate motor cortex. J. Neuroscience 2, 1527–1537 (1982)

12. Kalaska, J.F., Cohen, D., Hyde, M.L., Prud'Homme, M.: A comparison of movement direction-related versus load direction-related activity in primate motor cortex, using a two-dimensional reaching task. J. Neuroscience 9, 2080–2102 (1989)
13. Todorov, E.: Cosine tuning minimizes motor errors. Neural Computation 14, 1233–1260 (2002)
14. Matthews, P.: Relationship of firing intervals of human motor units to the trajectory of post-spike after-hyperpolarization and synaptic noise. J. Physiol-London 492, 597–628 (1996)
15. Harris, C.M., Wolpert, D.M.: Signal-dependent noise determines motor planning. Nature 394, 780–784 (1998)
16. Izawa, J., Shadmehr, R.: Learning from Sensory and Reward Prediction Errors during Motor Adaptation. PLoS Comput. Biol. 7, e1002012 (2011)
17. Hogan, N., Krebs, H.I., Rohrer, B., Palazzolo, J.J., Dipietro, L., Fasoli, S.E., Stein, J., Hughes, R., Frontera, W.R., Lynch, D.: Motions or muscles? some behavioral factors underlying robotic assistance of motor recovery. Journal of Rehabilitation Research & Development 43, 605–618 (2006)
18. Schultz, W., Dayan, P., Montague, P.R.: A neural substrate of prediction and reward. Science 275, 1593–1599 (1997)
19. Casadio, M., Morasso, P., Sanguineti, V., Giannoni, P.: Minimally assistive robot training for proprioception enhancement. Exp. Brain Res. 194, 219–231 (2009)
20. Emken, J.L., Benitez, R., Sideris, A., Bobrow, J.E., Reinkensmeyer, D.J.: Motor adaptation as a greedy optimization of error and effort. J. Neurophysiol. 97, 3997–4006 (2007)
21. Volpe, B.T., Huerta, P.T., Zipse, J.L., Rykman, A., Edwards, D., Dipietro, L., Hogan, N., Krebs, H.I.: Robotic devices as therapeutic and diagnostic tools for stroke recovery. Arch. Neurol. 66, 1086 (2009)
22. Marchal-Crespo, L., Reinkensmeyer, D.J.: Review of control strategies for robotic movement training after neurologic injury. Journal of Neuroengineering and Rehabilitation 6, 20 (2009)
23. Casadio, M., Sanguineti, V.: Learning, Retention, and Slacking: A Model of the Dynamics of Recovery in Robot Therapy. IEEE Transactions on Neural Systems and Rehabilitation Engineering 20, 286–296 (2012)

Real Time SVM for Health Monitoring System

Fahmi Ben Rejab, Kaouther Nouira, and Abdelwahed Trabelsi

BESTMOD, Institut Supérieur de Gestion de Tunis
Université de Tunis
41 Avenue de la Liberté, 2000 Le Bardo, Tunisie
{fahmi.benrejab,abdel.trabelsi}@gmail.com, kaouther.nouira@planet.tn

Abstract. In this paper, we propose a new health monitoring system (HMS) based on a new classification method consisting of the real time support vector machines (RTSVM). The new HMS denoted by RTSVM-MS deals with problems of monitoring systems in intensive care unit (ICU). The main aim of this new system is to considerably reduce the rate of false alarms and keep a high and stable level of sensitivity. Besides, it overcomes the main issue of the existing HMS by proposing a classification model that considers the variation of the patient states over time. In addition, the thresholds set has to be modified when patients are getting better. However, thresholds are stable and do not translate the states of patients over time since, all existing systems in ICU do not take into account of the patients' states evolution. Our proposal has the ability to generate an initial model that classifies states of patients to normal and abnormal (critical) using the LASVM. Then, it updates its model by considering the evolution in the states of patients using RTSVM. As a result, the new system gives what the medical staff wants as information and alarms relative to monitored patient.

Keywords: Health monitoring system, Real Time SVM, Intensive care unit.

1 Introduction

Intensive care unit (ICU) is a special department in hospital devoted to patients whose conditions are life threating. It provides intensive care to patients and try to control critical states. Unfortunately, the experience and clinical skills of the medical staff and care-givers are not always enough to give the best treatment or action to patients. To this end, ICU is equipped by sophisticated monitoring devices such as health monitoring system (HMS). The principal aim of HMS is to measure and alert medical staff when patient has a critical state. The current HMS function is based on threshold set by care-givers. An alarm is trigged when its limits are violated. Current monitoring systems are developed to especially provide a high sensitivity and do not miss true alarms.

In many research studies [9],[21] authors prove that there were an excessive number of alarms trigged by the HMS. This can affect the working conditions and make the patient state worst. The most trigged alarms are considered as

D. Ślęzak et al. (Eds.): BIH 2014, LNAI 8609, pp. 301–312, 2014.
© Springer International Publishing Switzerland 2014

false alarms. Studies have demonstrated that the presence of false or clinically insignificant alarms ranges from 80% to 99% [19]. The myriad of the alarm number creates a bad environment in ICU and reduces trust of care-givers to this system. Besides, it causes a continuous stress to both medical staff and patients. To avoid the noise of false alarms, the medical staff may silence, disable or even ignore the alarms [1]. By this behavior, true alarms are missed and patient will be in real danger. Furthermore, in [13] authors have reported that in Massachusetts General Hospital in 2010 the result of turning off alarms have caused the death of a patient.

Improving the HMS in ICU, reducing the number of false alarms, and increasing the positive ones have attracted the intention of many researchers over the past ten years. Several researchers have focused on this problem in ICU. We can mention the use of the digital signal processing in [7] where there is also a clinical validation study for two recently developed on-line signal filters, the use of trend extraction methodology based on the time evolution of signals in [11], and the use of the intelligent monitoring [18] detailed through the time series technology and multi-agent sub-systems. Moreover, there were several other studies [3], [20] that have reported and detailed this issue and how to overcome it.

To this end, we propose in this paper a new HMS based on a new machine learning technique which is the real time support vector machines (RTSVM). The RTSVM is a modified version of the standard SVM which can improve the model of classification in the test phase. Our proposal reduces the number of ignored or ineffective alarms, conserves the important sensitivity and simulates the expert reasoning. Besides, it takes into account of the evolution of the patient states over time.

The rest of the paper is structured as follows: Section 2 describes the health monitoring system in ICU. Section 3 provides an overview of the support vector machines and the LASVM. Section 4 illustrates our proposal which is the monitoring system based on RTSVM. Section 5 presents and analyzes the experimental results. Section 6 concludes the paper.

2   Health Monitoring System in ICU

Monitoring patient in critical care environments such as intensive care units (ICUs) and operating rooms involves estimating the status of the patient, reacting to events that may be life-threatening, and taking actions to bring the patient to a desired state. There is the use of medical devices when monitoring patients. Besides, the current HMS generates important data and information relative to the monitored patient. Physiological variables such as heart rate, blood pressure, temperature, ventilation, and brain activity are measured and constantly monitored on-line. Each variable has a practical limits or threshold, when a parameter exceeds its limits an alarm is trigged.

Table 1 shows an example of some measured parameters with their thresholds.

Alarms are generated by crossing a given limit. Unfortunately, it is not the best method to indicate the patient states. There is not a consideration of the

Table 1. Some measured parameters

Medical parameters	Min. value	Max. value
Heart Rate	50	120
Respiratory rate	5	25
Pulse rate	65	115
Saturated percentage of Oxygen in the blood	90	130

simultaneous evolution of different parameters. The information that the medical staff generally wants is the detection of critical changes in a patient conditions.

To guarantee patient safety, a high sensitivity in detecting clinically relevant situations is desired. However, this requirement causes the high number of alarms generated by the HMS. Studies have demonstrated that the majority of alarms created by patient monitoring systems have no clinical relevance. Borowski et al. [7] recorded monitoring data of 68 patients in a medical ICU. As a result, only 15 % of all alarms were clinically relevant. Furthermore, there were two other studies that have illustrated this problem. The first one is the survey of German ICUs detailed in [1] where authors conclude that more than 50 % of all alarms were irrelevant. The second one, is the national on-line survey on the effectiveness of clinical alarms which have reported the same results in [17]. Moreover, in [13], only 10 % of all alarms were taken into account by care-givers and 50% of all relevant alarms were not correctly identified.

With the large number of false alarms, care-givers do not trust the used monitoring system anymore and are becoming desensitized. As a results, care-givers ignore the majority of alarms and consider this system as a measurement tool not as a monitoring one. Due to the high rate of false alarms, the sensitivity of the current HMS is not close to 100%. There were 75 life-threating situations, where no alarm occurred, reported in the Federal Institute for Drugs and Medical Devices (BfArM) in Germany. Besides, missing true alarms caused, between 2002 and 2004, 237 deaths related to device alarms [14]. New solutions are needed to manage and process the continuous flow of information and to provide efficient and reliable decision support tools. The reduction of false alarms and keeping a high rate of sensitivity are the main purpose of many researches. We can mention the monitoring based on machine learning [4], [5].

As a result, the future patients monitoring system has to allow the medical staff to be more confident in the HMS. It has not to be a simple measurement tool but a monitoring one by providing important medical information. In order to avoid the issues indicated above, the monitoring system should be improved. To this end, we propose a new HMS based on real time support vector machines. This latter makes it possible to detect different patients' states as desired and needed by medical staff. The RTSVM is trained from expert decisions and can simulate the expert task for new observations.

3   Support Vector Machines and Its Incremental Version

3.1   The Standard SVM

Support vector machines (SVM) is a very popular method for binary classification data. It has been introduced by Vapnik in 1995 [12]. The basic idea was to find an hyperplane which separates data into its two classes with a maximization of the margin.

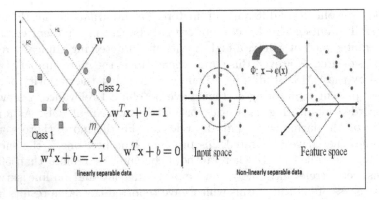

Fig. 1. The optimal hyperplane

1. **Case of linearly separable data:** Given a training set of observations $(x_i, y_i), i = \{1....m\}$ where $x_i \in R^n$ and $y \in \{1, -1\}$ (as illustrated in Figure 1, left). Training SVM means solving the following optimization problem.

$$\begin{cases} \min \frac{1}{2}||w||^2 + C, w \in R^d, b \in R, \\ subject\ to \\ y_i(x_i w + b) \geq 1 for\ i = 1, ..., m. \end{cases} \tag{1}$$

After finding the w and b, we use the decision rule to classify the new observations:

$$f_{w,b}(x) = sign(w^T x_i + b). \tag{2}$$

2. **Case of non-linearly separable data:** SVM can also be used to separate classes that cannot be separated with a linear classifier (as shown in Figure 1, right). In this case, the original observations are mapped into a feature space (high dimensional may be infinite) using non-linear functions called feature functions ϕ. In the new space, the two classes can be separated with a linear classifier.

The data mapping is defined through the function Φ. This latter is presented by $R^d \rightarrow R^D(D \succ\succ d)$, with R^D is HILBERT space.

To detect the hyperplane, we have to solve the optimization problem defined as follows using the slack variable ξ_i:

$$\min \frac{1}{2}||w||^2 + C \sum_{i=1}^{m} \xi_i, w \in R^d, b \in R, \tag{3}$$

subject to

$$y_i(x_i w + b) \geq 1 - \xi_i, \xi_i \geq 1 \, for \, i = \{1, ..., m\}. \tag{4}$$

In a previous work, we have proposed a monitoring system based on the SVM [2] and interesting results have been obtained. However, the system was tested in batch mode and it needs a high execution time to be trained with a large dataset. To overcome the SVM limitations, we have improved the proposed HMS based on a new incremental and on-line versions of SVM which is the LASVM [6]. The following subsection describes the LASVM technique used in our proposal.

3.2   The Improved Version of SVM: The LASVM

The LASVM proposed in [6] presents a well-known incremental algorithm. It is a modified and improved version of the SVM. It solves the problem of large data in the training phase that are added over time.

Besides, the LASVM is considered as an efficient incremental method successfully applied in several works such as in [15], [22].

The LASVM algorithm is based on the sequential minimal optimization (SMO) implemented by the libsvm tool [10]. Actually, the LASVM algorithm contains two main procedures mainly the process and reprocess procedures. The main advantages that the LASVM offers is being faster and using less memory than the SVM. The monitoring system based on the LASVM (LASVM-MS) [5] has shown efficient results by decreasing the number of false alarms and keeping a high level of sensitivity. In addition, it uses the same model for all new observations. However, patient's states change over time and medical staff needs a model that takes into account of this change. To this end, we propose a new technique consisting of the RTSVM.

4   Monitoring System Based on Real Time SVM

This section presents our proposal consisting of the monitoring system using real time SVM (RTSVM-MS). We explain the RTSVM algorithm then, we move to presenting our new system.

4.1   RTSVM Algorithm

The real time SVM (RTSVM) algorithm is presented as follows.

```
Begin

for each new observation X_i do
    Y_i ← LASVM(X_i)
    if X_i is not a candidate then
        AddErrorSet(X_i)
    else
        AddCandidate (X_i, Y_i) at the CandidateSet.
    end if
    for each time interval do
        Print CandidateSet
        Update CandidateSet from Expert Decision
        LASVM ← Update(LASVM, parameters)
    end for
end for
End
```

Based on the pseudo code of RTSVM algorithm, we notice that the RTSVM takes as input the original model of classification obtained in training phase using LASVM. When we have a new vector (set of measured variables), RTSVM assigns to this vector a label equal to -1 if this vector represents an alarm or $+1$ otherwise. In back office, RTSVM checks the nature of the new vector, if it is a candidate (may be a support vector), the RTSVM adds it to the CandiateSet. During the classification of new medical data, the expert should validate the CandidatesSet. The validation consists of proving or modifying the label assigned by the RTSVM.

After the validation of the CanditatesSet, we update the original model parameters. This step has many advantages mainly reducing the execution time of training by re-training the LASVM with only the CandidatesSet (and not using the whole dataset). In addition, it improves the original model over time to adapt it to the new patient states.

4.2   Description of the Proposed System

Actually, SVM classification and the majority of classification techniques, use the model built in the training phase to classify all new observations in test phase. However, there are always an evolution and change of data over time. In real-world situations, data dynamically change and the class of their labels could change from one class to another over time. Data are often continuously collected in time and, more importantly, the concepts to be learned may also evolve in time. It is necessarily to take into account of the evolution of data in both training and test phases. As a result, real-time systems are needed to better analyze data over time. In [23], authors have recently proposed a real time system applied in medical field for integrating simultaneous rtfMRI and EEG data streams. In our case, we focus on the improvement of the ICU by proposing a new real time monitoring system. The RTSVM-MS uses as input the model produced by the

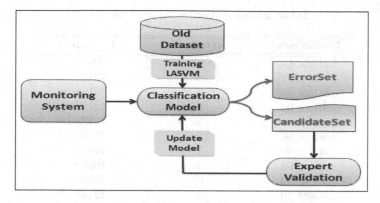

Fig. 2. The architecture of the RTSVM-MS

LASVM technique in the training phase. Then, it starts classification of new observations arriving from the monitoring system device. Finally, it improves the current model through the validation of the expert. Figure 2 reports the structure of our proposed system as described in the RTSVM algorithm.

In our case, data describe the measured medical parameters of patients that dynamically change and their states could be more or less critical over time. It is necessarily to take into account of the evolution of data in both training and test phases. Our new monitoring system RTSVM-MS is characterized by taking into account of all new states of patients over time. It also updates the model built by the LASVM each time interval. These updates avoid the missing of important information and guarantee an easier and more effective monitoring.

5   Experiments

5.1   The Framework

For the evaluation of our proposal (RTSVM-MS), we test it using real datasets from MIMICII database taken from Physiobank [16]. This database includes data from hemo-dynamically unstable patients hospitalized in 1996 in ICU of the cardiology division in the Teaching Hospital of Harvard Medical School.

We used 14 databases relative to several patients containing different physiological parameters. From these parameters, we can mention the Heart Rate (HR), Oxygen Saturation (SpO_2), Non-Invasive Blood Pressure (NBP), Respiratory rate (Resp), and Artery Blood Pressure (ABP). Table 2 details real-world databases taken from MIMICII where #Attributes and #Instances denote respectively the total number of measured parameters and the total number of instances for a specific database.

Table 2. Description of the used datasets

Databases	#Attributes	#Instances
Patient 01	6	4101
patient 02	8	42188
patient 03	8	42188
patient 04	7	42188
patient 05	9	42188
patient 06	9	5350
patient 07	7	11300
patient 08	7	10600
patient 09	12	5700
patient 10	5	42188
patient 11	7	42188
patient 12	7	42188
patient 13	9	42188
patient 14	7	42188

5.2   Evaluation Criteria

To test our new monitoring system i.e. RTSVM-MS, we essentially use three evaluation criteria described as follows.

1. The false alarm reduction rate (FARR) [7] defined by:

$$FARR = \frac{Suppressed \ false \ alarms}{Total \ number \ of \ false \ alarms}. \tag{5}$$

2. The sensitivity (S) that represents the ability of the system to detect positive results. It is defined by:

$$S = \frac{TP}{TP + FN}. \tag{6}$$

3. True positive (TP) defined as critical states that people correctly diagnosed it as critical.

5.3   Results and Discussion

In this section, we report the results of our proposal using the evaluation criteria and then, we detail all obtained results. As follows, the main steps followed to get the final results are illustrated.

1. We divide the patient dataset into two sets: training set and test set.
2. We build the initial model through the LASVM by using the training set.
3. In test phase, we start classifying the observations using the model obtained in training phase to alert medical staff when a patient has a critical state.

4. For each interval time fixed a priori by care-givers, the expert validates the candidate set (probably a support vector).
5. Based on the candidate set, RTSVM generates the new model.
6. We continue the classification of the remaining observations in the test phase.

The main problem of the current monitoring system is the high number of false alarms. The results obtained in Table 3 shows the rate of suppressed alarms by the different proposed systems.

Table 3. Suppressed false alarms for different patients' datasets

Databases	FARR SVM-MS	FARR LASVM-MS	FARR RTSVM-MS
patient 01	95,14	96,59	98,84
patient 02	98,89	99,42	99,75
patient 03	99,3	99,42	99,95
patient 04	96,46	98,34	98,96
patient 05	96,84	97,83	99,55
patient 06	95,68	97,64	98,83
patient 07	99,05	99,36	99,64
patient 08	96,15	97,68	98,68
patient 09	96,89	97,99	99,59
patient 10	80,23	87,2	95,35
patient 11	97,96	99,02	99,31
patient 12	96,87	98,83	99
patient 13	95,6	97,22	99,6
patient 14	98,41	98,84	99,89

Based on the first criterion, we remark that the new system RTSVM-MS has the highest rate of suppressed false alarms for all datasets. The improvement in the results is due to taking into account of the evolution of patient states over time. In fact, reducing false alarms is very important however, keeping a high level of sensitivity is needed. Lives of patients depend on trigged alarms and missing a true alarm can present a real threat for their lives.

Table 4 illustrates the sensitivity of the RTSVM-MS compared to the other monitoring systems that used LASVM, SVM, and the current system (CS). We can notice from Table 4 that the RTSVM-MS has a stable and high sensitivity compared to the other systems. Despite the high number of trigged alarms, the current system looses its sensitivity especially for patients 08 (23.3%) and 09 (4.6%) due to the bad setting of thresholds.

To proves the performance of the new system, true positive alarms are compared to the expert opinions. Note that true alarms consist of alarms generated by the monitoring system and indicating a real critical state of the patient. Table 5 shows the results.

From table 5, we can remark that the RTSVM-MS gives very similar results to the expert who indicates the critical cases where alarms should be generated.

Table 4. Sensitivity of the RTSVM-MS, LASVM-MS, SVM-MS, and the current system

Databases	CS	SVM-MS	LASVM-MS	RTSVM-MS
patient 01	100	86,41	94,17	99,68
patient 02	100	80,76	87,08	98,14
patient 03	100	68,24	79,05	97,7
patient 04	97,78	88,63	97,33	99,2
patient 05	97,34	66,32	79,4	98,1
patient 06	48,36	85,87	87,68	95,56
patient 07	100	94,44	94,44	94,44
patient 08	23,3	81,55	89,32	94,17
patient 09	4,6	67,97	71,21	96,25
patient 10	87,01	87,96	92,7	99,78
patient 11	36,28	85,8	94,43	89,54
patient 12	95,5	77,6	88,45	90,23
patient 13	100	88,12	90,17	99,51
patient 14	100	63,41	70,59	98,42

Table 5. Number of true positive alarms of the monitoring systems vs. the expert

Databases	TA-CS	TA-SVM-MS	TA-LASVM-MS	TA-RTSVM-MS	Expert
patient 01	309	267	291	308	309
patient 02	1076	869	937	1056	1076
patient 03	740	505	585	723	740
patient 04	4533	4109	4512	4599	4636
patient 05	1942	1323	1584	1957	1995
patient 06	883	1568	1601	1745	1826
patient 07	54	51	51	51	54
patient 08	24	84	92	97	103
patient 09	27	399	418	565	587
patient 10	2002	2024	2133	2296	2301
patient 11	378	894	984	933	1042
patient 12	1232	1001	1141	1164	1290
patient 13	6909	6088	6230	6875	6909
patient 14	697	442	492	686	697

In addition, we remark that in contrast to the new monitoring system, the current system has a trouble to detect true positive alarms. This is obvious especially for patients 06, 08, and 09.

6   Conclusion

In this paper, we have avoided the main problems of monitoring system in intensive care unit (ICU). We have presented a new technique based on the SVM consisting of real time SVM (RTSVM). This new technique is used to propose a new monitoring system more efficient than the current one. The new system significantly improves the working conditions in ICU by detecting true positive alarms and reducing the frequency of false alarms. In addition, our proposal has the capacity to identify patients' critical states over time. It updates the initial classification model through new observations in order to follow patient states evolution. As a result, the new system based on the RTSVM offers to the medical staff better working conditions and makes trigged alarms more significant. Furthermore, it helps care-givers to take the best decisions.

References

1. Adamski, P.: About the Healthcare Technology Safety Institute. HTSI Webinar Series on Alarm Systems Management,
   https://www.aami.org/meetings/webinars/2013/092513_HTSI_TJC_NPSG.html
   (accessed Januray 11, 2014)
2. Ben Rejab, F., Nouira, K., Trabelsi, A.: Support Vector Machines versus Multilayer Perceptrons for Reducing False Alarms in Intensive Care Units. International Journal of Computer Applications, Foundation of Computer Science 49, 41–47 (2012)
3. Ben Rejab, F., Nouira, K., Trabelsi, A.: Incremental Support Vector Machines for Monitoring Systems in Intensive Care Unit. In: SAI 2013, pp. 496–501 (2013)
4. Ben Rejab, F., Nouira, K., Trabelsi, A.: On the use of the incremental support vector machines for monitoring systems in intensive care unit. In: TAEECE 2013, pp. 266–270 (2013)
5. Ben Rejab, F., Nouira, K., Trabelsi, A.: Health Monitoring Systems Using Machine Learning Techniques. Intelligent Systems for Science and Information, 423–440 (2014)
6. Bordes, A., Ertekin, S., Weston, J., Bottou, J.: Fast Kernel Classifiers With Online And Active Learning. Journal of Machine Learning Research 6, 1579–1619 (2005)
7. Borowski, M., Siebig, S., Wrede, C., Imhoff, M.: Reducing false alarms of intensive care online monitoring systems: An evaluation of two signal extraction algorithms. Computational and Mathematical Methods in Medicine, vol. 2011 (2011)
8. Cauwenberghs, G., Poggio, T.: Incremental and decremental support vector machine learning. In: Adv. Neural Information Processing Systems (NIPS 2000), vol. 13, pp. 409–415 (2000)
9. Chambrin, M., Ravaux, P., Calvelo-Aros, D., Jaborska, A., Chopin, C., Boniface, B.: Multicentric study of monitoring alarms in the adult intensive care unit (ICU): a descriptive analysis. Intensive Care Med., 1360–1366 (1999)
10. Chang, C., Lin, C.: LIBSVM: A library for support vector machines. Transactions on Intelligent Systems and Technology 2, 1–27 (2011)
11. Charbonnie, S., Gentil, S.: A trend-based alarm system to improve patient monitoring in intensive care units. Control Engineering Practice 15, 1039–1050 (2007)
12. Cortes, C., Vapnik, V.: Support vector networks. Machine Learning 20, 273–297 (1995)
13. Cvach, M.: Monitor alarm fatigue: an integrative review. Biomed. Instrum. Technol. 46, 268–277 (2012)
14. Food and Drug Administration: Alarming Monitor Problems: Preventing Medical Errors. FDA Patient Safety News (January 2011),
    www.accessdata.fda.gov/scripts/cdrh/cfdocs/psn/
    transcript.cfm?show=106#7 (accessed July 27, 2011)

15. Frasconi, P., Passerini, A.: Predicting the geometry of metal binding sites from protein sequence. IEEE/ACM Transactions on Computational Biology and Bioinformatics 9, 203–213 (2012)

16. Goldberger, A., Amaral, L., Glass, L., Hausdorff, J., Ivanov, P., Mark, R., Mietus, J., Moody, G., Peng, C., Stanley, H.: PhysioBank, PhysioToolkit, and PhysioNet: Components of a New Research Resource for Complex Physiologic Signals 101, e215–e220 (2000)

17. Korniewicz, D., Clark, T., David, Y.: A national online survey on the effectiveness of clinical alarms. American Journal of Critical Care, 36–41 (2008)

18. Nouira, K., Trabelsi, A.: Intelligent monitoring system for intensive care units. Journal of Medical Systems 36, 2309–2318 (2011)

19. Schmid, F., Goepfert, M.S., Kuhnt, D., Eichhorn, V., Diedrichs, S., Reichenspurner, H., Goetz, A.E., Reuter, D.A.: The wolf is crying in the operating room: patient monitor and anesthesia workstation alarming patterns during cardiac surgery. Anesth Analgesia, 78–83 (2011)

20. Siebig, S., Kuhls, S., Imhoff, M., Langgartner, J., Reng, M., Scholmerich, J., Gather, U., Wrede, C.E.: Collection of annotated data in a clinical validation study for alarm algorithms in intensive care-a methodologic framework. Journal of Critical Care 25, 128–135 (2010)

21. Tsien, C.: Reducing False Alarms in the Intensive Care Unit: A Systematic Comparison of Four Algorithms. In: Proceedings of the AMIA Annual Fall Symposium. American Medical Informatics Association (1997)

22. Wang, Z., Vucetic, S.: Online training on a budget of support vector machines using twin prototypes. Statistical Analysis and Data Mining 3, 149–169 (2010)

23. Zotev, V., Phillips, R., Yuan, H., Misaki, M., Bodurka, J.: Self-regulation of human brain activity using simultaneous real-time fMRI and EEG neurofeedback. NeuroImage 85, 985–995 (2014)

Augmenting Cognitive Reserve of Dementia Patients with Brain Aerobics

Ahmad Zmily[1] and Ehab Mashal[2]

[1] School of Information Technology and Engineering
German Jordanian University, Amman, Jordan
ahmad.zmily@gju.edu.jo
[2] Darat Samir Shamma
Shafa Badran, Amman, Jordan
info@daratsamirshamma.com

Abstract. Dementia is the loss of cognitive brain functioning including thinking, remembering, and reasoning to such an extent that it interferes with a person's daily life and activities. Individuals with high levels of intelligence, educational, and occupational attainment may sustain greater brain damage before demonstrating functional deficit. This is mainly contributed to their cognitive reserve, the mind's resistance to damage of the brain. This paper proposes brain aerobics, a set of stimulating mental exercises that aims at building the cognitive reserve to protect elderly people from developing dementia's symptoms. Brain aerobics exercises are developed for mobile devices for ease of use. Experimental results demonstrate the benefits of the proposed brain aerobics in increasing IQ levels by 7.2% for elderly people who have dementia high risk factors.

Keywords: Dementia, Brain Aerobics, Mental Exercises, Alzheimer's Disease.

1 Introduction

Dementia is a degenerative condition that affects brain functions and mental ability severely enough to interfere with a person's daily activities. Dementia is normally associated with memory loss, cognitive dysfunction, and difficulty of thinking and communication. According to World's Alzheimer's 2013 Report, there are more than 35 million people worldwide living with Alzheimer condition, and the number is expected to double by 2030 [1]. In its 2012 report, World Health Organization (WHO) has called upon governments and policy makers to give dementia a global public health priority, calling on countries to develop health care systems to look after people living with dementia conditions [15].

Dementia is mainly attributed to brain cells damage that impedes the communication between these cells, causing brain not to carry out its functions normally. Damage of brain cells is mainly associated with normal aging, however, that doesn't mean that everyone develops dementia with aging. Despite the fact that aging is a significant risk factor for dementia and Alzheimer's disease,

D. Ślęzak et al. (Eds.): BIH 2014, LNAI 8609, pp. 313–322, 2014.

yet many seem to keep excellent memories and perform challenging mental tasks while in their 80s age and beyond.

Interestingly, autopsy studies have found that sizable number of cognitively normal old people have shown brain abnormalities similar to those of Alzheimer's decease patients [7, 5]. This was mainly explained by the concept of Cognitive Reserve which has been defined as the ability of an individual to tolerate progressive brain pathology without demonstrating clinical cognitive symptoms. Studies have suggested that susceptibility to age-related memory changes and dementia are related to many variables such as education, literacy, IQ and engagement in leisure activities [13, 9]. Later studies [12] theorize that brain may have the ability to develop connections that maintain extra neurons and connections to compensate for the rise in dementia.

In this paper, we propose brain aerobics, a set of stimulating brain exercises and activities to help in building a Cognitive Reserve to protect from developing Alzheimer's symptoms. We have developed a mobile device application for the brain aerobics exercise. Users can exercise using the application any time they like. We have evaluated our proposed brain aerobics on thirty different individuals, ten of them are with high AD risk factors. We have measured the participants' IQ before and after using the brain aerobics exercises. Results showed a 16.1% average improvement of IQ test results for all the participants and a 7.2% average improvement for the ten participants who have AD high risk factors.

The remainder of this paper is organized as follows: Section 2 describes the brain aerobics exercises. Section 3 presents the experimental setup and results. In Section 4, we discuss the related research that this work is based on. We conclude with final comments in Section 5.

2   Exercises

Our approach focuses on building the cognitive reserve for people with high AD risk factors. An application, named brain aerobics, with several exercises is developed for handheld mobile devices to support this approach. The application is designed to help the users exercising their brains and building their cognitive reserve on daily bases. The application provides an option that allows the user to specify the times he/she likes to exercise and to remind him/her with an alarm at the specified times.

2.1   Cubes Exercise

In this exercise, the tablet's screen is divided into 16 cubicles organized in four rows by four columns. Randomly, some of the 16 cubicles are selected and a single small red cube is inserted in each of them. Figure 1 shows a sample screenshot. The screen is displayed for thirty seconds where the user is required to memorize the exact locations of all the red cubes. The application then displays on the screen the same 16 cubicles but without the red cubes as shown in Figure 2. The user is required to tap on the cubicles that had the red cubes. Once the user is done, he/she can tap on the submit button. If the user managed to successfully remember the locations of all the red cubes, the exercise is repeated but with the red cubes randomly placed on different locations. In case the user failed to tap on the correct cubicles, the exercise with the same layout is repeated again. The total number of red cubes varies from 1 to 15 and adjusted so the complexity of the layout increases after each successful try. The application keeps track of the total score giving one point for each successful try. The user can pause and continue the exercise at any time.

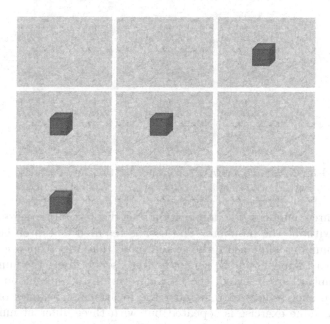

Fig. 1. Sample screenshot for the Cubes exercise

The cubes exercise comes in three levels. The number of small red cubes that may be inserted in a cubical is increased with each level. In level-2, one or two small red cubes can be inserted in a cubical. Figure 3a is a sample screenshot of cubes exercise level-2. In level-3, up to four small red cubes can be inserted in a cubical. Figure 3b shows a sample screenshot of the level-3 cubes exercise. The user advances to a higher level after managing to get a score of 30 in the previous level.

2.2   Numbers Exercise

In this exercise, the tablet's screen is divided into 16 cubicles. Three two digit numbers are randomly generated. Each number is placed randomly on a cubical. Figure 4 shows a sample screenshot. The screen is displayed for thirty seconds where the user is required to memorize the exact location and the exact value of

Fig. 2. Sample answers screenshot for the Cubes exercise

each of the three numbers. The application then displays on the screen the same 16 cubicles without the numbers. The user is required to tap on each cubical that had a number and insert the exact value that was displayed before. A popup keyboard appears on the screen for the user to insert the number. Once the three numbers are inserted, the user can tap on the submit button. If the user managed successfully to remember the locations and values of the three numbers, the same exercise is repeated but with three different numbers that are randomly placed on different locations. In case the user failed to tap on the correct cubicles and insert the correct values, the same exercise with the same numbers is repeated again. The application keeps track of the score giving one point for each successful recall. The number exercise comes in three levels. Three digit numbers can be inserted in a cubical for Level-2 and four digit numbers can be inserted in a cubical for level 3. The user moves to the next level after managing to get a score of 30 in the previous level.

2.3   Shapes Exercise

In this exercise, the tablet's screen is divided into 12 cubicles. Three shapes from a large group of shapes are randomly selected. In each of the 12 cubicles, one of the three shapes is displayed. Figure 5 shows a sample screenshot. The screen is displayed for thirty seconds where the user is required to memorize the exact locations and shapes. The application then displays on the screen the same 12 cubicles without shapes in them. The application also displays the three shapes where the user is required to drag one of them and place it in a cubical that

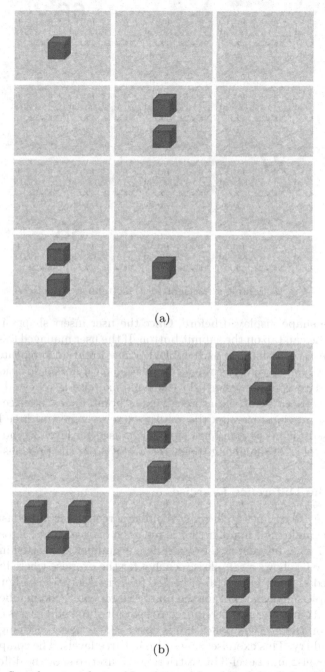

(a)

(b)

Fig. 3. Sample screenshots of Level-2 and Level-3 of the Cubes Exercise

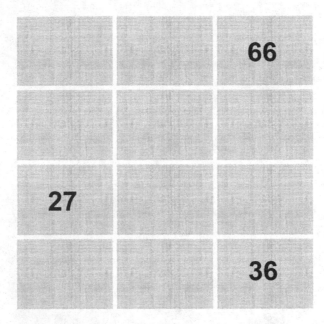

Fig. 4. Sample screenshot for the Numbers exercise

had the same shape displayed before. Once the user insert shapes in all of the cubicles, he/she can tap on the submit button. If the user managed to successfully remember the correct shape in each cubical, a new iteration is repeated but with three different shapes that are randomly placed on different locations. In case the user failed to complete the task, the same exercise is repeated again. The application keeps track of the score giving 1 point for each successful recall. Similar to the previous exercise, the shapes exercise comes in three levels. Four shapes are used for Level-2 and five shapes are used for level 3. The user moves to the next level after managing to get a score of 30 in the previous level.

2.4   Spot the Difference Exercise

In this exercise, 6 text lines are displayed on the screen. Each line consists of a single letter or a single digit number that is repeated over and over across the whole line. In each line, a different letter or a different number is inserted in various locations. Figure 6a shows a sample screenshot for the exercise where lines of letter **o** are displayed and few letter **c** are injected in various locations. Figure 6b shows a similar sample screenshot but for the number 5 repeated and number 2 injected in various locations. The user is required to spot all of the odd letters or odd numbers and tap on them. The application keeps track of the score giving 1 point for each successful try. This exercise comes also in three levels. The complexity is increased for Level-2 and Level-3 by restricting the user to spot the different letters or numbers in a specific time interval. Similar to the previous exercises, the user moves to higher levels after successfully getting 30 points.

Fig. 5. Sample screenshot for the Shapes Exercise

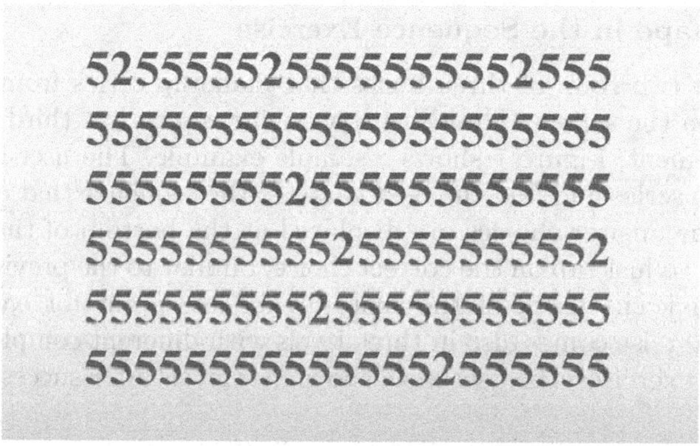

525555525555555552555
555555555555555555555
555555552555555555555
555555555525555555552
555555552555555555555
555555555555552555555

(a)

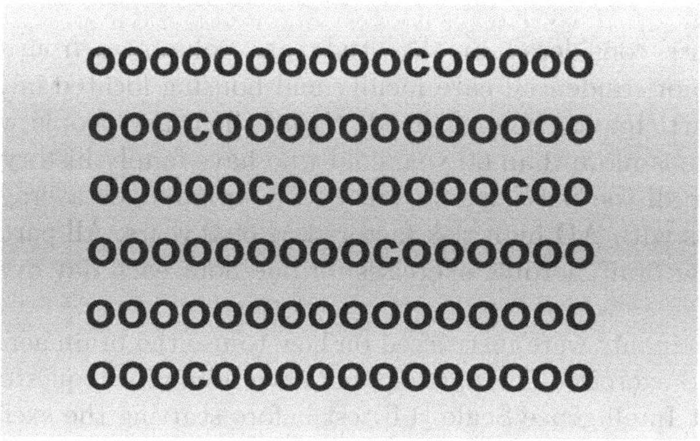

OOOOOOOOOOOCOOOOO
OOOCOOOOOOOOOOOOO
OOOOOCOOOOOOOOCOO
OOOOOOOOOCOOOOOOO
OOOOOOOOOOOOOOOOO
OOOCOOOOOOOOOOOOO

(b)

Fig. 6. Sample screenshots for Spot the Difference Exercise

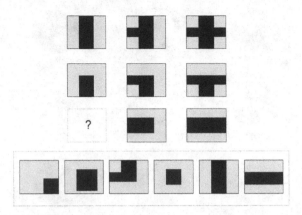

Fig. 7. Sample screenshot for the Next Shape in the Sequence Exercise

2.5 Next Shape in the Sequence Exercise

In this exercise two rows of three boxes that make up series from right to left are displayed on the screen. The third row on the screen is a third series that is missing one element. Figure 7 shows a sample example. The user is required to analyze the two series and find the next shape in the sequence that completes the third series. The answer choices are displayed at the bottom of the screen. The user is required to just tap on the correct choice. Similar to the previous exercises, the application keeps track of the score giving one point for each successful answer. This exercise comes also in three levels with different complexity. Similar to the previous exercises, the user moves to higher levels after successfully getting 30 points.

3 Results

The participants considered in the study are volunteers from Darat Samir Shamma, a senior residential care facility and housing located in Amman, Jordan. Thirty participants were selected, ten of them are people with AD high risk factors (age is more than 60 years old who have family history of AD). The average age for all the participants was 51.7 years and the average age for the ten participants with AD high risk factors was 69.3 years. All participants were asked to use the brain aerobic exercises for one hour each day over a period of two months.

All the participants were instructed on how to use the brain aerobics application and how to exercise. The participants have been also requested to take the Wechsler Adult Intelligence Scale [14] test before starting the exercises and the Raven's Matrices [11] test after the two months exercising period. On average, participants showed a 16.1% improvement of their IQ test results. The ten participants who have AD high risk factors showed a 7.2% average improvement of their IQ test results.

4 Related Work

Many researchers have focused on mental exercises for the care and prevention of dementia. Kawashima [8] proposed Learning Therapy based on using systematized problems in arithmetic and Japanese language as training tasks to improves the cognitive functions of dementia patients and healthy seniors. Breton et al. [4] proposed a computer-based tool for the elderly to improve their memory by performing mental activities and physical exercise at the same time using Kinect sensors. Guan-Feng et al. [6] proposed gesture recognition based on 3D serious games to prevent dementia by increasing brain usage and physical activities of users.

Other research focused on building cognitive reserve to delay the onset of the dementia symptoms. For example, Antoniou et al. [2] proposed using foreign language learning programs aimed at older populations for building cognitive reserve as language learning engages an extensive brain network that is known to overlap with the regions negatively affected by the aging process. Pike [10] suggested art therapy treatment to improve cognitive performance of elderly people.

Some research has also focused on using mobile devices for dementia patients. Coppola et al. [3] suggested utilizing tablets and iPads with dementia patients to portray favorite music and family photographs via apps developed in close partnership with geriatric facilities.

5 Conclusions

In this paper, we have presented brain aerobics, a mobile device application that can be used for mental exercising. Brain aerobics aims at building cognitive reserve for people who have dementia high risk factors to delay the manifest of the disease's symptoms. Evaluation results indicate that brain aerobics simplifies mental exercising and improves IQ levels of the participants. The simplicity of running brain aerobics would hopefully increase the adoption of mental exercising among elderly people.

Acknowledgements: The authors would like to thank Darat Samir Shamma's staff, especially Ms. Miaad Tarabsha, for their assistance and support.

References

[1] ADI. World alzheimer report. Journey of Caring, Alzheimer's Disease International (2013)

[2] Antoniou, M., Gunasekera, G.M., Wong, P.: Foreign language training as cognitive therapy for age-related cognitive decline: A hypothesis for future research. Neuroscience & Biobehavioral Reviews 37(10), 2689–2698 (2013)

[3] Coppola, J., Kowtko, M.A., Yamagata, C., Joyce, S.: Applying mobile application development to help dementia and alzheimer journal = Wilson Center for Social Entrepreneurship, number = 16, patients (2013)

[4] de Urturi Breton, Z.S., Zapirain, B.G., Zorrilla, A.M.: Kimentia: Kinect based tool to help cognitive stimulation for individuals with dementia. In: IEEE 14th International Conference one-Health Networking, Applications and Services, pp. 325–328. IEEE (2012)

[5] Reiman, E.M., Chen, K.: Fibrillar amyloid-beta burden in cognitively normal people at 3 levels of genetic risk for alzheimer's disease. Proc. Natl. Acad. Sci. U S A 106(16), 6820–6825 (2009)

[6] He, G.-F., Park, J.-W., Kang, S.-K., Jung, S.-T.: Development of gesture recognition-based serious games. In: 2012 IEEE-EMBS International Conference on Biomedical and Health Informatics (BHI), pp. 922–925. IEEE (2012)

[7] Aizenstein, H.J., Nebes, R.D.: Frequent amyloid deposition without significant cognitive impairment among the elderly. Arch. Neurol. 65(11), 1509–1517 (2008)

[8] Kawashima, R.: Mental exercises for cognitive function: clinical evidence. Journal of Preventive Medicine and Public Health 27(suppl. 1), S22–S27 (2013)

[9] Meng, X., D'Arcy, C.: Education and dementia in the context of the cognitive reserve hypothesis: A systematic review with meta-analyses and qualitative analyses. PLoS ONE 7(6) (2012)

[10] Pike, A.A.: The effect of art therapy on cognitive performance among ethnically diverse older adults. Art Therapy 30(4), 159–168 (2013)

[11] Raven, J.C.: Mental tests used in genetic studies: The performance of related individuals on tests mainly educative and mainly reproductive. MSc Thesis. PhD thesis (1936)

[12] Stern, Y.: What is cognitive reserve? theory and research application of the reserve concept. Journal of the International Neuropsychological Society 8, 448–460 (2002)

[13] Stern, Y., Zarahn, E.: A common neural network for cognitive reserve in verbal and object working memory in young but not old. Cereb. Cortex 18(4), 959–967 (2008)

[14] Wechsler, D.: Wechsler Adult Intelligence Scale. Pearson (2008)

[15] WHO. Dementia: a public health priority (2012)

Intraoperative Decision Making
with Rough Set Rules
for STN DBS in Parkinson Disease

Konrad Ciecierski[1], Zbigniew W. Raś[1,2], and Andrzej W. Przybyszewski[3,4]

[1] Warsaw Univ. of Technology, Institute of Comp. Science, 00-655 Warsaw, Poland
[2] Univ. of North Carolina, Dept. of Comp. Science, Charlotte, NC 28223, USA
[3] UMass Medical School, Dept. of Neurology, Worcester, MA 01655, USA
[4] Polish-Japanase Institute of Information Technology, 02-008 Warsaw, Poland
K.Ciecierski@ii.pw.edu.pl, ras@uncc.edu,
Andrzej.Przybyszewski@umassmed.edu

Abstract. In neurosurgical treatment of the Parkinson Disease (PD) the target is a small (9 x 7 x 4 mm) deep within brain placed structure called *SubthalamicNucleus* (STN). The goal of the Deep Brain Stimulation (DBS) surgery is the permanent precise placement of the stimulating electrode within target nucleus. As this structure poorly discriminates in CT[1] or MRI[2] it is usually stereotactically located using microelectrode recording. Several microelectrodes are parallelly inserted into the brain and in measured steps they are advanced towards expected location of the nucleus. At each step, from 20 mm above the target, the neuronal activity is recorded. Because STN has a distinct physiology, the signals recorded within it also present specific features. By extracting certain features from recordings provided by the microelectrodes, it is possible to construct a classifier that provides useful discrimination. This discrimination divides the recordings into two classes, i.e. those registered within the STN and those registered outside of it. Using the decision tree based classifiers, the best results have been obtained using the Random Forest method. In this paper we compared the results obtained from the Random Forest to those provided by the classification based upon rules extracted by the rough set approach.

Keywords: Parkinson's disease, DBS, STN, Decision Tree, Random Forest, Rough Set, Classification Rule, RSES.

1 Introduction

Recordings obtained by means of microrecording during PD DBS surgeries can be discriminated into those obtained from the STN and from structures adjacent to it. It is possible due to specific physiology of the STN. This physiology manifests in the activity that differs from that observed in neuronal structures

---

[1] Computer Tomography.
[2] Magnetic Resonance Imaging.

D. Ślęzak et al. (Eds.): BIH 2014, LNAI 8609, pp. 323–334, 2014.
© Springer International Publishing Switzerland 2014

being both dorsal[3] and ventral[4] to this structure [1][2]. Authors in [3][4][5] provided computational basis for calculation of attributes that when calculated for neurophysiological recordings can be successfully used for their discrimination. Those attributes have been used for construction of various decision tree based classifiers. The clinical database presently contains 16377 recordings obtained during 153 surgeries. In the case of both Random Forest and C4.5 the obtained sensitivity is above 0.9 and specificity above 0.98. Such results clearly fulfill the requirements for medical appliance [6] and allowed us to develop a recommender system that is currently in clinical use during neurosurgeries at Warsaw Institute of Psychiatry and Neurology. The goal of this paper if to compare results obtained from Random Forest to those generated by the classification based upon rules extracted by the rough set approach.

2   Methods

Parkinson Disease (PD) is a chronic and progressive movement disorder. The risk factor of the disease increases with the age. As the average human life span elongates also the number of people affected with PD steadily increases. According to the present medical knowledge, the PD disease is caused by low levels of the neurotransmitter: dopamine. Dopamine is produced by specific cells in deep placed brain region called *Substantia Nigra pars compacta* (SNc). The main cause of PD is cell-death of those cells. As the main cause of death of those cells is not clear, different treatments focus on symptom's improvements. The main treatment for the disease is the pharmacological one. Unfortunately, as more SNc cells are dying, the level of the dopamine is fast changing. PD patients have to take medications more often which may result in strong symptoms fluctuations (ON / OFF states). In such cases, patients may be qualified for the surgical treatment of the PD.

2.1   STN DBS Surgery in PD

STN DBS surgery stands for Deep Brain Stimulation of the Subthalamic Nucleus. Goal of the surgery is the placement of the permanent stimulating electrode into the STN. This nucleus is a small – deep in brain placed – structure that unfortunately does not show well neither in CT[5] nor MRI[6] scans. Above techniques allow only for approximate localization of the STN. Stimulating electrode, when properly placed disrupts overactive neural circuits that are responsible for the forming of the rigidness which is typical for the advanced stage of the PD disease. Incorrect placement of the stimulating electrode might evoke various serious adverse side effects such as severe emotional imbalance [7].

---

[3] Anatomically located above.
[4] Anatomically located beneath.
[5] Computer Tomography.
[6] Magnetic Resonance Imaging.

During the process of selection of the part of the STN into which the permanent electrode will be implanted a series of test stimulations are performed. During those stimulations the improvement of the patient condition is assessed. Care is also taken to exclude any areas which when stimulated produce side effects. As these procedures require interaction between patient and neurologist, the general anesthesia cannot be used during the neurosurgical phase of the STN DBS surgery. Patient must be conscious and is only locally anesthetized.

Having only an approximate location of the STN, during DBS surgery a precise localization of the STN is achieved by means of stereotactic navigation and intra-operative mapping based on microrecording. During the surgery, by means of probing microelectrodes, brain activity in areas near the expected STN location is recorded. Typically neurosurgeons use 3 to 5 parallel microelectrodes. Electrodes are advanced to a position that is about 10 mm above expected STN location. Later electrodes are advanced for about 15 mm with 1 mm steps. At each step a 10 s long recording of brain tissue activity is obtained. All recordings analyzed in this paper were sampled with 24 KHz.

Computer classification of recordings performed during surgery at operation theatre gives neurosurgeons valuable information about which of the electrodes and at which depths passed through the STN. In this way a precise dorsal and ventral boundaries of the STN are obtained and finally the stimulating electrode can safely be implanted.

Main advantages given by the recommender (decision support) system during STN DBS surgery are:

- From classification of the recordings it is possible to obtain information, which of the electrodes passed through the STN. It is also possible to obtain depth at which given electrode entered and exited this structure. When taking into account that information from all electrodes, the rough dorsal and ventral boundaries of the STN can be estimated.
- Besides the results of classification, values of the attributes give additional information that can be used to estimate the brain activity at any electrode inspected depth. Usually the best treatment results are obtained when the stimulating electrode is placed in one of the most active areas [7].
- One of the risks of the STN DBS surgery involves incorrect placement of the stimulating electrode. As part of the STN is involved in the control of emotions (limbic part), and in the vicinity of the STN – among others – are structures involved in emotions, eye movement and sight (OP - optic tract), wrong placement of the stimulating electrode might lead to life threatening situations. Additional computer based verification of the STN boundaries reduces risk of improper placement of the stimulating electrode.
- Any surgery is in some measure stressful for the patient. Recommender system allows faster selection of right areas for test stimulations. This shortens the time of the surgery when patient has to be awake.

2.2   Attributes Description

Attributes extracted from DBS recordings can be divided into two groups:

Spike based attributes are calculated basing on the occurrence of the neuronal action potentials i.e. spikes. The neural tissue is electrically active and
its information processing involves generation and transmission of electrical
impulses. Those impulses – spikes – are generated in neurones mainly by the
sodium (calcium) membrane channels activations. Microelectrode registers
the spiking activity from neurons that are within the 50 μm radius around
its recording lead. As shape of spikes generated by a single cell is characteristic, derived from its morphology [1] and mostly unchanging, it is possible
to calculate those attributes for all cells within 50 μm radius or for any of
them separately.

Background based attributes are calculated basing upon the signal's background noise. Cells that are farther than 50 μm away from electrode's lead
are too far away for their spikes to be clearly registered. Their summary
electrical activity creates the background noise ever present in signals obtained from microrecording. This background activity is a rough measure of
amount and activity of neuron cells in the broader vicinity of the electrode.

There is one decision attribute that has value STN for recordings from the STN
and value $MISS$ for all other recordings. For each 10 s long recording there are
five spike based attributes, four background attributes and four attributes being
the five element wide moving average of background attributes.

AvgSpkRate is the average number of spikes detected per second
AvgSpkRateScMax maximal $AvgSpkRate$ observed for single cell
BurstRatio percentage of intervals between spikes that are smaller than 33 ms
BurstRatioScMax maximal $BurstRatio$ observed for single cell
MPWR power of the derived meta signal, explained in detail in [5]

RMS Root Mean Square of the signal
PRC80 80th percentile of amplitude's module
LFB power of the signal's background in range $0 - 500\,Hz$
HFB power of the signal's background in range $500 - 3000\,Hz$

MRMS five element wide moving average of RMS
MPRC80 five element wide moving average of PRC80
MLFB five element wide moving average of LFB
MHFB five element wide moving average of HFB

In Table 1 one can observe, that for all background attributes and for 3 out
of 5 spike based attributes the Q3 for $MISS$ class is below Q1 for STN class.

Out of 16377 recordings, 3736 (22.8 %) recordings have decision attribute
STN. 12641 (77.2 %) have decision attribute $MISS$.

Table 1. Statistics for attributes

Attributes	Class	Q1	Q2	Q3	μ	σ
AvgSpkRate	MISS	0.000	0.000	7.400	5.555	9.859
	STN	10.700	18.900	29.225	21.509	15.181
AvgSpkRateScMax	MISS	0.000	0.000	4.700	3.578	6.334
	STN	6.500	11.300	18.000	13.261	9.597
BurstRatio	MISS	0.238	0.414	0.596	0.195	0.262
	STN	0.458	0.603	0.727	0.551	0.230
BurstRatioScMax	MISS	0.194	0.333	0.510	0.165	0.231
	STN	0.361	0.495	0.632	0.469	0.221
MPWR	MISS	0	0	858	448.025	546.937
	STN	1023	1315	1595	1275.836	485.373
RMS	MISS	0.939	1.006	1.153	1.064	0.230
	STN	1.757	2.069	2.493	2.190	0.598
PRC80	MISS	0.962	1.011	1.137	1.064	0.196
	STN	1.702	1.982	2.362	2.087	0.530
LFB	MISS	0.825	1.005	1.284	1.164	0.741
	STN	2.592	3.833	5.851	4.778	3.725
HFB	MISS	0.909	1.032	1.339	1.185	0.532
	STN	3.028	4.205	6.009	4.942	3.021
MRMS	MISS	0.998	1.020	1.195	1.111	0.212
	STN	1.653	1.929	2.254	1.997	0.466
MPRC80	MISS	0.999	1.022	1.183	1.106	0.190
	STN	1.614	1.852	2.145	1.916	0.427
MLFB	MISS	0.976	1.027	1.400	1.304	0.735
	STN	2.512	3.566	5.107	4.180	2.559
MHFB	MISS	0.997	1.056	1.496	1.336	0.623
	STN	2.903	3.861	5.184	4.341	2.267

2.3 Rough Set Approach

All above data can be stored as a decision table. Such table would have 16377 rows – objects. For each object there are defined 13 condition attributes i.e. $AvgSpkRate$ ... $MHFB$ and one decision attribute $Class$.

Together they form a decision system $S = (U, A)$ where U is the set of objects and A is the set of attributes. For any attribute $a \in A$ and object $u \in U$ the value of attribute a for object u is denoted as $a(u)$.

Crucial to the rough set is the definition of the *indiscernibility relation*. Indiscernibility relation is defined for a subset of attributes $B \subseteq A$ and is denoted as I_B. Two elements are in relation I_B iff for any attribute from B, its value is equal for both of them [8][9].

$$x\ I_B\ y \iff \forall_{a \in B}\ a(x) = a(y) \tag{1}$$

This relation obviously is reflexive, symmetric and transitive. From this, relation I_B is an equivalence relation and partitions the set U into equivalence classes.

Now, we define $IND(B)$ as:

$$IND(B) = \{(x, y) \in U^2 : x\ I_B\ y\} \tag{2}$$

Having defined the IND one can provide the definition of the reduct of information system. $B \subset A$ is said to be a reduct of information system if IND(B) = IND(A) and no proper subset of B has this property. $B \subset A$ is a decision reduct if IND(B) = IND(d) where d is a decision attribute.

Those reducts can further be used for obtaining attribute dependencies [10] and finally, rules that lead from the values of the conditional attributes to value of the decision attribute [11].

In information system the set of attributes A consists of set of conditional attributes C and decision attribute d. If $C = \{c_1, ..., c_m\}$ is the set of conditional attributes then decision rule can be formulated as

$$(c_{i_1} = v_1) \wedge\ ...\ \wedge\ (c_{i_k} = v_k) \implies (d = v_d) \tag{3}$$

where

$$1 \leq i_1 < ... < i_k \leq m$$

If any object has conditional attributes that satisfy the left hand site of a rule, its outcome gives value of the decision attribute of that object.

While rules basing on equality of attributes to certain values might have a very big confidence, they may have low support and as such are poorly suited for generalization and for further classification.

Much more general rules can be obtained when conditional attributes are not expected to be equal to certain values but to fall into certain ranges. This ranges are obtained by cutting the initial range of the attributes into intervals.

Fox example let's inspect the following rule

$$(PRC80 < 1.15279) \wedge (MRMS < 1.22111) \implies (CLASS = MISS)$$

which applies to 7854 recordings and states that they have not been recorded within the STN.

In contrast to decision tree classification, not every $u \in U$ must be matched by some rule. This leads to possible existence of objects for whom there are no fitting rules and which cannot be classified using given rule set. This feature is measured by the *coverage* of the rule set which gives the fraction of the tested objects that can be classified.

Classification Results

The following results were obtained using the Random Forest method and by means of classification based upon rules extracted by the rough set approach.

For Random Forest the Weka[7] v. 3.7.9 implementation has been used. Rough Set based classification has been done using RSES[8] v. 2.2.2 software [12]. All classifiers were run on unconstrained database containing described attributes for 16377 DBS recordings from 153 neurosurgeries.

Random Forest Classification Results

Random Forest Classification for All Objects with Division into 90% for Training and 10% for Testing Purposes

		Human classification		
		STN	$MISS$	Total
RF classification	STN	353	20	373
	$MISS$	29	1236	1265
	Total	382	1256	1638

$$sensitivity = \frac{353}{353+29} \approx 0.924 \qquad specificity = \frac{1236}{1236+20} \approx 0.984$$

$$accuracy = \frac{353+1236}{353+29+1236+20} \approx 0.970$$

For training of this classifier a random subset containing 90 % of objects have been chosen. Classifier has then been tested on remaining 10 % of objects. Both sensitivity and specificity are very good and above 0.9. The *Kappa* statistic was also very good: 0.916. Coverage for level 0.95 was 99.451 % of objects.

Random Forest Classification for All Objects with Division into 60% for Training and 40% for Testing Purposes

		Human classification		
		STN	$MISS$	Total
RF classification	STN	1317	79	1396
	$MISS$	110	5045	5155
	Total	1427	5124	6551

$$sensitivity = \frac{1317}{1317+110} \approx 0.923 \qquad specificity = \frac{5045}{5045+79} \approx 0.985$$

$$accuracy = \frac{1317+5045}{1317+110+5045+79} \approx 0.971$$

For training of this classifier a random subset containing 60 % of objects have been chosen. Classifier has then been tested on remaining 40 % of objects. Both sensitivity and specificity are very good and above 0.9. The *Kappa* statistic was also very good: 0.915. Coverage for level 0.95 was 99.435 % of objects.

---

[7] www.cs.waikato.ac.nz/ml/weka
[8] logic.mimuw.edu.pl/~rses/start.html

Random Forest Classification for All Objects With Ten Fold Cross–Validation

		Human classification		
		STN	$MISS$	Total
RF classification	STN	3473	169	3642
	$MISS$	263	12472	12735
	Total	3736	12641	16377

$$sensitivity = \tfrac{3473}{3473+263} \approx 0.930 \qquad specificity = \tfrac{12472}{12472+169} \approx 0.987$$

$$accuracy = \tfrac{3473+12472}{3473+263+12472+169} \approx 0.974$$

Both sensitivity and specificity are very good and above 0.9. Especially good is the specificity 0.987 which is very important in case of DBS[5]. The *Kappa* statistic was also very good: 0.924. Coverage for level 0.95 was 99.432 % of objects. This classifier is currently in clinical use during neurosurgeries.

RSES Rule Based Classification Results

RSES Rule Classification for All Objects with Division into 90% for Training and 10% for Testing Purposes

		Human classification		
		STN	$MISS$	Total
$RSES$ classification	STN	153	133	286
	$MISS$	119	740	859
	Total	272	873	1145

$$sensitivity = \tfrac{153}{153+119} \approx 0.562 \qquad specificity = \tfrac{740}{740+133} \approx 0.848$$

$$accuracy = \tfrac{153+740}{153+119+740+133} \approx 0.780 \qquad coverage = \tfrac{1145}{1638} \approx 0.699$$

In this case the specificity is acceptable but the sensitivity is very poor. Classifier failed to adequately detect objects from the STN class. It is also evident that resulting rules fail to classify over 30% of the objects.

RSES Rule Classification for All Objects with Division into 60% for Training and 40% for Testing Purposes

		Human classification		
		STN	$MISS$	Total
$RSES$ classification	STN	607	504	1111
	$MISS$	516	2720	3236
	Total	1123	3224	4347

$$sensitivity = \tfrac{607}{607+516} \approx 0.541 \qquad specificity = \tfrac{2720}{2720+504} \approx 0.844$$

$$accuracy = \tfrac{607+2720}{607+516+2720+504} \approx 0.765 \qquad coverage = \tfrac{4347}{6550} \approx 0.664$$

In this case the specificity is acceptable and the sensitivity is even worse than in previous case. Classifier failed to detect almost half of objects from the STN class. Resulting rules fail to classify over 33% of the objects.

RSES Rule Classification for All Objects with Ten Fold Cross–Validation

<table>
<tr><td></td><td></td><td colspan="3">Human classification</td></tr>
<tr><td></td><td></td><td>STN</td><td>$MISS$</td><td>Total</td></tr>
<tr><td rowspan="2">$RSES$ classification</td><td>STN</td><td>155.5</td><td>131.5</td><td>287</td></tr>
<tr><td>$MISS$</td><td>127.9</td><td>709.8</td><td>837.7</td></tr>
<tr><td></td><td>Total</td><td>283.4</td><td>841.3</td><td>4347</td></tr>
</table>

$$sensitivity = \frac{155.5}{155.5+127.9} \approx 0.548 \qquad specificity = \frac{709.8}{709.8+131.5} \approx 0.844$$

$$accuracy = \frac{155.5+709.8}{155.5+127.9+709.8+131.5} \approx 0.769 \qquad coverage = \frac{1124.7}{1637} \approx 0.687$$

In this case the specificity is acceptable and the sensitivity is as poor as in two previous cases. Classifier failed to detect almost half of objects from the STN class. Resulting rules fail to classify over 33% of the objects.

Classifications based on rules extracted from raw attributes by the rough set approach give good specificity. Still the sensitivity is very poor and over 30 % of objects are not matched by any rule.

RSES Rule Based Classification Results for Discretized Attributes

In following classifications, the conditional attributes have all been discretized i.e. cut into adjacent intervals. Cuts were made automatically by the RSES package. Number of intervals produced per attribute ranged from two for $AvgSpkRate$ up to eight for $MHFB$. Resulting cuts were not of uniform size.

RSES Rule Classification with Attribute Cut Done for All Objects with Division into 90% for Training and 10% for Testing Purposes

<table>
<tr><td></td><td></td><td colspan="3">Human classification</td></tr>
<tr><td></td><td></td><td>STN</td><td>$MISS$</td><td>Total</td></tr>
<tr><td rowspan="2">$RSES$ classification</td><td>STN</td><td>359</td><td>38</td><td>397</td></tr>
<tr><td>$MISS$</td><td>24</td><td>1216</td><td>1240</td></tr>
<tr><td></td><td>Total</td><td>383</td><td>1254</td><td>1637</td></tr>
</table>

$$sensitivity = \frac{359}{359+24} \approx 0.937 \qquad specificity = \frac{1216}{1216+38} \approx 0.970$$

$$accuracy = \frac{359+1216}{359+24+1216+38} \approx 0.962 \qquad coverage = \frac{1637}{1637} = 1.000$$

In this case both specificity and sensitivity are very good and above 0.9. Classifier has also perfect coverage. In comparison to analogous Random Forest results RSES provided slightly better sensitivity and slightly worse specificity.

RSES Rule Classification with Attribute Cut Done for All Objects with Division into 60% for Training and 40% for Testing Purposes

		Human classification		
		STN	$MISS$	Total
RSES classification	STN	1446	160	1606
	$MISS$	79	4865	4944
	Total	1525	5025	6550

$sensitivity = \frac{1446}{1446+79} \approx 0.948$ $specificity = \frac{4865}{4865+160} \approx 0.968$

$accuracy = \frac{1446+4865}{1446+79+4865+160} \approx 0.964$ $coverage = \frac{6550}{6550} = 1.000$

In this case also both specificity and sensitivity are very good and above 0.9. Classifier has also perfect coverage. In comparison to analogous Random Forest results RSES provided better sensitivity and worse specificity.

RSES Rule Classification with Attribute Cut Done for All Objects with Ten Fold Cross–Validation

		Human classification		
		STN	$MISS$	Total
RSES classification	STN	355.7	35.7	391.4
	$MISS$	17.7	1227.9	1245.6
	Total	373.4	1263.6	1637

$sensitivity = \frac{355.7}{355.7+17.7} \approx 0.953$ $specificity = \frac{1227.9}{1227.9+35.7} \approx 0.972$

$accuracy = \frac{355.7+1227.9}{355.7+17.7+1227.9+35.7} \approx 0.967$ $coverage = \frac{1637}{1637} = 0.687$

In this case specificity and sensitivity are very good and above 0.95. Classifier has perfect coverage. In comparison to analogous Random Forest results RSES provided better sensitivity and worse specificity. Still in case of both classifiers the sensitivity and specificity were above 0.93.

3   Summary

As shown in Table 2, in all tested cases the rough set rule based classification did not perform well when run on raw nondiscretized attributes. That was due to the continuous nature of all conditional attributes. Sets of rules produced by RSES for continuous attributes were huge and most of those rules matched only single objects. For example, rule generation for 90 % (14739 objects) subsample of objects with continuous attributes resulted in 154651 rules basing on equality of attributes. Not surprisingly such rule set had poor coverage during the test phase, more than 30 % of test object were not classified at all.

However when rules were produced basing on the discretized attributes, the obtained results were very good and in some aspects they outperformed those produced by the Random Forest. In all test scenarios (i.e. 90 % train & 10 % test; 60 % train & 40 % test; 10 fold cross–validation) while the RSES provided better sensitivity the Random Forest approach gave better specificity. On average the RSES sensitivity was better by 0.02 and Random Forest specificity was better by 0.015.

In conclusion it must be stated that both methods, i.e. Weka implementation of Random Forest and RSES implementation of rough set rule based classification for discretized attributes gave very good and comparable results. Also in both cases after the classifier / rule set has been constructed, the classification of new objects is very fast and certainly feasible for use at the operation theatre.

Table 2. Sensitivity, specificity and coverage

		Sensitivity	Specificity	Coverage
90% train; 10% test	Weka RF	0.924	0.984	1.000
	RSES	0.562	0.848	0.699
	Cut RSES	0.937	0.970	1.000
60% train; 40% test	Weka RF	0.923	0.985	1.000
	RSES	0.541	0.844	0.664
	Cut RSES	0.948	0.968	1.000
10 fold cross–validation	Weka RF	0.930	0.987	1.000
	RSES	0.548	0.844	0.687
	Cut RSES	0.953	0.972	1.000

Acknowledgements. This work was partially supported by DEC-2011/03/B/ST6/03816 from the Polish National Science Centre.

References

1. Nolte, J.: The Human Brain, An Introduction to Its Functional Anatomy. Elsevier (2009)
2. Israel, Z., Burchiel, K.J.: Microelectrode Recording in Movement Disorder Surgery. Thieme Medical Publishers (2004)
3. Ciecierski, K., Raś, Z.W., Przybyszewski, A.W.: Foundations of Recommender System for STN Localization during DBS Surgery in Parkinson's Patients. In: Chen, L., Felfernig, A., Liu, J., Raś, Z.W. (eds.) ISMIS 2012. LNCS, vol. 7661, pp. 234–243. Springer, Heidelberg (2012)
4. Ciecierski, K., Raś, Z.W., Przybyszewski, A.W.: Discrimination of the Micro Electrode Recordings for STN Localization during DBS Surgery in Parkinson's Patients. In: Larsen, H.L., Martin-Bautista, M.J., Vila, M.A., Andreasen, T., Christiansen, H. (eds.) FQAS 2013. LNCS, vol. 8132, pp. 328–339. Springer, Heidelberg (2013)

5. Ciecierski, K., Raś, Z.W., Przybyszewski, A.W.: Foundations of automatic system for intrasurgical localization of subthalamic nucleus in Parkinson patients. In: Web Intelligence and Agent Systems, 2014/1, pp. 63–82. IOS Press (2014)
6. Walker, H.K., Hall, W.D., Hurst, J.W. (eds.): Clinical Methods: The History, Physical, and Laboratory Examinations, 3rd edn. Butterworths, Boston (1990)
7. Israel, Z., Burchiel, K.J.: Microelectrode Recording in Movement Disorder Surgery. Thieme Medical Publishers (2004)
8. Pawlak, Z.: Rough sets: Theoretical aspects of reasoning about data. Kluwer, Dordrecht (1991)
9. Pawlak, Z.: Theoretical Aspects of Reasoning about Data Series. Theory and Decision Library D 9 (1991)
10. Pawlak, Z.: Rough sets and information systems. Podstawy Sterowania 18(3-4), 175–200 (1998)
11. Bazan, J., Skowron, A., Synak Dynamic, P.: Dynamic reducts as a tool for extracting laws from decisions tables. In: Raś, Z.W., Zemankova, M. (eds.) ISMIS 1994. LNCS, vol. 869, pp. 346–355. Springer, Heidelberg (1994)
12. Bazan, J., Szczuka, M.S.: RSES and RSESlib - A Collection of Tools for Rough Set Computations. In: Ziarko, W.P., Yao, Y. (eds.) RSCTC 2000. LNCS (LNAI), vol. 2005, p. 106. Springer, Heidelberg (2001)

The Analysis of Correlation between MOCAP-Based and UPDRS-Based Evaluation of Gait in Parkinson's Disease Patients

Magdalena Lachor[1], Adam Świtoński[1], Magdalena Boczarska-Jedynak[3], Stanisław Kwiek[4], Konrad Wojciechowski[2], and Andrzej Polański[1]

[1] Institute of Informatics, Silesian University of Technology
ul. Akademicka 16, 44-100 Gliwice, Poland
{Magdalena.Lachor,Adam.Switonski,Andrzej.Polanski}@polsl.pl
[2] Polish-Japanese Institute of Information Technology Aleja Legionów 2,
41-902 Bytom, Poland
{Konrad.Wojciechowski}@pjwstk.pl
[3] Department of Neurorehabilitation, Departament of Neurology, Medical University of Silesia, Central University Hospital, ul.Medyków 14, 40-752 Katowice, Poland
m.boczarska@gmail.com
[4] Departament of Neurosurgery, Medical University of Silesia, Central University Hospital, ul. Medyków 14, 40-752 Katowice, Poland
skwiek@csk.katowice.pl

Abstract. The most common method used by neurologist to evalute the Parkinson's Disease patients are different rating scales. They give overall picture of the PD patient, but are not objective and different experts can make different observations. In this article the results of correlation between UPDRS evaluation and different quality measures calculated based on MOCAP data recorded during walking for group of PD patients with implanted DBS stimulator have beed presented. This is a continuation of our previous research related to analysis of gait in Parkinson's Disease Patients.

Keywords: Parkinson's disease, UPDRS, gait, MOCAP.

1 Introduction

Diagnosis of medical disorders and rehabilitation therapy can significantly benefit from multimodal measurement and analysis of human gait with motion capture technology (MOCAP). With huge concentration on MOCAP technology and the constant improvement of quality and exactness of registered movement medical fields like physical therapy, orthopedics, neurology and neurosurgery start not only benefit but to relay on data acquired through MOCAP technology. This is all possible with the high level of accuracy and precision with which MOCAP systems measure the kinematics and geometrics of human gait. Important to notion is that along with kinematics of movement such approach allows additionally to record video, ground reaction forces and EMG signal, which form

D. Ślęzak et al. (Eds.): BIH 2014, LNAI 8609, pp. 335–344, 2014.

a synchronized multimodal measurement. Such collected data can be assessed with all clinical data already collected about the patient and thus significantly increase the quality of diagnostics and therapy. In the referenced publications [1][2][3][4] a wide scope of studies have been applied to the problem of use of MOCAP analysis of human gait among neurological disease patients. In those publications a research was conducted to obtain several indices, that could assess the neurological patients and the severity of their illness. The quality of those indices and their evaluation were measured among neurological patients and were proved to be meaningful. Those indices however where evaluated using different MOCAP system technology and with different approach to the asset of processing MOCAP data results. Moreover the patients, who were target of those experiments have different neurological disorders.

The Parkinson's disease (PD) is one of the most common neurodegenartive and movement disorder, which affects with the highest probability the older people, although the cases of the young pearsons with diagnosed PD are also known. The Parkinson's disease is manifested by several different symptoms and increases with time. The reason of this illness is not known so far and due to methods of treatments are symptomatic and not causal. Up to date exist two types of treatment methods rely on medication or surgical operations. The motor symptoms of Parkinson's disease are caused by the deficiency of dopamine in the brain, therefore used drugs are intended to supplement the lack of this key neurotransmitter. Unfortunately, with the progresses of the disease the medication are insufficient and due to this fact the increased emphasis on alternative methods of treatments has been placed. One of such a method is the deep brain stimulation (DBS for short). The DBS is a surgical procedure, which aims to implant the medical device into targeted brain area. However, the issue how to select this specific place in the brain to eliminate as much as possible symptoms with whom patient is struggling the most is still not clear. The DBS blocks electrical impulses from a targeted parts of the brain. It brings the greatest benefit in the treatment of symptoms associated with movement disorders such as bradykinesia, dyskinesia, muscle rigidity, tremor or gait disturbances.

In order to evelute the level of Parkinson's disease severity, the neurologists use different rating scales to make their observations unified. The developed assessment methodologies take into account motor or non-motor skills or both of them. There exists several different approaches but one of the most widely used is the Unified Parkison Disease Rating Scale (UPDRS)[17]. The UPDRS consists of six parts, which allows to rate different aspects of PD patient's quality of life. The III part is dedicated to motor symptoms and contains 18 questions and each item is measured on a five-point scale. Evaluation carried in this way allows to give the complete picture of the patient illustrating his/her response to treatment. However, the main disadvantage of such methods is subjectivity due to the fact, that two evaluators can make various observations of the same patient. In this article we would like to analyse the correlation between the subjective evaluation of PD patients group based on III part of UPDRS scale related to gait and quantitative indices calcualted based on MOCAP data.

2   Experiment and Methods

The experimental scenario assumed analysis of movement during different types of walking under four experimental conditions denoted as sessions. The studied group consists of five subjects.

2.1   Patients

Research was conducted on a subset of 4 male and 1 female patients with idiopathic Parkinson disease. Detailed clinical data are provided in Table 1.

Table 1. Clinical data

Patient	Gender	DBS side	Age at DBS [years]	Age at PD onset [years]	PD duration till DBS [years]	Time between DBS and MOCAP [months]	Daily LED before DBS	Daily LED after DBS
P1	Male	Bilateral	61	43	18	38	675	825
P2	Male	Bilateral	50	39	11	40	833	800
P3	Female	Right	50	42	8	32	563	675
P4	Male	Bilateral	65	57	8	32	1000	450
P5	Male	Bilateral	56	46	10	14	900	3375
Mean value			56,4	45,4	11	31,2	794,2	1225
DBS - Deep Brain Stimulation, PD - Parkinson's disease, MOCAP - Motion Capture, LED - levodopa equivalent dose								

Every patient in studied group was subjected to the DBS surgery at Parkinson's Disease Treatment Centre in Medical University of Silesia, Katowice. Surgeries where performed between November 2005 and September 2011. Patients were classified using CAPSIT [10] recommendations for a DBS treatment by a team of specialists in a field of Parkinson disease. The process and methodology of stereotactic surgery performed during DBS implantation as well as the complications, where widely described and can be found in [7][12][13][14][15]. The DBS electrode (Model 3389, Medtronic, Mineapollis) and internal pulse generators (Soletra, Medtronic, Mineapollis) were implanted in those subset of patients [8][9][10].

2.2   Experimental Procedures

The participants who took part in the experiment were asked to perform four types of walking along a five-meter path (Fig. 1B). The tasks were based on walking in normal way, walking faster then normal, but with caution, without running, along the line and tandem (the top of one foot should touch the heel of the opposite foot). The line and tandem types of walking have been performed along black line located in the middle of the walking path. The walking tasks were repeated during four experimental conditions called sessions. Before the experiment each PD patient was asked to not taking medication for 12 hours before the test. During first session subjects were without medication and the stimulator was turned off (S1 - MedOFF StimOFF). During second session the subjects were still without medication but the stimulator was turn on (S2 - MedOFF StimON). The next session was recorded after taking by the subjects suprather-apeutic dose of L-dopa, the stimulator was turn off (S3 - MedON StimOFF). The last session was performed, when the subjects were under the influence of drugs and with stimulator turned on (S4 - MedON StimON). After each session the overall condition of the patient was evalueted by neurogolist according to III part of the UPDRS scale.

2.3   Data Recording

All measurement have been performed in multimodal human motion laboratory located in Polish-Japanese Institute of Information Technology (Bytom, Poland). The laboratory is equipped in 10-camera, 3D motion capture system (Vicon) for kinematic data analysis, two Kistler platforms for ground reaction forces mea-surement (GRF), Dynamic Electromyography System (EMG) from Noraxon en-abling 16-channel measurement of muscle potentials and 4 video cameras with HD 1080. The computations were performed on data written in c3d files contain-ing spatial positions of all body markers during a MOCAP session and asf/amc files containing parameters of the skeletal model such as angles, velocities and orientations [11]. The spatial position of the patient was obtained based on 39 reflective body markers located on all body segments (4 on Head, 5 on Torso, 14 on left and right side of upper limbs, 16 on left and right side of lower body) as presented in Fig. 1A [16].

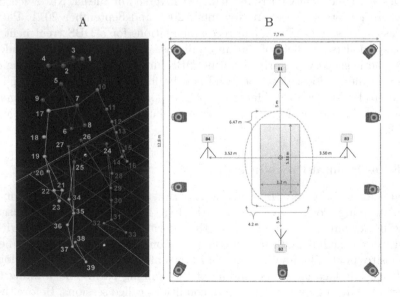

Fig. 1. A. 3D position of the patient B. Laboratory system

2.4   Gait Abnormality Indices

Based on the literature review three different quantitative measures have been selected to evalute the gait abnormalities among PD patients. Two indices (WDA and ASSS) reflect the assymetry between left and right side of the upper limbs, while DI parameter reflects the decomposition between pair of joints of the lower limbs during movement. The residual value of each parameter have been calculated for each patient across four sessions. The final value of each parameter was calcualted as artihmetic average across all strides during one trial, then average across all trials during session. The notion of single step has been defined as interval between foot off of one leg and heel strike of the ipsilateral leg, while stride as interval between foot off of one leg and heel strike of contralateral foot (two consecutive steps). The schematic illustraiton of differences between step and stride has been presented in Fig. 2. The detailed description of the parameters has been presented below.

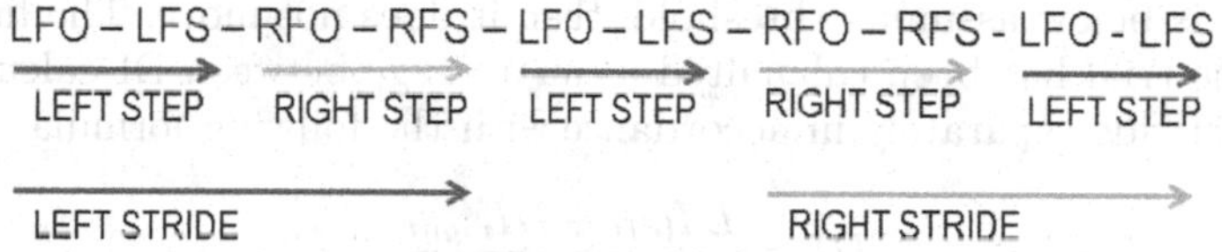

LFO – LFS – RFO – RFS – LFO – LFS – RFO – RFS - LFO - LFS

LEFT STEP   RIGHT STEP   LEFT STEP   RIGHT STEP   LEFT STEP

LEFT STRIDE   RIGHT STRIDE

Fig. 2. Illustration of consecutive events during walking. FO - foot off, FS - heel strike

Wrists Distance Asymmtery is used to reflect the assymetry between distances traveled by left and right wrists and has been proposed in [4] to evaluate gait abnormalities in the early stages of Parkinson's disease. This parameter has been denoted as WDA and defined in a following way:

$$WDA = \frac{(45 - arctan(\frac{WD_{larger}}{WD_{smaller}}))}{90} \cdot 100\% \qquad (1)$$

where variable $WD_{smaller}$ is related to shorter distance traveled by one of the wrist, while WD_{larger} to the grater wrist distance. The notion of wrist distance has been defined as the length of the marker trajectory. Let us assume that $P_i = (x_i, y_i, z_i)$ is a position of a joint in 3D space in the i - th frame, then distance between position in an i-th frame and the frame next in order will be calculated as:

$$\Delta P_i = \sqrt{(x_{i+1} - x_i)^2 + (y_{i+1} - y_i)^2 + (z_{i+1} - z_i)^2} \qquad (2)$$

The wrist distance has been calculted as a sum of marker shifts from the center of coordinate system and calcualted according to the following formula:

$$WD = \int f(P(t))dt \cong \sum_{i=1}^{n} \Delta P_i \qquad (3)$$

Arm Swing Size Symmetry is also dedicated to illustrate the difference between upper limbs. The Symmetry is calculated to measure the similarity between range of angle during arm swing [1]. The ASSS parameter is defined as:

$$ASSS = \frac{AS_{smaller}}{AS_{larger}} \cdot 100\% \tag{4}$$

The variable denoted as Arm Swing (AS) is calcualted for left and right side. The AS_{larger} and $AS_{smaller}$ relate to larger and smaller difference between maximum and minimum shoulder flexion/extension angles.

$$AS = maxSFE - minSFE \tag{5}$$

Decomposition Index has been proposed in [2] to analyse the decomposition between three pairs of joints as knee-hip, knee-ankle and hip-ankle. DI was defined as percentage of stride when one joint is moving while the another is not. When angular velocity of the joint is more than 5 [deg/s] then it is moving. If the velocity is below assumed threshold, then it does not move. The final value of DI for one trial has been calcualted as an average between DI calculated for left and right side separately in accordance with the follwing formula:

$$DI = \frac{DI_{left} + DI_{right}}{2} \tag{6}$$

The angular velocity can be represented as a three dimensional vector quantity (w_x, w_y, w_z) [6][5]. The elements w_x, w_y and w_z of vector W do not depend on each other and can be respectively defined as rates of change of rotation angle about the x, y and z axis. If the rotation represents by unit quaternion Q and treat quaternion Q as representing rotation relative to the neutral position of frames, angular velocity $W(t)$ can be computed based on the following equation:

$$W(t) = \frac{2}{Q(t)} * \frac{dQ}{dt} \tag{7}$$

3   Results

For each patient the mean value of five coefficients (WDA, ASSS and DI for knee-ankle, knee-hip and hip-ankle pairs of joints) during four sessions have been calculated as presented in Fig. 3 - 7 (the bar charts on the left side). The results were compared with gait evaluations obtained based on III part of UP-DRS scale related to gait. The UPDRS guidelines by which a gait assessment has been performed by neurologist, before each session are presented in Table 2. The Pearson's linear correlation coefficients between MOCAP quantitative measures and UPDRS evaluation for five PD patients are presented in Fig. 3 - 7 (the scatter plots on the right side). The correlation coefficient is equal to the slope of the least-squares reference line in the scatter plot. The calculated indices

Table 2. Criterions for the assessment of gait accordance with the UPDRS scale [17]

SCORE	CRITERIONS
0	Normal
1	Walks slowly, may shuffle with short steps, but no festination (hastening steps) or propulsion.
2	Walks with difficulty, but requires little or no assistance; may have some festination, short steps, or propulsion.
3	Severe disturbance of gait, requiring assistance.
4	Cannot walk at all, even with assistance.

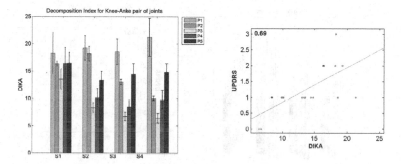

Fig. 3. RIGHT: Residual values of DI (Knee-Ankle) parameter calculated for five PD patients across four experimental conditions. LEFT: Scatter plot of MOCAP-based and UPDRS-based evaluations.

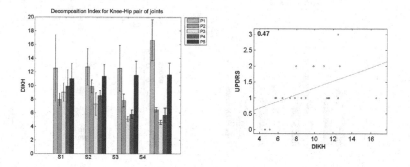

Fig. 4. RIGHT: Residual values of DI (Knee-Hip) parameter calculated for five PD patients across four experimental conditions. LEFT: Scatter plot of MOCAP-based and UPDRS-based evaluations.

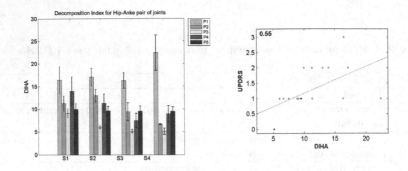

Fig. 5. RIGHT: Residual values of DI (Hip-Ankle) parameter calculated for five PD patients across four experimental conditions. LEFT: Scatter plot of MOCAP-based and UPDRS-based evaluations.

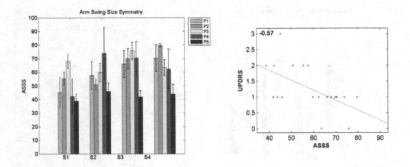

Fig. 6. RIGHT: Residual values of ASSS parameter calculated for five PD patients across four experimental conditions. LEFT: Scatter plot of MOCAP-based and UPDRS-based evaluations.

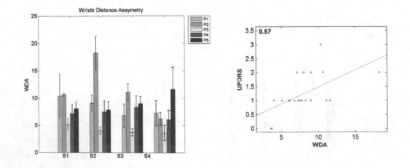

Fig. 7. RIGHT: Residual values of WDA parameter calculated for five PD patients across four experimental conditions. LEFT: Scatter plot of MOCAP-based and UPDRS-based evaluations.

and UPDRS evaluation analysed across four sessions reflect similar correlations, which absolute values ranging between 0.47-0.69. The best correlation has been obtained for the Decomposition Index calculated for knee-ankle pair of joints. The parameters ASSS and WDA showed the same level of interdependence with UPDRS, what is in accordance with the fact, that both of them reflect difference between movement of left and right side of upper limbs.

4 Conclusion

In this article the comparison between two different methods used to evaluate gait abnormalities in Parkinson's Disease Patients have been presented. For each patient the residual values of five quantitative measures calculated based on kinematic data during four experimental conditions have been obtained. The MOCAP-based evaluations have been compared with the UPDRS-based evaluations taking into account only score awarded to the patients based on gait observations. Despite the small group of investigated PD patients, the preliminary results reflect, that exists correlation between evaluation of gait based on MOCAP data and observations of neurologist based on UPDRS scale. However the usefulness of the proposed MOCAP-based method of gait evaluation need to be confirmed based on a larger group of examined subjects.

Acknowledgements. This work was supported by The National Science Center NN518289240 (K.W.), by the European Union from the European Social Fund grant agreement number: UDA-POKL.04.01.01-00-106/09 (M.L.), by POIG.02.03.01-24-099/13 grant: GCONiI - Upper-Silesian Center for Scientific Computation (A.P.).

References

1. Zifchock, R.A., Davis, I., Higginson, J., Royer, T.: The symmetry angle: a novel, robust method of quantifying asymmetry. Gait and Posture 27(4), 622–627 (2008)
2. Mian, O.S., Schneider, S.A., Schwingenschuh, P., Bhatia, K.P., Day, B.L.: Gait in SWEDDs patients: comparison with Parkinson's disease patients and healthy controls. Movement Disorders 26(7), 1266–1273 (2011)
3. Earhart, G.M.: Selection and Coordination of Hunlan Locomotor Forms Following Cerebellar Damage (2001)
4. Lewek, M.D., Poole, R., Johnson, J., Halawa, O., Huang, X.: Arm swing magnitude and asymmetry during gait in the early stages of Parkinson's disease. Gait and Posture 31(2), 256–260 (2010)
5. Coutsias, E.A., Romero, L.: The quaternions with an application to rigid body dynamics (2004)
6. Conway, J.H., Smith, D.A., Dixon, G.: On quaternions and octonions: Their geometry, arithmetic, and symmetry. The Mathematical Intelligencer 26(2), 75–77 (2004)

7. Kwiek, S.J., Boczarska, M., Świat, M., Kłodowska-Duda, G., Kukier, W., Ślusarczyk, W., Antonowicz-Olewicz, A., Szajkowski, S., Suszyński, K., Bażowski, P., Opala, G.: Deep brain stimulation for Parkinson's disease. Experience of Silesian Interdisciplinary Centre for Parkinson's disease treatment in Katowice, 39 Zjazd Polskiego Towarzystwa Neurochirurgów i Sekcji Pielegniarskiej PTNCh z udziałem Greckiego Towarzystwa Neurochirurgicznego. Mikołajki, 85–86 (September 17-20, 2009) (Poland)
8. Kwiek, S.J., Kłodowska-Duda, G., Wójcikiewicz, T., Ślusarczyk, W., Kukier, W., Bażowski, P., Zymon-Zagórska, A., Buszta, H., Konopka, M., Giec-Lorenz, A., Opala, G.: Stereotactic stimulation and ablative procedures for therapy of movement disorders. Acta Neurochir. 148(10), 42 (2006)
9. Kwiek, S.J., Kłodowska-Duda, G., Wójcikiewicz, T., Ślusarczyk, W., Kukier, W., Bażowski, P., Zymon-Zagórska, A., Buszta, H., Konopka, M., Kiełtyka, A., Opala, G.: Simultaneous targeting and stimulation of STN and VIM in tremor predominant PD patients. Pro's and cons. Acta Neurochir. 148(10), 36 (2006)
10. Kwiek, S.J., Boczarska-Jedynak, M., Świat, M., Kłodowska-Duda, G., Ślusarczyk, W., Kukier, W., Błaszczyk, B., Doleżych, H., Szajkowski, S., Suszyński, K., Kocur, D., Bażowski, P., Opala, G.: DBS for Parkinson's disease treatment. Experience and results interdisciplinary Silesian Centre for Parkinson's Disease Treatment in Katowice. Neurol. Neurochir. Pol. 44(supl.1), S16–S17 (2010)
11. Meredith, M., Maddock, S.: Motion capture file formats explained. Department of Computer Science, University of Sheffield 211 (2001)
12. Kwiek, S.J., Bierzyńska-Macyszyn, G., Tarnawski, R., Maciejewski, B., Wolwender, A., Lewin-Kowalik, J., Właszczuk, P., Konopka, M., Baron, J., Zymon-Zagórska, A., Luszawski, J.: Stereotactic methods in interdisciplinary diagnosis and treatment of posterior fossa tumours. Folia. Neuropathol. 41(4), 241–244 (2003)
13. Kwiek, S.J., Wolwender, A., Bierzyńska-Macyszyn, G., Fijałkowski, M., Tarnawski, R., Bażowski, P., Maciejewski, B., Luszawski, J., Kukier, W., Ślusarczyk, W., Zymon-Zagórska, A., Konopka, M.: Analysis of goal achievement and failure reasons of stereotactic procedures. In: 12th European Congress of Neurosurgery (EANS) - Neurosurgery 2003, Lisbon, Portugal, pp. 1043–1046. Monduzzi Editore, Bologna (September 7-12, 2003)
14. Kwiek, S.J., Bierzyńska-Macyszyn, G., Właszczuk, P., Bażowski, P., Maciejewski, B., Tarnawski, R., Ślusarczyk, W., Kukier, W., Wójcikiewicz, T., Hayatullah, A., Duda, I., Larysz, D., Blamek, S.: Non-neoplastic, degenerative brain pathologies and fibroses diagnosed on the basis of ultra-small samples obtained by stereotactic biopsy. Folia Neuropathol. 42(4), 197–201 (2004)
15. Kwiek, S.J., Bierzyńska-Macyszyn, G., Właszczuk, P., Tarnawski, R., Maciejewski, B., Bażowski, P., Wolwender, A., Zymon-Zagórska, A., Konopka, M., Hayatullah, A., Ślusarczyk, W., Kukier, W., Jeziorska, A.: Diagnosis of ultra-small samples obtained from stereotactic biopsy as a key for brainstem, cerebellar, mesencephalic and thalamic region lesions interdisciplinary management. In: Soares, F., Vassallo, J., Bleggi Torres, L.F. (eds.) 2nd Intercontinental Congress of Pathology, Iguassu Falls, Brazil, pp. 113–116. Monduzzi Editore, Bologna (July 9-13, 2004)
16. Stawarz, M., Kwiek, S., Polański, A., Janik, Ł., Boczarska-Jedynak, M., Przybyszewski, A., Wojciechowski, K.: Algorithms for computing indexes of neurological gait abnormalities in patients after DBS surgery for Parkinson Disease based on motion capture data. Machine Graphics and Vision 20(3) (2011)
17. Movement Disorder Society Task Force on Rating Scales for Parkinson's Disease. The Unified Parkinson's Disease Rating Scale (UPDRS): status and recommendations. Movement Disorders: Official Journal of the Movement Disorder Society 18(7), 738 (2003)

Rough Set Rules Help to Optimize Parameters of Deep Brain Stimulation in Parkinson's Patients

Artur Szymański[1] and Andrzej W. Przybyszewski[1,2]

[1] Polish-Japanese Institute of Information Technology,
Koszykowa 86, 02-008 Warszawa, Poland
artur.szymanski@pjwstk.edu.pl
[2] University of Massachusetts Medical School, Dept. Neurology,
65 Lake Av., Worcester, MA01655, USA
andrzej.przybyszewski@umassmed.edu

Abstract. Deep brain stimulation (DBS) is a well established method used as treatment in patients with advanced Parkinson's disease (PD). Our main purpose is to increase precision of DBS method by determining which parts of cortex are stimulated in different set-ups. In this paper we have analyzed MRIs that are performed as a standard procedure before and after the DBS surgery. We have used 3D Slicer for registration of MRIs with anatomical brain atlas. In addition, we have generated trajectories of neural tracts (tractography) connecting STN with cortex using data colected by DTI (Diffusion Tensor Imaging). In the following step we have used Rougt Set Theory to compare MRI data with neurological findings acquired by neurologists. We have tested prediction of DBS electrode contact's position and stimulating parameters in individual patients on improvements of particular neurological symptoms. Our results may give a basis to set optimal parameters of stimulation and electrode's position in order to obtain the most effective PD treatment.

Keywords: Deep Brain Stimulation, Parkinson's disease, 3D image analysis, RSES, MRI, DTI.

1   Introduction

The treatment of PD by the DBS is now used worldwide as a method that improves patients' health when pharmacological treatments become ineffective. The first experiments were performed on monkeys treated with MPTP that caused Parkinson-like state [1]. In fact, the first tests of the compound MPTP were performed by a drug-dealer who synthetized meperidine analog that caused that young cocaine addicts after taking it, could not move anymore [2]. In the 1980's a French neurosurgeon at the UJL Hospital in Grenoble, Alim-Louis Benabid was routinely performing lessoning of the thalamus in the brains of severely affected patients with Parkinson'. On the animal experiments basis, Benabid, also a professor of biophysics, in 1987 performed the first stimulation of the thalamus and later in the 90's has changed the target to the Subthalamic nucleus (STN) [3]. Nowadays, the major targeted structures are: STN [4]

D. Ślęzak et al. (Eds.): BIH 2014, LNAI 8609, pp. 345–356, 2014.
© Springer International Publishing Switzerland 2014

and Globus Pallidus Interna (GPi) [3]. As the most surgeries are still aiming STN that is a small nucleus 3x5x9 mm localized in the midbrain, mostly invisible in MRI, there is a problem with finding the exact stereotactic coordinated of its borders. An approximate STN localization, from other MRI visible neighboring structures, is normally verified by the electrophysiological data obtained during the DBS surgery. Pattern recognition of the STN spike train characteristic is not an easy task. It needs experienced team of neurosurgeon – neurologist and/or an intelligent on-line software analysis [5]. There are also additional complications as different parts of the STN are taking parts in different pathways related to the following loops: somatic motor, oculomotor, prefrontal and limbic.

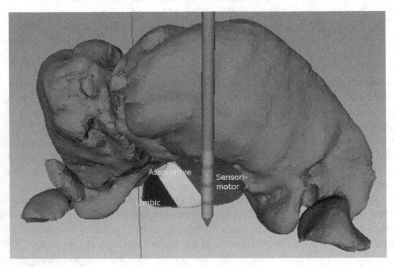

Fig. 1. The image of the thalamus with the STN (a small nucleus below the thalamus). A realistic model of the electrode with stimulating contacts was added as illustration of the DBS. Three parts of the STN were marked: sensorimotor, associative and limbic [6, 7]. Notice four contacts of the stimulating electrode that are near the STN.

In this study we are interested in the parallel STN signals processing. These signals are derived from the primary motor cortex (M1) and SMA (supplementary motor area) and related to the somatic motor circuit. Our interest is limited to the somatotopic organization of the connections between M1, SMA and STN (Fig. 1). By finding position of the electrode's contacts in relationship to different STN parts (loops), we can estimate possible motor effects that are related to stimulation of different contacts. In the near future, our method may give instructions to neurosurgeons where precisely should be placed stimulating electrodes in order to improve particular symptoms in each individual patient.

In the present study we have registered the position of the DBS electrode in relationship to the STN localization, and observed different neurological effects when the position electrode-STN and parameters of the stimulation were changed. In order to find how neurological effects are changing, we have used Rough Set Theory to generate rules for different electrode positions in all individual patients. On the basis anatomical position of the electrodes contact and parameters of stimulation we have proposed rules that can predict related neurological effects. In the next step, we have verified our predictions by comparing them with neurological diagnosis for each individual patient.

2 Methods

In this section we describe how to define relationship between electrode's position and STN. We have determined anatomical positions of important for our project structures by performing registration [8–10] of the individual patient's brain with the brain atlas [11, 12] and use postoperative imaging to locate exact position of implanted DBS electrodes. Then our experimental data are compared with an SPL-PNL atlas by localizing anterior and posterior commissure (AC-PC) line and brain's midline and aligning them with the atlas.

2.1 Data for Processing

In this project, we have processed the following sets of data: preoperative magnetic resonance imaging (pre-OP MRI), postoperative MRI (post-OP MRI), preoperative diffusion weighted imaging (pre-OP DWI), and 2008 SPL-PNL brain atlas. In several cases, in order to find DBS electrode, we have used the postoperative computer tomography (CT) instead of the post-OP MRI. It is important for our project that MRI data has small slice spacing and is performed in the 3D image acquire mode (equal spacing in all directions). We have analyzed data from nine patients with advanced Parkinson disease (PD), and with implanted DBS electrodes. The image processing in this work was performed by means of 3D Slicer, available as an open source-license from www.slicer.org. In the preparation for our analysis, we have performed the following steps as described below and illustrated as a diagram in Fig. 2.

2.2 MRI Registration

We have performed pre-OP versus post-OP images registration in order to mark electrode's contacts positions according to the post-OP MRI. The registration procedure has to be performed separately for each patient. As normally many images are taken from the same subject, only a simple linear registration using Slicer "BRAIN FIT" module had to be applied. Parameters for the registration were as follows: use center of head align, only rigid registration phase, 100 000 samples, and 1500 iterations. A quality of the registration was evaluated by comparing structures' surface coverage of the MRI measurements with the atlas.

After post-OP MRI to pre-OP MRI registration, the output transform was applied to the post-OP MRI images. Thanks to this transformation, DBS electrode became visible in preoperative images. In the next step electrode trajectory was marked with a ruler tool, setting its parameters to 0.5 mm point spacing and 1.5 mm point size.

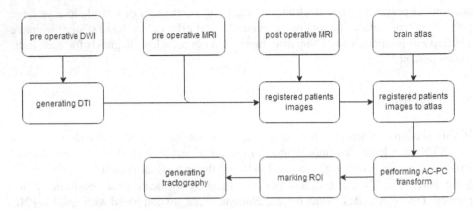

Fig. 2. In our procedures we have used different registration phases. First we have performed a linear registration of pre- to post-operative imaging. Next we apply local nonlinear registration to brain atlas followed with ROI selection and DTI generation.

These parameters were used in order to estimate exact positions of Medtronic (type 3389) electrode's contacts. As different Medtronic stimulating electrodes have different parameters, and DBS contacts are not visible in MRI, we used the following electrode's parameters: distance from the tip to the first contact – 1.5 mm, contact spacing - 0.5 mm, and length of each contact -1.5 mm. The key point was to find out and to mark the distal tip of the electrode at the beginning of the visible in MRI electrode trajectory (see below Fig. 5). The 0.1 mm slice step was used to achieve sufficient accuracy when marking the starting point. The end of the trajectory was marked toward the dorsal part of brain, as close as possible to the skull. Having marked the electrode trajectory, the contacts positions could be marked using the fiducial points on the ruler according to the electrode's specification.

2.3   Generation of the Tractography

In the following step, a tractography separately for each contact was generated on the basis of DTI data from the pre-OP DWI. The DWI to diffuse tensor-imaging (DTI) data was estimated by the least squares approximation.

Following the DTI estimation, it was possible to generate tracts specific for a given contact. At this step it was necessary to use the "Tractography Interactive Seeding" module (3D Slicer). Previously created fiducial points were used with the following module parameters: linear measure start point: 0.3, minimum path length: 20 mm, maximum path length: 800 mm, stopping criteria: fractional anisotropy, stopping track curvature: 0.7 and integration step length: 0.5. According to the generated tractography for a given contact, the seed spacing was increased and the stopping value was decreased until it was possible to record connections to the dorsal parts of brain.

The next step, after acquiring tractography for a given contact, was to normalize the brain's position. For this purpose anterior (AC) and posterior (PC) commissures had to be marked by patient's MRI registration to so-called AC-PC transform. In all procedures, we have used the SPL PNL brain atlas from 2008 [11]. In the registration procedure, we have performed a local registration of the brain's region of interest, to minimize errors that may occur when the whole brain registration is used. At this step, the appropriate brain parts were selected and cropped using relevant modules in 3DSlicer. The same procedure was applied in all cases, paying attention to select a similar region of interest as in the brain atlas. After the registration process the resulting linear transform was applied to AC-PC models and marked with fiducial points, one point per each structure.

Afterwards, brain's midline was marked with at least three fiducial points. Preferred method for this procedure was to use axial planes of MRIs where the midline is visible. When both the AC-PC and the midline annotation structures were selected, the AC-PC transform module (3DSlicer) was used to generate relevant linear transform that was applied to the whole brain MRI.

When brain images were aligned to AC-PC line we have marked regions of interest (ROI) by tracing tractography from the given electrode's contacts. In this paper, we have focused on three somatotopic areas representing lip, foot and hand in each hemisphere [13, 14]. These areas have variable positions in different patients, but there are some anatomical structures that help their identifications: anterior-posterior commiserates when projected to the cortex determine area of interest - AC position separates pre-SMA from SMA, as well as Cingulate, central and precentral sulci (Fig. 5). After registering we have estimated how many tracts are leading in proximity of each ROI.

2.4 Rough Set Approach

Our experimental data have been analyzed with the Rough Set Exploration System (RSES) version 2.2 [14] based on rough set theory proposed by Pawlak[15].

The structure of data is an important point of our analysis. It is represented in the form of information system or a decision table. We define after Pawlak [15] an information system as $S = (U, A)$, where U, A are nonempty finite sets called the *universe of objects* and the *set of attributes*, respectively. If $a \in A$ *and* $u \in U$, the value $a(u)$ is a unique element of V (where V is a value set). The *indiscernibility relation* of any subset B of A or $I(B)$, is defined [15] as follows:

$$I(B) = \{(x, y) \in A \cup B \mid \forall a \in B, a(x) = a(y)\} \tag{1}$$

Having in discernibility relation we define the notion of reduct $B \subset A$ is a reduct of information system if $IND(B) = IND(A)$ and no proper subset of B has this property. In case of decision tables decision reduct is a set $B \subset A$ of attributes such that it cannot be further reduced and $IND(B) \subset IND(D)$. All reduct set in the system consists of set of attributes C – conditional attributes, and attribute D – decision attribute. In general if any object in a set satisfies given set of C attributes it returns value of given D attribute, which is the result of classification process.

In our experiment we build attributes type C from neurological data acquired by doctor and visual analysis data acquired during our experiments in Slicer. Basing on this data we can create decision rules.

These rules are created based on training set and are later evaluated to classify test subset of data. By using only such rules we would end having a lot of redundant data for all of the patients with similar results. In order to limit number of rules we reduce them to reducts. It can be accomplished by different techniques for example by using discretization function on data, creating ranges of values for given decision class for given attribute. There are different algorithms available for creating those, among them LEM2 algorithms, covering algorithms, genetic algorithms and exhaustive algorithms. In this stage of project with yet limited data for analysis best results were acquired using exhaustive algorithm.

Since not all data was complete for patients analyzed during this research some objects appeared with *MISSING* values. In RSES we have possibility to choose how to approach such data, we can:

- fill empty values with most common value for given attribute
- fill empty values with most common value for given decision class
- analyze data without taking into account empty values
- treating missing values as information

3   Results

As described in the Methods section registered and processed MRI/DTI data were put as objects with their attributes in the decision table (see below). Fig. 3 illustrates the DTI tractography generated for whole STN after registration patient's imaging data to the brain atlas. There are placed registered thalamus and electrode on MRI patient's data (Fig. 3). There are many neuronal tracts in this figure showing connections of different cortical areas with STN, but normally DBS electrode activates only a small number of these connections. Which connections are activated it depends on the exact position of the electrode in relationship to the STN. In Fig. 4 is shown an example of the electrode's contact position in STN. The electrode trajectory and electrode's contacts served as points of interest for generating target tracts. Using this approach we were able to determine number of tracts leading to given ROI and use this data in decision table described later in this section. In this project, we have studied effects of the selected contact on both neurological effects and results of our analysis from 3DSlicer. In order to do this we have prepared different data sets as input for RSES and performed different experiments changing sets of parameters in order to determine the most efficient and accurate method.

At the first step, we have selected a single electrode's contact for each patient's scan. In the next step, we have marked characteristic brain structures and areas, which we have used for counting tracts generated with particular stimulation amplitude. It gave us a quantitative relationship between the stimulation amplitude to stimulated region. When this data was gathered we applied RSES to a set of objects organized into decision table, based mainly on neurological and Slicer data (Tab. 1).

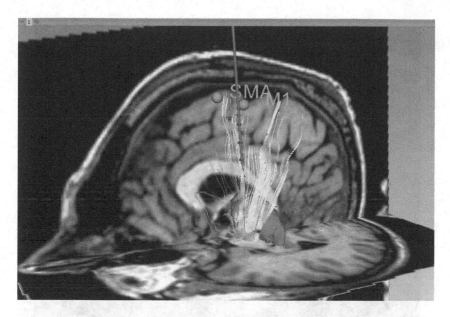

Fig. 3. An example of the tractography that was generated from the whole STN. The thalamus and electrode are marked in dark gray in the sagittal view of the brain. There are put together sagittal (vertical in this figure) and coronal (horizontal) views of the right brain MRIs.

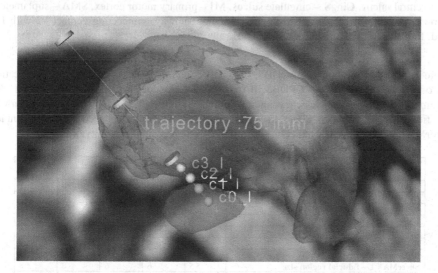

Fig. 4. A sagittal view of MRI registered to anatomical atlas. Two structures are visible in this picture: thalamus as a large structure and under it smaller STN. Electrode's contacts are labeled as c0_l,..., c3_I. The thin line represents trajectory of implanted electrode. In this example, two lower contacts are in STN, and the upper contact is in the thalamus.

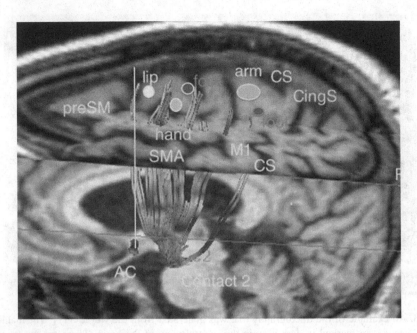

Fig. 5. Above image present ROI classification of patient's brain with marked major brain structures that helped in determining ROI used in our experiments, AC- anterior commiserate, CS – central sulcus, CingS – cingulate sulcus, M1 – primary motor cortex, SMA – suplamentary motor area, preSMA – pre SMA. Notice neural pathways connecting contact #2 with lip, hand, foot areas of SMA, and foot area of M1.

Table 1. A part of the input table. DBS: 0/1 - DBS   on/off; BMT: 0/1 – L-DOPA medication was on/off; UPDRS <code> - UPDRS III/for particular movement; L/R selected - contact L/R; L/R amplitude of contact - selecte contact amplitude for left/right side; SlicerMAX / SlicerMIn L/R fiducial region size – Slicer tractography radius in mm for selected electrode contact; SlicerMAX / SlicerMIn L/R tracts lip – number of tractc reaching proximity of lip ROI.

Patient #	20	10	10	25	25
DBS	0	0	1	0	1
BMT	1	1	1	0	1
UPDRS III	7	13		16	
UPDRS 30 - Postural Stability	3	3		1	
L - selected contact	2	1	1	1.5	1.5
L - amplitude of contact	2.5	2	2	1.5	1.5
R - selected contact	2	1	1	1.5	1.5
R - amplitude of contact	2.5	3.2	3.2	1.5	1.5
SlicerMAX L - fiducial region size	5.5	6	6	8	8
SlicerMAX L - tracts lip	2	20	20	22	22
SlicerMAX R - fiducial region size	5	5	5	8.5	8.5
SlicerMAX R – tracts lip	4	15	15	35	35

Table 2. We have compared statistics for choosing selected contact (the upper table) and selected amplitude(the lower table) for the right side for UPDRS III with all data from slicer. Notice that prediction for selecting proper amplitude was more accurate.

Results of experiments by cross-validation method: PD_slicer_UPDRSIII_minmax_...

Actual		Predicted						
		0.5	2	1	1.5	2.5	No. of obj.	Accuracy
	0.5	0.5	0	0	0	0	0.5	0.5
	2	0	0.75	0	0.25	0	1	0.5
	1	0	0	0.75	0.5	0	1.25	0.5
	1.5	0	0	0.5	0.75	0.5	1.75	0.583
	2.5	0	0	0	0	0.5	0.5	0.5
	True positive rate	0.5	0.5	0.5	0.46	0.33		

```
Total number of tested objects: 5
Total accuracy: 0.65
Total coverage: 1
```

Results of experiments by cross-validation method: PD_slicer_UPDRSIII_minmax_...

Actual		Predicted							
		1	2.5	2	1.5	3.7	2.8	2.2	No. of c
	1	0.5	0	0	0	0	0	0	0.5
	2.5	0	1.25	0	0	0	0	0	1.25
	2	0	0	0.75	0	0	0	0	0.75
	1.5	0	0	0.25	0	0	0.25	0	0.5
	3.7	0	0.25	0	0	0.75	0	0	1
	2.8	0	0	0	0	0	0.5	0	0.5
	2.2	0	0	0	0	0	0.5	0	0.5
	True positive rate	0.5	0.67	0.62	0	0.75	0.5	0	

```
Total number of tested objects: 5
Total accuracy: 0.75
Total coverage: 1
```

In order to get decision rules rows and columns of Table 1 must be exchanged so that measurements of different objects (patients) are in rows and their attributes (measurements results) are in columns. Then we can get equivalent rule to each row, for example the first raw gives:

$$('Pat\#'=20)\&('DBS'=0)\&('BMT'=1)\&('UPDRS\_III'=2)\&('UPDRS\_30'=3)\&...$$
$$\&('SlicerMAX\_region\_size\_L'=5.5)\&('SlicerMAX\_lip\_tracts\_L'=2)\&('SlicerMAX\_r$$
$$egion\_size\_R'=5.5)\&('SlicerMAX\_lip\_tracts\_R'=2)=>'selected\_contact'=2 \qquad (2)$$

In all experiments we used neurological data based on Unified Parkinson Disease Rating Scale (UPDRS). In an early stage of this research we reduced the number of attributes to UPDRS III, which refers to the Motor Examination [16]. For each patient neurological data consists of few series of measurements, containing data set with and without medications or before and after DBS procedure. From interactive DTI label seeding in Slicer we have added parameters for generating tracts for given patient, namely region size, stopping value, number of tracts in proximity of each ROI – lip, foot and hand. In Slicer for each patient we have collected two measurements, first using parameters that allowed us to show only few tracts leading into the ROI, described with tag MIN in our data set and second where number of tracts to the ROI's is close to 30-40, this measurement was tagged as MAX.

Having defined the data set we have performed following case scenarios. In first scenario we used exhaustive algorithm, and split of 60% to 40% of learning to testing part of data set (Tab 2). In the rest of scenarios we used 4 fold cross validation method (Tab 2 and 4).

First we tried to analyze full data set consisting of 53 attributes and 20 objects. For this data set we have conducted studies to choose as decision attribute for each experiment: left contact, left contact amplitude, right contact and right contact amplitude. In cases where there were two contacts involved we use notation 1.5 to mark that both contact 1 and 2 were used in a given case.

Table 3. This are an example results generated for choosing the left contact from data set containing all attributes related to motoric functions of patients. As we can see with this set up we were able to achieve 62.5% of accuracy with full result set coverage.

Results of experiments by train&test method: PD_slicer_UPDRSIII_minmax...

Actual		Predicted					
		0	2	1	No. of obj.	Accuracy	Coverage
	0	0	0	0	0	0	0
	2	0	2	1	3	0.667	1
	1	2	0	3	5	0.6	1
	True positive ...	0	1	0.75			

Total number of tested objects: 8
Total accuracy: 0.625
Total coverage: 1

Other test cases included ability to predict both selected contacts and amplitude chosen for given case based on reduced data set. It included testing for:

- selecting left electrode contact giving only neurological data for right side described by UPDRS like rigidity of right lower extremities, right hand tremor, etc.
- selecting left electrode contact for giving UPDRS III .

Both data sets included as well as previous experiments 20 objects and respectively 32 and 15 attributes. Our preliminary results demonstrated that accuracy of prediction of selected contact is greater in case when we have used UPDRS III with data acquired from Slicer. Moreover it can be further seen that we were able to better predict amplitude for given contact that selecting one.

Table 4. In the upper part are results of predicting selection of left side contact amplitude based on attributes from UPDRS III, and the lower part we have used the only right side specific UPDRS for given disorder to determine the same contact amplitude. Notice an increase in accuracy when attributes and decision parameters were for specific UPDRS.

Results of experiments by cross-validation method: PD_slicer_UPDRSIII_minmax_...

		Predicted							
		1	2.5	2	1.5	3.7	2.8	2.2	No.
Actual	1	0.5	0	0	0	0	0	0	0
	2.5	0	1.25	0	0	0	0	0	1
	2	0	0	0.75	0	0	0	0	0
	1.5	0	0	0.25	0	0	0.25	0	0
	3.7	0	0.25	0	0	0.75	0	0	
	2.8	0	0	0	0	0	0.5	0	0
	2.2	0	0	0	0	0	0.5	0	0
	True positive rate	0.5	0.67	0.62	0	0.75	0.5	0	

Total number of tested objects: 5
Total accuracy: 0.75
Total coverage: 1

Results of experiments by cross-validation method: PD_slicer_UPDRSIII_minmax_c...

		Predicted							
		1	2.5	2	1.5	3.7	2.8	2.2	No. of
Actual	1	0.5	0	0	0	0	0	0	0.5
	2.5	0.25	0.75	0	0.25	0	0	0	1.25
	2	0	0	0.75	0	0	0	0	0.75
	1.5	0	0.25	0	0	0	0.25	0	0.5
	3.7	0	0	0	0	1	0	0	1
	2.8	0	0	0	0	0	0.5	0	0.5
	2.2	0	0	0	0	0	0	0.5	0.5
	True positive rate	0.38	0.5	0.5	0	0.75	0.38	0.5	

Total number of tested objects: 5
Total accuracy: 0.8
Total coverage: 1

4 Conclusions

We have analyzed MRI data of patients who underwent the DBS surgery in order to determine if data mining may help to increase precision of this method. We have applied rough set theory to standard data recorded before and after surgery in order to determine whether we were able to optimize selection of proper stimulating parameters in an individual patient. Our results showed that this approach is more accurate in prediction of used stimulating amplitude for given electrodes than in selecting a contact. We are planning to apply our method to larger population of patients in order to introduce it in the clinical practice.

Acknowledgements. This work was partly supported by Grant DEC-2011/03/B/ST6/03816 from the Polish National Science Centre.

References

1. Aziz, T.Z., Peggs, D., Sambrook, M.A., Crossman, A.R.: Lesion of the subthalamic nucleus for the alleviation of 1-methyl-4-phenyl-1,2,3,6-tetrahydropyridine (MPTP)-induced parkinsonism in the primate. Mov. Disord. Off. J. Mov. Disord. Soc. 6, 288–292 (1991)

2. Langston, J.W., Ballard, P., Tetrud, J.W., Irwin, I.: Chronic Parkinsonism in humans due to a product of meperidine-analog synthesis. Science 219, 979–980 (1983)
3. Plaha, P., Ben-Shlomo, Y., Patel, N.K., Gill, S.S.: Stimulation of the caudal zona incerta is superior to stimulation of the subthalamic nucleus in improving contralateral parkinsonism. Brain 129, 1732–1747 (2006)
4. Limousin, P., Pollak, P., Benazzouz, A., Hoffmann, D., Le Bas, J.-F., Perret, J.E., Benabid, A.-L., Broussolle, E.: Effect on parkinsonian signs and symptoms of bilateral subthalamic nucleus stimulation. The Lancet. 345, 91–95 (1995)
5. Ciecierski, K., Raś, Z.W., Przybyszewski, A.W.: Selection of the Optimal Microelectrode during DBS Surgery in Parkinson's Patients. In: Kryszkiewicz, M., Rybinski, H., Skowron, A., Raś, Z.W. (eds.) ISMIS 2011. LNCS, vol. 6804, pp. 554–564. Springer, Heidelberg (2011)
6. Mallet, L., Schüpbach, M., N'Diaye, K., Remy, P., Bardinet, E., Czernecki, V., Welter, M.-L., Pelissolo, A., Ruberg, M., Agid, Y., Yelnik, J.: Stimulation of subterritories of the sub-thalamic nucleus reveals its role in the integration of the emotional and motor aspects of behavior. Proc. Natl. Acad. Sci. 104, 10661–10666 (2007)
7. Lambert, C., Zrinzo, L., Nagy, Z., Lutti, A., Hariz, M., Foltynie, T., Draganski, B., Ashburner, J., Frackowiak, R.: Confirmation of functional zones within the human subthalamic nucleus: patterns of connectivity and sub-parcellation using diffusion weighted imaging. NeuroImage 60, 83–94 (2012)
8. Tosun, D., Rettmann, M.E., Prince, J.L.: Mapping techniques for aligning sulci across multiple brains. Med. Image Anal. 8, 295–309 (2004)
9. Fischl, B., Sereno, M.I., Tootell, R.B., Dale, A.M.: High-resolution intersubject averaging and a coordinate system for the cortical surface. Hum. Brain Mapp. 8, 272–284 (1999)
10. Lester, H., Arridge, S.R.: A survey of hierarchical non-linear medical image registration. Pattern Recognit. 32, 129–149 (1999)
11. Talos, I.-F., Jakab, M., Kikinis, R., Shenton, M.E.: SPL-PNL Brain Atlas. SPL (2008)
12. Krauth, A., Blanc, R., Poveda, A., Jeanmonod, D., Morel, A., Székely, G.: A mean three-dimensional atlas of the human thalamus: Generation from multiple histological data. NeuroImage 49, 2053–2062 (2010)
13. Cauda, F., Giuliano, G., Federico, D., Sergio, D., Katiuscia, S.: Discovering the somatotopic organization of the motor areas of the medial wall using low-frequency BOLD fluctuations. Hum. Brain Mapp. 32, 1566–1579 (2011)
14. Mayer, A.R., Zimbelman, J.L., Watanabe, Y., Rao, S.M.: Somatotopic organization of the medial wall of the cerebral hemispheres: a 3 Tesla fMRI study. Neuroreport 12, 3811–3814 (2001)
15. Pawlak, Z.: Rough Set Theory and Its Applications to Data Analysis. Cybern. Syst. 29, 661–688 (1998)
16. Movement Disorder Society Task Force on Rating Scales for Parkinson's Disease: The Unified Parkinson's Disease Rating Scale (UPDRS): status and recommendations. Mov. Disord. Off. J. Mov. Disord. Soc. 18, 738–750 (2003)

Morphometric Basis of Depression in Parkinson's Disease and the Possibility of Its Prediction

Aleksandr Efimtsev, Vladimir Fokin, Andrei Sokolov,
Leonid Voronkov, and Artem Trufanov

Military Medical Academy, Radiology Department, Saint-Petersburg, Russian Federation
{atralf,vladfokin,falcon,saloforever}@mail.ru,
trufanovart@gmail.com

Abstract. One of the most common variants of mood disorders is depression. According to various authors, the incidence of depression in the population is 3-10 %, in Parkinson's disease (PD) – 40-50 % of patients. Most researchers are considering depression in PD as endogenous and finds it to be an important and independent component of the disease manifestations. We examined 49 patients with PD complicated by depression. All patients underwent MRI followed by postprocessing using FreeSurfer (http://surfer.nmr.mgh.harvard.edu). When depression occurs it affects lingual area, parahippocampal areas on both sides and straight gyrus. Regression analysis showed a predominant involvement of the frontal and temporal brain lobes. Prognostically three most important areas involved in the formation of depression were revealed - right and left parahippocampal area and the average occipital-temporal sulcus. The risk of depression manifestation, against the background of left parahippocampal cortex thinning at rates below 2,597 mm, increases 46.8 times.

Keywords: Parkinson's disease, depression, MRI, voxel based morphometry.

1 Introduction

There are motorized and non-motorized isolated symptoms of Parkinson's disease (PD). Motor symptoms include hypokinesia, rigidity, resting tremor and postural instability in the later stages of the drug attached dyskinesias and motor fluctuations. Non-motor symptoms in PD are autonomic disorders, affective (anxiety, depression) and psychotic disorders (nightmares, hallucinations, illusions, and, rarely, delusions) and sleep disorders [2,3].

One of the most common types of mood disorders is depression. According to various authors, frequency of depression in the population is 3-10 %, while in the PD patients it occurs in 40-50 % of cases (avg.) [4].

Depression – is mental disorder that significantly impacts social adjustment and quality of life, characterized by abnormally low mood with a pessimistic assessment of themselves and their position in reality, inhibition of intellectual and motor activity, reduced motivation [1].

D. Ślęzak et al. (Eds.): BIH 2014, LNAI 8609, pp. 357–365, 2014.

Depression in PD may be of endogenous and exogenous origin. Endogenous depression is associated with a deficit of monoamines to the specific disease; exogenous depression is associated with the patient's response to steadily progressive chronic disease. However, most researchers currently understand depression in PD as endogenous and considers it an important and independent component of disease manifestations. This view is supported by several facts: first – in 15-25 % of cases depression occurs before the motor symptoms, often for a year, and second – depression accompanies PD more often than other chronic physical and neurological pathologies that lead to comparable disability, and the third – depression does not usually correlate with the severity of PD [7,8]. Moreover, the presence of depression is an independent risk factor for PD [11].

Depression in PD is associated with physiological changes in brain metabolism. Perhaps the lack of dopamine production plays a role in emotion regulation disorder. Moreover, impaired noradrenalin and serotonin output might play significant role [1], [20].

Depression in PD is explained by frontostrial dysfunction, with a key role in its development being withdrawn to caudate nuclei involvement into pathological process. Mesocorticolimbic and serotonergic systems, that modulate frontostrial and limbic structures state, may play important role in PD pathogenesis [12], [15]. It is believed that dysfunction of serotoninergic system is responsible for anxiety and aggression occurrence in PD patients with depression [17].

Depression can occur at any stage of PD, but often it (30 %) precedes first clinical motor manifestations (like hypokinesia, rigidity, resting tremor) [19]. In general most patients with PD severity of depressive symptoms can be mild or moderate and meets the criteria of "minor depression" or "dysthymia". Only in 3-8 % of patients depression is severe and reaches the level of a psychotic [3], but it usually does not end with suicide attempts [7].

For depression diagnostics in PD they usually use focused and careful questioning basing on special scales (Hamilton Depression Rating Scale, Beck, Montgomery - Berg et al.) It has been suggested that prolonged PD treatment with levodopa is likely to cause depression, possibly due to the influence of DOPA - containing drugs on serotonin metabolism [6].

Depression in PD does not depend on age, duration and severity of illness or cognitive impairment. Maximum frequency of depression is observed in patients with stage 1 by Hoen/Yahr, then it is being reduced by two steps, re- increases in step 3-4, and finally reduced in patients with stage 5. The incidence of depression is higher with the debut of the disease at a younger age (under 55 years) and akinetic - rigid form of PD in female patients, and at fast temp of disease progression [9].

According to various authors, depressive symptoms in PD impair the quality of life to a greater extent than the severity of motor disorders [21]. Depression in PD affects activities of daily living, quality of life, reduces patient compliance (willingness to carry a doctor's prescription), aggravates the course of the underlying disease, often turnes to be a risk factor for dementia in PD. In addition, depression in PD patients significantly impairs the quality of life for families living with the patient or care for him [18].

In 2008, American and Hungarian researchers have published a joint work of voxel- based morphometry in patients with Parkinson's disease complicated by depression [10]. The study included 23 patients with depression and 27 without it. The analysis showed an inverse score proportion according to MADRS depression scale and severity of morphological changes in the right medial temporal gyrus, anterior and medial cingulate gyri, and the parahippocampal gyrus. Researchers have found that depression in Parkinson's disease is associated with orbitofrontal, right temporal region and limbic system volume decrease.

In 2010, a group of Dutch scientists have performed a study to compare the severity of depressive disorders in PD with brain gray matter volume indicators [16]. Totally 53 patients were included. It has been shown that the severity of apathy was associated with decrease of gray matter in several areas of the cerebral cortex: precentral gyrus, inferior parietal gyrus and inferior frontal gyrus on both sides, cingulate gyrus, and right precuneus. Cingulum and the inferior frontal gyrus involvement corresponded to the results of earlier studies on depression in patients with Alzheimer's disease. In the same year, and then in 2011, these data were confirmed by their Serbian colleagues [13 ,14].

However, to date the estimate is not the thickness of the cerebral cortex in depression in patients with PD and no attempts were made to identify prognostically important parameters that may be allowed to predict the development of depressive disorders in these patients.

The goal of this study was thickness determination of the morphometric characteristics of the cerebral cortex in Parkinson's disease complicated by depression and to establish their prognostic significance.

2   Materials and Methods

Total we examined 49 patients with idiopathic Parkinson's disease, according to the British Brain Bank criteria. [4] The study included patients with stage 3 by Hoen/Yahr, 31 patients had an akinetic -rigid form of the disease (63.3 %), others had a mixed form of PD (36.7%). Assessment of mental function was carried out using Beck Depression questionnaire. The main group consisted of patients with a total score greater than 16 (29 patients), which corresponded to the depression of moderate severity and higher. The control group were patients with PD with a total score of less than 9, what means – there was no depression (20 patients). General characteristics of the patients are presented in Table 1.

Table 1. General patients characteristics

Patients groups	Number of patients	Age, avg.	Beck score	Disease duration
Depression	29	62,7±6,3	19,3±2,7	6,3±3,3
No depression	20	58,4±8,1	5,5±2,7	5,2±3,6

The examination consisted of a clinical evaluation of patients with disease staging, MR imaging (Siemens 1.5T), obtaining T1-WI , T2-WI, coronal, axial sagittal slices. Additionally T1 MPRAGE was obtained and postprocessed using FreeSurfer software. 243 were subjected to statistical analysis of right and left hemispheres brain structures. Correlations were calculated using Spearman's test. Data processing was performed using Statistica 8.0 of package StatSoft using Mann-Whitney test.

3   Results

We have identified significant differences in cortical thickness in both left and right hemispheres (Table 2,3)

Table 2. Cortical thickness differences (mm) in left hemisphere between patients with and without depression (M - median ; LQ - lower quartel, UQ - top quartel)

Localization	Depression (Beck>16) M [LQ;UQ]	No depression (Beck<9) M [LQ;UQ]	p-value
Parahippocampal area	2,465 [2,265;2,559]	2,824 [2,493;3,046]	0,0393
G. frontalis inferior orbitalis	2,449 [2,257;2,506]	2,736 [2,449;2,871]	0,0492
G. temporalis superior, part polaris	3,232 [3,155;3,367]	3,592 [3,409;3,744]	0,0245
G. temporalis superior, part temporalis	2,100 [2,065;2,163]	2,388 [2,257;2,527]	0,0148
S. occipitalis medial temporalis, part Lingualis	1,913 [1,882;1,968]	2,109 [1,962;2,241]	0,0192

Table 3. Cortical thickness differences (mm) in right hemisphere between patients with and without depression (M - median ; LQ - lower quartel, UQ - top quartel)

Localization	Depression (Beck>16) M [LQ;UQ]	No depression (Beck<9) M [LQ;UQ]	p-value
Parahippocampal area	2,395 [2,321;2,466]	2,649 [2,582;2,775]	0,0087
G. occipitalis medial temporalis, part parahippocampalis	2,879 [2,782;3,132]	3,244 [3,115;3,332]	0,0245
G. rectus	2,033 [1,926;2,348]	2,333 [2,252;2,396]	0,0236
S. occipitalis medial temporalis, part Lingualis	1,816 [1,778;1,889]	2,054 [1,957;2,208]	0,0148

After statistical analysis we performed graphical processing for visual confirmation (Fig. 1, 2).

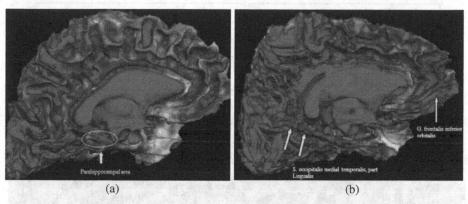

(a)   (b)

Fig. 1. Medial surface of cerebral hemisphere with the most important areas involved in the pathogenesis of depression in PD (a – patients with depression, b – patients without depression).

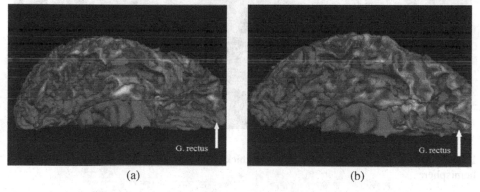

(a)   (b)

Fig. 2. Caudal surface of cerebral hemisphere with the most important areas involved in the pathogenesis of depression in PD (a – patients with depression, b – patients without depression)

Table 4. Correlation of cortical thickness and BDI points in the left hemisphere of depressed patients ($p < 0,05$)

Localization	L
Lingual area	-0,703
G. occipital-temporal medial, part Lingualis	-0,729
S. occipitalis anterior	-0,657
S. temporalis inferior	-0,735
Broadman area VI	-0,637

Table 5. Correlation of cortical thickness and BDI points in the right hemisphere of depressed patients (p <0,05)

Localization	R
Lingual area	-0,709
Pericalcarine area	-0,683
S. calcarinus	-0,644
S. occipitalis middle and Lunatus	-0, 762
S. orbitalis lateralis	-0,716
Broadman area VI	-0,755

Graphical representation of cortical thickness on the degree of depression in PD dependence was formed using the regression coefficient (Fig.3).

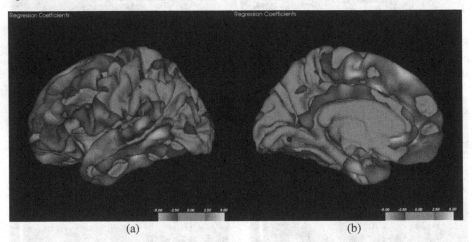

(a)   (b)

Fig. 3. Regression dependence of cortical thickness on the severity of depression in left hemisphere

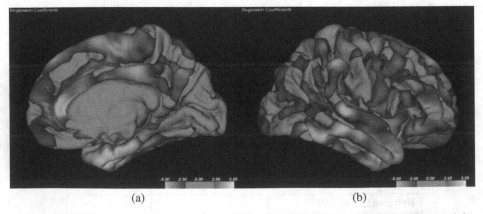

(a)   (b)

Fig. 4. Regression dependence of cortical thickness on the severity of depression in right hemisphere

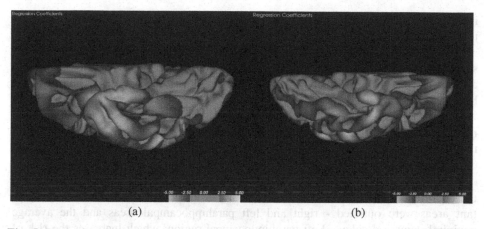

(a) (b)

Fig. 5. Regression dependence of cortical thickness on the severity of depression in temporal lobes of right and left hemispheres (a – right hemisphere, b – left hemisphere)

To determine the risk of depression occurance depending on cortical thickness in most important, outlined above, zones odds ratio was calculated (Table 6). Median was used as critical values.

Table 6. The odds ratio for depression in patients with PD, depending on the thickness of the cerebral cortex

Brain structure	Critical value (median, mm)	Odds ratio (OR)	95% confidence interval (CI)
Left parahippacampal area	2,597	46,8	11,14-106,1
Right parahippacampal area	2,395	9,1	1,77-46,77
S. occipital-temporal medial – part Lingualis	1,913	9,6	1,89-49,33

4   Discussion

Our data indicate the presence of a relatively small number of structures involved in the pathogenesis of depression in PD patients. First of all, you should pay attention to the lesions of lingual area and some of its components, in particular S. occipital-temporal medial, pars Lingualis, which has significantly reduced thickness of cortical layer in both hemispheres. In addition, we observed strong negative correlation between lingual cortical areas on both sides and total BDI points. The combination of these facts allows to use lingual cortex thickness of the middle occipital- temporal sulcus as a predictor of depression in PD patients.

The results reflect not only clinical syndrome of dementia in PD, but also the existing morphological component. This is shown in parahippocampal regions lesions on both sides and connection of the main structures that are affected in PD depression, that is, lingual region of the middle occipital- temporal sulcus, and the main structure involved in the formation of dementia - the lingual region of the middle occipital-temporal gyrus [5].

An interesting fact is straight gyrus lesion, which was also found by Bulgarian researchers. The function of this structure is not currently established yet, so, taking into account the data from both studies, we can assume that it participates in human mood background formation.

Taking into account performed regression analysis, we can say that depression mainly affects the structures of frontal and temporal lobes. The most important of these structures have significant differences from the control group and a negative correlation with the BDI.

One of the most important aspects of the study was to identify markers predicting the occurrence of depression in patients with Parkinson's disease. Three most important areas were outlined - right and left parahippocampal areas and the average occipital- temporal sulcus. Left parahippocampal region, which increases the risk of depression in patients (46,8%) with cortical thinning below 2,597 mm, represents the greatest value.

This work not only confirms the data obtained by foreign researchers, but also reveals new evidence of brain damage in PD patients with depression. Considering the ongoing debate about the nature of depression in Parkinson's disease, it is worth saying that our study confirms the endogenous cause of this complication. Besides, we obtained new tools for prediction of this complication development and, as a result, it becomes possible to monitor patients more carefully and administer appropriate therapy in time.

References

1. Vein, A.M., Voznesenskaya, T.G., Golubev, V.L., Duykova, G.M.: Depression in neurological practice. M., p. 126 (1998)
2. Glozman, J.M., Schtock, V.M., Saltykova, N.M., Fedorova, N.V.: Clinical psychological assessment of depression in parkinsonism.Vestnik MGU. Psycology, 29–36 (1995)
3. Golubev, V.L.: Depression and parkinsonism. M., pp. 1–3 (2000)
4. Smulevich, A.B.: 4r4rDepression: clinics and system in patients. RMM (2), 10–15 (1998)
5. Trufanov, A.G., Litvinenko, I.V., Voronkov, L.V.: Depression in Parkinson Disease: cortical atrophy and prognostic possibilities using MRI. Vestnin of Russian MMA 3(39), 116–122 (2012)
6. Aarsland, D., Larsen, J.P., Karlsen, K., et al.: Mental symptoms in Parkinson's disease are important contributors tu caregiver distress. Int. J. Geriatr. Psychiatry 14, 866–874 (1999)
7. Brooks, D.J., Doder, M.: Depression in Parkinson's disease. Curr. Opin. Neurol. 14, 456–470 (2001)
8. Burn, D.J.: Depression in Parkinson's disease. Eur. J. Neurol. (suppl. 3), 44–54 (2002)
9. Dooneief, G., Mirabello, E., Bell, K., et al.: An estimate of the incidence of depression in idiopathic Parkinson's disease. Arch. Neurol. 49, 305–307 (1992)
10. Feldmann, A.: Morphometric changes of gray matter in Parkinson's disease with depression: a voxel-based morphometry study. Mov. Disord. 23(1), 42–46 (2008)
11. Hubble, J.P., Cao, T., Hassanein, R.E., et al.: Risk Factors for Parkinson's disease. Neurology 43, 1693–1697 (1993)

12. Mayberg, H.S., Brannan, S.K., Jerabek, P.A., et al.: Cingulate function in depression: a potential predictor of treatment response. Neuroreport 8, 1057–1061 (1997)
13. Kostić, V.S.: Regional patterns of brain tissue loss associated with depression in Parkinson disease. Neurology 75(10), 857–863 (2010); Epub August 4, 2010
14. Kostić, V.S., Filippi, M.: Neuroanatomical correlates of depression and apathy in Parkinson's disease: magnetic resonance imaging studies. J. Neurol. Sci. 310(1-2), 61–63 (2011)
15. Mayeux, R., Stern, Y., Williams, J.B., et al.: Clinical and biochemical features of depression in Parkinson's disease. Am. J. Psychiatry 143, 756–759 (1986)
16. Reijnders, J.S.: Neuroanatomical correlates of apathy in Parkinson's disease: A magnetic resonance imaging study using voxel-based morphometry. Mov. Disord. 25(14), 2318–2325 (2010)
17. Richard, I.H., Schiffer, R.B., Kurlan, R.: Anxiety and Parkinson's disease. J. Neuropsychiatry Clin. Neurosci. 8, 383–392 (1996)
18. Schrag, A.: Depression in Parkinson's disease. In: Abstracts of the 4th International Scientific Symposium, Italy, pp. 56–57 (2005)
19. Starkstein, S.E., Berthier, M.L., Bolduc, P.L., et al.: Depression in patients with early versus late onset of Parkinson's disease. Neurology 39, 1441–1445 (1989)
20. Starkstein, S.E., Preziosi, T.J., Bolduc, P.L., Robinson, R.G.: Depression in Parkinson's disease. J. Nerv. Mental Dis. 178, 27–31 (1990)
21. Starkstein, S.E., Mayberg, H.S., Leiguarda, R., et al.: A prospective longitudinal stady of de-pression, cognitive decline, and physical impairments in patients with Parkinson's disease. J. NeurolNeurosurg Psychiatry 55, 377–382 (1992)

An Approach to Detect Negation
on Medical Documents in Spanish

Roberto Costumero[1], Federico Lopez[2], Consuelo Gonzalo-Martín[1],
Marta Millan[2], and Ernestina Menasalvas[1]

[1] Universidad Politécnica de Madrid - Centro de Tecnología Biomédica,
Madrid, Spain
{roberto.costumero,consuelo.gonzalo,ernestina.menasalvas}@upm.es
[2] Universidad del Valle, Colombia
{federico.lopez,marta.millan}@correounivalle.edu.co

Abstract. The adoption of hospital EHR technology is significantly
growing and expected to grow. Digitalized information is the basis for
health analytics. In particular, patient medical records contain valuable
clinical information written in narrative form that can only be extracted
after it has been previously preprocessed with Natural Language Processing techniques. An important challenge in clinical narrative text is
that concepts commonly appear negated. Though worldwide there are
nearly 500 million Spanish speakers, there seems to be no algorithm for
negation detection in medical texts written in that language.

Thus this paper presents an approach to adapt the NegEx algorithm
to be applied to detect negation regarding clinical conditions in Spanish
written medical documents. Our algorithm has been trained with 500
texts where 422 different sentences and 267 unique clinical conditions
were identified. It has been tested for negated terms showing an accuracy
obtained is of 83,37%. As in the detection of definite affirmed conditions,
the results show an accuracy of 84,78%.

Keywords: Natural Language Processing, Negation Detection, Medical
texts.

1 Introduction

Health data analytics highly relies on the availability of Electronic Health Records
(EHRs). The adoption of hospital EHR technology is significantly growing and
is expected to continue growing. While one third of the US hospitals (35%) had
already implemented some kind of EHR technology in 2011, it is expected that
by 2016 nearly every US hospital (95%) will use EHR technology.

EHR contains both structured and not structured information such as: the
patient's medical history, diagnoses, medications, treatment plans, immunization
dates, allergies, radiology images, and laboratory and test results. This information is being collected and managed by a health care provider or organization.
Analysis of this information can make it possible to develop evidence-based decision making tools that providers can use to improve patient's care.

D. Ślęzak et al. (Eds.): BIH 2014, LNAI 8609, pp. 366–375, 2014.

However technology for health care data analysis is not mature enough due to, among other reasons, a lack of standards, interoperable data schemas and natural text and image processing tools. In particular in this paper we focus on natural text processing.

Patient medical records contain valuable clinical information written in narrative form. Thus, in order to find relevant information it is often necessary to extract it from free-texts in order to support clinical and research processes. An important feature of the clinical narrative text is that it commonly encloses negation concepts. According to Chapman et al. [1], around half of all clinical conditions in narrative reports are negated.

Several systems and methods have been proposed for negation detection [1], [2], [3], [4], [5] [6], [7], [8], [9], [10], [11], [12].

NegEx is introduced in [2] to identify negation terms. In order to identify negated finding and diseases, NegEx algorithm uses regular expressions to determine the scope of trigger terms. A clinical condition is marked as negated whether within the scope of a trigger term. NegEx was applied to selected sentences from discharge summaries with a 94.5% specificity, 84.5% precision and 78% sensivity.

In [1], NegEx' performance is analyzed taking into account different kinds of clinical reports. The study uses three types of negation phrases: pre-UMLS, post-UMLS and pseudo-negation. Negation phrases were extracted from previous analysis of NegEx on discharge summaries, a system called SymText and also negation phrases were added by the authors. NegEx obtained an average precision of 97%. However, precision ranged from 84% to 19% depending on the section of the pathology report.

Recently, challenges in translation of negation triggers from English negation lexicon (NegEx) to Swedish, French and German have been analyzed in [3]. OWL and RDF multilingual lexicon version were developed based on an extended NegEx version proposed in [4].

Elkin et al. [5] introduce a method based on NegEx to identify the scope of the negation trigger. The method is applied to small segments generated by isolating sentences from health records. Precision and recall values of 91.2% and 97.2%, were respectively obtained.

The extended NegEx version, called ConText [4], is based on regular expressions and helps to determine whether a clinical condition not only is negated, but also if it is hypothetical, historical or experienced by someone other than the patient. To do this, several contextual properties (hypothetical, historical or the experiencer) are taken into account to modify clinical conditions.

In [6] Negfinder, a program to identify negated patterns present in medical documents, is described. Documents are preprocessed replacing a concept by its UMLS concept ID. Then, negations are distinguished and grammar rules are used to associate them with single or multiples concepts preceding or succeeding them. The sensivity and specificity obtained from evaluation when Negfinder was applied to medical documents to detect negations were between 91% and 96%.

A hybrid approach was proposed in [7]. The approach combines regular expression matching with grammatical parsing to automatically detect negations in radiology reports. Negated phrases were identified with sensitivity and precision values of 92.6% and 98.6%, respectively.

Skeppstedt [8], [9], [13] adapted the English rule-based negation detection system, NegEx to Swedish. The results [8] showed lower precision and recall values than results obtained for the English version. In [9], NegEx system adapted to Swedish is analyzed to a subset of free-text entries from the Stockholm EPR corpus. Particularly, the study has been centered in SNOMED CT terms having the semantic categories 'finding' or 'disorder'. Recently, in [14] Swedish health records are studied emphasizing the analysis on four entities: Disorder, Finding, Pharmaceutical Drug and Body Structure. The study investigated how well named entity recognition methods work on clinical texts written in Swedish and whether to divide the Medical Problem category into more specific entities could be meaningful.

On the other hand, several methods based on machine learning techniques have been proposed [10], [11], [12]. A machine learning system, consisting of two classifiers to determine the scope of negation in biomedical texts, is introduced in [10]. The classifiers determine if the tokens in a sentence are negation signals and find the full scope of these negation phrases. An error reduction of 32.07% w.r.t similar systems was obtained [11] in different text types.

In [12] a pattern learning method is proposed in order to automatically identify negations in medical narrative texts. According to the authors, the accuracy is improved with respect to other methods based on a machine learning approach. Four steps integrate the method: corpus preparation, regular expression pattern learning, patterns selection and classifier training.

Though there are 500 million Spanish speakers worldwide (According to [15]) as far as our knowledge there is no learning method for negation detection in medical text written in Spanish.

Thus in this paper we present an approach to adapt the NegEx algorithm to be applied to detect negation regarding diseases in Spanish written medical documents. The paper contributions are as follows: i) a list of terms for Spanish is compiled from clinical reports containing those terms that identify negation; ii) the frequency of the terms has been calculated on a corpus to compare the values to the corresponding ones in English for which the analysis has already been performed; iii) an implementation of the NegEx algorithm for Spanish and iv) the evaluation of the algorithm with Spanish texts.

The rest of the paper has been organized as follows: in section 2 we present the adaptation of the method proposed by [3] to work with Spanish texts. In this section we also present the list of terms that have been identified in Spanish as triggers for negation. In section 3 we present the results of applying the implementation of our approach over 500 medical texts, containing 422 different sentences and 267 unique clinical conditions. To end with, section 4 presents the main conclusions obtained so far as well as the future lines of development.

2   Method

In this section we present the approach we have followed to adapt NegEx algorithm for Spanish texts. The approach we present is similar to the one presented in [3].

In order to do so the processes depicted in figure 1 have been performed:

1. **Medical texts annotation.** Several medical texts have been manually annotated to detect situations in which terms appear to be negated.
2. **Labelling of terms.** The terms from NegEx are extracted and translated into Spanish. The list of terms is enriched with those that have been previously detected in the annotated medical texts and known synonyms.
3. **Frequency calculation.** Using a corpus the frequency of negated terms is calculated to categorize them according to their appearance (frequency). This makes it possible to compare the most frequently used terms in Spanish in comparison to those in English.
4. **Evaluation.** The NegEx algorithm is adapted to Spanish using the list of terms previously categorized and evaluated with a set of real clininal texts.

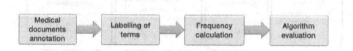

Fig. 1. Steps of the approach

In the following sections we detail these processes.

2.1   Medical Documents Annotation

In order to be able to detect negation, one of the requirements of the algorithm is to have a Gold Standard or a corpus of Spanish expressions. This is the first problem to be overcome as there is not such standard for Spanish texts. Consequently, the first step is to build such a corpus. The result of this process will be a set of annotated sentences to act as Gold Standard to test the performance of the negation detection algorithm.

2.2   Labelling of Terms

Another required process is to generate the translation to Spanish of the concepts found in the original NegEx lexicon as negation terms (see an example in table 1). Next, the lexicon has to be enriched with synonyms and clinical related common phrases in Spanish. Translation was done by a team composed by Computer Science Researchers, Physicians and Computational Linguists experts. It is interesting to note that not only terms used in [2] were translated but also the terms of the lexicon in the implementation of ConText [4] were translated.

Table 1. Example of translated terms

Term in English	Term in Spanish
can be ruled out	se puede descartar
can rule him out	
can rule out	
no, not	no
no evidence	sin evidencia
	no evidencia
no new	sin novedad
no support for	no hay soporte para
no suspicion of	ninguna sospecha de

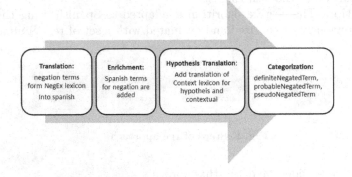

Fig. 2. Phases of the labelling process

According to [3], each translated term is assigned a certain category: i) Definite Negated Term, ii) Probable Negated Term, iii) Pseudo Negated Term.

This process of terms labelling is depicted in figure 2 and includes the depicted steps.

2.3 Frequency Calculation

Once all the sentences of the corpus are categorized, the frequency of each term of the lexicon on the corpus is calculated. The median value of the frequency for each term is also calculated and then the terms are categorized as follows:

- **No appearance:** For those terms with frequency equal to zero.
- **Infrequent:** Used to categorize those terms which frequency is greater than zero but lesser than the median value.
- **Frequent:** Those terms that appear with frequencies higher than the median value.

2.4 Evaluation

In order to validate the Spanish approach for negation detection a test dataset composed by pieces of previously (manually) annotated text written in Spanish is required. The testing corpus was generated by spliting into sentences the texts in the corpus previously described. This sentences were indexed using Apache Lucene [16]. For the indexing process the ICD-10 standard [17] is used to identify the sentences with an underlying clinical condition. After this process was completed, the set of sentences selected is manually annotated. Then the performance of the algorithm will be tested on the set of testing examples and results are shown. It is important noting that the NegEx algorithm has not been changed in its essence and only the terms used as triggers have been changed. Our aim is to show that due to the different structure of spanish language in comparison to that of english the performance of the algorithm should not be too high and consequently extensions of NegEx to deal with the morpho-sintatic struture of spanish is required to improve results. In what follows we present the results of applying the process in a set of selected texts.

3 Results

The Spanish approach has been programmed in Java, and it has been tested using 500 reports obtained from SciELO [18] as input corpus. In the extraction process the entitled sections: "Reporte de caso" (Case report), "A proposito de un caso" (About a case), "Caso clinico" (Clinical case) and similar ones were used. The resulting corpus is composed of 1,164,712 words, 65,605 out of which are different words.

In order to validate the approach the calculation of the frequency of terms for negation in Spanish texts has been performed to compare the obtained frequencies with those reported in the literature for English. In what follows we present the results obtained, in detail.

3.1 Frequency of Terms in Spanish

The frequencies shown in this section were calculated using the algorithm presented in Section 2.3. The results of the application of this algorithm are presented in the following section.

3.2 Lexical Analysis

Tables 2, 3 and 4 show the relative frequencies for terms both in Spanish and English which demonstrate Definite Negated Existence, Probable Negated Existence and Pseudo Negated Existence, respectively.

Note that the frequencies for frequent Definite and Probable Negated terms are higher in Spanish, whether Pseudo Negated terms are more frequent in English. Generally speaking, infrequent terms perform similarly in both languages,

Table 2. Definite Negated Terms frequencies in Spanish and English

Spanish (58)			English (60)		
Frequent	Infrequent	No appearance	Frequent	Infrequent	No appearance
14	20	23	4	24	32

Table 3. Probable Negated Terms frequencies in Spanish and English

Spanish (50)			English (78)		
Frequent	Infrequent	No appearance	Frequent	Infrequent	No appearance
4	17	29	3	37	38

Table 4. Pseudo Negated Terms frequencies in Spanish and English

Spanish (18)			English (16)		
Frequent	Infrequent	No appearance	Frequent	Infrequent	No appearance
1	13	4	2	13	1

though Probable and Pseudo Negated Terms appear more frequently in English (see table 5). It is important to note that some of the terms that were obtained in the labelling process do not appear in the corpus that has been used for testing and evaluating the algorithm which may affect the quality of the results.

3.3   Validation of NegEx implementation for Spanish

The Spanish version has been tested with 500 reports where we have identified 422 different sentences and 267 unique clinical conditions. Our experiments show the following performance values: A precision of 49.47%, a recall of 55.70% and a F-Measure of 52.38% were obtained when using the Definite Negated terms as the positive set in the classification task. This process also showed an accuracy of 83.37%. When the Definite Existence terms were used as the positive set, a precision of 86.86%, a recall of 95.2% and a F-Measure of 90.84% were obtained. In this case, the accuracy is similar to the previous one with a value of 84.78%.

We observed that the number of False Positives is high and that makes the precision of the algorithm to go very low for the cases specially of negation detection. The reason behind this result was expected as we firstly showed as the structure of Spanish differs from that of English and the rules implemented to calculate the scope of negation in English not always agrees with those to analyze negation in Spanish. Consequently, future research will be done in order to adapt Negex not only by translating triggering terms but also by adding rules after a deeper analysis of the negation process in Spanish grammar.

Table 5. Comparison of frequencies in Spanish and English

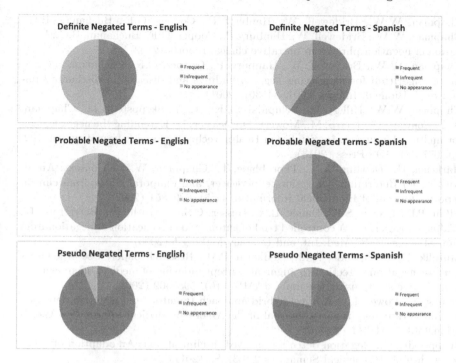

4   Conclusions

In this paper we have presented an adaptation of the NegEx algorithm to be used for clinical texts written in Spanish. First, a list of terms has been identified both from the translation of those identified previoulsy in NegEx and later enriched with synonyms and terms from manual annotation of medical texts in Spanish. Second, the frequency of terms in Spanish has been calculated and compared to that of the terms in English. The differences in frequencies of the terms in both languages suggests that the corpus can be biased an should be enlarged to contain appearances of those terms that do not appear. Finally, an implementation of NegEx algorithm adapted for Spanish has been evaluated and values of accurary and recall sugest that the results can yet be improved if the scope is properly adapted. On the other hand some of the terms that were identified as negated terms did not appear in the corpus that has been used suggesting also that the corpus has to be enlarged to contain all the possible negated terms. Thus as future work we propose to generate an improved version of the Spanish corpus and to annotate more sentences to be used for evaluation with a new implementation of the algorithm. Besides as it has also been mentioned, improvement of NegEx with rules that govern the negation process in spanish should improve results obtained so far.

References

1. Chapman, W.W., Bridewell, W., Hanbury, P., Cooper, G.F., Buchanan, B.G., Chapman, W.W., Bridewell, W., Hanbury, P., Cooper, G.F., Buchanan, B.G.: Evaluation of negation phrases in narrative clinical reports (2002)
2. Chapman, W.W., Bridewell, W., Hanbury, P., Cooper, G.F., Buchanan, B.G.: A simple algorithm for identifying negated findings and diseases in discharge summaries. J. Biomed. Inform. 2001, 34–301 (2001)
3. Chapman, W.W., Hillert, D., Velupillai, S., Kvist, M., Skeppstedt, M., Chapman, B.E., Conway, M., Tharp, M., Mowery, D., Deleger, L.: Extending the negex lexicon for multiple languages. In: Studies in Health Technology and Informatics, vol. 192, pp. 677–681. IOS Press (2013)
4. Harkema, H., Dowling, J.N., Thornblade, T., Chapman, W.W.: Context: An algorithm for determining negation, experiencer, and temporal status from clinical reports. Journal of Biomedical Informatics 42(5), 839–851 (2009)
5. Elkin, P.L., Brown, S.H., Bauer, B.A., Husser, C.S., Carruth, W., Bergstrom, L., Wahner-Roedler, D.: A controlled trial of automated classification of negation from clinical notes. BMC Med. Inf. and Decision Making 5 (2005)
6. Mutalik, P., Deshpande, A.M., Nadkarni, P.M.: Research paper: Use of general-purpose negation detection to augment concept indexing of medical documents: A quantitative study using the umls. JAMIA 8(6), 598–609 (2001)
7. Huang, Y., Lowe, H.J.: A novel hybrid approach to automated negation detection in clinical radiology reports. Journal of the American Medical Informatics Association 14(3), 304–311 (2007)
8. Skeppstedt, M.: Negation detection in swedish clinical text: An adaption of negex to swedish. J. Biomedical Semantics 2(S-3), S3 (2011)
9. Skeppstedt, M., Dalianis, H., Nilsson, G.H.: Retrieving disorders and findings: Results using snomed ct and negex adapted for swedish. In: LOUHI 2011 Health Document Text Mining and Information Analysis 2011: Proceedings of LOUHI 2011 Third International Workshop on Health Document Text Mining and Information Analysis Bled, Slovenia, vol. (744), pp. 11–17 (2011)
10. Morante, R., Liekens, A., Daelemans, W.: Learning the scope of negation in biomedical texts. In: Proceedings of the Conference on Empirical Methods in Natural Language Processing, EMNLP 2008, pp. 715–724 (2008)
11. Morante, R., Daelemans, W.: A metalearning approach to processing the scope of negation. In: Proceedings of the Thirteenth Conference on Computational Natural Language Learning, CoNLL 2009, pp. 21–29. Association for Computational Linguistics (2009)
12. Rokach, L., Romano, R., Maimon, O.: Negation recognition in medical narrative reports. Inf. Retr. 11(6), 499–538 (2008)
13. Skeppstedt, M.: Negation detection in swedish clinical text. In: Proceedings NAACL HLT Second Louhi Workshop on Text and Data Mining of Health Documents, pp. 53–60 (2010)
14. Nilsson, G.H., Dalianis, H., Skeppstedt, M., Kvist, M.: Automatic recognition of disorders, findings, pharmaceuticals and body structures from clinical text: An annotation and machine learning study. Journal of Biomedical Informatics (in press, 2014)

15. Instituto Cervantes. Electronic references (2013)
16. The Apache Foundation. Lucene. Programa de Computador (March 2000)
17. World Health Organization. International Statistical Classification of Diseases and Related Health Problems, 10th Revision. Version for 2006, ICD-10 (2006)
18. Packer, A.L.: Scielo - an electronic publishing model for developing countries. In: Smith, J., Ardö, A., Linde, P. (eds.) ELPUB. ICCC Press, Washington, DC (1999)

Are Some Brain Injury Patients Improving More Than Others?

Zaigham Faraz Siddiqui[1], Georg Krempl[1], Myra Spiliopoulou[1],
Jose M. Peña[2], Nuria Paul[3], and Fernando Maestu[4]

[1] Otto-von-Guericke University Magdeburg, Germany
{siddiqui,krempl,myra}@iti.cs.uni-magdeburg.de
[2] Technical University of Madrid, Spain
jmpena@fi.upm.es
[3] Complutense University of Madrid, Spain
jpaul68@hotmail.com
[4] Complutense & Technical University of Madrid, Spain
fernando.maestu@ctb.upm.es

Abstract. Predicting the evolution of individuals is a rather new mining task with applications in medicine. Medical researchers are interested in the progress of a disease and in the evolution of individuals subjected to treatment. We investigate the evolution of patients on the basis of medical tests before and during treatment after brain trauma: we want to understand how similar patients *can* become to healthy participants. We face two challenges. First, we have less information on healthy participants than on the patients. Second, the values of the medical tests for patients, even after treatment started, remain well-separated from those of healthy people; this is typical for neurodegenerative diseases, but also for further brain impairments. Our approach encompasses methods for modelling patient evolution and for predicting the health improvement of different patient subpopulations, dealing with the above challenges. We test our approach on a cohort of patients treated after brain trauma and a corresponding cohort of controls.

1 Introduction

Data mining is increasingly used on clinical data for purposes of diagnosis and treatment. In the context of neurodegenerative diseases and of events that disrupt mental functions, like traumatic brain damage and vascular brain lesions, medical researchers want to understand the *evolution* of the patients and to know whether a similar state as for healthy people can be reached. We propose a mining method that captures the evolution of patients subjected to treatment after brain trauma and juxtaposes them to the participants of a control cohort.

The context of our work is the monitoring of patients with a disease or impairment that affects their mental abilities, e.g. Parkinson, brain trauma or coma after excessive alcohol consumption. While there are treatments known to improve patient state, at least for some patients, it is also evident in many cases

D. Ślęzak et al. (Eds.): BIH 2014, LNAI 8609, pp. 376–387, 2014.
© Springer International Publishing Switzerland 2014

that the mental abilities of healthy controls are not recovered. Hence, our task is to identify subpopulations of patients, whose mental abilities become closer to those of some controls. We face two challenges. First, the results of the medical tests on the mental abilities of patients, even after treatment, are still very different from those of the controls, so that a direct comparison between treated patients and healthy cohort participants is not conclusive. Second, we have a lot of clinical data on the patients but much less on the controls, so that the evolution of patients can be modelled but the evolution of the controls cannot. To deal with these challenges, we model the evolution of the patients and identify subpopulations that become (asymptotically) similar to controls.

The study of patient evolution on the basis of timestamped clinical data has been largely influenced by the seminal work of Cox [1] on censored failure times and age-specific failure rates. As pointed out by Fitzmaurice et al., [1] "... was followed by a rich and important body of work that established the conceptual basis for the modern *survival analysis*" [2]. Survival analysis is not applicable to this problem, because there is neither a well-defined target event, nor explicit timepoints to guide the learner. Although there is a control population to juxtapose to the patients, there are no target values to predict, because the assessments of the controls are very different from those of the patients. Hence, we resort to unsupervised approaches to model the evolution of individuals.

The contributions of our EvolutionPredictor are as follows. We model the evolution of subpopulations of patients, on whom only two moments are available, where these two moments are not defined as timestamps[1]. We use this model to compute a future/target state for each patient. We show that the projected target state of patients allows a reasonable comparison to a control population, the recordings of which are very different from the patient recordings.

The paper is organized as follows. In Sec. 2 we discuss related work. In Sec. 3 we present our materials and the mining workflow for modelling evolution and projection of patients after treatment. In Sec. 4, we report on the results of our experiments on brain trauma patients. The last section concludes our study.

2   Related Work

Data mining methods are only recently deployed for analysis of brain pathologies or injury conditions. The authors of [3] analyse data from neuropsychological tests (concerning attention, memory and executive function tests) from 250 subjects before and after a treatment instrumented by a cognitive tele-rehabilitation platform. Their objective is to predict the expected outcome based on the cognitive affectation profile and the performance on the rehabilitation tasks. Our objective is not the prediction of a well-defined outcome, but rather of the future similarity between treated patients and a population of healthy people.

In [4], the authors present an artificial neural network model that predicts in-hospital survival following traumatic brain injury according to 11 clinical inputs.

---

[1] The one moment is "before" the treatment began, the other moment is "after" the treatment began, but without knowing when exactly the treatment began or ended.

A similar approach was taken by Shi et al [5], who also consider neural networks and logistic regression, but rather study recovery from brain surgery. Andrews et al. discuss methods for prediction of recovery from brain injury, including short-term evolution of patients [6]. The effect of cognitive therapies along longer periods (6 months to 1 year) is studied in [7,8]. Brown et al. learn decision trees on variables that include physical examinations and indices measuring injury severity, as well as gender, age and years of education [7]. Rovlias and Kotsou further consider pathological markers and the output of computer tomography, and learn CART trees [8]. Our study is different from the aforementioned ones, because we do not learn a model on patient recovery (we do not have recovery data), but rather study the evolution of the patients *towards a control population*.

Close to our work are the works [9,10], which predict the progression of glaucoma from cross-sectional (rather than longitudinal) data. The methods learn temporal models on trajectories. A trajectory is built by fitting so-called "partial paths" upon the cross-sectional data: path construction involves selecting one healthy individual and one patient, labelling them as start and end and then re-ordering the remaining cross-sectional instances based on the shortest path from start to end. Our approach shares with [9,10] the need to construct a trajectory of evolution: in principle, we could construct a "partial path" by combining the recordings of the controls and the recordings of the patients during treatment. But this would imply ignoring part of the already avaialble temporal information (pre-treatment data). Moreover, the Trauma Brain Injury dataset of [11], which we use, shows that the control individuals are too different from the patients: this might lead to long and unrealistic partial paths. Thus, we rather build a single projected *moment*, using data before and after the begin of treatment, and do not involve the recordings of the controls in our learning process.

A separate thread of work models and monitors how sub-populations (clusters) evolve over time. The framework MONIC [12] encompasses a set of 'transitions' that a cluster may experience, a set of measures and a cluster comparison mechanism that assesses whether a cluster observed at some timepoint has survived, disappeared, merged or become split at the next timepoint. Later frameworks [13,14] build upon MONIC to explain evolution: they model the clusters and their transitions as nodes, resp. edges of an *evolution* graph. In [15], we build upon [14] to learn a Mixture of Markov chains that capture the evolution of different subpopulations. We take up the idea of subpopulations here, but our goal is to predict rather than model the evolution of the subpopulations.

3   Materials and Methods

Given is a cohort of patients $\mathcal{X}$, for which we measure a set of *assessments A*, e.g. performance at cognitive tests, results of laboratory tests etc, before (t_{pre}) and after (t_{post}) the treatment started. Our goal is to predict *how close* the assessment values of these patients can become to the assessments of a control cohort $\mathcal{Y}$, assuming that the treatment continues. We pursue this goal by first building clusters of patients that evolve similarly from t_{pre} to t_{post}. Then, we compute a *projection* of each patient's future assessments, using (a) the patient's assessments, and (b) assessments observed in the cluster to which the patient belongs. Finally, we compare these projected assessment values to the values observed in the control cohort. In the following, we first describe the materials of our analysis, then we present the work flow of EvolutionPredictor.

Notation: For each moment t and patient $x \in \mathcal{X}$, x_t is the vector of assessments of x at t: the *instantiation of x at t* or *patient x at t*. The set of moments is $T = \{t_{pre}, t_{post}, t_{proj}\}$, where t_{pre} stands for instantiations before treatment, t_{post} for instantiations after the treatment started and t_{proj} for a future moment, not further specified. Hereafter, we skip the index t, i.e. $x_{t_{pre}} \equiv x_{pre}$.

It is stressed that t_{pre}, t_{post} and t_{proj} are moments ordered in time, but not timepoints in the strict sense, since we do not define a distance among them. The reason is that the duration of treatment among the patients varies, and so does the elapsed time between the incident (traumatic brain injury) and the commence of the treatment. As with many cohorts, the data (cf. subsection 3.1) are too few, so we cannot afford to distinguish among different treatment durations and elapsed time intervals.

3.1   Materials: The TBI Dataset

The **T**raumatic **B**rain **I**njury dataset (TBI) contains assessments on cognitive tests for 15 patients with brain injury and for 14 controls [11]. These tests are recorded once for the controls and twice for the patients – at moments t_{pre} and t_{post}. The cognitive tests are listed on Table 1 (cf. for details [11]).

3.2   The EvolutionPredictor Work Flow

The tasks of our workflow are: (1) bootstrap sampling over the set of patients $\mathcal{X}$; (2) clustering the patient instantiations at each $t \in \{t_{pre}, t_{post}\}$, building a clustering ζ_t; (3) building an evolution graph $G(\zeta_{pre}, \zeta_{post})$ of patients evolving similarly; (4) using the topological space of $G(\zeta_{pre}, \zeta_{post})$ to compute the projection, i.e. the projected instantiation of each $x \in \mathcal{X}$ into the future x_{proj}.

Bootstrap Sampling and Clustering at Each Moment. Our Evolution-Predictor learns from the set of patients $\mathcal{X}$. Since $\mathcal{X}$ is small (as is the case for many cohort datasets), we perform bootstrap aggregation [16] over $\mathcal{X}$. Subsequent instance of each out-of-sample patient (i.e., x_{pre}, x_{post}) are removed. We apply K-Means over the instances at each moment t, and build a set of clusters ζ_t.

Building a Cluster Evolution Graph. We use the concepts of MONIC [12,17] to build a graph of cluster transitions from t_{pre} to t_{post}. For each $c \in \zeta_{pre}$ and $c' \in \zeta_{post}$, we define their intersection as: $c \cap c' = \{x \in \mathcal{X} : x_{pre} \in c \wedge x_{post} \in c'\}$. If $c \cap c' \neq \emptyset$, we draw an edge (c, c') and assign to it the weight $w_{(c,c')} = \frac{|c \cap c'|}{|c \cup c'|}$.

Table 1. Acronyms and description of cognitive tests[2] from the TBI dataset from [11]

Name	Description
TMT-B	Train Making Test-Part B: measures cognitive flexibility (frontal lobe)
BTA	Brief Test of Attention (total score).
WCST-NC	Wisconsin Card Shorting Test: Percentage total score of conceptual level (#categories correctly achieved); also measures cognitive flexibility
WCST-RP	Wisconsin Card Shorting Test: # preservative responses (represent error)
FAS	Phonetic fluency test which uses as cues letters F, A, and S as the initial letters for the patients to start the production of words
ICP	Measures ability to perform daily activities, and awareness of the disease
CIV	Verbal Intelligent Quotient: measures ability to handle verbal material
CIM	Performance IQ: ability to handle visio-spatial/non-verbal material
CV	Verbal comprehension index (VCI)
MT	Working memory (WM): measures the subject's ability to maintain information in short-term memory and recall it
OP	Perceptual organization (PO)
VP	Processing Speed Index (PSI)
IAC	Attention/Concentration Index (ACI)
IMG	General Memory Index (GMI)
IRD	Delayed Recall Index (DRI)

We thus build a directed transition graph $G(\zeta_{pre}, \zeta_{post})$, where the weights of the edges emanating from the same cluster add to 1.0. We define:

$$firstmatch(c) = argmax_{c' \in \zeta_{post}} w(c, c') \qquad (1)$$

i.e. the *first match* of a pre-treatment cluster c is the post-treatment cluster with the highest weight among the clusters linked to c.

On Figure 1(a), we show the instantiations of example individuals at time-points t_{pre} (yellow) and t_{post} (aubergine); the corresponding clusters are in (b); the transition arrows and weights are in (c). The yellow star indicates the "projection" of the individual marked as a red star; projections are explained next.

Projecting Patient Assessments into the Future. Let $x \in \mathcal{X}$ be a patient, $c \in \zeta_{pre}$ be the cluster containing x_{pre} ,and c_{fm} be the *firstmatch(c)* (Eq. 1.) Further, we denote the centroid of an arbitrary cluster clu as $\widehat{clu}$. We define the *hard projection* of x from t_{pre} to t_{proj} as the instantiation of x such that the value of each $a \in A$ is determined by the values in x_{pre} and in $\widehat{c}, \widehat{c_{fm}}$:

$$projH(x, t_{pre}, t_{post}) = x_{pre}(a) + (\widehat{c_{fm}}(a) - \widehat{c}(a)) \text{ for each } a \in A \qquad (2)$$

---

[2] The acronyms were derived from the original Spanish names. Therefore, the textual descriptions do not reflect the acronyms. We also provide the English acronyms in parentheses.

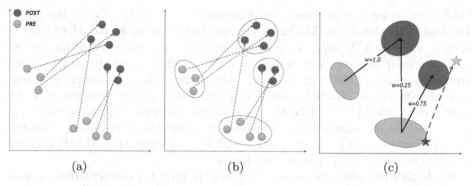

Fig. 1. Clustering, Evolution Graph, Soft Projection: (a) the nodes are patient instantiations at t_{pre} (yellow) and t_{post} (aubergine) – instantiations of the same individual are linked with dashed arrows; (b) clustering is done at each moment and (c) the evolution graph is built by connecting pre- and post-treatment clusters that share individuals; the edge weights are used to compute soft projections, as for the red-star instance

We define the *soft projection* of x from t_{pre} to t_{proj} as an instantiation, the values of which are influenced by all clusters in ζ_{post} that are linked to c:

$$projS(x, t_{pre}, t_{post}) = x_{pre}(a) + \sum_{c' \in \zeta_{post}} \left(\widehat{c'}(a) - \widehat{c}(a) \right) \cdot w_{c,c'} \text{ for each } a \in A \quad (3)$$

where $w_{c,c'}$ is the weight of a transition edge.

Hence, we learn models ζ_{pre} and ζ_{post} on some individuals and then assess the projection location of other (or the same) individuals. On Figure 1(c) we show the *soft projection* of an individual (red star): the projected position is outside both post-treatment clusters, since the individual is located at the rim of the pre-treatment cluster.

4 Experiments

We evaluate our method by first testing whether the projection captures the evolution of the patients reliably. To this purpose, we project from t_{pre} to t_{post}, i.e. on known instances. Then, we show the results of the projection from t_{post} to t_{proj}, which we juxtapose to the controls from TBI dataset. We have no ground truth for this projection, so we rely on the validity of the first projection. We first describe the framework and then discuss our findings.

4.1 EvaluationFramework

To evaluate the performance of the projections we are inspired by the Mean Absolute Scaled Error (MASE) [18], which was originally designed to alleviate the scaling effects of Mean Absolute Error(MAE). To define our variation of

MASE, we assume an arbitrary set of moments $\mathcal{T} = \{t_1, t_2, \ldots, t_n\}$. For an individual x, we define the MASE of the last instantiation x_n as: $MASE(x) = d(x_{proj}, x_n) / \frac{1}{n-1} \sum_{i=2}^{n-1} d(x_i, x_{i-1})$, where $d()$ is the function computing the distance between two consecutive instantiations of the same individual x. This function normalizes the error of EvolutionPredictor at the last moment t_n (nominator) to the error of a naive method (denominator), which predicts that the next instantiation of x will be the same as the previous (truly observed) one. If the average distance between consecutive instantiations is smaller than the distance between the last instantiation and its projection, then MASE is larger than 1. Obviously, smaller values are better.

We further compute the number of times ($Hits()$) the correct cluster is predicted for a patient x. Assume that instantiation x_{pre} belongs to cluster c_{pre} and let c_{proj} denote the $firstmatch(c_{pre})$ (cf. Eq. 1) at the projection moment t_{proj}. We define: $Hits(x) = 1$, if c_{proj} is same as c_{post} (i.e., cluster closest to x_{post}), otherwise $Hits(x) = 0$. Higher values are better.

For model purity, we compute the entropy of a cluster c towards a set of classes ξ, where the entropy is minimal if all members of c belong to the same class, and maximal if the members are equally distributed among the classes. We aggregate this to an entropy value for the whole set of clusters ζ, $entropy(\zeta, \xi)$.

In general, lower entropy values are better. However, the labels used by the EvolutionPredictor are $\underline{C}$ontrol and $\underline{P}$atient: if a clustering cannot separate well between patient instantiations and controls, this means that the patient instantiations (which are the result of the projection done by our EvolutionPredictor) have become very similar to the controls. Hence, high entropy values are better.

For learning evolutionary prediction model, we use a bootstrap sampling [16] with a sample size of 85% and 10,000 replications. Model validation is done with the help of out-of-sample data. For clustering the union of projected instances and the controls, we use K-Means clustering. We use bootstrap sampling with a sample size of 75% and 1000 replications, and vary $K = 2, \ldots 8$.

4.2   Findings

Validation of the Projection from t_{pre} to t_{post}. In the first experiment, we project the patient instantiations from t_{pre} to t_{post}. Since the true instantiations at t_{post} are known, we use these projections to validate EvolutionPredictor, whereupon evaluation is done with the MASE and Hits measures (cf. subsection 4.1). Figure 2 depicts the hard and soft projections of the pre-treatment patient instantiations, while Table 2 depicts the MASE and Hits values for each patient separately. We perform 10,000 runs and average the values per run.

On Figure 2, we see that the hard projection (yellow) and soft projection (green) behave very similarly. Both predict the patient instantiations at t_{post} very well: the mean values for the projected patient instantiations are almost identical to the true instantiations, and the shaded regions (capturing the variance around the mean) overlap with the variance of the true values almost completely.

The first row of Table 2 enumerates the 15 patients in the TBI dataset, the subsequent rows show the MASE values for the hard, respectively the soft

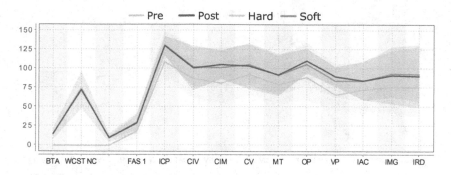

Fig. 2. Variance plots for patient projections, where t_{proj} is set to predict the (already known) instances at t_{post}: the solid lines represent the mean values of the true patient instantiations at moment t_{pre}, t_{post} and of the projected patient instantiations, while the surrounding regions (same color as the solid line) represent the variance of the instantiations; the two projections overlap almost completely with the true distribution at t_{post}, both with respect to the line of the mean and to the region of the variance

Table 2. Hard and soft projection of patients from t_{pre} towards t_{post}, with MASE and Hits per patient: low MASE is better, values larger than 1 are poor; high Hits are better, 1.0 is best; averages over all patients exclude outlier patient #14

IDs	#1	#2	#3	#4	#5	#6	#7	#8	#9	#10	#11	#12	#13	#14	#15	Avg
MASE																
Soft	0.29	0.14	0.12	0.19	0.24	0.83	0.13	0.22	0.15	0.21	0.58	0.22	0.37	3.24	0.34	**0.27**
Hard	0.22	0.09	0.10	0.14	0.16	0.90	0.07	0.17	0.13	0.20	0.29	0.23	0.34	3.49	0.42	**0.24**
Hits	0.86	0.62	0.93	0.62	0.95	0.99	0.86	0.89	0.96	0.96	0.54	0.87	0.77	0.81	1.00	**0.83**

projection. The last row shows the Hits value per patient. The last column averages the MASE and Hits values over all but one patients: patient #14 is excluded from the computation, because prior inspection revealed that this patient is an outlier, for whom few assessments are available. All other patients exhibit low MASE values (lower is better), indicating that our projection mechanisms predict well the patient assessments at t_{post}.

Projection from t_{post} to the Future t_{proj}. In the second experiment, our EvolutionPredictor projects the patients after treatment start towards a future moment t_{proj}, which corresponds to an ideal final set of assessments that the patient might ultimately reach through continuation of the treatment. We do not have a ground truth to evaluate the quality of our projections. Rather, we use a juxtaposition of patients and controls, depicted on Figure 3. We show the averages of values per population through a solid line, around which we expand to the variance of values for each variable. The cyan line and surrounding cyan shaded region stands for the moment t_{pre}, denoted as "Pre" in the legend; the

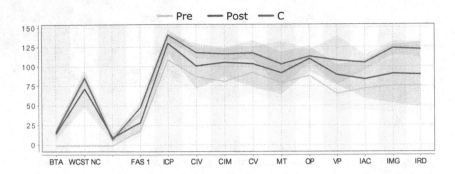

Fig. 3. Average assessment values and variance regions for controls and for patients before (Pre) and after treatment start (Post) for 16 variables: despite some overlaps, lines and regions of patients are mostly distinct from those of the controls

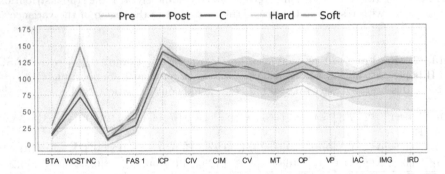

Fig. 4. Average assessment values and variance regions for controls and for patients before (Pre) and after treatment start (Post), and as result of Hard (yellow) and Soft (green) projection: the projected patient assessments are closer to the controls

blue line and region stand for the moment t_{post} ("Post"), while the "Controls" are marked by the red line and red shaded region. Except for Gender and Age, for which controls have been intentionally chosen to be similar to the patients, patients differ from controls. Even where we see overlap between the red area and the cyan (Pre) or the blue (Post) area of the patients, as for assessments CIM and CV, we also see that the average values are different.

Figure 4 shows the same lines and areas for assessments before and after treatment start (Pre:cyan, Post:blue) as the reference Figure 3, but also the projected assessment values (Proj: green/yellow). These projected assessments are closer to the controls, indicating that at least for some of the assessments (FAS1, ICP, CIM, CV, MT, VP), treatment continuation may lead asymptotically to similar values as for the controls.

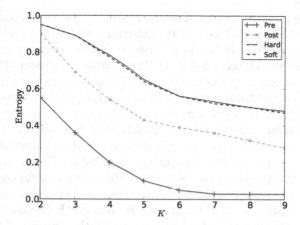

Fig. 5. Controls clustered with the patients before treatment (Pre: red), after treatment start (Post: yellow), with the Hard projection (green) and the Soft one (blue dashed): entropy drops as the number of clusters increases, but has higher (better) values for the projected instantiations, indicating that these are closer to the controls

Clustering Patients with Controls. We investigate whether the patients can be separated from the control population through clustering. We skip the assessments TMT-B, BTA, WCST-NC and WCST-RP, which have been recorded only for some patients. We cluster the controls with the patient instantiations before treatment (Pre: red line), after treatment start (Post: yellow line), with the Hard projected instantiations (green line) and with the Soft projection (blue dashed line). We use bootstrapping with a sample size of 75% with 1000 replications. On Figure 5, we show the entropy, as we vary the number of clusters K. *Higher* values are better, because they mean that the clustering cannot separate controls from patients. High values are achieved only for the projected instantiations.

On Figure 5, the entropy values are very high for the clusters containing controls together with projected patients, whereby soft projection and hard projection behave identically. The high values mean that the clustering algorithm cannot separate between projected patients and controls on similarity; the instances are too similar. This should be contrasted with the clusters containing controls and patients before treatment (red line): entropy is low and drops fast as the number of clusters increases, indicating that patients before treatment are similar to each other and dissimilar to controls. After the treatment starts, the separation between patients and controls on similarity (yellow line) is less easy, but an increase in the number of clusters leads to fair separation. In contrast, projected patients are similar to controls, even when the number of clusters increases: the small clusters contains still both controls and patients.

5   Conclusion

We investigated the problem of predicting the evolution of patients being treated after brain injury and we propose a mining workflow.

Key points: The mining workflow EvolutionPredictor clusters patients on similarity (of their assessments) before and after the treatment began, and then it tracks how each cluster evolves. It builds a cluster evolution graph that captures the transitions of patient clusters before (PRE) to after treatment (POST). Then, our EvolutionPredictor uses the cluster transitions to project each patient to a future moment, on the basis of what is known on the patient's thus far. The core of our approach is the projection mechanism, for which we propose two variants.

We have experimentally validated EvolutionPredictor on the Trauma Brain Injury dataset [11]. We have first applied the method on known data and have shown that the projected values are almost identical to the true ones. Then, we have compared the projected assessments to those of a control population, and we have shown that some patient assessments are projected close to the controls.

We studied treatment after brain trauma, but our EvolutionPredictor is applicable to any impairment, where progression or the process of recovery is of interest. The clusters we find may be of use in personalized medicine.

Shortcomings and Future Work: The projected assessments have not yet be evaluated against the assertions of a human expert about the patients' health state after treatment. We are currently in the process of acquiring such data for an additional evaluation. A further shortcoming is that we ignore the duration of treatment; this is planed as future step.

The evolution of brain trauma or impairment conditions is difficult to measure at the functional level. However, the scholars anticipate that the use of neuroimaging, e.g., MEG, could lead to the detection of progressive changes in the connectivity patterns even *before* they translate into changes at the memory, movement or orientation functions. Regularly recording MEG images before and during treatment of patients, allow a more effective evaluation of treatment by providing hints and indicators about the effectiveness of a particular therapy. A next step for our work will be the integration of MEG data into our mining workflow, to check whether the evolution of patients towards the subcohort of controls can be modelled more effectively with the MEG images.

Acknowledgements. Part of this work was supported by the German Research Foundation project SP 572/11-1 "IMPRINT: Incremental Mining for Perennial Objects".

The dataset used in this work was made available through the cooperation "Data Mining and Stream Mining for Epidemiological Studies on the Human Brain" (StreaMED) between the Centre of Biomedical Technology (CTB) of the Uni. Polytecnica de Madrid and the Otto-von-Guericke Uni. Magdeburg.

References

1. Cox, D.: Regression models and life-tables. Journal of the Royal Statistical Society. Series B (Methodological) 34(2), 187–220 (1972)
2. Fitzmaurice, G.M., Laird, N.M., Ware, J.H.: Applied longitudinal analysis, vol. 998. John Wiley & Sons (2012)

3. Marcano-Cedeño, A., Chausa, P., García, A., Cáceres, C., Tormos, J., Gómez, E.: Data mining applied to the cognitive rehabilitation of patients with acquired brain injury. Journal of Expert Systems with App. 40, 1054–1060 (2013)
4. Rughani, A.I., Dumont, T.M., Lu, Z., Bongard, J., Horgan, M.A., Penar, P.L., Tranmer, B.I.: Use of an artificial neural network to predict head injury outcome: clinical article. Journal of Neurosurgery 113, 585–590 (2010)
5. Shi, H.Y., Hwang, S.L., Lee, K.T., Lin, C.L.: In-hospital mortality after traumatic brain injury surgery: a nationwide population-based comparison of mortality predictors used in artificial neural network and logistic regression models: clinical article. Journal of Neurosurgery 118, 746–752 (2013)
6. Andrews, P.J.D., Sleeman, D.H., Statham, P.F.X., McQuatt, A., Corruble, V., Jones, P.A., Howells, T.P., Macmillan, C.S.A.: Predicting recovery in patients suffering from traumatic brain injury by using admission variables and physiological data: a comparison between decision tree analysis and logistic regression. Journal of Neurosurgery 97, 326–336 (2002)
7. Brown, A., Malec, J., McClelland, R., Diehl, N., Englander, J., Cifu, D.: Clinical elements that predict outcome after traumatic brain injury: a prospective multi-center recursive partitioning (decision-tree) analysis. Journal of Neurotrauma 22, 1040–1051 (2005)
8. Rovlias, A., Kotsou, S.: Classification and regression tree for prediction of outcome after severe head injury using simple clinical and laboratory variables. Journal of Neurotrauma 21, 886–893 (2004)
9. Tucker, A., Garway-Heath, D.: The pseudotemporal bootstrap for predicting glaucoma from cross-sectional visual field data. IEEE Trans. on Inf. Tech. in Biomedicine 14(1), 79–85 (2010)
10. Li, Y., Swift, S., Tucker, A.: Modelling and analysing the dynamics of disease progression from cross-sectional studies. Journal of Biomedical Informatics 46(2), 266–274 (2013)
11. Castellanos, N.P., Paul, N., Ordonez, V.E., Deuynck, O., Bajo, R., Campo, P., Bilbao, A., Ortiz, T., del-Pozo, F., Maestu, F.: Reorganization of functional connectivity as a correlate of cognitive recovery in acquired brain injury. Brain 133, 2365–2381 (2010)
12. Spiliopoulou, M., Ntoutsi, I., Theodoridis, Y., Schult, R.: MONIC – modeling and monitoring cluster transitions. In: Proc. of 12th Int. Conf. on Knowledge Disc. and Data Mining (KDD 2006), pp. 706–711. ACM (August 2006)
13. Ntoutsi, I., Spiliopoulou, M., Theodoridis, Y.: Summarizing cluster evolution in dynamic environments. In: Murgante, B., Gervasi, O., Iglesias, A., Taniar, D., Apduhan, B.O. (eds.) ICCSA 2011, Part II. LNCS, vol. 6783, pp. 562–577. Springer, Heidelberg (2011)
14. Oliveira, M., Gama, J.: A framework to monitor clusters evolution applied to economy and finance problems. Intelligent Data Analysis 16(1), 93–111 (2012)
15. Siddiqui, Z., Oliveira, M., Gama, J., Spiliopoulou, M.: Where are we going? predicting the evolution of individuals. In: Hollmén, J., Klawonn, F., Tucker, A. (eds.) IDA 2012. LNCS, vol. 7619, pp. 357–368. Springer, Heidelberg (2012)
16. Breiman, L.: Bagging predictors. Machine Learning 24(2), 123–140 (1996)
17. Ntoutsi, E., Spiliopoulou, M., Theodoridis, Y.: FINGERPRINT – summarizing cluster evolution in dynamic environments. Int. Journal of Data Warehousing and Mining (IJDWM) 8(3), 27–44 (2012)
18. Hyndman, R.J., Koehler, A.B.: Another look at measures of forecast accuracy. International Journal of Forecasting 22(4), 679–688 (2006)

An Adaptive Expert System for Automated Advices Generation-Based Semi-continuous M-Health Monitoring

Mohamed Adel Serhani[1], Abdelghani Benharref[2], and Al Ramzana Nujum[1]

[1] College of Information Technology, UAE University
{serhanim,ramazana}@uaeu.ac.ae
[2] University of Wollongong in Dubai
abdelgha@uow.edu.au

Abstract. Chronic diseases such as diabetes and hypertension have been recognized in the last decade among the principal causes of death in the world. Mitigating and controlling the elicited risks necessitate a continuous monitoring to produce accurate recommendations for both patients and physicians. For patient, it will help in adjusting his/her lifestyles, medications, and sport activities. However, for physicians, it helps in taking guided therapy decision. In this paper, we propose an adaptive Expert System (ES) that relies, not only on a set of rules validated by experts, but also linked to an intelligent continuous monitoring scheme that copes with semi-continuous data streams by implementing smart sensing and pre-processing of data. In addition, we implemented an iterative data analytic technique that learns from the past ES experience to continuously improve clinical decision-making and automatically generates validated advices. These advices are visualized via an application interface. We experimented the proposed system using different scenarios of monitoring blood sugar and blood pressure parameters of a population of patients with chronic diseases. The results we have obtained showed that our ES combined with the intelligent monitoring and analytic techniques provide a high accuracy of collected data and evident-based advices.

Keywords: Expert System, continuous monitoring, analytics, diabetes, blood pressure, healthy advice generation.

1   Introduction and Related Work

With the advances in emerging technologies such as biosensors, mobile devices, and communication networks, remote monitoring of patients with chronic diseases is being considered as an efficient and cost-effective solution to reduce the burden on patients as well as on governments. It allows monitoring of patients wearing biosensors connected to their mobile devices and enabled with network connection to relay the collected vital signs (i.e. readings) to a back-end server. To cope with the high speed and volume of continuous data streams collected from sensors, a couple of challenges should be addressed. These challenges cover data acquisition, data processing, data analytics and visualization.

D. Ślęzak et al. (Eds.): BIH 2014, LNAI 8609, pp. 388–399, 2014.
© Springer International Publishing Switzerland 2014

Many works have been conducted to address independently each one of the above challenges and proposed solution for M-health monitoring. In data analytics, there are some interesting works on the design of expert systems for automatic decision taking. In [1], the authors present a decision support system where the final aim is to provide a patient with a health score that reflects the expert system engine's interpretation of readings coming from clinical measurements. The final score (medium, average, or low priority) is then conveyed to medical staff to further assess the case and take any appropriate action. The authors in [2] present a rule-based decision support system. Decisions are taken using decision trees, rules, and transformation of rules into fuzzy logic. In [3], authors present a remote server that provides clinical decision support. Once this server receives data and data date stamps over the Internet, it will provide automated analysis to assist doctors in decision taking.

For diabetes, METABO [4] is a monitoring and management system that aims at recording and interpreting patient's context as well as providing decision support to both patient and doctor. This is based on a glucose meters, and physical activity sensors. The authors in [5] propose a fuzzy expert system for blood pressure and hypertension. This is a rule-based system that simulates an expert-doctor behavior for diagnosis. For the same class of patients (i.e. diabetes), authors in [6] present another system to support patients and doctors to determine their diet plans.

The authors in [7] present a case-based and rule-base reasoning system for combined therapies, in this case for lifestyle and pharmacology. The knowledge base in this system is constructed using fuzzified input values, which are subsequently de-fuzzified after reasoning to produce concise outputs. Another use of fuzzy logic in health-related diagnosis is presented in [8] where authors claim that fuzzy logic is an effective tool for accurate diagnosis of heart and blood pressure measurements.

Most of research initiatives in expert systems and DSS do not cope with the continuous monitoring generating a high volume of data which, makes it very challenging in retrieving accurate data, processing this data, and generating validated clinical decision. Also, none of the works above tackles closing the loop and further checks if the proposed clinical recommendations will impact the patient's future readings collected in the next cycle.

In this paper, we tried to address few of the above challenges by providing an end-to-end solution that implements the following:

- An adaptive continuous monitoring scheme that copes with semi-continuous data streams and implements smart sensing and pre-processing of data.
- An iterative data analytic technique that learns from the past ES experiences to continuously improve the knowledge base, the rules, thus automatically generates validated clinical advices for better decision-making.
- A visualization dashboard that displays generated advices.
- Closing the loop and further evaluates that the suggested advices impacted the readings collected in the next monitoring cycle. Therefore, it will allow continuous improvements and optimization of rules, knowledge base, and advices.

2   Architecture

2.1   Overview

The monitoring system depicted in Fig. 1 describes the set of entities involved in an end-to-end M-health monitoring of patients. These include key processes such as data acquisition, data processing and analytics, recommendation generation and visualization.

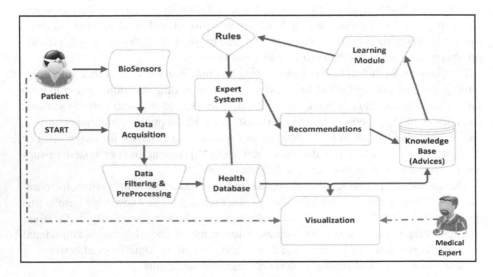

Fig. 1. End-to-End M-Health Monitoring Overview

Fig. 1 illustrates the overall M-health monitoring lifecycle scheme that starts with collecting data from *sensors* by the *data acquisition* module. Then data is *filtered* and *pre-processed* before being stored in the *database*. In addition to these readings, the database includes also patient's profile and other historical clinical data. These data are used as input to the *expert system,* which maps these data on a set of rules that are validated a priory by human medical experts. The generated output is mapped to a set of *recommendations* stored in a database and *visualized* by patients and physicians. Recommendations are food intake, medications, lifestyle and exercises. The physicians have the right to validate, update, and or extend these advices through the visualization interface before they are stored in the knowledge base database. Finally, the knowledge retrieved from physician's recommendations is used by the *learning module* to enrich the set of rules with new rules and or to update existing rules.

2.2   Rules Description and Validation

We have developed a set of rules for each monitored parameter. For instance, rules for blood sugar, blood pressure and a composition of rules for both vital signs. The table below provides a sample for each category of these rules.

Table 1. Rules Description

Rules	Description
Blood Sugar (BS)	1. **IF** (Fasting BloodSugar is *>=200*) **THEN** (fbglucose is *very high*) 2. **IF** (Fasting BloodSugar is *>=125*) **THEN** (fbglucose is *High*) 3. **IF** (Fasting BloodSugar is 50 - 70) **THEN** (fbglucose is *Low*) 4. **IF** (Fasting BloodSugar is < *50*) **THEN** (fbglucose is very *Low*) 5. **IF** (Fasting BloodSugar is *>=70*) **THEN** (fbglucose is *Normal*)
Blood Pressure (BP)	1. **IF** (SYSTOLIC is < 90) AND (DIASTOLIC is <60) **THEN** (BP is *low*) 2. **IF** (SYSTOLIC is 90 - 120) AND (DIASTOLIC is 60-80) **THEN** (BP is *normal*) 3. **IF** (SYSTOLIC is 120 - 139) AND (DIASTOLIC is 80 -90) **THEN** (BP is *preHigh*) 4. **IF** (SYSTOLIC is *140 -160*) AND (DIASTOLIC is *90 - 100*) **THEN** (BP is *stage1High*) 5. **IF** (SYSTOLIC is *>160*) AND (DIASTOLIC is > 100) **THEN** (BP is *stage2High*)
Composite (BP & BS)	1. **IF** (BP is *normal*) AND (fbglucose is *normal*) **THEN** (FoodIntake is *normal*) AND (Lifestyle & Exercise is *regular*) AND (Medication is *NoChange*) 2. **IF** (BP is *preHigh*) AND (fbglucose is *high*) **THEN** (FoodIntake is *strict*) AND (Lifestyle & Exercise is *moderate*) AND (Medication is *Consult & Change*) 3. **IF** (BP is *stage1High*) AND (fbglucose is *high*) **THEN** (FoodIntake is *strict*) AND (Lifestyle & Exercise is *regular*) AND (Medication is *Consult & Change*) 4. **IF** (BP is *stage2High*) AND (fbglucose is *high*) **THEN** (FoodIntake is *strict*) AND (Lifestyle & Exercise is *stop*) AND (Medication is *Consult & Change*) 5. **IF** (BP is *stage2High*) AND (fbglucose is *vLow*) **THEN** (FoodIntake is *strict*) AND (Lifestyle & Exercise is *stop*) AND (Medication is *Consult & Change*)

2.3   Smart Data Sensing and Acquisition

Data acquisition involves usage of sensors, mobile devices, and backend servers. Streams of continuous data collection from sensors induce a set of challenges including for instance the significance of collected data, its consistency, and its accuracy. Therefore, we implemented some smartness at different levels mentioned above. At the sensor, we re-program it to report only changes in collected data, also move to sleep mode if recorded readings are stable/normal over a period of time, then resume sensing if patient context changes. At the mobile device retrieving the sensory data, pre-processing functions were implemented such as data filtering and cleansing. These intelligent features implemented in sensors, and mobile devices reduced considerably the volume of collected data and insured a better data accuracy. In addition, the data gathered are seamlessly exposed as a Web service (Sensing as a Service) after being deployed on an application server that authorized applications can access and use (e.g. Expert System).

2.4   Adaptive Expert System for Data Analytics

For the adaptive expert system, we have developed two main features: 1) adapts to the volume of data streams received from continuous monitoring and 2) adapts to the updated knowledge gathered from different monitoring cycles. Data are filtered and pre-processed for the purpose of reducing their quantity and improving their quality. The data analytic scheme closes the loop and further evaluates if the suggested advices impacted the readings collected in the next monitoring cycle. Therefore, it will allow continuous improvements and optimization of rules, generated knowledge base, and advices.

2.5   Advice Processing and Validation

The expert system generates a set of outputs in form of high, low, very high, etc.
These outputs are mapped to a set of concrete recommendations covering the following areas: food intake, medications, and lifestyle and exercises. Recommendations are
generated automatically based on the results of the expert system and validated by
medical human expert through a visualization interface, then stored into a database.
Further validations are done to compare if the advices have adjusted the level of BS
and BP readings collected in the next monitoring cycle.

3   Implementation

3.1   Experimental Setup

Fig. 2 describes the experimentation setup we have used to validate our approach.
This implementation is for semi-continuous monitoring of patients with BS and BP.

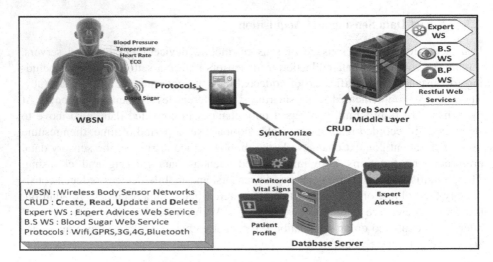

Fig. 2. M-Health Monitoring Setup

The following is the implementation details of the main components involved in
the end-to-end monitoring:

- WBSN: Wireless Body Sensor Networks consists of sensors placed in the body,
  which communicate and synchronize with the backend using various protocols
  (e.g. Bluetooth, Wi-Fi). The sensors we have used include Zephyr BioHarness-3,
  iBGStar® Blood Glucose Meter for iPhone, and Zephyr HxM heart Rate
  sensor.
- Mobile devices: iPhone 4S, Android tablet.

- Database server: MySQL server.
- Expert system: (Jess) Jess is a rule engine and scripting environment written entirely in Java. Using Jess APIs, we built Java application that reason using knowledge we supply in the form of declarative rules as in Table 1.
- Web Server / Middle Layer: Web Server acts as the middle layer, which serves the Restful Web Services.

3.2   Data Collection, Filtering, and Pre-processing

We used a total of 13650 readings, which were related to Blood Sugar (BS) and Blood Pressure (BP). Data were recorded from semi-continuous monitoring of 70 patients for a period of 6 months. The BP readings include two values namely: Systolic and Diastolic, and the BS readings include five readings that are: fasting, preprandial, after meal, bedtime, and random.

Collected data is processed at the source before being sent to the mobile device and to the database. Filters were implemented to remove irrelevant readings (e.g. damaged measurements, redundant readings, and incomplete data). Also, pre-processing was made to remove inaccurate readings, insignificant readings, or sensors' errors.

3.3   Implementations

We have implemented components to support data collection, processing, and visualization. These include a couple of restful Web services, Expert System, and visualization module:

Restful Web services: three Web services were implemented to help in the processing of collected readings. The BP and BS web services provide an interface with a required set of operations to create, read, update, and delete BP and BS readings. The third Web service is Expert System Web service that provides an interface to the visualization module to retrieve readings from the database.

Expert System implementation: it is developed using JESS, a Java based engine. Rules were specified using Common LISP (CLISP) type syntax, and then readings are inferred using JESS engine to generate a set of advices.

Visualization Interface: the generated advices include Food Intake, Medication, exercises and Lifestyle advices. They are visualized through an E-health portal where the patient has a read-only access while the physician has read-write access to be able to edit and update these advices.

3.4   Test Scenarios

We describe hereafter the key scenarios we have experienced within our monitoring scheme.

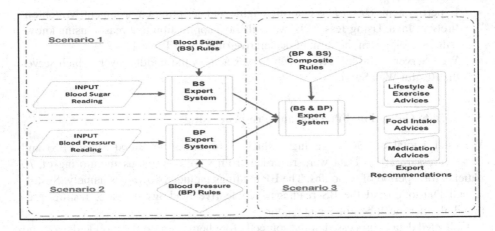

Fig. 3. Scenarios configuration

Fig. 3 illustrates the configuration of three scenarios we have developed to evaluate our semi-monitoring scheme using readings collected from 70 patients:

Scenario 1: blood sugar monitoring: the expert system gets the BS readings as inputs, infers those readings on the set of BS rules described in table 1 to generate a set of outputs in form of (*Fluctuating High, High, Low, Fluctuating Low, Fluctuating, Normal, VHigh*). In this scenario, we calculate the average matching readings to generated outputs. The result of this experiment is reported in Fig. 4 and Fig. 5.

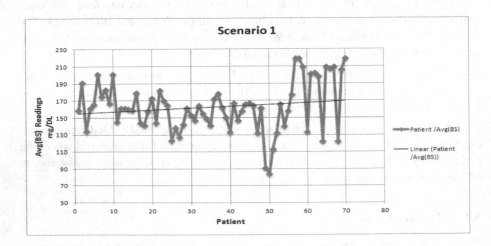

Fig. 4. BS readings inputted to the expert system

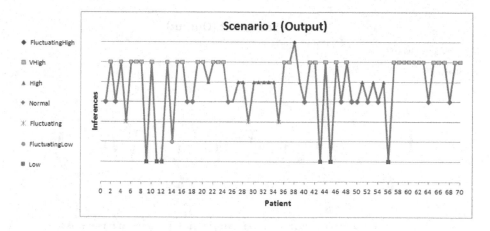

Fig. 5. Generated inferences of BS readings

Scenario 2: blood pressure monitoring: the expert system gets the BP readings as inputs, infers these on the set of BP rules described in table 1 to generate a set of output in form of: *Normal, Low, PreHigh, Stage1High, and Stage2High*. In this scenario, we calculate the average matching readings to generated outputs. The result of this experiment is reported in Fig. 6 and Fig. 7.

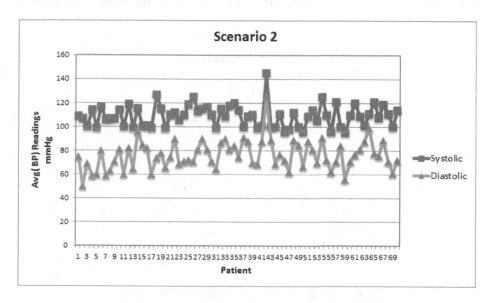

Fig. 6. BP readings inputted to the expert system

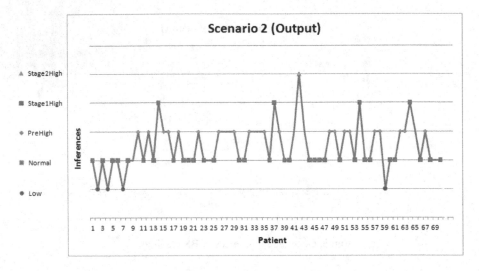

Fig. 7. Generated inferences of BP readings

<u>Scenario 3</u> (Combination BS and BP): the expert system uses, as input, the outputs generated from scenario 1 and 2. Then, it infers them on the set of composite rules of BS and BP as described in table 1 to generate outputs in the form of recommendations on life style, exercise, medication, and food intake. The result of this experiment is reported in Fig. 8.

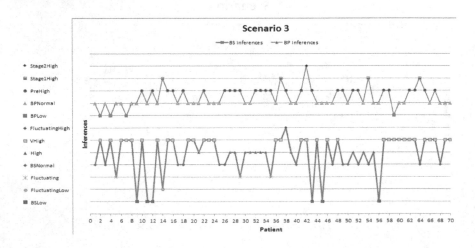

Fig. 8. Generated inferences for both BP and BS readings

3.5   Automated Advices

As mentioned above, advices are generated automatically based on the ES recommendations and considered lifestyle, medications, exercises and food intake. The advices below are related to patient number 38 in Fig. 8, for which a high BS and BP readings were recorded over a period of 6 months.

Very High: Bloor Sugar and Blood Pressure.

Your blood sugar and blood pressure is very high.
Symptoms: Dry mouth, thirst, frequent urination, tiredness, blurred vision, and over time.
Diagnosis: Reasons for high blood sugar include eating too much, being less active than usual, being sick or under stress, or needing an adjustment in your diabetes medicine.
Precautions: Your blood sugar may be too high to exercise safely, putting you at risk of ketoacidosis.
Lifestyle: lifestyle modifications are recommended for you. Postpone your workout until your blood sugar drops to a safe pre-exercise range.
Medications: You may need to increase the dose of current medications to adjust your blood sugar and blood pressure. Please consult with an expert.
Food in Take: Adjust your food and follow a strict diet by dietician.
Sport activities: Do not start any sport activity.
Short-term Risks: Risk of cardiovascular attacks (Stroke, Heart attack)
Long-term Risks: High blood sugar levels over a long period can lead to organ damage, commonly referred to as diabetic complications.
Action: Consult urgently with your doctor.

---

4   Results and Discussion

The results reported from the above scenarios evaluated three main characteristics of our semi-continuous monitoring scheme: (1) the ability to conduct semi-continuous monitoring of different parameters (e.g. BS and BP) and generate the appropriate decisions based on the adaptive expert system, (2) generates automated recommendations from monitoring composite parameters namely BP and BS, and (3) validates whether the automated recommendations matches at certain level the recommendations of medical experts.

Fig. 4 and Fig. 5 illustrate the inputs and outputs of the BS expert system. Fig. 4 shows the readings obtained from semi-continuous monitoring of 70 patients. It calculates the average BS obtained over a monitoring period of 6 months. Fig. 5 illustrates the output generated after inferring the reading of Fig. 4 on a set of BS rules. The results show fluctuating BS readings with around 80% are high, very high, to fluctuating high, 10% low to fluctuating low, and the rest are normal readings. These results prove that the BS expert system is able to provide accurate outputs correlated with the received readings. The risk in this monitoring situation of vascular complications due to high BS is significantly high.

Fig. 6 and Fig. 7 illustrate the inputs and outputs of the BP expert system. Fig. 6 shows the readings obtained from semi-continuous monitoring of 70 patients. It calculates the average BP obtained over a monitoring period of 6 months. The obtained values of BP are consistently normal. Fig. 7 illustrates the output generated after inferring the readings of Fig. 6 on a set of BP rules. The results show an average BP readings with around 50% as normal, 35% PreHigh, 10% Stage1High and Stage2High, and the rest of readings are low. These results prove that the BP expert system is able to provide accurate outputs correlated with the entered readings.

According to the generated outputs, it is unlikely that these patients will have a risk of vascular complications.

Finally, Fig. 8 illustrates the output of a composite BP and BS readings and the related recommendations. For each patient, two outputs are generated: one records the result of BP monitoring and the second records the result of BS monitoring. A good percentage of patients whose BP and BS are high, necessary urgent actions should be taken in order to react to such situation; this includes for example, consulting immediately with a physician, take overdose medication.

5   Conclusion

Continuous sensing and monitoring of health metrics generate a massive amount of data. Generating clinically validated recommendations to patients under monitoring is of prime importance to protect them from the risk of falling into severe health degradations. Physicians also can be supported with automated recommendations that gain from historical data and increasing learning cycles.

In this paper, we proposed an adaptive ES supported by a smart monitoring and an iterative data analytics techniques. Smart monitoring implemented, for instance, preprocessing of data and intelligent sensing (e.g. stop/resume sensing based on patient's context: sleeping, in activity). However, iterative data analytics implemented the loopback feature that continuously improved rules, knowledge base, and generated advices. Both techniques reduced data quantity and improved data quality. The advices generated are visualized via an application interface.

We conducted a series of experiments using different scenarios of monitoring blood sugar and blood pressure parameters of a population of patients with chronic diseases. We obtained interesting results that prove that our ES combined with the intelligent monitoring and analytic techniques provide a high accuracy of collected data and appropriate advices. As future work, we are planning to complete the other features of our proposed system mainly the loopback evaluation, and then continuously compare the recommendations generated from our ES with those of medical experts. This will require a close collaboration with medical expert for validating the accuracy of ES recommendations. We are also planning to experiment other classification techniques for data analytics and decision-making.

References

1. Basilakis, J., Lovell, N.H., Celler, B.G.: A decision support architecture for telecare patient management of chronic and complex disease. In: 29th Annual International Conference of the IEEE Engineering in Medicine and Biology Society, EMBS 2007, pp. 4335–4338. IEEE (2007)
2. Tsipouras, M.G., Exarchos, T.P., Fotiadis, D.I., Kotsia, A., Naka, A., Michalis, L.K.: A decision support system for the diagnosis of coronary artery disease. In: 19th IEEE International Symposium on Computer-Based Medical Systems, CBMS 2006, pp. 279–284. IEEE (2006)

3. Ramesh, M.V., Anu, T., Thirugnanam, H.: An intelligent decision support system for enhancing an m-health application. In: Ninth International Conference on Wireless and Optical Communications Networks (WOCN), pp. 1–5. IEEE (2012)
4. Georga, E., Protopappas, V., Guillen, A., Fico, G., Ardigo, D., Arredondo, M.T., et al.: Data mining for blood glucose prediction and knowledge discovery in diabetic patients: The METABO diabetes modeling and management system. In: Annual International Conference of the IEEE Engineering in Medicine and Biology Society, EMBC 2009, pp. 5633–5636. IEEE (2009)
5. Azian Azamimi, A., Zulkarnay, Z., Nur Farahiyah, M.: Design and development of Fuzzy Expert System for diagnosis of hypertension (2011)
6. Pintér, P., Vajda, L., Kovács, L.: Developing a decision support system to determine carbohydrate intake of diabetic patients. In: IEEE 10th International Symposium on Applied Machine Intelligence and Informatics (SAMI), pp. 427–430. IEEE (2012)
7. Nnamoko, N., Arshad, F., England, D., Vora, J.: Fuzzy Expert System for Type 2 Diabetes Mellitus (T2DM) Management Using Dual Inference Mechanism. In: 2013 AAAI Spring Symposium Series (2013)
8. Morsi, I., El Gawad, A., Zakria, Y.: Fuzzy logic in heart rate and blood pressure measuring system. In: IEEE Sensors Applications Symposium (SAS), pp. 113–117. IEEE (2013)

Application of Artificial Neural Networks for the Diagnosis of the Condition of the Arterio-venous Fistula on the Basis of Acoustic Signals

Marcin Grochowina[1], Lucyna Leniowska[1], and Piotr Dulkiewicz[2]

[1] Institute of Technology, University of Rzeszów,
al. Rejtana 16, 35-310 Rzeszów, Poland
{gromar,lleniow}@ur.edu.pl
http://www.kmia.ur.edu.pl/
[2] Nefron Sp z o.o., Rzeszów, Poland
http://www.nefron.eu

Abstract. The paper presents an innovative method for the diagnosis of the arterio-venous fistula based on recorded acoustic signals. A fistula is an artificial connection between an artery and a vein made to obtain a suitably large blood flow for haemodialysis. If the fistula does not work properly, thrombosis or other health- or life-threatening conditions may develop. Based on the analysis of sound generated by blood flowing through the fistula, the occurrence of pathological conditions may be diagnosed. An artificial neural network implemented using an FANN (Fast Artificial Neural Network) library has been used to evaluate the fistula condition.

Keywords: artificial neural networks, arterio-venous fistula, telemedicine.

1 Introduction

Acoustic emission is an effect used in the diagnostics of constructions, food, tools, in the surveillance of the condition of equipment and constructions, in testing fatigue and cracking in materials, detection of material defects, etc. [1][2]. The propagation of acoustic waves for diagnostic purposes may also be successfully used in medicine, because the human body emits a number of sounds, specific for biological processes. Physiological processes, such as breathing, digestion or blood circulation, generate acoustic waves, frequently used in history taking as a primary source of information about the patients health condition. Furthermore, following surgical interventions, new and non-natural connections between tissues or organs may be formed in the human body. They are sources of acoustic waves as well, and their characteristics may provide additional diagnostic information. The surgical procedure to make an arterio-venous fistula is an example of such an intervention. Analysis of sounds emitted by the fistula can be used to diagnose its condition. An artificial neural network is a convenient tool which supports the analysis as it helps to detect pathological changes with an uncomplicated algorithm.

D. Ślęzak et al. (Eds.): BIH 2014, LNAI 8609, pp. 400–411, 2014.

2   Analysis of Fistula Condition Based on the Sounds It Generates

The term "fistula" originates from a Latin word and when used in medicine, it means connecting two or more organs due to pathological processes, treatment-related complications or intentionally by a surgical procedure.

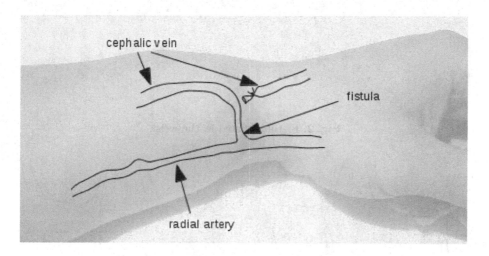

Fig. 1. Scheme of the arterio-venous fistula

The arterio-venous fistula is defined here as an artificially formed connection between an artery and a vein, usually located in the wrist in which it provides a bypass for blood flow in one of the two arteries which supply blood to the hand. However, other locations of the fistula are also possible, such as on the collar bone or the thigh. Due to the intervention, a vessel forms just beneath the skin (Fig.2.) in which needle insertion provides access to arterial blood with a flow rate of up to 1000 ml/min, being crucial for patients with renal disorders in need of dialysis [3].

When a fistula is formed correctly, it provides smooth and continuous blood flow; however, to maintain this condition, the patient has to perform certain activities, such as appropriate physical exercises involving the hand, the wrist and the forearm. Furthermore, the dialysis access should be treated with utmost care and protected. Any person with an arterio-venous fistula must adjust their life style to new requirements this element involves. The fundamental aspect of this is to examine the arterio-venous fistula on ones own daily. The examination entails gently pressing ones fingers to the fistula and checking blood pulsation throughout the length of the arterio-venous fistula. When the fistula works properly, a noticeable and distinct pulsation noise can be detected, usually in one, specific section. When a patient fails to be attentive and disciplined in this aspect, the fistula lumen may be gradually stenosed until it is completely occluded and, in extreme cases, blood flow completely ceases (Fig.3.) .

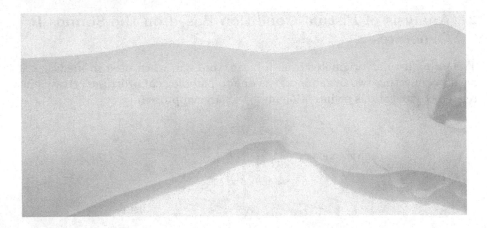

Fig. 2. Fistula located in the wrist

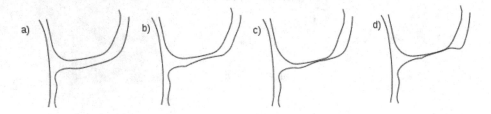

Fig. 3. Arterio-venous fistula: normal (a), stenosed (b), extremely stenosed (c), completely occluded (d)

Such situations usually occur in patients after a kidney transplant procedure in whom the fistula is no longer used and who, therefore, stopped to take care of it, even though its maintenance is in their interest. Fistula stenosis leads to reduced blood flow or turbulent flow, which can be monitored using an ultrasonic flow meter with a feature of flow measurement based on the Doppler effect (Fig.4.). In the case of extreme stenosis, blood flows through the vessel only when systolic pressure exceeds a certain limit value; this means that if the patients arterial pressure is low for a certain period, blood flow in the fistula may cease completely. Such situations are conducive to the formation of thrombi or, in a longer perspective, adhesions which lead to the complete and permanent occlusion of the fistula [4].

As the fistula vessel is located just beneath the skin, it is possible to detect the characteristic pulsation related to the rhythm of arterial pressure fluctuations due to heartbeat by touching. Furthermore, the characteristic, pulsating hum of blood flowing through the vessel can be heard using a stethoscope. To record the sound generated by the fistula, the only operation needed is to accommodate a microphone in the stethoscope and connect it to an analogue-to-digital converter. Based on the characteristic features of signals recorded this way, the condition of the fistula can be determined and, in particular, its possible stenosis which

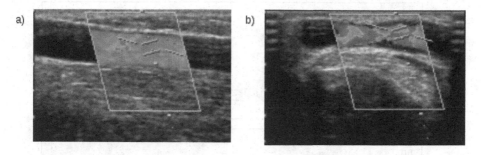

Fig. 4. Ultrasonic image with marked blood flow in a normal (a) and a stenosed (b) fistula

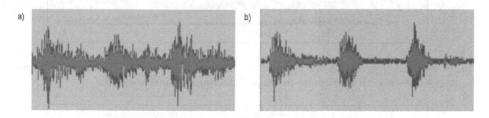

Fig. 5. Temporal sound profile for a normal fistula (a) and a fistula with significant pathological changes (b)

may lead to occlusion. The signal profile for a fistula without any pathological conditions has an amplitude higher than zero throughout the cardiac cycle and it is maintained constant between the maxima when the heart contracts.

Fistula stenosis leads to changes in the acoustic signal it generates (Fig.5.). Its amplitude between the maxima is no longer constant, but it is reduced instead the more, the larger fistula stenosis is; it may even be zero when the vessel becomes temporarily occluded. In the case of considerable pathology, differences with respect to a normal signal are so large that they can be heard. However, sound analysis in the time domain is rather difficult in terms of algorithms to be used, in particular with respect to recording signals from fistulae with less significant pathological changes, and an evident solution is to transfer the signal to the frequency domain and process it further in this form. The frequency spectrum of a signal from a normal fistula has a very minor contribution of low frequencies (up to approx. 50 Hz), with its maximum in the 150-250 Hz range. Subsequently, the amplitude of the components gradually declines to approx. 1 kHz (Fig.6.).

The acoustic signal typical of a pathological fistula (Fig.7.) has a large contribution of components around 150 Hz and in the 350-400 Hz range, increased contribution of components below 50 Hz and minor effects of components around 200 Hz. In moderately pathological cases, the characteristic sign is that the contribution of low-frequency components is increased with slight only changes of the spectrum profile compared to the normal shape.

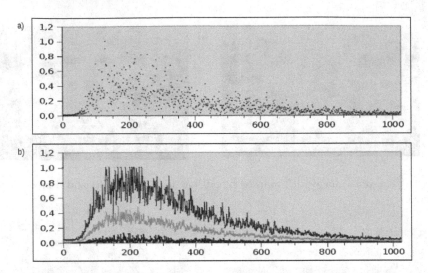

Fig. 6. Frequency spectrum for a signal of a normal fistula: a) single patient, b) synthesis of 64 cases with maximum, mean and minimum values marked

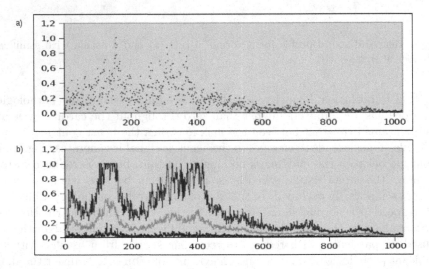

Fig. 7. Frequency spectrum for a signal of a strongly pathological fistula: a) single patient, b) synthesis of 64 cases with maximum, mean and minimum values marked

3   FANN Library

An FANN (Fast Artificial Neural Network) library was used in this project [5]. It is a C-programming language library distributed with a GPL licence which provides a programmers interface for the comprehensive use of artificial neural networks from their generation through training using several available algorithms to their use in users applications.

The input layer contains a number of neurons corresponding to the number of inputs to the network, while the number of neurons in the output layer is usually equal to the number of parameters to be recognised by the network. However, it is less simple to determine the number of hidden layers and neurons they contain. There are no rules to define those parameters and they are selected experimentally. The definition of the neuron activation function is important for the network to train and work properly. This is usually a unipolar sigmoid function

$$y(x) = \frac{1}{1 + e^{-\beta x}} \tag{1}$$

or bipolar

$$y(x) = \frac{2}{1 + e^{-\beta x}} - 1 \tag{2}$$

its slope can be determined using parameter β (Fig.8.). When $\beta \to \infty$, the function becomes a threshold function.

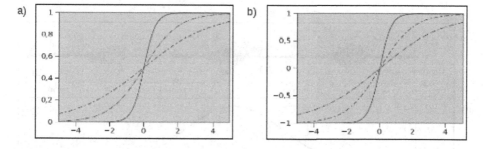

Fig. 8. Examples of three unipolar (a) and bipolar (b) sigmoid functions with different slopes

The FANN library can be used to determine the slope of a function separately for each layer; usually, however, it is set as identical for all layers. When the activation function has a large slope, the result of network operation is close to extreme values (0 or 1), while smaller slope functions yield intermediate values. The training process may use one of the available algorithms. Training algorithms are usually based on backward error propagation; however, network error values are computed in different ways. The FANN library has several solutions available.

The "FANN_TRAIN_INCREMENTAL" algorithm computes the error and changes the values of weights in the neuron for each training model. Therefore, the weights are changed more than once during one epoch to avoid situations whereby the training process is stopped, because a minor change in the weights has led to an increased mean squared error, even though the optimum solution has not been achieved.

Algorithms of the FANN_TRAIN_BATCH family compute the mean squared error for all training models and the resulting values are propagated backward in the network being trained from its outputs to inputs once per epoch. This method is much faster and enables the use of additional built-in global optimisation mechanisms; however, it may lose certain characteristic features found in a minor fraction of training models only.

4   Developing a Classification System for Sounds Generated by the Fistula

Approx. 200 model signals were used in the neural network training process from more than ten different patients with different physiological conditions of their bodies, in particular before and after dialysis, with different pulse and arterial pressure values. Five different mobile telephone models were used to acquire the training material: Sony Xperia Mini, Samsung Chat 335, Samsung Galaxy S3, LG Swift L5 and myPhone a210. Distortions of frequency characteristics due to audio systems of different telephones were irrelevant for the problem in question when the noise removal mode was switched off.

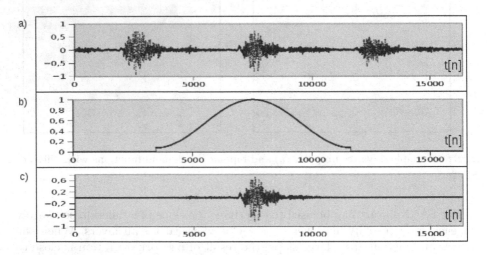

Fig. 9. Signal processing before spectral analysis: input signal (a), window function (b) and signal prepared for analysis (c)

The KissFFT library [7] available based on the BSD licence was used for signal frequency analysis; it enables fast Fourier transform to be computed through a programmers interface based on the mixed-radix algorithm [8]. Local maxima of sound intensity are marked in the data string which overlap the maximum systolic pressure values. The centre of the time window function is located in those points. (Fig.9.). To compensate for the spectral broadening effect, the Hamming window was used.

The spectral range to be analysed was limited to 1 kHz, because the fraction of higher-frequency components was negligible and irrelevant for the analysis. Information about spectral components in the 1-1024 Hz range with 1 Hz resolution is fed to 1024 neural network inputs. The number of network layers was set to 3, while the number of neurons in the hidden layer was experimentally determined to be 32. When the number of neurons in the hidden layer was lower than 21, it was impossible to train the network in the defined period of 200 epochs, while when increased above 32, no reduction in the number of epochs necessary for appropriate training was seen (Fig.10.).

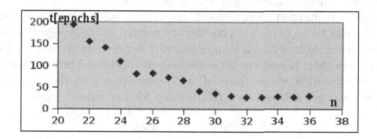

Fig. 10. Relationship between network training time and number of neurons in the hidden layer

Before analysis in the neural network, the spectrum is normalised as this process appeared to be necessary (Fig.11.). The result of network operation is the degree of consistency between the recorded signal and average reference signals during the network training process.

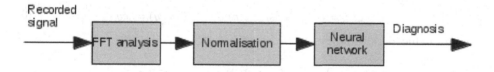

Fig. 11. Data flow in the diagnostic system

It appeared within testing that additional determination of the noise level in the recorded signal was necessary. When a signal other than that emitted by the fistula was fed to the system, pathology was diagnosed, while normal signals were frequently diagnosed as pathological due to noise and unwanted environmental signals. To prevent this, the neural network was modified so that it determined the degree of consistency not only with respect to normal reference signals, but also to pathological reference signals. Therefore, the extended version of the neural network has two outputs. They show values which indicate the degree of consistency with normal and pathological signals. An additional decision block

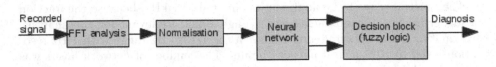

Fig. 12. Data flow in the system with additional classification of pathological signals

in which fuzzy logic was used finally determines whether the profile tested has recorded a normal or pathological acoustic signal from a fistula or else whether the noise level makes diagnosis impossible (Fig.12.).

Each output from the neural network may have a value in the ¡0; 1¿ range. As any signal needs to be explicitly classified as normal or pathological, only those cases are acceptable in which a value close to 1 is one output value and a value close to 0 is another. If not, the measurement is considered inconclusive. ex-nor is the logical function whose table of truth corresponds to those criteria. The function was compiled based on a relationship for two-valued logic:

$$x \odot y = \overline{x}\,\overline{y} + xy \tag{3}$$

Initially, the simplest definitions for s-norms and t-norms were assumed:

$$S(x,y) = max(x,y) \qquad and \qquad T(x,y) = min(x,y) \tag{4}$$

As a result, given that $\overline{x} = 1 - x$, the result was:

$$exNor(x,y) = max(min(1 - x, 1 - y), min(x,y)) \tag{5}$$

Considering the algorithm, it proved more straightforward to describe the function with the following assumptions

$$S(x,y) = x + y - xy \qquad and \qquad T(x,y) = xy \tag{6}$$

when reduced:

$$exNor(x,y) = 1 - x - y + 2xy + (x - x^2)(y^2 - y) \tag{7}$$

Finally, when simplified, which does not have any significant impact on the form of the function, the following function was used [6]

$$exNor(x,y) = 1 - x - y + 2xy \tag{8}$$

For the network training process to be correct, noise signals without any sounds emitted by the fistula were included among the training models together with normal and pathological signals. To eliminate any cases of wrong diagnosis, the system was extended with a pulse signal detection unit. If the signal to be analysed contains a characteristic, cyclic pulse signal within the defined limits, the subsequent part of the system based on FFT transform and the neural network is activated. When pulse cannot be detected, the input signal is rejected.

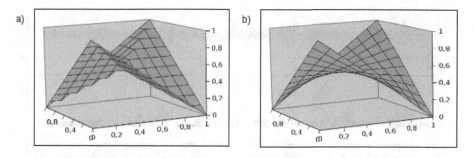

Fig. 13. Graphic visualisation of ex-nor functions given by relationships (5) (a) and (8) (b)

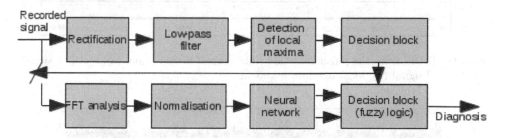

Fig. 14. Data flow in the system (version with pulse detection)

The pulse detection algorithm has a digital low-pass filter with an infinite impulse response (IRR) (Fig.14.) whose limit frequency is at a level of several hertz, preceded by a block which rectifies the signal tested.

On the subsequent stage, local maxima in the profile are detected and their distance is calculated. For an acoustic signal from a fistula, the maxima are distributed at regular distances and indicate the maximum values of systolic pressure. For signals without pulse, the result is an image of maxima distributed quite randomly, and the constant period of their occurrence cannot be determined (Fig.15. Fig.16.).

When maxima which occur at regular intervals are found, the signal is transferred to further processing using the neural network.

5   Summary

The possibility of reliable, fast and relatively simple diagnosis of the condition of the arterio-venous fistula is an important issue for many patients undergoing dialysis. As there are considerable differences in the signal generated by the fistula, pathological conditions can be diagnosed and avoided. The paper presents an original method for the diagnosis of the arterio-venous fistula based on acoustic signals recorded e.g. using a mobile phone. Because a neural network is used

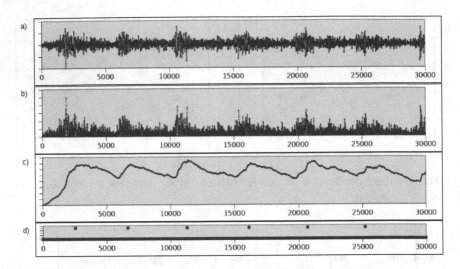

Fig. 15. Result from the pulse detection unit: normal fistula signal (a), rectified signal (b) filtered signal (c), local maxima found (d)

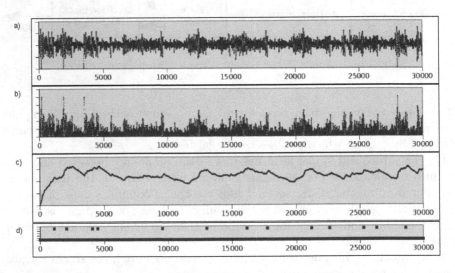

Fig. 16. Result from the pulse detection unit: noise signal (a), rectified signal (b) low-pass filtered signal (c), local maxima found (d)

for the diagnostics, it can be clearly stated whether any risk due to fistula stenosis exists. As continuous wavelet transform is used to analyse signals, the pulse detection process can be simplified and additional features of the signal to be analysed can be revealed which cannot be found in the analysis in the frequency domain. Longer observations of the same patient indicate that slow but systematic changes in the fistula signal spectrum are not directly related to the fistula condition. Therefore, further studies may be useful to identify reasons for such changes and to obtain further information which can be used for extended diagnostics based on the analysis of acoustic signals emitted by the arterio-venous fistula.

References

1. Ranachowski, Z.: Metody pomiaru i analiza sygnau emisji akustycznej. Prace IPPT PAN, 1, Warszawa (1997)
2. Grosse, C., Ochtsu, M. (eds.): Acoustic Emission Testing. Basic for Research - Applications in Civil Engineering. Springer, Berlin (2008)
3. Rutowski, B.: Dializoterapia w praktyce lekarskiej MAKmedia, Gdask (2004)
4. Daugirdas, J.T., Blake, P.G., Ing, T.S.: Handbook of dialysis. Lippincott Williams & Wilkins (2007)
5. Steffen Nissen, FANN reference manual
6. Bedregal1, B.C., Reiser, R.H.S., Dimuro, G.P.: Xor-Implications and E-Implications: Classes of fuzzy implications based on fuzzy Xor LSFA (2008)
7. http://sourceforge.net/projects/kissfft
8. Chu, E., George, A.: Inside the FFT BLACK BOX - Serial and Parallel Fast Fourier Transform. CRC Press LLC (2000)

On the Statistical Performance of Connectivity Estimators in the Frequency Domain

Koichi Sameshima[1], Daniel Y. Takahashi[2], and Luiz A. Baccalá[3]

[1] Department of Radiology and Oncology, Faculdade de Medicina,
University of São Paulo, São Paulo, SP, 01246-903, Brazil
ksameshi@usp.br
[2] Psychology Department, Neuroscience Institute,
Princeton University, Princeton, NJ, USA
[3] Department of Telecommunications and Control Engineering, Escola Politécnica,
University of São Paulo, São Paulo, SP, Brazil

Abstract. This paper studies the performance of recently introduced asymptotic statistics for connectivity inference in the frequency domain, namely via information partial directed coherence (iPDC) and information directed transfer function (iDTF) and compares them to the behaviour of a classic time domain multivariate Granger causality test (GCT) by using Monte Carlo simulations of three widely used toy-models under varying the simulated data record lengths. In general, the false-positive rates for non-existing connections and the false-negative rates for existing connections are found to decrease with longer record lengths.

Keywords: Partial Directed Coherence, Directed Transfer Function, Granger Causality, Null hypothesis test performance.

1 Introduction

This paper examines the comparative statistical performance of the connectivity detection problem [1] for three popular neural connectivity estimators that enjoy rigorously known description of their asymptotic behaviour. In addition to the Granger causality test (GCT) from [2], we recently derived rigorous results [3,4] about the asymptotic behaviour of information partial directed coherence (iPDC) and information directed transfer function (iDTF) [5] which are quantities that respectively generalize *partial directed coherence* (PDC) [6] and *directed transfer function* (DTF) [7] to correctly describe coupling effect size issues.

Exploiting three widely used toy models selected from the literature, we carried out Monte Carlo simulations to verify the performance of the connectivity null hypothesis under their derived optimum rejection criteria as a function of data record length (K) showing them compatible with their expected large sample behaviour. We complemented the study by computing false-positive and false-negative test rates for each estimator alternative.

D. Ślęzak et al. (Eds.): BIH 2014, LNAI 8609, pp. 412–423, 2014.

2   Methods and Results

2.1   Monte Carlo Simulations

Following our recently proposed the information PDC and information DTF [5], and their corresponding rigorous asymptotic statistics for both measures (see [3] and [4] for details) we here examine their statistical performance against that of the well-established time-domain GCT [2]. We do so via Monte Carlo simulations performed in the MATLAB environment by using its "normally distributed pseudorandom number" generator to simulate system innovation noise processes, which were furthermore assumed zero mean unit variance and uncorrelated. To test the performance of the latter three connectivity estimators, for each toy model and at each data record length we selected $K = \{100, 200, 500, 1\,000, 2\,000, 5\,000, 10\,000\}$ repeating $1\,000$ simulations for each case. For each simulation, the first $5\,000$ data points were discarded to eliminate possible transients. We used the Nuttal-Strand algorithm for multivariate autoregressive (MAR) model estimation and the Akaike information criterion (AIC) for model order selection [8]. iPDC and iDTF detection threshold was set for $\alpha = 1\%$ and p-values were computed at 32 uniformly separated normalized frequency points covering the whole interval.

A connection was deemed detected for a given pair of structures if its p-value resulted less than α for some frequency within the interval. This connectivity decision criterion is somewhat lax and tends to overestimate the presence connectivity for iPDC and iDTF. In particular for iPDC, it should detect connectivity more often than GCT does.

The reader may access our open MATLAB codes for both iPDC and iDTF asymptotic statistics used in this study at www.lcs.poli.usp.br/~baccala/pdc.

Next we describe and probe the toy models:

2.2   Model 1: Closed-Loop Model

Model 1 is an $\{N = 7\}$-variable model borrowed from [9] (Fig. 1). It has two distinct disconnected substructures: $\{x_1, x_2, x_3, x_4, x_5\}$ and $\{x_6, x_7\}$, which share a same common frequency of oscillation. The set of equations that describes the model is:

$$\begin{cases} x_1(t) = 0.95\sqrt{2}x_1(t-1) - 0.9025x_1(t-2) + 0.5x_5(t-2) + w_1(t) \\ x_2(t) = -0.5x_1(t-1) + w_2(t) \\ x_3(t) = 0.4x_2(t-2) + w_3(t) \\ x_4(t) = -0.5x_3(t-1) + 0.25\sqrt{2}x_4(t-1) + 0.25\sqrt{2}x_5(t-1) + w_4(t) \\ x_5(t) = -0.25\sqrt{2}x_4(t-1) + 0.25\sqrt{2}x_5(t-1) + w_5(t) \\ x_6(t) = 0.95\sqrt{2}x_6(t-1) - 0.9025x_6(t-2) + w_6(t) \\ x_7(t) = -0.1x_6(t-1) + w_7(t) \end{cases} \quad (1)$$

with w_i standing for innovation noises.

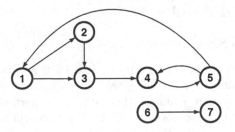

Fig. 1. Diagram depicting the essential elements of Model 1 represented by Eq. 1 from [9]. The elements x_1 to x_5 establish closed-loop connections, with short and long connected paths, while x_6 and x_7 are part of completely separate substructure, i.e. disconnected from $\{x_1, .., x_5\}$, but sharing a common frequency of oscillation.

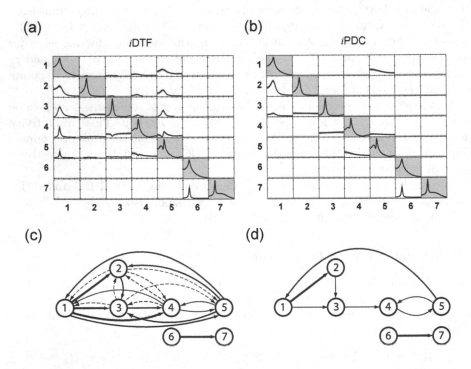

Fig. 2. This figure depicts the result of (**a**) iDTF and (**b**) iPDC estimations obtained with a data simulation of Model 1, given by Eq. 1, with $K = 2\,000$ points and $\alpha = 1\%$, where standard subplotting lay-out with variables in columns representing the source and in rows the target structures is used, and in each subplot the x-axis represents the frequency and y-axis the iDTF and iPDC scaled in [0 1] interval. The main-diagonals with grayed-background subplottings contain the power spectra. (**c**) Note, as theoretically expected, that according to iDTF estimation nodes can reach one another among $\{x_1, x_2, x_3, x_4, x_5\}$, as although some magnitudes of iDTF are very small, they are all statistically significant. (**d**) While iPDC estimate shows immediate adjacent node connectivity pattern.

A single trial example of iDTF and iPDC connectivity estimation in the frequency domain are respectively depicted in Figs. 2a and b, with significant values, at $\alpha = 0.01$, represented by black solid lines. The corresponding connectivity graph diagrams are contained in Figs. 2c and d, where arrow thickness represents estimate magnitude. Note that iPDC reflects adjacent connections Fig. 2b and d, while iDTF represents reachability aspects of the directed structure [10].

Granger Causality Test for Model 1. Fig. 3 summarizes the performance of Granger causality test for data record lengths $K = \{100, 200, 500, 1\,000, 2\,000, 5\,000\}$. As expected, for $K > 200$, GCT properly detects the connectivity presence and absence.

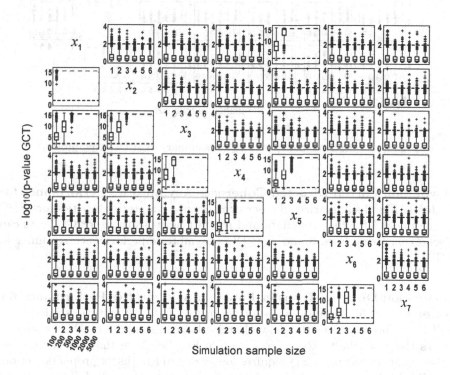

Fig. 3. In this and all the figures that follow, the pattern contains subplots with variables in columns representing the sources and while the target structures lie in rows. Each subplot possesses boxplots of the distribution of $-log_{10}(p$-value) for Granger causality test for 1 000 Monte Carlo simulations over different record lengths $K = \{100, 200, 500, 1\,000, 2\,000, 5\,000\}$, marked as 1, 2, 3, 4, 5 and 6, respectively, on the x-axis of each subplot. Since $\alpha = 0.01$ values above 2 (dashed-line) indicate rejection of the null-hypothesis of connectivity absence.

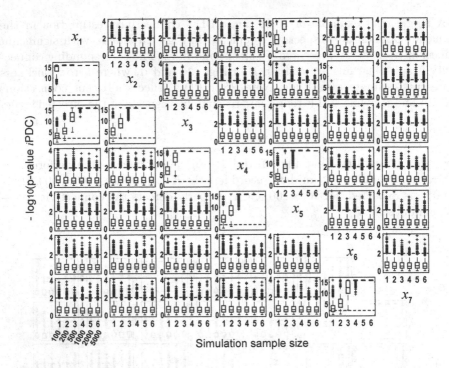

Fig. 4. Model 1 boxplot performance summary of iPDC asymptotics

Information Partial Directed Coherence Asymptotics Performance for Model 1. Fig. 4 summarizes the performance of asymptotic statistics for iPDC for the Model 1 for the same data and record lengths as those for GCT. As can be seen comparing Figs. 3 and 4, iPDC's asymptotic performance is similar to GCT's.

Information Directed Transfer Function Asymptotics Performance for Model 1. Fig. 5 summarizes the performance of the asymptotic statistics for iDTF. The boxplots clearly show that for larger sample size iDTF correctly detects the reachability structure shown in Fig. 2c. Note that the weakest or farthest connection ($x_2 \rightarrow x_1$) requires longer record lengths for proper detection. A modified DTF measure combined with partial coherence, called direct directed transfer function (dDTF) [11], was not explored here as its asymptotic statistics are not yet available.

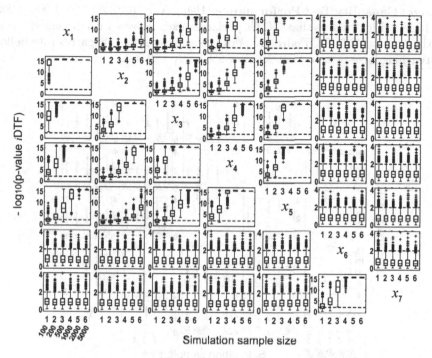

Fig. 5. Model 1 boxplot performance summary of iDTF asymptotics

2.3 Model 2: Five-Variable Model

Model 2 is graphically represented in Fig. 6 with its corresponding set of defining equations:

$$\begin{cases} x_1(t) = 0.95\sqrt{2}x_1(t-1) - 0.9025x_1(t-2) + w_1(t) \\ x_2(t) = 0.5x_1(t-2) + w_2(t) \\ x_3(t) = -0.4x_1(t-3) + w_3(t) \\ x_4(t) = -0.5x_1(t-2) + 0.25\sqrt{2}x_4(t-1) + 0.25\sqrt{2}x_5(t-1) + w_4(t) \\ x_5(t) = -0.25\sqrt{2}x_4(t-1) + 0.25\sqrt{2}x_5(t-1) + w_5(t) \end{cases} \quad (2)$$

where w_i stand for unit variance uncorrelated zero mean Gaussian innovations.

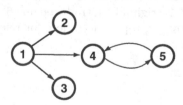

Fig. 6. Diagram depicting the essential elements of Model 2 introduced by [6]

Granger Causality Test Performance. Using $K = \{100, 200, 500, 1\,000, 2\,000\}$ for Model 2, Fig. 7 shows that GCT's performance improves with increased record length. At $K = 200$, GCT already performs well with false-negative rate bellow 5%, reaching false-negative rates below 2% for $K = 2\,000$.

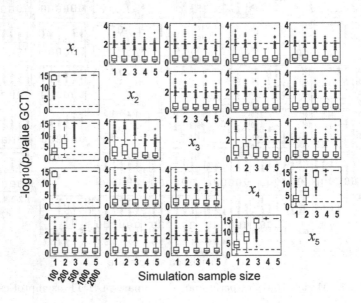

Fig. 7. GCT performance for Model 2

***i*PDC Asymptotics Performance for Model 2.** For Model 2, as seen in Fig. 8, the pattern of *i*PDC performance is similar to GCT's. Yet *i*PDC's false-negative rates are slightly higher than GCT's. For example its performance for $K = 2\,000$ is between 3.0% and 5.5%. False-negative rates are practically negligible when $K > 200$ for both GCT and *i*PDC.

2.4 Model 3: Modified Five-var Model

To further probe the statistical behaviour of GCT and *i*PDC, we simulated the five-channel toy model originally introduced in [6] under a variant of its formulation as proposed by [12] reproduced here for reference in Fig. 9.

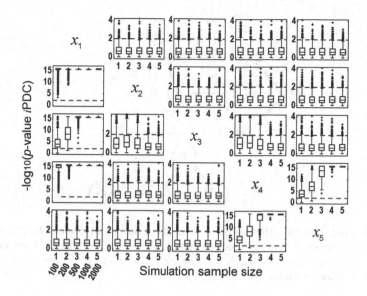

Fig. 8. iPDC performance for Model 2

The corresponding set of equations is given by

$$\begin{cases} x_1(t) = 0.95\sqrt{2}x_1(t-1) - 0.9025x_1(t-2) \\ \qquad + e_1(t) + a_1e_6(t) + b_1e_7(t-1) + c_1e_7(t-2) \\ x_2(t) = 0.5x_1(t-2) \\ \qquad + e_2(t) + a_2e_6(t) + b_2e_7(t-1) + c_2e_7(t-2) \\ x_3(t) = -0.4x_1(t-3) \\ \qquad + e_3(t) + a_3e_6(t) + b_3e_7(t-1) + c_3e_7(t-2) \\ x_4(t) = -0.5x_1(t-2) + 0.25\sqrt{2}x_4(t-1) + 0.25\sqrt{2}x_5(t-1) \\ \qquad + e_4(t) + a_4e_6(t) + b_4e_7(t-1) + c_4e_7(t-2) \\ x_5(t) = -0.25\sqrt{2}x_4(t-1) + 0.25\sqrt{2}x_5(t-1) \\ \qquad + e_5(t) + a_5e_6(t) + b_5e_7(t-1) + c_5e_7(t-2) \end{cases} \qquad (3)$$

additionally containing the large exogenous input $e_6(t)$ and the latent variable $e_7(t)$. In the simulations $e_i(t)$ were uncorrelated zero mean unit variance Gaussian innovation noises and the parameters were chosen $a_i \sim U(0,1)$, $b_i = 2$ and $c_i = 5$, $i = 1,\ldots,5$ as in [12]. Also for reference, $n_s = 2\,000$ data length were used in [12].

The proposal in [12] of introducing exogenous/latent variables is an interesting idea which allows investigating the influence of large common additive noise

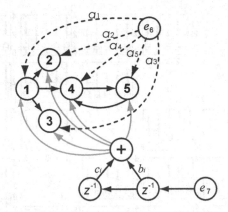

Fig. 9. Diagram depicting the essential elements of model introduced by [12] modified from [6]. For each simulation, the parameters a_i were chosen randomly from uniformly distributed [0 1] interval, and all $b_i = 2$ and $c_i = 5$, while the innovations, e_i, were drawn from random variables with $N\{0, 1\}$

sources on the performance of GCT and iPDC. Here, in order to assess the impairment that the extra exogenous/latent variables possibly inflict on null hypothesis testing, we repeated the procedure not just under the same conditions of [12], but also using a broader range of data record sizes:

$$K = \{100, 200, 500, 1\,000, 2\,000, 5\,000, 10\,000\}.$$

GCT Performance in the Presence of Exogenous Noise, Model 3. The GCT performance for Model 3 can be appreciated in Fig. 10. When compared with Model 2, GCT's performance deteriorates in the presence of exogenous noise. Interestingly its performance with respect to detecting existing connections increases with longer data records, while in absence of connections, the false-positive rate increases sharply for the $K = 10\,000$ case. For $K = 500$ the false-positive rates are around 5%, and increase to almost 40% for $K = 10\,000$. False-negative rates are negligible.

iPDC Performance in the Presence of Exogenous Noise. As seen in Fig. 11, iPDC performance in detecting connectivity is similar to GCT's. As noted before, iPDC tends to have higher false-positive rates compared to GCT due to possibly the chosen frequency domain detection criterion of using a single-frequency with significant p-value as indicative of a valid connection.

The false-positive rates go from 10% for $K = 100$ up to 48% for $K = 10\,000$.

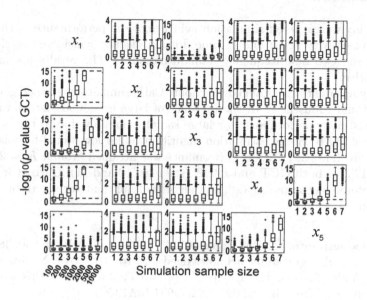

Fig. 10. GCT performance on Model 3

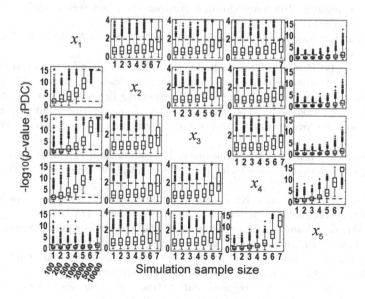

Fig. 11. iPDC performance on Model 3

3   Discussion

In this study we gathered simulation evidence of the performance of three statistical connectivity tests: one in time domain, usually considered as the gold-standard and two new frequency domain measures. The results are mutually corroborative.

The asymptotic results gauged via Monte Carlo simulations showed good large sample fit and robustness. In the presence of large exogenous/latent variables, we observed poor performance for large samples possibly due to the poor performance of MAR model estimation algorithm under low signal-to-noise ratio. Interestingly, however, a good performance was attained around $K = 2\,000$, as used by [12], for both GCT and iPDC (see Figs. 10 and 11). Current investigation is centered on comparing different algorithms for multivariate autoregressive estimation.

Acknowledgements. CNPq Grants 307163/2013-0 to L.A.B. and 309381/2012-6 to K.S. are also gratefully acknowledged and to NAPNA - Núcleo de Neurociência Aplicada from the University of São Paulo. Part of this work took place during FAPESP Grant 2005/56464-9 (CInAPCe).

References

1. Baccalá, L.A., Sameshima, K.: Brain Connectivity: An Overview. In: Methods in Brain Connectivity Inference through Multivariate Time Series Analysis, pp. 1–9. CRC Press (2014)
2. Lütkepohl, H.: New Introduction to Multiple Time Series Analysis. Springer, New York (2005)
3. Baccalá, L., De Brito, C., Takahashi, D., Sameshima, K.: Unified asymptotic theory for all partial directed coherence forms. Philosophical Transactions of the Royal Society A: Mathematical, Physical and Engineering Sciences 371, 1–13 (2013)
4. Baccalá, L.A., Takahashi, D.Y., Sameshima, K.: Consolidating a link centered neural connectivity framework with directed transfer function asymptotic. Biological Cybernetics (submitted, 2014)
5. Takahashi, D., Baccalá, L., Sameshima, K.: Information theoretic interpretation of frequency domain connectivity measures. Biological Cybernetics 103, 463–469 (2010)
6. Baccalá, L.A., Sameshima, K.: Partial directed coherence: a new concept in neural structure determination. Biological Cybernetics 84, 463–474 (2001)
7. Kamiński, M., Blinowska, K.J.: A new method of the description of the information flow in brain structures. Biological Cybernetics 65, 203–210 (1991)
8. Marple Jr., S.: Digital Spectral Analysis. Prentice Hall, Englewood Cliffs (1987)
9. Baccalá, L.A., Sameshima, K.: Overcoming the limitations of correlation analysis for many simultaneously processed neural structures. Progress in Brain Research, Advances in Neural Population Coding 130, 33–47 (2001)

10. Baccalá, L.A., Sameshima, K.: Multivariate Time Series Brain Connectivity: A Sum Up. In: Methods in Brain Connectivity Inference through Multivariate Time Series Analysis, pp. 245–251. CRC Press, Boca Raton (2014)
11. Korzeniewska, A., Mańczak, M., Kamiński, M., Blinowska, K.J., Kasicki, S.: Determination of information flow direction among brain structures by a modified directed transfer function (dDTF) method. Journal of Neuroscience Methods 125, 195–207 (2003)
12. Guo, S., Wu, J., Ding, M., Feng, J.: Uncovering interactions in the frequency domain. PLoS Computational Biology 4, e1000087 (2008)

Causality and Influentiability: The Need for Distinct Neural Connectivity Concepts

Luiz A. Baccalá[1] and Koichi Sameshima[2]

[1] Escola Politécnica, University of São Paulo,
São Paulo, SP, 05508-900, Brazil
baccala@lcs.poli.usp.br
http://www.lcs.poli.usp.br/~baccala/en
[2] Department of Radiology and Oncology, Faculdade de Medicina,
University of São Paulo, São Paulo, Brazil

Abstract. We employ toy models to re-examine the notion of causality and its implications in unravelling networks in neuroscience. We conclude that even though multivariate representations of neural dynamic data is indispensable, current popular terminologies for addressing connectivity are insufficiently precise and may even be misleading for fully describing the breadth of information multivariate models now provide. This imposes the need to consider a brand new link centered paradigm of network description where the directed nature of the links plays a central role.

Keywords: G-connectivity, G-influentiability, Link-Centered Networks, Partial Directed Coherence, Directed Transfer Function.

1 Introduction

From its usage and meaning at large, given its inherent character as a 'directed' binary relation, this paper discusses 'causality's' insufficiency as a notion for neuroscience applications.

Together with other means for quantifying dependence between observations such as correlation, it offers the possibility of characterizing neural systems in terms of their 'connectivity', a subject of much recent attention [1,2].

Because of their conceptual importance and appeal, 'connectivity' and 'causality' have upsurged in all sorts of contexts, some inappropriate. Offering a fair and comprehensive critical review of all such contending proposals is perhaps premature given the reigning conceptual confusion. We think that setting a positive agenda is more productive. Here we do so by proposing a fresh and brand new classification for interpreting connectivity networks that aims at clarifying issues and which puts former conceptual conflicts to rest. We began to address this matter in the epilogue to [3], a book collecting state-of-the-art estimators of neural connectivity based on multivariate time series analysis.

The recent establishment of rigorous quantitative asymptotics [4,5] for multivariate frequency domain connectivity estimators has provided operational

D. Ślęzak et al. (Eds.): BIH 2014, LNAI 8609, pp. 424–435, 2014.

criteria to probe for two complementary multivariate concepts: 'G-connectivity' and 'G-influentiability' introduced in [4], which we now further elaborate.

After a brief conceptual review of why one cannot dispense with multivariate descriptions, we show that the simple statement of connectivity as causality is insufficient and must be replaced by more fundamental descriptions which shift the current paradigm of network analysis from its 'node activity' centered basis to a new standpoint stressing the nature of the links between structures. A number of examples are used in the exposition. For conciseness, details about them are consigned to notes at the end.

Partial directed coherence (PDC) [6] and Directed Transfer Function (DTF) [7] are used throughout the text as illustrative tools under their recently derived asymptotics [4,5].

2 Causality

Having permeated history since Aristotle, causality can be summed up by the latin phrase: *Sublata causa, tollitur effectus* - i.e. *Doing away with cause, suppresses the effect* which works as its operational definition. To determine what constitutes a cause: remove it and see what else also disappears. It is easy to see why it permeates experimental science: researchers learn by interacting with their objects of inquiry. This is an old discipline whose debate is classical [8,9]. Most importantly, causality entails a binary relation where cause readily implies effect.

Recently the word causality has been employed in probabilistic reasoning to describe changes in conditional probabilities that underlie Bayesian networks [10,11]. But it is from physics and system theory that causation has become inextricably associated with time and the impossibility of effects prior to the inception of causes with many technically specific consequences like the Kramers-König relations to mention just one [12].

In neuroscience, usage of the term is relatively new, hardly much older than a couple of decades, and it is on the increase. Because of its traditional gist involving several epistemic issues from different areas, it is common to see it misused. Whereas the above classical notion is entirely appropriate in experimental contexts where the experimenter is able to intervene severing some nerve or knocking out a gene, the word in neuroscience is hardly, if ever, applied that way. Rather it is often applied to situations where one must infer the mechanisms at play solely from the evolution of measured quantities. This is rather common either because precise targeted intervention is impractical or due to *anima nobilis* constraints. The technically correct term in this case is 'Granger' causality - or G-causality, for brevity. Despite its ultimate early roots in Wiener's work [13], it was made practical while addressing empirical economic relationships thru bivariate time series analysis. In neuroscience, G-causality has been employed to the full spectrum of neural activity signals.

2.1   The Bivariate Case

As originally proposed, a time series $x_1(n)$ G-causes $x_2(n)$ if knowledge of its past helps predict $x_2(n)$ [14]. In contrast to correlation, an older albeit still popular measure of dependence, G-causality is unreciprocal, i.e. if $x_1(n)$ G-causes $x_2(n)$ it does not necessarily follow that $x_2(n)$ G-causes $x_1(n)$. This lends it its strictly *directed* nature as a connectivity measure.

When $x_1(n)$ G-causes $x_2(n)$ but $x_2(n)$ does not G-cause $x_1(n)$, one may speak of feedback free dependence [15]. As it rests on the ability to predict, its inference is contingent on how prediction is performed. First, the class of predictive models must be chosen, many add designations like linear or nonlinear to G-causality to stress this. The next issue is how to evaluate prediction improvement, for example, via least-mean-square-error (MMSE) prediction reduction [16].

Linear models under MMSE criteria remain popular for several reasons: (a) their merits and limitations are well known, (b) their appropriateness is easily diagnosed, (c) they are able to encode the same information that underlies the existence of correlation and (d) they can be easily expressed in the frequency

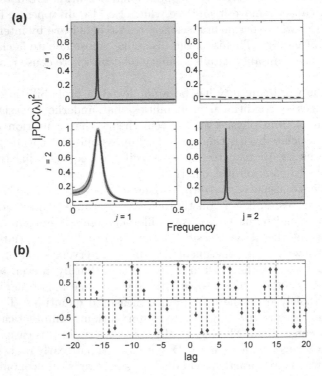

Fig. 1. (a) PDC showing $x_1 \to x_2$ influence corroborated by the delay of -2 lags in x_2 with respect to x_1 shown (with some difficulty) by the cross-correlation function maximum (b) for the model in Note 2

domain, a convenient property, given the ready physiological interpretability of quantities like the EEG over frequency bands [17].

Whether in the time or frequency domain, comparative statistical performance issues apart, all bivariate methods practically yield the same result as long as an adequate model can be fit. A good early example of this equivalence may be found in [6] for frequency domain descriptions and is true of both whether one is addressing the G-causality *detection* problem or tackling its *quantification* problem [18]

In this sense, bivariate modeling factorizes the cross-correlation/spectrum function in view of the autocorrelation/spectrum functions of the observed series. In the process, correlation information becomes exposed in its directed coupling quality. This can be appreciated in Fig. 1 which portrays the pairwise directional coupling as immediately evident from PDC computation even though directionality may also be deduced from estimating relative signal latency. Another interesting example where PDC works but correlation/coherence inference is less immediate can be appreciated in Ex. 7.4 (Fig. 7.6) from [19].

Use of computed pairwise G-causality to deduce the connectivity structure for networks of more than two simultaneously time varying quantities fails. This is readily apparent from in Fig. 2 where, despite a very definite coupling structure (contained and correctly captured by Fig. 3 (d) - see further details in Note 3), leads erroneously to active links between almost all first five variables. The exceptions are the $x_2 \rightarrow x_1$ and $x_3 \rightarrow x_1$ links. The x_6 and x_7 variables are detached from the others and the sole relation of x_6 towards x_7 is correctly captured.

It is failure in scenarios like this that demand considering multivariate approaches.

2.2   The Multivariate Case

A general possible signal representation of a multivariate time series is via autoregression:

$$
\begin{bmatrix} x_1(n) \\ \vdots \\ x_N(n) \end{bmatrix} = \sum_r \mathbf{A}_r \begin{bmatrix} x_1(n-r) \\ \vdots \\ x_N(n-r) \end{bmatrix} + \begin{bmatrix} w_1(n) \\ \vdots \\ w_N(n) \end{bmatrix} \tag{1}
$$

where the dynamics of the $\mathbf{x}(n) = [x_1(n) \ \ldots \ x_N(n)]^T$ process depends on its associated $\mathbf{w}(n) = [w_1(n) \ \ldots \ w_N(n)]^T$ *innovations* process whose white nature, i.e. the fact that observations at different time instants are uncorrelated, is such that the dependence structure among the x_i's are encoded in the $\mathbf{A}(r)$ matrices whose $a_{ij}(r)$ coefficients represent the linear interaction effect of the past r-th lagged $x_j(n-r)$ observation onto $x_i(n)$. In the $N = 2$ case $a_{ij}(r) = 0$ for all r implies absence of G-causality [14]. This criterion for G-causality determination is also popular in the $N > 2$ case [20].

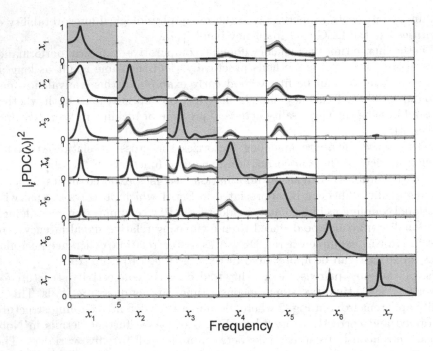

Fig. 2. The use of pairwise PDC to estimate G-causality for the model described in Note 5 shows links between almost all of the first five pairs of variables and does not reflect the correct dependence structure that multivariate PDC in Fig. 3(d) captures. Note that x_6 and x_7 are detached from the rest of the network.

An alternative to (1) is the *moving average* representation:

$$\mathbf{x}(n) = \sum_r \mathbf{H}_r \mathbf{w}(n - r) \tag{2}$$

where the dependence structure is encoded in the $h_{ij}(r)$ coefficients of the $\mathbf{H}_r$ matrices. In the $N = 2$ case, $h_{ij}(r) = 0$ for all r is equivalent to the $a_{ij}(r) = 0$ for all r condition and may be used for detecting G-causality. For $N > 2$, however, this is not the case.

Under very general conditions, (1) and (2) constitute equally valid representations, their choice dictated in practice by modeling convenience under model parsimony and estimation ease.

The frequency domain renditions of (1) and (2) constitute respectively what became known as PDC [6] and DTF [7] which we have shown [21] can be expressed in terms of more fundamental processes associated with $\mathbf{x}(n)$. When $N \leq 3$ there is only one such fundamental process: the innovations $\mathbf{w}(n)$ process. This is what underlies the above theoretical equivalence of G-causality's determination for $N = 2$. When $N > 2$ it is possible to define the so-called *partial processes* whereby one subtracts the effect of all the time series from $x_i(n)$, i.e.:

$$\eta_i(n) = x_i(n) - E[x_i(n)|\mathbf{x}^i] \tag{3}$$

where $E[x_i(n)|\mathbf{x}^i]$ is the conditional expectation of $x_i(n)$ on the collective of all other processes $\mathbf{x}^i$ that exclude $x_i(n)$. Explicit consideration of (3) is what has allowed generalizing PDC and DTF to quantities that are readily interpreted in terms of information theory [21] and whose full generality adequately addresses coupling effect size issues [19].

The values of the information scaled DTF and PDC for the data generating model of Fig. 2 leads respectively to the results in Figs. 3(a) and (b) whose connectivities are summed up by allied directed graph diagrams in Figs. 3(c) and 3(d). The actual imposed system structure is accurately recovered by the 3(d) diagram (see Note 3).

Some features in Fig. 3 are immediate to realize. The arrows indicating coupling differ markedly between Figures 3(c) and 3(d), except for $x_6(n)$ and $x_7(n)$ connections which are detached from the other structures but whose mutual coupling is essentially bivariate and unidirectional confirming PDC/DTF/pairwise G-causality equivalence when $N = 2$.

Though not readily apparent from the latter discussion, it is easy to show that PDC and DTF constitute inverse functions of sorts. In fact, DTF is usually computed using models like (1) which are inverted into a frequency domain representation resembling (2). Topological structure representation under DTF and PDC result identical if and if only their defining matrices are invariant under inversion. In fact, the latter topological structures constitute *digraphs* in graph theory where significant connecting arrows are representable by boolean '1' values and absent ones by '0'. PDC connections reflect the so-called graph *adjacency* matrix (and thus also the imposed model connectivity structure in Fig. 2) and its inverse, under boolean operations is the graph *reachability* matrix [22] which portrays whether a given graph node may be reached from the starting node even if intermediate nodes must be traversed. Once more, when only pairs of structures are under analysis, adjacency and reachability are equal. DTF is theoretically nonzero whether a direct adjacent link is active or if there is active indirect signal coupling via other pathways towards the signal target. PDC is nonzero only when immediate adjacent links are non zero but not otherwise. In the example of Fig. 3 signals from any of the first five structures reach one another albeit loosely in some cases whereas x_6 and x_7 are disconnected from the latter first five ones.

Further insight into reachability may be obtained from the following example in Fig. 4 (adapted from [23] and also discussed in[24] with a slightly different interpretation). The structure is an exclusively feedforward one. In it, PDC reflects the structure (Fig. 4a) at all frequencies, but DTF does not, because the coupling from $x_1(n)$ to $x_3(n)$ occurs via a filter that exactly delays the signal to match that which flows from $x_1(n)$ through $x_2(n)$ cancelling it upon reaching $x_3(n)$. Though the 'physical connection' from $x_1(n)$ to $x_3(n)$ exists and is active, it has no ultimate influence on $x_3(n)$. Messing with any link, or even better yet, under the *'sublata'* clause above, removing $x_1(n)$ changes everything: $x_2(n)$'s oscillations disappear but $x_3(n)$'s spectrum only changes slightly. It is important to convince oneself that intervening on the links, rather than on the structures, also disrupts the observed balance. As such, the often overlooked role of the exact nature of the links must also be taken objectively into account.

Coupled with the latter observations and because PDC and DTF provide different and complementary views on time series coupling by describing the links we introduced the terminology we discuss next.

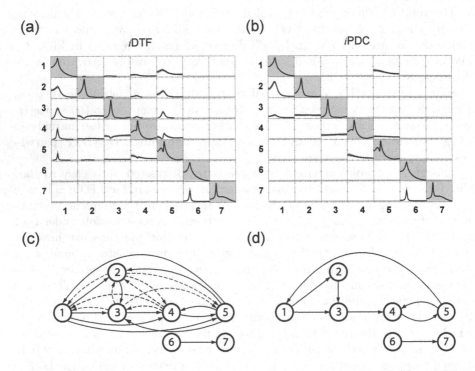

Fig. 3. Simulation results for the information scaled versions of DTF (a) and PDC (b) using 2000 data points under an $\alpha = 1\%$ decision threshold [5,4] using the model described in Note 3. The respective connectivity graph representations reveal PDC's (d) estimates closely mirror the imposed model 'anatomy' whereas to varying degrees of strength DTF's (c) show how much net directed influence exists between variables. x_6 and x_7 are unconnected to the other variables. See further remarks in Note 5.

3   G-Connectivity and G-Influentiability

The sum total of the examples so far is that the notion of G-causality alone is insufficient for a clear understanding of the dependence network between observed variables. For this reason, under the need to consider multivariate couplings, we proposed the concepts of *G*-connectivity (GC) and *G*-influentiability

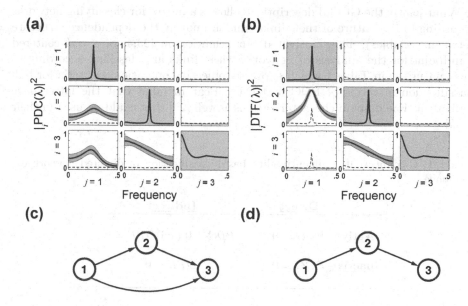

Fig. 4. iPDC (a) and iDTF (b) results for the simulated model from Note 4, and their respective graphical representations (c) which reflects G-connectivity and (d) which mirrors G-influentiability whereby $x_1(n)$'s influence on $x_3(n)$ results fully cancelled out

(GI) in [4]. GC reflects the $a_{ij}(r)$ coefficient/PDC/adjacency status and manages to pinpoint the active immediate directed coupling between time series but excludes active interactions taking place via intermediate observed structures which are captured by GI using $h_{ij}(r)$ coefficient/DTF/reachability representations. The G-designation, albeit dispensable, in addition to an homage to Granger, is a reminder that these properties are derived from the predictive multivariate ($N > 2$) modeling of simultaneously observed dynamical magnitudes; GC/GI do not necessarily reflect the intervention based causation of Sec. 2. Note that despite the employment of linear models, the concepts herein are in principle applicable in absolute generality.

A network using G-connectivity (GC) information describes the network's 'perceived' anatomy as in Fig. 3(d), whereas its G-influentiability (GI) network reflects the net totals of directed influence. GC networks contain those links that are *direct* and *active* whereas GI networks are made of links that are *active* regardless of whether the signal must flow through some structure in between for its effect to be felt or not, i.e. it contains both *direct* plus *indirect* active pathways. It is important to have in mind that the network analysis procedures that have of late become so popular [1,25,26] may lead to very different results depending on whether analysis algorithms are fed with GC or GI structures calling for the need to interpret the results accordingly.

What jointly the GC/GI descriptions allow is a means for classifying networks according to the nature of their links (and ultimately the dependence structure between variables). This motivated our definition in [23,4] of a *link*-centered standpoint for the analysis of networks where links are classified according to their nature as in Table 1 which expresses objective operational criteria for link classification in terms of PDC and DTF. Bear in mind that the latter have equivalent time domain characterizations as well [20] that could be used in their stead.

Table 1. G-connectivity/influentiability based classification of directed network dependence

	Direct	Indirect
Active	$PDC \neq 0$	$PDC = 0$ and $DTF \neq 0$
Inactive	$PDC = 0$	$DTF = 0$

4   Conclusions and Final Remarks

Thus far we have deliberately avoided some of the applicable technical time series jargon, like 'impulse response' function [20] and Sims-causality [27,28] because they evoke little to those uninitiated, but for whom the present network ideas are, nonetheless, important.

Other ideas like dDTF [29] which combines DTF and partial coherence were not explicit considered since jointly PDC and DTF achieves similar goals in more generality. Another reason for stressing PDC/DTF, besides their fundamental character [21], is their recent generalization to describe the interaction over blocks of variables [30,31] and the introduction of canonical decompositions for further addressing block interactions [32].

Sometimes (pairwise) *G*-causality is described as a measure of temporal signal precedence. This is questionable even in the bivariate case when feedback is present. In the multivariate case, relationships as we have shown are far more complex and this interpretation becomes untenable.

Today's prevailing paradigm for talking about how brain areas interrelate is dominated by the notions of 'functional'/'effective' connectivity [33]. Much of their popularity is due to the prevalence of correlation measures for the former and 'ad hoc' modelling for the latter [34]. Whereas some measure of structure is loosely implicit in 'effective', the more immediate notion of functional connectivity is very limited as it leads to undirected networks when compared to the directed network description tools of PDC/DTF whose estimation reveals so much more.

The overall conclusion from our argument is that connectivity analysis, as we have come to understand it, cannot dispense with jointly examining the dynamics of neural signals through modeling their multivariate behavior. The dependence structure of multivariate signals has two complementary aspects to it - one of connectivity and another of influentiability whose nature must always be precisely kept in mind.

The possibility of describing links in some detail via tools like DTF/PDC speaks in favour of a new paradigm for network description/comparison. Under this paradigm, it is the active/inactive nature of links that matters, and whether they are direct or indirect is what becomes something of a central concern.

Acknowledgements. CNPq Grants 307163/2013-0 to L.A.B. and 309381/2012-6 to K.S. are also gratefully acknowledged and to NAPNA - Núcleo de Neurociência Aplicada from the University of São Paulo. Part of this work took place during FAPESP Grant 2005/56464-9 (CInAPCe).

Notes and Comments

1. All results here were obtained by processing data simulated from 'toy' examples with 2000 time samples with model order estimates obtained via Akaike's criterion. Null hypothesis thresholds assumed $\alpha = 1\%$. All innovations $w_i(n)$ were zero mean uncorrelated unit gaussian. Computations used the package AsympPDC package from

$$\texttt{http://www.lcs.poli.usp.br/~baccala/pdc}$$

   which is to harbour scripts for the examples herein.

2. The toy $x_1 \to x_2$ G-causal system simulated in Fig. 1 is:

$$x_1(n) = 1.96 \, cos(\pi/4) \, x1(n-1) - (.98)^2 x_1(n-2) + w_1(n)$$
$$x_2(n) = 0.5 \, x_2(n-1) + x_1(n-1) + \sqrt{20} w_2(n)$$

3. The simulations used in Figs. 2 and 3 come directly from Model I with addition of Eq. (5) in [35].

4. The simulations behind the example in Fig. 4 were performed via the following equations:

$$x_1(n) = -(.98)^2 x_1(n-2) + w_1(n)$$
$$x2(t) = 0.5 x_2(n-1) + x_1(n-1) + w_2(n)$$
$$x3(n) = -0.1 \, x_3(n-1) + \sum_{k=0}^{+\infty} (.5)^k x_1(n-2-k) + x_2(n-1) + w_3(n)$$

The summation in the last equation was simulated using an internal hidden variable.

5. It is instructive to compare Fig. 2 to Fig. 3(a), DTF differs markedly from pairwise G-causality. At the common resonance frequency, DTF becomes zero for some pairs, i.e. there is no directed influentiability at those frequencies, something we imposed by design [35]. This lack of influentiability is brought about by the existence of multiple pathways that cancel one another as in the example of Fig. 4 but only at the resonance frequency. The model was designed to do exactly this.

References

1. Sporns, O.: Networks of the Brain. MIT Press (2011)
2. Seung, S.: Connectome: How the brain's wiring makes us who we are. Houghton Mifflin Harcourt (2012)
3. Sameshima, K., Baccalá, L.A. (eds.): Methods in Brain Connectivity Inference through Multivariate Time Series Analysis. CRC Press (2014)
4. Baccalá, L.A., Takahashi, D.Y., Sameshima, K.: Consolidating a link centered neural connectivity framework with directed transfer function asymptotic. Biological Cybernetics (submitted, 2014)
5. Baccalá, L., De Brito, C., Takahashi, D., Sameshima, K.: Unified asymptotic theory for all partial directed coherence forms. Philosophical Transactions of the Royal Society A: Mathematical, Physical and Engineering Sciences 371(2013), 1–13 (1997)
6. Baccalá, L.A., Sameshima, K.: Partial directed coherence: a new concept in neural structure determination. Biol. Cybern. 84(6), 463–474 (2001)
7. Kamiński, M., Blinowska, K.J.: A new method of the description of the information flow in brain structures. Biological Cybernetics 65(3), 203–210 (1991)
8. Coventry, A.: Hume's Theory of Causation. Bloomsbury (2006)
9. Ott, W.: Causation and Laws of Nature in Early Modern Philosophy. Oxford University Press, USA (2009)
10. Pearl, J.: Causality: Models, Reasoning, and Inference. Cambridge University Press (2000)
11. Neapolitan, R.E.: Learning Bayesian Networks. Prentice Hall (2004)
12. Nussenzveig, H.M.: Causality and Dispersion Relations. Academic Press, New York (1972)
13. Wiener, N.: Theory of Prediction. In: Modern Mathematics for the Engineer, pp. 165–190. McGraw-Hill, New York (1956)
14. Granger, C.W.J.: Investigating causal relations by econometric models and cross-spectral methods. Econometrica 37(3), 424–438 (1969)
15. Sims, C.A.: Money, income, and causality. The American Economic Review, 540–552 (1972)
16. Kay, S.M.: Modern spectral estimation. Prentice-Hall, Englewood Cliffs (1988)
17. Basar, E.: Memory and Brain Dynamics: Oscillations Integrating Attention, Perception, Learning, and Memory. CRC Press (2004)
18. Baccalá, L.A., Sameshima, K.: Brain Connectivity: An Overview. In: Methods in Brain Connectivity Inference through Multivariate Time Series Analysis, pp. 1–9. CRC Press (2014)
19. Sameshima, K., Takahashi, D., Baccalá, L.A.: Asymptotic PDC Properties. In: Methods in Brain Connectivity Inference through Multivariate Time Series Analysis, pp. 113–131. CRC Press (2014)

20. Lütkepohl, H.: New Introduction to Multiple Time Series Analysis. Springer, New York (2005)
21. Takahashi, D., Baccalá, L., Sameshima, K.: Information theoretic interpretation of frequency domain connectivity measures. Biological Cybernetics 103, 463–469 (2010)
22. Harary, F.: Graph Theory. Addison-Wesley Series in Mathematics. Perseus Books (1994)
23. Baccalá, L.A., Sameshima, K.: Multivariate Time Series Brain Connectivity: A Sum Up. In: Methods in Brain Connectivity Inference through Multivariate Time Series Analysis, pp. 245–251. CRC Press, Boca Raton (2014)
24. Eichler, M.: On the evaluation of information flow in multivariate systems by the directed transfer function. Biol. Cybern. 94, 469–482 (2006)
25. Barabasi, A.L., Frangos, J.: Linked: The New Science of Network. Basic Books (2002)
26. Caldarelli, G., Vespignani, A.: Large Scale Structure and Dynamics of Complex Networks: From Information Technology to Finance and Natural Science. World Scientific (2007)
27. Kuersteiner, G.M.: Granger-sims causality. In: Durlauf, S.N., Blume, L.E. (eds.) The New Palgrave Dictionary of Economics. Palgrave Macmillan, Basingstoke (2008)
28. Eichler, M.: Causal inference with multiple time series: principles and problems. Philosophical Transactions of the Royal Society A: Mathematical, Physical and Engineering Sciences 371, 20110613 (2013)
29. Korzeniewska, A., Mańczak, M., Kaminski, M., Blinowska, K.J., Kasicki, S.: Determination of information flow direction among brain structures by a modified directed transfer function (ddtf) method. Journal of Neuroscience Methods 125, 195 207 (2003)
30. Takahashi, D.Y.: Medidas de fluxo de informação com aplicação em neurociência. PhD thesis, University of São Paulo (2009), http://www.teses.usp.br/teses/disponiveis/95/95131/tde-07062011-115256/en.php
31. Faes, L., Nollo, G.: Measuring frequency domain Granger causality for multiple blocks of interacting time series. Biological Cybernetics 107(2), 217–232 (2013)
32. Takahashi, D., Baccalá, L.A., Sameshima, K.: Canonical information flow decomposition among neural structure subsets. Front. Neuroinform. 8, 49 (2014), 10.3389/fninf.2014.00049
33. Aertsen, A.M.H.J., Gerstein, G.L., Habib, M.K., Palm, G.: Dynamics of neuronal firing correlation: modulation of "effective connectivity". J. Neurophysiol. 61(5), 900–917 (1989)
34. Friston, K.: Functional and effective connectivity in neuroimaging: A synthesis. Human Brain Mapping 2, 256–278 (1994)
35. Baccalá, L.A., Sameshima, K.: Overcoming the limitations of correlation analysis for many simultaneously processed neural structures. Progress in Brain Research, Advances in Neural Population Coding 130, 33–47 (2001)

Local Dimension-Reduced Dynamical Spatio-Temporal Models for Resting State Network Estimation

Gilson Vieira[1], Edson Amaro Jr.[1], and Luiz A. Baccalá[2]

[1] Inter-institutional Grad Program on Bioinformatics,
University of São Paulo,
São Paulo, SP, 05508-050, Brazil
[2] Escola Politécnica, University of São Paulo,
São Paulo, SP, 05508-900, Brazil
baccala@lcs.poli.usp.br
http://www.lcs.poli.usp.br/~baccala/en

Abstract. Resting-state Functional Magnetic Resonance Imaging (FMRI) analysis has consistently shown the presence of specific spatial activation patterns. Independent component analysis (ICA) has been the analysis algorithm of choice even though its underlying assumptions preclude deeper connectivity analysis. By combining novel concepts of group sparsity with contiguity-constrained clusterization, we developed a new class of Local dimension-reduced Dynamical Spatio-Temporal Models (LDSTM) for estimating whole-brain dynamical models whereby the causal relationships between well localized spatial components can be identified. Experimental results of LDSTM on group resting-state FMRI data reveal physiologically plausible spatio-temporal brain connectivity patterns among participants.

Keywords: Resting-State FMRI, Spatio-Temporal Models, Brain Connectivity, Multiscale Analysis and Sparsity.

1 Introduction

In resting-state FMRI data analysis there is an ever growing and pressing need for accurately describing how brain regions are dynamically interrelated [3]. Due to the neuro-physiological nature of the BOLD signal, resting-state interactions are inseparable (in space and time) so that splitting the problem into separate space and time approaches is unrealistic specially if the focus lies in characterizing large spatial scale changes due to subtle interactions originating from a small number of regions of interest. The chief challenge is that any Dynamical Spatio-Temporal Model (DSTM) of FMRI data sets demands many parameters to describe what also is a large number of observed variables that nonetheless enjoy a great deal of spatial redundancy. In addition, most DSTMs in current use are problematic when it comes to estimating the spatial origin of signal variability as often only a relatively small sample size is available under largely unfavourable SNR (Signal-to-Noise) conditions [6,16,20,23].

Here we examine new classes of dimension-reduced DSTMs for resting-state network estimation. Dimension-reduced DSTMs were introduced by Wikle and Cressie

D. Ślęzak et al. (Eds.): BIH 2014, LNAI 8609, pp. 436–446, 2014.

[22] to capture nonstationary spatial dependence under an optimal state representation via the Kalman filter thereby turning them into effective tools for modelling spatially continuous phenomena that change rapidly in space. In the original Wikle-Cressie formulation, the DSTM invokes an *a priori* defined orthogonal basis to expand the redistribution kernel of a discrete time/continuous space linear integro-difference equation (IDE) in terms of a finite linear combination of spatial components [22]. This idea was further supported in [11] and extended in [18] who considered parameterized redistribution kernels of arbitrary shape that meet homogeneity conditions in space and time. Even though the change of basis proposed in [22] improve one's understanding of high-dimensional processes, it by no means ensures sparse solutions which are key to achieving statistically robust dynamical descriptions.

Robustness is frequently sought by indirect means as in LASSO regression [21], in basis pursuit for model selection and denoising [4], in sparse component analysis for blind source separation [27] and in iterative thresholding algorithms for image deconvolution and reconstruction [9,14]. These methods promote sparsity by maximizing a penalized loss function via a compromise between the goodness of fit and the number of basis elements that make up the signal. Recently, more attention has been given to group sparsity, where groups of variables are selected/shrunken simultaneously rather than individually (for a review see [2]) by minimizing an objective function that includes a quadratic error term added to a regularization term that considers *a priori* beliefs or data-driven analysis to induce group sparsity [25,24,26].

This paper presents a state-space formulation suited to data sets of high dimensionality, such as FMRI, by taking advantage of spatial wavelet analysis to provide a data representation requiring fewer significant parameters. We combine group sparsity and contiguity-constrained clusterization to initialize an Expectation Maximization (EM) algorithm constructed especially to identify Local dimension-reduced DSTMs (LD-STMs) whose columns of the observation matrix act as point-spreading functions. We used simulated data to evaluate our approach's ability for signal recovering and model estimation detection compared to the traditional EM algorithm. Our new method was also used to study resting-state patterns of brain activation in real group FMRI data from healthy volunteers under a Multiplexed Echo Planar Imaging sequence [13] (allowing very short repetition time).

2   Problem Formulation

DSTM problems may be formulated as state space models where space-related measurements z_t depend on the dynamical evolution of a suitably defined state x_t through a linear gaussian model

$$\mathbf{x}_t = \mathbf{H}\mathbf{x}_{t-1} + \mathbf{w}_t \tag{1}$$
$$\mathbf{z}_t = \mathbf{A}\mathbf{x}_t + \mathbf{v}_t, \tag{2}$$

where z_t is an M dimensional column vector of observed signals at time t, x_t is an K dimensional column vector of unknown states, $\mathbf{A}$ is an unknown $M \times K$ observation matrix, $\mathbf{H}$ is an unknown $K \times K$ state-transition matrix, $\mathbf{w}_t$ is an innovation process and

$\mathbf{v}_t$ is additive noise. Both $\mathbf{w}_t$ and $\mathbf{v}_t$ are assumed zero mean gaussian respectively with covariance $\mathbf{Q}$ and $\mathbf{R}$. The state-transition matrix $\mathbf{H}$, the observation matrix $\mathbf{A}$ together with $\mathbf{Q}$ and $\mathbf{R}$ and the state $\mathbf{x}_t$ must be inferred from $\mathbf{z}_t$.

For years, the Expectation Maximization (EM) algorithm has been the favourite tool to tackle the problem of estimating the system states and the model parameters from (1,2) [19], since they have been proved to at least converge to a local maximum of the overall log-likelihood function of (1,2) [10]. The traditional EM algorithm starts with a randomly generated solution and then proceeds by re-iterating its two main steps until the maximum conditional expected likelihood is achieved. The E-step consists of re-placing the unknown states by their expected value given the data and current model parameter estimates. Under gaussian assumptions the expected system states are obtained by the so called Rauch-Tung-Striebel (RTS) smoother [17]. This is followed by the M-step which estimates the model parameters by maximizing the conditional expected likelihood from previous E-step. However, for high dimensional systems, the model (1,2) becomes indeterminate and using the EM algorithm without proper initialization usually greatly deteriorates estimate quality.

3   Algorithm Details

3.1   Sparsifying Orthogonal Transformation

The goal of this paper is to solve (1,2) by assuming that the columns of $\mathbf{A}$ act as point-spreading functions. This hypothesis means that $\mathbf{a}_k$, where $\mathbf{a}_k$ is the k-th column of $\mathbf{A}$, can be perfectly described by few wavelet coefficients forming localized spatial patterns. Given $\{\phi_k\}_{1 \le k \le M}$ an wavelet basis in $\mathbf{R}^M$, the first step is to calculate the wavelet representation of the matrix of observations $\mathbf{Z} \equiv (z_{k,t})_{k,t}$

$$\hat{\mathbf{Z}} \equiv (\langle \mathbf{z}_t, \phi_k \rangle)_{k,t} = \Phi \mathbf{Z}, \tag{3}$$

where Φ is the $M \times M$ orthonormal matrix, whose rows are the ϕ_k's. Since $\mathbf{Z} = \mathbf{AX} + \mathbf{V}$, this notation satisfies $\hat{\mathbf{Z}} = \hat{\mathbf{S}} + \hat{\mathbf{V}}$, where $\hat{\mathbf{S}} = \Phi \mathbf{AX}$.

3.2   Signal Denoising

The transform Φ should be chosen such that an contiguity-constrained clustering of the rows of $\hat{\mathbf{Z}}$ provides the elements that approximate of the rows of $\hat{\mathbf{X}}$. But before clustering the rows of $\hat{\mathbf{Z}}$, we should denoise it based on the sparsity assumption. This is the second and most important step of our algorithm. To do so we consider that $\mathbf{s}_t = \mathbf{A}\mathbf{x}_t$ admits a sparse representation lying in a particular Besov space $\mathbf{B}_{1,1}^s$, chosen for containing smooth functions with localized singularities [15], so that the problem of approximating $\mathbf{z}_t$ by $\mathbf{s}_t \in \mathbf{B}_{1,1}^s$ can be expressed by adding a penalization term to $\|\mathbf{z}_t - \mathbf{s}_t\|_2^2$ requiring that $\|\mathbf{s}_t\|_{s,1}$ be small, where $\|\mathbf{s}_t\|_{s,1}$ is the $\mathbf{B}_{1,1}^s$ norm of $\mathbf{s}_t$. In other words, we want to minimize the following functional

$$f(\mathbf{s}_t) = \|\mathbf{z}_t - \mathbf{s}_t\|_2^2 + \|\mathbf{s}_t\|_{s,1} = \|\mathbf{z}_t - \mathbf{s}_t\|_2^2 + \sum_k \lambda_k |\hat{s}_{k,t}|, \tag{4}$$

where $\hat{s}_{k,t} = \langle \mathbf{s}_t, \phi_k \rangle$ [9]. The above functional is coercive and strictly convex which implies that it has a unique global minimum for each t. If $\lambda_k = \lambda$, for all k, the minimum value of (4) is obtained via the soft-thresholding operator [12]

$$\hat{s}_{k,t} = \text{sign}(\hat{z}_{k,t}) \max(|\hat{z}_{k,t}| - \lambda, 0). \tag{5}$$

The problem of using the estimator (5) for all t is that those coefficients set to zero for some values of t may not be so for other values of t even for large λ values. To overcome this problem we propose tying the $\hat{s}_{k,t}$'s together for different values of t and using the recently introduced group-separable regularizer [24]

$$\min_{\hat{s}^k} \frac{1}{2} \|\hat{z}^k - \hat{s}^k\|_2^2 + \lambda_k \|\hat{s}^k\|_2, \tag{6}$$

where $\hat{z}^k$ and $\hat{s}^k$ be the k-th row of $\hat{Z}$ and $\hat{S}$ respectively, whose solution is attained by the vector soft-thresholding operator [5]

$$\hat{s}^k = \frac{\max(\|\hat{z}^k\|_2 - \lambda_k, 0)}{\|\hat{z}^k\|_2} \hat{z}^k. \tag{7}$$

3.3   Clusterization

The third step consists in estimating $\mathbf{s}^k = a_k \mathbf{x}^k$, where $\mathbf{x}^k$ is the k-th row of $\mathbf{X}$, by clustering the rows of $\hat{S}$ and then applying the inverse transform of Φ

$$\mathbf{s}^k = \sum_{i \in I_k} \phi_i^{-1} \hat{s}^i, \tag{8}$$

where ϕ_i^{-1} is the i-th column of Φ^{-1} (Φ^T, for wavelet transforms) and I_k contains the indexes of the k-th group. The clustering algorithm uses a measure of dissimilarity which enforces cluster spatial contiguity by combining the instantaneous correlation between the rows of $\hat{S}$ and the physical distance between the ϕ_ks' centers of mass. The algorithm begins defining each time series $\hat{s}^k$, $1 \le k \le M$ as a singleton cluster. At each step, we join the pairs of clusters (A, B) which minimize the following criterion

$$\max \{ \text{dist}(\hat{s}^i, \hat{s}^j) : i \in A, j \in B \}, \tag{9}$$

where

$$\text{dist}(\hat{s}^i, \hat{s}^j) = \begin{cases} \infty, & \|\bar{\phi}_i - \bar{\phi}_j\|_2 > r \\ 1 - |\text{cor}(\hat{s}^i, \hat{s}^j)|, & \text{otherwise,} \end{cases} \tag{10}$$

where $\bar{\phi}_i = \int_{\mathbb{R}^d} s |\phi_i|^2 ds / \int_{\mathbb{R}^d} |\phi_i|^2 ds$ defines de center of mass of ϕ_i.

Though the measure of dissimilarity (9) already embodies much of the structure behind the spatial components in (1,2), deciding the tree cut level (i.e. how many clusters to consider) remains a problem. To address this we note that the height of a node is related to the correlation between the coefficients within the node. The correlation coefficient r has a well-known statistic whose upper limit with an $(1 - \alpha/2)\%$ confidence for the transformation $0.5 \log_e(\frac{1+r}{1-r})$, under the null hypothesis of independence, is approximately given by

$$u = z_{(1-\alpha/2)} \sqrt{1/(N-3)} \tag{11}$$

where $z_{(1-\alpha/2)}$ is the standard normal distribution.

Hence we set the value for cutting the tree as $h = (\exp(2u) + 1)/(\exp(2u) - 1)$. This is an interesting quantity since it enables estimating the number of spatial components and yet depends neither on the actual noise level nor on the number of variables but solely on sample size.

3.4 LDSTM Estimation

The last step consists of estimating the system states of (1,2) using the scores produced by the first component of a Principal Component Analysis (PCA) of $\mathbf{s}^k$. The remainder of the algorithm follows the steps of traditional EM algorithm for state space estimation [19] except that the $\mathbf{A}$ matrix estimation is modified to accommodate linear equality constraints ensuring well localized $\mathbf{a}_k$'s. The least squares problem we solve is as follows

$$\min_{\mathbf{a}_k} \| \mathbf{a}_k \mathbf{x}^k - \mathbf{Z} \|_2^2$$
$$\text{subject to } \mathbf{C} \mathbf{a}_k = 0, \tag{12}$$

where $\mathbf{C} = (c_{i,j})_{i,j}$ is an $M \times M$ matrix with $c_{i,i} = 1$ if $\mathrm{VAR}(s_{i,t}^k) > 0$ and $c_{i,j} = 0$ otherwise.

4 Numerical Illustration

4.1 Model Description

Based on a simulated data we examine how the algorithm presented in this paper performs under different conditions. We created a vector time series measured over an one dimensional space, sampled regularly in space ($\Delta s = 0.30$ e $M = 256$) and time ($\Delta t = 1$ e $N = 500$). The observation matrix that we used is drawn on Fig. 1 (A) which shows the columns of

$$\mathbf{A} = [\mathbf{f}_{80} \mathbf{f}_{180} \mathbf{f}_{100}],$$

where $\mathbf{f}_\mu = [f_{1,\mu}, \dots, f_{M,\mu}]^\mathrm{T}$ with $f_{i,\mu} = f(i\Delta s - \mu)$ and f is the Gaussian density function. The observations were corrupted by white Gaussian noise with covariance matrix

$$\mathbf{R} = \sigma^2 \mathbf{I}_{128,128},$$

with σ^2 accounting for the SNR level defined as $\mathrm{SNR} = 10 \log_{10}(\mathrm{VAR}(\mathbf{s})/\sigma^2)$ where $\mathbf{s} = \mathrm{vec}([\mathbf{A}\mathbf{x}_1 \cdots \mathbf{A}\mathbf{x}_N])$ and vec stands for the column stacking operator. The dynamics of the spatial components evolved according to the transition matrix

$$\mathbf{H} = \begin{bmatrix} .5 & -.5 & 0 \\ 0 & .5 & 0 \\ 0 & 0 & 0 \end{bmatrix},$$

and a zero mean Gaussian innovation process with covariance matrix

$$\mathbf{Q} = \begin{bmatrix} 1 & .5 & 0 \\ .5 & 2 & 0 \\ 0 & 0 & 2 \end{bmatrix}.$$

Fig. 1 (B) shows the sample variance for a simulated DSTM using the above parameters with SNR $= -19$db.

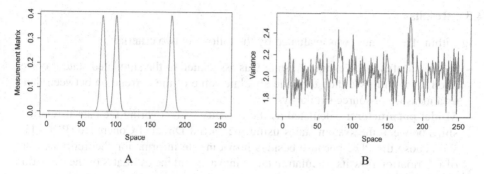

A   B

Fig. 1. (A) Measurement matrix $\mathbf{A}$ and (B) sample variance of the example model with $N = 500$ and SNR $= -19$db

4.2 Algorithm Setup

We used Daubechies (D2) functions to transform the data and studied the performance of our method by executing 100 Monte Carlo simulations, where we took the statistics of those runs (mean and variance). We define the values for λ_k based on an estimate for σ^2 presented next. If $\mathbf{R} = \sigma^2 \mathbf{I}_{M \times M}$, then $\hat{\mathbf{v}}^k \sim \mathcal{N}\left(\mathbf{0}, \sigma^2 \mathbf{I}_{N \times N}\right)$, where $\hat{\mathbf{v}}^k$ is the k-th row of $\hat{\mathbf{V}}$, since $\boldsymbol{\Phi}$ is orthogonal. By assumption $\mathbf{z}_t$ is sparse under $\boldsymbol{\Phi}$, so most of $\{\hat{s}_{k,t}\}_{\forall k}$ are zero. Provided that fifty percent of $\{\hat{s}_{k,t}\}_{\forall k}$ are zero, we define the following unbiased estimator for σ^2

$$\hat{\sigma}^2 = \text{median}_{\forall k} \hat{\text{VAR}}\{\hat{z}_{k,t}\}, \tag{13}$$

where $\hat{\text{VAR}}$ denotes temporal sample covariance.

If $\text{VAR}\{\hat{s}_{k,t}\} = 0$, we have that $\hat{z}_{k,t}$ are i.i.d normal variables, so

$$\frac{(N-1)\hat{\text{VAR}}\{\hat{z}_{k,t}\}}{\sigma^2} \sim \chi^2_{N-1} \tag{14}$$

implies that an interval with $(1 - \alpha)$ confidence for σ^2 is given by

$$\left[\frac{(N-1)\hat{\sigma}^2}{\chi^2_{1-\alpha/2, N-1}}, \frac{(N-1)\hat{\sigma}^2}{\chi^2_{\alpha/2, N-1}}\right], \tag{15}$$

where $\chi^2_{\alpha/2,N-1}$ is the $\alpha/2$-th percentile of the chi-square distribution with $N-1$ degrees of freedom.

Using the fact that $\|\hat{z}^k\|_2 = (N-1)\text{VÂR}\{\hat{z}_{k,t}\}$, the equation (15) provides the value of λ_k we set

$$\lambda_k = \frac{(N-1)^2\hat{\sigma}^2}{\chi^2_{\alpha/2,N-1}}, \tag{16}$$

with $\alpha = 0.05/M$.

We set the clustering parameter r to 3 although results are similar for $r = 1, 3$ and 5.

4.3   Results

Algorithm effectiveness was evaluated by the following two criteria:

- **System states:** each estimated state was associated to the simulated state it correlated most with. We then took the absolute value of the correlation between them as a measure of source similarity.
- **Model parameters:** calculated as the capacity of recovering the causal relationships between the system states using the Partial Directed Coherence (PDC) [1]. We choose the PDC because besides providing an information theoretic measure of information flow its calculation takes into account the estimates of the transition matrix **H** and the innovation processes' covariance matrix **Q**.

The mean absolute values of the correlation coefficient between the simulated and estimated states versus SNR are shown in Fig. 2 (A) for LDSTM and traditional EM. We observe that LDSTM outperforms EM and gave very good results for all the three channels even under very unfavourable SNR. Fig. 2 (B) shows the PDC of x_2 towards x_1 for different SNR levels compared to EM estimates. There is a clear pattern which shows that PDC magnitude decreases as SNR decreases, but fortunately, the estimated shape remains perfectly preserved.

5   Experimental Results

For illustration, we used FMRI images from seven healthy volunteers under a resting-state protocol. The study was approved by local ethical committee and written informed consents from all participants were obtained.

5.1   Image Data Acquisition

Whole brain FMRI images (TR = 600ms, TE = 33ms, 32 slices, FOV = 247×247 mm, matrix size 128×128, in plane resolution 1.975×1.975 mm, slice thickness 3.5mm with 1.8mm of gap) were acquired on a 3T Siemens system using a Multiplexed Echo Planar Imaging sequence (multi-band accelerator factor of 4) [13]. To aid in the localization of functional data, high-resolution T1-weighted images were also acquired with an MPRAGE sequence (TR = 2500 ms, TE = 3.45 ms, inversion time = 1000 ms, 256×256 mm FOV, 256×256 in-plane matrix, $1 \times 1 \times 1$ mm voxel size, $7°$ flip angle).

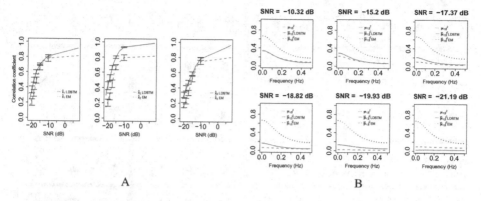

Fig. 2. LDSTM (solid lines) versus EM (dashed lines) comparison of efficiency in recovering source temporal information and estimating model parameters. (A) Lines represent the mean correlation between the simulated hidden state $x_{k,t}$ and the estimated hidden state $\hat{x}_{k,t}$ across 100 simulations. Vertical error bars denote the 95% confidence interval of the mean value. (B) Dotted lines represent the theoretical PDC of $\mathbf{x}_2$ towards $\mathbf{x}_1$. Others represent the estimated PDC of $\mathbf{x}_2$ towards $\mathbf{x}_1$ using LDSTM (solid) and EM (dash).

5.2   Preprocessing

Motion and slice time correction and temporal high pass filtering (allowing fluctuations above 0.005Hz) were carried out using FEAT v5.98. The FMRI data was aligned to the grey-matter mask via FreeSurfer's automatic registration tools (v. 5.0.0) resulting in extracted BOLD signals at regions with preponderantly neuronal cell bodies. To further group analysis by temporal concatenation, individual gray matter images were registered to MNI stereotactic standard space using a 12 parameter affine transform.

5.3   Results

Using 3D Daubechies (D2) functions to generate the spatial wavelet transform up to level 3 (other parameters as in Section 4.2), the LDSTM analysis identified thirty nine well localized spatial components comprise cortical (18), subcortical (2) and cerebellar (19) regions. Spatial components ($\mathbf{a}_k$'s) of the cortical and subcortical regions are shown in Figure 3. We are not showing cerebellar regions due to space constraints, even though they also form well localized bilateral activity patterns. Let us identify the region in the i-th row and j-th column of the Figure 3 as $e_{i,j}$. Regions include occipital pole ($e_{1,1}$ and $e_{1,2}$), lateral and superior occipital gyrus ($e_{2,1}$ and $e_{2,2}$), superior temporal gyrus ($e_{3,1}$ and $e_{3,2}$), motor (precentral gyrus ($e_{4,1}$ and $e_{4,2}$)) and sensory cortices (superior parietal gyrus ($e_{5,1}$ and $e_{5,2}$)), default mode network (precuneus and posterior cingulate ($e_{1,3}$ and $e_{1,4}$)), inferior frontal gyrus and anterior cingulate ($e_{2,3}$, $e_{2,4}$, $e_{3,3}$ and $e_{3,4}$)) and thalamus ($e_{4,3}$ and $e_{4,4}$).

Unsurprisingly these spatial components reflecting most of the data variability coincide with traditional resting-state regions observed across different individuals, data acquisition and analysis techniques [7,3]. The results draw attention to the fact that they

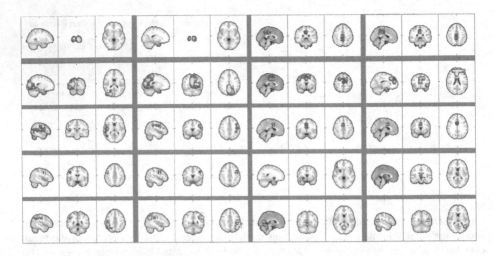

Fig. 3. Cortical and subcortical components identified by LDSTM (see text)

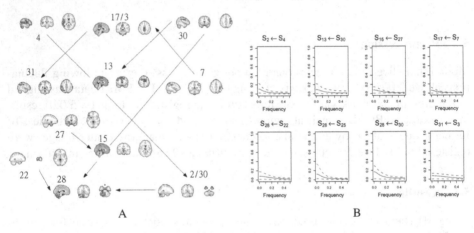

Fig. 4. FMRI resting-state analysis using LDSTM. Numbers represent different components. Components numbered twice represent two components located at the same region. (A) Connectivity map showing components whose system states are connected via the PDC. (B) PDC plots for each arrow drawing in (A). Dashed lines denote the 95% confidence interval of the mean value (solid lines).

were obtained without any additional assumption, such as independent or stationary sources, apart from requiring a_k spatial localization. Interest in this finding was stressed by [8] who suggested that FMRI analysis tools should highlight other mathematical characteristics rather than independence.

Furthermore, the lack of any artificial stochastic model constraints allows us studying the brain connectivity between the identified components. Fig. 4A shows the connectivity network estimated by PDC based on the reconstructed system states. In addition to showing that the connectivity is present mainly in low frequencies, a fact that has already been observed in several studies [3], the results shown in Fig. 4 B describe the existence of dynamic causal interactions between resting-state regions.

6 Conclusions

In this work, an EM-based algorithm was presented for LDSTM identification. More specifically, our method uses vector soft-thresholding operators to project high dimensional datasets into smoothness spaces where we can represent the system's spatial components with a reduced number of parameters. This is achieved by introducing a contiguity-constrained hierarchical clustering algorithm to group time series of wavelet coefficients characterizing the spatio-temporal variability of the data. PCA and constrained least squares provided initial estimates for the system states and the transition matrix, respectively. Finally, we presented simulated results showing that the LDSTM can outperform the traditional EM-algorithm even under mild conditions. The worst case scenario happened when we dealt with very large data such as FMRI in which it would be impossible to use the traditional EM-algorithm. In this case the LDSTM showed encouraging experimental results suggesting that this new technique can parcelate the human brain into well localized regions with physiologically plausible spatio-temporal brain activation patterns.

Acknowledgements. CNPq Grants 307163/2013-0 to L.A.B. We also thank NAPNA - Núcleo de Neurociência Aplicada from the University of São Paulo and FAPESP Grant 2005/56464-9 (CInAPCe) during which time part of this work took place.

References

1. Baccala, L.A., de Brito, C.S.N., Takahashi, D.Y., Sameshima, K.: Unified asymptotic theory for all partial directed coherence forms. Phil. Trans. R. Soc. A 371(1997), 20120158 (2013)
2. Bach, F., Jenatton, R., Mairal, J., Obozinski, G.: Structured sparsity through convex optimization. arXiv e-print 1109.2397 (September 2011)
3. Biswal, B.B., et al.: Toward discovery science of human brain function. Proc. Natl. Acad. Sci. U.S.A. 107(10), 4734–4739 (2010), PMID: 20176931
4. Chen, S.S., Donoho, D.L., Saunders, M.A.: Atomic decomposition by basis pursuit. SIAM Journal on Scientific Computing 20(1), 33–61 (1998)
5. Combettes, P.L., Wajs, V.R.: Signal recovery by proximal forward-backward splitting. Multiscale Modeling & Simulation 4(4), 1168–1200 (2005)
6. Cortes, J.: Distributed kriged kalman filter for spatial estimation. IEEE Transactions on Automatic Control 54(12), 2816–2827 (2009)
7. Damoiseaux, J.S., Rombouts, S.A.R.B., Barkhof, F., Scheltens, P., Stam, C.J., Smith, S.M., Beckmann, C.F.: Consistent resting-state networks across healthy subjects. PNAS 103(37), 13848–13853 (2006), PMID: 16945915
8. Daubechies, I., Roussos, E., Takerkart, S., Benharrosh, M., Golden, C., D'Ardenne, K., Richter, W., Cohen, J.D., Haxby, J.: Independent component analysis for brain fMRI does not select for independence. Proc. Natl. Acad. Sci. U. S. A. 106(26), 10415–10422 (2009), PMID: 19556548 PMCID: PMC2705604

9. Daubechies, I., Defrise, M., De Mol, C.: An iterative thresholding algorithm for linear inverse problems with a sparsity constraint. arXiv e-print math/0307152 (July 2003)

10. Dempster, A.P., Laird, N.M., Rubin, D.B.: Maximum likelihood from incomplete data via the EM algorithm. Journal of the Royal Statistical Society, Series B 39(1), 1–38 (1977)

11. Dewar, M., Scerri, K., Kadirkamanathan, V.: Data-driven spatio-temporal modeling using the integro-difference equation. IEEE Transactions on Signal Processing 57(1), 83–91 (2009)

12. Donoho, D.L., Johnstone, I.M., Kerkyacharian, G., Picard, D.: Wavelet shrinkage: Asymptopia? Journal of the Royal Statistical Society. Series B (Methodological) 57(2), 301–369 (1995), ArticleType: research-article/Full publication date: 1995/Copyright 1995 Royal Statistical Society

13. Feinberg, D.A., Moeller, S., Smith, S.M., Auerbach, E., Ramanna, S., Glasser, M.F., Miller, K.L., Ugurbil, K., Yacoub, E.: Multiplexed echo planar imaging for sub-second whole brain FMRI and fast diffusion imaging. PLoS ONE 5(12), e15710 (2010)

14. Figueiredo, M.A.T., Nowak, R.D.: An EM algorithm for wavelet-based image restoration. IEEE Transactions on Image Processing 12(8), 906–916 (2003)

15. Mallat, S.G.: A wavelet tour of signal processing the Sparse way. Elsevier/Academic Press, Amsterdam (2009)

16. Mardia, K.V., Goodall, C., Redfern, E.J., Alonso, F.J.: The kriged kalman filter. Test 7(2), 217–282 (1998)

17. Rauch, H.E., Striebel, C.T., Tung, F.: Maximum likelihood estimates of linear dynamic systems. Journal of the American Institute of Aeronautics and Astronautics 3(8), 1445–1450 (1965)

18. Scerri, K., Dewar, M., Kadirkamanathan, V.: Estimation and model selection for an IDE-Based spatio-temporal model. IEEE Transactions on Signal Processing 57(2), 482–492 (2009)

19. Shumway, R.H., Stoffer, D.S.: An approach to time series smoothing and forecasting using the em algorithm. Journal of Time Series Analysis 3(4), 253–264 (1982)

20. Theophilides, C.N., Ahearn, S.C., Grady, S., Merlino, M.: Identifying west nile virus risk areas: The dynamic continuous-area space-time system. Am. J. Epidemiol. 157(9), 843–854 (2003), PMID: 12727678

21. Tibshirani, R.: Regression shrinkage and selection via the lasso. Journal of the Royal Statistical Society, Series B 58, 267–288 (1994)

22. Wikle, C.K., Cressie, N.: A dimension-reduced approach to space-time kalman filtering. Biometrika 86(4), 815–829 (1999)

23. Woolrich, M.W., Jenkinson, M., Brady, M., Smith, S.M.: Fully bayesian spatio-temporal modeling of FMRI data. IEEE Trans. Med. Imaging 23(2), 213–231 (2004), PMID: 14964566

24. Wright, S.J., Nowak, R.D., Figueiredo, M.A.T.: Sparse reconstruction by separable approximation. IEEE Transactions on Signal Processing 57(7), 2479–2493 (2009)

25. Yuan, M., Lin, Y.: Model selection and estimation in regression with grouped variables. Journal of the Royal Statistical Society: Series B (Statistical Methodology) 68(1), 49–67 (2006)

26. Zhao, P., Rocha, G., Yu, B.: The composite absolute penalties family for grouped and hierarchical variable selection. arXiv e-print 0909.0411 (September 2009), Annals of Statistics 37(6A), 3468–3497 (2009)

27. Zibulevsky, M., Pearlmutter, B.A.: Blind source separation by sparse decomposition in a signal dictionary. Neural Computation 13(4), 863–882 (2001)

A Family of Reduced-Rank Neural Activity Indices for EEG/MEG Source Localization

Tomasz Piotrowski[1], David Gutiérrez[2],
Isao Yamada[3], and Jarosław Żygierewicz[4]

[1] Dept. of Informatics,
Faculty of Physics, Astronomy and Informatics,
Nicolaus Copernicus University,
Grudziądzka 5, 87-100 Toruń, Poland
tpiotrowski@is.umk.pl
[2] Center for Research and Advanced Studies,
Monterrey's Unit, Apodaca,
N.L., 66600, México
dgtz@ieee.org
[3] Dept. of Communications and Computer Engineering,
Tokyo Institute of Technology,
Tokyo 152-8550, Japan
isao@sp.ce.titech.ac.jp
[4] Biomedical Physics Division,
Institute of Experimental Physics, Faculty of Physics,
University of Warsaw,
Hoża 69, 00-681 Warsaw, Poland
Jaroslaw.Zygierewicz@fuw.edu.pl

Abstract. Localization of sources of brain electrical activity from electroencephalographic and magnetoencephalographic recordings is an ill-posed inverse problem. Therefore, the best one can hope for is to derive a source localization method which is guaranteed to find sources belonging to the set of possible solutions to this problem. Recently, a few methods with this property have been proposed as a non-trivial generalizations of the classical neural activity index based on the linearly constrained minimum-variance (LCMV) spatial filtering technique. In this paper we propose a family of reduced-rank activity indices achieving maximum value when evaluated at true source locations for uncorrelated dipole sources and any nonzero rank constraint. This fact shows in particular that this key property is not confined to a selected few activity indices. We present a series of numerical simulations evaluating localization performance of the proposed activity indices. We also give an overview of areas of future research which should be considered as an extension of the results of this paper. In particular, we discuss how new families of activity indices can be derived based on the proposed technique.

Keywords: Electroencephalography, magnetoencephalography, beamforming, reduced-rank signal processing, dipole source localization.

D. Ślęzak et al. (Eds.): BIH 2014, LNAI 8609, pp. 447–458, 2014.
© Springer International Publishing Switzerland 2014

1   Introduction

The problem of localization of sources of brain electrical activity from electroencephalographic (EEG) and magnetoencephalographic (MEG) recordings continues to attract researchers' and practitioners' attention. A myriad of solutions have been proposed, with the neural activity index (AI) introduced in [1] being a prime example of a successful approach to this problem. The AI is a function of the output of the linearly constrained minimum-variance (LCMV) filter [2] evaluated at the locations within region of interest (ROI), with the assumption that it is maximized when evaluated at true source locations. However, for the AI, this assumption has not been confirmed by the proof.

Recently, a new paradigm has emerged in spatial filtering community, which focuses on localization of sources from EEG and MEG recordings based on dual- and multi-source extensions of classical LCMV filter, see [3, 4] and references therein. In particular, the work [4] introduced four new multi-source activity indices, which were proved to achieve maximum value when evaluated at true source locations irrespective of signal-to-noise ratio (SNR), assuming that observed signal and noise covariance matrices are known exactly, and provided that an exhaustive search within ROI is performed.

In this paper we propose a family of activity indices, which are reduced-rank extensions of the multi-source activity index (MAI) introduced in [4], which itself can be seen as an extension of the AI to multi-source case. We prove that the proposed indices achieve maximum value when evaluated at true source locations for any SNR *and* any nonzero rank constraint, under the same assumptions made in the previous paragraph for the (full-rank) activity indices introduced in [4]. This result shows in particular that this key property is not confined to a selected few activity indices, which opens the question whether a certain optimization problem can be designed to select the optimal activity index for a given experiment.

Indeed, it shall be emphasized that the desirable properties of the activity indices described above hold under the assumption of perfect model knowledge. When conditions are not ideal, we can still count on getting closer to the correct solution compared with other localizers. In practice, signal and noise covariance matrices are unknown, thus they are estimated from the measurements. This estimation introduces perturbation in the values of activity indices, and this problem is especially acute if the sources are closely positioned, possibly correlated, and if the background activity is high. From a mathematical standpoint, such settings yield forward models in EEG and MEG ill-conditioned. Thus, we shall expect the proposed family of reduced-rank neural activity indices to be especially useful in such settings, as the reduced-rank methods have been established as powerful tools which are robust against ill-conditioned systems, see, e.g., [5–9] and references therein.

The paper is organized as follows: in Section 2 we introduce the EEG/MEG measurement model considered along with the AI and MAI indices. In Section 3 we introduce the proposed family of reduced-rank neural activity indices, and in Section 4 we show, through a series of numerical examples, its applicability in dipole source localization in ill-conditioned settings using realistically simulated MEG data. We close with Section 5 where areas of future research are discussed.

A short version of this paper has been presented at conference [10].

2 Preliminaries

We consider the case of EEG/MEG measurements produced by l dipole sources using an array of m sensors, and assume that the sources' activity changes in time, but their positions $\boldsymbol{\theta} = (\theta_1, \ldots, \theta_l)^t$ remain the same during the measurement period, where θ_i denotes the position of the i-th source. Then, the vector $\mathbf{y}$ composed of the measurements by m sensors at a given time instant can be modeled as [11]:

$$\mathbf{y} = A(\boldsymbol{\theta})\mathbf{q} + \mathbf{n}, \tag{1}$$

where $A(\boldsymbol{\theta})$ is the $m \times 3l$ array response matrix representing material and geometrical properties of the medium in which the sources are submerged relevant for EEG or MEG measurements; $\mathbf{q}$ represents dipole moments at locations $\boldsymbol{\theta}$ at a given time instant:

$$\mathbf{q} = \begin{pmatrix} \mathbf{q}_x(\theta_1) \\ \mathbf{q}_y(\theta_1) \\ \mathbf{q}_z(\theta_1) \\ \vdots \\ \mathbf{q}_x(\theta_l) \\ \mathbf{q}_y(\theta_l) \\ \mathbf{q}_z(\theta_l) \end{pmatrix} \in \mathbb{R}^{3l}, \tag{2}$$

where $(\mathbf{q}_x(\theta_i), \mathbf{q}_y(\theta_i), \mathbf{q}_z(\theta_i))^t$ are the Cartesian components of the dipole moment at i-th source location, and the zero-mean random vector $\mathbf{n}$ represents measurement noise and spontaneous background brain activity. The array response matrix $A(\boldsymbol{\theta})$ is of full-column rank $3l$ and we assume that $\mathbf{q}$ and $\mathbf{n}$ are uncorrelated.

In terms of (1), spatial filtering allows for estimation of dipole source moments $\mathbf{q}$ (when source locations $\boldsymbol{\theta}$ are known), and for source localization by defining a neural activity index as a function of $\boldsymbol{\theta}$, with the assumption that the maximum value of the activity index is achieved if evaluated at true source locations. It is the latter source localization problem in which we focus on in this paper.

The idea of using a neural activity index as a localizer originates in [1], where the following activity index (AI) has been proposed for the single-source case, i.e., $l = 1$ in (1):

$$\mathrm{AI}(\boldsymbol{\theta}) := \frac{\mathrm{tr}\{S(\boldsymbol{\theta})^{-1}\}}{\mathrm{tr}\{G(\boldsymbol{\theta})^{-1}\}}, \tag{3}$$

where $\mathrm{tr}\{\cdot\}$ indicates the trace of the matrix,

$$S(\boldsymbol{\theta}) := A(\boldsymbol{\theta})^t R_{\mathbf{y}}^{-1} A(\boldsymbol{\theta}), \tag{4}$$

and

$$G(\boldsymbol{\theta}) := A(\boldsymbol{\theta})^t R_{\mathbf{n}}^{-1} A(\boldsymbol{\theta}), \tag{5}$$

where $R_{\mathbf{y}}$ and $R_{\mathbf{n}}$ are covariance matrices of $\mathbf{y}$ and $\mathbf{n}$, respectively. However, it has been unclear whether $\mathrm{AI}(\boldsymbol{\theta})$ achieves its maximum value when evaluated at true source locations.

To circumvent this difficulty, a multi-source extension of $\mathrm{AI}(\boldsymbol{\theta})$ has been recently proposed in [4] for the general case $l \geq 1$:

$$\mathrm{MAI}(\boldsymbol{\theta}) := \mathrm{tr}\{G(\boldsymbol{\theta})S(\boldsymbol{\theta})^{-1}\} - 3l_x, \tag{6}$$

where l_x is the unknown number of concurrently active sources. The key properties of $\mathrm{MAI}(\boldsymbol{\theta})$ are summed up in the following theorem [4, p. 485]:

Theorem 1. *The $\mathrm{MAI}(\boldsymbol{\theta})$ in (6) is a non-negative and bounded function of $\boldsymbol{\theta}$, which achieves maximum value for $\boldsymbol{\theta} = \boldsymbol{\theta}_0$, where $\boldsymbol{\theta}_0$ are the true source locations, in which case $l_x = l$, where l is the number of active sources.*

The applicability of the $\mathrm{MAI}(\boldsymbol{\theta})$ has been already demonstrated in [4]. In particular, a practical method for determining the number of active sources can be deducted from Theorem 1 as follows: initiate the search with $l_x = 1$, find $\max_{\boldsymbol{\theta}} \mathrm{MAI}(\boldsymbol{\theta})$, and increase l_x until the value of $\max_{\boldsymbol{\theta}} \mathrm{MAI}(\boldsymbol{\theta})$ saturates. Thus, from now on we assume that the number of active sources l has been identified.

It shall be noted that the maximum of $\mathrm{MAI}(\boldsymbol{\theta})$ is achieved for $S(\boldsymbol{\theta}_0)^{-1}$. Thus, small changes in $S(\boldsymbol{\theta}_0)$ may cause huge changes in $S(\boldsymbol{\theta}_0)^{-1}$ if the former is ill-conditioned [12]. In our case, this could be the result of closely positioned sources and high background activity. In such situations, $G(\boldsymbol{\theta}_0)$ will be ill-conditioned as well.

Let us now introduce the following estimate:

$$\widehat{\mathrm{MAI}}(\boldsymbol{\theta}) := \mathrm{tr}\{\widehat{G(\boldsymbol{\theta})}\widehat{S(\boldsymbol{\theta})}^{-1}\} - 3l_x, \tag{7}$$

where

$$\widehat{G(\boldsymbol{\theta})} := A(\boldsymbol{\theta})^t \widehat{R_{\mathbf{n}}}^{-1} A(\boldsymbol{\theta}), \tag{8}$$

and

$$\widehat{S(\boldsymbol{\theta})} := A(\boldsymbol{\theta})^t \widehat{R_{\mathbf{y}}}^{-1} A(\boldsymbol{\theta}), \tag{9}$$

where $\widehat{R_{\mathbf{y}}}$ and $\widehat{R_{\mathbf{n}}}$ are the estimates of $R_{\mathbf{y}}$ and $R_{\mathbf{n}}$, respectively. Obviously, the value of (7) will differ from (6) for a given $\boldsymbol{\theta}$. More crucially, its argument of the maximum is likely to change from $\boldsymbol{\theta} = \boldsymbol{\theta}_0$ due to sensitivity of $S(\boldsymbol{\theta}_0)^{-1}$ to even smallest changes of an ill-conditioned $S(\boldsymbol{\theta}_0)$. This is a fundamental problem as it makes source localization using $\mathrm{MAI}(\boldsymbol{\theta})$ very prone to errors in ill-conditioned settings. In the next section, we provide a solution that allows for robust source localization in ill-conditioned settings by introducing the reduced-rank extension of $\mathrm{MAI}(\boldsymbol{\theta})$.

3   Proposed Activity Indices

In this section we propose first a family of reduced-rank activity indices achieving maximum value when evaluated at true source locations for uncorrelated dipole sources and any nonzero rank constraint.

We introduce the reduced-rank extension of MAI$(\boldsymbol{\theta})$ in (6) as:

$$\text{RR-MAI}_{T1}(\boldsymbol{\theta}, r) := \text{tr}\{G(\boldsymbol{\theta}) P_{\mathcal{R}(G(\boldsymbol{\theta})_r)} S(\boldsymbol{\theta})^{-1}\} - r, \tag{10}$$

where r is a natural number such that $1 \leq r \leq 3l$, and $P_{\mathcal{R}(G(\boldsymbol{\theta})_r)}$ is the orthogonal projection matrix onto $\mathcal{R}(G(\boldsymbol{\theta})_r)$, i.e., the subspace spanned by the r eigenvectors corresponding to the r largest eigenvalues of $G(\boldsymbol{\theta})$. The following theorem establishes the key properties of the RR-MAI$_{T1}(\boldsymbol{\theta}, r)$:

Theorem 2. *Let us fix a rank constraint r such that $1 \leq r \leq 3l$, and consider uncorrelated sources such that*

$$R_q = I_{3l}. \tag{11}$$

Then RR-MAI$_{T1}(\boldsymbol{\theta}, r)$ *in (10) is a non-negative and bounded function of $\boldsymbol{\theta}$, which reaches its global maximum for $\boldsymbol{\theta} = \boldsymbol{\theta}_0$, where $\boldsymbol{\theta}_0$ are the true source locations.*

Proof: To simplify notation, we denote below $G := G(\boldsymbol{\theta})$, and $S := S(\boldsymbol{\theta})$, with $G_0 := G(\boldsymbol{\theta}_0)$ and $S_0 := S(\boldsymbol{\theta}_0)$, where $\boldsymbol{\theta}_0$ are the true source locations. Such shortened notation does not introduce ambiguity, one needs to keep in mind however that G and S depend on $\boldsymbol{\theta}$, and G_0 and S_0 on $\boldsymbol{\theta}_0$.

Let us pick $r \in \{1, \ldots, 3l\}$, and consider $EVD(G) = M\Gamma M^t$ with $M = (m_1, \ldots, m_{3l})$ and eigenvalues organized in nonincreasing order, so that $P_{\mathcal{R}(G_r)}$ in (10) can be expressed as:

$$P_{\mathcal{R}(G_r)} = M_r M_r^t, \tag{12}$$

where $M_r := (m_1, \ldots, m_r)$ are the eigenvectors corresponding to the r largest eigenvalues of G. Then one has:

$$\text{tr}\{G P_{\mathcal{R}(G_r)} S^{-1}\} = \text{tr}\{G M_r M_r^t S^{-1}\}. \tag{13}$$

Using matrix inversion lemma, we express S^{-1} as {*cf.* (A3) in [4, Appendix A.]}:

$$S^{-1} = G^{-1} + G^{-1}K(R_q^{-1} + G_0 - K^t G^{-1} K)^{-1} K^t G^{-1}, \tag{14}$$

where $K := A(\boldsymbol{\theta})^t R_n^{-1} A(\boldsymbol{\theta}_0) \in \mathbb{R}^{3l \times 3l}$. Denote

$$Z = R_q^{-1} + G_0 - K^t G^{-1} K. \tag{15}$$

Insertion of (14) into (13) yields

$$\text{tr}\{G M_r M_r^t S^{-1}\} = \text{tr}\{M_r M_r^t\} + \text{tr}\{G M_r M_r^t G^{-1} K Z^{-1} K^t G^{-1}\} =$$
$$r + \text{tr}\{Z^{-1} (K^t M_r M_r^t G^{-1} K)\}. \tag{16}$$

Denote

$$Y_r := K^t M_r M_r^t G^{-1} K, \tag{17}$$

so that

$$tr\{GM_r M_r^t S^{-1}\} = r + tr\{Z^{-1} Y_r\}. \tag{18}$$

Consider now Z in (15). The matrix $G_0 - K^t G^{-1} K$ therein is shown below (A4) in [4, Appendix A.] to be positive semidefinite for any $\boldsymbol{\theta}$ and $\boldsymbol{\theta}_0$. Thus, Z is positive definite and satisfies the following relationship:

$$Z \succeq R_{\mathbf{q}}^{-1}, \tag{19}$$

where $\succeq$ denotes Loewner ordering, i.e., $Z - R_{\mathbf{q}}^{-1}$ is positive semidefinite. Note also that Y_r is positive semidefinite, because $M_r M_r^t G^{-1}$ is positive semidefinite. Hence, the value of $tr\{GM_r M_r^t S^{-1}\}$ is always at least r, and consequently, (10) is a non-negative function.

Next, relationship (19) is equivalent to [13, p.471]

$$R_{\mathbf{q}} \succeq Z^{-1}. \tag{20}$$

Using relationship (20) in (18) we have:

$$tr\{GM_r M_r^t S^{-1}\} = r + tr\{Z^{-1} Y_r\} \leq r + tr\{R_{\mathbf{q}} Y_r\}, \tag{21}$$

with equality if $\boldsymbol{\theta} = \boldsymbol{\theta}_0$. We now employ assumption (11) to simplify (21) to

$$tr\{GM_r M_r^t S^{-1}\} = r + tr\{Z^{-1} Y_r\} \leq r + tr\{Y_r\}. \tag{22}$$

Consider now

$$SVD(R_{\mathbf{n}}^{-1/2} A(\boldsymbol{\theta})) = U\Sigma V^t$$

and

$$SVD(R_{\mathbf{n}}^{-1/2} A(\boldsymbol{\theta}_0)) = U_0 \Sigma_0 V_0^t,$$

with singular values organized in both cases in nonincreasing order, so that Y_r (17) can be expressed as

$$Y_r := (V_0 \Sigma_0^t U_0^t U \Sigma V^t)(M_r M_r^t G^{-1})(V \Sigma^t U^t U_0 \Sigma_0 V_0^t). \tag{23}$$

We can also express G as

$$G = V\Sigma^t U^t U \Sigma V^t = V\Sigma^t \Sigma V^t, \tag{24}$$

and

$$P_{\mathcal{R}(G_r)} = V_r V_r^t = V I_{3l}^r V^t, \tag{25}$$

where I_{3l}^r contains as its $r \times r$ principal submatrix the identity matrix of size r and zeros elsewhere. Thus, Y_r takes the form

$$Y_r = (V_0 \Sigma_0^t U_0^t U \Sigma V^t)(V I_{3l}^r V^t V (\Sigma^t \Sigma)^{-1} V^t)(V \Sigma^t U^t U_0 \Sigma_0 V_0^t) =$$
$$V_0 \Sigma_0^t U_0^t U \Sigma I_{3l}^r (\Sigma^t \Sigma)^{-1} \Sigma^t U^t U_0 \Sigma_0 V_0^t = V_0 \Sigma_0^t U_0^t U I_{3l}^r U^t U_0 \Sigma_0 V_0^t. \tag{26}$$

Therefore, one has

$$tr\{GM_r M_r^t S^{-1}\} \leq r + tr\{Y_r\} = r + tr\{V_0 \Sigma_0^t U_0^t U I_{3l}^r U^t U_0 \Sigma_0 V_0^t\} =$$
$$r + tr\{U_0 \Sigma_0 \Sigma_0^t U_0^t U I_{3l}^r U^t\} = r + tr\{B_0 C\}, \quad (27)$$

where $B_0 = U_0 \Sigma_0 \Sigma_0^t U_0^t$ and $C = U I_{3l}^r U^t$. Matrices B_0 and C are symmetric with eigenvalues organized in nonincreasing order. Thus, from [14] we obtain

$$tr\{GM_r M_r^t S^{-1}\} \leq r + tr\{B_0 C\} \leq r + tr\{\Sigma_0 \Sigma_0^t I_{3l}^r\}. \quad (28)$$

In particular, the form of U and U_0 for which equality is achieved in the second inequality is satisfied if $\boldsymbol{\theta} = \boldsymbol{\theta}_0$ in view of [14]. Note that $tr\{\Sigma_0 \Sigma_0^t I_{3l}^r\}$ is a fixed positive number for a given $\boldsymbol{\theta}_0$. Thus, one has

$$tr\{GM_r M_r^t S^{-1}\} \leq r + tr\{\Sigma_0 \Sigma_0^t I_{3l}^r\}, \quad (29)$$

with equality achieved if $\boldsymbol{\theta} = \boldsymbol{\theta}_0$. This fact proves that (10) reaches its global maximum for $\boldsymbol{\theta} = \boldsymbol{\theta}_0$, where $\boldsymbol{\theta}_0$ are the true source locations. $\square$

The above Theorem demonstrates that the key properties of MAI($\boldsymbol{\theta}$), as given in Theorem 1, are attained by the whole family of indices of the form (10), provided the sources are uncorrelated. A natural question is whether we can design other families of activity indices achieving maximum value when evaluated at true source locations. This will be discussed in Section 5.

Furthermore, based on the above considerations, we take the liberty of proposing another reduced-rank activity index:

$$\text{RR-MAI}_{\text{T2}}(\boldsymbol{\theta}, r) := tr\{G(\boldsymbol{\theta}) P_{\mathcal{R}(S(\boldsymbol{\theta})_r)} S(\boldsymbol{\theta})^{-1}\} - r, \quad (30)$$

for $1 \leq r \leq 3l$. This alternative index has the desirable property of being fully independent from the $m - r$ smallest eigenvalues of $S(\boldsymbol{\theta})$ for any $\boldsymbol{\theta}$. This fact can be easily observed from the eigenvalue decomposition $EVD(S(\boldsymbol{\theta})) = N\Lambda N^t$ with $N = (n_1, \ldots, n_{3l})$ and eigenvalues organized in nonincreasing order, as $P_{\mathcal{R}(S(\boldsymbol{\theta})_r)} S(\boldsymbol{\theta})^{-1}$ can be expressed as:

$$P_{\mathcal{R}(S(\boldsymbol{\theta})_r)} S(\boldsymbol{\theta})^{-1} = N_r N_r^t S(\boldsymbol{\theta})^{-1} = N_r N_r^t N \Lambda^{-1} N^t = N \Lambda_r^{\dagger} N^t, \quad (31)$$

where $N_r := (n_1, \ldots, n_r)$ are the eigenvectors corresponding to the r largest eigenvalues of $S(\boldsymbol{\theta})$, and the diagonal matrix $\Lambda_r^{\dagger}$ contains on its diagonal the vector $(\lambda_1^{-1}, \ldots, \lambda_r^{-1}, 0, \ldots, 0)$.

This property suggests that one should expect better performance of the activity index RR-MAI$_{\text{T2}}(\boldsymbol{\theta}, r)$ in (30) compared with RR-MAI$_{\text{T1}}(\boldsymbol{\theta}, r)$ in (10), specially for closely positioned sources and high background activity. To verify this hypothesis, we will consider both families of activity indices in the numerical simulations in Section 4. Note that a similar proof of Theorem 2 for the RR-MAI$_{\text{T2}}(\boldsymbol{\theta}, r)$ in (30) is currently being developed.

4   Numerical Example

We consider the case of estimating the position of $l = 3$ dipole sources through the indices previously described. Let us assume that the dipole source components are allowed to change in time as $\mathbf{q}(t) = (\mathbf{q}_1(t), \ldots, \mathbf{q}_9(t))^t$, where $\mathbf{q}_i(t) = \sin(i\pi(t/150 - 1))$, for $i = 1, \ldots, 9$, and $t = 0, 1, \ldots, 300$. Then, $\mathbf{Q}$ is defined as

$$\mathbf{Q} = [\mathbf{q}(0), \mathbf{q}(1), \ldots, \mathbf{q}(300)] = \begin{bmatrix} \mathbf{q}_1(0) & \cdots & \mathbf{q}_1(300) \\ \vdots & & \vdots \\ \mathbf{q}_9(0) & \cdots & \mathbf{q}_9(300) \end{bmatrix}. \tag{32}$$

Note that, under these conditions, $R_{\mathbf{q}} = I$.

MEG measurements were generated using the Helsinki BEM library [15] with a head model composed by three tessellated meshes which were nested one inside the other in order to approximate the geometry of the scalp, skull, and brain. Such head model was created based on the anatomical information of "Subject # 1" of the MEG-SIM portal, which is a repository that contains an extensive series of real and simulated MEG measurements for testing purposes [16]. In particular, the volume modeling the brain was constructed with 11520 triangles, and it is shown in Figure 1. There, we show the centroids of the triangles under which the dipole sources were located, as well as the centroids of 100 neighboring triangles which define a region-of-interest (ROI) around the sources. The large number of triangles used to approximate the head's anatomy in BEM guarantees that the modeling errors are negligible.

Fig. 1. Tessellated mesh of the brain showing the dipoles' positions (in red) and the ROI around them (in blue)

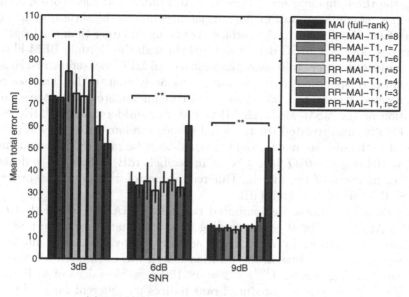

(a) MAI($\boldsymbol{\theta}$) compared against RR-MAI$_{\text{T1}}(\boldsymbol{\theta}, r)$

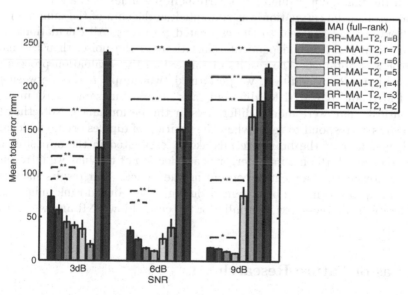

(b) MAI($\boldsymbol{\theta}$) compared against RR-MAI$_{\text{T2}}(\boldsymbol{\theta}, r)$

Fig. 2. Mean localization errors as a function of SNR and rank. The vertical lines on top of the bars indicate the ($\pm$) standard error, while horizontal lines indicate those groups with significant differences ($^{*}p < 0.05$, $^{**}p < 0.01$).

Next, the three dipole sources were located 2 mm below their corresponding triangle (i.e., going downward in the normal direction to the surface). Since the distances from the dipoles to the surface are not much larger than the length of the triangles sides, the MEG data generated through the Helsinki BEM library can be considered a very close approximation to real MEG measurements. Hence, MEG data corresponding to the simultaneous activation of the three sources were generated using an array of $m = 275$ magnetometers with the spatial distribution of the VSM MedTech MEG system considered in the MEG-SIM portal. Finally, uncorrelated (in time and space) random noise $\mathbf{N} \sim \mathcal{N}(0, \sigma^2)$ was added to the measurements, and the signal-to-noise ratio (SNR) was defined as SNR $= 10 \log_{10} \| A(\boldsymbol{\theta})\mathbf{Q} \|_F / \| \mathbf{N} \|_F$ in decibels (dB), where $\| \cdot \|_F$ denotes the Frobenius norm of the matrix. Different values of σ^2 were set in order to obtain SNR levels of 3, 6, and 9 dB.

Under these conditions, we computed the indices $\mathrm{MAI}(\boldsymbol{\theta})$, $\mathrm{RR\text{-}MAI}_{\mathrm{T1}}(\boldsymbol{\theta}, r)$, and $\mathrm{RR\text{-}MAI}_{\mathrm{T2}}(\boldsymbol{\theta}, r)$, for $\boldsymbol{\theta}$ corresponding to a combination of three positions chosen from the centroids in the ROI, but actually located 2, 4, and 6 mm below the surface (i.e., a small bias in the position search was introduced). Therefore, we evaluated each index for $\binom{100}{3} \times 3 = 485100$ possible values of $\boldsymbol{\theta}$. Furthermore, we tested our proposed reduced-rank indices for different rank values. In all cases, the estimated positions (denoted by $\hat{\boldsymbol{\theta}}$) were taken as the value of $\boldsymbol{\theta}$ for which the maximum value of the corresponding index was achieved. Then, the total error in the estimation was computed as the sum of the minimum distances from each of the real to the estimated positions. All calculations were repeated for at least 50 independent realizations of the noise, then the mean total error was obtained. The results of this exhaustive evaluation process are shown in Figure 2. In addition, we performed two-sample t-tests between the errors of MAI and RR-MAI for different rank values (but same SNR) in order to establish if there were indeed differences in the performance. Note that the largest errors correspond to cases when the position of dipoles originally located in one hemisphere of the brain are mistakenly estimated in the opposite side. On the other hand, the minimum error is a reflection of the bias we introduced in the position at the moment of computing the indices. Our results show that significant improvement can be obtained through the reduced-rank indices with a considerable rank reduction, specially for the case of low SNR and when using $\mathrm{RR\text{-}MAI}_{\mathrm{T2}}$.

5   Areas of Future Research

The family of reduced-rank activity indices introduced in Theorem 2 are guaranteed to get true source locations irrespective of the SNR, for *any* nonzero rank constraint. Thus, at first sight it may appear that there is no trade-off usually associated with reduced-rank methods. However, such trade-off becomes visible if we note that the assumption (11) is necessary for inequality (29) to hold, with equality if $\boldsymbol{\theta} = \boldsymbol{\theta}_0$. This fact leads to rather subtle algebraical considerations, which reveal that for arbitrarily correlated sources, the less correlated the sources are, the lower the rank r_0 may be chosen such that $\text{RR-MAI}_{\text{T}1}(\boldsymbol{\theta}, r)$ will get true source locations for all rank constraints r such that $r_0 \leq r \leq 3l$.

Moreover, the proof of Theorem 2 may be readily modified to prove that other families of reduced-rank localizers have the key property established in Theorem 2 for $\text{RR-MAI}_{\text{T}1}(\boldsymbol{\theta}, r)$. For example, one may introduce the reduced-rank extensions of the event-related localizers, which were introduced in [4] along with $\text{MAI}(\boldsymbol{\theta})$. It will be specially interesting to see which family of the reduced-rank activity indices will perform best in a given practical setup, where theorems such as Theorem 1 and Theorem 2 hold only approximately. More generally, one will perhaps need to consider a hierarchical optimization problem, where the aim may be to maximize the steepness of the activity index in vicinity of the argument of the maximum $\boldsymbol{\theta} = \boldsymbol{\theta}_0$, among rank constraints *and* form of the index. Whether such optimization problem is feasible remains to be seen.

On the other hand, in the present form, a brute-force search over a region of interest is needed to implement the proposed activity indices in practice. To ease the computational load, a recursive source localization procedure approximating $\text{RR-MAI}_{\text{T}1}(\boldsymbol{\theta}, r)$ (or $\text{RR-MAI}_{\text{T}2}(\boldsymbol{\theta}, r)$) needs to be derived. An example of such algorithm is given in [4]. Indeed, it can be readily applied to the proposed family of reduced-rank activity indices. Moreover, such recursive procedure should be extended in the future to the adaptive case, where the positions of the sources $\boldsymbol{\theta} = (\boldsymbol{\theta}_1, \ldots, \boldsymbol{\theta}_l)^t$ are time-dependent. In such a case, one will have to take into consideration also the possible change in the number of active sources l.

Acknowledgment. D. Gutiérrez was supported by the National Council of Science and Technology (CONACyT-México) under Grant 220145.

References

1. Van Veen, B.D., Van Drongelen, W., Yuchtman, M., Suzuki, A.: Localization of Brain Electrical Activity via Linearly Constrained Minimum Variance Spatial Filtering. IEEE Transactions on Biomedical Engineering 44(9), 867–880 (1997)
2. Frost, O.T.: An Algorithm for Linearly Constrained Adaptive Array Processing. Proceedings of the IEEE 60(8), 926–935 (1972)
3. Diwakar, M., Huang, M.-X., Srinivasan, R., Harrington, D.L., Robb, A., Angeles, A., Muzzatti, L., Pakdaman, R., Song, T., Theilmann, R.J., Lee, R.R.: Dual-Core Beamformer for Obtaining Highly Correlated Neuronal Networks in MEG. NeuroImage 54(1), 253–263 (2011)
4. Moiseev, A., Gaspar, J.M., Schneider, J.A., Herdman, A.T.: Application of Multi-Source Minimum Variance Beamformers for Reconstruction of Correlated Neural Activity. NeuroImage 58(2), 481–496 (2011)
5. Yamada, I., Elbadraoui, J.: Minimum-Variance Pseudo-Unbiased Low-Rank Estimator for Ill-Conditioned Inverse Problems. In: IEEE ICASSP 2006, pp. 325–328 (2006)
6. Piotrowski, T., Yamada, I.: MV-PURE Estimator: Minimum-Variance Pseudo-Unbiased Reduced-Rank Estimator for Linearly Constrained Ill-Conditioned Inverse Problems. IEEE Transactions on Signal Processing 56(8), 3408–3423 (2008)

7. Piotrowski, T., Cavalcante, R.L.G., Yamada, I.: Stochastic MV-PURE Estimator: Robust Reduced-Rank Estimator for Stochastic Linear Model. IEEE Transactions on Signal Processing 57(4), 1293–1303 (2009)
8. Piotrowski, T., Zaragoza-Martinez, C.C., Gutiérrez, D., Yamada, I.: MV-PURE Estimator of Dipole Source Signals in EEG. In: IEEE ICASSP 2013, pp. 968–972 (2013)
9. Piotrowski, T., Yamada, I.: Performance of the Stochastic MV-PURE Estimator in Highly Noisy Settings. Journal of the Franklin Institute (in press)
10. Piotrowski, T., Gutiérrez, D., Yamada, I., Żygierewicz, J.: Reduced-Rank Neural Activity Index for EEG/MEG Multi-Source Localization. In: IEEE ICASSP 2014 (in press, 2014)
11. Mosher, J.C., Leahy, R.M., Lewis, P.S.: EEG and MEG: Forward Solutions for Inverse Methods. IEEE Transactions on Biomedical Engineering 46(3), 245–259 (1999)
12. Golub, G.H., Van Loan, C.F.: Matrix Computations. The Johns Hopkins University Press, Baltimore (1996)
13. Horn, R.A., Johnson, C.R.: Matrix Analysis. Cambridge University Press, New York (1985)
14. Theobald, C.M.: An Inequality for the Trace of the Product of Two Symmetric Matrices. Math. Proc. Camb. Phil. Soc. 77, 265–267 (1975)
15. Stenroos, M., Mantynen, V., Nenonen, J.: A MATLAB Library for Solving Quasi-Static Volume Conduction Problems Using the Boundary Element Method. Computer Methods and Programs in Biomedicine 88(3), 256–263 (2007)
16. Aine, C.J., Sanfratello, L., Ranken, D., Best, E., MacArthur, J.A., Wallace, T., Gilliam, K., Donahue, C.H., Montano, R., Bryant, J.E., Scott, A., Stephen, J.M.: MEG-SIM: A Web Portal for Testing MEG Analysis Methods Using Realistic Simulated and Empirical Data. Neuroinformatics 10(2), 141–158 (2012)

Neurologically Inspired Computational Cognitive Modelling of Situation Awareness

Dilhan J. Thilakarathne

Agent Systems Research Group, Department of Computer Science,
VU University Amsterdam, De Boelelaan 1081, 1081 HV Amsterdam, The Netherlands
d.j.thilakarathne@vu.nl
http://www.few.vu.nl/~dte220/

Abstract. How information processes in the human brain relate to action formation is an interesting research question and with the latest development of
brain imaging and recording techniques more and more interesting insights
have been uncovered. In this paper a cognitive model is scrutinized which is
based on cognitive, affective, and behavioural science evidences for situation
awareness. Situation awareness has been recognized as an important phenomenon in almost all domains where safety is of highest importance and complex
decision making is inevitable. This paper discusses analysis, modelling and simulation of three scenarios in the aviation domain where poor situation awareness plays a main role, and which have been explained by Endsley according to
her three level situation awareness model. The computational model presented
in this paper is driven by the interplay between bottom-up and top-down
processes in action formation together with processes and states such as: perception, attention, intention, desires, feeling, action preparation, ownership, and
communication. This type of cognitively and neurologically inspired computational models provide new directions for the artificial intelligence community to
develop systems that are more aligning with realistic human mental processes
and for designers of interfaces of complex systems.

Keywords: Situation Awareness, Perception, Attention, Intention, Bottom-Up,
Top-Down, Cognitive Modelling and Simulation.

1 Introduction

Situation Awareness (SA) describes the subjective quality of awareness of a situation
a person is engaged in. The construct of SA is a nontrivial challenge mainly because
of poor understanding in the scientific area of human cognition and the associated
complexity in practical areas where SA is relevant, for example: aviation, air traffic
control, maintenance, healthcare, intelligence, power systems, transportation, etc. The
latest findings from brain imaging and recording techniques in the last decade provide
the opportunity to uplift the understanding of cognitive processes in the human brain
and more specifically the interplay among those for action selection. It seems that
most of the basic actions are pre-stored as habitual tasks through the effects of prior

D. Ślęzak et al. (Eds.): BIH 2014, LNAI 8609, pp. 459–470, 2014.

learning, and will activate unconsciously when a relevant stimulus is perceived [1]. Nevertheless, it is an innate ability of human beings to control in a conscious manner habitual actions adhering to a situation and/or to react in novel situations where no prior learning or experience exists. Conscious action formation turns out to be complicated; especially the complex interplay among bottom-up and top-down processes behind it has to be addressed to provide more insight in action selection [2–5]. Furthermore, there are various viewpoints about conscious awareness and it seems from the latest findings that we develop awareness of action selection related to a situation just before the action execution, and it may be the case that this awareness has a decisive effect on actually executing the action, but it may equally well be the case that the awareness state has no effect on whether the action is performed (cf. [2, 6, 7]). Therefore, from the current evidences from cognitive, affective, and behavioural sciences, the process behind SA in parallel to action formation can be reformed together with considering the factors explained in well known past SA models.

With the lessons learned from tragic events that have occurred in the aviation domain, more attention has been given to the importance of SA in the aviation domain (cf. [8, 9]). There are more than fifteen definitions for SA in the literature [10], and still it is debate over what SA actually is, what it comprises, what factors impact it. Mica R. Endsley in [11] put forward a working definition which became the most widely used definition among many researches. According to Endsley, SA is:

"the perception of the elements in the environment within a volume of time and space, the comprehension of their meaning, and the projection of their status in the near future" ([12], pp. 36).

Based on this definition Endsley highlighted three elements 1) perception, 2) comprehension, and 3) projection, as the necessary conditions for SA which are three levels of which one is followed by the other to develop complete (subjective) awareness. Furthermore, it has been found that based on the safety reports in the aviation domain for the period of 1986 to 1992, 76% of errors related to SA were because of Level 1 (i.e., failure to correctly perceive information), 20.3% were Level 2 (i.e., failure to comprehend the situation), and 3.4% were Level 3 (i.e., failure to project situation into future) [8, 9]. Therefore, this statistical information provides an indication of the importance of those three factors on SA. Furthermore, Endsley has indicated how attention, goals, expectations, mental models, long-term memory, working memory and automaticity contribute to situation assessment as cognitive processes [12, 13]. To get a more detailed picture of such interplay, in this paper both the insights derived from Endsley's SA model and the latest neurocognitive findings have been utilized and brought together.

Research like this may have benefits especially for the artificial intelligence community to consider more natural computational models for complex systems where emergent behaviours need to be analyzed and simulated. Furthermore, through such simulations, system (or interface) designers can validate the quality of their designs and may come up with fine-tuned designs which are guaranteed with better action selection minimizing data related errors. Below, in Section 2 introduces the SA model by Endsley. Section 3 explains the proposed neurologically inspired cognitive model mainly by adapting the work in [14], and three simulation experiments are discussed in Section 4. Finally concludes the paper with a discussion.

2   Situation Awareness by Endsley

System automation has been rapidly improved, and has facilitated more robust systems. Therefore, obtaining information is not difficult though finding the relevant and most important information is more challenging due to information overloading [13]. Developing operator interfaces, automation concepts and training programs are important areas where theoretical SA models can contribute to minimize human errors in complex systems [12, 13]. As mentioned in the previous section, Endsley's model with three levels of SA has obtained the highest attention (though some are not fully accepting this definition (e.g., [15])). According to Endsley, Level 1 is the first step to achieve the SA which concerns to perceiving status, attributes, and dynamics of relevant elements in the environment [12, 13, 15]. It is the most important factor for better SA and having a wrong perception always ends up with poor SA. As reasons to have poor Level 1 SA are indicated: data not available, data hard to detect, failure to monitor/observe data, misperception of data, and memory loss [8, 9]. Level 2 takes the awareness beyond being sensitive to the perceptual information but to develop the understanding by binding the relevant perceptual information to ones goals through comprehension [12]. Incomplete or incorrect mental models and over-reliance on default values have been identified as reason for poor Level 2 SA [8, 9]. Level 3 further extends the awareness so that it will obtain the ability to project the future actions [12]. According to Endsley each higher level of SA depends on the success of the lower level [12, 13]. Incomplete/poor mental models and over-projection of current trends have been noted as the main reasons behind poor Level 3 SA [8, 9]. More descriptive information about each level with examples from the aviation domain can be found in [16]. Furthermore, this model includes more mechanisms behind information processing (based on information processing theory in [17]) that includes attention, goals, expectations, mental models, long-term memory, working memory and automaticity for situation assessment (cf. [13]). According to Endsley's view SA and situation assessment are different: product and process respectively [13]. The summary from Endsley in [12], p. 49 provides some useful indications of how this model can be related with neurocognitive literature (in Section 3):

3   Description of the Computational Model

This section presents a computational cognitive model for SA based on the latest findings and evidence from cognitive, affective, and behavioural sciences. The underlying research evidence behind this model has been separately explained in [14]; there also the role of cognitive control in action formation is illustrated in more detail. Therefore, here only a condensed summary will be provided as a theoretical basis.

3.1   Overview of the Model

Fig. 1 below highlights the adapted cognitive model for SA from [14] and in Table 1 listed abbreviations for the state labels in it. The model uses two world states WS(s) and WS(b) as inputs, for stimulus s and effect b. The stimulus s represents any external (or even internal) change that may lead to an action execution. To reduce the complexity of computations in this model it is assumed to be that stimulus s is a compound input (alternatively it is possible to use s as a vector s_k, $k = 1, 2, \ldots$ where k inputs are taken in parallel).

The effect b_i represents the effects of the execution of an action a_i. The input world states WS(s), and WS(b) lead to sensor states SS(s), and SS(b), and subsequently to sensory representation states SR(s), and SR(b), respectively. This model includes the aspects of both conscious (through a top-down process: internally guided based on prior knowledge, intentions, and long-term desires [5, 18]) and unconscious (through a bottom-up process: mainly driven by salient features of external stimuli [18]) processes behind action formation. Automaticity concerns the unconscious behaviour according to Endsley [13]. The unconscious process of action formation has been modelled in here in a causal manner by combining an as-if body loop (see Damasio [19]) and a body loop (see James [20]); for more details see [14]. According to

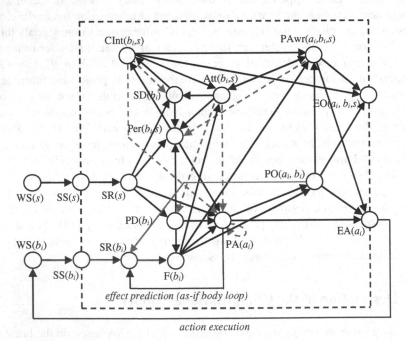

Fig. 1. Overview of the computational cognitive agent model. The arrow ➜ represent a direct activation to state B from state A, arrow ⇥ represent a direct suppression to state B from state A, arrow ⤍ represent a suppression to all the complements of 'ith' state on B$_i$ from state A$_i$ (where 'i' presents an instance of a perticuler state), and ⤍ represent a direct activation to state B$_i$ from state A$_i$ while supressing all the complements of 'ith' state on B$_i$ from state A$_i$.

Table 1. Nomenclature for Fig. 1

WS(W)	world state W (W can be either stimulus s, or effect b)	PAwr(a,b,s)	prior-awareness state for action a with b and s
SS(W)	sensor state for W	Att(b,s)	attention state for s on b
SR(W)	sensory representation of W	CInt(b,s)	conscious intention state for s on b
PD(b)	performative desires for b	EA(a)	execution of action a
SD(b)	subjective desires for b	Per(s,b)	perception state for s on b
PA(a)	preparation for action a	F(b)	feeling for action a and its effects b
PO(a,b)	prior ownership state for action a with b	EO(a,b,s)	communication of ownership of a with b and s

Damasio the cognitive process of action selection is based on an internal simulation process prior to the execution of an action. Effects of each relevant action option $PA(a_i)$ (a stimulus s will have many options i=1..n) are evaluated (without actually executing them) by comparing the feeling-related valuations associated to their individual effects. Each option on $PA(a_i)$ suppresses its complementary options on a_i for all $PA(a_j)$ with j≠i (see Fig. 1), and therefore by a kind of winner takes it all principle naturally the option that has the highest valued effect felt will execute through the body loop (for more details see [14]).

- as-if body loop: $PA(a_i) \rightarrow SR(b_i) \rightarrow F(b_i)$
- body loop: $PA(a_i) \rightarrow EA(a_i) \rightarrow WS(b_i) \rightarrow SS(b_i) \rightarrow SR(b_i) \rightarrow F(b_i)$

In parallel to action preparation prior ownership (in how far does a person attribute an action to him or herself or to another person) of the action will be developed, as explained in [21]. Ownership and performative desires states also relate to the unconscious processes (for more details see [14]). PD(b) facilitates short-term desire effects on action execution. Furthermore, in this model $Per(b_i,s)$ gets a direct effect from the stimulus s and therefore it will enable to develop bottom-up perception which further leads to strengthen action preparation (see Fig. 1) [22]. This phenomenon is particularly useful in a fight-or-flight situation. Therefore a suddenly developed very strong perception (due to salient features in a stimulus) may execute an action without enabling top-down control (cf. [14]).

In this model action formation is initiated through the as-if body loop and because of the limited capacity of the human brain to process all action options, bottom-up attention will play its role as described in [18] (see [14]). Due to this bottom-up attention, higher-order cognitive processes will enable and start to control current action formation. Here an important role is played by the internally activated subjective intentions on cognitive content [18, 23, 24]. This is in line with the idea of transforming Level 1 SA to Level 2 SA in Endsley's model in terms of a process. The prefrontal cortex (PFC) has a higher-order connectivity with other cortical and subcortical areas and therefore, when sensory inputs need more attention in top-down driven controlling, it plays a role of integrator [25, 26]. Furthermore, brain circuits related to cognitive control seem to consist of loops rather than linear chains (cf. [4]) and this can be clearly seen from the associations among states in Fig. 1. Posterior parietal cortex

(PPC) and PFC seem to be playing unique roles in bottom-up and top-down attentional systems respectively and a close interaction among these two has been observed when orienting the attention [18]. This explains the possible interplays among these two and how such an interaction will contribute to sophisticated cognitive control with suppression mechanisms (for more details see [14]). In Fig. 1 to model bottom-up attention an effect from $F(b)$ to $Att(b,s)$ is provided, and then top-down attention modulates $PA(a_i)$ (i.e., increasing the activation of option a_i while suppressing all its complementary options $PA(a_j)$ for all $j{\neq}i$). This leads to a cyclic dependency and eventually with the other states ($SD(b)$, $CInt(b,s)$ and $Per(b,s)$) this will select an option from the competing set through a cognitive bias.

In literature intentional actions are related to a brain network that involves SMA proper and pre-SMA and further an increase of activation of pre-SMA has been observed when participants attend to their intention [4, 27]. Therefore, attention to intention has been hypothesized as one mechanism for control of actions and this has been modelled through a loop: $Att(b,s)$, $SD(b)$ and $CInt(b,s)$. Subjective desires (or constitutive desires) $SD(b)$ is essential in top-down control to facilitate alternative interpretations (or even to further extend the meaning) on performative desires [3].

Awareness is one of the challenging phenomena in human cognition, and as highlighted in the introduction there are various viewpoints related to this. Based on many evidences it is assumed to be that we develop awareness of action selection related to a situation just before the action execution [2, 6, 7]. Nevertheless, Moore and Haggard have highlighted that this awareness may have a decisive effect on actually executing the action [2] (therefore in Fig. 1 there is a direct relation between $EA(a)$ and $PAwr(a,b,s)$). More importantly, the cognitive processes behind this development of awareness are important, which is why they have been given more weight in this model. Therefore, based on such recent research finding the choice was made to let the model deviate from the traditional idea of first developing a proper awareness before getting to decision making (as highlighted, for example, by Endsley). With this difference and by having cyclic loops, the model proposed here deviates from what Endsley proposed, and more attention has been given to the action selection as a wider process covering decision making. Furthermore, Moore and Haggard have highlighted the interplay between prior and retrospective (relative to action execution) awareness of action [2], but for the simplicity of this model retrospective awareness was not included. Finally through $EO(a,b,s)$ the agent can communicate its information to the outside. In addition to the highlighted relations among states all the remaining dependencies (including suppression processes) have been explained in more detail in [14].

3.2   Dynamics of the Model

The computational model was mathematically compiled as proposed in [28] to simulate situations. Each connection between states have been given a weight value (ω_{ji}: weight of state j to i) that varies between +1 and -1. Weight values are non negative in general, except if it is a suppressive (or inhibiting) link (see Fig. 1 caption). To model the dynamics following the connections between the states as temporal–causal relations, a dynamical systems perspective is used as explained in [28]. Therefore, each state includes an additional parameter called speed factor γ_i, indicating the speed by which an activation level is updated upon received input from other states to the state 'i'. Two different speed factor values are used as fast and slow: fast value is for internal states and slow value is for external states (i.e., for WS(W), SS(W), EA(a), and EO(a,b,s)). Activation of a state is depending on multiple other states that are directly attached to it. Therefore incoming activation levels from other states are combined to some aggregated input and affect the activation level according to a differential equation as in (1). As the combination function for each state a continuous logistic threshold function is used as in equation (2), where σ is the steepness, and τ the threshold value. When the aggregated input is negative, (3) is used. To achieve the temporal behaviour of each state as a dynamical system, a difference equation is used in the form of equation (4) (where Δt is the time step size). More details about the dynamics of the model can be found in [14].

$$\frac{dy_i}{dt} = \gamma_i\left[f\left(\sum_{j \in S(i)} \omega_{ji} y_j\right) - y_i\right] \tag{1}$$

$$f(X) = th(\sigma, \tau, X) = \left(\frac{1}{1+e^{-\sigma(X-\tau)}} - \frac{1}{1+e^{\sigma\tau}}\right)(1 + e^{\sigma\tau}) \text{ when } X > 0 \tag{2}$$

$$f(x) = 0 \text{ when } X \leq 0 \tag{3}$$

$$y_i(t + \Delta t) = y_i(t) + \gamma_i\left[th\left(\sigma, \tau, \sum_{j \in S(i)} \omega_{ji} y_j\right) - y_i(t)\right]\Delta t \tag{4}$$

4   Analysis of SA on the Proposed Model Based on Simulations

In this section by simulations it will be explained how situation awareness related incidents can be explained through this proposed model. For this, three situations were selected from the document 'Enhancing Situational Awareness[1]' in 'Flight Operations Briefing Notes' from the Airbus Company. They have provided 3 generic examples for each of the three levels of the SA described by Endsley:

- For Level 1 SA: *'Focusing on recapturing the LOC and not monitoring the G/S'*
- For Level 2 SA: *'Applying a fuel imbalance procedure without realizing it is an engine fuel leak'*
- For Level 3 SA: *'Expecting an approach on a particular runway after having received ATIS information and being surprised to be vectored for another runway'*

These three generic examples were modelled as an implementation in Java, based on the mathematical basis explained in the previous section. For each scenario, three different sets of input data were used in XML format with dedicated parameter values. All the input information and parameter values (step size (Δt), speed factor (γ), total time slots, steepness (σ), threshold (τ), and weight values) for each state can be found in an external appendix[2].

---

[1] http://www.airbus.com/fileadmin/media_gallery/files/
safety_library_items/AirbusSafetyLib_-FLT_OPS-HUM_
PER-SEQ06.pdf

[2] http://www.few.vu.nl/~dte220/BIH14Appendix.pdf

4.1   Simulation for a Level 1 SA Example Incident

The reason behind this example incident is poor SA due to a failure to monitor/observe data, as highlighted in Section 2. A pilot has observed only one device (LOC) though he/she was supposed to take into consideration data from two devices (LOC and G/S). Due to these missing data, the pilot has developed a strong perception related to action selection only based on LOC, while his perception should have been for action selection in line with the integrated reading of LOC and G/S. Due to this incomplete input the appropriate perception was unable to develop and as a consequence of that the pilot has not developed the 'right' situation awareness, but instead of an awareness based on incomplete situation information. For the sake of simplicity of the simulation it is assumed that the current stimulus includes salient features of the LOC device but not strong data from the G/S device. From that stimulus agent will prepare for two action options $PA(a_1)$ and $PA(a_2)$ where action a_1 is based on information from the device LOC and action a_2 is based on information from both devices. Fig. 2 provides simulation results for this scenario; more enlarged graphics can be found (for all simulations) in the previously mentioned external appendix. It can be clearly seen from these that from the given input stimulus the agent has obtained sufficiently large effects on $SR(s_i)$ and $PD(b_i)$ for both options (i.e. for i={1,2}). Nevertheless, it clearly shows that the agent has developed very strong $PA(a_1)$ (with a max of 0.86) and $Per(b_1,s)$ (with a max of 0.86). For action option a_2 it has a relatively weak $Per(b_2,s)$ (max of 0.25) that contributes to develop a poor $PA(a_2)$ (max of 0.17). Therefore, merely through this effect of incomplete perception (as Endsley highlighted) the agent has not developed the right situation awareness (in this case it would have been $PAwr(a_2,b_2,s)$) but the situation awareness $PAwr(a_1,b_1,s)$ (max of 0.74) based on wrong perception; note that SA is a subjective term and always the agent will develop an awareness and the argument is whether that's the right

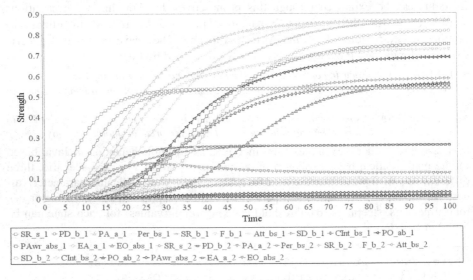

Fig. 2. Simulation details for Level 1 SA example

awareness for that situation. Subsequently the agent has shown sufficient strengths for all the other states related with option a_1, and finally has executed the action $EA(a_1)$ (max of 0.81) with a $PAwr(a_1,b_1,s)$ of max 0.74.

4.2 Simulation for a Level 2 SA Example Incident

In this situation the problem is with the Level 2 SA and according to the incident the reason may be due to an incorrect mental model. In this situation the pilot has observed all the necessary data with a correct and complete perception, and noted a problem with fuel usage. Nevertheless, the pilot was unable to realize that the reason was a fuel leak in the engine, and therefore he has decided to follow fuel imbalance procedure, whereas the recommendation is not to apply fuel imbalance procedure if fuel leak is suspected [29]. Fig. 3 provides the simulation information for this scenario. Here for the given stimulus the agent will internally prepare for two action options: a_1 is to execute the fuel imbalance procedure and a_2 is to deal with a fuel leak in the engine. For this simulation all the states involve identical parameter values for the action options 1 & 2 separately, except for $SD(b_i)$ and $CInt(b_i,s)$. This shows the impact of subjective desires and intention of top-down control on other states. The agent starts action formation with the input stimulus that triggers two action options as mentioned. At the beginning it clearly shows that the rate of activation for $Per(b_1,s)$ and $Per(b_2,s)$ are almost the same (similarly the other pairs: $PA(a_i)$, $SR(b_i)$, and $F(b_i)$), but the development of $SD(b_1)$ and $CInt(b_1,s)$, the rates of increase related to action option a_2 have been significantly declined. The states $SD(b_2)$ and $CInt(b_2,s)$ have not been activated with sufficient strength (which was assumed to be the relevant mental model to interpret the situation as an engine fuel leak) and therefore the state $Att(b_1,s)$ has increased rapidly (with a max of 0.85) due to the cyclic dependency highlighted among $SD(b_1)$, $CInt(b_1,s)$ and $Att(b_1,s)$. Therefore, naturally the agent has been led to

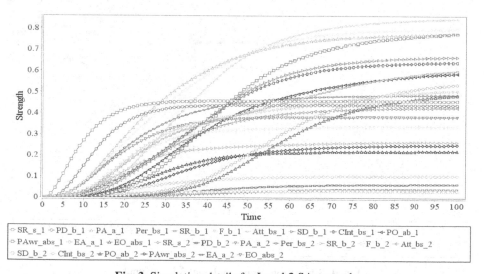

Fig. 3. Simulation details for Level 2 SA example

select option a_1: s/he developed a strong prior awareness PAwr(a_1,b_1,s) (with a max of 0.77) and has executed option a_1 (i.e., EA(a_1)) with a maximum activation value of 0.54. Having the same parameter values for each state on the respective action options but only different values for each option on SD(b_i), CInt(b_i,s) has sufficiently explained the behavior of SA in Level 2: inability of binding the perceptual information relevance to the subjective goals through comprehension.

4.3   Simulation for a Level 3 SA Example Incident

In this scenario a pilot was expecting an approach on a particular runway (let's say R14) and while he is preparing for that he gets an instruction from the air traffic controller (ATC) to be vectored for a different runway (let's say R35). Here it is assumed that landing on R14 is the most common action and therefore without getting a direct request from ATC the pilot was preparing for the habitual task. Due to this new ATC instruction now the pilot may be unable to immediately adjust for this new situation as he may have not loaded the necessary mental model to execute the new instruction. This may go together with the effect of 'over-projection of current trends' as mentioned in Section 2 as one of the possible reasons behind poor Level 3 SA. Therefore, it is assumed here that due to this over-projection of current trends, the pilot is unable to immediately project the necessary future actions. Therefore first s/he needs to internally suppress current action execution and needs to get ready for the relevant action choice for the new ATC instruction. Simulated behaviour of this situation is presented in Fig. 4. Two stimuli were used for this scenario but they occur at different time points: one at time t=0 and the other one at time t=100. More specifically, it has been assumed that at t=100 the agent is getting the ATC instruction and by that time the agent was already performing an action with the intention of approaching to R14 (labelled as action option a_1, whereas the new action after t=100 is labelled as a_2). From Fig. 4 it shows that the agent has initiated action formation for option a_1 and has

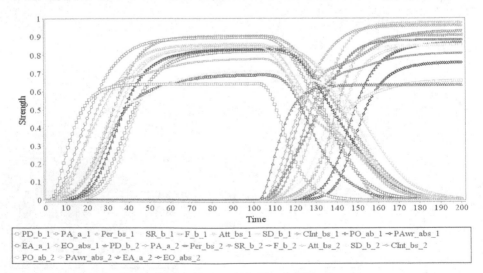

Fig. 4. Simulation details for Level 3 SA example

developed sufficiently high activation of $PD(b_1)$ (max of 0.64), $PA(a_1)$ (max of 0.89), $Per(b_1,s)$ (max of 0.85), $SR(b_1)$ (max of 0.70), $F(b_1)$ (max of 0.77), $Att(b_1,s)$ (max of 0.84), $SD(b_1)$ (max of 0.82), $CInt(b_1,s)$ (max of 0.90), $PO(a_1,b_1)$ (max of 0.68), $PAwr(a_1,b_1,s)$ (max of 0.82), $EA(a_1)$ (max of 0.81), and $EO(a_1,b_1,s)$ (max of 0.82) (in the order mentioned here). Nevertheless, having a new instruction at t=100, the agent has started to suspend its current action and enabling the relevant states to execute option a_2. Related to option a_2, the respective states have obtained slightly higher activation values in the same order as for option a_1. Furthermore, it can be clearly observed that to fully execute action a_1, the agent has taken roughly 60 time intervals but for a_2 to be fully activated it has taken more than 80 time intervals (due to the mental overload: to suppress the current action and to form the new action selection).

5   Discussion

This paper has presented a neurologically inspired cognitive model (which was adapted from [14]) and has provided simulation results for 3 incident examples where poor SA was expected as put forward by Endsley. The obtained results explain the different scenarios. The model has been designed according to the latest neurocognitive evidence, and therefore it deviates a bit from the somewhat linear model that Endsley proposed originally. More specifically, this research shows how models that were designed according to the earlier cognitive science tradition and often assume linear causal cascades from sensory input to behavioural output, can be refined and enriched by incorporating more recent evidence on actual brain processes in which cyclic processes play a major role. Such model refinement often leads to dynamic systems style models with cyclic causal cascades instead of linear ones, as is clearly shown here (see also [28]). This work can be further extended to explain more specific scenarios in the aviation domain and also to other areas that are applicable.

Acknowledgment. I wish to thank Prof. Jan Treur and Dr. Tibor Bosse at VU University Amsterdam, for their great support and supervision in all the phases of this work. This work is part of the SESAR WP-E programme on long-term and innovative research in ATM. It is co-financed by Eurocontrol on behalf of the SESAR Joint Undertaking (SJU).

References

1. Monsell, S.: Task switching. Trends Cogn. Sci. 7, 134–140 (2003)
2. Moore, J., Haggard, P.: Awareness of action: Inference and prediction. Conscious. Cogn. 17, 136–144 (2008)
3. Engel, A.K., Fries, P., Singer, W.: Dynamic predictions: Oscillations and synchrony in top–down processing. Nat. Rev. Neurosci. 2, 704–716 (2001)
4. Haggard, P.: Human volition: towards a neuroscience of will. Nat. Rev. Neurosci. 9, 934–946 (2008)
5. Kiefer, M.: Top-down modulation of unconscious "automatic" processes: A gating framework. Adv. Cogn. Psychol. 3, 289–306 (2007)
6. D'Ostilio, K., Garraux, G.: Brain mechanisms underlying automatic and unconscious control of motor action. Front. Hum. Neurosci. 6 (2012)

7. Haynes, J.-D.: Decoding and predicting intentions. Ann. N. Y. Acad. Sci. 1224, 9–21 (2011)
8. Endsley, M.R., Garland, D.G.: Pilot situation awareness training in general aviation. In: Proceedings of the 14th Triennial Congress of the International Ergonomics Association and the 44th Annual Meeting of the Human Factors and Ergonomics Society, pp. 357–360. Human Factors and Ergonomics Society, Santa Monica (2000)
9. Endsley, M.R.: Situation Awareness and Human Error: Designing to Support Human Performance. In: Proceedings of the High Consequence Systems Surety Conference, Albuquerque, NM (1999)
10. Dominguez, C.: Can SA be defined? In: Vidulich, M., Dominguez, C., Vogel, E., McMillan, G. (eds.) Situation awareness: Papers and annotated bibliography (AL/CFTR- 1994-0085), pp. 5–15. Armstrong Laboratory, Wright-Patterson AFB, OH (1994)
11. Endsley, M.R.: Design and evaluation for situation awareness enhancement. In: Proceedings of the Human Factors Society 32nd Annual Meeting, pp. 97–101. Human Factors Society, Santa Monica (1988)
12. Endsley, M.R.: Toward a Theory of Situation Awareness in Dynamic Systems. Hum. Factors J. Hum. Factors Ergon. Soc. 37, 32–64 (1995)
13. Endsley, M.R.: Theoretical underpinnings of situation awareness: a critical review. In: Endsley, M.R., Garland, D.J. (eds.) Situation Awareness Analysis and Measurement. Lawrence Erlbaum Associates, Mahwah (2000)
14. Thilakarathne, D.J.: Modeling Dynamics of Cognitive Control in Action Formation with Intention, Attention, and Awareness. In: Proc. of the International Joint Conferences on Web Intelligence (WI) and Intelligent Agent Technologies (IAT). IEEE Press (to appear)
15. Uhlarik, J., Comerford, D.A.: A Review of Situation Awareness Literature Relevant to Pilot Surveillance Functions: Final Report. General Books LLC (2011)
16. Endsley, M.R.: Designing for Situation Awareness: An Approach to User-Centered Design. CRC Press (2011)
17. Wickens, C.D.: Engineering Psychology and Human Performance. Harper Collins, New York (1992)
18. Katsuki, F., Constantinidis, C.: Bottom-Up and Top-Down Attention: Different Processes and Overlapping Neural Systems. The Neuroscientist (2013)
19. Damasio, A.R.: Self Comes to Mind: Constructing the Conscious Brain. Pantheon Books, NY (2010)
20. James, W.: What is an Emotion? Mind 9, 188–205 (1884)
21. Treur, J.: A computational agent model incorporating prior and retrospective ownership states for actions. Biol. Inspired Cogn. Archit. 2, 54–67 (2012)
22. Pessoa, L.: How do emotion and motivation direct executive control? Trends Cogn. Sci. 13, 160–166 (2009)
23. Tallon-Baudry, C.: On the Neural Mechanisms Subserving Consciousness and Attention. Front. Psychol. 2 (2012)
24. Baluch, F., Itti, L.: Mechanisms of top-down attention. Trends Neurosci. 34, 210–224 (2011)
25. Miller, E.K., Cohen, J.D.: An integrative theory of prefrontal cortex function. Annu. Rev. Neurosci. 24, 167–202 (2001)
26. Miller, E.K.: The prefontral cortex and cognitive control. Nat. Rev. Neurosci. 1, 59–65 (2000)
27. Rigoni, D., Brass, M., Roger, C., Vidal, F., Sartori, G.: Top-down modulation of brain activity underlying intentional action and its relationship with awareness of intention: an ERP/Laplacian analysis. Exp. Brain Res. 229, 347–357 (2013)
28. Treur, J.: An integrative dynamical systems perspective on emotions. Biol. Inspired Cogn. Archit. 4, 27–40 (2013)
29. Cramoisi, G.: Air Crash Investigations: Running Out of Fuel, How Air Transat 236 Managed to Fly 100 Miles without Fuel and Land Safely. Mabuhay Publishing (2010)

Dealing with the Heterogeneous Multi-site Neuroimaging Data Sets: A Discrimination Study of Children Dyslexia

Piotr Płoński[1], Wojciech Gradkowski[1,3], Artur Marchewka[2],
Katarzyna Jednoróg[2], and Piotr Bogorodzki[1]

[1] Institute of Radioelectronics, Warsaw University of Technology,
Nowowiejska 15/19,00-665 Warsaw, Poland
[2] Department of Neurophysiology, Nencki Institute of Experimental Biology,
Pasteur 3, 02-093 Warsaw, Poland
[3] Imagilys SPRL,
Rue Maurice Lietart 60, 1150 Brussels, Belgium
pplonski@ire.pw.edu.pl

Abstract. Neuroimaging studies of rare disorders, such as dyslexia, require long term, multi-centre data collection in order to create representative disease specific cohorts. However, multi-site data have inherent heterogeneity caused by site specific acquisition protocols, scanner setup, etc. The aim of this study was the analysis of the influence of the two confounding factors: site location and field strength on feature selection procedure. We propose two methods: site-dependent whitening and site-dependent extension and compare with naive approach using classification accuracy as a quality measure of selected features subset. The proposed methods outperform the naive approach, and significantly improves the classification performance of developmental dyslexia.

Keywords: dyslexia, multi-site data, MRI, feature selection, classification.

1 Introduction

Currently high-resolution magnetic resonance (MR) images of the human brain especially non-quantitative T1-weighted are available in several large-scale multi-centre data repositories. This provides great opportunity to study large number of subjects, resulting in increased sensitivity for detection of subtle anatomical patterns but poses several methodological issues. Up to date it was demonstrated with voxel-based morphometry (VBM) [3] that despite the MR scanner differences in hardware [18] and magnetic field strength [11] multi-centre data can be classified using Support Vector Machine (SVM) [1] as one cohort in Alzheimer Disease studies. However, to our knowledge, there are only two published studies using multivariate approaches on developmental dyslexia performed on anatomical images of adults (39 dyslexic and 38 controls, [13]) and on fMRI children

D. Ślęzak et al. (Eds.): BIH 2014, LNAI 8609, pp. 471–480, 2014.

data (13 dyslexic who showed reading gain and 12 who did not gain from intervention, [7]). Univariate analyses with VBM based on datasets used in this
paper have been published before for the French [2], [8], [12], and the Polish
children [9].

In this paper, we analyzed neuroimaging data of developmental dyslexia (106
control and 130 dyslexic children) aquired at 3 different countries. The image
data were pre-processed using standard pipelines to extract cortical features.
This included an unbiased within-subject template space and image creation using robust, inverse consistent registration, then obtained information was used
in skull stripping, Talairach transform, atlas registration and spherical surface
mapping and parcellation [14],[15]. The significant dependency between data
distribution and site location and field strength was observed. We examine how
feture selection and in consequence a classification accuracy is affected by this
effect. We propose two methods that incorporate the site-specific information
during discrimination, namely: site-dependent whitening and site-dependent extension. They were compared with naive approach, which assumes homogeneity
of the data. The significant improvement in discrimination performance was observed when site-dependent information were used.

The rest of this paper is organized as follows: firstly, we describe data aqusition
and procedure of cortical features extraction; secondly, the classification and
feature selection algorithms are described; then, we present methods for dealing
with site-dependent data; finally, the comparison results of proposed methods
with naive approach are presented and disscussed.

2   Materials and Methods

2.1   Participants

The analyzed dataset consists of 236 T1-weighted, children images coming from
3 countries: 81 Polish children – 35 control (22 girls) and 46 dyslexic (20 girls);
84 French children – 45 control (23 girls) and 39 dyslexic (14 girls); 71 German
children – 26 control (10 girls) and 45 dyslexic (22 girls). Participants came from
diverse social backgrounds and finished at least one and a half years of formal
reading instruction to differentiate serious problems in reading acquisition from
early delays that are not always persistent. Dyslexic participants were either
identified in school, or were specifically requesting clinical assessment of their
reading problems. Participants were recruited following the criteria below: age
between 8,5 and 13,7 years; IQ higher than 85, or an age-appropriate scaled
score of at least 7 on WISC Block Design, and 6 on WISC Similarities, no
formal diagnosis of ADHD, no reported hearing, sight or neurological problems.
The inclusion criterion for dyslexic children was defined as more than 1.5 SD
below grade level on a standardized test of word reading, whereas for controls it
was less than 0.85 SD below grade level.

All studies were approved by local ethics committees (CPP Bicêtre in France; Medical University of Warsaw in Poland; Uniklinik RWTH Aachen in Germany). The children and their parents gave informed written consent to participate in the study.

2.2   Imaging Procedure

High-resolution T1-weighted images were acquired in 3 different countries, the brief summary of data set is in Table 1, details of aqusition are described below:

French Sample. For 13 control and 11 dyslexic children, whole brain images were acquired on a 3 Tesla (3T) Siemens Trio Tim MRI platform with either 12-channels head coil with the following parameters: acquisition matrix: $256 \times 256 \times 176$, TR=2300 ms, TE=4.18 ms, flip angle=9 deg, FOV=256 mm, voxel size: $1 \times 1 \times 1$ mm, and for 32 control and 28 dyslexic with 32-channels head coil with the following parameters: acquisition matrix=$230 \times 230 \times 202$, TR=2300 ms, TE=3.05 ms, flip angle=9 deg, FOV=230 mm, voxel size=$0.9 \times 0.9 \times 0.9$ mm.

German Sample. For 11 control and 35 dyslexic children, whole brain images were acquired on a 3T Siemens Trio Tim scanner using a standard birdcage head coil with the following specifications: acquisition matrix: $256 \times 256 \times 176$, TR=1900 ms, TE=2.52 ms, flip angle=9 deg, FOV=256 mm, voxel size: $1 \times 1 \times 1$ mm. For 15 control and 10 dyslexic, T1-weighted images were acquired on a 1.5T Siemens Avanto scanner using a standard birdcage head coil with the following parameters: acquisition matrix: $256 \times 256 \times 170$, TR=2200 ms, TE=3.93ms, flip angle=15 deg, FOV=256 mm, voxel size: $1 \times 1 \times 1$ mm.

Polish Sample. For 35 control and 46 dyslexic whole brain images were acquired on a 1.5T Siemens Avanto platform with 32-channels phased array head coil. T1-weighted images had the following specifications: acquisition matrix: $256 \times 256 \times 192$; TR $= 1720$ msec; TE $= 2.92$ msec; flip angle=9 deg, FOV $= 256$, voxel size $1 \times 1 \times 1$ mm.

Table 1. The number of considered control and dyslexic children in the analysis coming from three countries and two different field strengths

Field strength	French sample	German sample		Polish sample
	3T	3T	1.5T	1.5T
# Control	45	11	15	35
# Dyslexic	39	35	10	46

2.3   Data Pre-processing and Feature Extraction

The MR images data were pre-processed in order to retrieve features, which later would be used for the purpose of classification. We were interested in cortical metrics of subject's brain such as thickness and volume of particular brain regions. To extract reliable volume and thickness estimates, images where automatically processed with the longitudinal stream [15] in FreeSurfer image analysis suite, which is documented and freely available for download online (http://surfer.nmr.mgh.harvard.edu/). Specifically an unbiased within-subject template space and image is created using robust, inverse consistent registration [14]. Several processing steps, such as skull stripping, Talairach transforms, atlas registration as well as spherical surface maps and parcellations are then initialized with common information from the within-subject template, significantly increasing reliability and statistical power [15]. Procedures for the measurement of cortical thickness have been validated against histological analysis [16] and manual measurements [10], [17]. Freesurfer morphometric procedures have been demonstrated to show good test-retest reliability across scanner manufacturers and across field strengths [5], [15]. For each subject we obtained a vector of features constituted of cortical measures. We used the Destrieux Atlas [4] to extract 742 features used for further analysis. These included fold index, average thickness, surface area, grey volume and mean curvature for 74 brain structures for left and right hemisphere.

2.4   Classification and Feature Selection

Let's denote data set as $\mathcal{D} = \{\mathbf{X}_1, \mathbf{X}_2, ..., \mathbf{X}_N, \mathbf{C}\}$, where $\mathbf{X}_i$ is a i-th feature vector, $\mathbf{X}_i \in \mathcal{R}^M$, where $N = 742$ is a feature number and $M = 236$ is a sample count, $\mathbf{C}$ is a vector with discrete class number, where class value is from set $\{control, dyslexic\}$. Additionally, for each sample there is information about location and field strength, noted as $\mathbf{X}_l$ and $\mathbf{X}_s$ respectively.

As a discrimination method the logistic regression (LR) algorithm was used [6]. To measure the discrimination power the Area Under Curve (AUC) computed on 10-fold cross validation (CV) was employed. The features selection was performed with step-forward manner [6]. The pseudocode of applied procedure is described in the Algorithm 1 listing. As an optimal number of features in the subset we select the number of features from which the classification performance is constant or is starting to decrease with gearter features number [6]. It is worth to note that, in feature selection procedure CV folds were drawn before testing every new candidate subset of features to improve generalization ablitity.

2.5   Cofounding Factors Correction

In order to deal with the influence of site location and scanner field strength variability we investigate two approaches. Their performance will be compared with **naive** approach, which assumes homogeneity of the data.

Algorithm 1: The applied feature selection procedure.

---

input : $\mathcal{D} = \{\mathbf{X}_1, \mathbf{X}_2, ..., \mathbf{X}_N, \mathbf{C}\}$,

         L number of maximal features to consider in selection.

output: The selected optimal subset S of features.

begin

    Let's denote as $S_0 = \{\}$ an empty feature subset

    for k *in 1 .. L* **do**

        for i *in 1 .. N* **do**

            Build a classifier K_i using as a feature subset $\{S_{k-1}, \mathbf{X}_i\}$

            Draw folds for CV

            Compute perfomance of classifier K_i with AUC on 10-fold CV

        Select classifier K_j with highest ACU on 10-fold CV

        Set $S_k = \{S_{k-1}, \mathbf{X}_j\}$

    Among candidate subsets S_k select one which statisfy selection criteria.

Site-Dependent Extension (SDE). We included the information about the site location and field strength by adding them as additional features into the subjects' set of features. Thus, we expand the attributes space used by the classification algorithm. The starting subset of features in feature selection procedure is $S_0 = \{\mathbf{X}_l, \mathbf{X}_s\}$. We called this approach as site-dependent extension (SDE).

Site-Dependent Whitening (SDW). Each measured i-*th* feature $\mathbf{X}_i$ can be expressed as sum of true feature value $\mathbf{X}_i^{true}$ and site-dependent vector $\mathbf{\Gamma}$:

$$\mathbf{X}_i = \mathbf{X}_i^{true} + \mathbf{\Gamma}, \tag{1}$$

The site-dependent vector $\mathbf{\Gamma}$ can be approximated with linear combination of site-dependent features:

$$\mathbf{\Gamma} = \beta_1 \mathbf{X}_l + \beta_2 \mathbf{X}_s. \tag{2}$$

The β parameters can be computed with linear regression by solving the equation:

$$\mathbf{X}_i = \beta_1 \mathbf{X}_l + \beta_2 \mathbf{X}_s + \beta_0, \tag{3}$$

where β_0 is representing an expected value of $\mathbf{X}_i^{true}$. The estimate of $\mathbf{X}_i^{true}$ can be found by substracting from measured value the site-dependent factors value, as desribed in the following equation:

$$\hat{\mathbf{X}}_i^{true} = \mathbf{X}_i - \beta_1 \mathbf{X}_l - \beta_2 \mathbf{X}_s. \tag{4}$$

Applying this procedure to each feature will remove the site dependency from the data. After using the SDW, the feature selection procedure is performed with estimated true feature vectors $\hat{\mathbf{X}}_i^{true}$. We called this approach as site-dependent whitening (SDW).

3   Results

From 742 features describing the cortical properties of the analyzed subjects, the 462 features are significantly dependent (p-value < 0.05) from at least one of the factors: site location or scanner field strength. To visualize the site-dependency the boxplots with respect to site factors are presented in the Fig.1 for one selected feature (with the lowest p-values). After applying the SDW, all features were independent from site loction and scanner field strength (p-values > 0.999). In the Fig.1 are presented results of SDW transformation on selected feature.

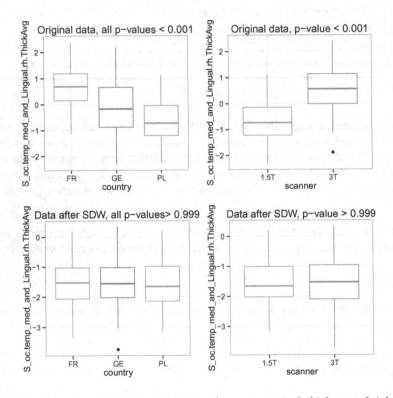

Fig. 1. The dependency of a selected feature (average cortical thickness of right hemisphere gyrus occipitotemporalis medialis) on the country and scanner field strength. The upper plots present the original feature values, lower with the SDW applied. For each plot a p-value computed with t-test is provided.

The procedure of feature selection was performed for each approach: naive, SDW, SDE. The discrimination power measured as AUC on 10-fold CV for number of feaures varying from 1 to 50 is presented in the Fig.2. As an optimal subset size a solution with 25 features was selected for each approach[1]. It

---

[1] For SDE method there were 25 cortical features desciting a brain structures and two additional describing the site-dependend factors.

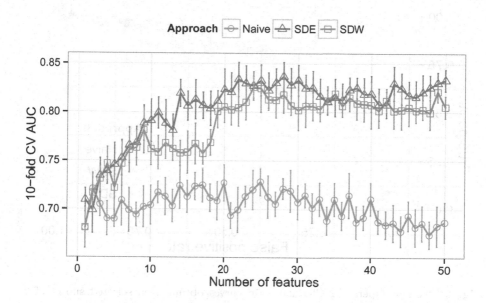

Fig. 2. Classification accuracy during step-forward feature selection presented as mean and standard error over 10-fold CV for approaches: naive, SDW, SDE

can be observed from the Fig.2, that for more than 25 features in the subset the classification performance does not increase or even decrease for all examined methods. The AUC for examined methods for selected optimal subset of features is presented in the Table 2. The performance of the SDW and SDE is approximately 12% higher than naive approach, while SDW and SDE has very similar results (with higher standard deviation of SDW method). The all proposed methods with selected optimal features give significantly better results than performing disrimination on all available features, which give 0.61 ± 0.10, 0.56 ± 0.06, 0.62 ± 0.08 AUC on 10 fold-CV for using naive, SDW and SDE approaches respectively. In the Fig.3 a Receiver Operating Characteristic curve (ROC) for selected 25 features subset is presented for each method. From ROC curves we can observe that SDW and SDE give similar performance, and they overcome the naive approach.

For selected the optimal subset of 25 features the performance of other than LR algorithms: Random Forest and linear Support Vector Machine (SVM) was tested. The obtained results of AUC on 10-fold CV are presented in the Table 2. The SDW and SDE gained higher results than naive approach for all used classifiers. However, there is an increase in the difference between performance of SDW and SDE on Random Forest and SVM classifiers. It is the highest for SVM, where SDW is better than SDE by 0.086 on average.

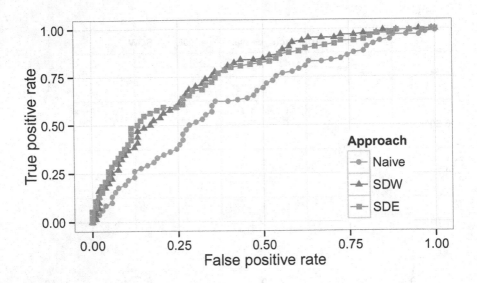

Fig. 3. Receiver Operating Characteristic curves obtained on selected subset of 25 features for three approaches

Table 2. The performance of different classifiers on selected subset of 25 features computed as mean and standard deviation of AUC computed on 10-fold CV for different approaches: naive, SDW, SDE

	LR	Random Forest	SVM
Naive	0.728 ± 0.089	0.640 ± 0.130	0.616 ± 0.090
SDW	0.824 ± 0.155	0.690± 0.076	0.737 ± 0.081
SDE	0.832 ± 0.098	0.660 ± 0.082	0.651 ± 0.090

4   Discussion

The analysis of neuroimaging data of developmental dyslexia was presented. The data consists of 106 controls and 130 dyslexic subjects and each of them was described with 742 cortical features. There were two difficulties in analysis of this data which we overcame. Firstly, the analyzed data is highly dimensional, in our case a number of features is three times larger than number of subjects - it is so-called 'large p, small n' problem. Thus, using all available features can lead to poor classification performance. The logistic regression classifier obtains a 0.61 AUC performance with all available features and treating homogeneously features from all locations. We applied the step-forward feature selection which optimize the AUC on 10-fold CV to select a subset of 25 featues, which is only a 3.4% of all features. After feature selection the classifier performance increase to 0.73 (with naive approach). The second problem, is data dependency to site location and scanner field strength. In our case, 62% of features significantly depend on at least one of the site factors (with p-value < 0.05). We propose two methods to cope with this problem, namely: site-dependent whitening (SDW) and site-dependent extension (SDE). The SDW method approximates and substracts a site-dependent part from feature value. The all features after SDW were independent to site factors (p-value > 0.999). The SDE method extends the features space by adding the site factors. For each of the proposed method a procedure of feature selection was repeated. This increase the discrimination accuracy on 25 selected features to 0.82 and 0.83 for SDW and SDE, respectively. This is an improvement by about 12% (in AUC difference) over naive approach after feature selection and over 25% better than naive approach with all features used in classification. What is more, without site-dependency correction the selection of optimal features number will be ambiguous. For naive approach the increase in classfication performance with increasing the feature number from 1 to 25 is not as clearly visible as for SDW or SDE.

To conclude, the first attempt to classify anatomical T1-weighted data of dyslexic and control children acquired at 3 different countries was made. The high dimensionality and dependency to site specific factors of the data were overcome with feature selection and proposed methods: SDW and SDE. This significantly improves the discrimination performance. The performed study showed that feature selection and including the information about site factors are important in analysis of neuroimaging data.

Acknowledgements. This study was supported by the Polish Ministry of Science grants: IP2010 015170 and IP2012 025272. PP has been supported by the European Union in the framework of European Social Fund through the Warsaw University of Technology Development Programme. WG has been supported by Imagilys SPRL, Brussels, Belgium.

References

1. Abdulkadir, A., Mortamet, B., Vemuri, P., Jack Jr., C.R., Krueger, G., Klöppel, S.: Effects of hardware heterogeneity on the performance of SVM alzheimer's disease classifier. NeuroImage 58(3), 785–792 (2011)
2. Altarelli, I., Monzalvo, K., Iannuzzi, S., Fluss, J., Billard, C., Ramus, F., Dehaene-Lambertz, G.: A functionally guided approach to the morphometry of occipitotemporal regions in developmental dyslexia: Evidence for differential effects in boys and girls. The Journal of Neuroscience 33(27), 11296–11301 (2013), PMID: 23825432
3. Ashburner, J., Friston, K.J.: Voxel-based Morphometry—The methods. NeuroImage 11(6), 805–821 (2000)
4. Desikan, R.S., Ségonne, F., Fischl, B., Quinn, B.T., Dickerson, B.C., Blacker, D., Buckner, R.L., Dale, A.M., Maguire, R.P., Hyman, B.T.: An automated labeling system for subdividing the human cerebral cortex on MRI scans into gyral based regions of interest. Neuroimage 31(3), 968–980 (2006)

5. Han, X., Jovicich, J., Salat, D., van der Kouwe, A., Quinn, B., Czanner, S., Busa, E., Pacheco, J., Albert, M., Killiany, R., Maguire, P., Rosas, D., Makris, N., Dale, A., Dickerson, B., Fischl, B.: Reliability of MRI-derived measurements of human cerebral cortical thickness: The effects of field strength, scanner upgrade and manufacturer. NeuroImage 32(1), 180–194 (2006)
6. Hastie, T., Tibshirani, R., Friedman, J., Hastie, T., Friedman, J., Tibshirani, R.: The elements of statistical learning, vol. 2. Springer (2009)
7. Hoeft, F., McCandliss, B.D., Black, J.M., Gantman, A., Zakerani, N., Hulme, C., Lyytinen, H., Whitfield-Gabrieli, S., Glover, G.H., Reiss, A.L., Gabrieli, J.D.E.: Neural systems predicting long-term outcome in dyslexia. Proceedings of the National Academy of Sciences 108(1), 361–366 (2011), PMID: 21173250
8. Jednoróg, K., Gawron, N., Marchewka, A., Heim, S., Grabowska, A.: Cognitive subtypes of dyslexia are characterized by distinct patterns of grey matter volume. Brain Structure and Function, 1–11
9. Jednoróg, K., Marchewka, A., Altarelli, I., Monzalvo, K., van Ermingen-Marbach, M., Grande, M., Grabowska, A., Heim, S., Ramus, F.: How reliable are grey matter disruptions in developmental dyslexia? insights from a large-scale voxel-based morphometry study
10. Kuperberg, G.R., Broome, M., McGuire, P.K., David, A.S., Eddy, M., Ozawa, F., Goff, D., West, W.C., Williams, S.C.R., van der Kouwe, A., Salat, D., Dale, A., Fischl, B.: Regionally localized thinning of the cerebral cortex in schizophrenia. Archives of General Psychiatry 60, 878–888 (2003)
11. Marchewka, A., Kherif, F., Krueger, G., Grabowska, A., Frackowiak, R., Draganski, B.: Influence of magnetic field strength and image registration strategy on voxel-based morphometry in a study of alzheimer's disease. Human Brain Mapping (2013)
12. Monzalvo, K., Fluss, J., Billard, C., Dehaene, S., Dehaene-Lambertz, G.: Cortical networks for vision and language in dyslexic and normal children of variable socioeconomic status. NeuroImage 61(1), 258–274 (2012)
13. Pernet, C.R., Poline, J.B., Demonet, J.F., Rousselet, G.A.: Brain classification reveals the right cerebellum as the best biomarker of dyslexia. BMC Neuroscience 10(1), 67 (2009), PMID: 19555471
14. Reuter, M., Rosas, H.D., Fischl, B.: Highly accurate inverse consistent registration: A robust approach. NeuroImage 53(4), 1181–1196 (2010)
15. Reuter, M., Schmansky, N.J., Rosas, H.D., Fischl, B.: Within-subject template estimation for unbiased longitudinal image analysis. NeuroImage 61(4), 1402–1418 (2012)
16. Rosas, H.D., Liu, A.K., Hersch, S., Glessner, M., Ferrante, R.J., Salat, D.H., van der Kouwe, A., Jenkins, B.G., Dale, A.M., Fischl, B.: Regional and progressive thinning of the cortical ribbon in huntington's disease. Neurology 58(5), 695–701 (2002)
17. Salat, D., Buckner, R.L., Snyder, A.Z., Greve, D.N., Desikan, R.S., Busa, E., Morris, J.C., Dale, A., Fischl, B.: Thinning of the cerebral cortex in aging. Cerebral Cortex 14, 721–730 (2004)
18. Stonnington, C.M., Tan, G., Klöppel, S., Chu, C., Draganski, B., Jack Jr., C.R., Chen, K., Ashburner, J., Frackowiak, R.S.J.: Interpreting scan data acquired from multiple scanners: A study with alzheimer's disease. NeuroImage 39(3), 1180–1185 (2008)

K-Surfer: A KNIME Extension for the Management and Analysis of Human Brain MRI FreeSurfer/FSL Data

Alessia Sarica[1,*], Giuseppe Di Fatta[2], and Mario Cannataro[1]

[1] Bioinformatics Laboratory, Department of Medical and Surgical Sciences,
Magna Graecia University of Catanzaro, Italy
sarica,cannataro@unicz.it
[2] School of Systems Engineering, University of Reading, UK
g.difatta@reading.ac.uk

Abstract. Human brain imaging techniques, such as Magnetic Resonance Imaging (MRI) or Diffusion Tensor Imaging (DTI), have been established as scientific and diagnostic tools and their adoption is growing in popularity. Statistical methods, machine learning and data mining algorithms have successfully been adopted to extract predictive and descriptive models from neuroimage data. However, the knowledge discovery process typically requires also the adoption of pre-processing, post-processing and visualisation techniques in complex data workflows. Currently, a main problem for the integrated preprocessing and mining of MRI data is the lack of comprehensive platforms able to avoid the manual invocation of preprocessing and mining tools, that yields to an error-prone and inefficient process. In this work we present K-Surfer, a novel plug-in of the Konstanz Information Miner (KNIME) workbench, that automatizes the preprocessing of brain images and leverages the mining capabilities of KNIME in an integrated way. K-Surfer supports the importing, filtering, merging and pre-processing of neuroimage data from FreeSurfer, a tool for human brain MRI feature extraction and interpretation. K-Surfer automatizes the steps for importing FreeSurfer data, reducing time costs, eliminating human errors and enabling the design of complex analytics workflow for neuroimage data by leveraging the rich functionalities available in the KNIME workbench.

Keywords: MRI, DTI, FreeSurfer, FSL, Data Workflows, Data Mining.

1 Introduction

Neuroimages are produced by several techniques such as positron emission tomography (PET), magnetic resonance imaging (MRI), functional MRI (fMRI) and diffusion tensor imaging (DTI). Nowadays, neuroimaging methods are the

---

* The author is funded by the *European Commission, European Social Fund* and *Regione Calabria*. The Author had full control of the design of the study, methods used, outcome parameters and results, analysis of data and production of the manuscript.

D. Ślęzak et al. (Eds.): BIH 2014, LNAI 8609, pp. 481–492, 2014.

primary source of information in neuroscience and the further processing of brain images has exponentially increased the quantity of data to be analysed. In [1], the authors discuss the complexity of the knowledge discovery process for human brain data, especially when it requires information fusion from heterogeneous sources, e.g. age, genders, genetic makers, EEG, morphological measures, etc. Neuroimages need to be processed to extract relevant features before it is possible to perform any kind of analysis [2] together with clinical and genomics information. This phase generates segmented and reconstructed 3D images and numerical summaries, such as areas, volumes, thicknesses, signal intensities, probability distributions and diffusion values [1].

It is often desirable to process neuroimages of a large number of subjects in an almost fully automated pipeline. Although this may introduce some overestimations [1], this approach is definitely faster than manual segmentation and is leading to a high-throughput data generation. As a consequence, managing, filtering and, in general, pre-processing large volumes of data from many horizontal and vertical surveys has become a critical component of the knowledge discovery process of brain data. For example, neuroscientists often need to convert and import neuroimage data from several sources into a single table format for an integrated analysis in their preferred analytical platform [3]. This data preparation phase is clearly a time consuming task, which is also error prone when carried out manually. Moreover, the choice of the appropriate tools for statistical analysis and data mining is often critical for a fast prototyping of complex data workflows, their documentation and deployment. The Konstanz Information Miner (KNIME) [4,5] is a popular open-source software for data analysis workflows. KNIME has a very intuitive and user-friendly interface, an elegant and powerful extension mechanism based on the plug-in technology of the Eclipse rich client platform, and a seamless integration of other platforms such as Weka and R. Several KNIME extensions are available for specific algorithms and application domains, many of which are contributed by scientific communities, such as Cheminformatics and Bioinformatics.

In this paper, a novel and unique KNIME plug-in for Neuroscience, K-Surfer[1], is presented. K-Surfer facilitates the design and deployment of fully automated workflows for extracting, managing and analysing statistical measures produced by FreeSurfer and FSL. K-Surfer reduces time costs for importing and merging neurological data and eliminates human errors from this process. K-Surfer is unique in the sense that it allows neuroscientists to integrate in a unique environment the preprocessing and mining tasks of the neuroimage analysis pipeline.

This paper has been organized in the following way. Section 2 gives an overview of the process and tools for brain MRI data acquisition, processing and analysis. In Section 3, the main characteristics of KNIME are briefly presented. Section 4 provides a detailed description of the proposed KNIME extension, K-Surfer. A case study is illustrated in Section 5 using the FreeSurfer tutorial data. Finally, conclusions and future works are discussed in the Section 6.

---

[1] https://sourceforge.net/projects/ksurfer/

2   Background on Brain MRI Data Analysis

Diagnostic imaging of the human brain provides in vivo images related both to its structures and its functionalities. Several brain imaging techniques exist; Magnetic Resonance Imaging (MRI) is well known for its high image quality in terms of spatial resolution and signal to noise ratio (SNR) [6]. Moreover, MRI does not use ionizing radiation (X-rays) or radioactive tracers and thus it is safer than other methods such as Computed Tomography (CT).

Magnetic resonance is able to provide static anatomical information (structural MRI), dynamic physiological information (functional Magnetic Resonance - fMRI) or diffusion indices (Diffusion Tensor Imaging - DTI). Different amounts of diffusion weighting (Diffusion Weighted Imaging - DWI) return diffusion coefficients such as Mean Diffusivity (MD) or Fractional Anisotropy (FA). These diffusion indices, which show the main moving direction of water molecules, allow performing tractography, a technique for tracing fibre bundles within white matter [6].

Software for neuroimaging processing could be roughly categorized into monolithic and modular implementations. Examples of the monolithic approach are SPM [7], BrainVoyager [8], and Caret [9], while modular software examples are 3DSlicer [10], Camino [11], FreeSurfer [12] and FSL [13]. Rex et al. [14] list advantages and disadvantages of monolithic and modular software. FreeSurfer and FSL are popular examples of the modular approach: their tools and scripts can be used in conjunction for obtaining best results.

FreeSurfer [12] is an open-source suite of tools for conducting both volume-based and surface-based analysis. FreeSurfer users are able to drive the default processing stream for anatomical analysis by the UNIX shell script *recon-all*. Moreover, FreeSurfer provides the tool TRACULA (*TRActs Constrained by UnderLying Anatomy*) for performing tractography, that is the reconstruction of a set of 18 major white-matter pathways from DWI data. TRACULA workflow is managed by the UNIX shell script *trac-all*, which is composed of three steps: a pre-processing phase, the *ball-and-stick* diffusion model fitting and the generation of the probability distributions for each white-matter bundle. For the *ball-and-stick* model fitting, TRACULA uses *bedpost*, a tool from FSL's library. The FMRIB Software Library (FSL) [13] provides freely available image analysis and statistical tools for fMRI, MRI and DTI brain data. Similarly to FreeSurfer, FSL is composed of several modules for three main tasks: structural, functional and diffusion analysis.

Merging, managing and analysing the multi-dimensional data generated by FreeSurfer and FSL is not straightforward and requires an accurate and detailed knowledge of their tools, conventions and file formats.

There have been a few attempts to automatize commands writing for exporting FreeSurfer data[2]. For example, Matlab/Octave scripts are provided by default installation. FreeSurfer provides three command-line tools for extracting measures of interest into a table format: *asegstats2table*, *aparcstats2table* and

---

[2] https://surfer.nmr.mgh.harvard.edu/fswiki/UserContributions/Scripts

tractstats2table. Since each of the three default scripts is able to extract a specific type of data only, joining together volume, thickness and diffusion values requires additional work. Manually merging this data with demographical/clinical data and finally importing them into an analytics platform, makes the process slow and may add a source of errors that should not be in fact ignored.

Neuroimaging in Python Pipelines and Interfaces (Nipype)[3] is one of the attempts to automatize the writing process of FreeSurfer/FSL scripts. Nipype provides a Python interface for wrapping specific FreeSurfer functionalities such as the reconstruction, but it does not provide any wraps or tools for importing, visualising or analysing numerical data from FreeSurfer. *PySurfer*[4] is another example of Python library intended for use with FreeSurfer. However, its aim is giving a simpler interface than FreeSurfer scripts for displaying neuroimages, e.g. fMRI Activation or Volume, Conjunction Map.

This paper introduces a novel tool, K-Surfer, for automatically importing, managing and analysing FreeSurfer/FSL data into KNIME, a modern, user-friendly and extendible data analytics platform.

3   The Konstanz Information Miner (KNIME)

Several commercial and open-source software implementing data mining algorithms exist. The Konstanz Information Miner (KNIME) [4,5], along with STATISTICA, SAS JMP and IBM SPSS Modeler, has received high satisfaction ratings in the last edition of the largest survey of data mining, data science and data analytics professionals in the industry [15]. Some commercial and widely used software provide robust tools for statistical analysis. However, apart from the cost for their license, they cannot be easily extended with new functionalities, nor easily integrated with external tools. KNIME provides an easy-to-use platform for data analysis, manipulation, visualisation and reporting. KNIME is developed in Java and is based on Eclipse, an integrated development environment (IDE) for programmers. KNIME seamlessly integrates R and Weka, making it a good choice for completeness and user-friendliness at the same time. However, the most interesting aspect in KNIME is the use of a graphical representation of the data workflows: KNIME manages the analysis process using workflows made by nodes (*processes*) linked by edges (*data flows*). Each node encapsulates a specific algorithm, such as database integration, pre-processing techniques, descriptive and predictive model learners, statistical tests, visualisation: hundreds of nodes are provided in the base installation and many more can be easily downloaded and installed when required. Nodes can have one or two inputs and output ports: inputs and outputs are managed by means of an internal data table format which is optimised for sequential access and can scale up with the use of the secondary memory when the main memory is not sufficient. Nodes may also provide data visualisation (*Views*), which supports an interactive data exploration approach. In particular, the *Hiliting* functionality,

---

[3] http://nipy.org/nipype
[4] http://pysurfer.github.io/

a unique characteristic supported by KNIME, allows sharing data selection in different nodes and views. This functionality is particularly effective for the interactive exploration of data.

4   K-Surfer

K-Surfer is a novel KNIME plug-in that contributes a number of nodes and meta nodes to integrate neuroimage data formats (FreeSurfer and FSL) into KNIME and to allow their further data mining analysis with the KNIME algorithms. K-Surfer simplifies the importing of multi-dimensional data for group analysis based on the volume, thickness and diffusion data of neuroimages. Its user-friendly nodes configuration dialogues do not require the user to write UNIX shell commands and scripts. K-Surfer uses the configuration to generate and execute appropriate commands and scripts transparently to the user. In particular, K-Surfer automatically detects the file system structure generated by FreeSurfer and the files of interest, and manages the environment variables required by the various FreeSurfer tools. K-Surfer automatizes the selection and importing of neuroimages data for further analysis, thus reducing time costs and eliminating potential human errors. K-Surfer allows importing any set of measures of interest for any set of subjects in a table format into KNIME workflows, ready for any analysis process with other KNIME nodes. For example, K-Surfer makes it possible to quickly build a workflow for statistical analysis and data mining for longitudinal studies and for merging neuroimage data to other heterogeneous data (information fusion), such as demographic, behavioural, clinical, genomics and proteomics data. K-Surfer also integrates the FreeSurfer tool for the visualisation of 3D brain tracts into KNIME, to allow an immediate comparison of numerical and visual findings.

4.1   Requirements and Software Architecture

The main purpose of K-Surfer is to provide a communication interface between KNIME and FreeSurfer/FSL that complies to several functional requirements. In particular, for assuring the data quality, software for this goal must:

- automatize steps for importing measures FreeSurfer/FSL data (volume, thickness, diffusion measures);
- prepare data in a table format for statistical analysis and data mining;
- provide a graphical user interface for selecting subjects of interest and parameters;
- automatically detect folders and files from the installation root of FreeSurfer;
- automatically set environment variables, such as FreeSurfer home and subjects directory;
- be able to import data from both local and remote machines;
- avoid the use of intermediate and supporting files;
- ensure the uniqueness of row IDs in the generated data tables;
- provide name conventions for attributes following FreeSurfer specifications;

– guide the user to the data management;
– extend current functionalities of FreeSurfer scripts for converting text files into table format and, in particular, allow:
  • importing measures related to one or more brain tracts as a single step;
  • selecting subjects of different studies stored in different directories;
  • merging volume, thickness and diffusion data tables;
– provide a graphical user interface to visualize the probability distribution of single white-matter pathways.

K-Surfer is developed in Java as an Eclipse plug-in for KNIME SDK v2.8.2 under MacOS and Linux[5]. It is compatible with FreeSurfer v5.3, FSL v5.0 and KNIME Desktop v2.9. K-Surfer is distributed as a jar archive (350 kB) and it is installed by simply moving the archive into the *dropins* folder of KNIME/Eclipse. Before using any K-Surfer node, the FreeSurfer home path must be set in the *Preference* menu of KNIME. Figure 1 depicts the K-Surfer software architecture. The text files produced by FreeSurfer/FSL, e.g. pathstats.overall.txt and aseg.stats.txt, are stored in the Data Layer. K-Surfer is integrated to the KNIME environment to provides functionalities at the Application Layer by means of FreeSurfer tools. Other KNIME nodes also provide data preprocessing, data fusion, data analysis and visualization at the Application Layer. For example, it is straightforward to import and integrate other kind of information such as behavioural data.

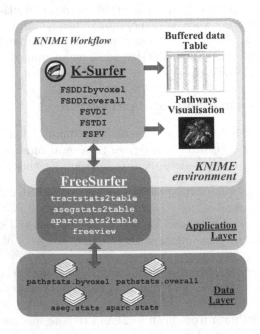

Fig. 1. K-Surfer software architecture

---

[5] FreeSurfer and FSL are only available for UNIX.

K-Surfer nodes can be combined with other KNIME nodes to build complete data workflows of brain MRI data for preprocessing-analysis-visualization tasks. The next section describes the features of K-Surfer nodes and their configuration options in detail.

4.2   K-Surfer Nodes and Meta Nodes

After the installation, K-Surfer nodes are available in the *Node Repository* of KNIME under the root category *K-Surfer* (area (a) in Fig. 2). The subcategory *Meta Nodes* contains meta nodes (see below for a description of meta nodes) that provide sub-workflows, i.e. single nodes containing workflows with nodes and even other meta nodes. These meta nodes combine K-Surfer nodes and KNIME nodes to provide complex workflows for specific tasks as single nodes (modularization). The area (b) of Fig. 2 shows a simple KNIME workflow project to showcase all K-Surfer nodes and meta nodes, while the area (c) in Fig. 2 shows the *Node Description* of a selected node. The current implementation of K-Surfer includes 5 nodes and 2 meta nodes described in the following:

- **FSDDIoverall - FreeSurfer Diffusion Data Import overall**. This node extracts anisotropy and diffusivity values averaged over an entire pathway as calculated by TRACULA. The FSDDIoverall node uses the FreeSurfer script *tractstats2table* to import the measures into a data table. The configuration dialog contains a tab *Options* for selecting one or more subjects and a tab *Tracts and Attributes* for selecting one tract and one or more metrics, such as Mean Diffusivity or Fractional Anisotropy.
- **FSDDIbyvoxel - FreeSurfer Diffusion Data Import by voxel**. This node extracts diffusion measures as a function of the position along the trajectory of the pathway, as calculated by TRACULA. The FSDDIbyvoxel node uses the FreeSurfer script *tractstats2table* to import the measures into a data table. The configuration dialog contains a tab *Options* for selecting one subject and a tab *Tracts and Attributes* for selecting one tract and one metric, such as Mean Diffusivity or Fractional Anisotropy.
- **FSVDI - FreeSurfer Volume Data Import**. This node extracts the volumes of specific structures, calculated during the FreeSurfer processing stream (*recon-all*). The FSVDI node uses the FreeSurfer script *asegstats2table* to import the statistics of the subcortical segmentation into a data table. The configuration dialog contains a tab *Options* for selecting one or more subjects.
- **FSTDI - FreeSurfer Thickness Data Import**. This node extracts the thickness and other measures of specific structures, calculated during the FreeSurfer processing stream (*recon-all*). The FSTDI node uses the FreeSurfer script *aparcstats2table* to import the statistics of the cortical segmentation into a data table. The configuration dialog contains a tab *Options* for selecting one or more subjects and a tab *Measures* for selecting the left or right hemisphere and one measure among *Surface Area*, *Gray matter volume*, *Average Thickness* and *Thickness Standard Deviation*.

- **FSPV - FreeSurfer Pathways Viewer.** This node visualises the probability distribution of single white-matter pathways or all white-matter pathways simultaneously as calculated by TRACULA. The FSPV node uses the FreeSurfer tool *freeview* adding, for each chosen tract, default values for visualisation.

The two K-Surfer meta nodes combine and extend the nodes listed above. Thanks to these meta nodes unique functionalities are provided:

- **Add Class Attribute (overall).** This meta node uses two FSDDIoverall nodes to add a new column containing the class attribute to a diffusion table. E.g., for group analysis, the user may need to add a class attribute, such as healthy control patient and affected patient.
- **Select multiple tracts (overall).** This meta node allows importing the diffusion values of multiple tracts at once by using the FSDDIoverall node. In the next section, a simple case study for analysing FreeSurfer tutorial data is presented to provide a step-by-step guide for using K-Surfer.

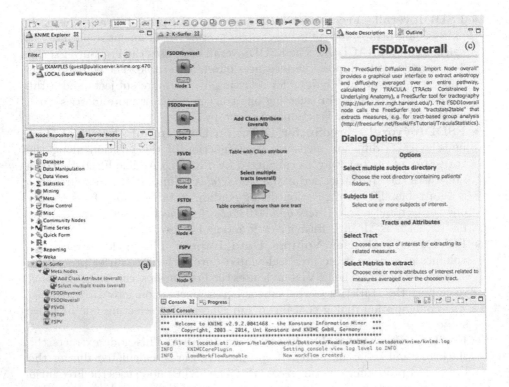

Fig. 2. Screenshot of KNIME workbench (a) K-Surfer nodes category, (b) Workspace containing K-Surfer nodes, (c) Node Description for FreeSurfer Diffusion Data Import overall

5 A Case Study Using FreeSurfer Tutorial Data

K-Surfer makes FreeSurfer data analysis simpler and faster. This simple case study uses the tutorial data[6] provided by FreeSurfer. The tutorial dataset contains MRI data of a small set (ten) of healthy subjects generated by recon-all and trac-all scripts. Furthermore, a text file containing information about age and gender is available. For the sake of a demonstration, here it is hypothesized that the first five subjects are affected patients (PAT) and the remaining five are control patients (HC). The choice of measures to analyse depends on the particular neurodegenerative disease to investigate. For example, Parkinson's disease is well known for affecting the volumes of encephalic areas. In this case of study the class "PAT" is treated as affected by a disease that influences the diffusion indices (e.g. Amyotrophic Lateral Sclerosis). Thus, only nodes for extracting this kind of measures are used, but similar workflows can be designed for investigating volumes or volumes and diffusion measures together. The workflow in Figure 3 is designed for the task of accepting or rejecting the hypothesis that the means of diffusion indices in *Left Anterior Thalamic Radiations* are equal between PAT and HC subjects. It contains two FSDDIoverall nodes, one for importing PAT subjects (orange area) and the other for HC subjects (green area). Fig. 4.a shows the *Options* tab of the configuration panel of the node FSDDIoverall for selecting subjects of interest. Fig. 4.b depicts the tab *Tracts and Attributes*, for selecting the tract of interest and the attributes (in this case *Left Anterior Thalamic Radiations* and *Fractional Anisotropy, Mean Diffusivity, Axial Diffusivity* and *Radial Diffusivity*). Once executed, the FSDDIoverall node generates an output table in which the columns are named following the convention: `coded_name_of_tract:attribute`, where `coded_name_of_tract` is the standard abbreviation for the tract used by FreeSurfer. The KNIME node *Joiner* is used to join the output of the FSDDIoverall node to a table containing data about gender, age and diagnosis, which is imported from a text file with the *CSV Reader* node, for both PAT and HC subjects. Using the *Concatenate* node the data tables of the PAT and HC subjects are merged and a node *Color Manager* associates a color to each class. The yellow area of Fig.3 shows a subworkflow for a simple statistical analysis. The node *Scatter Matrix* provides a graphical representation of the data and a box plot about Fractional Anisotropy of each class is generated with the node of type *Conditional Box Plot*. This latter node also returns Robust Statistics (Lower Quartile, Upper Quartile, etc.). The *Statistics* node calculates statistical moments such as minimum, maximum, mean, standard deviation, variance and median. A node of type *Independent groups t-test* is added for performing a Levene-test, used for assessing the equality of variance between two groups, and an independent groups t-test. The *Test statistics* view of this node gives an overview of the results of the test in term of p-values. Since tutorial data consisting all in healthy control subjects, the t-test result leads to accept the null hypothesis. In brown areas of Fig.3, two FSPV nodes are added for visualizing and comparing the reconstructed tracts

---

[6] https://surfer.nmr.mgh.harvard.edu/fswiki/FsTutorial/Data/

of *PAT_1* and *HC_1* subjects. The differences related to diffusion indices of the *Left Anterior Thalamic Radiations* in the two groups can be investigated using a Data Mining approach. The output provided by concatenating the two groups, is the input for a *k-Means node* (red area of Fig.3). The *Crosstab* node gives the contingency table related to the clusters and chi-square test statistics. Regarding classification, in the blue area of Fig.3 the workflow for Decision Tree learner is showed. A *Partitioning* node is added to split the data in two sets, 67% for the training set and the rest for the test set. A *Scorer* node at the end of the workflow provides the Confusion Matrix and a table of accuracy statistics. Using K-Surfer nodes together with other standard KNIME nodes, it is possible to perform even more complex analysis. For example the Add Class Attribute (overall) meta node can be used in combination with the Select multiple tracts (overall) meta node for obtaining a data table containing multiple tracts and their relative attributes.

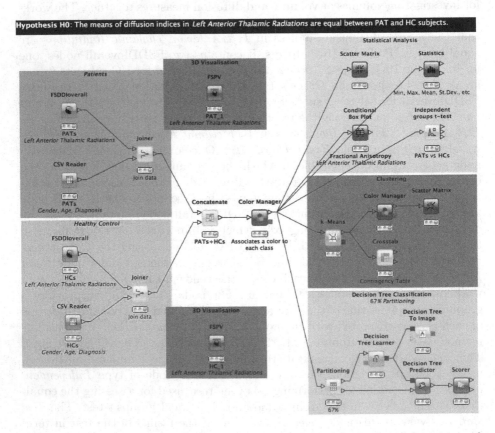

Fig. 3. Case Study workflow for confuting the null hypothesis that "the means of diffusion indices in *Left Anterior Thalamic Radiations* are equal between PAT and HC subjects"

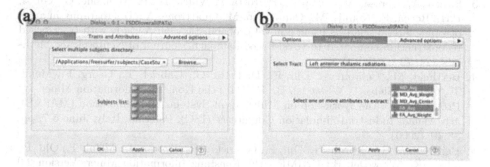

Fig. 4. (a) Tab *Options* and (b) tab *Tract and Attributes* of the configuration panel of FSDDIoverall node for the case study

6   Conclusion

High resolution and a non-invasive approach make MRI technologies both a very accurate and desirable diagnostic tool. Mining neuroimage data represents a promising approach for supporting diagnosis, monitoring treatment and discovering new knowledge about brain functions and neurological deficits [16]. However, the overwhelming availability of experimental data and the complexity of the preprocessing and data selection phases, is a main bottleneck in brain MRI data analysis. Surprisingly, a comprehensive data analytics environment for managing and analysing neurological data does not exist yet.

Among several well-known and general-purpose analytics platforms, KNIME stands out for its usability, friendliness and extendibility. The main goal of this study was to extend its functionalities by designing and implementing K-Surfer, a bundle of new KNIME nodes for importing, managing and analysing neuroimage data generated by FreeSurfer and FSL. K-Surfer automatizes the overall process and helps to reduce time costs and human errors by removing the need for low-level data manipulation. With K-Surfer importing multiple measures from many neuroimage surveys and integrating heterogeneous data sources are straightforward and automatic operations.

As future work, further K-Surfer nodes will be developed, for example, for visualising cortical and subcortical segmentation. Since FreeSurfer easily interoperates with other tools, like Caret and 3D Slicer, K-Surfer could also be extended to support their data formats.

References

1. Cannataro, M., Guzzi, P.H., Sarica, A.: Data mining and life sciences applications on the grid. WIREs Data Mining Knowl. Discov. 3, 216–238 (2013)
2. Megalooikonomou, V., Ford, J., Shen, L., Makedon, F., Saykin, A.: Data Mining in Brain Imaging. Stat Methods Med. Res. 9, 359–394 (2000)

3. Sarica, A., Cerasa, A., Vasta, R., Perrotta, P., Valentino, P., Mangone, G., Guzzi, P.H., Rocca, F., Nonnis, M., Cannataro, M., Quattrone, A.: Tractography in amyotrophic lateral sclerosis using a novel probabilistic tool: A study with tract-based reconstruction compared to voxel-based approach. Journal of Neuroscience Methods 224, 79–87 (2014)

4. Berthold, M., Cebron, N., Dill, F., Di Fatta, G., Gabriel, T., Georg, F., Meinl, T., Ohl, P., Sieb, C., Wiswedel, B.: KNIME: the Konstanz Information Miner. In: Proceedings of the Workshop on Multi-Agent Systems and Simulation (MAS&S), 4th Annual Industrial Simulation Conference (ISC), Palermo, Italy, June 5-7, pp. 58–61 (2006)

5. Berthold, M.R., Cebron, N., Dill, F., Gabriel, T.R., Kotter, T., Meinl, T., Ohl, P., Thiel, K., Wiswedel, B.: KNIME - the Konstanz Information Miner: Version 2.0 and Beyond. SIGKDD Explor. Newsl. 11, 26–31 (2009)

6. Symms, M., Jager, H.R., Schmierer, K., Yousry, T.A.: 'A Review of Structural Magnetic Resonance Neuroimaging'. J. Neurol. Neurosurg. Psychiatry 75, 1235–1244 (2004)

7. Friston, K.J., Holmes, A.P., Worsley, K.J., Poline, J.P., Frith, C.D., Frackowiak, R.S.J.: Statistical parametric maps in functional imaging: a general linear approach. Hum. Brain Mapp. 2, 189–210 (1994)

8. Goebel, R.: Brainvoyager–Past, Present, Future. Neuroimage 62, 748–756 (2012)

9. Van Essen, D.C., Dickson, J., Harwell, J., Hanlon, D., Anderson, C.H., Drury, H.A.: An Integrated Software System for Surface-based Analyses of Cerebral Cortex. Journal of American Medical Informatics Association 8(5), 443–459 (2001)

10. Pieper, S., Halle, M., Kikinis, R.: 3D SLICER. In: Proc. IEEE Int. Symp. Biomed. Imaging., pp. 632–635 (2004)

11. Cook, P.A., Bai, Y., Nedjati-Gilani, S., Seunarine, K.K., Hall, M.G., Parker, G.J., Alexander, D.C.: Camino: Open-Source Diffusion-MRI Reconstruction and Processing. In: 14th Scientific Meeting of the International Society for Magnetic Resonance in Medicine, Seattle, WA, USA, pp. 27–59 (May 2006)

12. Dale, A.M., Fischl, B., Sereno, M.I.: Cortical surface-based analysis. I. segmentation and surface reconstruction. NeuroImage 9, 179–194 (1999)

13. Smith, S.M., Jenkinson, M., Woolrich, M.W., Beckmann, C.F., Behrens, T.E.J., Johansen-Berg, H., Bannister, P.R., De Luca, M., Drobnjak, I., Flitney, D.E., Niazy, R., Saunders, J., Vickers, J., Zhang, Y., De Stefano, N., Brady, J.M., Matthews, P.M.: Advances in functional and structural MR image analysis and implementation as FSL. Neuroimage 23(S1), 208–219 (2004)

14. Rex, D.E., Ma, J.Q., Toga, A.W.: The Loni Pipeline Processing Environment. Neuroimage 19, 1033–1048 (2003)

15. Rexer, K.: Rexer Analytics 2013 Data Miner Survey (2013), http://www.rexeranalytics.com/Data-Miner-Survey-2013-Intro.html

16. Sarica, A., Critelli, C., Guzzi, P.H., Cerasa, A., Quattrone, A., Cannataro, M.: Application of Different Classification Techniques on Brain Morphological Data. In: Proc. of the 26th IEEE Inter. Symposium on Computer-based Medical Systems (CBMS), Porto, Portugal, pp. 425–428 (June 2013)

Practice and Task Experience Change the Gradient Organization in the Resting Brain

Jun Zhou[1,2], Haiyan Zhou[1,2], Chuan Li[1,2], JiaLiang Guo[1,2],
Xiaojing Yang[1,2], Zhoujun Long[1,2], Yulin Qin[1,2,3], and Ning Zhong[1,2,4]

[1] International WIC Institute, Beijing University of Technology, China
[2] Beijing Key Laboratory of MRI and Brain Informatics, China
[3] Dept. of Psychology, Carnegie Mellon University, USA
[4] Dept. of Life Science and Informatics, Maebashi Institute of Technology, Japan
`910092147@emails.bjut.edu.cn, zhouhaiyan@bjut.edu.cn`

Abstract. A kind of metacognitive and cognitive activity patterns in the brain have been found in the task state, showing the gradient distribution from abstract to concrete processing in the frontal and parietal cortex especially. In our early study, it is observed that this kind of gradient organization is intrinsic and prepared in the resting state. Learning experience is a process from metacognitive to cognitive processing, which might change the spontaneous activity patterns in the resting brain. This study is to explore how the learning experience, including both long-term practice and short-term task experience, influences the intrinsic gradient organization in the human brain. Focused on the task-evoked metacognitive and cognitive pattern regions, by comparing four resting state data, before and after task performing in Day 1 before practice named pre-pre and pre-post respectively, and before and after task in Day 7 after 5-day's practice, named post-pre and post-post respectively, we investigated the change of gradient organization in the human brain with the approach of functional connectivity (FC) analysis. The result showed that the gradient organization is quite stable across the four resting states, which is similar with our previous finding. Task performance enhanced the correlation between cognitive and mixed functional network, especially after long-time practice, suggesting the key role of cognitive network in the task execution. Moreover, after long practice, the internal connectivity within the metacognitive network and the connection between mixed and cognitive functional network were both weakened, which suggested a functional modulation and separation when task performance became more and more skilled and automatic.

1 Introduction

Recent researches suggest that the gradient organization from concrete to abstract processing is widely distributed in the frontal and parietal cortex using functional MRI (fMRI) in the task state [1–6]. And our previous study shows that this kind of gradient organization is observed in the resting brain. It is intrinsic and prepared in the resting state [7]. This distribution is divided into three layers:

D. Ślęzak et al. (Eds.): BIH 2014, LNAI 8609, pp. 493–501, 2014.
© Springer International Publishing Switzerland 2014

metacognition, mixed and cognition. Cognitive processing is relative specific, and the main function comprises information extraction, characterization and operations. Metacognitive processing is the function of monitoring and reflection, which is more abstract and can be seen as the cognition of cognition [1, 8]. In addition, some researches also show cognition is related to task-positive voxels and metacognition is related to task-negative voxels in the task-state [7, 9, 10]. This study focuses on the change of gradient organization influenced by short time task performance and long-time practice.

Researches find the problem-solving strategies would be changed after a long-time practice or learning (for example, see [11]). In addition, the human brain networks will be dynamic configuration during the learning phase, and the functional connectivity is dynamic to support the consolidation of previous experience [12, 13]. It is suggested that the dynamic characteristics of the human brain played a key role in stability and plasticity [13].

This study is to explore how the learning experience, including both long-term practice and short-term task experience, influences the intrinsic gradient organization in the human brain. Since learning experience includes the process from metacognitive to cognitive processing, we hypothesized as following: before the long-time learning, the connection between the metacognitive and cognitive network would be stronger; but after practice, the connection between them would weakened because of the skilled processing. According to the task-evoked pattern [1, 14, 15] and our previous study, we predefined six regions of interest (ROIs) to focus on in this study. Two regions are related to metacognitive processing: angular gyrus (ANG) and Brodmann Area 10 (BA10), the regions of lateral inferior prefrontal cortex (LIPFC) and posterior parietal cortex (PPC) are related to mixed processing, and the regions of horizontal intraparietal sulcus (HIPS) and posterior superior parietal lobule (PSPL) belong to the cognitive network.

2   Material and Methods

2.1   Subjects

Twenty-one subjects (15 males, 6 females, and 23.14 ± 1.32 years old) from Beijing University of Technology participated in the study. All of the participants were right-handed and reported with no history of neurological or psychiatric disorders. Written informed consent was obtained from each participant.

2.2   Data Acquisitions

Participants were scanned on 3.0 Tesla Siemens MRI scanner with the parameters: repetition time/echo time = 2000/31 ms, thickness/gap = 3.2/0 mm, matrix = 64×64, axial slices number = 32 and field of view = $200 \times 200 \ mm^2$. Voxel size: $3.125 \times 3.125 \times 3.2 \ mm^3$. The whole brain functional images using an echo planar imaging (EPI) sequence were acquired over all sessions. There were five-days practices and the practice lasted for one hour in each day in order to improve the proficiency. Each participant was scanned including both a 4×4 Sudoku task [16] and two resting states in Day 1 and Day 7 (Fig.1). During the rest scans, each participant was instructed to relax with their eyes closed and move as little as possible and each participant took part in two fMRI scans that lasted approximately 90 min.

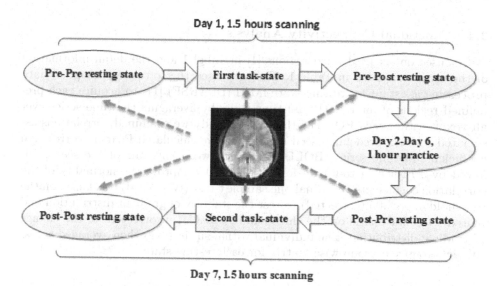

Fig. 1. This study compared four resting state: two resting states scanning in the first day before and after task, named pre-pre and pre-post respectively; after five days practice, two resting states scanning in the seventh day before and after task, named post-pre and post-post respectively. The present study aimed to reveal short time tasks and long-term practice or learning effect on functional organization in four resting state.

2.3   Preprocessing of Functional Data

Images were firstly preprocessed using data processing assistant for resting-state fMRI (DPARSF, http://rfmri.org/DPARSF) over sessions respectively. FMRI preprocessing steps included: first, the first 7 images were discarded for magnetization equilibrium; second, all the images were corrected for the acquisition time delay by slice timing; third, those were realigned to the first volume for head-motion correction in each session; fourth, all the images were spatially normalized to the Montreal Neurological Institute (MNI) EPI template and resampled to 3.0 mm cubic voxels. Subjects (2 subjects) with head motion more than 3.0 mm of maximal translation (in any direction of x, y or z) or 1.5° of maximal rotation throughout the course of scanning were excluded from further analysis. After those, data were spatially smoothed (4 mm full width at half maximum Gaussian blur) and temporally band-pass filtered into the frequency range of 0.01-0.08 Hz to reduce the effects of low-frequency drift and high-frequency noise, followed by a multiple linear regression analysis to remove several sources of spurious variances [10]: (i) six parameters obtained by rigid body correction of head motion, (ii) global brain signal, (iii) signal from a ventricular region of interest, and (iv) signal from a region centered in the white matter. The residual of the linear regression was considered the neuronal-induced signal of each corresponding region.

2.4   Functional Connectivity Analysis

We focused on six predefined regions [1] in Tabel 1 and the detail information of the seeds was listed in Table 1. Then, we used the software package of data processing assistant for resting-state fMRI (DPARSF) [17] to acquire each predefined regions of interest (ROIs) time series by averaging the time series over all voxels within each ROI. For the current study we examined correlations associated with six predefined seed regions and we calculated Pearson correlation coefficients of time series (BOLD signals) between any pair of the seeds, followed by a Fisher's r-to-z transformation [18] to improve the normality of the correlation coefficients. The final one sample t-test (two-tailed) was based on the threshold of $p < .05$ (corrected) to test the stability of gradient distribution and paired t-test was based on the threshold of $p < .05$ (uncorrected) to the change of gradient distribution. The individual within-subject was then averaged across subjects to give a group-wise matrix for each resting state.

Table 1. The Talairach coordinates of the centers of six predefined regions of interest

Seed	Size	Talairach Coordinates		
		x	y	z
ANG	$4*4*4$	-41	-65	37
BA10	$4*4*4$	-35	49	7
LIPFC	$5*5*4$	-43	23	24
PPC	$5*5*4$	-23	-63	40
HIPS	$4*4*4$	-34	-49	45
PSPL	$4*4*4$	-19	-68	55

3   Results

3.1   The Stability of the Gradient Distribution

With different thresholds, we found that six brain regions showed stable gradient distribution (Fig.2: under FDR both 0.05, Fig.3: under FDR both 0.01 and Bonferroni both 0.05/15). And this gradient organization mainly shows the regions from ANG and BA10 networks to LIPFC and PPC networks to HIPS and PSPL networks in human brain cortex.

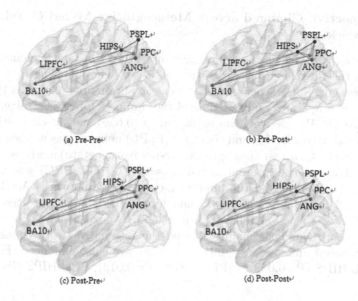

Fig. 2. The functional connectivity between the predefined ROIs with the threshold of FDR corrected $p < 0.05$. The red line denotes metacognitive network, green one denotes mixed network, blue one denotes cognitive network, gray one denotes the connection between networks.

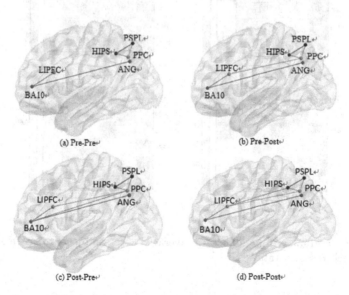

Fig. 3. The functional connectivity between the predefined ROIs with the threshold of FDR corrected $p < 0.01$ and Bonferroni corrected $p < 0.05/15$. The result of two corrective methods are the same. The red line denotes metacognitive network, green one denotes mixed network, blue one denotes cognitive network, gray one denotes the connection between networks.

3.2   Connective Changed across Metacognitive-Mixed-Cognitive Network

By comparing the difference within the four resting state data, change within or between the functional networks were observed. The following four pictures (Fig.4) shows correlation coefficient between each brain area. Contrast (pre-post vs. pre-pre resting state) analysis showed the connection between mixed (PPC) and cognitive (PSPL) network was enhanced (p=0.056) and the connectivity between metacognitive (BA10) and cognitive (PSPL) network was weakened significantly (p=0.04). Contrast (post-pre vs. pre-pre resting state) analysis indicated the connectivity of the internal mixed network (LIPFC, PPC) was increased significantly (p=0.052) and the internal metacognitive network (ANG, BA10) was weakened marginally (p=0.087) and mixed (PPC) and cognitive (HIPS) networks was weakened significantly (p=0.022). Contrast (post-post vs. post-pre resting state) analysis mainly showed the internal network connectivities changed: between mixed and cognitive networks were also enhanced (For example: LIPFC-HIPS (P=0.052), LIPFC-PSPL (P=0.013), PPC-HIPS (P=0.034)).

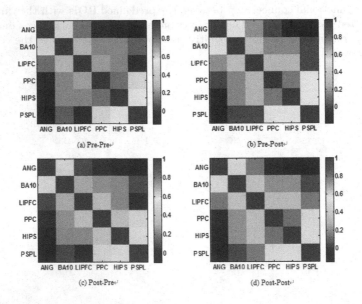

Fig. 4. The individual within-subject was averaged across subjects to give a group-wise matrix for each resting state

4   Discussion

By comparing the four resting states with different thresholds, we found there is a stable gradient organization in the resting brain, which is consistent with the result found in task-evoked or resting state data [1, 14]. There is a great deal of evidence to suggests that the possibility of the existence of gradient organization in the resting state: (I) the coordinates of the gradient organization's intrinsic networks in spatial terms is similar to two anticorrelated intrinsic functional networks in human brain [10]. For example our predefined seed of PPC (-23, -63, 40), HIPS (-34, -49, 45) and PSPL (-19, -68, 55) is near to the task-positive seed of IP (-25, -57, 46). Our predefined seed of ANG (-41, -65, 37) is near to the task-negative seed of LP (-45, -67, 36) [7]. Here, in this study , we find LIPFC was involved in the task-positive networks. As to the our predefined seed of BA10 (-35, 49, 7), the connectivity with other networks was observed. This Brodmann Area 10 (BA10) is special in being exclusively connected only with supramodal regions of the cortex [19]. It indicates that that region is involved in the information and communication from multiple regions [1]. This is consistent with the results of our study; (II) with the process of human evolution and learning, the organization of the human brain networks would be changed by the change of experience [20–22]. Besides, brain was not only limited to the gradient distribution but also there are some uncertain connection between brain areas.

In addition, the result indicates that the gradient organization is changed by the learning experience, including long time practice and short term task experience. The result showed that task performance enhanced the correlation between cognitive and mixed functional networks, especially after long time practice suggesting the key role of cognitive network in the task execution. Moreover, the connection within network weakened (PPC and HIPS: p=0.022) in the post-pre resting state, and the internal network of metacognition weakened, the internal network of mixed enhanced (LIPFC and PPC: p=0.052), which suggests a functional brain networks separation and modulation after long time practice and no task effects. The change of the gradient organization indicates the human brain has a certain plasticity. The word 'plastic' comes from the Greek language and the main ingredient is resin which means the ability to undergo a change such as a structure or a shape change and so on. Alvaro Pascual-Leone et al stress plasticity is an obligatory result of all neural activity (even mental practice), and also stress environmental pressures, functional significance, and experience are critical factors [21]. But beyond that, it indicates learning and plasticity of the brain are inseparable. Human brain networks will be dynamic configuration during the learning phase [12]. Also studies show that functional connectivity in the brain function are dynamic to support the consolidation of previous experience [23].

It could be with the increase of number of practice, the division of labor between networks becomes clearer and more modular, and presents function separation. Metacognition is more abstract and can guide the establishment of the new rules. When the participant was solving the task problems, especially in the early stage with nonproficiency, the metacognition played a key role to perform the task efficiently [1]. When after reaching a certain proficiency, metacognition may reduce the level of involvement, while some brain regions such as cognitive regions can finish the work alone, in order to achieve a high degree of automation [24, 25]. This result is similar to a triarchic theory of learning [20] and it indirectly reflects the brain is capable of a kind of plasticity.

In addition, some researches suggest the whole brain has certain stability, adaptive and dynamic optimal balance under the interference of the task in time [13]. So the next job is the further exploratory analysis to investigate the change of gradient organization in the whole brain under the interference of the task in time and long-term task.

Acknowledgements. This work was supported by the National Basic Research Program of China (2014CB744605, 2014CB744603), International Science and Technology Cooperation Program of China (2013DFA32180), National Natural Science Foundation of China (61272345), and also supported by Beijing Municipal Commission of Education and Beijing Key Laboratory of Magnetic Resonance Imaging and Brain Informatics.

References

1. Anderson, J.R., Betts, S., Ferris, J.L., Fincham, J.M.: Cognitive and metacognitive activity in mathematical problem solving: prefrontal and parietal patterns. Cognitive, Affective, Behavioral Neuroscience 11, 52–67 (2011)
2. Asari, T., Konishi, S., Jimura, K., Miyashita, Y.: Multiple components of lateral posterior parietal activation associated with cognitive set shifting. NeuroImage 26, 694–702 (2005)
3. Badre, D.: Cognitive control, hierachy, and the rostro-caudal organization of the frontal lobes. Trends in Cognitive Sciences 12(5), 193–200 (2008)
4. Buckner, R.L.: Functional-anatomic correlates of control processes in memory. The Journal of Neuroscience 23(10), 3999–4004 (2003)
5. Christoff, K., Gabrieli, J.D.E.: The frontopolar cortex and human cognition: Evidence for a rostrocaudal hierarchical organization within the human prefrontal cortex. Psychology 28(2), 168–186 (2000)
6. Nee, D.E., Brown, J.W.: Rostral-caudal gradients of abstraction revealed by multivariate pattern analysis of working memory. NeuroImage 63(3), 1285–1294 (2012)
7. Zhou, H.Y., Wang, Z.J., Yang, J., Qin, Y.L., Li, K.C., Zhong, N.: The gradient cognitive and metacognitive organization in the resting brain (2013) (Preparation)
8. Kitchner, K.S.: Cognition, Metacognition, and Epistemic Cognition. Human Development 26(4), 222–232 (1983)
9. Buckner, R.L., Andrews-Hanna, J.R., Schacter, D.L.: The brain's default network. Annals of the New York Academy of Sciences 1124, 1–38 (2008)
10. Fox, M.D., Snyder, A.Z., Vincent, J.L., Corbetta, M., Van Essen, D.C., Raichle, M.E.: The human brain is intrinsically organized into dynamic, anticorrelated functional networks. Proceedings of the National Academy of Sciences 102(27), 9673–9678 (2005)
11. Qin, Y.L., Carter, C.S., Silk, E.M., Stenger, V.A., Fissell, K., Goode, A., Anderson, J.R.: The change of the brain activation patterns as children learn algebra equation solving. Proceedings of the National Academy of Sciences 101(15), 5686–5691 (2004)

12. Bassett, D.S., Wymbs, N.F., Porter, M.A., Mucha, P.J., Carlson, J.M., Grafton, S.T.: Dynamic reconfiguration of human brain networks during learning. Proceedings of the National Academy of Sciences 108(18), 7641–7646 (2011)
13. Wang, Z.J., Liu, J.M., Zhong, N., Qin, Y.L., Zhou, H.Y., Li, K.C.: Changes in the brain intrinsic organization in both on-task state and post-task resting state. NeuroImage 62, 394–407 (2012)
14. Wintermute, S., Betts, S., Ferris, J.L., Fincham, J.M., Anderson, J.R.: Brain networks supporting execution of mathematical skills versus acquisition of new mathematical competence. PLoS ONE 7(12), 1–16 (2012)
15. Rosenberg-Lee, M., Lovett, M.C., Anderson, J.R.: Neural correlates of arithmetic calculation strategies. Cognitive, Affective, Behavioral Neuroscience 9(3), 270–285 (2009)
16. Qin, Y.L., Xiang, J., Wang, R.F., Zhou, H.Y., Li, H.C., Zhong, N.: Neural bases for basic processes in heuristic problem solving: Take solving Sudoku puzzles as an example. PsyCh Journal 1(2), 101–117 (2012)
17. Yan, C.G., Zang, Y.F.: DPARSF: a MATLAB toolbox for "pipeline" data analysis of resting-state fMRI. Neuroscience 4(13), 1–7 (2010)
18. Jenkins, G.M., Watts, D.G.: Spectral Analysis and Its Applications. Holden-Day Series in Time Series Analysis (1968)
19. Ramnani, N., Owen, A.M.: Anterior prefrontal cortex: Insights into function from anatomy and neuroimaging. Nature Reviews Neuroscience 5, 184–194 (2004)
20. Chein, J.M., Schneider, W.: The Brain's Learning and Control Architecture. Psychological Science 21(2), 78–84 (2012)
21. Pascual-Leone, A., Amedi, A., Fregni, F., Merabet, L.B.: The plastic human brain cortex. Annual Review of Neuroscience 28, 377–401 (2005)
22. Hill, N.M., Schneider, W.: Brain Changes in the Development of Expertise: Neuroanatomical and Neurophysiological Evidence about Skill-Based Adaptations. In: The Cambridge handbook of expertise and expert performance, pp. 653–682. Cambridge University Press, NY (2006)
23. Lewis, C.M., Baldassarre, A., Committeri, G., Romani, G.L., Corbetta, M.: Learning sculpts the spontaneous activity of the resting human brain. Proceedings of the National of Sciences 106(41), 17558–17563 (2009)
24. Shiffrin, R.M., Schneider, W.: Controlled and automatic human information processing: II. Perceptual learning, automatic attending and a general theory. Psychological Review 84(2), 127–190 (1977)
25. Schneider, W., Shiffrin, R.M.: Controlled and automatic human information processing: I. Detection, search, and attention. Psychological Review 84(1), 1–66 (1977)

Extravaganza Tutorial on
Hot Ideas for Interactive Knowledge Discovery
and Data Mining in Biomedical Informatics

Andreas Holzinger[1,2]

[1] Research Unit Human–Computer Interaction, Institute for Medical Informatics,
Statistics & Documentation, Medical University Graz, Austria
`a.holzinger@hci4all.at`
[2] Institute for Information Systems and Computer Media
Graz University of Technology, Austria

Abstract. Biomedical experts are confronted with "Big data", driven
by the trend towards precision medicine. Despite the fact that humans
are excellent at pattern recognition in dimensions of ≤ 3, most biomedical
data is in dimensions much higher than 3, making manual analysis often
impossible. Experts in daily routine are decreasingly capable of dealing
with such data. Efficient, useable and useful computational methods,
algorithms and tools to interactively gain insight into such data are a
commandment of the time. A synergistic combination of methodologies
of two areas may be of great help here: Human–Computer Interaction
(HCI) and Knowledge Discovery/Data Mining (KDD), with the goal of
supporting human intelligence with machine learning. Mapping higher
dimensional data into lower dimensions is a major task in HCI, and
a concerted effort including recent advances from graph-theory and algebraic topology may contribute to finding solutions. Moreover, much
biomedical data is sparse, noisy and time-dependent, hence entropy is
also amongst promising topics. This tutorial gives an overview of the
HCI-KDD approach and focuses on 3 topics: graphs, topology and entropy. The goal of this intro tutorial is to motivate and stimulate further
research.

Keywords: Knowledge Discovery, Data Mining, HCI-KDD, Graph-
based Text Mining, Topological Data Mining, Entropy-based Data
Mining.

1 Introduction and Motivation

Experts in the life sciences have to deal with large amounts of complex, high-
dimensional, heterogenous, noisy, and weakly structured data sets and massive
sets of unstructured information from various sources [1], [2]. "Big Data" [3]
in the medical domain is driven by the trend towards precision P4-medicine
(Predictive, Preventive, Participatory, Personalized) and has resulted in an explosion in the amount of generated data sets, in particular "-omics" data, for

D. Ślęzak et al. (Eds.): BIH 2014, LNAI 8609, pp. 502–515, 2014.

example from genomics, proteomics, metabolomics, etc. [4]. Within such data, relevant *structural* patterns and/or *temporal* patterns ("knowledge") are often hidden and not accessible to the expert. The progressively trend towards data intensive science, which is nearly a reverse of the classical hypothetico-deductive approach, makes optimization of discovery tools imperative [5], and calls for visual data mining approaches [6]. This paper is organized as follows: In section 2 some key terms are briefly explained. In section 3 the basic idea of the HCI-KDD approach is presented, along with the seven research areas involved, however, in the following we concentrate briefly on only three of them: In section 4 on graph-based data mining, in section 5 on topological data mining and in section 6 on entropy-based data mining, concluding by emphasizing that the *combination* of such approaches may bring added values. In the limited space given, such vast topics can only be touched, so the goal of this tutorial is to provide a coarse overview, to motivate and stimulate further research and to encourage to test crazy ideas.

2   Glossary and Key Terms

Algebraic Topology: is concerned with computations of homologies and homotopies in topological spaces [7].

Alpha Shapes: family of piecewise linear simple curves in the Euclidean plane associated with the shape of a finite set of points [8]; i.e. α-shapes are a generalization of the convex hull of a point set: Let **S** be a finite set in $\mathbb{R}^3$ and α a real number $0 \leq \alpha \leq \infty$; the u-shape of **S** is a polytope that is neither necessarily convex nor necessarily connected. For $\alpha \to \infty$ the α-shape is identical to the convex hull of **S** [9]; important e.g. in protein-related interactions [10].

Betti Number: can be used to distinguish topological spaces based on the connectivity of n-dimensional simplicial complexes: In dimension k, the rank of the k-th homology group is denoted β_k, useful in the presence of noisy shapes, because Betti numbers can be used as shape descriptor admitting dissimilarity distances stable under continuous shape deformations [11].

Graph mining: is the application of graph-based methods to structural data sets [12], a survey on graph mining can be found here [13].

Homomorphism: is a function that preserve the operators associated with the specified structure.

Homotopy: Given two maps $f, g : X \to Y$ of topological spaces, f and g are homotopic, $f \simeq g$, if there is a continuous map $H : X \times [0, 1] \to Y$ so that $H(x, 0) = f(x)$ and $H(x, 1) = g(x)$ for all $x \in X$ [14].

Homology: (and cohomology) are algebraic objects associated to a manifold, which give one measure of the number of holes of the object. Computation of the homology groups of topological spaces is a central topic in topology; if the simplicial complex is small, the homology group computations can be done manually; to solve such problems generally a classic algorithm exists [15].

Human–Computer Interaction: study, design and development of the interaction between end users and computers; this classic definition goes back to
the work of Alan Newell and Herbert Simon, and HCI research has in the
last decades focused almost exclusively on ergonomics of the user interface,
while the HCI-KDD approach concentrates almost exclusively on human–
data interaction.

Information Entropy: is a measure of the uncertainty in a random variable.
This refers to the Shannon entropy, which quantifies the expected value of
the information contained in a message.

Manifold: is a fundamental mathematical object which locally resembles a line,
a plane, or space.

Network: Synonym for a graph, which can be defined as an ordered or un-
ordered pair (N, E) of a set N of nodes and a set E of edges [16]. Engineers
often mention: Data + Graph = Network, or call at least directed graphs as
networks; however, in theory, there is no difference between a graph and a
network.

Pattern discovery: subsumes a plethora of machine learning methods to detect complex patterns in data sets [17]; applications thereof are, for instance,
graph mining [18] and string matching [19].

Persistent Homology: Persistent homology is an algebraic tool for measuring
topological features of shapes and functions. It casts the multi-scale organization we frequently observe in nature into a mathematical formalism [20].

Simplicial Complex: is made up of simplices, e.g. a simplicial polytope has
simplices as faces and a simplicial complex is a collection of simplices pasted
together in any reasonable vertex-to-vertex and edge-to-edge arrangement.
A graph is a 1-dim simplicial complex.

Small world networks: are generated based on certain rules with high clustering coefficient [16, 21] but the distances among the vertices are rather
short in average, hence they are somewhat similar to random networks and
they have been found in several classes of biological networks, see [22].

Topological Entropy: is a nonnegative real number that is a measure of the
complexity of a dynamical system [23].

3   The HCI-KDD Approach

Humans are very good at pattern recognition in the low-dimensional space, although humans do not see in three spatial dimensions directly, but rather via
sequences of planar projections integrated in a manner that is *sensed* if not
comprehended. Humans spend a lot of their life time to learn how to infer three-
dimensional spatial data from paired planar projections. Years of practice have
tuned a remarkable ability to extract global structures from representations in
lower dimension. On the other hand, computers can be used to deal with high-
dimensional data, where we can make use of the benefits of computational topology [24], e.g. by replacing a set of point cloud data with a simplicial complex,
which converts the data into global topological objects. To combine the most

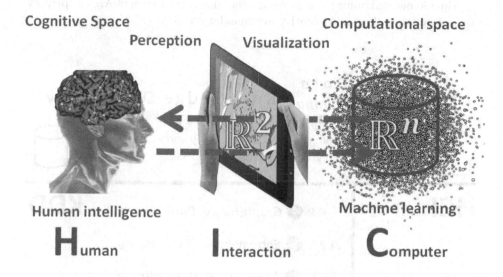

Cognitive Space   Computational space
        Perception   Visualization

Human intelligence   Machine learning

Human   **I**nteraction   **C**omputer

Fig. 1. This image, created originally by A. Holzinger as logo for his group, emphasizes the importance of the interaction between high-dimensional computational spaces in $\mathbb{R}^n$ and highlights the reality that current devices only allow data visualization in $\mathbb{R}^2$. Consequently, the major task of Human–Computer Interaction is to map data from high-dimensional spaces into lower-dimensional spaces, hence enabling interaction, which is the most difficult and challenging task in this field.

desirable of these formidable talents might highly benefit the knowledge discovery process [25]. The most critical and not easy endeavour is in interaction and visualization (see Figure 1).

The original idea of the HCI-KDD [26] approach (Figure 2) is in combining aspects of the best of two worlds: Human–Computer Interaction (HCI), with emphasis on perception, cognition, interaction, reasoning, decision making, human learning and human intelligence, and Knowledge Discovery/Data Mining (KDD), dealing with data processing, computational statistics, artificial intelligence and particularly with machine learning [27].

Whilst interactive knowledge discovery encompasses the horizontal process ranging from physical aspects of data (left in Figure 2) to the human aspects of information processing (right in Figure 2), data mining can be seen vertically and deals specifically with methods, algorithms and tools for finding patterns in the data. In the HCI-KDD approach, seven (the new magical number 7) essential research areas can be determined as outlined in Figure 2, including: Area 1: Data integration, data fusion and data mapping; Area 2: mining algorithms and Area 6: data visualization [28], [29], [30]. This tutorial focuses on three hot topics:

Area 3: Graph-based Data Mining (GDM) [31], [32], [33],[34].
Area 4: Entropy-based Data Mining (EDM) [35], [36].
Area 5: Topological Data Mining (TDM) [37].

In the biomedical domain as in some other domains issues of Area 7: privacy, data protection, safety and security are mandatory [38].

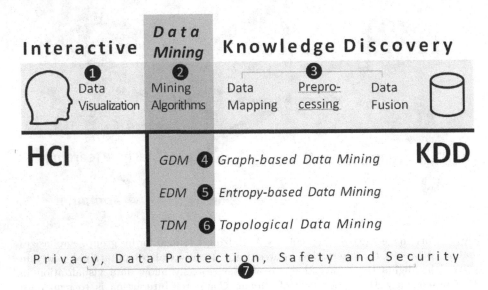

Fig. 2. The big picture of the HCI-KDD approach: KDD encompasses the whole horizontal process chain from data to information and knowledge; actually from physical aspects of raw data, to human aspects including attention, memory, vision, interaction etc. as core topics in HCI, whilst DM as a vertical subject focuses on the development of methods, algorithms and tools for data mining (Image taken from the hci4all.at website, as of May, 2014)

4   Graph-Based Data Mining

Graph-Theory [39] provides powerful tools to map data structures and to find novel connections between single data objects [16, 40]. The inferred graphs can be further analyzed by using graph-theoretical, statistical and machine learning techniques [41]. A mapping of already existing and in medical practice approved *knowledge spaces* as a conceptual graph (as e.g. demonstrated in [32] and a subsequent visual and graph-theoretical analysis can bring novel insights on hidden patterns in the data, which exactly is the goal of knowledge discovery. Another benefit of a graph-based data structure is in the applicability of methods from network topology and network analysis and data mining, e.g. small-world phenomenon [42, 43], and cluster analysis [44, 45]. However, the first question is "How to get a graph?", or simpler "How to get point sets?", because point cloud data sets (PCD) are used as primitives for such approaches. The answer to this question is not trivial (see [46]), apart from "naturally available" point clouds, e.g. from laser scanners, protein structures [47], or text mapped into a set of points (vectors) in $\mathbb{R}^n$. Sticking on the last example, graphs are intuitively more informative as example words/phrase representations [48], and graphs are the best studied data structures in computer science, with a strong relation to logical languages [49]. The beginning of graph-based data mining approaches was two decades ago, some pioneering work include [50–52]. According to [49] there are five theoretical bases of graph-based data mining approaches such as (1) subgraph categories, (2) subgraph isomorphism, (3) graph invariants, (4) mining measures and (5) solution methods. Furthermore, there are five groups of different graph-theoretical approaches for data mining such as (1) greedy search based approach, (2) inductive logic programming based approach, (3) inductive database based approach, (4) mathematical graph theory based approach and (5) kernel function based approach [53]. However, the main disadvantage of graph-theoretical text mining is the computational complexity of the graph representation, consequently the goal of future research in the field of graph-theoretical approaches for text mining is to develop efficient graph mining algorithms which implement effective search strategies and data structures [48].

In [54] a graph-theoretical approach for text mining is used to extract relation information between terms in "free-text" electronic health care records that are semantically or syntactically related. Another field of application is the text analysis of web and social media for detecting influenza-like illnesses [55].

Moreover there can be content-rich relationship networks among biological concepts, genes, proteins and drugs developed with topological text data mining like shown in [56]. According to [57] network medicine describes the clinical application field of topological text mining due to addressing the complexity of human diseases with molecular and phenotypic network maps.

5 Topological Data Mining

Closely related to graph-based methods are topological data mining methods; for both we need point cloud data sets - or at least distances - as input. A set of such primitives forms a space, and if we have finite sets equipped with proximity or similarity measure functions $sim_q : S^{q+1} \rightarrow [0,1]$, which measure how "close" or "similar" $(q+1)$-tuples of elements of S are, we speak about a *topological space*. A value of 0 means totally different objects, while 1 corresponds to equivalent items. Interesting are manifolds, which can be seen as a topological space, which is locally homeomorphic (that means it has a continuous function with an inverse function) to a real n-dimensional space. In other words: X is a d-manifold if every point of X has a neighborhood homeomorphic to $\mathbb{B}^d$; with boundary if every point has a neighborhood homeomorphic to $\mathbb{B}$ or $\mathbb{B}^d_+$ [58].

A topological space may be viewed as an abstraction of a metric space, and similarly, manifolds generalize the connectivity of d-dimensional Euclidean spaces $\mathbb{B}^d$ by being locally similar, but globally different. A d-dimensional chart at $p \in X$ is a homeomorphism $\phi : U \rightarrow \mathbb{R}^d$ onto an open subset of $\mathbb{R}^d$, where U is a neighborhood of p and open is defined using the metric. A d-dimensional manifold (d-manifold) is a topological space X with a d-dimensional chart at every point $x \in X$ [59].

For us also interesting are simplicial complexes ("simplicials") which are spaces described in a very particular way, the basis is in Homology. The reason is that it is not possible to represent surfaces precisely in a computer system due to limited computational storage; thus, surfaces are sampled and represented with triangulations. Such a triangulation is called a simplicial complex, and is a combinatorial space that can represent a space. With such simplicial complexes, the topology of a space from its geometry can be separated. Zomorodian [59] compares it with the separation of syntax and semantics in logic.

Topological techniques originated in pure mathematics, but have been adapted to the study and analysis of data during the past two decades. The two most popular topological techniques in the study of data are *homology* and *persistence*. The connectivity of a space is determined by its cycles of different dimensions. These cycles are organized into groups, called homology groups. Given a reasonably explicit description of a space, the homology groups can be computed with linear algebra. Homology groups have a relatively strong discriminative power and a clear meaning, while having low computational cost. In the study of persistent homology the invariants are in the form of persistence diagrams or barcodes [60].

In data mining it is important to extract significant features, and exactly for this, topological methods are useful, since they provide robust and general feature definitions with emphasis on global information, for example Alpha Shapes [9].

A recent example for topological data mining is given by [61]: Topological text mining, which builds on the well-known vector space model, which is a standard approach in text mining [62]: a collection of text documents (corpus) is mapped into points (=vectors) in $\mathbb{R}^n$. Moreover, each word can be mapped into so-called term vectors, resulting in a very high dimensional vector space. If there are n words extracted from all the documents then each document is mapped to a point (*term vector*) in $\mathbb{R}^\kappa$ with coordinates corresponding to the weights. This way the whole corpus can be transformed into a point cloud data set. Instead of the Euclidean metric the use of a similarity (proximity) measure is sometimes more convenient; the *cosine similarity measure* is a typical example: the cosine of the angle between two vectors (points in the cloud) reflects how "similar" the underlying weighted combinations of keywords are. Amongst the many different text mining methods (for a recent overview refer to [63]); topological approaches are promising, but need a lot of further research.

Due to finding meaningful topological patterns greater information depth can be achieved from the same data input [64]. However, with increasing complexity of the data to process also the need to find a scalable shape characteristic is greater [65]. Therefore methods of the mathematical field of topology are used for complex data areas like the biomedical field [65], [60]. Topology as the mathematical study of shapes and spaces that are not rigid [65], pose a lot of possibilities for the application in knowledge discovery and data mining, as topology is the study of connectivity information and it deals with qualitative geometric properties [66].

One of the main tasks of applied topology is to find and analyse higher dimensional topological structures in lower dimensional spaces (e.g. point cloud from vector space model as discussed in [64]). A common way to describe topological spaces is to first create simplicial complexes, because a simplicial complex structure on a topological space is an expression of the space as a union of simplices such as points, intervals, triangles, and higher dimensional analogues. Simplicial complexes provide an easy combinatorial way to define certain topological spaces [66]. A simplical complex K is defined as a finite collection of simplices such that $\sigma \in K$ and τ, which is a face of σ, implies $\tau \in K$, and $\sigma, \sigma' \in K$ implies $\sigma \cap \sigma'$ can either be a face of both σ and σ' or empty [67]. One way to create a simplical complex is to examine all subsets of points, and if any subsets of points are close enough, a p-simplex (e.g. line) is added to the complex with those points as vertices. For instance, a Vietoris-Rips complex of diameter ϵ is defined as $VR(\epsilon) = \sigma | diam(\sigma) \leq \epsilon$, where $diam(\epsilon)$ is defined as the largest distance between two points in σ [67]. A common way a analyse the topological structure is to use persistent homology, which identifies cluster, holes and voids therein. It is assumed that more robust topological structures are the one which persist with increasing ϵ. For detailed information about persistent homology, see [67], [68], [69].

6   Entropy-Based Data Mining

In the real medical world, we are confronted not only with complex and high-dimensional data sets, but usually with sparse, noisy, incomplete and uncertain data, where the application of traditional methods of knowledge discovery and data mining always entail the danger of modeling artifacts. Originally, information entropy was introduced by Shannon (1949), as a measure of *uncertainty in the data*. To date, there have emerged many different types of entropy methods with a large number of different purposes and applications. Here we mention only two:

Graph Entropy was described by [70] to measure structural information content of graphs, and a different definition, more focused on problems in information and coding theory, was introduced by Körner in [71]. Graph entropy is often used for the characterization of the structure of graph-based systems, e.g. in mathematical biochemistry, but also for any complex network [72]. In these applications the entropy of a graph is interpreted as its structural information content and serves as a complexity measure, and such a measure is associated with an equivalence relation defined on a finite graph; by application of Shannons Equation with the probability distribution we get a numerical value that serves as an index of the structural feature captured by the equivalence relation [41].

Topological Entropy (TopEn), was introduced by [73] with the purpose to introduce the notion of entropy as an invariant for continuous mappings: Let (X, T) be a topological dynamical system, i.e., let X be a nonempty compact

Hausdorff space and $T : X \to X$ a continuous map; the TopEn is a nonnegative number which measures the complexity of the system [74].

Hornero et al. [75] performed a complexity analysis of intracranial pressure dynamics during periods of severe intracranial hypertension. For that purpose they analyzed eleven episodes of intracranial hypertension from seven patients. They measured the changes in the intracranial pressure complexity by applying ApEn, as patients progressed from a state of normal intracranial pressure to intracranial hypertension, and found that a decreased complexity of intracranial pressure coincides with periods of intracranial hypertension in brain injury. Their approach is of particular interest to us, because they proposed classification based on ApEn tendencies instead of absolute values.

Pincus et al. took in [76] heart rate recordings of 45 healthy infants with recordings of an infant one week after an aborted sudden infant death syndrom (SIDS) episode. They then calculated the ApEn of these recordings and found a significant smaller value for the aborted SIDS infant compared to the healthy ones.

Holzinger et al. (2012) [77] experimented with point cloud data sets in the two dimensional space: They developed a model of handwriting, and evaluated the performance of entropy based slant and skew correction, and compared the results to other methods. This work is the basis for further entropy-based approaches, which are very relevant for advanced entropy-based data mining approaches.

7   Conclusion and Future Outlook

Discovering knowledge in complex, high-dimensional data sets needs a concerted effort of various topics, ranging from data preprocessing, data fusion, data integration and data mapping to interactive visualization within a low-dimensional space. For this reason, graph-based and topological methods are very useful, since they provide robust and general feature definitions and may support a "global information view". A promising area of future research is in graph-theoretical approaches for text mining, in particular to develop efficient graph mining algorithms which implement robust and efficient search strategies and data structures [48]. Such approaches could be combined with techniques from machine learning, e.g. multi-agents and evolutionary algorithms [78]. However, there remain many open questions, for example about the graph characteristics and the isomorphism complexity [49], to mention just only one. A further promising research route is to combine such methods with entropy-based approaches, which have extensively been applied for analyzing sparse and noisy time series data, but so far have not yet been applied to weakly structured data in combination with techniques from computational topology. Consequently, the inclusion of entropy measures for discovery of knowledge in high-dimensional biomedical data is a big future issue, opening a lot of challenging research routes [35].

The grand vision for the future is to effectively support human learning with machine learning. The HCI-KDD network of excellence is proactively supporting this vision in bringing together people with diverse background - sharing a common goal: finding solutions for dealing with big and complex data sets. A recent output of the network can be found here [79] (for more information please refer to www.hci4all.at).

Acknowledgments. The author is very grateful for the friendly support of Dominik Slezak, Jerzy Stefanowski, Juzhen Dong and Andrzej Skowron.

References

1. Holzinger, A., Dehmer, M., Jurisica, I.: Knowledge discovery and interactive data mining in bioinformatics - state-of-the-art, future challenges and research directions. BMC Bioinformatics 15, I1 (2014)
2. Holzinger, A.: Biomedical Informatics: Discovering Knowledge in Big Data. Springer, New York (2014)
3. Wu, X.D., Zhu, X.Q., Wu, G.Q., Ding, W.: Data mining with big data. IEEE Transactions on Knowledge and Data Engineering 26, 97–107 (2014)
4. Huppertz, B., Holzinger, A.: Biobanks – A source of large biological data sets: Open problems and future challenges. In: Holzinger, A., Jurisica, I. (eds.) Knowledge Discovery and Data Mining. LNCS, vol. 8401, pp. 317–330. Springer, Heidelberg (2014)
5. Mattmann, C.A.: Computing: A vision for data science. Nature 493, 473–475 (2013)
6. Otasek, D., Pastrello, C., Holzinger, A., Jurisica, I.: Visual data mining: Effective exploration of the biological universe. In: Holzinger, A., Jurisica, I. (eds.) Knowledge Discovery and Data Mining. LNCS, vol. 8401, pp. 19–33. Springer, Heidelberg (2014)
7. Hatcher, A.: Algebraic Topology. Cambridge University Press, Cambridge (2002)
8. Edelsbrunner, H., Kirkpatrick, D., Seidel, R.: On the shape of a set of points in the plane. IEEE Transactions on Information Theory 29, 551–559 (1983)
9. Edelsbrunner, H., Mucke, E.P.: 3-dimensional alpha-shapes. ACM Transactions on Graphics 13, 43–72 (1994)
10. Albou, L.P., Schwarz, B., Poch, O., Wurtz, J.M., Moras, D.: Defining and characterizing protein surface using alpha shapes. Proteins-Structure Function and Bioinformatics 76, 1–12 (2009)
11. Frosini, P., Landi, C.: Persistent betti numbers for a noise tolerant shape-based approach to image retrieval. Pattern Recognition Letters 34, 863–872 (2013)
12. Cook, D., Holder, L.B.: Mining Graph Data. Wiley Interscience (2007)
13. Chakrabarti, D., Faloutsos, C.: Graph mining: Laws, generators, and algorithms. ACM Computing Surveys (CSUR) 38, 2 (2006)
14. Whitehead, G.W.: Elements of homotopy theory. Springer (1978)
15. Munkres, J.R.: Elements of algebraic topology, vol. 2. Addison-Wesley Reading (1984)
16. Dorogovtsev, S., Mendes, J.: Evolution of networks: From biological nets to the Internet and WWW. Oxford University Press (2003)
17. Duda, R.O., Hart, P.E., Stork, D.G.: Pattern Classification, vol. 2. Wiley, New York (2000)
18. Cook, D.J., Holder, L.B.: Graph-based data mining. IEEE Intelligent Systems and their Applications 15, 32–41 (2000)

19. Gusfield, D.: Algorithms on Strings, Trees, and Sequences: Computer Science and Computational Biology. Cambridge University Press (1997)

20. Edelsbrunner, H., Harer, J.: Persistent homology - a survey. Contemporary Mathematics Series, vol. 453, pp. 257–282. Amer Mathematical Soc., Providence (2008)

21. Watts, D.J., Strogatz, S.H.: Collective dynamics of 'small-world' networks. Nature 393, 440–442 (1998)

22. Emmert-Streib, F., Dehmer, M.: Networks for systems biology: Conceptual connection of data and function. IET Systems Biology 5, 185–207 (2011)

23. Koslicki, D.: Topological entropy of dna sequences. Bioinformatics 27, 1061–1067 (2011)

24. Ghrist, R.: Barcodes: the persistent topology of data. Bulletin of the American Mathematical Society 45, 61–75 (2008)

25. Holzinger, A.: Human-computer interaction and knowledge discovery (HCI-KDD): What is the benefit of bringing those two fields to work together? In: Cuzzocrea, A., Kittl, C., Simos, D.E., Weippl, E., Xu, L. (eds.) CD-ARES 2013. LNCS, vol. 8127, pp. 319–328. Springer, Heidelberg (2013)

26. Holzinger, A.: On knowledge discovery and interactive intelligent visualization of biomedical data - challenges in human–computer interaction and biomedical informatics. In: DATA 2012, Rome, Italy, pp. 9–20 (2012)

27. Holzinger, A., Jurisica, I.: Knowledge discovery and data mining in biomedical informatics: The future is in integrative, interactive machine learning solutions. In: Holzinger, A., Jurisica, I. (eds.) Knowledge Discovery and Data Mining. LNCS, vol. 8401, pp. 1–18. Springer, Heidelberg (2014)

28. Holzinger, A., Bruschi, M., Eder, W.: On interactive data visualization of physiological low-cost-sensor data with focus on mental stress. In: Cuzzocrea, A., Kittl, C., Simos, D.E., Weippl, E., Xu, L. (eds.) CD-ARES 2013. LNCS, vol. 8127, pp. 469–480. Springer, Heidelberg (2013)

29. Wong, B.L.W., Xu, K., Holzinger, A.: Interactive visualization for information analysis in medical diagnosis. In: Holzinger, A., Simonic, K.-M. (eds.) USAB 2011. LNCS, vol. 7058, pp. 109–120. Springer, Heidelberg (2011)

30. Wiltgen, M., Holzinger, A., Tilz, G.P.: Interactive analysis and visualization of macromolecular interfaces between proteins. In: Holzinger, A. (ed.) USAB 2007. LNCS, vol. 4799, pp. 199–212. Springer, Heidelberg (2007)

31. Preuss, M., Dehmer, M., Pickl, S., Holzinger, A.: On terrain coverage optimization by using a network approach for universal graph-based data mining and knowledge discovery. In: Proceedings of the Active Media Technology - 10th International Conference, AMT 2014, Warsaw, Poland, August 11-14. LNCS, vol. 8610, Springer, Heidelberg (2014)

32. Holzinger, A., Ofner, B., Dehmer, M.: Multi-touch graph-based interaction for knowledge discovery on mobile devices: State-of-the-art and future challenges. In: Holzinger, A., Jurisica, I. (eds.) Knowledge Discovery and Data Mining. LNCS, vol. 8401, pp. 241–254. Springer, Heidelberg (2014)

33. Holzinger, A., Malle, B., Aigner, R., Giuliani, N.: On graph extraction from image data. In: Slezak, D., Schaefer, G., Vuong, T.S., Kim, Y.S. (eds.) Active Media Technology AMT 2014. LNCS, vol. 8610, Springer, Heidelberg (2014)

34. Holzinger, A., Ofner, B., Stocker, C., Calero Valdez, A., Schaar, A.K., Ziefle, M., Dehmer, M.: On graph entropy measures for knowledge discovery from publication network data. In: Cuzzocrea, A., Kittl, C., Simos, D.E., Weippl, E., Xu, L. (eds.) CD-ARES 2013. LNCS, vol. 8127, pp. 354–362. Springer, Heidelberg (2013)

35. Holzinger, A., Hörtenhuber, M., Mayer, C., Bachler, M., Wassertheurer, S., Pinho, A.J., Koslicki, D.: On entropy-based data mining. In: Holzinger, A., Jurisica, I. (eds.) Interactive Knowledge Discovery and Data Mining in Biomedical Informatics. LNCS, vol. 8401, pp. 209–226. Springer, Heidelberg (2014)

36. Holzinger, A., Stocker, C., Bruschi, M., Auinger, A., Silva, H., Gamboa, H., Fred, A.: On applying approximate entropy to ECG signals for knowledge discovery on the example of big sensor data. In: Huang, R., Ghorbani, A.A., Pasi, G., Yamaguchi, T., Yen, N.Y., Jin, B. (eds.) AMT 2012. LNCS, vol. 7669, pp. 646–657. Springer, Heidelberg (2012)

37. Holzinger, A.: On topological data mining. In: Holzinger, A., Jurisica, I. (eds.) Interactive Knowledge Discovery and Data Mining in Biomedical Informatics. LNCS, vol. 8401, pp. 331–356. Springer, Heidelberg (2014)

38. Kieseberg, P., Hobel, H., Schrittwieser, S., Weippl, E., Holzinger, A.: Protecting anonymity in data-driven biomedical science. In: Holzinger, A., Jurisica, I. (eds.) Interactive Knowledge Discovery and Data Mining in Biomedical Informatics. LNCS, vol. 8401, pp. 301–316. Springer, Heidelberg (2014)

39. Harary, F.: Structural models. An introduction to the theory of directed graphs. Wiley (1965)

40. Strogatz, S.: Exploring complex networks. Nature 410, 268–276 (2001)

41. Dehmer, M., Mowshowitz, A.: A history of graph entropy measures. Information Sciences 181, 57–78 (2011)

42. Barabasi, A.L., Albert, R.: Emergence of scaling in random networks. Science 286, 509–512 (1999)

43. Kleinberg, J.: Navigation in a small world. Nature 406, 845–845 (2000)

44. Koontz, W., Narendra, P., Fukunaga, K.: A graph-theoretic approach to nonparametric cluster analysis. IEEE Transactions on Computers 100, 936–944 (1976)

45. Wittkop, T., Emig, D., Truss, A., Albrecht, M., Boecker, S., Baumbach, J.: Comprehensive cluster analysis with transitivity clustering. Nature Protocols 6, 285–295 (2011)

46. Holzinger, A., Malle, B., Bloice, M., Wiltgen, M., Ferri, M., Stanganelli, I., Hofmann-Wellenhof, R.: On the generation of point cloud data sets: Step one in the knowledge discovery process. In: Holzinger, A., Jurisica, I. (eds.) Knowledge Discovery and Data Mining. LNCS, vol. 8401, pp. 57–80. Springer, Heidelberg (2014)

47. Canutescu, A.A., Shelenkov, A.A., Dunbrack, R.L.: A graph-theory algorithm for rapid protein side-chain prediction. Protein science 12, 2001–2014 (2003)

48. Jiang, C., Coenen, F., Sanderson, R., Zito, M.: Text classification using graph mining-based feature extraction. Knowledge-Based Systems 23, 302–308 (2010)

49. Washio, T., Motoda, H.: State of the art of graph-based data mining. ACM SIGKDD Explorations Newsletter 5, 59 (2003)

50. Cook, D.J., Holder, L.B.: Substructure discovery using minimum description length and background knowledge. J. Artif. Int. Res. 1, 231–255 (1994)

51. Yoshida, K., Motoda, H., Indurkhya, N.: Graph-based induction as a unified learning framework. Applied Intelligence 4, 297–316 (1994)

52. Dehaspe, L., Toivonen, H.: Discovery of frequent DATALOG patterns. Data Mining and Knowledge Discovery 3, 7–36 (1999)

53. Windridge, D., Bober, M.: A kernel-based framework for medical big-data analytics. In: Holzinger, A., Jurisica, I. (eds.) Knowledge Discovery and Data Mining. LNCS, vol. 8401, pp. 197–208. Springer, Heidelberg (2014)

54. Zhou, X., Han, H., Chankai, I., Prestrud, A., Brooks, A.: Approaches to text mining for clinical medical records. In: Proceedings of the 2006 ACM symposium on Applied computing - SAC 2006, p. 235. ACM Press, New York (2006)

55. Corley, C.D., Cook, D.J., Mikler, A.R., Singh, K.P.: Text and structural data mining of influenza mentions in Web and social media. International journal of environmental research and public health 7, 596–615 (2010)

56. Chen, H., Sharp, B.M.: Content-rich biological network constructed by mining PubMed abstracts. BMC bioinformatics 5, 147 (2004)

57. Barabási, A., Gulbahce, N., Loscalzo, J.: Network medicine: a network-based approach to human disease. Nature Reviews Genetics 12, 56–68 (2011)

58. Cannon, J.W.: The recognition problem: what is a topological manifold? Bulletin of the American Mathematical Society 84, 832–866 (1978)

59. Zomorodian, A.: Chapman & Hall/CRC Applied Algorithms and Data Structures series. In: Computational Topology, pp. 1–31. Chapman and Hall, Boca Raton (2010), doi:10.1201/9781584888215-c3.

60. Epstein, C., Carlsson, G., Edelsbrunner, H.: Topological data analysis. Inverse Problems 27, 120201 (2011)

61. Wagner, H., Dlotko, P.: Towards topological analysis of high-dimensional feature spaces. Computer Vision and Image Understanding 121, 21–26 (2014)

62. Kobayashi, M., Aono, M.: Vector space models for search and cluster mining. In: Berry, M.W. (ed.) Survey of Text Mining: Clustering, Classification, and Retrieval, pp. 103–122. Springer, New York (2004)

63. Holzinger, A., Schantl, J., Schroettner, M., Seifert, C., Verspoor, K.: Biomedical text mining: State-of-the-art, open problems and future challenges. In: Holzinger, A., Jurisica, I. (eds.) Interactive Knowledge Discovery and Data Mining in Biomedical Informatics. LNCS, vol. 8401, pp. 271–300. Springer, Heidelberg (2014)

64. Wagner, H., Dlotko, P., Mrozek, M.: Computational topology in text mining. In: Ferri, M., Frosini, P., Landi, C., Cerri, A., Di Fabio, B. (eds.) CTIC 2012. LNCS, vol. 7309, pp. 68–78. Springer, Heidelberg (2012)

65. Nicolau, M., Levine, A.J., Carlsson, G.: Topology based data analysis identifies a subgroup of breast cancers with a unique mutational profile and excellent survival. Proceedings of the National Academy of Sciences of the United States of America 108, 7265–7270 (2011)

66. Carlsson, G.: Topology and Data. Bull. Amer. Math. Soc. 46, 255–308 (2009)

67. Zhu, X.: Persistent homology: An introduction and a new text representation for natural language processing. In: Rossi, F. (ed.) IJCAI. IJCAI/AAAI (2013)

68. Cerri, A., Fabio, B.D., Ferri, M., Frosini, P., Landi, C.: Betti numbers in multidimensional persistent homology are stable functions. Mathematical Methods in the Applied Sciences 36, 1543–1557 (2013)

69. Bubenik, P., Kim, P.T.: A statistical approach to persistent homology. Homology, Homotopy and Applications 9, 337–362 (2007)

70. Mowshowitz, A.: Entropy and the complexity of graphs: I. an index of the relative complexity of a graph. The Bulletin of Mathematical Biophysics 30, 175–204 (1968)

71. Körner, J.: Coding of an information source having ambiguous alphabet and the entropy of graphs. In: 6th Prague Conference on Information Theory, pp. 411–425 (1973)

72. Holzinger, A., Ofner, B., Stocker, C., Calero Valdez, A., Schaar, A.K., Ziefle, M., Dehmer, M.: On graph entropy measures for knowledge discovery from publication network data. In: Cuzzocrea, A., Kittl, C., Simos, D.E., Weippl, E., Xu, L. (eds.) CD-ARES 2013. LNCS, vol. 8127, pp. 354–362. Springer, Heidelberg (2013)

73. Adler, R.L., Konheim, A.G., McAndrew, M.H.: Topological entropy. Transactions of the American Mathematical Society 114, 309–319 (1965)

74. Adler, R., Downarowicz, T., Misiurewicz, M.: Topological entropy. Scholarpedia 3, 2200 (2008)

75. Hornero, R., Aboy, M., Abasolo, D., McNames, J., Wakeland, W., Goldstein, B.: Complex analysis of intracranial hypertension using approximate entropy. Crit. Care Med. 34, 87–95 (2006)

76. Pincus, S.M.: Approximate entropy as a measure of system complexity. Proceedings of the National Academy of Sciences 88, 2297–2301 (1991)

77. Holzinger, A., Stocker, C., Peischl, B., Simonic, K.M.: On using entropy for enhancing handwriting preprocessing. Entropy 14, 2324–2350 (2012)

78. Holzinger, K., Palade, V., Rabadan, R., Holzinger, A.: Darwin or lamarck? Future challenges in evolutionary algorithms for knowledge discovery and data mining. In: Holzinger, A., Jurisica, I. (eds.) Knowledge Discovery and Data Mining. LNCS, vol. 8401, pp. 35–56. Springer, Heidelberg (2014)

79. Holzinger, A., Jurisica, I.: Knowledge discovery and data mining in biomedical informatics: The future is in integrative, interactive machine learning solutions. In: Holzinger, A., Jurisica, I. (eds.) Interactive Knowledge Discovery and Data Mining in Biomedical Informatics. LNCS, vol. 8401, pp. 1–18. Springer, Heidelberg (2014)

Characterization of Subgroup Patterns from Graphical Representation of Genomic Data

Sangkyun Lee

Fakultät für Informatik, LS VIII
Technische Universität Dortmund, 44221 Dortmund, Germany
sangkyun.lee@tu-dortmund.de

Abstract. High-throughput genomic profiling technology provides us detailed information of biological systems. However, it also increases the dimensionality in data, which makes it harder to identify key features and their relations to other features hidden in feature spaces. In this paper we propose a new idea based on the structure learning for the Gaussian Markov random field, which provides us an efficient way to represent a feature space as a collection of small graphs, where nodes represent features and edges represent conditional dependency between features. In our approach a collection of small graphs is created for each subgroup of a cohort, where our interest lies in finding characteristic patterns in each subgroup graph compared to the other subgroup graphs. A simple but effective method is proposed using polarized adjacency matrices to find topological differences in collections of graphs.

Keywords: Graph Patterns, Adjacency Matrix, Gaussian Markov Random Field, Structure Learning, Sparse Inverse Covariance Matrix.

1 Introduction

Modern high-throughput genomic profiling technologies provide us fine details about biological systems. For example, whole-transcript microarrays or next generation sequencing provide information on thousands or millions subsequences of human DNA and their products. As these technologies become more accessible at lower cost, they become a popular basis for modern computational biology studies [15].

One of the goals in computational biology studies using high-throughput genomic profiles is to identify so-called biomarkers from a large amount of features representing genes, exons, miRNAs, etc., that contribute to the development of certain diseases. These biomarkers are also studied in terms of their relations to other features, so that we can hopefully identify controllable parts of biochemical circuits that may affect disease development. However, when the number of features to be considered is very large, it becomes challenging to find biomarkers and their relations so to understand the underlying systems.

Structure learning of feature space can help identify the relations among features, and especially a graphical representation of such structure can be useful

D. Ślęzak et al. (Eds.): BIH 2014, LNAI 8609, pp. 516–527, 2014.

since graphs provide decomposable view of structures. For this purpose, a simple probabilistic graphical model, called the *Gaussian Markov random field* (Gaussian MRF or GMRF), fits well, for which efficient structure learning methods are also available.

Gaussian MRFs have been quite popular in various areas such as biostatistics [10, 14, 41] and image analysis [6, 11, 26]. The first idea of structure learning of GMRFs goes back to covariance selection [8] and model selection problems for the Gaussian concentration graphs [5]. However, efficient methods for structure learning of GMRFs have been appeared only recently beginning with [29], and finally a convex optimization framework combining parameter estimation and model selection steps was first proposed in [43], which became a focus of many research areas including machine learning, statistics, and optimization [1,12,13,43].

Since the outcome of structure learning is a graph, it is natural to consider visualizing the graphical structure to aid our understanding and to better use our insights toward comprehending complex systems. This is also the key element in the HCI-KDD approach [16, 31, 38], which searches for a tight integration of computer analysis with human interpretation.

2 Structure Learning of Gaussian MRFs

2.1 Gaussian Markov Random Field (GMRF)

Briefly speaking, the Markov random field (MRF) is a collection of p random variables represented as nodes in a graph, where the conditional dependency structure of nodes is represented by undirected edges between nodes. We denote a graph by $G = (V, E)$, where V is the set of all nodes ($|V| = p$ in our setting) and E is the set of all edges. A graph is an MRF if its elements satisfy the Markov properties [34], which also enable us to compute the joint probability function of the random variables in a factorized form.

The Gaussian MRF (GMRF) is a special type of MRFs, where the random variables, collected as elements in a vector $\mathbf{x} \in \Re^p$, follow the multivariate Gaussian distribution $\mathcal{N}(\mu, \Sigma)$ with a mean vector μ and a covariance matrix Σ, whose probability density function is expressed as

$$p(\mathbf{x}) = (2\pi)^{-p/2} \det(\Sigma)^{-1/2} \exp\left(-\frac{1}{2}(\mathbf{x} - \mu)^T \Sigma^{-1}(\mathbf{x} - \mu)\right).$$

For the Gaussian MRF, the Markov properties simplify to the condition that whenever the (i, j)th entry of the inverse covariance matrix (also known as the precision matrix) $\Sigma_{ij}^{-1} = 0$, then there exists no edge between the two nodes i and j [34]. The condition $\Sigma_{ij}^{-1} = 0$ also implies that the two random variables $\mathbf{x}_i$ and $\mathbf{x}_j$ associated with the nodes i and j are *conditionally independent* given all the other nodes [20], i.e.,

$$\Sigma_{ij}^{-1} = 0 \quad \Leftrightarrow \quad \begin{aligned} &P(\mathbf{x}_i, \mathbf{x}_j | \{\mathbf{x}_k\}_{k \in \{1,2,...,p\} \setminus \{i,j\}}) \\ &= P(\mathbf{x}_i | \{\mathbf{x}_k\}_{k \in \{1,2,...,p\} \setminus \{i,j\}}) P(\mathbf{x}_j | \{\mathbf{x}_k\}_{k \in \{1,2,...,p\} \setminus \{i,j\}}). \end{aligned} \tag{1}$$

This can be summarized as that the graph G of a GMRF represents the conditional (in)dependence structure of a feature space from which the vectors $\mathbf{x}$ are sampled.

In general, the entries of the inverse covariance matrix represent conditional correlation between the corresponding random variables [20]. When the underlying distribution is the Gaussian, $\Sigma_{ij}^{-1} = 0$ also implies conditional independence of the two random variables $\mathbf{x}_i$ and $\mathbf{x}_j$, giving our statement in (1).

2.2   Structure Learning of GMRFs

As we discussed, the graphical structure of a GMRF is determined by the nonzero patterns in the inverse covariance matrix Σ^{-1}. To estimate such a matrix, we use the framework of the maximum likelihood estimation as described in the following. Let us denote a collection of n feature vectors $\mathbf{x}^1, \mathbf{x}^2, \ldots, \mathbf{x}^n$, each with length p, sampled independently and identically from a multivariate Gaussian distribution $\mathcal{N}(\mathbf{0}, \Sigma^{-1})$, whose distribution function is given by,

$$p(\mathbf{x}) = (2\pi)^{-p/2} \det(\Sigma)^{-1/2} \exp\left(-\frac{1}{2}\mathbf{x}^T \Sigma^{-1} \mathbf{x}\right).$$

The mean of the Gaussian is assumed to be the zero vector without loss of generality (the observations can be simply centered to achieve this). The likelihood function to describe the chance to observe the collection of the n feature vectors $\mathcal{D} = \{\mathbf{x}^1, \mathbf{x}^2, \ldots, \mathbf{x}^n\}$ from $\mathcal{N}(\mathbf{0}, \Sigma^{-1})$ is written as,

$$L(\Sigma^{-1}, \mathcal{D}) = \prod_{i=1}^{n} p(\mathbf{x}^i) \sim \prod_{i=1}^{n} \det(\Sigma)^{-1/2} \exp\left(-\frac{1}{2}(\mathbf{x}^i)^T \Sigma^{-1} \mathbf{x}^i\right).$$

Therefore the log likelihood function (omitting constant terms and scaled by $2/n$) becomes,

$$LL(\Sigma^{-1}, \mathcal{D}) = \log\det(\Sigma^{-1}) - \mathrm{tr}(S\Sigma^{-1}), \tag{2}$$

where $S := \frac{1}{n}\sum_{i=1}^{n} \mathbf{x}^i(\mathbf{x}^i)^T$ is the sample covariance matrix and $\mathrm{tr}(A)$ is the trace (the sum of diagonal elements) of a square matrix A. Our task is then finding a matrix $\Sigma^{-1} \in \Re^{p \times p}$ that maximizes the log likelihood function.

2.3   Sparsity in the Inverse Covariance Matrix

Amongst the inverse covariance matrices that maximize the log likelihood function in (2), we prefer to finding a matrix that is as sparse as possible, in other words, having as many zero entries as possible. The reason is that otherwise the resulting graphical structure of the GMRF will be densely connected, in which case interpretation or visualization becomes difficult.

A typical way to obtain a sparse Σ^{-1} is to minimize the ℓ_1 norm of the matrix (as defined below) together with maximizing the log likelihood function. A convex minimization problem achieving both goals can be described as follows,

$$\min_{\Theta \in \Re^{p \times p}} \quad -LL(\Theta, \mathcal{D}) + \lambda\|\Theta\|_1$$

$$\text{subject to } \Theta \succ 0, \ \Theta^T = \Theta. \tag{3}$$

Here Σ^{-1} has been replaced by Θ for notational convenience. We use the ℓ_1 norm of Θ defined by

$$\|\Theta\|_1 := \sum_{i=1}^{p} \sum_{j=1}^{p} |\Theta_{ij}|,$$

whose value becomes small when Θ is sparse. The parameter $\lambda > 0$ in (2) therefore controls how sparse the matrix Θ will be, that is, large values of λ will produce sparser solutions. The constraints $\Theta = \Theta^T$ and $\Theta \succ 0$ specify that the matrix Θ should be symmetric and positive definite (that is, all of its eigenvalues are strictly positive). These are required to be consistent with the fact that Σ is a covariance matrix (which is symmetric positive semidefinite) and that Σ^{-1} should be invertible so that $S = (\Sigma^{-1})^{-1}$ is well defined. Regularizing the ℓ_1 norm is known to induce sparsity in solutions and used in many recent applications such as penalized regression with the lasso [37] or the elastic net [45] regularizer, online manifold identification [23], spatio-temporal Markov random fields [33], and compressed sensing [2, 22].

Collecting the formulations in (2) and (3), we can summarize the structure learning with GMRFs as follows:

$$\min_{\Theta \in \mathfrak{R}^{p \times p}} \quad -\log \det \Theta + \mathrm{tr}(S\Theta) + \lambda \|\Theta\|_1$$

$$\text{subject to } \Theta \succ 0, \; \Theta^T = \Theta. \tag{4}$$

In this optimization problem the sample covariance matrix $S := \frac{1}{n} \sum_{i=1}^{n} \mathbf{x}^i (\mathbf{x}^i)^T \in \mathfrak{R}^{p \times p}$ is the only input. Depending on the number of features p, the entire matrix S can be computed and given to the optimization, or its entries can be computed on-the-fly as required during optimization.

2.4   Polarized Adjacency Matrices

From the solution Θ^* of the optimization problem in (4), we can construct an adjacency matrix A as follows that represents the associated GMRF graph G,

$$A_{ij} = \begin{cases} 1 & \text{if } \Theta_{ij}^* \neq 0, \\ 0 & \text{if } \Theta_{ij}^* = 0 \text{ or } i = j, \end{cases} \quad \text{for } i, j = 1, 2, \ldots, p.$$

Here each row (and column) corresponds to a node, and when $A_{ij} = 1$ there is an edge between two nodes i and j, and no edge if $A_{ij} = 0$. The diagonal of A is set to zero since we do not consider self-connections of nodes.

For each entry A_{ij}, we also consider the associated *polarity* representing if the correlation between the two nodes i and j is positive or negative. Such information comes from the covariance matrix S which is already created as an input to the problem (4). Using this, we define the *polarized adjacency matrix* $\tilde{A}$,

$$\tilde{A}_{ij} = \begin{cases} +1 & \text{if } \Theta_{ij}^* \neq 0 \text{ and } S_{ij} > 0 \text{ for } i \neq j, \\ -1 & \text{if } \Theta_{ij}^* \neq 0 \text{ and } S_{ij} < 0 \text{ for } i \neq j, \\ 0 & \text{if } \Theta_{ij}^* = 0 \text{ or } i = j. \end{cases} \tag{5}$$

3   Finding Differences in Subgroup Graphs

With a cohort of n patients, suppose that there are K subgroups of patients according to clinical data, defined by grades or stages of a disease, age groups, genders, responds to a therapy, etc. The structure learning with GMRF problem (4) can be solve for each subgroup separately, to generate K polarized adjacency matrices $\tilde{A}^1, \tilde{A}^2, \ldots, \tilde{A}^K$ where $\tilde{A}^k$ represents the subgroup graph G^k of features.

Our interest is to characterize topological differences between two graphs corresponding to two different subgroups represented by $\tilde{A}^r$ and $\tilde{A}^s$, for $r \neq s$, in order to facilitate the identification of differences in features (nodes) and differences in feature relations (edges). The numbers of nodes and edges in "difference graphs" are expected to be smaller than the numbers in the original graphs, and therefore finding difference graphs will enable us to generate more understandable representations and visualizations.

Finding differences in graphs can be seen as an instance of the (sub)graph isomorphism problem checking if connected components from graphs G^r and G^s match or not. However, (sub)graph isomorphism problems are typically very costly to solve [36,39,42], and therefore we suggest a simple alternative algorithm comparing edges between two graphs based on the polarized adjacency matrices (5) and then consider only the connected components according to differences in edges.

3.1   Polarized Edge Difference

Before discussing a difference graph, we first define a matrix J that represents polarized edge differences, for which the meaning will be clear as we explain the definition. For two polarized adjacency matrices $\tilde{A}^r$ and $\tilde{A}^s$, $r \neq s$, we define

$$J^{rs} = |\tilde{A}^r - \tilde{A}^s|, \quad \text{for } r, s = 1, \ldots, K. \tag{6}$$

Here the absolute value operator is taken for each element of a matrix. The elements of this matrix satisfy the following properties:

$(i) \quad J_{ij}^{rs} = 0 \quad \Leftrightarrow \quad \tilde{A}_{ij}^r = \tilde{A}_{ij}^s,$

$(ii) \quad J_{ij}^{rs} = 1 \quad \Leftrightarrow \quad$ One of $|\tilde{A}_{ij}^r|$ or $|\tilde{A}_{ij}^s|$ is 1, the other is 0,

$(iii) \quad J_{ij}^{rs} = 2 \quad \Leftrightarrow \quad \tilde{A}_{ij}^r = -\tilde{A}_{ij}^s.$

The above three cases correspond to (i) if an edge is shared with the same polarity, (ii) if an edge exists only in one graph but not in the other graph, or (iii) if an edge exists in both graphs but with different polarities. Note that J^{rs} is symmetric in terms of the arguments r and s.

3.2   Polarized Graph Subtraction

Using the matrix J^{rs} in (6), we define our "difference graph" as the polarized graph subtraction $G^r - G^s$, defined in terms of its adjacency matrix $A(G^r - G^s)$,

$$A(G^r - G^s)_{ij} = \begin{cases} 1 & \text{if } A^r_{ij} = 1 \text{ and } J^{rs}_{ij} = 1, \\ \kappa & \text{if } J^{rs}_{ij} = 2, \\ 0 & \text{otherwise.} \end{cases} \qquad (7)$$

This matrix represents a graph having the edges from G^r which is not in G^s, and the edges shared between the two graphs but with different polarities (indicated by the value $\kappa \geq 1$). If $\kappa = 1$ is chosen then $A(G^r - G^s)$ becomes a regular adjacency matrix, but $\kappa > 1$ can be used to display the corresponding edges differently in visualization, for example. Note that when $J^{rs}_{ij} = 2$, then $A^r_{ij} = 1$ is implied and therefore the condition is omitted.

The time complexity of computing (7) is $\mathcal{O}(p^2)$, and therefore $(K^2 p^2)$ for all pairwise comparisons of K subgroup graphs. However, they can be drastically reduced by considering only the connected components in graphs, given that there are only a few small connected components in each graph. (In this case the above definitions have to be modified to consider the union of nodes from the connected components of two graphs.)

4   Experiments

To demonstrate our proposed approach, we used a genomic data set consisting of gene expression profiles of $p = 20492$ features (genes, more specifically, transcripts) from $n = 362$ breast cancer patients.

4.1   Data Preparation

Our data set was created by combining three publicly available gene expression data sets from the Gene Expression Omnibus (GEO)[1] with the accession IDs GSE1456, GSE7390, and GSE11121. All gene expression profiles in the three data sets were obtained with the Affymetrix GeneChip Human Genome HG-U133A microarray platform[2].

The raw data (CEL files) downloaded from the GEO website were normalized and summarized for gene features with the frozen RMA algorithm [28], the gene features of the "grade A" were chosen for further analysis according to the NetAffx probeset annotation v33.1 from Affymetrix (so that the total number of features is to be $p = 20492$ afterward), and the microarrays with low quality according to the GNUSE [27] error scores > 1 were discarded (so that $n = 392$ afterward).

---

[1] http://www.ncbi.nlm.nih.gov/geo
[2] http://www.affymetrix.com

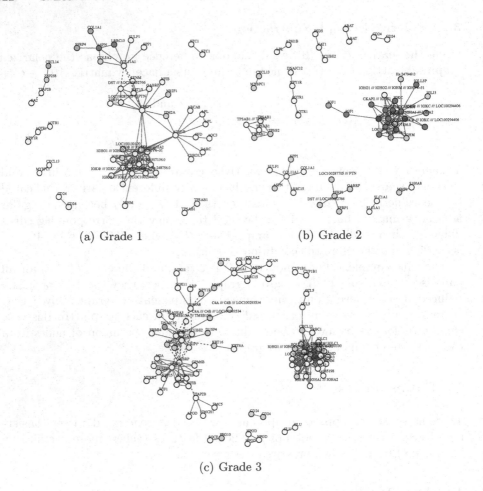

(a) Grade 1   (b) Grade 2

(c) Grade 3

Fig. 1. Graphical representation of feature spaces corresponding to grades 1, 2, and 3 breast cancer subgroups, obtained with the structure learning of GMRFs ($\lambda = 1.6$). Nodes are colored according to their p-value of predicting overall survival times as univariate predictors in Cox models for each subgroup (darker color = smaller p-value). Edge types represent polarity in correlation: solid = positive, and dashed = negative. Node labels show the corresponding gene symbols.

4.2   Subgroup Graphs

To generate subgroup graphs, we considered the "grades" of breast cancer (the following information is from http://www.macmillan.org.uk):

- Grade 1: the cancer cells look similar to normal cells and grow slowly.
- Grade 2: the cancer cells look different from normal cells and grow faster than grade 1 cells.
- Grade 3: the cancer cells look very different from normal cells and grow much faster than grade 1/2 cells.

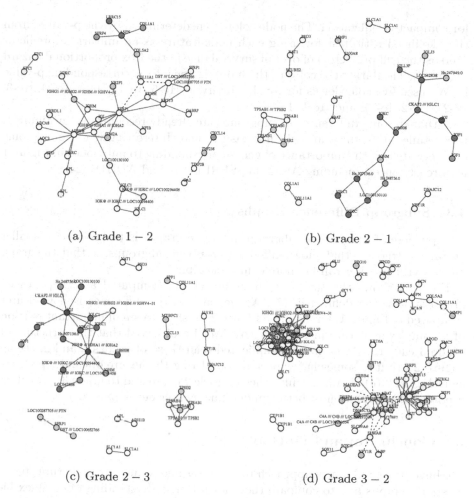

(a) Grade 1 − 2   (b) Grade 2 − 1

(c) Grade 2 − 3   (d) Grade 3 − 2

Fig. 2. Subgroup differences in graphical representation of feature spaces. Nodes are colored according to their p-value of predicting overall survival times as univariate predictors in Cox models for each subtype (darker color = smaller p-value). Edge types represent polarity in correlation: solid = positive, and dashed = negative. Node labels show the corresponding gene symbols. If shared edges have different polarities, then the edges are shown in thick lines (no such case here).

Using the clinical annotation of patients in our data, we split the expression data into three groups corresponding to the three grades, solved the structure learning problem with GMRFs (4) (the parameter $\lambda = 1.6$ was chosen for all cases which produced small numbers of connected components), and generated the polarized adjacency matrices $\tilde{A}^1$, $\tilde{A}^2$ and $\tilde{A}^3$ respectively to the cancer grades, according to the definition (5).

The graphs G^1, G^2, and G^3 represented by $\tilde{A}^1$, $\tilde{A}^2$ and $\tilde{A}^3$ are shown in Figure 1. Here, we showed only the connected components with at least two nodes for compact visualization. The node colors were determined by the p-values from the likelihood ratio test for using each node feature as an univariate predictor (versus the null predictor) of overall survival time in the Cox proportional hazard model [4]. The darker the color is, the more significant the corresponding p-value is. We used five color levels for p-value intervals: [1e-5, 1e-4), [1e-4, 1e-3), [1e-3, 1e-2), [1e-2, 1e-1), and [1e-1, 1).

Although some differences of subgroups are already recognizable in Figure 1, the detailed differences are still not easy to find. Interestingly, we found some evidences telling the importance of genes corresponding to hub nodes in Figure 1 for breast cancer, including ASPN [3], SFRP1 [19], and ADH1B [24].

4.3   Subgroup Difference Graphs

The purpose of computing subgroup difference graphs is to produce a smaller graphical structure that shows differences between subgroups, so that the graph and its visualization will be more comprehensible.

Figure 2 shows the subgroup difference graphs computed as the polarized graph subtraction defined in (7). As we can see, the difference is now clearer compared to Figure 1, for example Figure 2 (b) shows a small important portion of a complex structure in Figure 1 (b). We also observed that the structure of grade 3 cancer is much more complicated than these of grades 1 and 2, seeing Figure 2 (d): it is somewhat expected considering the nature of cancer progression. Figure 2 (c) shows the difference of grade 2 compared to grade 3, providing a potential information to better understand cancer development.

5   Conclusion and Outlook

We have presented a new approach to represent high dimensional feature spaces as sparse graphs and to compare them for better understanding of complex biological systems using a simple yet useful method based on polarized adjacency matrices. We demonstrated our method for characterizing subgroup graph patterns for difference grades of breast cancer, but our technique can be considered for comparing graphs from many other different subgroups.

Structure learning of GMRFs in (4) is a convex optimization, which was suggested by Yuan and Lin [43] and solved with an available interior point method [40] at the time. Later, more efficient optimization methods have been developed based on a dual formulation and a coordinate descent algorithm [1], another coordinate descent formulation together with the lasso algorithm [13], a projected gradient method [12], Nesterov's optimal first order methods and smoothing techniques [7, 25], alternating direction methods [35, 44], and proximal Newton methods [9] combined with curvature information to have faster convergence [17, 18, 32]. Although optimization methods have been improved to deal with large values of p efficiently, computing these for many subgroups of a sample is challenging in terms of memory and computation requirements, and therefore we still need to search for better methods for such settings.

The determination of the sparsity control parameter λ in (4) is not simple. It is closely related to a notion in statistics called *consistency in variable selection*, which relates the number of nonzero coefficients we can estimate with statistical power to the sample size n and the number of features p. When $p \gg n$, more care is needed for choosing λ. For more details, we refer to [21, 30].

As we see in Figures 1 and 2, the visualization of graphs can play a crucial role for identifying important genes and their relations to other genes in graphs. In particular, the coloring of nodes according to their predictive power and different types of edges according to positive/negative correlation make it easier to understand the underlying structure. This is a good example indicating that a tight integration of machine learning, data mining and visualization techniques will be necessary for successful understanding of complex systems.

Acknowledgments. This research was supported by Deutsche Forschungsgemeinschaft (DFG) within the Collaborative Research Center SFB 876 "Providing Information by Resource-Constrained Analysis", project C1.

References

1. Banerjee, O., Ghaoui, L.E., d'Aspremont, A.: Model selection through sparse maximum likelihood estimation for multivariate gaussian or binary data. Journal of Machine Learning Research 9, 485–516 (2008)
2. Candés, E.J., Romberg, J., Tao, T.: Stable signal recovery from incomplete and inaccurate measurements. Comm. Pure Appl. Math. 59, 1207–1223 (2005)
3. Castellana, B., Escuin, D., Peiró, G., Garcia-Valdecasas, B., Vázquez, T., Pons, C., Pérez-Olabarria, M., Barnadas, A., Lerma, E.: ASPN and GJB2 are implicated in the mechanisms of invasion of ductal breast carcinomas. Journal of Cancer 3, 175–183 (2012)
4. Cox, D.R., Oakes, D.: Analysis of Survival Data. Monographs on Statistics & Applied Probability. Chapman & Hall/CRC (1984)
5. Cox, D.R., Wermuth, N.: Multivariate Dependencies: Models, Analysis and Interpretation. Chapman and Hall (1996)
6. Cross, G.R., Jain, A.K.: Markov random field texture models. IEEE Transactions on Pattern Analysis and Machine Intelligence 5(1), 25–39 (1983)
7. d'Aspremont, A., Banerjee, O., El Ghaoui, L.: First-order methods for sparse covariance selection. SIAM Journal on Matrix Analysis and Applications 30(1), 56–66 (2008)
8. Dempster, A.P.: Covariance selection. Biometrika 32, 95–108 (1972)
9. Dinh, Q.T., Kyrillidis, A., Cevher, V.: A proximal newton framework for composite minimization: Graph learning without cholesky decompositions and matrix inversions. In: International Conference on Machine Learning (2013)
10. Dobra, A., Hans, C., Jones, B., Nevins, J.R., Yao, G., West, M.: Sparse graphical models for exploring gene expression data. Journal of Multivariate Analysis 90(1), 196–212 (2004)
11. Dryden, I., Ippoliti, L., Romagnoli, L.: Adjusted maximum likelihood and pseudo-likelihood estimation for noisy Gaussian Markov random fields. Journal of Computational and Graphical Statistics 11(2), 370–388 (2002)

12. Duchi, J., Gould, S., Koller, D.: Projected subgradient methods for learning sparse gaussians. In: Conference on Uncertainty in Artificial Intelligence (2008)
13. Friedman, J., Hastie, T., Tibshirani, R.: Sparse inverse covariance estimation with the graphical lasso. Biostatistics 9(3), 432–441 (2008)
14. Giudici, P., Green, P.: Decomposable graphical Gaussian model determination. Biometrika 86(4), 785–801 (1999)
15. Grunenwald, H., Baas, B., Caruccio, N., Syed, F.: Rapid, high-throughput library preparation for next-generation sequencing. Nature Methods 7(8) (2010)
16. Holzinger, A.: Human-computer interaction and knowledge discovery (HCI-KDD): What is the benefit of bringing those two fields to work together? In: Cuzzocrea, A., Kittl, C., Simos, D.E., Weippl, E., Xu, L. (eds.) CD-ARES 2013. LNCS, vol. 8127, pp. 319–328. Springer, Heidelberg (2013)
17. Jui Hsieh, C., Dhillon, I.S., Ravikumar, P.K., Sustik, M.A.: Sparse inverse covariance matrix estimation using quadratic approximation. In: Advances in Neural Information Processing Systems, vol. 24, pp. 2330–2338. MIT Press (2011)
18. Hsieh, C.J., Sustik, M.A., Dhillon, I., Ravikumar, P., Poldrack, R.: BIG & QUIC: Sparse inverse covariance estimation for a million variables. In: Advances in Neural Information Processing Systems, vol. 26, pp. 3165–3173. MIT Press (2013)
19. Klopocki, E., Kristiansen, G., Wild, P.J., Klaman, I., Castanos-Velez, E., Singer, G., Stöhr, R., Simon, R., Sauter, G., Leibiger, H., Essers, L., Weber, B., Hermann, K., Rosenthal, A., Hartmann, A., Dahl, E.: Loss of SFRP1 is associated with breast cancer progression and poor prognosis in early stage tumors. International Journal of Oncology 25(3), 641–649 (2004)
20. Lauritzen, S.L.: Graphical Models. Oxford University Press (1996)
21. Lee, S.: Sparse inverse covariance estimation for graph representation of feature structure. In: Holzinger, A., Jurisica, I. (eds.) Knowledge Discovery and Data Mining. LNCS, vol. 8401, pp. 227–240. Springer, Heidelberg (2014)
22. Lee, S., Wright, S.J.: Implementing algorithms for signal and image reconstruction on graphical processing units. Tech. rep., University of Wisconsin-Madison (2008)
23. Lee, S., Wright, S.J.: Manifold identification in dual averaging methods for regularized stochastic online learning. Journal of Machine Learning Research 13, 1705–1744 (2012)
24. Lilla, C., Koehler, T., Kropp, S., Wang-Gohrke, S., Chang-Claude, J.: Alcohol dehydrogenase 1B (ADH1B) genotype, alcohol consumption and breast cancer risk by age 50 years in a german case-control study. British Journal of Cancer 92(11), 2039–2041 (2005)
25. Lu, Z.: Smooth optimization approach for sparse covariance selection. SIAM Journal on Optimization 19(4), 1807–1827 (2009)
26. Manjunath, B.S., Chellappa, R.: Unsupervised texture segmentation using Markov random field models. IEEE Transactions on Pattern Analysis and Machine Intelligence 13(5), 478–482 (1991)
27. McCall, M., Murakami, P., Lukk, M., Huber, W., Irizarry, R.: Assessing affymetrix genechip microarray quality. BMC Bioinformatics 12(1), 137 (2011)
28. McCall, M.N., Bolstad, B.M., Irizarry, R.A.: Frozen robust multiarray analysis (fRMA). Biostatistics 11(2), 242–253 (2010)
29. Meinshausen, N., Bühlmann, P.: High-dimensional graphs and variable selection with the lasso. Annals of Statistics 34, 1436–1462 (2006)
30. Meinshausen, N., Bühlmann, P.: Stability selection. Journal of the Royal Statistical Society (Series B) 72(4), 417–473 (2010)

31. Otasek, D., Pastrello, C., Holzinger, A., Jurisica, I.: Visual data mining: Effective exploration of the biological universe. In: Holzinger, A., Jurisica, I. (eds.) Knowledge Discovery and Data Mining. LNCS, vol. 8401, pp. 19–33. Springer, Heidelberg (2014)

32. Oztoprak, F., Nocedal, J., Rennie, S., Olsen, P.A.: Newton-like methods for sparse inverse covariance estimation. In: Advances in Neural Information Processing Systems, vol. 25, pp. 764–772. MIT Press (2012)

33. Piatkowski, N., Lee, S., Morik, K.: Spatio-temporal random fields: compressible representation and distributed estimation. Machine Learning 93(1), 115–139 (2013)

34. Rue, H., Held, L.: Gaussian Markov Random Fields: Theory and Applications. Monographs on Statistics and Applied Probability, vol. 104. Chapman & Hall (2005)

35. Scheinberg, K., Ma, S., Goldfarb, D.: Sparse inverse covariance selection via alternating linearization methods. In: Advances in Neural Information Processing Systems, vol. 23, pp. 2101–2109. MIT Press (2010)

36. Spielman, D.A.: Faster isomorphism testing of strongly regular graphs. In: Proceedings of the Twenty-eighth Annual ACM Symposium on Theory of Computing, pp. 576–584 (1996)

37. Tibshirani, R.: Regression shrinkage and selection via the lasso. Journal of the Royal Statistical Society (Series B) 58, 267–288 (1996)

38. Turkay, C., Jeanquartier, F., Holzinger, A., Hauser, H.: On computationally-enhanced visual analysis of heterogeneous data and its application in biomedical informatics. In: Holzinger, A., Jurisica, I. (eds.) Knowledge Discovery and Data Mining. LNCS, vol. 8401, pp. 117–140. Springer, Heidelberg (2014)

39. Ullmann, J.R.: An algorithm for subgraph isomorphism. Journal of the ACM 23(1), 31–42 (1976)

40. Vandenberghe, L., Boyd, S., Wu, S.P.: Determinant maximization with linear matrix inequality constraints. SIAM Journal on Matrix Analysis and Applications 19(2), 499–533 (1998)

41. Verzelen, N., Villers, F.: Tests for gaussian graphical models. Computational Statistics and Data Analysis 53(5), 1894–1905 (2009)

42. Whitney, H.: Congruent graphs and the connectivity of graphs. American Journal of Mathematics 54(1), 150–168 (1932)

43. Yuan, M., Lin, Y.: Model selection and estimation in the gaussian graphical model. Biometrika 94(1), 19–35 (2007)

44. Yuan, X.: Alternating direction method for covariance selection models. Journal of Scientific Computing 51(2), 261–273 (2012)

45. Zou, H., Hastie, T.: Regularization and variable selection via the elastic net. Journal of the Royal Statistical Society (Series B) 67, 301–320 (2005)

Moduli Spaces of Phylogenetic Trees Describing Tumor Evolutionary Patterns

Sakellarios Zairis[1,2], Hossein Khiabanian[1,2],
Andrew J. Blumberg[3], and Raul Rabadan[1,2]

[1] Department of Systems Biology, Columbia University, New York, NY 10032
[2] Department of Biomedical Informatics, Columbia University, New York, NY 10032
[3] Department of Mathematics, University of Texas at Austin, Austin, TX 78712

Abstract. Cancers follow a clonal Darwinian evolution, with fitter subclones replacing more quiescent cells, ultimately giving rise to macroscopic disease. High-throughput genomics provides the opportunity to investigate these processes and determine specific genetic alterations driving disease progression. Genomic sampling of a patient's cancer provides a molecular history, represented by a phylogenetic tree. Cohorts of patients represent a forest of related phylogenetic structures. To extract clinically relevant information, one must represent and statistically compare these collections of trees. We propose a framework based on an application of the work by Billera, Holmes and Vogtmann on phylogenetic tree spaces to the case of unrooted trees of intra-individual cancer tissue samples. We observe that these tree spaces are globally nonpositively curved, allowing for statistical inference on populations of patient histories. A projective tree space is introduced, permitting visualizations of evolutionary patterns. Published data from four types of human malignancies are explored within our framework.

Keywords: phylogenetic tree, moduli space, tumor evolution, genomics.

1 Introduction

A tumor is the result of successive accumulation of genetic alterations. As alterations accumulate, clones of higher fitness are selected, which drives cancer progression. The clonal aspect of cancer is a unifying and defining characteristic of an otherwise diverse set of diseases. In the last five years, next generation sequencing has illuminated the landscape of genomic alterations in a large number of tumors. The Cancer Genome Atlas (TCGA) and the International Cancer Genome Consortium (ICGC) have led this effort, sequencing thousands of tumors spanning the spectrum of human malignancies, leading to the identification of recurrent alterations that indicate mechanisms of convergent evolution in certain genes and pathways. Large cross-sectional studies, however, are not designed to capture the dynamic nature of tumor evolution, and longitudinal NGS studies, sequencing a tumor at multiple time points within an individual are only emerging. [6,10,12,14] Key questions in tumor dynamics surround the mechanisms of

D. Ślęzak et al. (Eds.): BIH 2014, LNAI 8609, pp. 528–539, 2014.
© Springer International Publishing Switzerland 2014

acquired drug resistance, the emergence of subclones with metastatic potential, the clinical stratification of patients according to observed tumor evolution, and the design of personalized drug treatment regimens to steer tumor evolution.

The rise of dominant clones in a tumor can be inferred by sequential sequencing of an individual's disease. Successive genomic snapshots may represent defined temporal intervals, progression of disease through predefined stages, or successive anatomic sites to which a cancer has spread. In all of these scenarios we make observations about an evolutionary process and can represent the relationships between genomic snapshots as a phylogenetic tree. When large cohorts of cancer patients are studied, yielding a forest of such phylogenetic trees, we require a mathematical framework in which to reason about aggregate evolutionary behaviors. We must be able to, at a minimum, directly compare two evolutionary histories. Here, we apply the work of Billera, Holmes and Vogtmann [3] and Sturm [13] on geometric spaces of phylogenetic trees to provide a framework for statistical inference and visualization of evolutionary histories. Our work provides a compact language for cancer biologists and oncologists to use in describing longitudinal NGS data.

2 Description of the Space of Trees

We can understand the relation between m different genomes following clonal evolution as a phylogenetic tree with m leaves. A phylogenetic tree is a weighted, connected graph with no circuits, having m distinguished vertices of degree 1 labelled $\{1, \ldots, m\}$, and all other vertices of degree ≥ 3. Edges that terminate in leaves are "external" edges and the remaining edges are "internal".

When the external branches all have length 0, the tree space we have described (where the nonzero weights are on the internal branches) was introduced and studied by Billera, Holmes, and Vogtmann. Specifically, the structure of the internal branches is captured by the BHV_{m-1} construction (where the $m-1$ index arises from the fact that they consider rooted trees). Allowing potentially nonzero weights for the m external leaves corresponds to crossing with an m-dimensional orthant. Therefore, the space we wish to study is simply

$$\Sigma_m = \mathrm{BHV}_{m-1} \times (\mathbb{R}^{\geq 0})^m.$$

We refer to Σ_m as the evolutionary moduli space.

2.1 The Metric Geometry of Evolutionary Moduli Spaces

As described above, the space Σ_m is just a set of points. The key insight of Billera, Holmes, and Vogtmann is that this space is equipped with a natural metric that endows the space with an intrinsic geometry.

The metric on BHV_{m-1} is induced from the standard Euclidean distance on each of the orthants, as follows. For two trees t_1 and t_2 which are both in a given orthant, the distance $d_{\mathrm{BHV}_{m-1}}(t_1, t_2)$ is defined to be the Euclidean distance between the points specified by the weights. For two trees which are in different quadrants, there exist (many) paths connecting them which consist of straight lines in each quadrant. The length of such a path is the sum of the lengths of these lines, and the distance $d_{\mathrm{BHV}_{m-1}}(t_1, t_2)$ is then the minimum length over all such paths. There is an analogous metric on Σ_m, which can be regarded as induced from the metric on BHV_{m-1}. Specifically, for a tree t, let $t(i)$ denote the length of the external edge associated to the vertex i. Then

$$d_{\Sigma_m}(t_1, t_2) = \sqrt{d_{\mathrm{BHV}_{m-1}}(\bar{t}_1, \bar{t}_2) + \sum_{i=1}^{m}(t_1(i) - t_2(i))^2},$$

where $\bar{t}_i$ denotes the tree in BHV_{m-1} obtained by forgetting the lengths of the external edges (e.g., see [11]).

The metric space (Σ_m, d_{Σ_m}) allows us to talk meaningfully about the distance between two evolutionary histories. But more importantly, d_{Σ_m} allows us to describe the geometry of Σ_m, specifically curvature. Curvature can be seen in the behavior of triangles; given side lengths $(\ell_1, \ell_2, \ell_3) \subset \mathbb{R}^3$, a triangle with these side lengths on the surface of the Earth is "fatter" than the corresponding triangle on a Euclidean plane. We can be more precise about this by looking at the distance from a vertex of the triangle to a point p on the opposite side — in a fat triangle, this distance will be larger than in the the corresponding Euclidean triangle.(Thin triangles are defined analogously.)

Alexandrov observed that this perspective makes sense in any geodesic metric space [2]. A metric space M is a geodesic metric space if any two points x and y can be joined by a path with length precisely $d(x, y)$. Then given points p, q, r, we have the triangle $T = [p, q, r]$ with edges the paths connecting each pair of vertices. These paths specify edge lengths, and so we can find a corresponding triangle $\tilde{T}$ in Euclidean space. Given a point z on the edge $[p, q]$, a comparison point in $\tilde{T}$ is a point $\tilde{z}$ on the corresponding edge $[\tilde{p}, \tilde{q}]$ such that $d(\tilde{z}, \tilde{p}) = d(p, z)$.

We say that a triangle T in M satisfies the CAT(0) inequality if for every pair of points x and y in T and comparison points $\tilde{x}$ and $\tilde{y}$ on $\tilde{T}$, we have $d(x, y) \leq d(\tilde{x}, \tilde{y})$. If every triangle in M satisfies the CAT(0) inequality then we say that M is a CAT(0) space. More generally, let M_κ denote the unique two-dimensional Riemannian manifold with curvature κ. Then we say that a geodesic metric space M is CAT(κ) if every triangle in M satisfies the inequality above for the comparison triangle in M_κ. Gromov gave a condition for a cubical complex to be CAT(0), and using this condition Billera, Holmes, and Vogtmann showed that BHV_{m-1} is CAT(0). An immediate generalization of their argument yields the analogous result for Σ_m.

Theorem 1. *The space Σ_m is a CAT(0) space.*

2.2   Statistics on Evolutionary Moduli Spaces

Sequencing longitudinal cancer samples can be regarded as sampling from a distribution on the evolutionary moduli space. Differences between the distributions associated with different tumors can be used to predict different evolutionary trajectories. First, we must justify the use of distributions on Σ_m. One can set up many aspects of the formal apparatus of probability theory on any complete metric space with a countable dense subset (i.e., a Polish spaces).

Theorem 2. *The space Σ_m is a Polish space.*

There are many natural distributions on Σ_m (e.g., uniform selection of tree topology followed by uniform selection of edge weights from a range $[a, b]$). The principal virtue of establishing that Σ_m is a CAT(0) space is that in this context, there exist well-defined notions of mean and variance. An account of basic statistical procedures for such spaces has recently been given by Sturm [13]. The correct notion of the mean of a set of points is a generalization of a centroid: we define the Fréchet mean and variance in Σ_m.

Definition 1. *Given a fixed set of n trees $\{T_0, \ldots T_{n-1}\} \subseteq \Sigma_m$, the Fréchet mean T is the unique tree that minimizes the quantity*

$$E = \sum_{i=0}^{n-1} d_{\Sigma_m}(T_i, T)^2.$$

The variance of T is the ratio $\frac{E}{n}$.

Sturm's work provides an iterative procedure for computing the mean in Σ_m, and by exploiting the local geometric structure of Σ_m, Miller, Owen, and Provan produce somewhat more efficient algorithms for computing the mean.

There are many natural test statistics defined in terms of the Fréchet mean. One can use resampling and Monte Carlo simulation to obtain confidence intervals and perform inference, but practical study of such procedures and the development of the theoretical foundations for inference are both work in progress.

2.3   The Projective Evolutionary Moduli Spaces

We are primarily interested in classifying and comparing distinct evolutionary behaviors by understanding the relative lengths of edges: rescaling edge lengths does not change the relationship between the branches. Thus, we will also use the quotient space of Σ_m by the equivalence relation that for each orthant, the tree $\{t_i\}$ is equivalent to the rescaled tree $\{\lambda t_i\}$, i.e., the subspace of Σ_m consisting of the points $\{t_i\}$ in each orthant for which the constraint $\sum_i t_i = 1$ holds. We will denote this quotient by $\mathbb{P}\Sigma_m$, the evolutionary projective moduli spaces.

This space of trees (without external edges) of fixed length was studied by Boardman and is denoted by τ_{m-1}. The space of m external branches that sum to a fixed length is an $m - 1$ dimensional simplex, which we denote T_{m-1}. As we are requiring that the length of internal branches plus the external branches sum to a fixed constant, we can describe our space as the join of τ_{m-1} and T_{m-1}:

$$\mathbb{P}\Sigma_m = \tau_{m-1} \star T_{m-1}.$$

Since for the applications we describe herein the trees have either 3 or 4 leaves, it is instructive to describe explicitly the spaces $\mathbb{P}\Sigma_3$ and $\mathbb{P}\Sigma_4$. In the case of 3 leaves all structure is in the external branches and $\mathbb{P}\Sigma_3$ is a triangle. The triangle has three vertices and 3 edges; below we provide biological interpretations for these regions of the space in the context of different experiments. In the case of four leaves, τ_3 is a set of 3 points reflecting the three possible topologies of unrooted 4-trees and $\mathbb{P}\Sigma_4$ becomes a richer space in which to compare and visualize evolutionary modes.

There is a natural projection map $\Sigma_m \to \mathbb{P}\Sigma_m$ given by rescaling. However, a number of warnings apply to the use of this projection. Notably, $\mathbb{P}\Sigma_m$ is not a CAT(0) space (it is a CAT(1) space). As a consequence, we cannot compute meaningful averages or variances in general. Moreover, the metric structure on $\mathbb{P}\Sigma_m$ is complicated. Even for a single simplex Δ_n, treating Δ_n as a subspace of $\mathbb{R}^n$ does not lead to sensible statistical procedures. In this case, an approach to inference was introduced by Aitchison [1]. In work in progress we are studying the integration of Aitchison's transformation with $\mathbb{P}\Sigma_m$.

2.4   Triplet Data

In the context of cancer patients, triplet samples are often comprised of 1) **normal** tissue, 2) malignant tissue at **diagnosis**, and 3) malignant tissue at a later clinical time point such as local **relapse**. The moduli space of unrooted phylogenetic 3-trees, Σ_3, is a Euclidean 3-orthant whose basis vectors represent the 3 external edge lengths (l_n, l_d, l_r). We project each tree onto $\mathbb{P}\Sigma_3$, the space formed by the intersection $\mathbb{R}^{3+} \cap S^2$, by rescaling the branch lengths. This space is visualized in Figure 1

The general case of three nonzero external branch lengths is called branched evolution and such phylogenetic trees will be found far from the boundary of $\mathbb{P}\Sigma_3$. We would also like to understand the possible singular cases that occur when one or more branches degenerate. If all branch lengths are zero then we have the trivial situation of no evolution among the three samples.

The edges of $\mathbb{P}\Sigma_3$ represent trees in which a single branch has collapsed to zero. As $l_n \to 0$ we have the situation where the diagnosis and the relapse are completely distinct tumors whose earliest common ancestor is in fact normal tissue. We call this divergent evolution. As $l_d \to 0$ we have the situation where the diagnosis is a perfect intermediate between the normal and relapse genotypes, the well known case of linear evolution. Lastly, as $l_r \to 0$ we have the situation where the relapse sample is actually the intermediate between normal and diagnosis genotypes, indicating the emergence of an ancient clone that was not dominant at the time of diagnosis. We call this revertant evolution.

The vertices of $\mathbb{P}\Sigma_3$ represent trees in which two branches have collapsed to zero. Near the "shared" vertex is the case where the tumor genomics are almost identical between diagnosis and relapse samples with respect to normal tissue. From a clinical perspective, no further mutations are needed beyond the diagnosis stage for the disease to relapse, and we term this scenario frozen evolution. Near the "diagnosis" vertex is the case where the relapsed tumor is almost

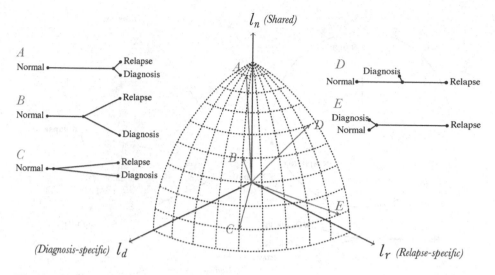

Fig. 1. Evolutionary modes in $\mathbb{P}\Sigma_3$. A: frozen evolution, B: branched evolution, C: divergent evolution, D: linear evolution, E: somatic hypermutation.

identical to normal, healthy tissue with respect to the lesion at diagnosis. This would be a highly unusual set of genotypes to observe since advanced cancers require some genomic deviation from normal. Near the "relapse" vertex is the case where the tumor at diagnosis is essentially the same as normal tissue compared to the number of mutations specific to the relapsed disease. Rapid accumulation of mutations can result from a shifting fitness landscape during medical therapy, and this region of the space can indicate somatic hypermutation. This scenario does not imply that the lesion at diagnosis has zero difference from normal tissue, but rather that the difference is dwarfed by the number of mutations accumulated in the relapsed sample.

2.5   Quadruplet Data

Quadruplet samples can arise from 1) **normal** tissue, 2) malignant tissue at **diagnosis**, and 3) malignant tissue at local **relapse** and 4) malignant tissue from distant **metastasis**. Unrooted trees constructed from quadruplet data contain a single internal edge, implying 3 possible tree topologies. We decompose the moduli space of unrooted phylogenetic 4-trees, Σ_4, into the product of spaces for its internal and external edges respectively, $BHV_3 \times \mathbb{R}^{4+}$. Upon rescaling of the branch lengths we project each tree onto $\mathbb{P}\Sigma_4$, the space formed by $\tau_3 \star T_3$, which is the join of a set of three points and a tetrahedron.

In Figure 2, we illustrate the two components of $\mathbb{P}\Sigma_4$. A quadruplet is represented by a point in the star plot and a point in the tetrahedron. The three arms of the star plot represent the three possible tree topologies, and they meet at an origin corresponding to the degenerate case of a length zero internal branch.

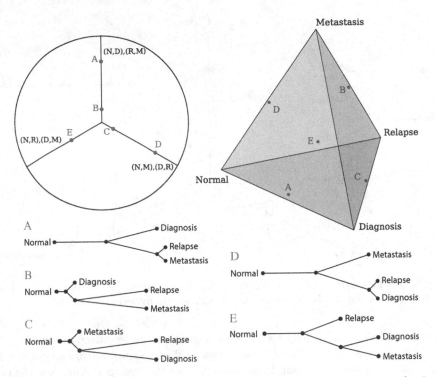

Fig. 2. Evolutionary modes in $\mathbb{P}\Sigma_4$. Each tree, A—E, is represented by a pair of points. The three arms of the star plot specify the internal branch, and thus the topology, while the tetrahedral plot describes the external branches.

The vertices of the tetrahedron correspond to trees having only one nonzero external branch, the edges to trees with two nonzero external branches, and the faces to trees with three nonzero external branches.

3   Case Studies

We now turn to the recent cancer genomics literature for examples of different patterns of tumor evolution. We examine the progression of two major hematologic malignancies for which there is abundant triplet data: acute myelogenous leukemia and follicular lymphoma. Then we shift to the highly aggressive solid tumors arising in the exocrine pancreas, pancreatic ductal adenocarcinoma, for which there is publicly available quadruplet data. In each case study we visualize aggregate evolutionary behavior and compute centroid trees via an implementation of Definition 1 (Section 2.2) given by [8]. Useful acronyms for the ensuing sections are WGS (whole genome sequencing) and WES (whole exome sequencing).

3.1   Relapsed Acute Myelogenous Leukemia

Acute myelogenous keukemia (AML) accounts for about 80% of acute leukemia in adults with a median survival time of less than three years, accounting for more than 1% of cancer deaths in the US. AML is caused by the abnormal rapid growth of myeloid progenitor cells interfering with normal hematopoeisis. Most patients die from relapse after chemotherapy and subsequent disease progression, with relapse free survival at only 40%. [9] The molecular mechanism of relapse in AML is not fully understood. In a recent study of relapsed AML, [6] the evolution to relapse was followed in 8 patients who received both induction and consolidation chemotherapy. The time to relapse varied between 235 - 961 days, and the investigators found that treatment did not eliminate the original cancer clone in any of the patients. WGS was performed on all 8 patients and an average of 21 protein changing mutations per patient were revealed.

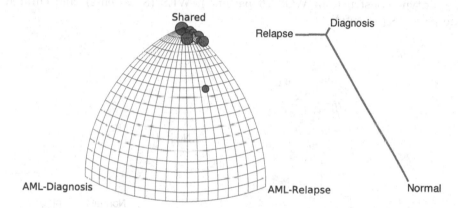

Fig. 3. Frozen linear evolution from diagnosis to relapse observed in 8 AML patients. Patients are represented by red circles, scaled by their total number of mutations. The centroid of the distribution is represented as a gold star, and its associated phylogenetic tree is visualized.

When mapped to $\mathbb{P}\Sigma_3$ all patients are near the "frozen evolution" vertex illustrating that very few mutations were specific to either diagnosis or relapse samples (Figure 3). Despite the genotypes being virtually shared between diagnosis and relapse, the latter is a far more dangerous clinical entity. Also worth noting is the recurrence of mutations in genes that regulate DNA methylation such as *DNMT3A*, *IDH1*, and *IDH2*. The combination of frozen evolution, mutations that could affect global methylation patterns, and clinical progression of disease hints that the majority of evolution in this cancer is occurring beyond the DNA level. Indeed, recent reports suggest that relapse in AML is driven by epigenetic deregulation. [7]

3.2   Follicular Lymphoma Transformation to Diffuse Large B-Cell Lymphoma

Follicular lymphoma (FL) is a common lymphoid cancer, comprising 13% of all mature B-cell neoplasms. Roughly 20% of FL cases undergo a histologic transformation to more aggressive lymphoma phenotype resembling diffuse large B-cell lymphoma. While the prognosis of FL as a whole is 80% at 5 years, the prognosis for tFL is far worse at 20% survival after 2 years. Two recent genomic studies independently analyze patients with FL–tFL sample pairs and assess the evolutionary behavior of the transformation. In the first paper, [12] WES was performed on 12 patients, only 4 of whom had matched normal tissue. For the 8 patients in which somatic mutations could not be reliably called, a panel of 52 genes with established roles in lymphomagenesis was used as a surrogate genotype. In the second paper, [10] WES was performed on 4 patients and WGS was performed on 6 patients. We pool this data into three distinct groups based on genotype construction: WGS (6 patients), WES (8 patients), and curated gene panel (8 patients).

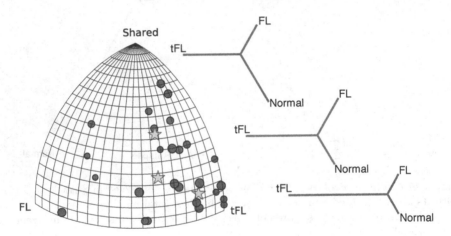

Fig. 4. Different degrees of branched evolution observed in patients with FL–tFL transformation. Colored circles are scaled by patients' total number of mutations. Genotype construction strategy affects the degree of branched vs. linear evolution observed in WGS (red), WES (green), and curated gene panel (blue). The centroids of the three distributions are represented as gold stars, and their associated phylogenetic trees are visualized.

The pooled data is visualized in Figure 5, with different colorings for the three groups. Until recently there was no consensus on the evolutionary mode of FL–tFL transformation, with some data even pointing to a linear process.[5] Figure 5, however, clearly demonstrates that the majority of the data fall in the bulk of $\mathbb{P}\Sigma_3$ and represent a branched evolutionary process. Comparison between the different genotype constructions further reveals that the degree of branched vs. linear evolution observed depends on the data curation strategy.

3.3 Metastatic Pancreatic Cancer

Cancer of the exocrine pancreas accounts for roughly 85% of all pancreatic malignancies and is the 4th leading cause of cancer-related deaths in the United States. In a recent study, [4] 13 cases of widely metastatic pancreatic ductal adenocarcinoma (PDAC) were studied at autopsy using a genome-wide detection method of structural rearrangements. The anatomic sites represented among the metastases include liver, lung, diaphragm, adrenal glands, peritoneum, and omentum.

We are interested in evolutionary histories involving distinct anatomical regions. To cast this data as quadruplets of successive anatomic sites of disease, we consider the hypothesis that the liver should represent the first metastatic location of PDAC. There is direct anatomical communication between the exocrine pancreas and the liver, via the common bile duct, while many of the other metastatic sites are only reachable via hematogenous spread of cancer cells. Furthermore, the liver receives a large fraction of cardiac output and might therefore be responsible for seeding the various more distant sites via the blood. For these reasons we are interested in differentiating between metastases to the liver vs. other sites. We partition the large number of samples per patient into the following disjoint subsets: normal tissue (1), primary pancreatic tumor (1), liver metastases ($\sim$ 5), non-liver metastases ($\sim$ 5).

All combinatorial 4-trees are inferred from this data and their mapping to $\mathbb{P}\Sigma_4$ is visualized in Figure 6. We denote the normal tissue sample by N, the primary pancreatic tumor by P, the liver metastases by LM, and the non-liver metastases by nLM. Contrary to our hypothesis that liver metastases give rise to metastases in other tissues, we find that the centroid of the data corresponds to

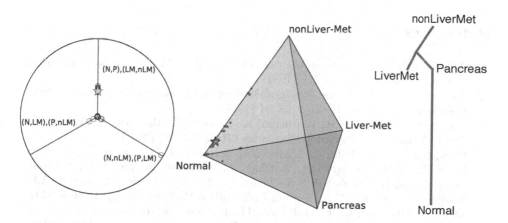

Fig. 5. Both linear and branching behavior observed in 10 cases of metastatic PDAC. A strong tendency toward (N,P),(LM,nLM) topology in is seen in the star plot on the left. The majority of genetic alterations are acquired at the primary tumor stage. Evolution to LM and nLM do not appear to be linearly related. The centroid of the distribution is represented as a gold star, and its associated phylogenetic tree is visualized.

a tree with branched ancestry between LM and nLM. Furthermore, we observe that there is no branching in the progression from normal tissue to primary disease to metastatic potential. In other words, the trajectory leading to the common ancestor of LM and nLM is a linear one.

4 Conclusions

A rigorous, quantitative study of clonal evolution in cancer requires a consistent mathematical formulation. Herein we present a natural application of the work on BHV spaces [3] to the setting of unrooted phylogenetic trees representing malignant tissue samples in individual patients. Exploring the distributions of evolutionary modes in different cancers has direct implications for personalized medical management and prognostication. For example, tuning the intensity of a patient's chemotherapeutic regimen requires an understanding of how treatment perturbs the natural evolutionary path of the cancer. As the collection of intra-individual, longitudinal genomic data sets accelerates, it will become unfeasible to directly reason about large forests of phylogenetic trees. Thus, we propose a framework for visual and statistical exploration of tumor evolutionary data that can augment the intuition of cancer biologists and oncologists.

Acknowledgments. The authors gratefully acknowledge the constructive feedback of Adolfo Ferrando, Teresa Palomero, Ricardo Dalla-Favera, Laura Pasqualucci, and Kevin Emmett. This work is supported by NIH grants R01 CA185486, R01 CA179044, and U54 CA121852, as well as the Stewart Foundation.

References

1. Aitchison, J.: The Statistical Analysis of Compositional Data. Journal of the Royal Statistical Society 44, 139–177 (1982)
2. Alexandrov, A.: Über eine verallgemeinerung der riemannschen geometrie. Schr. Forschungsinst. Math. Berlin 1, 33–84 (1957)
3. Billera, L.J., Holmes, S.P., Vogtmann, K.: Geometry of the Space of Phylogenetic Trees. Advances in Applied Mathematics 27(4), 733–767 (2001)
4. Campbell, P.J., Yachida, S., Mudie, L.J., Stephens, P.J., Pleasance, E.D., Stebbings, L.A., Morsberger, L.A., Latimer, C., McLaren, S., Lin, M.L., McBride, D.J., Varela, I., Nik-Zainal, S.A., Leroy, C., Jia, M., Menzies, A., Butler, A.P., Teague, J.W., Griffin, C.A., Burton, J., Swerdlow, H., Quail, M.A., Stratton, M.R., Iacobuzio-Donahue, C., Futreal, P.A.: The patterns and dynamics of genomic instability in metastatic pancreatic cancer. Nature 467(7319), 1109–1113 (2010)
5. Carlotti, E., Wrench, D., Matthews, J., Iqbal, S., Davies, A., Norton, A., Hart, J., Lai, R., Montoto, S., Gribben, J.G., Lister, T.A., Fitzgibbon, J.: Transformation of follicular lymphoma to diffuse large B-cell lymphoma may occur by divergent evolution from a common progenitor cell or by direct evolution from the follicular lymphoma clone. Blood 113(15), 3553–3557 (2009)

6. Ding, L., Ley, T.J., Larson, D.E., Miller, C.A., Koboldt, D.C., Welch, J.S., Ritchey, J.K., Young, M.A., Lamprecht, T., McLellan, M.D., McMichael, J.F., Wallis, J.W., Lu, C., Shen, D., Harris, C.C., Dooling, D.J., Fulton, R.S., Fulton, L.L., Chen, K., Schmidt, H., Kalicki-Veizer, J., Magrini, V.J., Cook, L., McGrath, S.D., Vickery, T.L., Wendl, M.C., Heath, S., Watson, M.A., Link, D.C., Tomasson, M.H., Shannon, W.D., Payton, J.E., Kulkarni, S., Westervelt, P., Walter, M.J., Graubert, T.A., Mardis, E.R., Wilson, R.K., DiPersio, J.F.: Clonal evolution in relapsed acute myeloid leukaemia revealed by whole-genome sequencing. Nature 481(7382), 506–510 (2012)
7. Li, S., Hricik, T., Chung, S.S., Bar, H., Brown, A.L., Patel, J.P., Rapoport, F., Liu, L., Sheridan, C., Ishii, J., Zumbo, P., Gandara, J., Lewis, I.D., To, L.B., Becker, M.W., Guzman, M.L., D'Andrea, R.J., Michor, F., Park, C.Y., Carroll, M., Levine, R.L., Mason, C.E., Melnick, A.M.: Epigenetic deregulation in relapsed acute myeloid leukemia. Blood 122(21), 2499 (2013)
8. Miller, E., Owen, M., Provan, J.S.: Polyhedral computational geometry for averaging metric phylogenetic trees (2014)
9. Ohtake, S., Miyawaki, S., Fujita, H., Kiyoi, H., Shinagawa, K., Usui, N., Okumura, H., Miyamura, K., Nakaseko, C., Miyazaki, Y., Fujieda, A., Nagai, T., Yamane, T., Taniwaki, M., Takahashi, M., Yagasaki, F., Kimura, Y., Asou, N., Sakamaki, H., Handa, H., Honda, S., Ohnishi, K., Naoe, T., Ohno, R.: Randomized study of induction therapy comparing standard-dose idarubicin with high-dose daunorubicin in adult patients with previously untreated acute myeloid leukemia: the JALSG AML201 Study. Blood 117(8), 2358–2365 (2011)
10. Okosun, J., Bödör, C., Wang, J., Araf, S., Yang, C.Y., Pan, C., Boller, S., Cittaro, D., Bozek, M., Iqbal, S., Matthews, J., Wrench, D., Marzec, J., Tawana, K., Popov, N., O'Riain, C., O'Shea, D., Carlotti, F., Davies, A., Lawrie, C.H., Matolcsy, A., Calaminici, M., Norton, A., Byers, R.J., Mein, C., Stupka, E., Lister, T.A., Lenz, G., Montoto, S., Gribben, J.G., Fan, Y., Grosschedl, R., Chelala, C., Fitzgibbon, J.: Integrated genomic analysis identifies recurrent mutations and evolution patterns driving the initiation and progression of follicular lymphoma. Nature Genetics 46(2), 176–181 (2014)
11. Owen, M., Provan, J.: A fast algorithm for computing geodesic distances in tree space. IEEE/ACM Transactions on Computational Biology, 1–18 (2011)
12. Pasqualucci, L., Khiabanian, H., Fangazio, M., Vasishtha, M., Messina, M., Holmes, A.B., Ouillette, P., Trifonov, V., Rossi, D., Tabbò, F., Ponzoni, M., Chadburn, A., Murty, V.V., Bhagat, G., Gaidano, G., Inghirami, G., Malek, S.N., Rabadan, R., Dalla-Favera, R.: Genetics of follicular lymphoma transformation. Cell Reports 6(1), 130–140 (2014)
13. Sturm, K.: Probability measures on metric spaces of nonpositive curvature. Contemporary Mathematics, 1–34 (2003)
14. Tzoneva, G., Perez-Garcia, A., Carpenter, Z., Khiabanian, H., Tosello, V., Allegretta, M., Paietta, E., Racevskis, J., Rowe, J.M., Tallman, M.S., Paganin, M., Basso, G., Hof, J., Kirschner-Schwabe, R., Palomero, T., Rabadan, R., Ferrando, A.: Activating mutations in the NT5C2 nucleotidase gene drive chemotherapy resistance in relapsed ALL. Nature medicine 19(3), 368–371 (2013)

Characterizing Scales of Genetic Recombination and Antibiotic Resistance in Pathogenic Bacteria Using Topological Data Analysis

Kevin J. Emmett[1] and Raul Rabadan[2]

[1] Department of Physics, Columbia University, New York, USA
kje2109@columbia.edu
[2] Department of Systems Biology and Department of Biomedical Informatics,
Columbia University, New York, USA
rr2579@c2b2.columbia.edu

Abstract. Pathogenic bacteria present a large disease burden on human health. Control of these pathogens is hampered by rampant lateral gene transfer, whereby pathogenic strains may acquire genes conferring resistance to common antibiotics. Here we introduce tools from topological data analysis to characterize the frequency and scale of lateral gene transfer in bacteria, focusing on a set of pathogens of significant public health relevance. As a case study, we examine the spread of antibiotic resistance in *Staphylococcus aureus*. Finally, we consider the possible role of the human microbiome as a reservoir for antibiotic resistance genes.

Keywords: topological data analysis, microbial evolution, antibiotic resistance.

1   Introduction

Pathogenic bacteria can lead to severe infection and mortality and presents an enormous burden on human populations and public health systems. One of the achievements of twentieth century medicine was the development of a wide range of antibiotic drugs to control and contain the spread of pathogenic bacteria, leading to vastly increased life expectancies and global economic development. However, rapidly rising levels of multidrug antibiotic resistance in several common pathogens, including *Escherichia coli*, *Klebsiella pneumoniae*, *Staphylococcus aureus*, and *Neisseria gonorrhoea*, is recognized as a pressing global issue with near-term consequences [15,23,26]. The threat of a post-antibiotic 21st century is serious, and new methods to characterize and monitor the spread of resistance are urgently needed.

Antibiotic resistance can be acquired through point mutation or through horizontal transfer of resistance genes. Horizontal exchange occurs when a donor bacteria transmits foreign DNA into a genetically distinct bacteria strain. Three mechanisms of horizontal transfer are identified, depending on the route by which foreign DNA is acquired [16]. Foreign DNA can be acquired via uptake from an

D. Ślęzak et al. (Eds.): BIH 2014, LNAI 8609, pp. 540–551, 2014.

external environment (transformation), via viral-mediated processes (transduction), or via direct cell-to-cell contact between bacterial strains (conjugation). Resistance genes can be transferred between strains of the same species, or can be acquired from different species in the same environment. While the former is generally more common, an example of the latter is the phage-mediated acquisition of Shiga toxin in *E. coli* in Germany in 2011 [18]. Elements of the bacterial genome that show evidence of foreign origin are called genomic islands, and are of particular concern when associated with phenotypic effects such as virulence or antibiotic resistance.

The presence of horizontal gene transfer precludes accurate phylogenetic characterization, because different segments of the genome will have different evolutionary histories. Bacterial species definitions and taxonomic classifications are made on the basis of 16S ribosomal RNA, a highly conserved genomic region between bacteria and archaea species [25]. However, the region generally accounts for less than 1% of the complete genome, implying that the vast majority of evolutionary relationships are not accounted for in the taxonomy [5]. Because of the important role played by lateral gene transfer, new ways of characterizing evolutionary and phenotypic relationships between microorganisms are needed.

Topological data analysis (TDA), and persistent homology in particular, has been shown to be an effective tool for capturing horizontal evolutionary processes at the population level by measuring deviations from treelike additivity. Initial work in this direction characterized recombination in viral evolution, particularly in influenza, where genomic reassortment can lead to the emergence of viral pandemics [3]. Further work established foundations for statistical inference in population genetics models using TDA [8]. We provide a brief overview of TDA and persistent homology in Section 2, for additional reviews see [2][7].

In this paper we explore topics relating to horizontal gene transfer in bacteria and the emergence of antibiotic resistance in pathogenic strains. We show that TDA can not only quantify gene transfer events, but also characterize the scale of gene transfer. The scale of recombination can be measured from the distribution of birth times of the H_1 invariants in the persistent barcode diagram. It has been shown that recombination rates decrease with increasing sequence divergence [9]. We characterize the rate and scale of intraspecies recombination in several pathogenic bacteria of public health concern. We select a set of pathogenic bacteria that are of significant public health interest based on a recently released World Health Organization (WHO) report on antimicrobial resistance [26]. Using persistent homology, we characterize the rate and scale of recombination in the core genome using multilocus sequence data. To extend our characterization to the whole genome, we use protein family annotations as a proxy for sequence composition. This allows us to compute a similarity matrix between strains. Comparing persistence diagrams gives us information about the relative scales of gene transfer at arbitrary loci. The species selected for study and the sample sizes in each analysis are specified in Table 1. Next, we explore the spread of antibiotic resistance genes in *S. aureus* using Mapper, an algorithm for partial clustering and visualization of high dimensional data [19]. We identify

Table 1. Pathogenic bacteria selected for study and sample sizes in each analysis

Species	MLST profiles	PATRIC profiles
Campylobacter jejuni	7216	91
Escherichia coli	616	1621
Enterococcus faecalis	532	301
Haemphilus influenzae	1354	22
Helicobacter pylori	2759	366
Klebsiella pneumoniae	1579	161
Neisseria spp.	10802	234
Pseudomonas aeruginosa	1757	181
Staphylococcus aureus	2650	461
Salmonella enterica	1716	638
Streptococcus pneumoniae	9626	293
Streptococcus pyogenes	627	48

two major populations of *S. aureus*, and observe one cluster with strong enrichment for the antibiotic resistance gene *mecA*. Importantly, resistance appears to be increasingly spreading in the second population. Finally, we consider the risk of horizontal transfer of resistance genes from the human microbiome into an antibiotic sensitive strain, using β-Lactam resistence as an example. In this environment, benign bacterial strains can harbor known resistance genes. We use a network analysis to visualize the spread of antibiotic resistance gene *mecA* into nonnative phyla. Each individual has a unique microbiome, and we speculate that microbiome typing of this sort may useful in developing personalized antibiotic therapies.

These results demonstrate the important role the HCI-KDD approach can play in tackling the challenges of large scale -omics data applied to clinical settings and personalized medicine: Interactive visualization through graph and network construction, data mining global invariants with topological algorithms, and knowledge discovery through data integration and fusion [11][10].

2   Topological Data Analysis and Persistent Homology

Topological data analysis computes global invariants from point cloud data. These global invariants represent loops, holes, and higher dimensional voids in data. A topological representation of the data is constructed by building a set of triangulated objects representing the connectivity of the data at different scales, called a filtration. Various constructions exist for triangulating data. The most efficient approach for large scale data is the Vietoris-Rips complex, which associates a simplex to a set of points if they are pairwise connected. In this way, the complex is specified purely by its 1-skeleton, which can be efficiently computed.

Given a filtration, persistent homology is an algorithm to associate homology groups to each scale, which give information about the invariants in the data. H_0

gives information about the connectivity, H_1 about loops, etc. The output of the algorithm is a set of intervals corresponding to toplogoical features present at different scales. The homology information can be compactly summarized as a barcode diagram, in which invariants are represented as horizontal line segments with the birth and death scales as the left and right edge of the line segment, respectively. Alternatively, the homology information can be represented as a persistence diagram, a 2-d plot in which intervals are represented as points on a (birth,death) plane.

For the purposes of studying biological sequence data, and horizontal evolutionary processes in particular, these approaches are widely useful, as it was shown in [3] that sequence datasets with treelike phylogeny will have vanishing higher homology. The observed homological features are therefore direct evidence for horizontal exchange amonst the sequences in a sample. These topological constructions become a natural way of reasoning about evolutionary relationships between organisms in cases where treelike phylogeny is not appopriate.

3   Evolutionary Scales of Recombination in the Core Genome

The genes comprising the bacterial genome can be largely paritioned into two groups: the core genome, consisting of those genes that are highly conserved and characteristic of a given species classification, and the accessory genome, consisting of those genes whose presence can be variable even within strains of the same species. We first sought to examine scales of recombination in the core bacterial genome using multilocus sequence typing (MLST) data. MLST is a method of rapidly assigning a sequence profile to a sample bacterial strain. For each species, a predetermined set of loci on a small number of housekeeping genes are selected as representative of the core genome of the species. As new strains are sequenced, they are annotated with a profile corresponding to the sequence type at each locus. If a sample has a previously unseen type at a given locus, it is appended to the list of types at that locus. Large online databases have curated MLST data from labs around the world; significant pathogens can have several thousand typed strains (over 10,000 in the case of *Neisseria spp.*). Because different species will be typed at different loci, examining direct interspecies genetic exchange with this data is unfeasible, however MLST provides a large quantity of data with which to examine intraspecies exchange in the core genome. However, because the selected loci are generally all housekeeping genes, this type of recombination analysis will be only informative about genetic exchange in the core genome. Mobile genetic elements will have separate rates of exchange.

We investigate horizontal exchange in the core genome for twelve pathogens using MLST data from PubMLST [13]. For each strain, a pseudogenome can be constructed by concatenating the typed sequence at each locus. Using a Hamming metric, we construct a pairwise distance matrix between strains and compute persistent homology on the resulting metric space. Because of the large

number of sample strains, we employ a Lazy Witness complex with 250 land-
mark points and $\nu = 0$ [6]. The computation is performed using javaplex [21].
An example of our output is shown in Figure 1, where we plot the H_1 barcode diagrams for *K. pneumoniae* and *S. enterica*. The two species have distinct
recombination profiles, characterized by the range of recombinations: *K. pneumoniae* recombines at only one short-lived scale, while *S. enterica* recombines
both at the short-lived scale and a longer-lived scale. We repeat this analysis for
each species, and plot the results as a persistence diagram in Figure 2. Among
the bulk of pathogens there appears to be three major scales of recombination,
a short-lived scale at intermediate distances, a longer-lived scale at intermediate
distances, and a short-lived scale at longer distances. *H. polyori* is a clear outlier,
tending to recombine at scales significantly lower than the other pathogens.

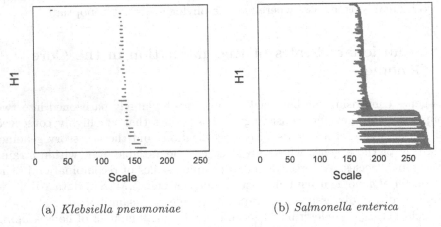

(a) *Klebsiella pneumoniae*   (b) *Salmonella enterica*

Fig. 1. Barcode diagrams reflect different scales of genomic exchange in *K. pneumoniae*
and *S. enterica*

We define a relative rate of recombination by counting the number of H_1 loops
across the filtration and dividing by the number of samples for that species. The
results are shown in Figure 3, where we observe that different species can have
vastly different recombination profiles. For example, *S. enterica* and *E. coli* have
the highest recombination rates, while *H. pylori* is substantially lower than the
others. Coupled with the smaller scale of recombinations suggests that the *H.
pylori* core genome is relatively resistant to recombination except within closely
related strains.

4   Protein Families as a Proxy for Genome Wide Reticulation

Protein family annotations cluster proteins into sets of isofunctional homologs,
i.e., clusters of proteins with both similar sequence composition and similar

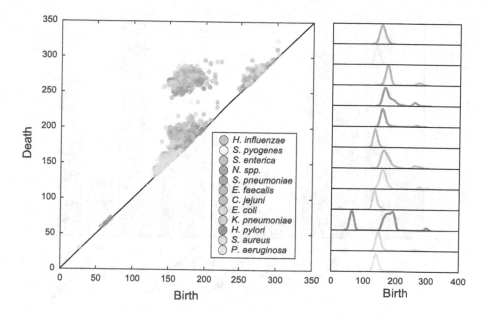

Fig. 2. The H_1 persistence diagram for the twelve pathogenic strains selected for this study using MLST profile data. There are three broad scales of recombination. To the right is the birth time distribution for each strain. *H. pylori* has an earlier scale of recombination not present in the other species.

function. A particular strain is represented as a binary vector indicating the presence or absence of a given protein family. Correlations between strains can reveal genome-wide patterns of genetic exchange, unlike the MLST data which can only provide evidence of exchange in the core genome. We use the FigFam protein annotations in the Pathosystems Resource Institute Center (PATRIC) database because of the breadth of pathogenic strain coverage and depth of genomic annotations [24]. The FigFam annotation scheme consists of over 100,000 protein families curated from over 950,000 unique proteins [14].

For each strain we compute a transformation into FigFam space. We transform into this space because the frequency of genome rearrangements and differences in mobile genetic elements makes whole genome alignments unreliable, even for strains within the same species. As justification for performing this step, it has been shown experimentally that recombination rates decrease with increasing genetic distance [9]. After transforming, we construct a strain-strain correlation matrix and compute the persistent homology in this space. In Figure 4 we show the persistence diagram relating the structure and scale between different species. We find that different species have a much more diverse topological structure in this space than in MLST space, and a wide variety of recombination scales. The large scales of exchange in *H. influenzae* suggest it can regularly acquire novel genetic material from distantly related strains.

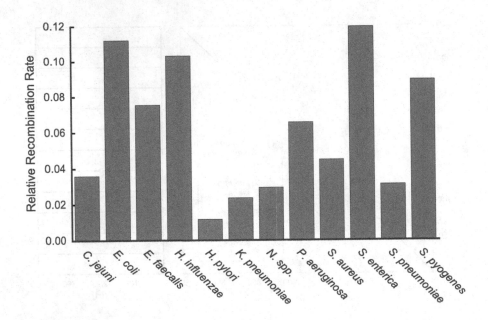

Fig. 3. Relative recombination rates computed by persistent homology from MLST profile data

5   Antibiotic Resistance in *Staphylococcus aureus*

S. aureus is a gram positive bacteria commonly found in the nostrils and upper respiratory tract. Certain strains can cause severe infection in high-risk populations, particulary in the hospital setting. The emergence of antibiotic resistant *S. aureus* is therefore of significant clinical concern. Methicillin resistant *S. aureus* (MRSA) strains are resistant to β-Lactam antibiotics including penicillin and cephalosporin. Resistance is conferred by the gene *mecA*, an element of the Staphyloccoccal cassette chromosome mec (*SCCmec*). *mecA* codes for a dysfunctional penicillin-binding protein 2a (PBP2a), which inhibits β-Lactam antibiotic binding, the primary mechanism of action [12]. Of substantial clinical importance are methods for characterizing the spread of MRSA within the *S. aureus* population.

To address this question, we use the FigFam annotations in PATRIC, as described in the previous section. PATRIC contains genomic annotations for 461 strains of *S. aureus*, collectively spanning 3,578 protein families. We perform a clustering analysis using the Mapper algorithm as implemented in Ayasdi Iris [1]. Principal and second metric singular value decomposition are used as filter functions, with a 4x gain and an equalized resolution of 30. This results in a graph structure with two large clusters, connected by a narrow bridge, as shown in Figure 5. The two clusters are consistent with previous phylogenetic studies using multilocus sequence data to identify two major population groups [4].

Of the 461 *S. aureus* strains in PATRIC, 142 carry the *mecA* gene. When we color nodes in the network based on an enrichment for the presence of *mecA*, we observe a much stronger enrichment in one of the two clusters. This suggests that β-Lactam resistance has already begun to dominate in that clade, likely due to selective pressures. More strikingly, we observe that while *mecA* enrichment is not as strong in the second cluster, there is a distinct path of enrichment emanating along the connecting bridge between the two clusters and into the less enriched cluster. This suggests the hypothesis that antibiotic resistance has spread from the first cluster into the second cluster via strains intermediate to the two, and will likely continue to be selected for in the second cluster.

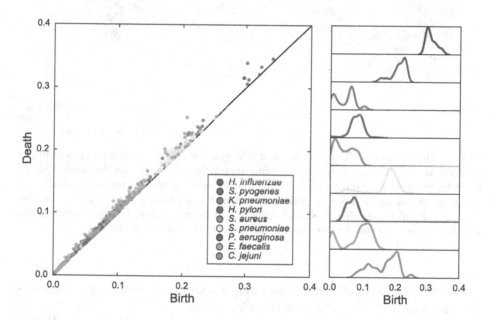

Fig. 4. Persistence diagram for a subset of pathogenic bacteria, computed using the FigFam annotations compiled in PATRIC. Compared to the MLST persistence diagram, the Figfam diagram has a more diverse scale of topological structure.

6 Microbiome as a Reservoir of Antibiotic Resistance Genes

While antibiotic resistance can be acquired through gene exchange between strains of the same species, it is also possible for gene exchange to occur between distantly related species. It has been recognized that an individual's microbiome, the set of microorganisms that exist symbiotically within a human host, can act as a reservoir of antimicrobial resistance genes [20,17]. It is of substantial clinical interest to characterize to what extent an individual's microbiome may pose

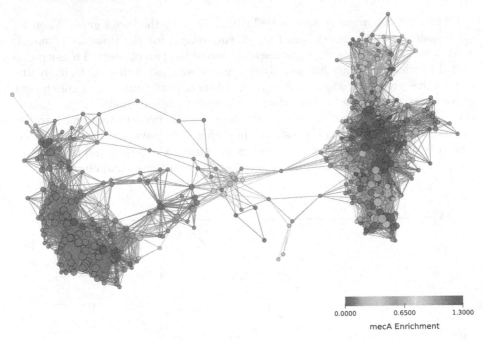

mecA Enrichment

Fig. 5. The FigFam similarity network of *S. aureus* constructed using Mapper as implemented in Ayasdi Iris. We use a Hamming metric and Primary and Secondary Metric SVD filters (res: 30, gain 4x, eq.). Node color is based on strain enrichment for *mecA*, the gene conferring β-Lactam resistance. Two distinct clades of *S. aureus* are visible, one of which has already been compromised for resistance. Of important clinical significance is the growing enrichment for *mecA* in the second clade.

a risk for a pathogenic bacteria acquiring a resistance gene through horizontal transfer from an benign strain in the microbiome.

To address this question, we use data from the Human Microbiome Project (HMP), a major research initiative performing metagenomic characterization of hundreds of healthy human microbiomes [22]. The HMP has defined a set of reference strains that have been observed in the human microbiome. We collect FigFam annotations from PATRIC for the reference strain list in the gastrointestinal tract. We focus on the gastrointestinal tract because it is an isolated environment and likely to undergo higher rates of exchange than other anatomic regions. Of the 717 gastrointestinal tract reference strains, 321 had FigFam annotations. We computed a similarity matrix as in previous sections, using correlation as distance. The resulting network is shown in Figure 6, where strains are colored by phyla-level classifications. While largely recapitulating phylogeny, the network depicts interesting correlations between phyla, such as the loop between Firmicutes, Bacteroides, and Proteobacteria.

Next, we searched for genomic annotations relating to β-Lactam resistance. 10 strains in the reference set had matching annotations, and we highlight those

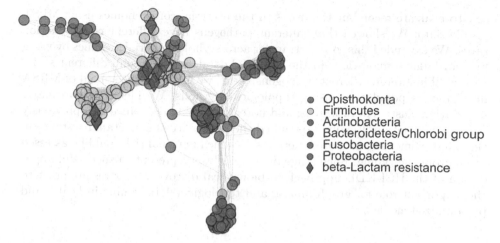

- ● Opisthokonta
- ○ Firmicutes
- ● Actinobacteria
- ● Bacteroidetes/Chlorobi group
- ● Fusobacteria
- ● Proteobacteria
- ◆ beta-Lactam resistance

Fig. 6. The FigFam similarity network of gastrointestinal tract reference strains identified in the Human Microbiome Project. The green diamond identifies the strains carrying resistance to β-Lactam antibiotics.

strains in the network with green diamonds. We observe resistance mostly concentrated in the Firmicutes, of which *S. aureus* is a member, however there is a strain of Proteobacteria that has acquired the resistance gene. Transfer of β-Lactam resistance into the Protebacteria is clinically worrisome. Pathogenic Proteobacteria include *S. enterica*, *V. cholerae*, and *H. pylori*, and emergence of β-Lactam resistance will severely impact currently used antibiotic drug therapies.

The species composition of each individual's microbiome can differ substantially due to a wide variety of poorly understood factors [22]. In this case, an individual's personal microbiome network will differ from the network we show in Figure 6, which was constructed from the set of *all* strains that have been reported across studies of multiple individuals. The relative risk for acquiring self-induced resistance will therefore vary from person to person and by the infectious strain acquired. However, a network analysis of this type can be used to assess risk and give clues as to possible routes by which antibiotic resistance may be acquired. In the clinical setting, this could assist in developing personalized antibiotic treatment regimens. We propose a more thorough expansion of this work, examining the full range of antibiotic resistance genes in order to quantify microbiome risk factors for treatment failure. We foresee an era of genomically informed infectious disease management in the clinical setting, based on an understanding of a patient's personal microbiome network profile.

7 Conclusions

In this paper we have brought some ideas from topological data analysis to bear on problems in pathogenic microbial genetics. First, we used persistent homology to evaluate recombination rates in the bacterial core genomes using MLST profile data. We showed that different pathogens have different recombination rates. We expanded this to gene transfer across whole bacterial genomes by using protein family annotations in the PATRIC database. We found different scales of recombination in different pathogens. Next, we explored the spread of MRSA in *S. aureus* populations using topological methods. We identified two major population clusters of *S. aureus*, and noted increasing resistance in a previously isolated population. Finally, we studied the emergence of β-Lactam resistance in the microbiome, and proposed methods by which personal risk could be assessed by microbiome typing. Each stage of this analysis represents a successful application of the HCI-KDD approach to biomedical discovery. Our results point to the important role for graph mining and topological data mining in health and personalized medicine.

Acknowledgements. The authors thank Gunnar Carlsson for access to the Ayasdi Iris platform. KJE thanks Chris Wiggins, Daniel Rosenbloom, and Sakellarios Zairis for useful discussions. KJE and RR were supported by NIH grant U54-CA121852, Multiscale Analysis of Genomic and Cellular Networks.

This publication made use of the PubMLST website (http://pubmlst.org/) developed by Keith Jolley [13] and sited at the University of Oxford. The development of that website was funded by the Wellcome Trust.

References

1. Ayasdi Inc.: Iris, http://www.ayasdi.com
2. Carlsson, G.: Topology and data. Bulletin-American Mathematical Society 46(2), 255 (2009)
3. Chan, J.M., Carlsson, G., Rabadan, R.: Topology of viral evolution. Proceedings of the National Academy of Sciences of the United States of America 110(46), 18566–18571 (2013)
4. Cooper, J.E., Feil, E.J.: The phylogeny of Staphylococcus aureus - which genes make the best intra-species markers? Microbiology 152(5), 1297–1305 (2006)
5. Dagan, T., Martin, W.: The tree of one percent. Genome Biol. 7(10), 118 (2006)
6. de Silva, V., Carlsson, G.: Topological estimation using witness complexes. In: Proceedings of the First Eurographics Conference on Point-Based Graphics, pp. 157–166. Eurographics Association (2004)
7. Edelsbrunner, H., Harer, J.: Computational topology: an introduction. American Mathematical Society (2010)
8. Emmett, K., Rosenbloom, D., Camara, P., Rabadan, R.: Parametric inference using persistence diagrams: A case study in population genetics. In: ICML Workshop on Topological Methods in Machine Learning (2014)
9. Fraser, C., Hanage, W.P., Spratt, B.G.: Recombination and the Nature of Bacterial Speciation. Science 315(5811), 476–480 (2007)
10. Holzinger, A., Dehmer, M., Jurisica, I.: Knowledge Discovery and interactive Data Mining in Bioinformatics-State-of-the-Art, future challenges and research directions. BMC Bioinformatics 15(suppl. 6), 11 (2014)

11. Holzinger, A.: Human-computer interaction and knowledge discovery (HCI-KDD): What is the benefit of bringing those two fields to work together? In: Cuzzocrea, A., Kittl, C., Simos, D.E., Weippl, E., Xu, L. (eds.) CD-ARES 2013. LNCS, vol. 8127, pp. 319–328. Springer, Heidelberg (2013)

12. Jensen, S.O., Lyon, B.R.: Genetics of antimicrobial resistance in *Staphylococcus aureus*. Future Microbiology 4(5), 565–582 (2009)

13. Jolley, K.A., Maiden, M.C.: BIGSdb: Scalable analysis of bacterial genome variation at the population level. BMC Bioinformatics 11(1), 595 (2010)

14. Meyer, F., Overbeek, R., Rodriguez, A.: FIGfams: yet another set of protein families. Nucleic Acids Research 37(20), 6643–6654 (2009)

15. Neu, H.C.: The Crisis in Antibiotic Resistance. Science 257(5073), 1064–1073 (1992)

16. Ochman, H., Lawrence, J.G., Groisman, E.A.: Lateral gene transfer and the nature of bacterial innovation. Nature 405(6784), 299–304 (2000)

17. Penders, J., Stobberingh, E.E., Savelkoul, P.H., Wolffs, P.F.: The human microbiome as a reservoir of antimicrobial resistance. Frontiers in Microbiology 4 (2013)

18. Rohde, H., Qin, J., Cui, Y., Li, D., Loman, N.J., Hentschke, M., Chen, W., Pu, F., Peng, Y., Li, J., Xi, F., Li, S., Li, Y., Zhang, Z., Yang, X., Zhao, M., Wang, P., Guan, Y., Cen, Z., Zhao, X., Christner, M., Kobbe, R., Loos, S., Oh, J., Yang, L., Danchin, A., Gao, G.F., Song, Y., Li, Y., Yang, H., Wang, J., Xu, J., Pallen, M.J., Wang, J., Aepfelbacher, M., Yang, R.: Open-source genomic analysis of shiga-toxin–producing E. coli O104:H4. New England Journal of Medicine 365(8), 718–724 (2011)

19. Singh, G., Mémoli, F., Carlsson, G.: Topological methods for the analysis of high dimensional data sets and 3d object recognition. In: Eurographics Symposium on Point-Based Graphics. The Eurographics Association, Prague (2007)

20. Sommer, M.O., Church, G.M., Dantas, G.: The human microbiome harbors a diverse reservoir of antibiotic resistance genes. Virulence 1(4), 299–303 (2010)

21. Tausz, A., Vejdemo-Johansson, M., Adams, H.: Javaplex: A research software package for persistent (co)homology (2011), Software available at http://code.google.com/javaplex

22. The Human Microbiome Project Consortium: Structure, function and diversity of the healthy human microbiome. Nature 486(7402), 207–214 (2012)

23. Thomas, C.M., Nielsen, K.M.: Mechanisms of, and Barriers to, Horizontal Gene Transfer between Bacteria. Nature Reviews Microbiology 3(9), 711–721 (2005)

24. Wattam, A.R., Abraham, D., Dalay, O., Disz, T.L., Driscoll, T., Gabbard, J.L., Gillespie, J.J., Gough, R., Hix, D., Kenyon, R., Machi, D., Mao, C., Nordberg, E.K., Olson, R., Overbeek, R., Pusch, G.D., Shukla, M., Schulman, J., Stevens, R.L., Sullivan, D.E., Vonstein, V., Warren, A., Will, R., Wilson, M.J.C., Yoo, H.S., Zhang, C., Zhang, Y., Sobral, B.W.: PATRIC, the bacterial bioinformatics database and analysis resource. Nucleic Acids Research 42(D1), D581–D591 (2013)

25. Woese, C.R., Fox, G.E.: Phylogenetic structure of the prokaryotic domain: the primary kingdoms. Proceedings of the National Academy of Sciences of the United States of America 74(11), 5088–5090 (1977)

26. World Health Organization: Antimicrobial Resistance: global report on surveillance 2014 (2014), http://www.who.int/drugresistance/documents/surveillancereport/en/

On Graph Extraction from Image Data

Andreas Holzinger, Bernd Malle, and Nicola Giuliani

Research Unit Human-Computer Interaction, Institute for Medical Informatics,
Statistics & Documentation, Medical University Graz, Austria
{a.holzinger,b.malle,n.giuliani}@hci4all.at

Abstract. Hot topics in knowledge discovery and interactive data mining from natural images include the application of topological methods and machine learning algorithms. For any such approach one needs at first a relevant and robust digital content representation from the image data. However, traditional pixel-based image analysis techniques do not effectively extract, hence represent the content. A very promising approach is to extract graphs from images, which is not an easy task. In this paper we present a novel approach for knowledge discovery by extracting graph structures from natural image data. For this purpose, we created a framework built upon modern Web technologies, utilizing HTML canvas and pure Javascript inside a Web-browser, which is a very promising engineering approach. Following on a short description of some popular image classification and segmentation methodologies, we outline a specific data processing pipeline suitable for carrying out future scientific research. A demonstration of our implementation, compared to the results of a traditional watershed transformation performed in Matlab showed very promising results in both quality and runtime, despite some open problems. Finally, we provide a short discussion of a few open problems and outline some of our future research routes.

Keywords: data preprocessing, image segmentation, graphs, graph-based algorithms, graph extraction, image analysis, image content analytics, knowledge discovery, data mining.

1 Introduction and Motivation

Big challenges in the biomedical domain are today in the development of new methods, algorithms and tools for the effective analysis and interpretation of complex biomedical data [1]. Within such data sets, relevant structural and/or temporal patterns ("knowledge") are often hidden, difficult to extract, thus not directly accessible to a biomedical expert, consequently, a major challenge is in interactive Knowledge Discovery and Data Mining which relies heavily on machine learning approaches. However, many of the classical methods are based on the assumption that the data objects under consideration are represented in terms of feature vectors, or collections of attribute values; Bunke (2003) [2], for example, argued that graphs have a representational power that is significantly higher than the representational power of feature vectors. Moreover,

D. Ślęzak et al. (Eds.): BIH 2014, LNAI 8609, pp. 552–563, 2014.

graph-theory provides powerful tools to map data structures and to find novel connections between data objects [3] and allow the application of statistical and machine learning techniques [4].

Methods from computational geometry and algebraic topology may also be of great help [5], and could be combined with machine learning approaches, e.g. evolutionary algorithms [6], [7]. Promising future research routes in this field are in interactive visual data mining together with graph-based data analysis [8], [9]. Another benefit of a graph-based data structure is in the applicability of methods from network topology and network analysis and data mining, e.g. small-world phenomenon [10], and cluster analysis [11] to mention only two.

The application of graph theory to image analysis (see e.g. [12]) is in the focus of research for some time and still poses a lot of challenges and calls for new approaches.

2 Definitions

In this work we are dealing with *natural images*, which includes every digital image taken from real world scenes, for example biomedical images from dermoscopy (epiluminescence microscopy). The starting point of our calculations is the conversion of such a digital image into a topographic map, which we need for graph extraction. Caselles et al. (1999) [13] provide some necessary definitions:

Definition 1 (digital image). *A digital image is modelled as a real function* $u(x)$*, where* x *represents an arbitrary point of the plane and* $u(x)$ *denotes the grey-level at* x*. Let* $u : \Omega \to \mathbb{R}$ *be an image, i.e., a bounded measurable function.*

Definition 2 (upper level set). *Given an image* u*, we call upper level set of* u *any set of the form* $[u \geq \lambda]$ *where* $\lambda \in \mathbb{R}$*.*

Definition 3 (connected component). *Let* X *be a topological space. We say that* X *is connected if it cannot be written as the union ot two nonempty closed (open) disjoint sets. A subset* C *of* X *is called a connected component id* C *is a maximal connected subset of* X*, i.e.,* C *is connected and for any conected subset* C_1 *of* X *such that* $C \subseteq C_1$*, then* $C_1 = C$*.*

Definition 4 (upper topographic map). *The upper topographic map of an image is the family of the connected components of the level sets od* u*,* $[u \geq \lambda]$*,* $\lambda \in \mathbb{R}$*.*

Definition 5 (topographic map). *If* u *belongs to a function space, such that each connected component of a level set is bounded by a countable or finite number of oriented Jordan curves, we call topographic map the family of these Jordan curves.*

3 Related Work

3.1 Traditional Image Classification

In the biomedical domain there has been a shift in demands, from software assisting in the production and processing of image data, analysed by humans alone, to software systems to represent, discover and evaluate knowledge. In [14] the authors describe a method of image classification which might be categorized as traditional, in the sense that it does not segment an image into logical substructures and attempts to compute relations among those. Instead, it uses metrics based on pixel values, divided into 1st order statistical parameters which describe the global structure of an image, and 2nd order statistical parameters which describe the neighborhoods of individual pixels.

- **1st order parameters.** Amongst the global parameters are those that use grey-value probabilities (histogram values) as the building blocks of their formulas. They include variance (as a measure of homogeneity), skewness (asymmetry of the value distribution), kurtosis (shape, either peaked or flat) and energy as well as entropy.
- **2nd order parameters.** In order to calculate those, the probability of grey-value co-occurrence is used as a basic concept. Using these values, the local / neighborhood parameters Energy, Entropy, Contrast, Homogeneity and Correlation are computed.

Once the needed metrics were taken, a C4.5 algorithm was used to build a decision tree and classify the images. Although the algorithm is not a segmentation approach as such and thus not immediately usable in the endeavour to extract graph structures out of image data, it could provide regional information usable as classifiers in tasks such as identifying structural / topographical primitives. Therefore it might constitute a building block in the preprocessing pipeline of a more extensive procedure.

3.2 Watershed Methods

Watershed algorithms [15] got their name from the fact that they treat images as topographic maps, that is as 'landscapes' with height structures. The segmentation of those landscapes into regions of pixels belonging together is then performed by assuming drops of water raining down on the map, following paths of descent into low areas until they form 'lakes', which in watershed terminology are called catchment basins. This can be thought of in one of various ways: by simulating drops raining from above, by immersing the whole landscape into an ocean (with holes punched into the deepest spots of the landscape, so the water can enter.), but also by using topographical distance measures like Minimum Spanning Trees (MST). A usual watershed processing pipeline consists of the following steps:

1. **Transformation into a topographic map.** The color or gray values of the pixels in an image are converted to height information; for example, if

given a grayscale from 0 (black) to 255 (white), one could assume 255 to be the highest possible peak in a landscape and 0 the deepest reachable point, thereby converting the image into a three-dimensional structure of voxels with coordinates (x, y, z). As a first step, the application of a gradient filter in order to produce continuous 'crests' throughout the landscape might be in order.

2. **Finding local minima.** In order to be able to fill a topographical relief with imaginary fluid by immersion, one first has to find the points through which the fluid can enter the landscape (or above which points it accumulates, depending on one's view). This is akin to finding the set of local minima in the image interpreted as topographical relief. This can easily be done in an image, by inspecting small regions of the image in sequence and finding the ones with the lowest value (one would probably use color or computed grey values). If such an operation would result in a significant percentage of all pixels marked as minima, which is often the case with watershed methods, a suitable subset of the computed minima (= seed points) can also be used instead.

3. **Finding catchment basins.** The main point in using watershed methods is finding regions that spatially belong together. They are usually seen as caverns or ditches separated by crests (the formations already extracted from color / grey value information earlier). This is done by using an algorithm to simulate flooding, so that the water accumulates in basins until it reaches a crest. At this point the basin can either 'flow over', filling an adjacent deep region as well, or the flooding can be stopped by erecting a virtual watershed. Another way to see this is by visualizing the voxels as vertices of a graph; based on this structure, the voxels belonging to a nearest minimum can be found by applying traditional, well-tested and well-understood graph algorithms such as Minimum Spanning Trees (MST). In order to find the voxels belonging to a catchment basin, the edges between them would first be assigned a weight corresponding to the distance they represent. By introducing auxiliary vertices connecting the first set of minimum points in the landscape via an edge of weight zero, a connected MST can be found which encompasses all the vertices in the graph. The individual subtrees starting at the set of minimum points then form the output of the algorithm.

4. **Erecting watersheds.** Functioning as an artificial divide between two adjacent catchment basins, watersheds provide the final segmentation lines of the process described. When to erect a watershed vs. letting two regions merge (by being overflowed from one side) is a question depending on how many segments are wanted, so no universal decision criterion exists. As watershed methods often produce over-segmented images, this is a very important point in implementing such a procedure.

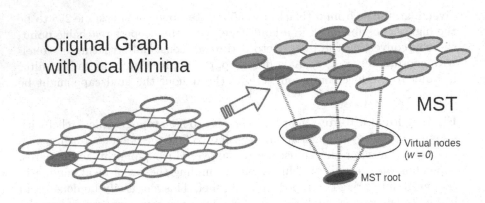

Fig. 1. MST view of finding catchment basins: According to [16] a minimum spanning tree can be computed using auxiliary (virtual) vertices. The weight of the edges represents a dissimilarity measure between pixels / voxels.

3.3   Region Merging

This section briefly describes a region merging algorithm which was published by [17]. This algorithm forms the basis of our own image segmentation implementation whose results will be discussed in a later section.

The original digital image can be interpreted as a directed, conservative weighted graph G, whose vertices V are the pixels themselves, where every (non-bordering) vertex has eight edges to its neighbouring nodes. Every edge $e \in E$ is weighted with the difference of the intensity values $i \in \{0 \dots 255\}$ of the pixels it connects. In this initial phase every pixel also constitutes its own region. To group similar pixels into a region R, where R is a subset of V, the following steps (written as pseudo algorithm) are needed:

1. Sort all edges $e \in E$ in ascending order.
2. For all edges e do:
    (a) Check if the pixels connected by e are already in the same region. If yes, continue to the next edge.
    (b) If not, check if there exists a boundary between the regions under observation. There exists a boundary if the minimum edge weight connecting those regions is greater than the minimum of the maximum internal MST-edges of the respective regions, where MST denotes the Minimum-Spanning Tree of the regions the pixels belong to.
    (c) If a boundary exists, continue to the next edge.
    (d) Else, merge the regions and update any pertinent properties (internal MST, avg color, gradients, etc.).

3.4   Segmentation Techniques Using Hybrid Approaches

Aside the rather traditional approaches mentioned earlier there has also been published some interesting work in methods using anterior knowledge about object primitives, employing supervised learning etc. An example of this is the approach described in [18]. First, they propose extracting known and unknown objects from an image - this of course presupposes the existance of such knowledge and an efficient lookup possibility in an object database. Once those primitives are established, they compute object histograms over several different distances for each single object previously found. Thus they strive to derive an understanding about the global image structure from individual regions. For instance, if an object were a tree, and its histograms of surrounding objects would comprise (in ascending order of distance): 3 trees, 7 tress, 25 trees..., one could infer that the image depicted a forest. If, however, the histograms would show: 3 trees and 3 windows, 5 trees and 5 windows, 7 trees and 7 windows..., the image might rather depict an alley. Although in our work we are not yet concerned about object recognition or category discovery, this modern approach is rather similar to ours and we are looking forward to seeing further advancement in the area.

4   Experimental Setup

Our overall goal is to establish a software framework for graph extraction and graph analysis which is open source and accessible via a Web site. Specifically, as technology in Virtual Machines has improved dramatically since the late 2000s, it is now feasible to conduct such computations client side in a language like Javascript, which would have been fantastic only a few years back. The advantages to this approach are manifold: First, the possibility of running a low-cost infrastructure as scaling is done automatically by users providing their own computational power. Second, we have to store only the compressed graph structure (in JSON) along with some metadata concerning the algorithms and parameters used; storing the complete images is no longer required. Third, the processing is done faster because the additional computation time necessary in Javascript is now less than the time it takes to upload an image. Fourth, we can thus make use of the amazing visualization capabilities now offered for free by modern Javascript libraries; this will allow our users to immediately see and interact with the results of our computations.

4.1   Processing Pipeline

In extracting a graph from a natural image, we generally follow 4 consecutive steps whose specific implementation may be switched and whose input and output datastructures may vary depending on the chosen segmentation algorithm. Nevertheless, they form a logical flow which we intend to formalize in later versions of our framework in order to provide a standard procedure that user extensions can be plugged into.

1. **Image Preprocessing.** As a first step we may need to apply some preprocessing operations, e.x. the conversion to an intensity (grayscale) image or a background separation step. In any case both input and output of this step are images.

2. **Algorithmic Preprocessing.** There exist a wide variety of image segmentation algorithms, some of which are graph-based (like the region merging approach described earlier), while others would use clustering, compression etc. Therefore, the second step in our pipeline consists of providing the datastructures needed by the particular class of segmentation method. For the example case in this paper, we transform the image to an initial graph structure, with every pixel forming it's own region, and provide an adjacency list and edge list representation for further computations.

3. **Image Segmentation.** The core of our processing pipeline consists of the actual image segmentation step, which transforms the datastructures provided to it into a label map denoting each pixels affiliation to a region. In this step users should be able to choose among different classes and specific implementations of algorithms. In the future we also intend to give users the opportunity to implement and upload their own code, which will be injected into the pipeline.

4. **Graph extraction.** Based on the label map produced in the preceding step we can now extract the graph structure by first computing the region centroids followed by a Delaunay triangulation on the resulting set of vertices. Additionally, depending on the chosen segmentation algorithm and implementation, a representative feature vector will be stored for each region. This might include information like average color, gradients, or environment histograms, and in the future will be adaptable by the user as well.

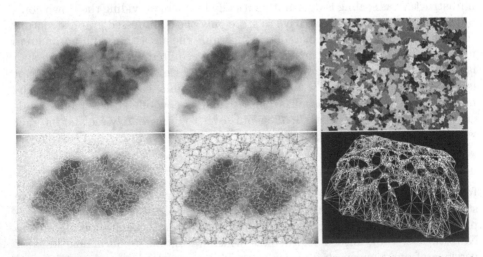

Fig. 2. A depiction of our computational pipeline: The input image (1) is transformed by a simple preprocessing step (2), then we segment the image using the Meyers 1994 watershed algorithm (Matlab implementation) [19] (3). Once the regions are obtained, centroids (4) as well as k-nearest neighbors (5) are computed and the graph is stored as a JSON datastructure visualized by the three.js Javascript framework (6).

5 Results

As we are building our graph extraction framework from the ground up, we have yet only implemented a single algorithm to demonstrate its feasability: We chose the Kruskal-based region merging algorithm described in [17] and implemented it in Javascript, adding two additional parameters to the algorithm: While the original paper only utilized k, which defined an input to the threshold computation above which two regions would be merged, we are also using s (size-threshold), the minimum size of pixels a region has to contain in order to be considered in the final graph construction phase, as well as m (max-merge-size) which gives the maximum amount of pixels a region may be grown to.

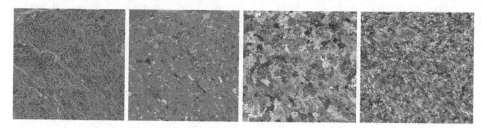

Fig. 3. Result of applying a Kruskal based region merging algorithm to an image of numerous small scale regular structures. (1) Input image, (2) Result with parameters $k = 1150, s = 0, m = \infty$, (3) Result with parameters $k = 150, s = 5, m = 500$, (4) Result with parameters $k = 50, s = 2, m = 150$.

In order to be able to compare our results, we performed a watershed-based segmentation plus graph extraction in Matlab as well. To that purpose, we chose a simple algorithm wich converts the RGB into an intensity image, performs a top hat filtering followed by a grey level threshold computation. It then converts the image to a binary matrix which the watershed is finally performed on. The algorithm only uses 1 parameter d to control its behavior - the size of the disk-shaped morphological structuring element that is used in the top hat filtering.

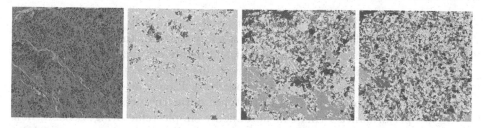

Fig. 4. Results of applying a Matlab Watershed algorithm to an image of numerous small scale regular structures. (1) Input image, (2) Result with parameter $d = 5$, (3) Result with parameter $d = 10$, (4) Result with parameter $d = 20$.

As we haven't implemented the watershed segmentation ourselves and there are diverse ways of doing this, we will not delve into details about the quality of the resulting images. However, we would like to compare the execution time of both algorithms for the different parameter settings as well as the resulting graph sizes, as those are important for any further computation. Our test system was equipped with a Core i5 Quad IvyBridge CPU, 8 GB of RAM and an SATA III SSD drive. No hardware acceleration was used in either case.

Table 1. Runtimes and graph sizes for different algorithms & parameter settings

Algorithm	k	s	m	d	Nr. Vertices	Runtime in ms
ML / Watershed				5	2,350	493
ML / Watershed				10	5,065	1,044
ML / Watershed				20	6,323	1,359
JS / Kruskal	1150	0	∞		3,952	3,178
JS / Kruskal	150	5	500		4,169	3,220
JS / Kruskal	50	2	150		13,916	3,863

Although at first glance it would seem that the Matlab based watershed algorithm clearly outperforms the Javascript based Kruskal segmentation, it is worth noting that the latter has only been in existence for about 2 weeks and no optimization has been performed on the code (see below). Moreover, since region merging depends on a sorted edge list for the original image graph, this base operation does not change with different parameters. Last, our Kruskal based method for the most extreme set of parameters produces a graph of about twice the number of vertices than the largest graph emitted by ML / Watershed.

6   Open Problems

Graph based analysis of image data on the Web (-browser) is still a novel topic. Consequently, there are many open issues to address, two of which will affect us in the immediate future.

- **Performance.** Even though our first results are already very promising and could not have been achieved only a few years ago, there is still a small gap in the performance of Javascript and highly optimized, Desktop-based compiled libraries. In order to address this issue, we propose to perform three improvements on our initial code base. First, our code currently uses generic Javascript data types, while typed datastructures allow significantly higher performance - this can be done by simple refactoring. Second, new technologies like asm.js would enable us to write low-level pieces of code in C and compile them to highly optimized Javascript. This requires special support by JS Virtual Machines, but has already shown the potential to speed up code execution to within 2x the runtime of native compiled C code. Third, a shift to parallel implementations of our algorithms would provide the opportunity to outsource those operations to a GPU (e.x. via WebGL), which could reduce runtime to a small fraction of today's.

— **Quality of extracted graphs.** At this point we can already extract graph structures of different sizes and forms, but we lack a metric to judge if the obtained graph is suitable for further computation towards a given goal. As there seem to be no scientific graph analysis libraries available in JS today, we will have to implement our own in order to compare the results to those obtained by traditional image segmentation or manual diagnosis [20].

7 Conclusion and Future Work

Hot and promising topics for future research in knowledge discovery and data mining from natural image data is in the application of sophisticated topological methods and machine learning approaches, where natural images are seen as topographical landscapes, or map structures, similar to a terrain network [21]. On such landscapes autonomous multi-agents [17] [22], e.g. ant-robots [23], can leave markings on "interesting" areas, where such markings can be sensed by all robots and allow them to cover the unknown terrain without direct communication with each other, e.g. to discover anomalies, similarities or dissimilarities in images - exactly the aim of knowledge discovery and data mining. In the near future we will focus on the following issues:

— **Multistage processing.** To get even better results on small scale regular structures, it could be useful to perform several passes of our methods. For instance, background separation could be achieved with certain parameters in a first step. Afterwards one can apply the method again in order to find similar structures within the remaining boundaries.

— **Compression / reconstruction of images via topographic maps.** When a digital image is converted to a topographic map, the whole image information could theoretically stay complete, in which case the image can be fully restored afterwards. This might lead to a new approach in image compression.

— **Similarity measure on graph structures.** One major problem of taking a single digital image is measurement errors (artefacts) stemming from electronic fluctuations in the picture taking device. We could avoid these mistakes by taking pictures in short sequence and merging them in a meaningful way. Furthermore identifying similarities and differences between these images could help to improve the quality and stability of the resulting graphs, thus enabling us to get more reliable results from the data.

— **Extendable Web based research platform.** In order to make our platform valuable to a variety of researchers, we not only need to implement a range of algorithms ourselves, but enable our users to easily exchange their results or even upload their own code to test it on predefined images. This would be interesting from our perspective as storing different *image − algorithm − parameter* sets opens up the way to meaningful comparisons of results as well as to applying machine learning techniques on the whole processing pipeline. Moreover, it is also desirable to our users as they could use our platform as a publishing service, making their research accessible / reproducible via simple bookmarking.

References

1. Holzinger, A., Dehmer, M., Jurisica, I.: Knowledge discovery and interactive data mining in bioinformatics state-of-the-art, future challenges and research directions. BMC Bioinformatics 15(suppl. 6), S1 (2014)
2. Bunke, H.: Graph-based tools for data mining and machine learning. In: Perner, P., Rosenfeld, A. (eds.) MLDM 2003. LNCS, vol. 2734, pp. 7–19. Springer, Heidelberg (2003)
3. Strogatz, S.: Exploring complex networks. Nature 410, 268–276 (2001)
4. Dehmer, M., Emmert-Streib, F., Mehler, A.: Towards an Information Theory of Complex Networks: Statistical Methods and Applications. Birkhaeuser, Boston (2011)
5. Holzinger, A.: On topological data mining. In: Holzinger, A., Jurisica, I. (eds.) Interactive Knowledge Discovery and Data Mining in Biomedical Informatics. LNCS, vol. 8401, pp. 331–356. Springer, Heidelberg (2014)
6. Holzinger, K., Palade, V., Rabadan, R., Holzinger, A.: Darwin or lamarck? future challenges in evolutionary algorithms for knowledge discovery and data mining. In: Holzinger, A., Jurisica, I. (eds.) Interactive Knowledge Discovery and Data Mining in Biomedical Informatics. LNCS, vol. 8401, pp. 35–56. Springer, Heidelberg (2014)
7. Holzinger, A., Blanchard, D., Bloice, M., Holzinger, K., Palade, V., Rabadan, R.: Darwin, lamarck, or baldwin: Applying evolutionary algorithms to machine learning techniques. In: The 2014 IEEE/WIC/ACM International Conference on Web Intelligence (WI 2014). IEEE (in print, 2014)
8. Holzinger, A., Jurisica, I.: Knowledge discovery and data mining in biomedical informatics: The future is in integrative, interactive machine learning solutions. In: Holzinger, A., Jurisica, I. (eds.) Knowledge Discovery and Data Mining. LNCS, vol. 8401, pp. 1–18. Springer, Heidelberg (2014)
9. Otasek, D., Pastrello, C., Holzinger, A., Jurisica, I.: Visual data mining: Effective exploration of the biological universe. In: Holzinger, A., Jurisica, I. (eds.) Knowledge Discovery and Data Mining. LNCS, vol. 8401, pp. 19–33. Springer, Heidelberg (2014)
10. Albert, R., Barabási, A.L.: Statistical mechanics of complex networks. Reviews of Modern Physics 74, 47–97 (2002)
11. Makrogiannis, S., Economou, G., Fotopoulos, S., Bourbakis, N.G.: Segmentation of color images using multiscale clustering and graph theoretic region synthesis. IEEE Transactions on Systems Man and Cybernetics Part A: Systems and Humans 35, 224–238 (2005)
12. Kropatsch, W.G., Burge, M., Glantz, R.: Graphs in image analysis. In: Kropatsch, W.G., Bischof, H. (eds.) Digital Image Analysis, pp. 179–197. Springer, New York (2001)
13. Caselles, V., Coll, B., Morel, J.M.: Topographic maps and local contrast changes in natural images. International Journal of Computer Vision 33, 5–27 (1999)

14. Ahammer, H., Kröpfl, J.M., Hackl, C., Sedivy, R.: Image statistics and data mining of anal intraepithelial neoplasia. Pattern Recognition Letters 29, 2189–2196 (2008)
15. Vincent, L., Soille, P.: Watersheds in digital spaces: an efficient algorithm based on immersion simulations. IEEE Transactions on Pattern Analysis and Machine Intelligence 13, 583–598 (1991)
16. Straehle, C., Peter, S., Köthe, U., Hamprecht, F.A.: K-smallest spanning tree segmentations. In: Weickert, J., Hein, M., Schiele, B. (eds.) GCPR 2013. LNCS, vol. 8142, pp. 375–384. Springer, Heidelberg (2013)
17. Felzenszwalb, P.F., Huttenlocher, D.P.: Efficient graph-based image segmentation. International Journal of Computer Vision 59, 167–181 (2004)
18. Lee, Y.J., Grauman, K.: Object-graphs for context-aware visual category discovery. IEEE Transactions on Pattern Analysis and Machine Intelligence 34, 346–358 (2012)
19. Meyer, F.: Topographic distance and watershed lines. Signal Processing 38, 113–125 (1994)
20. Holzinger, A., Malle, B., Bloice, M., Wiltgen, M., Ferri, M., Stanganelli, I., Hofmann-Wellenhof, R.: On the generation of point cloud data sets: Step one in the knowledge discovery process. In: Holzinger, A., Jurisica, I. (eds.) Knowledge Discovery and Data Mining. LNCS, vol. 8401, pp. 57–80. Springer, Heidelberg (2014)
21. Preuß, M., Dehmer, M., Pickl, S., Holzinger, A.: On terrain coverage optimization by using a network approach for universal graph-based data mining and knowledge discovery. In: Slezak, D., Peters, J.F., Ah-Hwee, T., Schwabe, L. (eds.) Brain Informatics and Health. LNCS (LNAI), vol. 8609, pp. 569–578. Springer, Heidelberg (2014)
22. Olfati-Saber, R., Fax, J.A., Murray, R.M.: Consensus and cooperation in networked multi-agent systems. Proceedings of the IEEE 95, 215–233 (2007)
23. Wagner, I., Bruckstein, A.: From ants to a(ge)nts: A special issue on ant-robotics. Annals of Mathematics and Artificial Intelligence 31, 1–5 (2001)

On Terrain Coverage Optimization by Using a Network Approach for Universal Graph-Based Data Mining and Knowledge Discovery

Michael Preuß[1], Matthias Dehmer[1], Stefan Pickl[1], and Andreas Holzinger[2,3]

[1] Institute for Theoretical Computer Science, Mathematics & Operations Research,
University of the German Federal Armed Forces Munich, Germany
michael.preuss@unibw.de, stefan.pickl@unibw.de,
matthias.dehmer@umit.at
[2] Research Unit HCI, Institute for Medical Informatics, Medical University Graz
[3] Institute for Information Systems and Computer Media,
Graz University of Technology, Austria
a.holzinger@hci4all.at

Abstract. This conceptual paper discusses a graph-based approach for on-line terrain coverage, which has many important research aspects and a wide range of application possibilities, e.g in multi-agents. Such approaches can be used in different application domains, e.g. in medical image analysis. In this paper we discuss how the graphs are being generated and analyzed. In particular, the analysis is important for improving the estimation of the parameter set for the used heuristic in the field of route planning. Moreover, we describe some methods from quantitative graph theory and outline a few potential research routes.

1 Introduction

The on-line terrain coverage problem is very important and can be found in many different real world applications in diverse areas ranging from farming [1] to search and rescue [2].

There are a few research attempts on terrain coverage based on genetic algorithms, in particular ant-robots [3], and in [4] a simultaneous on-line coverage strategy for multi-robots is presented, which assures robust coverage of the surface regardless of the shape of the unknown environment. This is very interesting as ant-robots can cover terrain by leaving "markings" in the terrain, similar as in nature, and these markings can be sensed by all robots and allow them to cover the unknown terrain without direct communication with each other. Such approaches can be used for knowledge discovery and interactive data mining [5, 6].

By means of smart autonomous single agents or a swarm, these applications pursue the main objective to cover an unknown environment without any a priori information. For the multi-agent case this problem is known as NP-hard [7]. The coordination of multi-agent systems have been investigated extensively

D. Ślęzak et al. (Eds.): BIH 2014, LNAI 8609, pp. 564–573, 2014.

[8]. There are examples for the coordination of multi-agent systems in biology [9, 10] and physics [11] inspired approaches as well as economic based control models [12, 13].

While the agents visit each location at least once, they create a graph to represent the actual information of the environment. Through continuous sensing and data collection, the graph will change during the whole run time. To optimize the coverage process the agents try to find suitable routes based on the actual graph. There are established heuristics to solve the route planning problem [14–18]. The quality of the determined solutions depends on the used parameter set of the heuristic. Therefore it is necessary to analyze the available graph before. As a result we are able to estimate and adjust the heuristic parameters to find optimized routes.

This paper is structured as follows. Firstly, the general terrain coverage assumptions and an overview of the graph building process are presented. Secondly, we describe the optimization process from the current coverage to Terrain networks through to the routes. Thereafter an introduction of quantitative analysis and the measurement of graphs are presented. The last section summarizes the advantages of a continuous graph analysis in the field of terrain coverage. Furthermore we will outline potential applications.

2   Graph-Based Terrain Coverage Model

The terrain coverage problem can be described with the help of a graph. In general the range of the sensors will determine the size of a cell which is represented by a node. The environment which is blocked by an obstacle is not transferred into the graph. The possible crossings between adjacent cells are represented by the edges. Consequently an undirected graph $G = (V, E)$ with the costs c_{v_i,v_j} represents the environment. In our case the costs are encoded on the considered property like energy consumption. The cost matrix is defined on the edges $(v_i, v_j) \in E$. Furthermore the agents can move between two connected cells within one time step. While the agents are visiting a cell they can sense two different things. They can check all eight adjacent cells for obstacles. Besides the components can sense the cost function for the current cell. Only for two adjacent and sensed vertices we are able to determine the true costs to traverse the referring edge.

For the on-line terrain coverage problem there is limited information of the environment. While the agents traverse the environment they collect new data of costs and general connections between the cells. Therefore the individual graph of each agent is changing during the run time in a continuous way. In addition the individual graph is used to exchange the actual information. As a result there is a global graph representing the combined information of all agents.

The swarm of autonomous agents is self-coordinated and organized by an auction based approach [13], [19]. There are different advantages using an auction based model without a central coordinator, called planning and control agent. On the one hand a decentralized and more robust behavior is expected. There is for example no need of direct and permanent communication links. Besides failures by the planning and control agent would affect the swarm in a negative way. In the worst case the whole swarm would collapse. On the other hand for a self-coordinated auction based approach, the agents try to maximize their individual profits in an opportunistic way. Consequently the global efficiency is increased.

The exploration of the swarm can be organized by different approaches [13], [20, 21]. In general there are tasks representing parts of the unknown environment. Each agent uses the currently available and matched graph for determining possible routes. In previous researches [22] a multi-objective ant colony algorithm [23] is used to determine routes considering multiple objectives. For example the agents are able to find good routes which are as safe, short, robust, most informative and economical as possible at the same time. This is a significant improvement for real world applications. For further information on the described terrain coverage approach we recommend [19].

3   Optimization Process

Next we explain our conceptional optimization process for an autonomous multi-agent system. First of all each agent creates an individual graph representing the information about the sensed environment only. As long as an agent does not have a current task, auctions will be initiated by this agent. Every agent within the same communication network participates with a bid. Before the agents determine their routes, they exchange the individual graphs. The auctioneer agent merges the graphs by determining the union of known vertices. Besides some additional costs to traverse the edges can be added to the graph.

Next the matched graph will be used to estimate missing information of vertices and edges/costs for unknown parts of the environment. The transformation from the coverage to the matched Terrain network for two agents at $t = 5$ and $t = 21$ is shown in Figure 1. The estimation is necessary to enlarge the solution space of possible routes. There are different approaches using intervals [24], probability distributions [25] or Fuzzy Logic [26] to describe and determine costs under uncertainties [27]. Already known cells are used to estimate the unknown cells. For this purpose we use the method of diffusion. The closer an unknown cell is to a known cell, the higher is the probability that the costs are similar. Therefore, a diffusion function is introduced which describes the influence of known costs as a function of distance. The diffusion function can be either constant or non-constant. For example interval boundaries for the costs $c_{i,j} \in [\underline{b}_{i,j}, \overline{b}_{i,j}]$ of unknown edges are determined by the weighted mean of all diffused costs starting from known cells. The resulting graph called Terrain network is the basis of further graph analysis. In general a Terrain network is an undirected multigraph which is connected and weighted. In Section 4 we present quantitative graph measurements which can be used for analysis. Because of the analysis results concerning the characteristics, structure and complexity of the graph, the understanding and optimization is facilitated in general. Furthermore the results are used to define a good parameter set for heuristics which solve the route planning problem. In addition the analysis can be used to define an autonomous decision maker for multi-objective optimization. The decision maker evaluates the influences of the different objectives to select one of the compromise solutions. Considered objectives may be the minimization of the energy consumption, directional changes and route length as well as the maximization of the information content described by the number of unknown vertices. For example at the beginning of the coverage process the route length should attach more weight. While the coverage process the weight for routes with higher information content should be increased.

Finally the agents use the optimized parameter set and decision maker to find a good solution for the route planning problem. The agent with the best bid concerning the objective function wins the auction. In Figure 2 we visualize the previous described generic optimization process using networks.

4   Quantitative Analysis of Terrain Networks

Graph analysis is currently ubiquitous and has been inspired by interdisciplinary applications such as the World Wide Web [28, 29] and Network Biology [30–32]. Triggered by the hype dealing with the analysis of complex networks, it turned out that besides exploring random networks the analysis of non-random graphs is crucial too [33–35]. Finally this insight led to the term *complex networks* [33], [36] representing graphs whose network topology is neither regular nor random. Besides investigating the topology of graph classes such as random graphs, small world graphs and various complex networks, the quantitative analysis of networks has been proven useful [37–39]. Instead of only describing structural information of networks [40, 41], quantitative graph theory relates to quantify structural information by using a measurement approach.

The simplest case is defining graph measures $M : \mathcal{G} \longrightarrow \mathbb{R}$ which capture structural information of the graphs. Those measures are called complexity measures [42, 43] that map graphs to the reals. Examples for simple graph complexity measures are the famous Wiener index and Randić index given by [44]

$$W(G) := \frac{1}{2} \sum_{i=1}^{N} \sum_{j=1}^{N} d(v_i, v_j) \tag{1}$$

and

$$R(G) := \sum_{(v_i, v_j) \in E} [k_{v_i} k_{v_j}]^{-\frac{1}{2}}, \tag{2}$$

respectively. We define $G = (V, E)$ and $d(v_i, v_j)$ is the shortest distance between the $(v_i, v_j) \in V$. Furthermore k_{v_i} is the vertex degree of v_i.

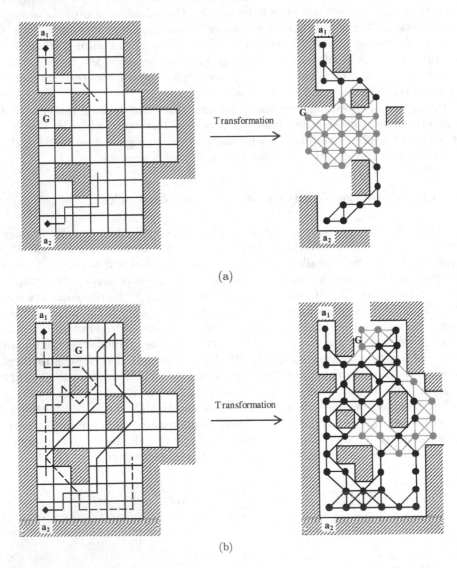

(a)

(b)

Fig. 1. Terrain network transformation for a) t=5 and b) t=21. Estimated vertices and edges are in gray.

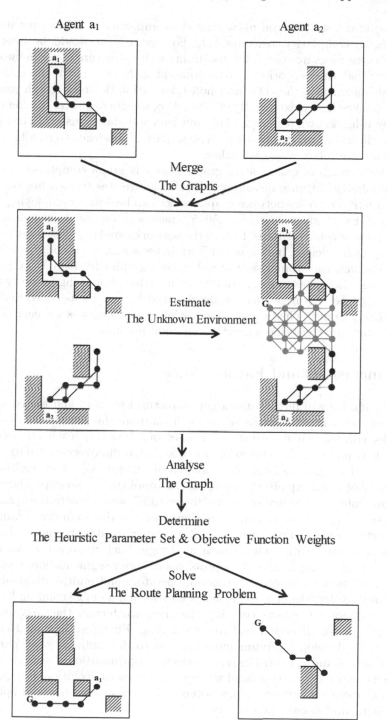

Fig. 2. Generic optimization process by using graph analysis of networks

In the future, we focus on measuring the complexity of Terrain networks by using known complexity measures [44]. For instance, it would be interesting whether these measures can fully discriminate the structure of the networks as it is likely that the networks are non-isomorphic. Note that the discrimination power of information-theoretic and non-information-theoretic graph measures have been investigated extensively [45–48]. Also, we aim to cluster the complexity values by using known techniques [49] and interpret those clusters. Then we get clusters which contain graphs for a given scenario. This leads to results how the graph may interrelate with each other.

Another branch of quantitative graph theory is graph comparison by using graph similarity/distance measures [50–52]. This relates to measure the structural similarity/distance between graphs which can be done by employing several paradigms. Exact graph matching [50–52] relates to determine isomorphic and subgraph isomorphic relations. In case the networks are large, the resulting measures may be inefficient. In case of our Terrain networks, we intend to use inexact graph matching that comprises the well-known graph edit distance (GED) [50] and various other measures, e.g., those which are based on using property strings [53, 54]. The Terrain networks can be classified by using supervised and unsupervised techniques. This would allow defining graph classes for each scenario and to determine their characteristic structural features.

5   Conclusions and Future Work

In the future we will further investigate structural features and the complexity of Terrain networks. In particular, we will compare the complexity of Terrain networks with those of other network classes and draw conclusions thereof. This approach is particularly interesting for knowledge discovery and data mining from natural images, e.g. complex biomedical images [55] where multi-agents, e.g. ant-robots can explore the image as an topological landscape and the autonomous robots leave markings on "interesting" spots, where these markings can be sensed by all robots and allow them to cover the unknown terrain without direct communication with each other, hence to discover anomalies, similarities or dissimilarities within such an image. Such approaches can also be useful for overcoming local optima problems in image segmentation, where such an approach takes advantage of random operators and multi-individual search algorithms, so that the best single agent tries to find a global solution [56]. During the autonomous agents covering the unknown terrain they have to make decisions on task allocation and route planning. First results show that there is a need to develop an autonomous process to determine a good parameter set for route planning heuristics, e.g. ant-colony optimization. Particularly, such approaches can be very beneficial when combined with evolutionary algorithms [57] which together have enormous potential in further research on graph-based data mining and knowledge discovery.

References

1. van Evert, F.K., van der Heijden, G.W.A.M., Lotz, L.A.P., Polder, G., Lamaker, A., de Jong, A., Kuyper, M.C., Groendijk, E.J.K., Neeteson, J.J., van der Zalm, T.: A mobile field robot with vision-based detection of volunteer potato plants in a corn crop. Weed Technology 20, 853–861 (2006)
2. Kumar, V., Rus, D., Singh, S.: Robot and sensor networks for first responders. IEEE Pervasive Computing 3, 24–33 (2004)
3. Dorigo, M., Maniezzo, V., Colorni, A.: Ant system: optimization by a colony of cooperating agents. IEEE Transactions on Systems, Man, and Cybernetics, Part B: Cybernetics 26, 29–41 (1996)
4. Senthilkumar, K.S., Bharadwaj, K.K.: Spanning tree based terrain coverage by multi robots in unknown environments. In: IEEE Annual IEEE INDICON Conference, pp. 120–125 (2008)
5. Holzinger, A., Ofner, B., Dehmer, M.: Multi-touch graph-based interaction for knowledge discovery on mobile devices: State-of-the-art and future challenges. In: Holzinger, A., Jurisica, I. (eds.) Knowledge Discovery and Data Mining. LNCS, vol. 8401, pp. 241–254. Springer, Heidelberg (2014)
6. Holzinger, A., Dehmer, M., Jurisica, I.: Knowledge discovery and interactive data mining in bioinformatics - state-of-the-art, future challenges and research directions. BMC Bioinformatics 15, I1 (2014)
7. Zheng, X., Koenig, S., Kempe, D., Jain, S.: Multirobot forest coverage for weighted and unweighted terrain. Transactions on Robotics 26, 1018–1031 (2010)
8. Olfati-Saber, R., Fax, J.A., Murray, R.M.: Consensus and cooperation in networked multi-agent systems. Proceedings of the IEEE 95, 215–233 (2007)
9. Arkin, R., Balch, T.: Cooperative multiagent robotic systems. In: Artificial Intelligence and Mobile Robots. MIT/AAAI Press (1998)
10. Wagner, I., Bruckstein, A.: From ants to a(ge)nts: A special issue on ant-robotics. Annals of Mathematics and Artificial Intelligence 31, 1–5 (2001)
11. Chevallier, D., Payandeh, S.: On kinematic geometry of multi-agent manipulating system based on the contact force information. In: Proceedings of the 6th International Conference on Intelligent Autonomous Systems (2000)
12. Gerkey, B., Mataric, M.: Sold!: auction methods for multirobot coordination. IEEE Transactions on Robotics and Automation 18, 758–768 (2002)
13. Zlot, R., Stentz, A., Dias, M., Thayer, S.: Multi-robot exploration controlled by a market economy. In: Proceedings of the IEEE International Conference on Robotics and Automation, vol. 3, pp. 3016–3023 (2002)
14. Dijkstra, E.W.: A note on two problems in connexion with graphs. Numerische Mathematik 1, 269–271 (1959)
15. Dorigo, M.: Optimization, Learning and Natural Algorithms. PhD thesis, Dipartimento di Elettronica, Politecnico di Milano, Milan, Italy (1992) (in Italian)
16. Floyd, R.W.: Algorithm 97: Shortest path. Communications of the ACM 5, 345 (1962)
17. Gen, M., Cheng, R., Wang, Q.: Genetic algorithms for solving shortest path problems. In: IEEE International Conference on Evolutionary Computation, pp. 401–406 (1997)
18. Hart, P.E., Nilsson, N.J., Raphael, B.: A formal basis for the heuristic determination of minimum cost paths. IEEE Transactions on Systems Science and Cybernetics 4, 100–107 (1968)

19. Preuß, M.: A multi-objective online terrain coverage approach. In: Proceedings of the International Conference on Operations Research. Springer (in print, 2014)

20. Hoog, J., Cameron, S., Visser, A.: Role-based autonomous multi-robot exploration. In: Proceedings of the International Conference on Advanced Cognitive Technologies and Applications (2009)

21. Ghoul, S., Hussein, A., Abdel-Wahab, M., Witkowski, U., Rückert, U.: A modified multiple depth first search algorithm for grid mapping using mini-robots khepera. Journal of Computing Science and Engineering 2, 321–338 (2008)

22. Preuß, M.: Terrain Coverage - Modelle und Algorithmen. Master's thesis, University of the German Federal Armed Forces Munich (2011)

23. Alaya, I., Solnon, C., Ghédira, K.: Ant colony optimization for multi-objective optimization problems. In: Proceedings of the IEEE International Conference on Tools with Artificial Intelligence, pp. 450–457 (2007)

24. Karasan, O., Pinar, M., Yaman, H.: The robust shortest path problem with interval data. Technical report, Bilkent University, Department of Industrial Engineering, Ankara (2001)

25. Bertsekas, D., Tsitsiklis, J.: An Analysis of Stochastic Shortest Path Problems. Mathematics of Operations Research 16 (1991)

26. Yao, J.S., Lin, F.T.: Fuzzy shortest-path network problems with uncertain edge weights. Journal of Information Science and Engineering 19, 329–351 (2003)

27. Sahinidis, N.: Optimization under uncertainty: state-of-the-art and opportunities. Computers & Chemical Engineering 28, 971–983 (2004); FOCAPO 2003 Special issue

28. Adamic, L., Huberman, B.: Power-law distribution of the world wide web. Science 287, 2115a (2000)

29. Chakrabarti, S.: Mining the Web: Discovering Knowledge from Hypertext Data. Morgan Kaufmann, San Francisco (2002)

30. Barabási, A.L., Oltvai, Z.N.: Network biology: Understanding the cell's functional organization. Nature Reviews. Genetics 5, 101–113 (2004)

31. Dehmer, M., Emmert-Streib, F., Graber, A., Salvador, A. (eds.): Applied Statistics for Network Biology. Quantitative and Network Biology. Wiley-Blackwell (2011)

32. Emmert-Streib, F., Dehmer, M. (eds.): Analysis of Microarray Data: A Network-based Approach. Wiley VCH Publishing (2010)

33. Dorogovtsev, S.N., Mendes, J.F.F.: Evolution of Networks. From Biological Networks to the Internet and WWW. Oxford University Press (2003)

34. Erdös, P., Rényi, P.: On the evolution of random graphs. Magyar Tud. Akad. Mat. Kutató Int. Közl 5, 17–61 (1960)

35. Watts, D.J., Strogatz, S.H.: Collective dynamics of 'small-world' networks. Nature 393, 440–442 (1998)

36. Estrada, E.: The Structure of Complex Networks. Theory and Applications. Oxford University Press (2011)

37. Dehmer, M., Emmert-Streib, F.: Quantitative Graph Theory. Theory and Applications. CRC Press (in press, 2014)

38. Mehler, A.: A quantitative graph model of social ontologies by example of wikipedia. In: Mehler, A., Sharoff, S., Rehm, G., Santini, M. (eds.) Genres on the Web: Computational Models and Empirical Studies. Springer (2009) (to appear)

39. Mehler, A.: Social ontologies as generalized nearly acyclic directed graphs: A quantitative graph model of social tagging. In: Dehmer, M., Emmert-Streib, F., Mehler, A. (eds.) Towards an Information Theory of Complex Networks: Statistical Methods and Applications, pp. 259–319. Birkhäuser, Boston/Basel (2011)

40. Halin, R.: Graphentheorie, Berlin, Germany. Akademie Verlag (1989)
41. Harary, F.: Graph Theory, Reading, MA, USA. Addison Wesley Publishing Company (1969)
42. Bonchev, D., Rouvray, D.H.: Complexity in Chemistry, Biology, and Ecology, New York, NY, USA. Mathematical and Computational Chemistry. Springer (2005)
43. Mowshowitz, A.: Entropy and the complexity of the graphs I: An index of the relative complexity of a graph. Bull. Math. Biophys. 30, 175–204 (1968)
44. Todeschini, R., Consonni, V., Mannhold, R.: Handbook of Molecular Descriptors, Weinheim, Germany. Wiley-VCH (2002)
45. Bonchev, D., Mekenyan, O., Trinajstić, N.: Isomer discrimination by topological information approach. J. Comp. Chem. 2, 127–148 (1981)
46. Dehmer, M., Emmert-Streib, F., Grabner, M.: A computational approach to construct a multivariate complete graph invariant. Inf. Sci. 260, 200–208 (2014)
47. Dehmer, M., Grabner, M., Varmuza, K.: Information indices with high discriminative power for graphs. PLoS One 7, e31214 (2012)
48. Konstantinova, E.V., Skorobogatov, V.A., Vidyuk, M.V.: Applications of information theory in chemical graph theory. Indian Journal of Chemistry 42, 1227–1240 (2002)
49. Jain, A.K., Dubes, R.C.: Algorithms for clustering data. Prentice-Hall, Inc., Upper Saddle River (1988)
50. Bunke, H.: Graph matching: Theoretical foundations, algorithms, and applications. In: Proceedings of Vision Interface 2000, pp. 82–88 (2000)
51. Sobik, F.: Graphmetriken und Klassifikation strukturierter Objekte. ZKI-Informationen, Akad. Wiss. DDR 2, 63–122 (1982)
52. Zelinka, B.: On a certain distance between isomorphism classes of graphs. Časopis pro pěst. Mathematiky 100, 371–373 (1975)
53. Dehmer, M., Emmert-Streib, F.: Comparing large graphs efficiently by margins of feature vectors. Applied Mathematics and Computation 188, 1699–1710 (2007)
54. Dehmer, M., Mehler, A.: A new method of measuring similarity for a special class of directed graphs. Tatra Mountains Mathematical Publications 36, 39–59 (2007)
55. Holzinger, A., Malle, B., Bloice, M., Wiltgen, M., Ferri, M., Stanganelli, I., Hofmann-Wellenhof, R.: On the generation of point cloud data sets: the first step in the knowledge discovery process. In: Holzinger, A., Jurisica, I. (eds.) Interactive Knowledge Discovery and Data Mining in Biomedical Informatics. LNCS, vol. 8401, pp. 57–80. Springer, Heidelberg (2014)
56. Kasaiezadeh, A., Khajepour, A.: Multi-agent stochastic level set method in image segmentation. Computer Vision and Image Understanding 117, 1147–1162 (2013)
57. Holzinger, K., Palade, V., Rabadan, R., Holzinger, A.: Darwin or lamarck? future challenges in evolutionary algorithms for knowledge discovery and data mining. In: Holzinger, A., Jurisica, I. (eds.) Knowledge Discovery and Data Mining. LNCS, vol. 8401, pp. 35–56. Springer, Heidelberg (2014)

Entropy-Based Data Mining on the Example of Cardiac Arrhythmia Suppression

Martin Bachler[1,2], Matthias Hörtenhuber[2], Christopher Mayer[1], Andreas Holzinger[3], and Siegfried Wassertheurer[1]

[1] AIT Austrian Institute of Technology, Health & Environment Department, Biomedical Systems, Donau-City-Str. 1, 1220 Vienna, Austria
{martin.bachler,christopher.mayer,siegfried.wassertheurer}@ait.ac.at
[2] Vienna University of Technology, Institute for Analysis and Scientific Computing, Wiedner Hauptstr. 8-10, 1040 Vienna, Austria
{martin.bachler,e0927120}@student.tuwien.ac.at
[3] Medical University Graz, Research Unit HCI, Institute of Medical Informatics, Statistics and Documentation Auenbruggerplatz 2/V, 8036 Graz, Austria
a.holzinger@hci4all.at

Abstract. Heart rate variability (HRV) is the variation of the time interval between consecutive heartbeats and depends on the extrinsic regulation of the heart rate. It can be quantified using nonlinear methods such as entropy measures, which determine the irregularity of the time intervals.

In this work, approximate entropy (ApEn), sample entropy (SampEn), fuzzy entropy (FuzzyEn) and fuzzy measure entropy (FuzzyMEn) were used to assess the effects of three different cardiac arrhythmia suppressing drugs on the HRV after a myocardial infarction.

The results show that the ability of all four entropy measures to distinguish between pre- and post-treatment HRV data is highly significant ($p < 0.01$). Furthermore, approximate entropy and sample entropy are able to differentiate significantly ($p < 0.05$) between the tested arrhythmia suppressing agents.

Keywords: Data Mining, Entropy, Heart Rate Variability, Cardiac Arrhythmia Suppression.

1 Introduction

Heart rate variability (HRV) is the variation of the time interval between consecutive heartbeats. It highly depends on the extrinsic regulation of the heart rate (HR) and reflects the balance between the sympathetic and the parasympathetic nervous system [1]. In studies of HRV, both time- and frequency-domain measures are typically used by practitioners and researchers [1,2]. Additionally, there exist non-linear measures such as the Poincaré Plot [3] and entropy measures [4]. The later one were used in this study. We applied the entropy measures on recordings from the Cardiac Arrhythmia Suppression Trial (CAST), a large postinfarction trial, with data before and after cardiac arrhythmia suppression

D. Ślęzak et al. (Eds.): BIH 2014, LNAI 8609, pp. 574–585, 2014.

treatments [5]. Our goal was to examine the effects of antiarrhythmic medication on various entropy measures.

2   Methods

2.1   Data and Study Population

All data used in this paper have been taken from Physionet.org [6], a free-access, on-line archive of physiological signals. Particularly, data are obtained from the CAST RR Interval Sub-Study Database [5], which consists of 1543 24-hour RR-interval records from 809 subjects. The database is divided into three sub-groups based on the cardiac arrhythmia suppression medication (Encainide, Flecainide and Moricizine) received by the subjects. For almost all subjects, there is a pair of records representing baseline and on-therapy data available. In total, 1464 records for 731 subjects (599 men and 132 women) have been used and 75 subjects have been excluded due to incompleteness of data (i.e., just baseline or just on-therapy data available), three subject were excluded additionally, because there were no recordings at the used time window. The age distribution of the subjects is represented in Figure 1. One-hour RR-intervals at 6pm have been extracted for all subjects to decrease computation time and to avoid daytime dependent variations. The Cardiac Arrhythmia Suppression Trial (CAST) was originally started to analyze the effect of suppressing ventricular arrhythmias by antiarrhythmic drugs after myocardial infarction (MI) on the survival rate [7]. The data are divided in three sub-groups depending on the treatment (Encainide, $N_E = 260$ (44 female, 216 male); Flecainide, $N_F = 207$ (43 female, 164 male); Moricizine, $N_M = 264$ (45 female, 219 male)).

2.2   Analysis of Heart Rate Variability

Heart rate variability is analyzed by the following entropy measures: approximate entropy (ApEn) [8], sample entropy (SampEn) [9], fuzzy entropy (FuzzyEn) [10] and fuzzy measure entropy (FuzzyMEn) [11].

2.3   Approximate Entropy (ApEn)

Approximate Entropy measures the logarithmic likelihood that runs of patterns that are close remain close on following incremental comparisons [12]. We state Pincus' definition [12,13], for the family of statistics $\text{ApEn}(m, r, N)$,:

Definition 1. *Fix m, a positive integer and r, a positive real number. Given a regularly sampled time series $u(t)$, a sequence of vectors $x(1)^m, x^m(2), \ldots, x^m$ $(N - m + 1)$ in $\mathbb{R}^m$ is formed, defined by*

$$x^m(i) := [u(t_i), u(t_{i+1}), \ldots, u(t_{i+m-1})] \quad . \tag{1}$$

Define for each i, $1 \leq i \leq N - m + 1$,

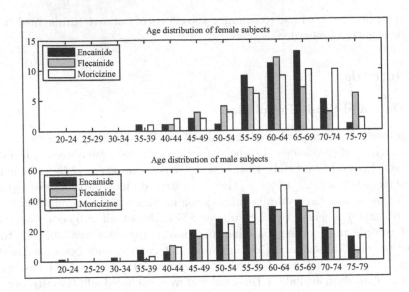

Fig. 1. Age distribution of subjects per gender

$$C_i^m(r) := \frac{number\ of\ j\ such\ that\ d[\boldsymbol{x}^m(i), \boldsymbol{x}^m(j)] \leq r}{N - m + 1} \ , \tag{2}$$

where $d[\boldsymbol{x}(i), \boldsymbol{x}(j)]$ *is the Chebyshev distance given by:*

$$d[\boldsymbol{x}^m(i), \boldsymbol{x}^m(j)] := \max_{k=1,2,\dots,m} \left(|u\left(t_{i+k-1}\right) - u\left(t_{j+k-1}\right)| \right) \ . \tag{3}$$

Furthermore, define

$$\phi^m(r) := (N - m + 1)^{-1} \sum_{i=1}^{N-m+1} \log C_i^m(r) \ , \tag{4}$$

then the **Approximate Entropy** *is defined as*

$$\text{ApEn}(m, r, N) := \phi^m(r) - \phi^{m+1}(r) \ . \tag{5}$$

2.4   Sample Entropy (SampEn)

Richman and Moorman showed in [14] that approximate entropy is biased towards regularity. Thus, they modified it to Sample Entropy. The main difference between the two is that sample entropy does not count self-matches, and only the first $N - m$ subsequences instead of all $N - m + 1$ are compared, for both ϕ^m and ϕ^{m+1} [14]. Similar to ApEn above, SampEn is defined as follows:

Definition 2. *Fix m, a positive integer and r, a positive real number. Given a regularly sampled time series $U(t)$, a sequence of vectors $\boldsymbol{x}^m(1), \boldsymbol{x}^m(2), \ldots, \boldsymbol{x}^m (N - m + 1) \in \mathbb{R}^m$ is formed, defined by eq. (1). Define for each i, $1 \leq i \leq N - m + 1$,*

$$C_i^m = \frac{number\ of\ j\ such\ that\ d[\boldsymbol{x}^m(i), \boldsymbol{x}^m(j)] \leq r\ and\ i \neq j}{N - m + 1} , \tag{6}$$

where $d[(i), (j)]$ is the Chebyshev distance (see eq. (3)). Furthermore, define

$$\phi^m(r) := (N - m)^{-1} \sum_{i=1}^{N-m} C_i^m(r) , \tag{7}$$

*then the **Sample Entropy** is defined as*

$$\mathrm{SampEn}(m, r, N) := \log(\phi^m(r)) - \log(\phi^{m+1}(r)) . \tag{8}$$

2.5 Fuzzy (Measure) Entropy (Fuzzy(M)En)

To soften the effects of the threshold value r, Chen et al. proposed in [15] Fuzzy Entropy, which uses a fuzzy membership function instead of the Heaviside function. FuzzyEn is defined the following way:

Definition 3. *Fix m, a positive integer and r, a positive real number. Given a regularly sampled time series $U(t)$, a sequence of vectors $\boldsymbol{x}^m(1), \boldsymbol{x}^m(2), \ldots, \boldsymbol{x}^m (N - m + 1) \in \mathbb{R}^m$ is formed, as defined by eq. (1). This sequence is transformed into $\overline{\boldsymbol{x}}^m(1), \overline{\boldsymbol{x}}^m(2), \ldots, \overline{\boldsymbol{x}}^m(N - m + 1)$, with $\overline{\boldsymbol{x}}^m(i) := \{u(l_i) - u0_i, \ldots, u(t_{i+m-1}) - u0_i\}$, where $u0_i$ is the mean value of $\boldsymbol{x}^m(i)$, i.e.*

$$u0_i := \sum_{j=0}^{m-1} \frac{u_{i+j}}{m}. \tag{9}$$

Next the fuzzy membership matrix is defined as:

$$D_{i,j}^m := \mu(d(\overline{x}_i^m, \overline{x}_j^m), n, r) , \tag{10}$$

with the Chebyshev distance d (see eq. (3)) and the fuzzy membership function

$$\mu(\boldsymbol{x}, n, r) := e^{-(\boldsymbol{x}/r)^n} . \tag{11}$$

Finally, with

$$\phi^m := \frac{1}{N - m} \sum_{i=1}^{N-m} \sum_{j=1, j \neq i}^{N-m} \frac{D_{i,j}^m}{N - m - 1} , \tag{12}$$

*the **Fuzzy Entropy** is defined as:*

$$\mathrm{FuzzyEn}(m, r, n, N) := \ln \phi^m - \ln \phi^{m+1} . \tag{13}$$

Liu et al. proposed in [16] **Fuzzy Measure Entropy**, which introduces a distinction between local entropy and global entropy, based on FuzzyEn. It is defined as:

$$\text{FuzzyMEn}(m, r_L, r_F, n_L, n_F, N) := \ln \phi_L^m - \ln \phi_L^{m+1} + \ln \phi_F^m - \ln \phi_F^{m+1} \ , \quad (14)$$

where the local terms ϕ_L^m and ϕ_L^{m+1} are calculated as in eq. (12) and the global terms ϕ_F^m and ϕ_F^{m+1} are calculated with eq. (10) and eq. (12), but with $\overline{x}^m(i) := \{u(t_i) - u_{\text{mean}}, \ldots, u(t_{i+m-1}) - u_{\text{mean}}\}$, where u_{mean} is the mean value of the complete sequence $u(t)$.

Parameters of all entropy measures were selected according to [17].

2.6 Statistical Analysis

For better comprehension we will call from here on the Encainide group recordings before treatment EA and after treatment EB, the recordings of the Flecainide group pretreatment will be marked with FA and the postreatment ones FB. The same scheme is used for MA and MB as abbreviations for the pre- and postreatment recordings of the group receiving a medication with Moricizine.

First differences in the entropies of the groups' pretreatment recordings, i.e. between EA, FA, and MA (the baseline), were tested using the Kruskal Wallis test, since the three groups are assumed to be independent but not normally distributed. Afterwards we tested again with a Kurskal Wallis test for differences between the groups' entropies after the treatment, i.e. between EB, FB, and MA. Subsequently, the effect of the treatment was tested with a Wilcoxon signed-rank test for paired samples without normal distribution, by comparing the entropies of EA with EB, FA with FB, and MA with MB.

Further on we tested if there was any sex-based difference in the entropy values. Therefore we used the Wilcoxon rank sum test to test the female members of the group EA against the male members of the same group. The same was done for FA, MA and EB, FB, MB.

Finally, the connection of the various entropy values was investigated using scatter plots and Pearson's linear correlation coefficient on the results before and after the treatment.

For all tests their implementation in *The MathWorks MATLAB* was used. The test results were declared significant for $p < 0.05$ and highly significant for $p < 0.01$.

3 Results

Figure 2 shows the distribution of entropy values of the groups before and after treatment. All posttreatment recordings show lower entropy values than their respective pretreatment counterparts. No significant difference between the three medication groups could be detected in the entropies of the pretreatment recordings, as can be seen in Table 1. The same table shows, that ApEn and SampEn were significantly different for the recordings after the treatment between the three groups ($p < 0.05$). This was not the case for FuzzyEn and FuzzyMEn. In the same table it can also be seen, that all four entropy measures show a highly significant difference between the subjects entropy of heart rate variability before and after treatment ($p < 0.01$ for all tests).

No significant difference was found between female and male subjects in the three groups before as well as after the treatment, see Table 2 for details.

Table 1. Results of the Kurskal-Wallis test and the Wilcoxon signed rank test of the recordings before and after treatment with different medications

	Entropy Measure	P-Value
EA vs. FA vs. MA:		
	ApEn	0.2974
	SampEn	0.1267
	FuzzyEn	0.2765
	FuzzyMEn	0.2635
EB vs. FB vs. MB:		
	ApEn	0.0307
	SampEn	0.0448
	FuzzyEn	0.1698
	FuzzyMEn	0.1055
EΛ vs. EB:		
	ApEn	< 0.01
	SampEn	< 0.01
	FuzzyEn	< 0.01
	FuzzyMEn	< 0.01
FA vs. FB:		
	ApEn	< 0.01
	SampEn	< 0.01
	FuzzyEn	< 0.01
	FuzzyMEn	< 0.01
MA vs. MB:		
	ApEn	< 0.01
	SampEn	< 0.01
	FuzzyEn	< 0.01
	FuzzyMEn	< 0.01

Figure 3 and Table 3 show the connection of the readings of the various entropy determining methods. Figure 3 contains scatter plots of the pairwise comparisons of the methods and the histogram for each method, respectively. It can be seen that the distribution of the results of all methods is highly asymmetrical. The scatter plots show that, in general, values of ApEn were higher than

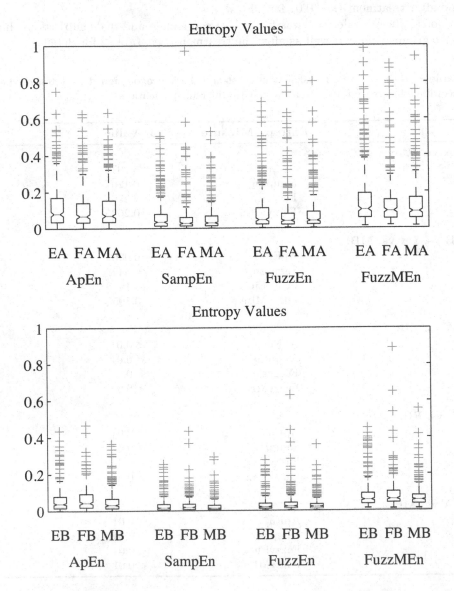

Fig. 2. Boxplot of the entropy values of the recordings before treatment (top) and afterwards (bottom)

Table 2. Results of the Wilcoxon rank sum test of the recordings before and after treatment with different medications separated by subject's sex

	Entropy Measure	P-Value
EA-female vs. EA-male:		
	ApEn	0.2080
	SampEn	0.1662
	FuzzyEn	0.4064
	FuzzyMEn	0.3250
FA-female vs. FA-male:		
	ApEn	0.3373
	SampEn	0.2893
	FuzzyEn	0.5245
	FuzzyMEn	0.3996
MA-female vs. MA-male:		
	ApEn	0.8994
	SampEn	0.6603
	FuzzyEn	0.7494
	FuzzyMEn	0.7204
EB-female vs. EB-male:		
	ApEn	0.8012
	SampEn	0.7465
	FuzzyEn	0.8820
	FuzzyMEn	0.7473
FB-female vs. FB-male:		
	ApEn	0.9715
	SampEn	0.9237
	FuzzyEn	0.4545
	FuzzyMEn	0.1055
MB-female vs. MB-male:		
	ApEn	0.7690
	SampEn	0.4302
	FuzzyEn	0.3772
	FuzzyMEn	0.3294

those of SampEn and FuzzyEn, whereas they are slightly lower than reading of FuzzyMEn. Results of SampEn tended to be lower then those of FuzzyEn and FuzzyMEn. The direct comparison of FuzzyEn and FuzzyMEn showed higher values for FuzzyMEn. Nevertheless, the scatter plots show a reasonably linear connection between all methods. Table 3 quantifies this observation, showing high correlation coefficients for the pairwise comparison of all methods.

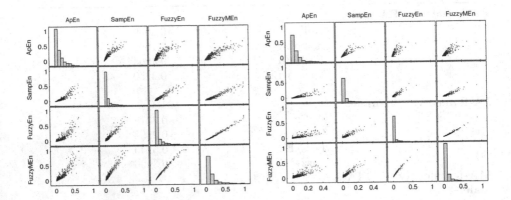

Fig. 3. Scatter plot matrix and histograms of the entropy values of the recordings before treatment (left) and afterwards (right) in order to visualize the connection between different entropy measures

Table 3. Pearson's linear correlation coefficients for entropy values before and after treatment (all $p < 0.01$)

| | Before Treatment (A) | | | | After Treatment (B) | | | |
	Ap	Samp	Fuzzy	FuzzyM	Ap	Samp	Fuzzy	FuzzyM
ApEn	1	0.9210	0.8822	0.9111	1	0.8736	0.8185	0.8601
SampEn	0.9210	1	0.9649	0.9750	0.8736	1	0.9341	0.9509
FuzzyEn	0.8822	0.9649	1	0.9936	0.8185	0.9341	1	0.9889
FuzzyMEn	0.9111	0.9750	0.9936	1	0.8601	0.9509	0.9889	1

4   Discussion

The results of the first test on the three pretreatment groups (EA vs. FA vs. MA) did not reveal any significant differences. Therefore the null-hypothesis of a consistent baseline population is accepted and further posttreatment comparisons are reasonable.

Testing the differences between the posttreatment groups (EB vs. FB vs. MB), though, yielded mixed results. While ApEn and SampEn showed significantly different results for the diverse treatments, FuzzyEn and FuzzyMEn did not. Further investigation of these methods is necessary to determine the cause of these differences.

Cardiac arrhythmias are a disruption in the regularity of the heart rhythm. Therefore, they cause a distinct alteration in the HRV and in all measures quantifying it. Sethuraman et al. reported, that even one single ectopic beat (a certain type of cardiac arrhythmia) causes a striking alteration of the HRV [18]. As Encainide, Flecainide and Moricizine aim to suppress cardiac arrhythmia, the prominent reduction of the irregularity and therefore the highly significant difference between pre- and posttreatment as seen in Figure 2 and Table 1 was expected. It remains an open question, however, if these differences can be attributed solely to the reduction of cardiac arrhythmias, or whether the heart's sinus rhythm is changed as well. Methods of ectopic beat correction will be necessary for further data mining regarding this matter [19].

The fourth test, which looked for differences due to the sex of the subjects, showed no significant results. This is in accordance with Beckers et al., who showed in [20] a difference in the entropy based on sex, but reported that this effect vanishes for subjects older than 40 years. This is the case for most of the subjects in our used data.

The qualitative investigation of the connection between the four entropy measures using scatter plots (Figure 3) revealed obvious pairwise linear relationships. Therefore, the usage of Pearson's linear correlation coefficient is justified. As listed in Table 3, the highest correlations where found between FuzzyEn and FuzzyMEn. These readings suggest that the extension of FuzzyEn by a global term influences the results only by a constant value. This similarity between FuzzyEn and FuzzyMEn is also in accordance with the findings of the second test. Again, the striking reduction in all entropy measures between pre- and posttreatment is visible.

In general, Mäkikallio et al. found in [21] higher ApEn values for postinfarction patients compared to a healthy age matched control group. In our data this effect seems to be reduced after the treatment with any of the three medications. However, simply reducing the amount of cardiac arrhythmias and therefore reducing the entropy of the HRV for patients after a myocardial infarction does not reduce mortality. In fact, the postinfarction treatment with (Na^+) channel blocking antiarrhythmic agents (class I, e.g. Encainide, Flecainide and Moricizine) is associated with increased mortality [22]. This suggests the presence of more extensive alterations of the HRV than cardiac arrhythmias alone. As stated above, ectopic beat correction will be necessary for further investigation.

4.1 Limitations

Due to the lack of availability of the related survival outcome data, we could not evaluate the predictability of the tested entropy measures on mortality.

5   Conclusion

In our study, all four entropy measures (approximate, sample, fuzzy and fuzzy measure entropy) are significantly different before and after antiarrhythmic treatment. However, as also addressed by Holzinger et al. in [4], the problem of how to use entropy measures for the classification of pathological and non-pathological data still remains, as a simple reduction of entropy in HRV does not necessarily reduce mortality after a myocardial infarction. Further research using ectopic beat correction for entropy-based data mining in HRV will be necessary.

References

1. Rajendra Acharya, U., Paul Joseph, K., Kannathal, N., Lim, C., Suri, J.: Heart rate variability: a review. Med. Biol. Eng. Comput. 44, 1031–1051 (2006)
2. American Heart Association Inc.: European Society of Cardiology: Guidelines – heart rate variability. Eur. Heart J. 17, 354–381 (1996)
3. Smith, A.L., Reynolds, K.J., Owen, H.: Correlated Poincaré indices for measuring heart rate variability. Australasian physical & engineering sciences in medicine / supported by the Australasian College of Physical Scientists in Medicine and the Australasian Association of Physical Sciences in Medicine 30, 336–341 (2007)
4. Holzinger, A., Hörtenhuber, M., Mayer, C., Bachler, M., Wassertheurer, S., Pinho, A.J., Koslicki, D.: On entropy-based data mining. In: Holzinger, A., Jurisica, I. (eds.) Knowledge Discovery and Data Mining. LNCS, vol. 8401, pp. 209–226. Springer, Heidelberg (2014)
5. Stein, P.K., Kleiger, R.E., Domitrovich, P.P., Schechtman, K.B., Rottman, J.N.: Clinical and demographic determinants of heart rate variability in patients post myocardial infarction: insights from the cardiac arrhythmia suppression trial (cast). Clinical Cardiology 23, 187–194 (2000)
6. Goldberger, A.L., Amaral, L.A., Glass, L., Hausdorff, J.M., Ivanov, P.C., Mark, R.G., Mietus, J.E., Moody, G.B., Peng, C.K., Stanley, H.E.: PhysioBank, PhysioToolkit, and PhysioNet: components of a new research resource for complex physiologic signals. Circulation 101, E215–E220 (2000)
7. Epstein, A.E., Bigger, J.T., Wyse, D.G., Romhilt, D.W., Reynolds-Haertle, R.A., Hallstrom, A.P.: Events in the cardiac arrhythmia suppression trial (cast): mortality in the entire population enrolled. Journal of the American College of Cardiology 18, 14–19 (1991)
8. Pincus, S.M.: Approximate entropy as a measure of system complexity. Proc. Natl. Acad. Sci. U.S.A. 88, 2297–2301 (1991)
9. Richman, J.S., Moorman, J.R.: Physiological time-series analysis using approximate entropy and sample entropy. Am. J. Physiol. Heart Circ. Physiol. 278, H2039–H2049 (2000)
10. Chen, W., Zhuang, J., Yu, W., Wang, Z.: Measuring complexity using FuzzyEn, ApEn, and SampEn. Med. Eng. Phys. 31, 61–68 (2009)
11. Liu, C., Li, K., Zhao, L., Liu, F., Zheng, D., Liu, C., Liu, S.: Analysis of heart rate variability using fuzzy measure entropy. Comput. Biol. Med. 43, 100–108 (2013)
12. Pincus, S.M.: Approximate entropy as a measure of system complexity. Proceedings of the National Academy of Sciences 88, 2297–2301 (1991)
13. Pincus, S.: Approximate entropy (apen) as a complexity measure. Chaos: An Interdisciplinary Journal of Nonlinear Science 5, 110–117 (1995)

14. Richman, J.S., Moorman, J.R.: Physiological time-series analysis using approximate entropy and sample entropy. Am. J. Physiol. Heart Circ. Physiol. 278, H2039–H2049 (2000)
15. Chen, W., Wang, Z., Xie, H., Yu, W.: Characterization of surface emg signal based on fuzzy entropy. IEEE Transactions on Neural Systems and Rehabilitation Engineering 15, 266–272 (2007)
16. Liu, C., Li, K., Zhao, L., Liu, F., Zheng, D., Liu, C., Liu, S.: Analysis of heart rate variability using fuzzy measure entropy. Comput. Biol. Med. 43, 100–108 (2013)
17. Mayer, C., Bachler, M., Hörtenhuber, M., Stocker, C., Holzinger, A., Wassertheurer, S.: Selection of entropy-measure parameters for knowledge discovery in heart rate variability data (in press)
18. Sethuraman, G., Ryan, K.L., Rickards, C.A., Convertino, V.A.: Ectopy in trauma patients: cautions for use of heart period variability in medical monitoring. Aviation, Space, and Environmental Medicine 81, 125–129 (2010)
19. Mateo, J., Laguna, P.: Analysis of heart rate variability in the presence of ectopic beats using the heart timing signal. IEEE Transactions on Biomedical Engineering 50, 334–343 (2003)
20. Beckers, F., Verheyden, B., Aubert, A.E.: Aging and nonlinear heart rate control in a healthy population. American Journal of Physiology-Heart and Circulatory Physiology 290, H2560–H2570 (2006)
21. Mäkikallio, T.H., Seppännen, T., Niemelä, M., Airaksinen, K.J., Tulppo, M., Huikuri, H.V.: Abnormalities in beat to beat complexity of heart rate dynamics in patients with a previous myocardial infarction1. Journal of the American College of Cardiology 28, 1005–1011 (1996)
22. Teo, K., Yusuf, S., Furberg, C.: Effects of prophylactic antiarrhythmic drug therapy in acute myocardial infarction: An overview of results from randomized controlled trials. JAMA 270, 1589–1595 (1993)

Characterizing Web User Visual Gaze Patterns: A Graph Theory Inspired Approach

Pablo Loyola and Juan D. Velásquez

Department of Industrial Engineering, University of Chile
Santiago, Chile
ployola@ing.uchile.cl, jvelasqu@dii.uchile.cl

Abstract. We propose a graph-based analysis framework to study the dynamics of visual gaze from web users. Our goal is to extract the main characteristics of the information foraging process from an attention-centric perspective. Our approach consists of modeling web objects, such as images and paragraphs, as nodes. The visual transitions are represented as edges. With the resulting graphs, several standard metrics were computed. We performed an initial empirical study with 23 subjects. The visual activity was captured using an eye tracking device. The results suggest that a graph based analysis can capture in a reliable way the dynamics of user behavior and the identification of salient objects within a web site.

Keywords: Web User Behavior, Visual Gaze Patterns, Graph Theory.

1 Introduction

The need for understanding the evolution of Web usage have led to incorporate new sources of data to the stack of standard analysis. As the Web is no longer a static ecosystem where users can only perform simple tasks, the idea of considering usage as an evolving, time-dependent phenomena emerges as a feasible alternative to disentangle the underlying factors that drive user's decision making.

Originally, common approaches have been exploiting the concept user sessions, which are extracted from the set of web logs stored on the server. For years, this approach has been the foundation of the Web Mining research. Although the results have showed several success cases, there are two main limitations that threaten the current reliability and future improvement [5,6].

Given the above, using only a click-stream-based data source, such as web logs, does not necessary reflect web user behavior [9]. Both academia and industry have addressed this issue and have put efforts into finding new sources that could support and improve the analysis.

Secondly, web sessions provide a estimation of the interests for a inter-page basis, but they do not give any insight about the actions and preferences within a web page. Given the dynamism and complexity of the current web applications, we consider that this issue is highly relevant and should be taken into

D. Ślęzak et al. (Eds.): BIH 2014, LNAI 8609, pp. 586–594, 2014.

consideration. For example, several web sites are single page application, which have leveraged the power of Javascript-based frameworks to improve user experience. In this case, the question is how to analyze user behavior when there is no explicit transition between pages?

One feasible alternative that has been considered is the analysis of the users visual gaze. Several approaches have been proposed in order to study of the user explore an interface and conduct the information foraging process. Therefore, applications for identification of salient objects and analysis of page layout have contributed to enrich the understanding and also provides new lines of research, specifically in Information Retrieval.

Although this line of research have shown important results and have contributed to improve the understanding of the users in a more detailed way, they have not acknowledged the relevance of the time component. Currently, the analysis is based on snapshots without considering the evolution of the variables over time.

In this work, our main goal is to support the understanding of the attention allocation process and propose ways to infer user interest. We obtained users data through a empirical study with 23 subjects whose navigation and visual activity was tracked using server-side and eye tracking devices.

Using a graph-based analysis framework, web objects within web pages are represented as nodes The edges are generated from the transitions extracted from the the visual gaze activity. This representation produces continuously growing graphs that encapsulate the user activity within a web page.

The initial results suggest that a graph based analysis can capture in a reliable way the dynamics of user behavior and the identification of salient objects within a web site.

2   Related Work

One of the most remarkable lines of research has been developed by Buscher et al. The main motivation comes from the need for understanding how people allocate visual attention on web pages, taking into account the relevance of this for both web developers and advertisers.

A study from 2009 performed an eye tracking-based analysis in which 20 users were shown 361 pages while performing information foraging and inspection tasks [3]. The main assumption was that gaze data could represent a proxy of attention. From that, an analysis framework was developed by first generating a tool that allows DOM elements to be characterized and a mapping performed between gaze data and the DOM elements. The second part involves the use of machine learning techniques to predict salient elements on a web page.

In this study, the concept of *fixation impact* is introduced. It allows the identification of which elements are under the gaze of the user at a certain time. It follows empirical studies that show that human vision is characterized by a narrow window of high acuity along with the standard gaze area. Thus, when visualizing an element, it also means that other elements in the surroundings are being considered. Therefore, given a fixation point, a DOM area is selected in order to identify every element under it. A distance score is given to each element based on its coverage, assuming a Gaussian distribution. The fixation impact is computed using this distance and also incorporating a time dimension, which means the fixation duration.

The information obtained in the previous step is used to predict salient elements. After performing a selection of the ten features that provide the highest information gain, Linear Regression was used in order to identify the measures that most influence the fixation impact scores. The results showed that positional features obtained the highest weights.

Another line of research has been developed by Velasquez et al., where the main goal is to identify the most relevant elements on a web site by using the concept of Website Keyobjects [8]. A web site object is considered as any group of words having some kind of structure, and in the same way, multimedia files which are shown on the web site pages, including all kinds of pictures, images, sound and animations. Objects based on word structure need to be inside a delimitation such as paragraphs, tables or other kinds of tag separation.

Then, from the definition of Website object, a Web site Keyobject is derived as follows: *One or a group of website objects that attract the user attention and characterize the content of a page or website* . This definition states which web objects get more attention and are more interesting to the user and therefore, identify which object types would help to improve the presentation, usability and content of the web site. The identification of the Keyobjects involved primarily the analysis of web logs and a measure of time spent. In order to validate the findings, surveys were conducted, which do not provide a strong level of confidence for the results. The authors addressed this issue, and in [7] they incorporated eye-tracking methodologies to replace the use of surveys. With this, they were able to validate the approach by having an objective measure of the user attention.

3 Methodology

We performed an exploratory analysis based on monitoring the visual activity during web user navigation. The experiment consists of asking a set of subjects to explore a defined web site based on a standard foraging task using an eye-tracking device that stores all the visual gaze activity. No specific instructions are given to the subjects.

The specific steps are described as follows:

1. The eye tracking device is calibrated according to the subject characteristics and the initial web page of the site is presented.
2. The subject begins the web exploration. His behavior is tracked with the eye tracking device and additionally the by the server, which stores the web session.
3. Two re-calibration procedures are performed during the experiment to verify the quality of the data extracted by the eye tracker.

3.1   Implementation

Experimental Group. For the experiment, a group of 23 people were chosen. The average age was 26.1 years (with a variance of 2.2 years). The group involved was mainly composed of university students and professionals, from different fields. According to their own experience (no test was developed for measuring this), one considered him/herself an expert on web navigation, 12 considered their knowledge as average and the other two think they are basic users.

Target Web Site. The analysis was performed on the website of the MBA program that is offered by the Industrial Engineering Department at the University of Chile[1]. This site has been running since January 2011 and provides information about the courses, the methodology of the plan, teachers, student profiles, etc., as well as some pages for applying to the program.

At the time of the analysis, the site was composed of 29 pages and 359 DOM objects, which appear 1014 times in total. This means that an object can appear on more than one page. This phenomena is usual with common objects as banners, menus, footers, headers, etc. The average number of objects per page is 31.9 and their average size is 418.6 pixels wide and 100.1 pixels high.

Tracking Device. To capture eye movements and to measure pupillary dilation an eye-tracker system was used, which is video-based combined pupil and corneal reflection. These kinds of devices are the most advanced system for measuring this kind of movements according to the degree of accuracy obtained with them. In particular the device corresponds to eye-tracker model Eyelink 1000, developed by SR Research. This device is composed of a main screen with a high speed camera and an infrared emitter, connected to a host computer which does the data processing. There is one more computer which is also connected to the host. This one allows the researcher to develop the experiments and get the data in an easy way. It also shows in real time the same stimulus that the participants see. The whole setup for a trial takes around 2 to 5 minutes.

4   Analysis

After collecting the data from each subject, we transformed it into a graph representation. Each web element from a web page, such an text paragraph or an image, is represented as a node, giving it an unique identification.

Links in the graph represent the transitions in the visual gaze reported by the eye tracking device. Figure 1 shows an example. In this case, suppose that an user fixes the attention initially on the green picture. Then, the user moves to the central paragraph. This transition is represented as a directed edge between two nodes.

---

[1] http://www.mbauchile.cl

Therefore, each transition adds a new node to the corresponding graph, which makes it a directed structure. One may think that instead of a graph representation, only sequence lists are being obtained, but the evidence shows that users tend to go return to previously seen elements, which generates directed cycles. All the data from the graph generation is stored, thus, it is feasible to inspect all the process.

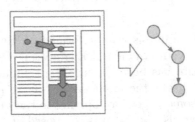

Fig. 1. Transformation from visual gaze activity to a graph representation

Each user generates a graph for each page he visits. Therefore, the maximum number of graphs per user is 29. The graphs for the same page vary from user to user, as the attention allocation process is different for each of them.

4.1   Salient Object Recognition

Salient object recognition is one the most relevant types of analysis tasks that can be performed when studying user attention. To achieve such task, we propose to use the concept of *Network Centrality*.

In Graph theory, Network Centrality metrics express the relevance of a node within a graph. This type of metrics originated from the Social Network Analysis field in order to identify the degree of influence within a group of individuals [4].

One of the most common measures of centrality is called *eigenvector centrality* [2,1]. Given the adjacency matrix A from a graph G, this centrality is defined as the principal eigenvector, given the following equation:

$$\lambda v = Av \tag{1}$$

where λ is the eigenvalue (constant) and v the eigenvector. The interpretation of this equation is that a node has a high eigenvector score if it is adjacent to nodes that are themselves high scorers. The intrinsic idea of this metric is the notion of influence: If a node influences just one other node, who subsequently influences several other nodes, then the first node in that chain is highly influential. Other interpretation that could be more related to control flow analysis, is that the eigenvector centrality provides a model for nodal risk, in the sense that a node long term equilibrium risk of receiving traffic is a function of the risk level of its neighbors.

Although the application of this metric appears promising in a data flow context, it must be noted that, given its nature, there some assumptions that need to be taken into account. Firstly, it assumes that traffic is able to move via unconstrained walks. Secondly, it assumes that a node influence all its neighbors at the same time.

Another measure of centrality is the degree centrality. Given a graph $G = (V, E)$, where V is the number of nodes and E the number of edges, the degree centrality for a node i is defined as $CD = deg(i)$, which means, the number of ties incident upon a node. The interpretation of this is that degree centrality represents immediate effect in a network. For example, if a certain proportion of nodes are infected, the probability of infection is a function of the number of nodes the node is adjacent to.

It can be seen that degree and eigenvector centrality metrics share certain aspects. But while degree centrality focuses on immediate risk/influence, eigenvector centrality is related to the long term risk/influence.

Closeness centrality is defined, for a given node, as the sum of all the graph-theoretic distances from all the other nodes. The notion of distance in this case is defined as the length of the shortest path between two nodes. In the data flow context, this metric is relevant in the sense that it can be interpreted as the expected time of arrival of data to a certain node. Nodes with a low closeness score have short distances from the rest, which allow them to receive data sooner.

It must be noted that the use of this metric implies a discussion on the concept of reachability, in the sense that closeness metric only provides meaningful results if the graph under study is a connected graph.

Finally, betweenness centrality. Freeman defined this metric as the share of times a node i needs a node k in order to reach a node j via the shortest path. If g_{ij} is the number of geodesic paths from i to j and g_{ikj} is the number of these geodesic paths that pass through node k, then the betweenness centrality is of node k is defined as :

$$C_B = \sum_i \sum_j \frac{g_{ikj}}{g_{ij}} \tag{2}$$

with $i \neq j \neq k$.

We applied the above metrics to resulting graphs for each page visited for each user. The main goal is to analyze if the nodes that have a high score are correlated with the ones in which the users spend more time.

In order to generate a comparison, each centrality metric was computed for each node in the graph, and the scores were aggregated along the group of users.

As a measure of the user attention, the time spent on each element was calculated, as a proxy for the visual fixation.

Therefore, for each node that was visualized by any user, there is a set of four centrality scores and also a measurement of the time spent.

Figure 2 shows the aggregated results for the salient element recognition for the 29 pages the conform the web site under study. The representation in the plot is the following: closeness (red), degree (blue), betweeness (green) and eigenvector (yellow). The time spent on each object is represented by the black line.

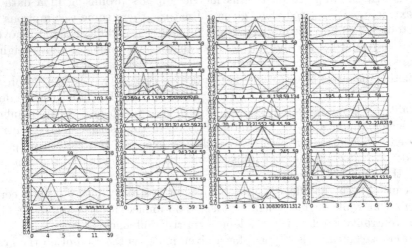

Fig. 2. Centrality metric and time spent scores for each node

We performed a comparison process in order to find which centrality metric behaves more similar to the time spent for each node. As this is an exploratory study, we chose two ways to compare centrality metrics to time spent.

The first way is to use the RMSE as a metric of closeness betweeen the centrality and the time. The idea is to find, an an aggregated way, which centrality curve has the lowest RMSE. Figure 3 shows, for one subject, the values of the RMSE for all centrality metrics along the web session.

We computed the average RMSE value for each centrality metric, and the results shows that the metric that has the lowest score is the eigenvector centrality, followed by the closeness centrality.

This result seems logical as the concept of *influence* in graphical interfaces, such as a web site, is related to how the attention to a specific element affects the attention to the rest. An example of this could be the following: A colorful image which is displayed in a web site eventually could guide the attention of the user to the elements that surrounds it. Therefore elements that are adjacent to this image, will receive more attention (in terms of time spent on a fixation), that elements that are far. Thus, an element will be influential if it is at the same time linked to other elements which are influential as well.

The second way to explore the results was to use a correlation metric between the centrality values and the time spent on each element. This analysis is different to the previous one in the sense it does not have as goal to find the level of fit between two curves. In this case, we would like to explore if there is a dependency between the variables.

We used the Pearson correlation coefficient for calculating a dependence score. Therefore we assumed the scenario of a linear correlation and that the data follows a Normal distribution.

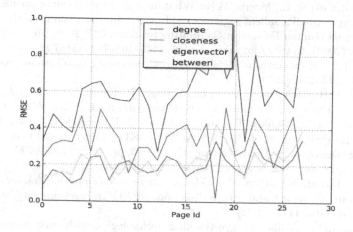

Fig. 3. Example of RMSE values for all centrality metrics for each page for one subject

The results showed that the highest value for correlation was obtained by the eigenvector centrality ($r = 0.41$), although the level of confidence is not statistically significant. No other centrality metric obtained a plausible correlation score.

5   Conclusions and Future Work

In this work, we have explored how the web user behaves from a visual gaze perspective. In order to formalize our analysis, we used a graph based framework, which allowed to computed several metrics. With these initial results, we are not able to generate strong conclusion, but we can use them as a motivation in the sense of showing that the centrality metrics can be used as a proxy to identify the salient objects from a web page. The tracked problem is relevant, as it is always desired to have an estimation of which elements the user will focus on.

Future work aims to continue refining the metrics and transforming the current set up into a prediction problem.

Acknowledgments. This work was supported by the FONDEF-CONICYT CA12I10061 - AKORI project.

References

1. Bonacich, P.: Factoring and weighting approaches to status scores and clique identification. Journal of Mathematical Sociology 2(1), 113–120 (1972)
2. Borgatti, S.P.: Centrality and network flow. Social networks 27(1), 55–71 (2005)

3. Buscher, G., Cutrell, E., Morris, M.R.: What do you see when you're surfing?: Using eye tracking to predict salient regions of web pages. In: Proceedings of the SIGCHI Conference on Human Factors in Computing Systems, CHI 2009, pp. 21–30. ACM, New York (2009), http://doi.acm.org/10.1145/1518701.1518705

4. Freeman, L.C.: Centrality in social networks conceptual clarification. Social networks 1(3), 215–239 (1979)

5. McMahan, H.B., Holt, G., Sculley, D., Young, M., Ebner, D., Grady, J., Nie, L., Phillips, T., Davydov, E., Golovin, D., Chikkerur, S., Liu, D., Wattenberg, M., Hrafnkelsson, A.M., Boulos, T., Kubica, J.: Ad click prediction: A view from the trenches. In: Proceedings of the 19th ACM SIGKDD International Conference on Knowledge Discovery and Data Mining, KDD 2013, pp. 1222–1230. ACM, New York (2013), http://doi.acm.org/10.1145/2487575.2488200

6. Pal, S.K., Talwar, V., Mitra, P.: Web mining in soft computing framework: Relevance, state of the art and future directions. IEEE Transactions on Neural Networks 13(5), 1163–1177 (2002)

7. Velasquez, J.D.: Combining eye-tracking technologies with web usage mining for identifying website keyobjects. Engineering Applications of Artificial Intelligence 26(5-6), 1469–1478 (2013),
http://www.sciencedirect.com/science/article/pii/S0952197613000134

8. Velasquez, J.D., Dujovne, L.E., L'Huillier, G.: Extracting significant website key objects: A semantic web mining approach. Engineering Applications of Artificial Intelligence 24(8), 1532–1541 (2011)

9. Won, S.S., Jin, J., Hong, J.I.: Contextual web history: using visual and contextual cues to improve web browser history. In: Proceedings of the SIGCHI Conference on Human Factors in Computing Systems, pp. 1457–1466. ACM (2009)

Author Index